COMPREHENSIVE HANDBOOK OF SOCIAL WORK AND SOCIAL WELFARE

Volume

1

COMPREHENSIVE HANDBOOK OF SOCIAL WORK AND SOCIAL WELFARE

THE PROFESSION OF SOCIAL WORK

Volume Editor

Barbara W. White

Editors-in-Chief

Karen M. Sowers **Catherine N. Dulmus**

John Wiley & Sons, Inc.

KH

This book is printed on acid-free paper. ♾

Published by John Wiley & Sons, Inc., Hoboken, New Jersey.
Published simultaneously in Canada.

For general information on our other products and services please contact our Customer Care Department within the United States at (800) 762-2974, outside the United States at (317) 572-3993 or fax (317) 572-4002.

Wiley also publishes its books in a variety of electronic formats. Some content that appears in print may not be available in electronic books. For more information about Wiley products, visit our web site at www.wiley.com.

Library of Congress Cataloging-in-Publication Data:

Comprehensive handbook of social work and social welfare /
editors-in-chief, Karen M. Sowers and Catherine N. Dulmus.
p. cm.
Includes bibliographical references.
ISBN 978-0-471-76997-2 (cloth) Volume 1: The Profession of Social Work
ISBN 978-0-471-76272-0 (cloth) Volume 2: Human Behavior in the Social Environment
ISBN 978-0-471-76280-5 (cloth) Volume 3: Social Work Practice
ISBN 978-0-471-76998-9 (cloth) Volume 4: Social Policy and Policy Practice
ISBN 978-0-471-75222-6 (cloth) 4-Volume set
1. Social service. 2. Social service—Practice. 3. Public welfare. 4. Social policy.
I. Sowers, Karen M. (Karen Marlaine) II. Dulmus, Catherine N.

HV40.C66 2008
361—dc22 2007026315

Printed in the United States of America.

10 9 8 7 6 5 4 3 2 1

10/5/09

To Tonja, Phaedra and John.
This book may help you better understand my work for these many years. You are my inspiration and my wish for your future is embedded in the mission of social work.

Contents

Handbook Preface

The profession of social work spans more than 100 years. Over this period, the profession has changed in scope and depth. Despite the varied functions and methods of our profession, it has always been committed to social justice and the promotion of well-being for all. The profession has made great strides and is experiencing a resurgence of energy, commitment, and advancement as we face new global realities and challenges and embrace new and innovative technologies.

In considering how the field of social work has evolved over the past century with the resulting explosion of new knowledge and technologies, it seemed imperative to create a resource (*Comprehensive Handbook of Social Work and Social Welfare*) that provides a manageable format of information for researchers, clinicians, educators, and students. Our editors at John Wiley & Sons, the volume editors (Ira Colby, William Rowe, Lisa Rapp-Pagglici, Bruce Thyer, and Barbara W. White) and we as editors-in-chief, developed this four-volume handbook to serve as a resource to the profession.

The *Comprehensive Handbook of Social Work and Social Welfare* includes four volumes (*The Profession of Social Work, Human Behavior in the Social Environment, Social Work Practice,* and *Social Policy and Policy Practice*). Each volume editor did an outstanding job of assembling the top social work scholars from around the globe to contribute chapters in their respective areas of expertise. We are enormously grateful to the chapter authors who have contributed their expert knowledge to this work. Each volume includes a Preface written by the respective volume editor(s) that provides a general overview to the volume. In developing the *Comprehensive Handbook,* we attempted to focus on evidence supporting our theoretical underpinnings and our practice interventions across multiple systems. Content was designed to explore areas critically and to present the best available knowledge impacting the well-being of social systems, organizations, individuals, families, groups, and communities. The content is contemporaneous and is reflective of demographic, social, political, and economic current and emerging trends. Authors have paid close attention to contextual factors that shape the profession and will have a future impact on practice. Our profession strives to understand the dimensions of human difference that we value and engage to ensure excellence in practice. These dimensions of diversity are multiple and include factors such as disability, religion, race, culture, sexual orientation, social class, and gender. Each of the volumes addresses how difference characterizes and shapes our profession and our daily practice. New knowledge, technology, and ideas that may have a bearing on contemporary and future social work practice are infused throughout each of the volumes.

We challenged the chapter authors to not only provide an overview of specific content, but to feel free to raise controversial issues and debates within the profession. In the interest of intellectual freedom, many of our chapter authors have done just that in ways that are intriguing and thought provoking. It was our objective to be comprehensive but not encyclopedic. Readers wishing to obtain even greater specificity are encouraged to access works listed in the references for each chapter.

The *Handbook*'s focus on evidence should assist the reader with identifying opportunities to strengthen their own understanding of the amount of science that does or does not support our social work theory and practice. Social work researchers must expand the scientific evidence that supports social work theory and practice as well as informing policy, and enhance their functional scope to overcome the more than 10-year lag between research and practice. We are rightfully proud of our social work history, and its future will be driven by our success in demonstrating that as a profession we can achieve credible and verifiable outcomes across the spectrum of services that utilize our skills. As a profession, we must assure we value science so that even the most vulnerable populations receive the best available services.

We hope that you find this *Handbook* useful. We have endeavored to provide you, the reader and user, with a comprehensive work that will serve as a guide for your own work in this wonderful profession. We welcome your comments and suggestions.

KAREN M. SOWERS
CATHERINE N. DULMUS

Acknowledgments

An endeavor of this magnitude required the efforts of many people, and we are indebted to their unique and valuable contributions. First, we would like to thank Tracey Belmont, our initial editor at John Wiley & Sons, for recognizing the importance of this project to the profession of social work and for her commitment to making it a reality. It was Tracey's vision that allowed this project to get off the ground, and we are grateful to her. A special thanks to Lisa Gebo, our current editor at John Wiley & Sons, who provided us with expert guidance and technical support to see this project to fruition. Others to thank at John Wiley & Sons include Isabel Pratt and Sweta Gupta who assisted us with all aspects of the contractual and prepublication processes. They were invaluable in assisting with a project of this size, and we are grateful to them.

Most important, we would like to thank the volume editors and contributors who made this *Handbook* a reality. The volume editors did an excellent job of developing their respective volumes. We particularly thank them for their thoughtful selection and recruitment of chapter contributors. The contributor lists for each volume read like a "Who's Who" of social work scholars. We are pleased that each contributor recognized the importance of a seminal piece such as this *Handbook* for the profession of social work and willingly contributed their time and knowledge. We extend a special debt of gratitude to these eminent contributors from around the globe who so graciously and willingly shared their expertise with us. It is the work of these scholars that continues to move our profession forward.

K. M. S.
C. N. D.

Preface

The compilation before you is a significant professional reference volume on the social work profession. As a complex, diverse, and licensed profession, the time for a publication such as this is long overdue.

Indeed, nearly a century ago, at the 1915 National Conference of Charities and Correction, Abraham Flexner infamously declared that while social work was a useful, mediating social activity, it was not a profession. In response to Flexner's assertion, the early practitioners of social welfare busied themselves with proving that, in fact, social work was a profession, and a necessary one at that. As a result, what began as charity organization societies and philanthropic assistance to those in need has grown in leaps and bounds.

Now fast-forward about 100 years. This Volume began as an idea between the senior editors several years ago, and after approaching experts from various fields and backgrounds across the country and the world, we are proud to present you a proficient, in-depth manual on various poignant aspects of the social work profession—past, present, and future.

Throughout its history, social work has remained a profession steadfast in its commitment to help improve the lives of the disenfranchised and oppressed, and in accordance with this commitment, the motivational characteristics of those who enter this profession have primarily remained the same. However, other elements of social work have changed, and in many respects matured. This Volume provides an overview of some of the significant areas of concern, responsibility, and investigation of scholars and practitioners that comprise contemporary professional social work practice and education. The history of the profession sets the background for understanding the complex nature of the professional mandate and evolution of the mission over time.

As the needs of the populations served have grown and become more complex, so has the profession. A number of professional issues occupy our attention today. We are paying due attention to gender, ethnicity, sexual identity, and socioeconomic characteristics of persons coming into professional education and practice in order to enhance diversity and cultural competence. The national structure of social work education and practice organizations are in question, as are the organizational structures in our individual colleges and universities. This is currently a salient issue ripe for discussion and debate. The financial structure and support of social work education and its students fluctuates with federal government priorities, regional needs, and political whims. Policies and financial support systems for professional social work practice have ebbs and flows that impact curriculum modifications and practice methodologies. Some of these forces include the chronic underfunding of prevention, intervention, and treatment services and gaps in the workforce, both in regard to personnel and in practice knowledge. The organized profession has identified and is addressing these forces through various milieus and platforms. These issues and challenges are being confronted, and the substance and tone of this dialogue is accurately reflected through the works of the distinguished authors in this comprehensive Volume. Through their individual and collective efforts, the authors provide an excellent source of information on the current state of the profession as viewed through select fields of practice.

The introductory chapters set the context by providing an in-depth overview of social work. The bulk of the Volume then offers insight into different fields of practice, such as child welfare, substance abuse, and international social work. The work then concludes with a chapter on issues that will inform the future of social work.

ACKNOWLEDGMENTS

I would like to thank our team of distinguished chapter authors, as well as the countless professionals who helped make this project a reality. Their expertise and countless hours of hard work and dedication cumulated not only in an excellent reference piece for this diverse profession, but their efforts represent the power and potential our profession has to offer.

I'd like to thank Julie Cunniff, my executive assistant at the University of Texas—Austin School of Social Work, for her patience and assistance as we worked through this volume. Her great heart and incredible service make me a better leader. This effort would not have happened without her tremendous support.

I am also grateful to Shireen Connor, MSSW, who was my talented graduate assistant at the University of Texas—Austin School of Social Work. Shireen's experience and skills were major assets that I generously used to complete this project.

BARBARA W. WHITE

Contributors

James G. Barber, MSW, PhD
Deputy Vice-Chancellor and Provost
RMIT University
Melbourne, Australia

Tricia B. Bent-Goodley, PhD
School of Social Work
Howard University
Washington, DC

Patricia Brownell, PhD
Graduate School of Social Services
Fordham University-Lincoln Center Campus
New York, New York

Iris B. Carlton-LaNey, PhD
School of Social Work
University of North Carolina
Chapel Hill, North Carolina

Amy Chanmugam, MSSW, LCSW
School of Social Work
University of Texas—Austin
Austin, Texas

Namkee Choi, PhD
School of Social Work
University of Texas—Austin
Austin, Texas

King Davis, PhD
Hogg Foundation for Mental Health
University of Texas—Austin
Austin, Texas

Donna DeAngelis, LICSW, ACSW
Association of Social Work Boards
Culpepper, Virginia

Elizabeth DePoy, PhD
Center for Community Inclusion and Disability Studies
University of Maine
Orono, Maine

Alberta J. Ellett, PhD
School of Social Work
University of Georgia
Athens, Georgia

Doreen Elliott, PhD
School of Social Work
University of Texas—Arlington
Arlington, Texas

Cynthia Franklin, PhD, LCSW, LMFT
School of Social Work
University of Texas—Austin
Austin, Texas

Beth Gerlach, MSSW, LCSW
School of Social Work
University of Texas—Austin
Austin, Texas

Stephen Gilson, PhD
School of Social Work
University of Maine
Orono, Maine

Roberta R. Greene, PhD
School of Social Work
University of Texas—Austin
Austin, Texas

Jessica Holmes, MSW
Council on Social Work Education
Alexandria, Virginia

June G. Hopps, PhD
School of Social Work
University of Georgia
Athens, Georgia

Roberta Rehner Iversen, PhD
School of Social Policy & Practice
University of Pennsylvania
Philadelphia, Pennsylvania

Leslie Leighninger, PhD
School of Social Work
Arizona State University
Tempe, Arizona

Gary R. Lowe, MSW, PhD
School of Social Work
Florida International University
Miami, Florida

Tony B. Lowe, PhD
School of Social Work
University of Georgia
Athens, Georgia

Samuel A. MacMaster, PhD
College of Social Work
University of Tennessee—Knoxville
Nashville, Tennessee

Jon Matsuoka, PhD
School of Social Work
University of Hawai'i—Manoa
Honolulu, Hawai'i

Hamilton I. McCubbin, PhD
School of Social Work
University of Hawai'i—Manoa
Honolulu, Hawai'i

Mary Jo Monahan, LCSW
Family Services Centers, Inc.
Clearwater, Florida

Robin E. Perry, PhD
Department of Social Work
Florida A&M University
Tallahassee, Florida

Albert Roberts, PhD
FAS-Criminal Justice
Rutgers-State University of New Jersey
Piscataway, New Jersey

Allen Rubin, PhD
School of Social Work
University of Texas—Austin
Austin, Texas

Dennis Saleebey, DSW
School of Social Welfare
University of Kansas
Lawrence, Kansas

Uma A. Segal, PhD
School of Social Work
University of Missouri—St. Louis
St. Louis, Missouri

Terry L. Singer, MSW, PhD
Kent School of Social Work
University of Louisville
Louisville, Kentucky

David W. Springer, PhD, LCSW
School of Social Work
University of Texas—Austin
Austin, Texas

Lori K. Holleran Steiker, PhD
School of Social Work
University of Texas—Austin
Austin, Texas

Kimberly Strom-Gottfried, LISW, PhD
School of Social Work
University of North Carolina
Chapel Hill, North Carolina

Barbara Thomlison, PhD
School of Social Work
College of Social Work, Justice, and Public Affairs
Florida International University
Miami, Florida

Julia M. Watkins, MSW, PhD
Council on Social Work Education
Alexandria, Virginia

Stanley L. Witkin, PhD
Department of Social Work
University of Vermont
Burlington, Vermont

Katherine van Wormer, PhD
Department of Social Work
University of Northern Iowa
Cedar Falls, Iowa

Chapter 1

THE HISTORY OF SOCIAL WORK AND SOCIAL WELFARE

Leslie Leighninger

Social work as a profession grew chiefly out of the development of social welfare policies and programs in the United States, Europe, and Muslim countries. Judeo-Christian and Muslim practices and beliefs underlie many of the early attempts to provide help to the poor, the sick, widows, orphans, the "insane" and "imbeciles" (as those with problems of mental illness and developmental disability used to be called) and the elderly. This history begins with a discussion of the development of social welfare in Middle Eastern and European countries and then moves to the transfer of social welfare policies and practices to the New World of the American colonies. We then discuss the transition from the work of government officials and "people of good will," who both helped and regulated those who were needy, to the creation of the profession of social work as we know it today.

Two thousand years before the birth of Christ, a ruler of Babylonia named Hammurabi made the protection of widows and orphans an essential part of his code. The Ancient Greeks and Romans were similarly concerned about helping the needy. The Roman statesman Cicero (106–43 B.C.) described man as a social animal who should "cooperate with and assist his fellow men." From Cicero we get the scripture that it is more blessed to give than to receive. As the social welfare historian Walter Trattner notes, "the words 'philanthropy' and 'charity' and the concepts for which they stand B love of mankind, love of humanity, brotherhood B are of Greek and Latin origin" (Trattner, 1999, pp. 1–2).

The Arab world has also contributed to charitable traditions. Islamic thought draws a distinction between social justice and charity. The faith has a strong tradition of social reform, based on the Prophet Muhammad's advocacy on behalf of women, children, and the disadvantaged. This tradition is operationalized through the requirement that all Muslims who are financially able shall contribute 2.5% of their net wealth each year for support of the needy. This practice, called *zakah*, is not considered to be charity but rather an act of social justice through the redistribution of wealth. Any contributions in addition are seen as charity, or *sadaqa*, which is one of the five pillars of Islam. The Koran lists eight categories of uses to which charitable contributions can be put: aid to the poor, the needy, those who collect the contributions, "those whose hearts must be reconciled," debtors, wayfarers, the redemption of captives, and "for God's cause" (Al-Krenawi & Graham, 2000; Augustine, 2002; Canda & Furman, 1999, pp. 137–138; Stillman, 1975).

Social historian Walter Trattner emphasizes the importance of Jewish tradition in the development of modern philanthropy. Ancient Jewish doctrines, he notes, teach the duty of giving and "equally important, the *right* of those in need to receive." Throughout the

Old Testament, we find commandments to give to others, particularly the old, the sick, those with handicaps, and the poor. This giving is not a matter of charity but a matter of justice. Not only do the Scriptures state that "one might break off his iniquities" (or acts of wickedness) by showing a compassionate face to the poor, but they also go on to command that "thou shalt not harden thy heart nor shut thy hand" to the unfortunate. "It is forbidden," according to the Scriptures, "to turn away a poor man . . . empty-handed." And in a phrase that social workers would appreciate, people should give such aid "with a friendly countenance, with joy, and with a good heart" (Trattner, 1999, p. 2).

The Jewish philosopher Maimonides set out the following eight degrees of charity:

> Give, but with reluctance and regret. This is the gift of the hand but not of the heart.
>
> The second is to give cheerfully, but not proportionately to the distress of the sufferer.
>
> The third is to give cheerfully and proportionately, but not until we are solicited.
>
> The fourth is to give cheerfully and proportionately, and even unsolicited; but to put it in the poor man's hand, thereby exciting in him the painful emotion of shame.
>
> The fifth is to give charity in such a way that the distressed may receive the bounty and know their benefactor, without being known to him.
>
> The sixth, which rises still higher, is to know the objects of our bounty, but remain unknown to them.
>
> The seventh is still more meritorious, namely, to bestow charity in such a way that the benefactor may not know the relieved persons, nor they the name of their benefactor.
>
> The eighth and most meritorious of all is to anticipate charity by preventing poverty; that is, to assist a reduced person so that he may earn an honest livelihood and not be forced to the dreadful alternative of holding up his hand for charity (Macarov, 1978, p. 6).

From these ideas and principles, the Jews developed many social welfare practices. These included the education of orphans, burial of the dead, consolation of the bereaved, visitation of the ill and infirm, and the care of widows, divorcees, and the aged. Provision for the poor was made primarily through various agricultural practices, which included "gleanings," or the practice of leaving grain dropped during the harvest which could be picked up by the hungry (Lowenberg, 2001).

Christianity carried on the charitable tradition, adding a particular emphasis on love and compassion. Since the founders of the Christian Church were Jews, it is not surprising that many parts of the New Testament focused on charity. The basic principle underlying early Christian approaches to social welfare was similar to the Hebraic idea that poverty was not a crime. Even though discretion should be observed in giving aid, and rules set up for discriminating between the various classes of poor people, evidence of need was still the paramount factor in offering help. It was assumed that need came about as a result of misfortune for which society should take responsibility.

At first, charity was an informal system of help, but as Christianity became more established as a religion, Church fathers felt it was important to set up a more formal system of charities. Beginning in the sixth century, monasteries began to serve as basic agencies of relief, particularly in rural areas. Some monastic orders were organized with a particular mission of serving the needy. These orders received income from donations, legacies, and collections, and used this to provide help to the poor who came to their doors. They also, in a forecasting of what we might now call "community outreach," carried food and other provisions to the sick and needy in their communities (Trattner, 1999).

During the First Crusade in the eleventh century, which called for the abolishment of the Muslim states, military monastic orders were developed to care for and provide protection for pilgrims and the sick. These orders were well-organized associations of devout Christians who cared for pilgrims, nursed the sick, and even eventually took part in the military defense of the "Crusader States." Once Jerusalem had been "reclaimed by the Crusaders, there was a dramatic increase in the numbers of Christian pilgrims making their way to the Holy City. These pilgrims were often old and ill, coming to die in the same city where Christ had died. One of the first formal orders of those ministering to them was the Hospitallers. The order set up the great pilgrim hospital in Jerusalem. In what we might now call a "multicultural" approach, they sometimes employed both Jewish and Muslim physicians to care for the sick (Jordan, 2001).

Other monasteries expanded on the work of the Hospitallers, providing a medieval system of hospitals for the sick poor, including lepers. These hospitals did not solely provide for the sick, however. They also housed "weary wayfarers," pilgrims, orphans, the elderly, and the destitute. Like the "community-based social services" of today, hospitals were found along main routes of travel and later in cities. Eventually, these hospitals were taken over by municipal authorities, creating a link between religious and secular charity. Trattner notes that by the middle of the 1500s there were more than 1,100 hospitals in England alone. Some took care of up to several hundred people (Trattner, 1999).

The evolution of feudalism in Europe in the eleventh century provided a system of government which, at least theoretically, dealt with poverty or distress among the population. By the late eleventh and twelfth centuries, most "common" people in Western Christian countries lived on feudal estates as serfs to the lords who owned the estates. While they had little freedom, serfs were to be protected by the landowners against the hazards of illness, unemployment, and old age. At the expense of individual freedom, serfs were thus provided a form of social insurance against the challenges of life. This might be considered a primitive form of social insurance (Trattner, 1999).

Those who were not serfs, and who lived in cities, were often helped by social, craft, and merchant guilds. Like labor unions today, guilds provided benefits for their members. They also provided some assistance to the town poor, such as the distribution of corn and other food and the provision of free lodging for poor travelers (Trattner, 1999).

As early as the Middle Ages, people were developing a distinction between the "deserving" and the "undeserving" poor. Monks praised poverty, generally meaning the voluntary poverty of those in religious orders. But they also spoke of the "blessed poor"—presumably meaning those who had not volunteered to be destitute. They saw people who worked hard, and yet still suffered deprivation, as worthy of pity. People who begged, did not work, or "drank themselves into torpor," and women and men who "hired out their bodies for sex" were the undeserving poor (Jordan, 2001, pp. 191–192).

The Black Death, or bubonic plague of the mid-1300s, and similar epidemics in the next two centuries, brought poverty and death to new heights in Europe and the Islamic world. The plague bacterium is a pathogen carried by fleas. The rat is the preferred host of fleas, and in the Middle Ages the plague spread to Europe and Asia through the fleas on shipboard rats. Once the host rat died of the disease, the fleas sought other hosts, such as cats or humans. The death rate from the disease, particularly in crowded urban areas, was extremely high. The Black Death, which occurred in England in 1348 to 1349, killed almost a third of the population. During the years of the plague, strangers who earlier might have been granted relief were seen as vagabonds "to whom the State prohibited almsgiving under pain of imprisonment" (Herlihy, 1997; Jordan, 2001; Trattner, 1999).

The first English "law of settlement" was established in 1388. Under this law, able-bodied beggars were subject to punishment, presumably because the state was in great need of workers. Social welfare historian Blanche Coll notes that in this period, "those seeking work at better wages and under freer conditions . . . were deemed criminal." In other words, poverty among the able-bodied was beginning to be seen as a crime, and people should deem themselves lucky to get any job available (Coll, 1969).

The problems of the fourteenth century also resulted in what can be described as the first step in the development of a social security system in England (and eventually the United States)—a law passed in 1349, called the Statute of Laborers. The law set a maximum wage and compelled workers to work for whomever needed them. It forbade laborers from traveling, and made it illegal for an able-bodied man to beg. Although this repressive act hardly seems like a first step toward social security, it was the beginning of an attempt to link labor problems to problems of poverty. It also foreshadowed a schizophrenic approach to poverty that was mirrored in the U.S. social security legislation centuries later. The public welfare portion of the Social Security Act has developed into a system that all too often focuses on potential "cheating" in the system (e.g., the possibility that people who are able to work are not trying hard enough to get a job), as opposed to giving people the necessary supports and skills to succeed (Popple & Leighninger, 2005).

Subsequent centuries brought new challenges and problems. In England, the feudal system was declining, mercantilism (or commitment to commerce and trade) was rising, new trade routes were being opened, and new industries were being developed. As the New World began to open up, the potential for increased prosperity grew. Systems like serfdom, however, which at least offered some protection to individuals by the lords of the land, went into decline. With the coming of industrialization and urbanization, many people no longer had any rights to the land they lived on nor to their dwellings. To make things worse, the Protestant Reformation brought about the expulsion of the Catholic Church from England in 1536. This meant the demise of the system of monasteries and their hospitals, which had carried much of the responsibility for helping the sick, the old, the traveler, and the poor in general (Popple & Leighninger, 2005).

Following the Statute of Laborers, various laws were passed that proposed to deal with the problems of labor, begging, and crime. These acts were eventually collected in one major piece of legislation, the Elizabethan Poor Law of 1601. This major law established "the first secure basis for public assistance to the poor." It required each parish or town to provide for the poor through levying rates on property held within the jurisdiction. The Elizabethan Poor Law, which would stand with only minor changes for almost 250 years, defined three major categories of dependents. These were the vagrant, the involuntary unemployed person, and the helpless. The law established ways for dealing with each. It also established the parish, "acting through the overseers of the poor appointed by local officials, as the administrative unit for executing the law" (Coll, 1969; Ziliak, 2005).

In a system that might seem familiar today, the parish was given the power to use the tax revenues to build and maintain almshouses, to supply help to the aged, the sick, and handicapped, and other helpless people in their own homes, and to "purchase materials with which to put the able-bodied unemployed to work." The law held parents, if they had the means, responsible for the support of their children and grandchildren. In turn, children were liable for the care of their "unemployable parents and grandparents." Those children whose parents could not provide for them "were to be set to work or bound out as apprentices." Finally, vagrants and able-bodied people refusing to work could be committed either to a "house of correction," a workhouse, or a common jail. Putting people into almshouses (or "poorhouses"), workhouses, or other institutions was considered "indoor relief." "Outdoor relief" referred to providing some sort of help to people in their homes. As we will see, these terms were later transplanted to the American colonies, and lingered in the parlance of the American social welfare system for some time (Coll, 1969; Marx, 2004).

Most of the institutions for indoor relief, even orphanages, were unpleasant, often punishing places. Many were not much more than sheds divided into tiny rooms with little heat. Sanitation facilities were rudimentary, and food was inadequate. Watery gruel was a staple. Those who refused to go into workhouses were harshly dealt with. Vagrants "not willing to work," could be sent to an institution, whipped, branded, stoned, or even put to death. Clearly all able-bodied, and thus "undeserving" poor were to be strictly and punitively controlled (Day, 2000; Dolgoff & Feldstein, 1998; Trattner, 1999).

Although it sounds like their work could be grim and often punitive, the overseers of the poor constituted an antecedent to modern-day social workers. Theirs was the job of identifying the poor, the vagrant and homeless, the unemployed, and others who were having difficulty surviving. They then decided what should happen with each of these groups of people. Moreover, they were part of a system that said that the government had an obligation to help people (at least the "deserving" ones) who could not provide for themselves and a responsibility to control the other groups in some way. As "government administrators," they might be compared to contemporary child welfare social workers and social workers in the criminal justice system.

By the 1800s, dissatisfaction with the Poor Law system was growing in England. The effectiveness and equity of the system were being questioned. The system of parish responsibility for responses to the poor often led to unequal and inadequate standards. A body of "unpaid, untrained, and often incompetent overseers of the poor . . . did not make for effective administration." Perhaps even more important, many of the poorer areas had "a higher proportion of needy residents and less money to spend on relief than the more prosperous ones." Thus, not only was treatment of the poor unequal from parish to parish, but "the communities that could least afford it usually had the highest poor rates," or taxes. And taxes went up even for richer parishes. Between 1760 and 1818, "poor relief expenditures throughout England increased sixfold, while the population about doubled" (Trattner, 1999).

This happened in part due to a law related to poor workers that was enacted in the late 1700s. During a period of economic distress in England in the mid-1790s, a new policy changed the sense of the Elizabethan Poor Law. This was an allowance system set up by what became known as the Speenhamland Law. In 1795, during a particularly bad period of poverty, the justices of Berkshire met at an inn in Speenhamland and declared that subsidies to help poor workers and their families should be based on the price of bread. When a "gallon loaf" of bread cost one shilling, every "poor and industrious person" would receive a relief allowance of three shillings weekly, based on his own or his family's labor. He would also receive one shilling six pence for the support of his wife and other family members. If the cost of bread rose, he would receive proportionately more money. The system was financed by taxpayers. Although never made a formal law, this practice was soon instituted throughout most of the countryside, and even in some manufacturing areas. By the 1830s, middle class critics saw this as an obstacle to the new capitalistic economy, and brought about the system's demise. However, as Trattner points out, the Speenhamland approach was actually a "forward looking measure that provided financial aid to the destitute according to need as determined by the cost of living" and family size (Polanyi, 1976; Trattner, 1999).

At the same time, the Poor Law itself was coming under attack by classical economists as well as by the manufacturing interests that were gaining power in England. The economists had come to believe that poverty was the natural state of the working class. They argued that the possession of property and wealth was a "natural right," not to be interfered with by the state. The Poor Law was an artificial creation of the state that taxed the well-to-do for the maintenance and care of the needy. Earlier proponents of the poor law system, members of the old landed aristocracy, had a sense of social responsibility and reasoned that the stability of the state required public action to regulate the affairs of mankind, including the discouragement of labor mobility. The rise of a business class and the emergence of a capitalist economy that substituted the price mechanism for the state in determining the status of labor led to the belief that interference with the normal operations of the market, which included a fluid labor force controlled by supply and demand, would threaten, if not overturn, the economic order. In essence, the Elizabethan Poor Law was being replaced by a self-regulating market economy (Trattner, 1999).

Under the poor laws, another important approach to the deserving poor was for families to take them in. For example, a widow might be sent to live with a family. Sometimes this was on a rotational basis: 2 weeks with one family, 2 weeks with another, back to the first, and so forth. Another practice was to place poor people with families, where they could help with farming, caring for children, or similar tasks. The town or other local government body would reimburse the family for the poor person's care. Consequently, unlike the practice of a normal auction, the care and services of the person being auctioned went to the lowest bidder—the family that could feed and clothe them for the smallest amount (Trattner, 1999).

Just as in the Old World, as time went on, states and communities turned to the use of various institutions, or indoor relief, to respond to the problems of the poor, sick, elderly, "idle beggars," and others with particular needs. Where previously they were run out of town, able-bodied beggars were sent to the poorhouse, or almshouse. The goal of this new practice was to decrease the expense of pauperism by establishing cheaper care; another advantage of this cheaper, less pleasant treatment was that it would discourage people from applying for help. One estimate was that the annual cost of a poor person on outdoor relief was $33 to $65 (even more if the person was sick or old). In contrast, the cost of sending that person to a poorhouse would be only $20 to $35 (Trattner, 1999).

Poorhouses would also build character. Work, especially farm labor, was required of all able-bodied inmates. Idleness and alcohol were prohibited. According to officials, pauper children would receive "an education to fit them for future usefulness." While conditions in the poorhouse might have constituted some improvement over the practice of auctioning individuals off to the lowest bidder, it was still basically a repressive system with the goal of deterring people from seeking relief except in cases of dire need (Trattner, 1999).

Another institution, the orphanage, has a long history in America. The Ursuline Convent in New Orleans established the first orphanage in 1727. This was set up to provide a home for children whose parents had been slain in an Indian raid. The next, and more permanent, orphanage was Bethesda. Founded in Savannah, Georgia, in 1740 by a priest. The first public orphanage was created in South Carolina 50 years later. Between 1860 and 1880, about 250 orphanages were founded, most by Catholic and Protestant organizations. Although an improvement over the poorhouse and other ways of dealing with orphaned children, these new institutions tended to be large structures in which rigid schedules and daily routines were stressed. Conjuring up pictures of Dickens' Oliver Twist asking "Please, sir, I want some more," the orphanages of the 1800s practiced harsh discipline and strove to suppress individuality among the children (Katz, 1986; Trattner, 1999).

Responses to those with mental illness also played a major role in the development of institutions. As early as 1689, the residents of Braintree, Massachusetts, agreed to finance the construction of a small house in which a man in the community could "secure his sister and goodwife" since both were "distracted." This decision was based on a Massachusetts statute that empowered town Selectmen to take care of unruly and distracted persons so that they would not "damnify [or annoy] others." But it was not until the well-publicized campaigns of Dorothea Dix that institutionalization of the mentally ill began in full force (Trattner, 1999).

Dix's campaign and its results are an excellent example of the phenomenon that one era's solution to a social welfare issue can deteriorate into another era's catastrophe. Dix is credited with the first major campaign to get the national government to provide funding for institutions that would provide for the mentally ill. In fact, when we ask students in a beginning social work or social welfare class to name important historic figures in the profession, the first name is often Dorothea Dix, the second Jane Addams. Dix was born in Maine in 1802 and moved at age 12 to Boston to live with her grandparents. There she received a good education and went on to become a teacher. After opening a private school for girls, and then a free school for poor children, she suffered a "mental collapse" in 1836. After her recovery, she became a Sunday school teacher for women inmates in the East Cambridge jail. During this life-changing experience, she witnessed the cruel treatment of prisoners, especially those who were mentally disturbed (Katz, 1986).

As Trattner (1999) notes, "Horrified by what she saw [Dix] apparently experienced a tremendous emotional reaction which led her to embark upon one of the most remarkable crusades of the century" (p. 64)—a campaign to ensure better treatment of the mentally ill. Since at the time private hospitals for those with mental illness were small, selective, and expensive, many of those deemed insane were placed in almshouses and jails. Others were held, often chained, in cabins, closets, and pens.

Eventually, individual states began taking on more responsibility for those with mental illness. Mental institutions were established in a number of states, and in 1890, the state of New York took over the complete care of all its "insane" poor. Much of this activity in the states was inspired by Dix, who was instrumental in the improvement of the state mental institution in Massachusetts and went on to inspire and cajole state legislatures to found hospitals for the mentally ill in nine other states. A genuine pioneer, she journeyed "by train, stagecoach, lumber wagon, and foot over muddy roads and swollen rivers" to get to remote facilities for those with mental illness (Katz, 1986).

Based on Dix's broad and detailed research, a bill was introduced in Congress in 1848 to provide millions of acres of land to the states to help pay for the construction of more state mental institutions. Dix lobbied hard for the bill, which had to be reintroduced a number of times and was not passed by Congress until 1854. Many prominent citizens, clergymen, and public and private organizations had lobbied for the measure. However, the measure was vetoed by President Franklin Pierce, on the grounds that he could not find any authority in the Constitution for making the federal government the great almoner of public charity throughout the United States (Crenson, 1998; Trattner, 1999).

Following the development of such institutions as orphanages and mental hospitals, the country began to swing back to more individualized approaches such as the "placing out" of poor and orphaned children and organized charity work with the needy. Matthew A. Crenson has developed a fascinating narrative of the connection between the abandonment of the orphanage and the development of a mothers' pension system that eventually led to the creation of the federal Aid to Families with Dependent Children (AFDC) program (Crenson, 1998; Trattner, 1999).

Crenson's thesis is that the states' creation of public orphanages or their subsidization of private orphanages made them responsible, either directly or indirectly, for the religious upbringing of their wards. "A generation of tense maneuvering . . . led to a general search to sidestep these hazards." A potential solution was the development of mothers' pensions, which would enable destitute mothers to keep their children at home through state payments for financial support. While this approach was not carried out in most places until the New Deal, reformers concerned about the needs of neglected children developed programs in which foster families were paid for caring for children, and systems for supervising these families (Crenson, 1998).

By the end of the 1800s, state and local institutions no longer seemed the most effective way to deal with problems of poverty and dependency. The system of state mental institutions championed by Dorothea Dix was an important improvement over its antecedents. Yet, in the 1870s, these institutions went into a dramatic decline. Patients were increasingly subjected to restraints and punishments and ordered routines of care broke down. Part of the change stemmed from underfunding, part from the basic difficulty of "curing" mental illness. In addition, the patient population was changing from the acutely mentally ill to the chronically mentally ill and the aged (Crenson, 1998).

Concerns about the effectiveness of large institutions swung the pendulum back toward individual approaches to dealing with poverty, dependency, and other social problems. Each of these movements had a major impact on the development of social work as a profession. The first was the development of the Charity Organization Society (COS), which was first established in England and then transported to the United States in 1877 (Katz, 1986; Trattner, 1999).

The COS in England was inspired in part by the work of a Scottish clergyman, Thomas Chalmers, who set up a district plan to organize relief in his Glasgow parish in the 1820s. Chalmers put the poor relief work of each district under the direction of a deacon. The system stressed "friendly visiting" with the poor and based the giving of alms on the needy person's "reformation of character." A similar organization, called the "London Society for Organizing Charitable Relief and Repressing Mendicancy" had been established in England in 1869 (Sapiro, 1990; Trattner, 1999).

Impressed by the work of the London Society, S. Humpreys Gurteen, an Episcopal clergyman in Buffalo, proposed the formation of a similar agency in his city. The Buffalo Charity Organization was established in 1877. Gurteen told the citizens of the city that charity organization was the solution to the city's problems of "indiscriminate relief policies" in which overlapping systems of private charities and municipal relief led to indolence, pauperism, and fraud (Crenson, 1998, pp. 240–250).

The idea of "organizing" charity spread widely throughout the United States in the late 1800s. The New York Association for Improving the Condition of the Poor, for example, set up a system of home visiting by volunteers, who would attend to the "moral deficits" of poor families as well as their economic needs. Basically the goal of the Association for Improving the Condition of the Poor was to ensure investigation of every appeal for assistance, to distinguish between the deserving and undeserving poor, and to blend this "with a judicious mixture of moral exhortation." The organization placed each city ward under the responsibility of an advisory committee which would coordinate provision of relief through a system of friendly visitors (Crenson, 1998, pp. 250–251).

Spokespeople for the new system saw it as a new benevolent gospel. They pictured charity organization as a "crusade to save the city from itself and from the evils of pauperism." Leaders of the movement saw themselves as missionaries in a holy cause. As the New York Charity Organization (which grew out of the Association for Improving the Condition of the Poor) put it, "if we do not furnish the poor with elevating influences, they will rule us by degrading ones" (Popple & Leighninger, 2005, pp. 71–75).

The COS movement reflected a conservative interpretation of the causes of poverty. According to one of its leaders, Josephine Shaw Lowell, individual dependency was one of the greatest evils of modern industrial life. Lowell was a reformer who came from a wealthy Boston family. She stressed that the poor were in need "largely because of their own shortcomings, including drunkenness and idleness." Haphazard charity must be avoided, as it contributed to their dependency. The solution to the problems of poverty and dependency was to provide patient, skilled visiting of the poor by "dedicated volunteers." Lowell felt that well-to-do visitors, generally women, could bring not alms, but "kind action," and could serve as good moral examples for the poor. Visitors should avoid giving money, but to provide loans and assistance in finding jobs to "deserving" families (Popple & Leighninger, 2005, p. 65).

Charity organization societies spread quickly among American cities in the late nineteenth century. However, the original goals of COS leaders proved difficult to sustain. Individual approaches to the complex problem of poverty failed to stop its growth. There was also an insufficient pool of volunteers to carry out an effective system of friendly visiting. Increasingly, charities turned to the use of paid staff to investigate applications and visit the poor (Lubove, 1969).

These paid agents were a major forerunner of professional social workers. Like the earlier charity volunteers, they were chiefly women. They also tended to be Protestant, White, and middle class. The job of charity worker offered an outlet for college-educated women at a time when taking care of a family "took center stage and career possibilities for women were few and far between." Charity work was a relatively acceptable job for women because it used traditional feminine characteristics such as caring for others (Lubove, 1969; Muncy, 1991).

Josephine Shaw Lowell was a good example of such a woman. She was born into a well-to-do Boston family in 1843. Her parents had a strong interest in social reform, imbuing in Lowell a belief in the importance of public service. The Lowells were abolitionists, and Josephine joined a women's relief organization that provided aid to Union soldiers. Widowed at a young age, Lowell turned to even greater involvement in social reform. Her work with the New York Charities Aid Association, including a statewide study of pauperism, led to her appointment by the governor of New York to the Commission of the State Board of Charities. She was the first female member of the board (Lubove, 1969; Popple & Leighninger, 2005).

Although she dressed in black and seemed the symbol of a self-sacrificing reformer, Lowell was also tough, shrewd, and pragmatic. She held strong views about the causes of poverty and the appropriate remedies for dealing with it. Many of her principles and ideas can be found in her book, *Private Charity and Public Relief*, published in 1884. Although sometimes portrayed as exhibiting a punitive, moralistic attitude toward the poor, Lowell had a mixture of values and beliefs regarding dependency. She viewed idleness as a major defect of the poor and government aid as a disincentive to honest work. Private charity, with its approach of friendly visiting, was necessary to elevate the moral nature of the poor. She had little sympathy for drunkards, vagrant women, and mothers of illegitimate children (Beatty, 1986).

Lowell also believed, however, that certain groups of people, including orphans, widows, and the sick, were poor through no fault of their own. In these instances, she felt public responses, such as institutions and widows' pensions, to be appropriate sources of relief. She realized that low wages were one source of poverty, and she fought to improve working conditions for women. Yet, while she appreciated the importance of environmental factors in poverty, Lowell also tended to apply such insights only to the "deserving poor," such as those clearly demonstrating a desire to work. In essence, she was convinced that personal character was the most significant element determining a person's position in life (Popple & Leighninger, 2005).

Charity organization workers such as Lowell were a major forerunner of professional social workers. Elements of the COS system, such as investigations by caseworkers and one-to-one work with mothers of poor families, also made their way into state and federal child welfare programs. The National Conference of Charities and Correction, founded by state boards of charity in 1874, was a precursor of the American Association of Social Workers, one of the organizations that helped found today's National Association of Social Workers (NASW; Popple & Leighninger, 2005).

Another forerunner of modern social welfare programs and professional social work was the settlement house. Like the COS, this was an idea imported from England. However, unlike the charity movement, with its stress on individual defects, the social settlement focused chiefly on the environmental factors in poverty.

While Jane Addams' Hull House is regarded as the inspiration of the settlement house movement in America, the first American settlement was actually founded in New York City by an organization of graduates from Smith College in 1887. But it was Addams' accomplishments in a poor immigrant community in Chicago's West Side that captured the imagination of American reformers (Popple & Leighninger, 2005).

Addams grew up in a comfortable home in the small town of Cedarville, Illinois. Her parents were part of the second wave of pioneers in America; her father came to what was then the frontier "to organize and develop what others had discovered and settled." He bought a sawmill and gristmill, and in an effort to help build a community, he planted the hill across from his mills with the seeds of Norway pines. He invested in railroads and banks and became a wealthy man. John Addams believed in hard work and had a strong religious faith. He served for many years as a Republican in the State Senate and was instrumental in the improvement of prisons, insane asylums, and the state industrial schools (Popple & Leighninger, 2005).

Jane Addams was one of eight children. Her mother died when she was 2 years old. While an older sister took over the management of the household, their father was the dominant force in the family. From him, Jane inherited a love of reading, but also a sense of ambition, purpose, and commitment. Her father's second wife encouraged Jane to think of herself as an intelligent woman. Like a growing number of young, well-to-do women of her generation, Addams attended college. Even though this was at a female seminary in Rockford, Illinois, rather than Radcliffe or Vassar, Addams and her friends at Rockford were "self-consciously aware that they were college women." One of her friends was Ellen Gates Starr, with whom she would later found Hull House (Davis, 2000, pp. 160–161).

Part of Addams' childhood had also included a series of illnesses. The most serious was tuberculosis of the spine, which left a slight curvature in her back and caused her to be pigeon-toed and to walk with her head slightly cocked to one side. This experience, along with the early loss of her mother and the death of one of her sisters when Addams was 6, may have increased her empathy for people facing difficulties in life (Davis, 2000, pp. 6–7).

After graduation from Rockford, Addams returned home to Cedarville, where she suddenly became ill and despondent. She had hoped to pursue a further degree at Smith College, but now this seemed out of the question. Her father and stepmother had not wanted her to go on to Smith anyway, and probably helped convince her that she was too ill to continue her academic work. The sudden death of her father threw her into deeper despondency, and she eventually entered a mental institution. Part of her difficulty stemmed from "her inability to reconcile her career ambitions, her need to study hard . . . with the sense of responsibility she felt toward her family" (Davis, 2000, pp. 9–16, 24–29).

After several months at the mental hospital, she felt well enough to return home. Here she struggled with regaining a purpose in life, something beyond managing a household. Her feelings were similar to many in the first generation of college women, who had difficulty finding a suitable career or goal in life beyond marriage. Her solution for this impasse was not atypical—she chose, like many other well-to-do young people of her times, to take a European tour (Davis, 2000, pp. 31–32).

In Europe, Addams visited the usual sites for the American visitor: museums, cathedrals, and the homes and graves of celebrated poets and political figures. Yet she also noted the poverty of the Irish countryside and the slums of London's East End. She met and talked with a variety of people, and noted in one of her letters home "I am more convinced all the time of the value of social life, of its necessity for the development of some of our best traits" (Davis, 2000, pp. 32–37).

After 2 more years at home, where she continued to struggle with her search for some useful purpose for her life, Addams embarked on a second European tour, this time accompanied by Ellen Starr and another friend. This is the tour most familiar to those interested in Jane Addams. This trip included her famous encounter with the bullfights in Spain. The cruelty of the bullfights, legend has it (a legend created by Jane herself), led her to devote her life to helping the poor. In her book *Twenty Years at Hull House*, Addams describes it this way:

> It is hard to tell just when the very simple plan which afterward developed into the settlement first began to form itself in my mind. It may have been even before I went to Europe for the second time, but I gradually became convinced that it would be a good thing to rent a house in a part of the city [of Chicago] where many . . . needs are found, in which young women who had been given over too exclusively to study might restore a balance of activity . . . and learn of life from life itself. . . . I do not remember to have mentioned this plan to anyone until we reached Madrid. . . .
>
> We had been to see a bullfight rendered in the most magnificent Spanish style, where greatly to my surprise and horror, I found that I had seen, with comparative indifference, five bulls and many more horses killed. . . .
>
> In the evening, the natural and inevitable reaction came, and in deep chagrin I found myself tried and condemned . . . by the entire moral situation which [this experience] revealed. (Addams, 1910/1960, p. 72)

In her autobiography, Addams then describes her conviction to carry out the plan of creating what would become Hull House. She recalls the "stumbling and uncertainty with which I finally set it forth to Miss Starr. . . . By the time we had reached the enchantment of the Alhambra [in Spain], the scheme had become convincing and tangible although still most hazy in detail" (Addams, 1910/1960, p. 73).

Addams' visit to Toynbee Hall in London was probably much more influential in the founding of Hull House. Two months after the famous bullfight, the future American settlement founder came to Toynbee Hall settlement in London carrying a letter of introduction from Canon Fremantle. She had high expectations that whatever challenges concerning the life of the poor were in store for her, she would at least know something at firsthand about how to respond to their needs. Addams felt that she had finally finished her "preparation for life" and was ready for the next stage (Davis, 2000, p. 49).

By the next January, Addams and Starr had located an old run-down mansion in a poor neighborhood on Chicago's West Side. The neighborhood was home to newly arrived Italian, Polish, German, Russian, and Bohemian immigrants. At that time, the Italian community was the largest in the neighborhood. When Addams and Starr first moved into Hull House, they had vague notions of becoming "good neighbors" to the poor around them, as well as studying the conditions in which they lived. As present-day social workers might observe, this idea of "meeting the client where he or she is" was not a bad idea. As Addams and her friend studied the conditions in which their new neighbors lived, they began to create a specific agenda of both services and reform. What they saw helped them to understand that exploitation of these newcomers from southern and eastern Europe, poor employment conditions and low wages, a lack of educational opportunities, substandard housing, and an inefficient city government (rather than personal deficiencies of the immigrants) were the major factors that led to the poverty of the area and called for specific responses (Popple & Leighninger, 2005).

Following the Toynbee House model of sharing their knowledge of arts and literature with members of the community, the two women began their work by inviting their new neighbors to visit the settlement to hear George Eliot's *Romola* read aloud in Italian and to see Addams' slides of Florentine art. As Allen Davis, one of Addams' biographers, notes, while some of the visitors may have appreciated the lecture and the novel, "more probably they were baffled by these two cultured ladies and their big house." One bewildered visitor called it the "strangest thing he had met in his experience" (Davis, 2000, pp. 67).

However, soon more neighbors came because they needed a welcoming place in this overcrowded neighborhood to simply sit and talk with their friends. Before long they were arriving at Hull House in great numbers, accompanied by their children. Addams and Starr's genius was to meet the needs of people in their adopted community in concrete ways, such as creating a nursery and a kindergarten. Responding to the need of the moment, they set the path toward a new kind of help. Women and men with similar goals came to live at Hull House in order to help carry out its work (Addams, 1910/1960; Davis, 2000, pp. 67–68, 75–81).

As they continued to observe the situation of their neighbors and the poverty of the area, the two Hull House founders began to create a specific agenda for reform. In addition to the nursery and kindergarten, they developed a club for working girls, a free labor bureau for both men and women, meeting spaces for neighborhood political groups, and a visiting nurse service. In addition, in a move that seems particularly refreshing in the context of today's frequent outbreaks of hysteria over the surge of Hispanic immigration to the United States, Addams and her cohorts created a Labor Museum at Hull House. This was a place where immigrants demonstrated their skills at spinning, making clothing, building furniture, and weaving baskets. The many outside visitors to Hull House were impressed by this "living" museum. But perhaps its greatest contribution was the pride instilled in immigrant children when they saw their parents in a situation in which they were recognized for their skills, rather than their poverty and difficulties in adjusting to a new land (Addams, 1910/1960; Popple & Leighninger, 2005).

Addams and her Hull House colleagues soon turned to reforms in the neighborhood itself. Noting the lack of vital services provided by the city, Addams lobbied Chicago's city officials for sanitary and housing reforms. Appalled by the trash piled up in streets and alleys, Addams became a city garbage inspector. She and her colleagues supported labor union activity and set up the Immigrants' Protective League in an attempt to fight the pervasive discrimination in employment and other exploitation of the newcomers (Addams, 1910/1960; Davis, 1973).

In a move that made Addams and her colleagues contributors to the developing field of sociology, Hull House also undertook an active program of research. The settlement's residents surveyed conditions in workplaces and tenement houses. They publicized their findings widely, attempting to create an atmosphere that would be conducive to governmental and legislative reform (Popple & Leighninger, 2005).

Following the Hull House example, a number of settlements were established in other American cities, such as New York City's Henry Street Settlement and Boston's South End House. Graham Taylor, a Dutch Reformed Church minister, founded the second settlement house in Chicago, the Chicago Commons. The Commons was located in an Irish-German-Scandinavian community. Taylor's wife and children joined him at the Commons, becoming the first American family to live in an American settlement. While most settlements were established in White neighborhoods, settlements were also developed by African Americans in African American areas. Lugenia Burns Hope started a settlement in Atlanta, Georgia. Both of Hope's parents came from racially mixed marriages. When her father died, Hope, as the oldest of seven, had to drop out of high school to become the family breadwinner. After working as a bookkeeper and a dressmaker, she took a position as a secretary in a charity organization called the Board of Directors of Kings Daughters. Burns was the first African American in this job. In 1897, Burns married John Hope, a college classics professor. The couple moved to Atlanta, where John became the president of what would become Morehouse College. In 1908, Lugenia Burns Hope led a group of women in establishing the Neighborhood Union. This was the first women's social welfare organization for African Americans in Atlanta. Through the Union, the women hoped to improve "the standard of living in the community and to make the West Side of Atlanta a better place to raise our children." By 1914, the Union had established branches throughout the city (Popple & Leighninger, 2005, p. 77).

A broad social movement in the United States, often labeled the Progressive Era, developed in the early 1900s and climaxed in the 1912 election of Theodore Roosevelt. As a Republican, Roosevelt had served as vice president under William McKinley and as president after McKinley's assassination in 1901. He served a second term in 1904 to 1908, and hoped his successor, William Taft, would carry out a series of reforms, Roosevelt had in fact left a lengthy "reform agenda" for the incoming president. However, Taft did not live up to Roosevelt's expectations. When Taft planned to run again in 1912, Roosevelt decided that he would also run for president, this time under the banner of a new party, called the Progressive Party.

Progressivism was a period of social and economic reform that began in America at the beginning of the twentieth century. According to historian Richard Hofstadter, a previous period of agrarian discontent "was enlarged and redirected by the growing enthusiasm of middle-class people for social and economic reform." This was not a cohesive movement, but a gathering of many impulses and suggestions for change. The movement was not confined to the Progressive Party, but affected all the various political parties and "the whole tone of American political life" (Hofstadter, 1955, pp. 133–135).

The movement took place during a rapid transition from the conditions of an agrarian society to those of modern urban life. Another stimulus for reform was the increasing heterogeneity in American society, caused in large part from the major migration of Europeans, mostly of peasant stock, whose traditions, religions, and languages seemed to make easy assimilation impossible. As Hofstadter (1955) notes in his classic book, *The Age of Reform:*

> In many ways the struggles of the Protestant Era were influenced by the conflict between the two codes elaborated on one side by the highly moral leaders of Protestant social reform and on the other by the bosses, political professionals, and immigrant masses. (p. 9)

Hofstadter draws a picture of a movement with much complexity, which combined desires to maintain some of the traditional values of agrarian life with the preservation of individual opportunity and personal entrepreneurship. These desires often clashed with the interests of political professionals, immigrant masses, and political bosses.

Absorbing at least part of the earlier Populist movement, Progressives championed and were able to enact laws that regulated the working conditions of women and children, improved working conditions in industry, set up community housing codes, limited patronage in the civil service system on the local and federal levels, established prohibition in various localities, regulated the reserve requirements of banks (the Depression of the 1930s was not the only time of bank failures), improved sewage and garbage disposal systems in many local communities, and restricted prostitution on the local level. There were also many attempts to pass federal laws to restrict immigration (just like today) and at both the national and local level, controls were put on people who hired the newcomers (Hofstadter, 1955, pp. 8–9, 181–184).

Many social workers were active in the Progressive Movement. Jane Addams and other settlement workers were particularly involved. In promoting better working conditions for young people, Addams noted how increasing industrialism had "gathered together multitudes of eager young creatures" from every part of the earth to serve as a labor supply "for the countless factories and workshops, upon which the present industrial city is based." In her first Christmas at Hull House, Addams offered Christmas candy to "a number of little girls [who] refused to take the candy," saying simply that they worked in a candy factory, and "could not bear the sight of it." This led to an investigation of child labor by Florence Kelley, a resident of Hull House. One result of the investigation was the first factory law in Illinois, which regulated the sanitary conditions of these factories and set 14 as the age at which children could be employed (Addams, 1910/1960, pp. 148–150).

Addams and other settlement reformers, as well as Charity Organization workers, also railed against the evils of "gin joints" and prostitution. For these reformers, the problems of prostitution were not just the rise of illegitimacy, the spread of venereal disease, and the destruction of families. They also included the use of a "white slave trade" to ensnare innocent young women. Likewise, establishments that sold alcohol helped fathers avoid the responsibility of supporting their wives and children (Davis, 1973).

Based on her involvement in issues such as child labor, prostitution, and other social problems, Addams joined the Progressive Party. She felt the goals and actions of the party seemed to be a "legitimate way . . . to bring social justice to America." Addams seconded the nomination of Theodore Roosevelt at the Progressive Party convention of 1912 (Davis, 1973).

Addams and at least some others in the settlement movement were concerned about justice and opportunity for African Americans. Addams was one of the founders of the National Association for the Advancement of Colored People (NAACP) and not only attended a conference of the National Association of Colored Women in Chicago, but also invited the delegates to Hull House for lunch. By 1910, there were 10 settlements around the country that specifically served African Americans, and at least a few more that reported having a mixed clientele (Davis, 1973; Popple & Leighninger, 2005; Trattner, 1999).

Amidst the ferment of social reform in the early 1900s, some social work leaders were turning their attention to the development of formal education in the field. By 1910, social work, as it was coming to be called, boasted five professional training schools. As early as 1897, Mary Richmond, who directed the Baltimore Charity Organization Society, had urged the establishment of formal training in social work. A leader in the charity organization movement, Richmond was interested in research and in establishing a "scientific" foundation for social work practice. It was time, she felt, "to get educated young men and women to make a life vocation of charity organization work" (Popple & Leighninger, 2005; Richmond, 2000).

Following calls for formal training by Mary Richmond and other COS leaders, the New York Charity Organization Society responded by establishing the New York Summer School of Applied Philanthropy in New York City in 1898. This initial series of courses for charity workers soon became a full-fledged school of social work (now the prestigious Columbia School of Social Work). In 1895, Graham Taylor, founder of the Chicago Commons settlement, launched a series of lectures at the Commons. The series grew into an institute, with courses offered through the University of Chicago's extension program. In 1908, the program became the free-standing Chicago School of Civics and Philanthropy. This was the start of today's well-known School of Social Service Administration at the University of Chicago (Leighninger, 2000).

Other schools quickly followed, including the psychiatrically oriented Smith College School for Social Work (which grew out of an early training program to prepare social workers to help patients at a state mental hospital in Boston), the Boston School for Social Workers (later housed in Simmons College), the St. Louis School of Philanthropy (which became part of the University of Missouri), and the Pennsylvania School for Social Service (Lubove, 1969).

African American social workers generally found little acceptance in the field. This led to the development of their own social agencies and training schools. George Haynes, a notable African American social worker, received a BA at Fisk University in 1903, an MA at Yale, and became a secretary of the Colored Men's Department of the International Committee of the YMCA. After becoming the first African American graduate of the New York School of Philanthropy, he helped form the National Urban League. In a creative effort to provide training for Black social workers, who would then help staff the League, Haynes set up a program at Fisk in which social science students would do field work at the League offices (Popple & Leighninger, 2005).

As social work education programs expanded, a desire to share ideas and deal with common problems led to the creation of the American Association of Schools of Social Work in 1919. These schools varied in their structure; some were undergraduate programs, others graduate schools, some tied to social work agencies, and others affiliated with universities. A movement to standardize schools in the 1930s, to promote the master's degree as the only qualifying degree for social work practice, led to a restriction of membership in the organization to schools that offered at least 1 year of graduate training and followed prescribed guidelines regarding course content (Leighninger, 2000).

Edith Abbott and Sophonisba Breckinridge were major figures in the establishment of the University of Chicago's School of Social Administration—a prestigious school that focused on education for both administration as well as casework practice in the field of public welfare. Edith's sister, Grace Abbott, had a more activist bent, and went to Washington, DC, in 1917 to head the U.S. Children's Bureau. The Bureau had been created to administer the first child labor law (Leighninger, 2000).

By the 1920s, charity workers, the directors and residents of settlement houses, social work educators, and "policy people" such as Grace Abbott were beginning to come together under the broad umbrella of the term *social work*. At the same time, this new entity was developing an increased sense of professionalization. Two important figures helped influence the move toward professionalism, Abraham Flexner and Porter Lee.

Flexner was the assistant secretary of the General Education Board of New York City. In 1915, the National Conference of Charities and Correction invited him to talk about social work's status as a new profession. The Conference had been organized in the 1880s by the various state charitable institutions serving the mentally ill, orphans, and the like; by the turn of the century, charity and settlement workers had also joined the group. Today, nearly every article or book about social work professionalism begins with a reference to this famous speech. At the time, Flexner was widely regarded as an authority on graduate professional education. His title "Is Social Work a Profession?" posed a major question for the field, and his listeners no doubt waited on the edge of their seats for his answer (Flexner, 1915, as cited in Leighninger, 2000).

To their dismay, Flexner's answer was no. His chilling words were:

> Is social work a profession in the ... strict sense of the term? ... I have made the point that all the established and recognized professions have definite and specific ends.... This is not true of social work. It appears not so much a defined field as an aspect of work in many fields. (pp. 37–39, pp. 43–46)

Flexner went on to explain that to "make a profession in the genuine sense," certain objective standards had to be formulated. The group's activities must be limited to those reflecting these standards. The activities should be "intellectual in character," based on "the laboratory and the seminar." He also assured them that professions were also "definitely practical." He saw social work falling short, however, not only in intellectual preparation but in the vagueness and "lack of specificity in aim." What was to be made of this amorphous group working in so many fields and types of organizations? The work called for "well-informed, well-balanced, tactful, judicious, sympathetic, and resourceful people" rather than those with a definite kind of technical skill. But, he reassured the group, social work was a needed endeavor. All that mattered was a "professional spirit," a humanitarian and spiritual approach, and unselfish devotion (Flexner, 1915, as cited in Leighninger, 2000, pp. 39–47).

Many in Flexner's audience were no doubt greatly disappointed in this assessment of their professional status. Yet, others took his words as a challenge. As they heeded his observations about the need for systematic technique and specialized education based on scientific knowledge, some felt that the "scientific charity" approach had been vindicated and that social work should turn away from its reform activities. "Scientific charity" was reinventing itself as social casework. Social reform was already becoming suspect in the more conservative and disillusioned years following World War I (Ehrenreich, 1985; Lubove, 1969).

The field's aspirations toward professionalism were also encouraged by another famous speech, this time by a social work academic. Porter Lee, director of the New York School of Social Work, addressed the National Conference of Social Work (a telling name change for the National Conference of Charities and Corrections) in 1929. In his presidential address, "Lee praised the achievements of pioneers in the field of social welfare, and heralded a new period about to unfold." Lee told the audience about the transition from "cause" to "function" in a modern society. Zeal would now give way to training and intelligence, and "sacrifice and flaming spirits" to methods and standards. Social work was changing from social reform to the organized provision of social casework and other help to individuals with problems (Leighninger, 1987, pp. 7–8).

Lee's address was no doubt disappointing to some of his listeners. Drawn to the field of Jane Addams and other prominent reformers, many were still eager to take up their role as bearers of a social conscience. But others were excited about the new theories of psychotherapy that had begun to filter into the profession, and the promise of a psychiatric social work. Perhaps social workers would finally find a new dignity as members of a skilled and legitimate profession (Leighninger, 1987).

This increased interest in professionalism helped fuel more consciously professional organizations in social work alongside broader groups such as the National Conference of Charities and Corrections. The American Association of Social Workers was founded in 1921. This was a broad organization that included social caseworkers in a variety of fields of practice, although it tended to exclude settlement and group workers, as they often lacked the formal specialized training required for membership. The 1920s brought an expansion of the kinds of settings in which social work was carried out. Many now worked in private family agencies, as most charity organizations were coming to be called. A new type of practice, social work with groups, was developing within settlement houses and the YMCA/YWCA. Social workers also staffed the Home Service Program created by the Red Cross soon after World War I. This program marked the beginnings of rural social work, providing services to the families of servicemen and disaster victims in small towns and rural areas as well as cities. However, the private social agency was still the major setting for social work practice (Popple & Leighninger, 2005).

All this was to be changed after the stock market crash of 1929 and the onset of the Great Depression. As the Depression spread, social workers were often the first to view its effects. In the various agencies and organizations where they worked, they encountered increasing numbers of the unemployed. Their clients were no longer just the traditional poor, but also growing numbers of working- and middle-class families. Gradually, as they looked at clients much like themselves, many social workers began to shift their perspective from a focus on individual defects back to an appreciation of the economic and social conditions causing dependency. Caseworkers had become interested in Freudian and other psychologically focused ideas in the 1920s and early 1930s; these ideas now seemed less salient in responding to widespread economic and social disaster (Popple & Leighninger, 2005).

President Hoover was slow to respond to the growing catastrophe, and social workers were among the earliest groups calling for a federal response to the problems of widespread unemployment. They testified in congressional hearings on relief and helped to draft social welfare legislation. Most of them supported President Franklin Roosevelt's creation of a federally funded relief program and the subsequent development of unemployment insurance and a Social Security system that was created to deal with the financial needs of the elderly, dependent children, and those with physical disabilities. President Roosevelt's emergency relief program was headed by social worker Harry Hopkins, and the public assistance segment was directed by another social worker, Jane Hoey (Popple & Leighninger, 2005).

Hoey had received her social work degree at the New York School of Social Work in 1916, and then worked in a variety of health and public welfare jobs in New York City. She had been Hopkins' assistant when he was secretary of the New York Board of Child Welfare. Hoey brought to this new position a sound knowledge of state and local government and a commitment to public social work. The new Bureau of Public Assistance was put in charge of developing congressionally mandated programs of federal aid for the poor. Among these were the dependent children of single mothers that earlier social reformers had tried to attend to. Hoey began her work with a staff of three: a small group, but eager to carry out the new and exciting ideas being generated in New Deal Washington. Hoey's task was to guide states in developing their own systems for administering these jointly funded programs. Some states, particularly in the South, had already developed child welfare programs, but many were starting from scratch (Coll, 1980; Popple & Leighninger, 2005).

Hoey promoted the use of professionally trained social workers in child welfare work on both the state and federal levels—not a widespread practice at the time. She fought vigorously against the attempts of many states to discriminate against African Americans and other minorities in providing welfare grants. She could be adamant in her cause to get important help to mothers and children. One state official complained strongly to the head of the Social Security Board: "That red-headed devil of yours is in my office. She's telling me certain things that I need to do. Do I have to?" "Yes sir," was the unwelcome answer. While Hoey was not always successful in her attempts to improve social welfare, she left her mark by bringing professionalism to most state welfare departments, and to the federal agency (Leighninger, 2000; Popple & Leighninger, 2005).

A radical social work movement also developed in the Depression Era. Socialist and Communist groups formed among Americans from various economic and political backgrounds. This version of social work was called the Rank and File Movement. The movement stemmed largely from the organization of low-paid and over-worked public relief workers, case aides, and clerical workers in Chicago, New York, and other cities into protective associations or unions to promote improved working conditions and salaries. The movement was soon joined by professionally trained social workers that were forming groups that focused on analyzing social problems and dealing with issues of unemployment from a social work perspective. Bertha Capen Reynolds, a well-known psychiatric social worker and the associate dean of the Smith College School of Social Work, was an important member of the Rank and File Movement. She credited her social activism to the effects of a keynote speech at the 1934 National Conference of Social Work in which Mary Van Kleeck of the Russell Sage Foundation spoke of the inherent conflict "between capital and labor" and the fact that social workers were often caught upholding the status quo (Leighninger, 1987; Popple & Leighninger, 2005).

In the early 1940s, a growing national backlash against New Deal reforms, as well as the escalation of war in Europe and Asia, contributed not only to the downfall of the Rank and File Movement, but also to social work's renewed interest in individual treatment. Many social workers came to view the provision of relief as the responsibility of public, rather than private agencies. Now, they felt, social workers could return to the more personal aspects of family and individual difficulties. They were free to deal with these issues in private family and children's agencies, expanding their services to a middle-class clientele. Sigmund Freud's theories had a tremendous appeal, and many social work educators incorporated them in their teachings (which this author experienced firsthand in her graduate education at the Syracuse University School of Social Work as late as the mid-1960s; Popple & Leighninger, 2005).

The 1950s brought new developments in social work professional and educational organizations, developments that reflected the wide variety of people now coming into social work education and practice as well as an impulse toward coordination within this large and varied profession. In 1955, five specialist social work organizations merged with the American Association of Social Workers to create a single voice for the profession: the NASW. This new group sought to solidify and strengthen social work's identity and recognition as a profession, to increase the group's impact on national social policy, and to attend to basic professional issues such as ensuring ethical practice, defining the skills and scope of social work practice, and helping to plan for adequate and appropriate staffing of social work agencies (Leighninger, 1987; Popple & Leighninger, 2005).

Shortly thereafter, the Council on Social Work Education grew out of a merger of the American Association of Schools of Social Work, which was made up of graduate schools only, and an organization of schools offering social work programs at the baccalaureate level. The latter, the National Association of Schools of Social Service Administration, was made up largely of programs in large state universities and some smaller institutions that saw their mission as preparing people to work in the new public social services first developed during the Depression. The group argued that social work's stress on graduate education as the only pathway into the profession was "elitist and impractical in a time of growing staffing needs" in the field (Leighninger, 1987).

Social work has never been a dull profession. In the 1960s, President John F. Kennedy brought a new conviction to creating a more equitable society. Inspired in part by influential books like Michael Harrington's *The Other America, Poverty in the United States*, poverty was "rediscovered" and the federal government tried anew to fashion a broad response to the problems of the poor. The major approach of the Kennedy administration was embodied in amendments to the Social Security Acts that provided increased federal funding to the states to improve and enlarge their services to recipients of public assistance. These services included intensive social services, and greatly increased the number of social workers in public welfare settings. The law promoted the use of workers with master's degrees in social work, and money was allocated to public welfare departments to send employees to graduate schools of social work. Kennedy also promoted a sense of personal contribution to others by establishing the Peace Corps program to send Americans, particularly young people, to other countries to help poor communities (Patterson, 1994; Popple & Leighninger, 2005).

After Kennedy's assassination, President Lyndon Johnson took over the war on poverty under the banner of the Great Society. Johnson significantly enlarged the federal partnership in American social welfare, including federal and state agencies as well as private institutions in administering the system. The Work Incentive Program (WIN to its supporters, WIP to its critics), funded training programs and child care for women on welfare. This was in many ways a punitive welfare reform, since clients could be cut off from AFDC if they refused to enroll in job training or to take any job offered. The program marked an important shift from the original Aid to Dependent Children system, which aimed to help mothers care for their children at home. WIN and subsequent welfare reform programs have failed to provide sufficient, good-quality child care programs, training for reasonably paid jobs, and other supports to make this type of approach a realistic response to poverty among women and children (Patterson, 1994).

Johnson also inherited a tumultuous situation in which the continued discrimination of African Americans had boiled over into racial tensions, boycotts, riots, and the development of a very effective civil rights movement. The Reverend Martin Luther King and "ordinary people" like Rosa Parks were joined by many White Americans in fighting institutionalized and ingrained prejudice. Under Johnson's leadership, Congress passed the 1965 Civil Rights Act (Rouse, 1989).

By the end of President Johnson's term in office, the country's mood had begun to shift to the right. In 1968, Republicans put Richard Nixon in the White House. Although he had been critical of Johnson's Great Society programs, he continued to expand the federal partnership in social welfare. According to historian James T. Patterson, Nixon sought welfare reform largely because northern governors were crying out for federal help in dealing with a rise in child welfare caseloads. In 1969, Nixon called for a Family Assistance Plan (FAP) that would guarantee all families with children a minimum of $500 per adult and $300 per child a year. Responding to the age-old concerns about individual responsibility for poverty, the program "promised especially to sustain the incentive to work and supplant welfare dependency." Critics quickly weighed in. They included social workers and advocates for the welfare poor organized under the banner of the National Welfare Rights Organization (NWRO). The advocacy group was set up by George Wiley, an African American professor of chemistry at Syracuse University. NWRO and other groups expressed concern about the workfare aspects of the program. Adult recipients (except for the disabled, aged, and mothers of preschool children) had to accept "suitable" training or work in order to maintain their grants. Yet, day care and other services were insufficient to support recipients and their families (Patterson, 1994).

President Ronald Reagan's administration built on and accelerated the conservative trend in social policy that began in Nixon's second term and was continued under Presidents Gerald Ford and Jimmy Carter. In the decade before Reagan's election, the economy had stagnated, inflation rates were high, and both taxes and the federal deficit were rising. Reagan's agenda included balancing the federal budget (through cuts in "wasteful government spending"), cutting taxes, and reducing government regulation. He also sought to diminish the federal government's role in supporting social welfare programs. The responsibility for many health and human services should revert back to the state and local level, were they had been lodged before the New Deal. The Omnibus Budget Reconciliation Acts of the early 1980s reduced support for programs such as Aid for Dependent Children, food stamps, unemployment insurance, and low income housing. Reagan's tax legislation, which cut taxes for the rich, ironically also resulted in raising taxes for the working poor (Popple & Leighninger, 2005; Trattner, 1999).

The Reagan years were challenging times for many social workers and their organizations. Ronald Reagan was a popular president, with public approval ratings higher than any president since Franklin Delano Roosevelt. As much as the profession tried to protect public programs for the disadvantaged, it often seemed like an uphill battle. The NASW frequently attacked the conservative positions of the Reagan administration and promoted national health insurance and other social reforms. NASW joined with other advocacy groups such as the Children's Defense Fund, and formed a political action arm, the Political Action Committee for Candidate Election, or PACE, which is still active today. PACE was set up to back candidates who supported social reforms (Katz, 1986).

Reagan's successor, George H. W. Bush, maintained much of Reagan's health and welfare agenda. Due to the large budget deficits he inherited from Reagan, it was difficult to fund new federal programs, especially since Bush had also pledged not to raise taxes. Bush did make two contributions that advanced social welfare: the enactment of the Child Care and Development Block Grant, which provided funding to local child care providers for staff training, administration, and direct care; and the enactment of the Americans with Disabilities Act. This important piece of legislation required employers to make "reasonable accommodations" for people with disabilities. It also made it illegal to discriminate against those with disabilities in areas such as employment, housing, and education (Popple & Leighninger, 2005; Trattner, 1999).

The election of Bill Clinton brought the Democratic Party back to the Presidential Office in 1992. However, Clinton shared Bush and Reagan's aversion to long-term and costly public assistance. While he came from a more modest background than Reagan and Bush, and had a personal style that enabled him to reach out to disadvantaged people and minorities, Clinton was wary of "long-term, costly assistance" to the poor. He promised to "scrap the current welfare system and make welfare a second chance" rather than a way of life. Accordingly, his major social welfare reform was the creation and passage of the Personal Responsibility and Work Opportunities Act (PRWOA). This replaced the AFDC entitlement with a block grant, called Temporary Assistance to Needy Families (TANF). Under TANF, people were not "entitled" to welfare. Instead, in the tradition of WIN and FAP, recipients had to participate in work activities and families were limited to a total of 5 years of assistance in a lifetime (Lindhorst & Leighninger, 2003; Popple & Leighninger, 2005).

Welfare reform under Clinton did not alleviate the problems of poverty. Many of the poor were simply moved from "welfare poverty" into "employment poverty." Former recipients often had a lower financial status as workers than they had had under public welfare, and few of their jobs provided good benefits, such as health insurance. Over half of those who left the welfare rolls for employment in 1999 still had jobs below the poverty level (Popple & Leighninger, 2005).

The current presidency of George W. Bush has brought back a more conservative approach to social issues and social welfare. Bush has used the argument that social welfare "is the historic mission of the churches" as a justification for cutting back on government programs. Under his "faith-based initiative," Bush proposed that religious groups should have the right to contract with federal agencies and to use federal dollars for a variety of services for people in need. By 2006, under the auspices of this initiative, millions of dollars in taxpayer funds have gone to groups that support the president's agenda on abortion and similar issues (Popple & Leighninger, 2005).

Social welfare has come a long way from its beginnings in early religious responses to the problems of poverty, famine, sickness, disability, community break-downs, and other vicissitudes of life. Social work as a profession has slowly emerged from the helping efforts of religious orders, good Samaritans, and the like. While some themes and structures have been repeated through the centuries, new ideas and variations on older approaches continue to emerge. By understanding the history of social welfare and social work, we can endeavor to put current situations into context and to think carefully about the results—intended and unintended—of our programs and actions.

REFERENCES

Addams, J. (1960). The spirit of youth in the city streets. In C. Lasch (Ed.), *The social thought of Jane Addams*. Indianapolis, IN: Bobbs-Merrill. (Original work published 1910)

Addams, J. (1960). *Twenty years at Hull House*. New York: Signet. (Reprinted from Phillips Publishing, 1910)

Al-Krenawi, A., & Graham, J. R. (2000). Islamic theology and prayer: Relevance for social work practice. *International Social Work*, *43*(3), 289–304.

Augustine, S. E. B. (2002, Spring). Islam and the peoples of the book: A social work perspective. *New Social Worker*, 18–20.

Beatty, B. R. (1986). *Josephine Shaw Lowell.* In W. Trattner (Ed.), *Biographical dictionary of social welfare in America* (pp. 511–515). Westport, CT: Greenwood Press.

Canda, E., & Furman, L. (1999). *Spiritual diversity in social work practice: The art of helping.* New York: Free Press.

Coll, B. D. (1969). *Perspectives in public welfare: A history.* Washington, DC: U.S. Government Printing Office, U.S. Department of Health, Education, and Welfare, Social and Rehabilitation Services.

Coll, B. D. (1980). Jane Margueretta Hoey. In B. Sicherman & C. H. Green (Eds.), *Notable American women: The modern period* (pp. 341–343). Cambridge, MA: Belknap Press.

Crenson, M. A. (1998). *Building the invisible orphanage.* Cambridge, MA: Harvard University Press.

Davis, A. F. (2000). *The life and legend of Jane Addams.* Chicago: Ivan R. Dee Press.

Day, P. J. (2000). *A new history of social welfare* (3rd ed.). Boston: Allyn & Bacon.

Dolgoff, R., & Feldstein, D. (1998). *Understanding social welfare* (5th ed.). Boston: Allyn & Bacon.

Ehrenreich, J. H. (1985). *The altruistic imagination: A history of social work and social policy in the United States.* Ithaca, NY: Cornell University Press.

Flexner, A. (1915). Is social work a profession? Proceedings of the National Conference of Charities and Correction. In L. Leighninger (Ed.), *Creating a new profession* (pp. 43–44). Alexandria, VA: Council on Social Work Education.

Herlihy, D. (1997). *The black death and the transformation of the west.* Cambridge, MA: Harvard University Press.

Hofstadter, R. (1955). *The age of reform.* New York: Vintage Books.

Jordan, W. C. (2001). *Europe in the high middle ages.* New York: Viking/Penguin.

Katz, M. B. (1986). *In the shadow of the poorhouse: A social history of welfare in America.* New York: Basic Books.

Leighninger, L. (1987). *Social work: Search for identity.* Westport, CT: Greenwood Press.

Leighninger, L. (2000). *Creating a new profession: The beginnings of social work education in the United States.* Alexandria, VA: Council on Social Work Education.

Lindhorst, T., & Leighninger, L. (2003). "Ending welfare as we know it" in 1960: Louisiana's suitable home law. *Social Service Review*, *27*, 564–584.

Lowenberg, F. M. (2001). *From charity to social justice: The emergence of communal institutions for the support of the poor in ancient Judaism.* New Brunswick, NJ: Transaction.

Lubove, R. (1969). *The professional altruist: The emergence of social work as a career, 1880–1930.* New York: Atheneum.

Macarov, D. (1978). *The design of social welfare.* New York: Holt, Rinehart and Winston.

Marx, J. D. (2004). *Social work: The American partnership.* Boston: Allyn & Bacon.

Muncy, R. (1991). *Creating a female dominion in American reform, 1890–1935.* New York: Oxford University Press.

Patterson, J. (1994). *America's struggle against poverty, 1900–1994.* Cambridge, MA: Harvard University Press.

Polanyi, K. (1976). "Speenhamland, 1795." In N. Gilbert & H. Specht (Eds.), *The emergence of social welfare and social work* (pp. 48–49). Itasca, IL: Peacock.

Popple, P. R., & Leighninger, L. (2005). *Social work, social welfare, and American society* (6th ed.). Boston: Allyn & Bacon.

Richmond, M. (2000). The need of a training school in applied philanthropy. In L. Leighninger (Ed.), *Creating a new profession* (pp. 7–10). Alexandria, VA: Council on Social Work Education.

Roosevelt named, shows emotion. (1912, August 8). *New York Times*, 1–3.

Rouse, J. A. (1989). *Lugenia Burns Hope: Black southern reformer*. Athens, GA: University of Georgia Press.

Sapiro, V. (1990). The gender basis of American social policy. In L. Gordon (Ed.), *Women, the state, and welfare* (p. 37). Madison, WI: University of Wisconsin Press.

Stillman, N. A. (1975). Charity and social service in medieval Islam. *Societas—A Review of Social History*, *5*, 105–115.

Trattner, W. A. (1999). *From poor law to welfare state: A history of social welfare in America* (6th ed.). New York: Free Press.

Ziliak, S. T. (2005). Poor law (United States). In J. M. Herrick & P. H. Stuart (Eds.), *Encyclopedia of social welfare history in North America* (p. 274). Thousand Oaks, CA: Sage.

Chapter 2

EDUCATING FOR SOCIAL WORK

Julia M. Watkins and Jessica Holmes

More than a century has passed since social work first emerged as both a profession and as a discipline. What began as an unorganized and undefined community developed into a distinct field with its own philosophy, knowledge base, and competencies. This development is a truly remarkable one that was accomplished in large part due to the early recognition of the need for education as a means for defining, validating, and carrying social work forward as a discipline.

Social work education has grown considerably since its beginnings. There are currently three levels of education in social work: baccalaureate, master's, and doctoral. The Council on Social Work Education (CSWE), the sole accrediting body for social work baccalaureate and master's programs, now accredits the 645 social work programs that graduated over 30,000 social work students in 2006 (see Figure 2.1). In that same year, the 69 doctoral social work programs (in the United States) graduated 293 students (Group for the Advancement of Doctoral Education [GADE], n.d.; CSWE, 2007). Social work education is currently represented by more than 8,000 faculty, with approximately 63.9% of full-time female and 24.5% of full-time racial or ethnic minorities (from category "Total Minorities," not including categories "Multiple Race/Ethnicity" or "Foreign"; CSWE, 2007). The social work field has grown, not just in the number of programs, faculty, and students, but also in quality—the training and qualifications of faculty and the breadth and depth of curriculum.

In preparing for the next century of social work, it is important to recall both the issues and successes of the past in social work education. Some of the challenges for social work education in the next century are similar to those faced by the early social work educators: the need to recruit qualified students and faculty and the need to promote understanding between social work programs, levels, and membership organizations. Other challenges are unique to this particular time: sustainability, accountability, and relevancy. Meeting these challenges requires recognition of the past, as well as collaboration and cooperation among all stakeholders in social work, in order to ensure continued growth and quality improvement.

NEED FOR TRAINED SOCIAL WORKERS

Although forms of social work were practiced for some time in the 1800s, near the turn of the nineteenth century, social work had moved beyond the point where simple apprenticeship was adequate—training and more formalized education in social work became imminently necessary (Leighninger, 2000; McCrea, 1911). In the United States, the demand for education first came from practitioners and the community as well as the philanthropic agencies

Figure 2.1 Number of baccalaureate and graduate social work programs by year 1980 to 2006. Data from *2006 Annual Survey of Social Work Programs: Research Brief,* by the Council on Social Work Education, 2007, Alexandria, VA: Author; *Statistics on Social Work Education in the United States: 1986–1987*, by J. Hidalgo, and E. C. Spaulding, 1987–1988, Washington, DC: Council on Social Work Education; *Statistics on Social Work Education in the United States: 1991–2002*, by T. Lennon, 1992–2004. Alexandria, VA: Council on Social Work Education; *Statistics on Social Work Education in the United States: 1980–1985*, by A. Rubin, 1981–1986, New York: Council on Social Work Education; *Statistics on Social Work Education in the United States: 1988–1990*, by E. C. Spaulding, 1989–1991, Alexandria, VA: Council on Social Work Education.

that employed social workers, then later from the government. Employers in the public and private sectors felt that their needs for training were disparate; these unreconciled differences resulted in the formation of two separate types of schools of social work (Kendall, 2002).

In the private sector, caseworkers and directors of social service organizations sought advanced training for practice specific to the work they were doing, including charity, social theory, and social service practice methods (Austin, 1997; Kendall, 2002; McCrea, 1911). In the late 1800s and early 1900s, philanthropic organizations began forming professional social work schools, which would eventually become graduate schools of social work, designed to meet the training needs of those workers (Kendall, 2002; Leighninger, 2000). These same graduate schools formed an accrediting organization, the American Association of Schools of Social Work (AASSW) that, in 1919, had 17 program members (Kendall, 2002).

In the public sector, a need arose to have trained social workers for the particular work and the growing number of public jobs in social service through the Social Security Administration and the Children's Bureau. The federal government determined that the schools of social work forged by the philanthropic organizations were not meeting their training needs and pressured public universities to begin social work programs focused on the public sector. Public universities formed these social work schools as undergraduate programs in social work or social welfare (Kendall, 2002) with the majority of the programs in rural areas (Stamm, 1972). These schools were organized under the National Association of Schools of Social Administration (NASSA), which also briefly served as an accrediting organization for programs in social work (Kendall, 2002).

The difference between the two types of schools—how they defined practice, training, and therefore curriculum for social work—caused increasing divisions in the field and continuous problems for social work students. The need to combine the two educational types into a single discipline for a comprehensive and united education was necessary for the survival of social work (Kendall, 2002). Social work education took nearly 50 years to consolidate and the continuing difficulties in reconciling the transition from baccalaureate to master's education in social work took even longer (Bernard, 1977). The consolidation of the two accrediting organizations and their programs was a slow process because both were concerned that the interests of their schools, students, and educational purposes would not be best represented in a combined education organization. The establishment of the Council on Social Work Education (CSWE) as the sole accrediting body for baccalaureate and master's social work programs helped solidify the unification (Austin, 1997; Kendall, 2002).

ACCREDITATION

The CSWE was established in 1952, formed from the accrediting organization of the graduate social work schools, AASSW, and the baccalaureate social work schools, NASSA (Austin, 1997; Kendall, 2002). At CSWE's inception, there were 59 graduate schools of social work and 19 undergraduate departments of social work (Kendall, 2002). CSWE was created to bring continuity to social work education while striving for and ensuring quality in schools of social work. CSWE does this, "by setting and maintaining national accreditation standards for baccalaureate and master's degree programs in social work, by promoting faculty development, and by advocating for social work education and research" (CSWE, 2006, p. 1). Priorities for CSWE in its early years included expanding graduate social work education, improving the quality of curriculum at all levels, recruiting academically well-prepared and committed students, recruiting teachers, and determining appropriate practice for different educational levels (Kendall, 1966).

The CSWE Commission on Accreditation (COA) is a semi-autonomous group that has the authority to make accreditation decisions based on a review of a program under the CSWE *Educational Policy and Accreditation Standards*. The COA is composed of social work faculty, deans, directors, and practitioners, as well as public members from outside the social work community. Members of the COA are nominated and appointed for 3-year terms by the president of CSWE (CSWE, 2004). The CSWE Office of Social Work Accreditation and Educational Excellence (OSWAEE) provides administrative support to the COA and the social work programs throughout the accreditation process, including arranging site visits to the programs, maintaining the accreditation database and web site, providing technical assistance to programs, reviewing program "self-studies," and arranging meetings. CSWE is recognized by the Council for Higher Education Accreditation (CHEA) as the sole accrediting body for social work education.

As of the June 2006 COA meeting, CSWE accredited 635 social work programs, including 179 graduate programs and 456 undergraduate programs, over eight times the number accredited in 1952. Figure 2.1 illustrates the continued trend of growth in social work baccalaureate and master's programs since 1980. The need for trained social workers has driven this growth in programs and the need for continued training has remained strong.

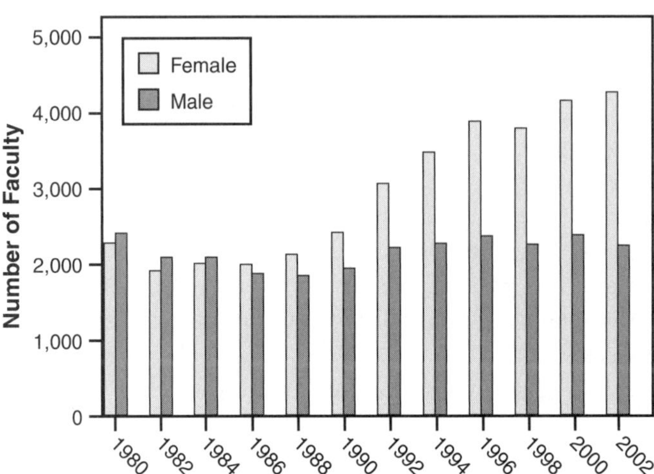

Figure 2.2 Social work faculty by gender (1980 to 2002). Data from Statistics on Social Work Education in the United States: 1980–1985, by A. Rubin, 1981–1986, New York: Council on Social Work Education; Statistics on Social Work Education in the United States: 1986–1987, by J. Hidalgo and E. C. Spaulding, 1987–1988, Washington, DC: Council on Social Work Education; Statistics on Social Work Education in the United States: 1988–1990, by E. C. Spaulding, 1989–1991, Alexandria, VA: Council on Social Work Education; Statistics on Social Work Education in the United States: 1991–2002, by T. Lennon, 1992–2004. Alexandria, VA: Council on Social Work Education. Reprinted with permission.

In fact, the U.S. Department of Labor cited social work as a field expected to "grow faster than average" (U.S. Department of Labor, 2006).

Social work education represents over 7,000 faculty, with over 65% female (Lennon, 2005). As indicated by Figure 2.2, female predominance in social work faculty is a relatively new development, in spite of the longtime predominance of women in the field of social work. Representation of women has not yet reached many areas of program administration, but groups such as the CSWE Volunteer Council on the Role and Status of Women in Social Work Education are working to call attention to and remedy remaining gaps. Racial and ethnic minorities comprise approximately 22% of social work faculty (Lennon, 2005). Increasing the representation of racial and ethnic minorities in social work is one of the priorities of work by the National Institute of Mental Health- and Substance Abuse and Mental Health Systems Administration-funded Minority Fellowship Program, which has been managed by CSWE for over 30 years, and a focus of the CSWE Volunteer Commission for Diversity and Social and Economic Justice.

PURPOSE OF SOCIAL WORK EDUCATION

There continue to be differences among schools of social work in terms of mission and goals for education at both the baccalaureate and master's levels, however, there is now a single accrediting body helping to define the basic knowledge and skills necessary in social work education. The first schools of social work seem to have depended more on the types of practice for which they were preparing students, rather than the overall purpose of preparing students for practice. This overall purpose for practice preparation is still the focus of both baccalaureate and master's social work programs. According to the CSWE *Educational Policy and Accreditation Standards* (2001):

> The purposes of social work education are to prepare competent and effective professionals, to develop social work knowledge, and to provide leadership in the development of service delivery systems. Social work education is grounded in the profession's history, purposes, and philosophy and is based on a body of knowledge, values, and skills. Social work education enables students to integrate the knowledge, values, and skills of the social work profession for competent practice. (p. 4)

The CSWE *Educational Policy and Accreditation Standards* (EPAS) is the basis for accreditation in social work at the baccalaureate and master's level. The EPAS (CSWE, 2001) "promotes academic excellence" and "specifies the curricular and educational context" (p. 2). The EPAS outlines not only the resources needed to operate a social work program (i.e., faculty, facilities), but also the specific content areas that must be included in the baccalaureate and master's program curriculum. The EPAS is written to maintain a balance between ensuring all social work graduates receive a particular education and allowing programs to innovate and specialize in the curriculum as pertains to their specific goals for the program and in the delivery methods for that education.

The EPAS is periodically reexamined (at least every 7 years) by the CSWE Commission on Curriculum and Educational Innovation (COCEI) and the COA (CSWE, 2001); the most recent iteration was approved by the CSWE board of directors in 2001. The commissions are composed of appointed members of the social work community including social work deans, directors, faculty members, and practitioners who contribute to the revision process by advising on the ever-changing educational environment, new developments in the field, as well as the underlying needs of students and the social work practice community.

In the 1950s, a group of private foundations and public offices funded a study for a comprehensive review of social work curriculum (Boehm, 1959). The resulting volumes, *Social Work Curriculum Study*, helped determine the necessary foundation of knowledge for social work graduates at the baccalaureate and master's level (Frumpkin & Lloyd, 1995). Subsequent reviews of the educational policy statement and accreditation standards have incorporated changes in the field and included emerging interests. Reviews have also adapted the structure of the policy statement to improve on the educational continuum (Austin, 1997) and to make the policy statement less prescriptive (Frumpkin & Lloyd, 1995). When the COCEI and the COA were tasked with reevaluating the EPAS for 2008, they were asked to study the educational policy and the current educational environment before developing and recommending changes. In the 2005 COCEI annual report to the CSWE board of directors, the commission mentions that the EPAS is still perceived as prescriptive and that the COCEI, in rewriting the educational policy, is interested in making it less so and more encouraging of innovation (Black, 2005). The commissions are currently rewriting the EPAS, which will be sent to the CSWE board of directors for approval in 2008.

Purposes of Baccalaureate Social Work Education

The baccalaureate degree in social work (BSW) is the first professional degree in social work. The main preparation goal for the BSW as stated in the EPAS is "generalist professional practice" (CSWE, 2001). The BSW usually includes 2 years of undergraduate education in liberal arts and 2 years in a social work major. Since the 1970s, the descriptions of BSW education purposes have been similar in the literature: preparation for practice, graduate study in social work, and exposure and recruitment of more students to the field of social work (Bernard, 1977; Frumpkin & Lloyd, 1995; Stamm, 1972; Witte, 1966). Recognition of the BSW as the first professional degree in social work was only fully realized in the 1970s. As indicated in a list of priorities for CSWE from the 1960s, many of the first years of CSWE were devoted to examining the social work continuum and attempting to determine what the purposes of education were at each level (Kendall, 1966).

In those early years of CSWE, baccalaureate social work education held an uncertain position. It was suggested that the social work education continuum would be 2 years at the undergraduate level and 2 years for the master's (Deasy, 1971; Kendall, 1966). For many years, however, the undergraduate-graduate continuum was not reconciled, rather curriculum at both levels overlapped and a baccalaureate degree in social work was not a prerequisite for master's education (Bernard, 1977; Witte, 1966). The tension in the relationship between master's and baccalaureate education is evidenced by a 1966 article by Ernest Witte, titled "The Purposes of Undergraduate Education for Social Welfare," which begins, "The title of this brief paper suggests that undergraduate education *has* acceptable purposes. A few years ago, the title might well have been phrased so as to raise a question as to whether this is so" (p. 53). Prior to the 1970s, baccalaureate programs in social work could hold membership in CSWE, but were not formally accredited (Bernard, 1977). In 1971, the CSWE finally recognized the bachelors in social work as the first practice degree and released recommendations for the baccalaureate curriculum (Kendall, 2002). After receiving approval from the U.S. Office of Education and the Council on Postsecondary Accreditation, the CSWE released standards for accreditation of baccalaureate programs in 1974 (Bernard, 1977).

The educational continuum was partially reconciled thereafter with the recognition of similarity in curriculum being taught in the baccalaureate-level advanced courses with curriculum in the master's foundation year (Frumpkin & Lloyd, 1995); recognition of the similarities in curriculum led to the emergence of "advanced standing" status. The other major change for baccalaureate social work education was the shift to field education as a component of curriculum. Previously, much of the field experience at the baccalaureate level had either been observational or included very few hours. The initial curriculum recommendations from the CSWE board of directors helped to make field experience a much larger part of the BSW program (Stamm, 1972). The EPAS now mandates a minimum of 400 hours in the field for baccalaureate social work students (CSWE, 2001).

Purposes of Master's in Social Work Education

A master's in social work prepares, "graduates for advanced professional practice in an area of concentration" (CSWE, 2001, p. 6). The goal of "advanced professional practice" remains constant to the original intentions of the philanthropic organizations that first developed the graduate schools of social work in the late 1800s (Bernard, 1977; Frumpkin & Lloyd, 1995). The master's program is typically 2 years in length with foundation and concentration level courses (time to degree is less for "advanced standing" students). Content for the foundation level of the master's programs is mandated through the EPAS, providing consistency across social work programs in what social work students learn before leaving the program. Master's programs have more flexibility in the concentration year, however, to determine the type of concentration and the curriculum to be used in meeting it. This degree of autonomy has allowed programs to dynamically reflect the changing scope, skill needs, and clientele of the profession through the concentrations and courses they provide in the second year.

While CSWE was focusing on the continuum from baccalaureate to master's education, changes were concurrently taking place with the educational structure beyond the master's degree. For many years, a third-year program was provided at some schools of social work for continued advanced practice training beyond the 2-year master's. However, as the number of doctorate programs grew, the third-year programs began to diminish (Frumpkin & Lloyd, 1995).

Purposes of Doctoral Education in Social Work

Doctoral social work preparation goals have been cited as preparation for leadership roles in administration and policy, more advanced and specialized practice, research and teaching (Bernard, 1977; Frumpkin & Lloyd, 1995). The doctoral degrees were at first split between the DSW and PhD, but over time the number of programs offering the DSW decreased and the PhD became the prevailing degree (Bolte, 1971). Doctoral programs in social work are not accredited; many doctoral program directors belong to the Group for the Advancement of Doctoral Education (GADE), which "provides a forum for sharing ideas and strategies and for strengthening members' efforts at enhancing doctoral education" (GADE, 2006). The GADE also publishes Quality Guidelines, which are recommendations for doctoral programs in social work as approved by the GADE membership. In 2006, there were 69 doctoral programs in social work in the United States, which graduated 293 students (CSWE, 2007).

Curriculum and Pedagogy

EPAS outlines the major components of social work curriculum and the content and structure for field education. EPAS states that, "the baccalaureate and master's levels of educational preparation are differentiated according to (a) conceptualization and design; (b) content; (c) program objectives; and (d) depth, breadth, and specificity of knowledge and skills" (CSWE, 2001, p. 6). EPAS specifies foundation level curriculum for baccalaureate and master's graduates and provides guidelines for advanced curriculum for master's graduates.

Baccalaureate social work education is based on a liberal arts foundation and provides content that includes the knowledge, skills, and values necessary for generalist social work practice. Both baccalaureate and master's graduates are expected to "demonstrate the capacity to meet the foundation objectives and objectives unique to the program" (CSWE, 2001, p. 7). The foundation level curriculum mandated for baccalaureate and master's students includes values and ethics, diversity, populations-at-risk, and social and economic justice, human behavior and the social environment, social welfare policy and services, social work practice, research, and field education (CSWE, 2001).

Master's education builds on the foundation of social work knowledge with advanced skills and knowledge for social work practice. Social work concentrations and specializations are taught in the second year of master's education. Schools of social work have the autonomy to determine the type of concentration and the curriculum in support of the concentration; EPAS only outlines, "frameworks and perspectives for concentration include fields of practice, problem areas, intervention methods, and practice contexts and perspectives" (CSWE, 2001, p. 6). The concentrations allow for a wide range of issues to be covered, from clinical practice to policy and administration.

Additionally, many infusion models have been used in social work curriculum. In the past, infusion models related to women and global social work have been encouraged by CSWE volunteer commissions and have been included as content areas in EPAS. For example, EPAS includes that its purposes are achieved by "Preparing social workers to recognize the global context of social work practice" (CSWE, 2001, p. 5). A more recent infusion effort has resulted from the John A. Hartford Foundation-funded National Center for Gerontological Social Work Education (Gero-Ed Center), which focuses on, and promotes, the infusion of gerontological social work training in social work curriculum, particularly in foundation content.

Although some of the original social work curriculum has changed since the early 1900s, field education has consistently remained a component of social work education. Field education has been an essential element of graduate social work education since its earliest articulation. Field education as observation, or as a short period of practice, was also commonly used at the baccalaureate level, until specific time mandates were issued by CSWE in 1974 (Bernard, 1977; Stamm, 1972). Field education is the connection between social work education—the knowledge, skills, and values that a social work student must learn—and social work practice, where a student must put the knowledge, skills, and values into practice. This connection in the educational process is critical to the development of competent social workers.

EDUCATION FOR PRACTICE

Throughout the growth of social work education, the relationship between social work practice and education has continued to be reciprocal, responding to the need to train social workers who are prepared for practice. This reciprocity has held true as social work developed a proprietary social work knowledge base and began building presence within the academy. The path of social work education is, in fact, a reflection of the growth and expansion of the entire social work field of practice. Specialization in practice has a corresponding specialization in education, evidenced by differentiation in social work graduate concentrations, dual-degree programs, certificate programs, and can be seen in curriculum and pedagogy. In 1977, Bernard cited specialization as a future trend, which was growing due to increasing complexity of practice and the expansion of fields of practice. The field of social work practice is continuing to diversify and specialize; the social work curriculum, concentrations, and specializations are diversifying and expanding concurrently to meet the changing and growing demand.

The necessity for reciprocity between education and practice is also built into EPAS. One way in which EPAS does this is by mandating an ongoing relationship between social work programs and the practice community. EPAS (CSWE, 2001) states, "Social work education remains vital, relevant, and progressive by pursuing exchanges with the practice community" (p. 6) and, "The program has ongoing exchanges with external constituencies that may include social work practitioners, social service recipients, advocacy groups, social service agencies, professional associations, regulatory agencies, the academic community, and the community at large" (p. 17). Field education also provides an exchange between education and practice and helps to establish long-term relationships between community organizations and the school. A third way that EPAS helps ensure reciprocity is by mandating that social work faculty teaching practice must have a master's in social work and 2 years postbaccalaureate or postmaster's practice experience (CSWE, 2001; Frumpkin & Lloyd, 1995).

The CSWE also has an established relationship with the National Association of Social Workers (NASW), the largest membership association of professional social workers. As an outcome of that relationship, CSWE mandates teaching the NASW *Code of Ethics* through foundation curriculum. The *Code of Ethics* outlines appropriate conduct for professional practice. CSWE has collaborated with the NASW and other sister organizations such as GADE, the Association of Baccalaureate Social Work Program Directors (BPD), the National Association of Deans and Directors of Schools of Social Work (NADD), and the Association of Social Work Boards (ASWB), to set goals and address problems in social work education and practice (NASW, 1999). Continued reflection of the needs of practice throughout the educational programs will ensure continued relevancy of social work education.

OPPORTUNITIES AND CHALLENGES

As Katherine A. Kendall, then executive director of CSWE, pointed out in 1966, many of the issues that social work education faces are the same ones social work had faced in the past. Her observation is still true today. Among these issues are the need to recruit social work students and faculty and the need for understanding between social work program levels and associated organizations (Austin, 1997; Kendall, 2002; Leighninger, 2000). Some of the challenges and opportunities are more particular to this time, including the need for funding or sustainability, the need for accountability and evaluation, education in a global environment, and the need for curriculum relevant to twenty-first century social work practice.

Recruitment

There is a continuous need for competent, trained social workers. The expansion of social work into new fields, continued specialization, and overall growth of social work practice ensures that need for some time to come (U.S. Department of Labor, 2006). Social work programs have had increasing difficulty attracting a diverse population, however, and those who do come do not necessarily practice in the field after graduation (Hoffman, 2006). Also, as the number of social work programs increases, so does the number of faculty needed to serve in those programs. However, though the number of social work doctoral programs has increased in recent years, the number of degree recipients has only increased slightly. This could make it difficult to meet the demand to fill academic positions requiring doctorates. This issue will be exacerbated as greater numbers of social work faculty retire over the next 5 years (Hoffman, 2006; Watkins & Pierce, 2005).

To address the pressing issue of recruitment, especially recruitment of doctoral students and social work faculty, a Task Force on Doctoral Education in Social Work was formed in 2005. The Task Force included leaders in social work education—representatives from GADE, CSWE, NASW, BPD, NADD, Society for Social Work Research (SSWR), Institute for the Advancement of Social Work Research (IASWR), as well as social work deans, directors, faculty, and doctoral students. Although the Task Force addressed many of the pressures on doctoral education (i.e., funding, curriculum), recruitment of qualified students and then recruitment of doctoral graduates to teach were repeatedly mentioned as most pressing. The Task Force formed an action plan and is continuing to work on initiatives to address these pressing concerns.

Understanding between Educational Levels and Member Associations

Issues of the social work educational continuum are still being addressed and tension is still present among the different education levels in social work (Austin, 1997; Kendall, 2002). This tension is evidenced, in part, by the separation of social work education membership organizations for deans and directors of baccalaureate (BPD), master's (NADD and the St. Louis Group), and doctoral (GADE) (Austin, 1997). However, these groups are beginning to recognize the interrelationship between challenges and solutions at each level. That is, recruitment of doctoral students is not just about marketing to master's graduates, but also about the need for mentoring programs to begin in undergraduate and master's social work programs that encourage doctoral education. The need for doctoral social work faculty in baccalaureate programs suggests the need for training in teaching in the doctoral programs.

Social work bachelors, master's, and doctoral education are interrelated and interdependent. The solution for issues at each level must, in part, begin with solutions at the other levels; it is only through cooperation and coordination of the efforts of all the stakeholders in social work education that social work will be able to move forward. The Leadership Roundtable, a group of the major association stakeholders in social work education (including CSWE, NASW, BPD, NADD, GADE, SSWR, IASWR, and the St. Louis Group), has been convening to discuss some of the continuum and representation issues. This group has begun a conversation about how to collaborate and potentially share goals, projects, and resources in the future. A Social Work Congress was also held in 2005, bringing together many leaders of the profession to focus on the common goals, called "imperatives," for social work in the next decade. The leadership will move forward individually and in collaboration for meeting the imperatives (NASW, 2005).

Funding

Another current issue common to all of social work education is limits in funding. It is striking to note the diversity of funding once made available for social work education, especially at the federal level (Kendall, 2002). There have been a number of cutbacks in funding in recent years for social work education initiatives that have been felt universally by social work programs and organizations (Austin, 1997). Universities have been forced to cut budgets to remain operational and small programs with low enrollments are especially at risk (Watkins & Pierce, 2005). EPAS requires that a program be financially stable to be accredited, stating, "The program has sufficient and stable financial supports that permit program planning and achievement of program goals and objectives. These include a budgetary allocation and procedures for budget development and administration" (CSWE, 2001, p. 14). These mandates, as well as the required faculty, suggested faculty-to-student ratio, and resource mandates, can prove problematic to programs with limited finances. In fact, lack of resources is one of the primary reasons that programs have been found out of compliance with accreditation standards and forced to close (Watkins & Pierce, 2005).

Accountability

All of the issues confronting social work education are presented in a context of increased public demand for greater educational accountability. This demand is evidenced in increased evaluation requirements for both public and private funding, the recent emphasis on "best practices," the creation of programs like "No Child Left Behind," and the work of groups like the Secretary of Education's Commission on the Future of Higher Education, which has called for more evaluation of higher education at the program, university, and accreditation levels. The necessity for higher education to meet the public's needs and the desire for accountability is, in part, a request for relevancy (Watkins & Pierce, 2005); students, employers, and funders want to know that what is being taught in social work is relevant to professional practice, that what is mandated for accreditation is being taught by the programs, and that what is necessary for practice is actually being learned by the students. Transparency in program design and outcomes measurement helps ensure responsiveness to all stakeholders in social work education.

CURRICULUM FOR THE TWENTY-FIRST CENTURY

Part of being responsive to the public's need includes continued reciprocity among social work education, practice, and research—the need to prepare students for the type of practice that is relevant to the twenty-first century. The social work field of practice is continually changing and expanding in response to the practitioners, researchers, and the changing environment. Social work education has the responsibility of anticipating what competencies are needed by social work practitioners in the coming years and in translating those competencies into curriculum (Watkins & Pierce, 2005). Collaboration and cooperation among all stakeholders in social work will ensure continued growth and progress in social work education through the next century.

REFERENCES

Austin, D. M. (1997). The institutional development of social work education: The first 100 years: And beyond. *Journal of Social Work Education, 33*(3), 599–612.

Bernard, L. D. (1977). Education for social work. In *Encyclopedia of social work* (17th ed., Vol. 1). Washington, DC: National Association of Social Workers Press.

Black, P. (2005). *Commission on curriculum and educational innovation annual report*. Retrieved September 5, 2006, from http://cswe.org.

Boehm, W. W. (1959). *Objectives of the social work curriculum of the future. The comprehensive report of the curriculum study* (Vol. 1). New York: Council on Social Work Education.

Bolte, G. L. (1971). Current trends in doctoral programs in schools of social work in the United States and Canada. In L. C. Deasy (Ed.), *Doctoral students look at social work education* (pp. 109–126). New York: Council on Social Work Education.

Council on Social Work Education. (2001). *Educational policy and accreditation standards*. Alexandria, VA: Author.

Council on Social Work Education. (2004). *Bylaws* (redlined version). Retrieved September 15, 2006, from http://cswe.org.

Council on Social Work Education. (2006). *Signs of success: The year in review* (annual report). Alexandria, VA: Author.

Council on Social Work Education. (2007). *2006 annual survey of social work programs: Research brief*. Alexandria, VA: Author.

Deasy, L. C. (1971). Some comments on education for social work. In L. C. Deasy (Ed.), *Doctoral students look at social work education*. New York: Council on Social Work Education.

Frumpkin, M., & Lloyd, G. A. (1995). Social work education. In *Encyclopedia of social work* (19th ed., pp. 2238–2246). Washington, DC: National Association of Social Workers Press.

Group for the Advancement of Doctoral Education. (n.d.). *Purpose of GADE*. Retrieved September 5, 2006, from http://web.uconn.edu/gade/.

Hidalgo, J., & Spaulding, E. C. (1987–1988). *Statistics on social work education in the United States: 1986–1987*. Washington, DC: Council on Social Work Education.

Hoffman, K. (2006). *CSWE and social work education's joint agenda* (Remarks based on the President's address at the 2006 CSWE Annual Program Meeting: Chicago). Retrieved August 8, 2006, from http://cswe.org.

Kendall, K. A. (1966). Issues and problems in social work education. *Social Work Education Reporter*, *14*(1), 15, 34–38, 48.

Kendall, K. A. (2002). *Council on social work education: Its antecedents and first twenty years*. Alexandria, VA: Council on Social Work Education.

Leighninger, L. (2000). *Creating a new profession: The beginnings of social work education in the United States*. Alexandria, VA: Council on Social Work Education.

Lennon, T. (1992–2004). *Statistics on social work education in the United States: 1991–2002*. Alexandria, VA: Council on Social Work Education.

Lennon, T. (2005). *Statistics on social work education in the United States, 2003*. Alexandria, VA: Council on Social Work Education.

McCrea, R. C. (1911). The professional school for social workers, its aims and methods. In A. Johnson (Ed.), *Proceedings of the national conference of charities and correction* (pp. 380–384). Fort Wayne, IN: Fort Wayne Printing.

National Association of Social Workers. (1999). *Code of ethics of the National Association of Social Workers*. Washington, DC: Author.

National Association of Social Workers. (2005). *Social work imperatives for the next decade*. Retrieved September 5, 2006, from http://cswe.org.

Rubin, A. (1981–1986). *Statistics on social work education in the United States: 1980–1985*. New York: Council on Social Work Education.

Spaulding, E. C. (1989–1991). *Statistics on social work education in the United States: 1988–1990*. Alexandria, VA: Council on Social Work Education.

Stamm, A. (1972). *An analysis of undergraduate social work programs approved by CSWE, 1971*. New York: Council on Social Work Education.

U.S. Department of Labor. (2006). *Social workers: Occupational outlook handbook*. Retrieved June 8, 2006, from www.bls.gov/oco/ocos060.htm.

Watkins, J. M., & Pierce, D. (2005). Social work education: A future of strength or peril. *Advances in Social Work*, *6*(1), 17–23.

Witte, E. F. (1966). The purposes of undergraduate education for social welfare. *Journal of Education for Social Work*, *1*(2), 53–60.

Chapter 3

THE SCOPE OF SOCIAL WORK PRACTICE

June G. Hopps and Tony B. Lowe

It is timely that the scope of social work practice be reviewed at the mid-point of the first decade of the twenty-first century. What must be considered is the expansion of professional social work boundaries brought on by forceful, dynamic biological, psychological, social, economic, political, and international dimensions that impact this contextual profession. These dynamics influence the profession's boundaries by expanding some and shrinking others at any given point in time and include purposes, auspices, settings, sanctions, roles/functions, populations, theoretical underpinnings, research, and interventions. The field is expected to respond to these ever-changing, dimensions and, at the same time, hold on to its core mission and values, develop, apply, and disseminate knowledge and demonstrate effectiveness of practice interventions.

This overview highlights the scope of postmodern social work practice including an ever-expanding number of goals, settings, roles, and approaches related to interventions at micro, mezzo, and macro levels of intervention. The emergence of a new science on genetic disorders, for example, has led to the utilization of social work practitioners serving individuals and families affected by the biopsychosocial realities associated with these issues. Thus, the term *practice* has broad meaning for social workers because the scope of professional social work practice is as wide as it is deep. Indeed, one of the current, bedeviling questions is whether there is an inverse correlation between expansion of the profession and problem resolution (Gambrill, 2003).

SUMMARY OF THE PROFESSION'S EVOLUTION

Throughout its history, social functioning and change have been the fundamental hallmarks of this contextual profession. Morris (2000) suggests the social work profession's history and consequences can be summarized as:

- The tradition initially was part of a much wider interest in social change and human needs that had been expressed since 1860 through the National Conference of Charities and Corrections and the American Social Science Association.
- The movement became a part of the later progressive movement.
- The early participants were multidisciplined, drawn from sociology, nascent economists, other social scientists, lay community leaders, clergy, and workers in agencies.

- Social work as a distinctive vocation soon concentrated on developing its position as a profession, with the apparatus of a social science: academic training to combine learning and practical experience and professional associations with accrediting authority.
- The twin aims of individual care and changing conditions have been retained in the expressed aims of the field, but after 1935 the development of the Great Depression and World War II forced the field to reconsider its future.
- A series of choices, some taken almost unwittingly, were reinforced by the popularity of new mental health thinking and the compatibility of psychological theory with social casework, along with the great social and economic changes following the Depression.
- By 1990, the field was primarily involved in interpersonal and mental health kinds of careers, while work to change conditions remained at the rhetorical level rather than providing jobs and institutional opportunities to work for change.
- At the same time, social work as a profession was identified mainly with counseling help to individuals or as adjunct staff for organizations, rather than becoming "the profession" associated with any one service system (pp. 44–45).

In sum, the scope of social work practice over the twentieth century has evolved as a result of internal and external forces that gave rise to this contextual profession. It may be evidentiary that external forces have played a stronger hand in defining practice than the former, since practice is defined by the profession's position in the environment at a particular period of time (Gibelman, 1999). Nonetheless, the field can be applauded for its flexibility in responding to urgent, unmet pressing human needs in times of crisis at various systems levels.

PURPOSE OF SOCIAL WORK PRACTICE

The purpose of social work practice in general is to enhance, maintain, and restore the social functioning and promote social justice of individuals, families, groups, communities, organizations, and society at-large with special emphasis on vulnerable populations. Given the dual purpose of enhancing social functioning and promoting social justice, the profession is challenged by the tapestry of human conditions and societal values juxtaposed by its mission. Services provided may be preventative, developmental, remedial, or transformative in nature, depending on the organization's purpose, setting, and need. Social work services are delivered at three practice levels: micro, mezzo, and macro.

The working definition notes that a "configuration of value, purpose, sanction, knowledge, and method" (Bartlett, 1961, p. 5) are the elements that constitute social work practice, as well as demark it from cognate professions and/or disciplines (e.g., psychiatric nursing, pastoral counseling, or psychology) which is or ought to be in social work's best interest given competition for increasingly scarce fiscal resources, clients, and students (Gambrill, 2003). Bartlett (1961) suggested that "Social work is always concerned with the same aspect, namely, the lessening of social stress and the improvement of social functioning" (p. 11). Pinderhughes (1995) states that the purpose of practice, both direct and indirect, includes efforts to facilitate the best possible adaptation between people and the social environment and initiate a process of change to enhance their problem solving, coping, and capacities for growth; to make appropriate linkages between these systems and resources, opportunities, and structures and to promote humanization and effectiveness of service delivery systems. The call to facilitate change in individuals, case by case, is well discussed; however, the social control dimension of practice is not widely articulated (Margolin, 1997). Practitioners must surely recognize the vagueness in constructs and the consequential difficulty in setting goals and measurement. As well, they realize that facilitating adaptation to the social environment in some situations may prove detrimental to the client as well as painful to themselves. This phenomenon occurs when the practice context is characterized by resource scarcity owing to reductions in taxes, budgets, and fiscal distributions for human service policies and programs. In other words, there are attempts to curtail costs and reduce deficits and debt by sacrificing the poor, disadvantaged, and oppressed; groups with limited power to affect change in their situation—personal or environmental. Practitioners often face tension and dilemmas between demands in service delivery to individuals, families, groups, organizations, and communities on one hand and resource deficits in the policy practice environment on the other. Value and ethnical imperatives are critical components of practice in this all-too-common contextual scenario.

VALUES

With contextual changes and ever-shifting professional boundaries, lack of conceptual clarity or high paradigm development, the profession's shared values have helped solidify the field and have held a pivotal position in social work since its inception. These humanistic values are based on concerns relative to human well-being and social justice. Multiple, generally cited, core values of the profession include "individual worth and dignity, respect of person, valuing individual's capacity for change, client self-determination, providing individual's common human needs, commitment to social change and social justice, confidentiality, seeking to provide individuals with adequate resources to meet their basic needs, client empowerment, equal opportunity, nondiscrimination, respect of diversity, and willingness to transmit professional knowledge and skills to others" (Reamer, 1995, p. 199). These values undergird the social work process covering the organization of services, the approach(s) used to engage and dialogue with clients, the method of problem assessment and goal determination, and what intervention strategies are utilized (Pinderhughes, 1995). Currently, social justice, embraced and increasingly advocated by social workers, has been described as the "organizing value" of the profession (Swenson, 1998). The latest edition of the profession's *Code of Ethics* (1994) seems to substantiate this position.

There is little, if any, question among practitioners regarding the centrality of values. There is a question, however, of the weight assigned to those influential values that can lead to dilemmas and conflicts relative to a boundless number of issues. For example, individual change or social change, individual assistance or family assistance, confidentiality or compromise of individual/public safety, design and allocation of service including structure and financing via managed care or design of structure of care reflective of client needs. What this suggests is that value questions and values clarification will probably remain a central part of practice construction and discourse well into the future. Practitioners need to continually examine and confront their personal and professional values and their own power and authority needs in the helping process, as documented in the literature (Hopps & Pinderhuges, 1999; Hopps, Pinderhuges, & Shankar, 1995). They also need to understand the value of ethical reasoning when challenged by situations encountered in practice when helping individual or community clients assess and transition through hot-button, unsettled, conflictual societal issues and policies; for example, same sex marriage, selective abortion, adoption by nontraditional couples, service to illegal immigrants, and privacy rights. Understanding and sorting out difficult issues are professional responsibilities required of all practitioners as they face ambiguities, contradiction, and even confusion rooted in dominant societal attitudes, policies, and laws.

ETHICAL ISSUES

When practitioners are confronted with competing responsibilities and principles, they often find themselves challenged by, and involved in, unavoidable ethical dilemmas. Reamer (1999) outlines three broad areas where ethical dilemmas are manifested: (1) those covering practice with individuals, families, and groups including questions surrounding client self-determination, confidentiality, truth-telling, and paternalism; (2) those covering policy development and program design and administration; and (3) those covering relationships among and between social workers. Moreover, the context for practice when challenged by the "diminution in confidentiality, informed consent, and privacy would create serious difficulties in client services and the value of regulatory compliance would define social workers' behavior more than the professional code" (Hayes & Mickelson, 2003, p. 48). Thus, given the seriousness of, as well as the expanse of, ethical dilemmas, it is understandable that guides for ethical decision making have gained attention in the professional literature (Holland & Kilpatrick, 1991; Mattison, 2000; Reamer, 1994; Simmons, 1978). Issues identified as posing the greatest ethical challenges to members of one professional direct service association, American Association of Marriage and Family Therapy (AAMFT), for example, were ranked by respondents as (1) reporting child abuse and (2) tensions related to individual versus family needs. The ranking was derived from a membership survey of the association (Green & Hansen, 1989, as cited in Kilpatrick & Holland, 2006).

Social workers are generally exposed to and inculcated with ethical grounding that promotes the interests of clients, their well-being, and growth. However, organizational culture in service delivery systems may demonstrate negativity toward the chronically needful (e.g., Katrina hurricane victims) or the expanding and sometimes illegal client populations (e.g., immigrants) as they struggle with mission and resource scarcity.

PROFESSION'S RELATION TO SOCIAL AND BIOLOGICAL SCIENCES

Traditionally, social work has undergirded many of its theoretical approaches from knowledge generated by the biological, psychological, and social sciences. These fields contribute knowledge and empirically derived research findings that are both important and relevant to the profession. However, they are disciplines having different sets of concerns that influence, if not dictate, the structure of inquiry, how thoughts are organized, questions are framed, studies conducted, and theories formulated (Meenaghan, 2001). Attention to application of theories and findings is not an expectation of the social scientist. In contrast, professionals, functioning as they do in complex environmental contexts, must focus on such imperatives as intervention and problem resolution. Unlike disciplines, professions have to address fluid, contextual policy and practice questions that imply political processes and generation of a "consequential ethic" (p. 44).

Social Sciences

"How" and "why" are questions social scientists attempt to answer through study and analysis. They provide much of the raw material often used in human behavior and social environment (HBSE) courses where BSW and MSW social work programs house a considerable segment of theory. The HBSE content includes extensive psychological, behavioral, and systems material often at the expense of information that influences the larger environment. Some sociological content is usually incorporated but what is clearly insufficient is both economic and political theories (Morris, 2000). These latter two areas often overlap and are linked in the political economy that drives social welfare policy and programs.

Biological Sciences

Important advances in biological sciences are providing new knowledge so that the "bio" part of the biopsychosocial perspective can be strengthened. Findings in cognitive neuroscience and neurobiology are available for integration with other psychosocial theories of human behavior that have been used in practice. A body of material from neuroscience postulates that brain structure and chemistry can be changed via social work interventions in ways that are helpful to the client (Gabboard, 1992; Schore, 1994). What this means is that there is little justification for the biological component of one of the professions' major theoretical perspectives receiving insufficient attention in both education and practice (Shapiro & Applegate, 2000).

Social work's self-generated content has grown both substantially and rapidly, owing to many facts including greater recognition of research methods courses in the curriculum, increased interest among schools of social work for improved scholarship, and the process of professional maturation. Even so, the profession will continue to rely on other professions for important knowledge, but at a cost (Tucker, 2000). What is important is for social work to continue developing and refining its theory, practice, and research so other professions will adopt more of its knowledge.

CONCEPTUAL FRAMEWORK OF PRACTICE

The nature of the profession's knowledge building is skewed toward mainly craft knowledge needed for expert action. Theoretical abstract knowledge is less developed but this is the type that provides a foundation for "an effective definition of a profession" (Abbott, as cited in Tucker, 2000, p. 247). Indeed the profession has been concerned about, and has invested talent and resources in, attempting to develop consensus relative to a working definition, framework, paradigm, and/or common base (i.e., purpose, values, knowledge, sanction, skills) for some time. Acknowledging that delimiting discussion is an effective route to articulate dialogue, several pivotal conversations and subsequent publications are noted for moving the profession toward a working definition and greater conceptual clarity. This longstanding, difficult but necessary initiative actually generated a history of its own. The genesis started early in the past century, with the establishment of Charitable Organization Societies (COS) and settlement houses followed by debates relative to scientific philanthropy and individual problems incorporating the Mary Richmond—Jane Addams positions on the case approach to individual problems versus structural reform to eradicate poverty. Opinion shapers include Flexner's 1915 paper, the 1928 Milford Conference papers, the Hollis-Taylor Report (1951), Bartlett's first working definition (1958), Boehm's Curriculum Study (1959), Bartlett's 1955 analysis, Gordon's working definition (1965), Bartlett's Common Base (1970), the 1976 National Association of Social Workers (NASW) meeting on conceptual frameworks and the follow-up meeting in 1979, and finally the Kentucky School of Social Work's 2001 Conference where the works noted were reexamined (Holosko, 2003).

Harriet Bartlett worked on this subject for several decades and through her foundation, two NASW conferences were funded. NASW's editorial board and the publication committee planned a conference in the mid-1970s to consider purposes and activities and what, if any, consensus could be developed related to all the profession's specialties (Brieland & Korr, 2000). Several questions were addressed:

- What is the mission of social work?
- What are social works objectives?
- What do social workers currently do?
- What should they do, or not do, to achieve their objectives?
- What sanctions should social workers have?
- What knowledge and skills are available that would enable social workers to achieve their objectives?
- What are the practical and educational implications of the mission in terms of the professions' objectives, interventions, sanctions, and knowledge? (p. 129)

In the conference summary, Briar (Minahan & Briar, 1977, as cited in Korr & Brieland, 2000) noted difficulty in shaping a mission/purpose statement, ongoing controversy regarding values relative to social change and individual change (the need for social change was acknowledged but also the role of social workers who help clients adapt to circumstances that need to be changed), and the generalist-specialist debate.

A second follow-up conference focusing on specialization was held in 1979. The question of whether the profession should support quality of life for all was an issue that cut across areas of practice. In the end, this conference, like its predecessor, failed to develop and promote consensus on mission and values. At the end of the first conference, Briar surmised that it "is not good when the profession cannot clearly and simply articulate what is common to the activities of all social workers" (Brieland & Korr, 2000, p. 130). Unfortunately, the subject has only been systematically addressed once since the 1979 conference.

The social work profession has long been celebrated for its breath of practice, while concurrently criticized for its lack of sufficient depth, fragmentation, and inadequate conceptual framework. Words of the late social work educator, Carol H. Meyer, "Whereas other professional specialists become expert by narrowing their knowledge parameters, social workers have had to increase theirs" (Meyer, 1976, p. 21) are as relevant as ever. As emerging knowledge from social science, science, neuroscience, and technology coupled with that created by the profession itself from its own research and theory testing, practice interventions, and monitoring for effectiveness or best practice to meet expanding human needs, the question becomes: What is most relevant and verifiable, and what can be categorized and organized into a taxonomy that is useful for practice?

Given challenges regarding boundaries, the core issue is really one of focus. A practitioner asked: "Are social workers supposed to be concerned about the poor, the middle class, and the wealthy? Should we be concerned with groups or individuals? Which issues define social work's true scope: Welfare, social policy, mental and physical health?. . . [S]hould we focus our attention on a broader scope, such as issues of racism and gender equality" (Glaser, 2001, p. 196)?

Does the lack of a cohesive element and reality of fragmented approaches to knowledge development and knowledge application cast a shadow over the profession (Gambrill, 2003; Tucker, 2000)? Recognizing this state of affairs, it seems imperative for the profession to continue to address inquiry relevant to its purpose and identity, and a unifying, coherent conceptual framework and supporting theories. In other words, what is common to the activities of social work (Briar, 1977, as cited in Brieland & Korr, 2000)? Not known for monopolistic theories or positions, what then is the field's "problematic" (Tucker, 2000)? That is "[a]n integrated framework of concepts, propositions, and practices that together define the central intellectual problems of a field" (p. 239). For this profession, the unit of analysis is the interaction of person-in-environment, which is hardly a problem. The goal is to have as strong and positive an interaction as possible between the two systems. A weakness, however, is the limitation in addressing problems that emanate from the environment, which impacts individual functioning (Tucker, 2000). Clearly, the profession prefers to discuss "individual variables" over "system variables" (Solomon, 2002). The profession has underaddressed and expended far less intellect in developing the necessary theories and technologies to be an effective player in the macro-domain, which requires understanding and knowledge of economic principles, than it has in direct practice (Morris, 2000). To change dominate attitudes, as well as educational models, hard issues, several of which were noted by Morris (2000), Solomon (2002), Tucker (2002) and Gambrill (2003), will have to be dealt with before the profession fully embraces its original dual goals of both individual and environmental change, which have been treated as dichotomous entities over much of the past century (Hayes, 1998).

Without a working definition, conceptual clarity and/or a cohesive element, there is a tendency for the field to generate numerous theories, technologies, methodologies, and intervention strategies—and perhaps even fads—all of which invites and enhances a proclivity toward eclecticism. However, there is an intellectual position that eclecticism is not a "free good" (Tucker, 2000), but rather, one that extracts a high cost, placing social work at a comparative disadvantage vis-à-vis those disciplines with higher paradigm development. Social work, as explained by Tucker, is therefore hampered in obtaining and maintaining resources, in the pace at which knowledge is developed and disseminated, the degree of power and autonomy it has amassed, and in the capacity for collaborative study and research. In addition to Briar and colleagues at the NASW conferences, others have also addressed this issue. Reamer (1994) stated, "we should not be encouraging random or undisciplined eclecticism but, rather, the purposeful conceptual viewpoint that define and serve as pillars for each social worker's understanding of and approach to practice" (p. 8). He did note, however, that the value of diversity can add richness to practice and no single approach should claim hegemony. Reynolds (1965) stated that "we have competing schools of thoughts, extremely valuable in the intensive study they give to one phase or another of the whole, but wasteful and destructive in their assumption that no one but themselves has the truth" (as cited in Reamer, 1994, p. 8). Voicing concern for practitioners who are flooded with a rich diversity of theories, Turner (1995) questioned the basis on which selections are made for intervention. Gambrill (2003) argued that the vagueness in the professions' purpose, as evidenced in the working definition, has hindered the development of a conceptual framework. Lofty, inspirational, largely unattainable goals are detractors that continue to nurture electism, mitigating against true, rigorous paradigm development.

The profession, in spite of Tucker's warning and Gambrill's assessment, as well as those of others, has not developed a "problematic" that might create a stronger, more cohesive conceptual framework. At the same time, it would be a mistake to suggest that the various professional initiatives toward a common base and working definition did not advance social work conceptually. They did. Bartlett's (1958) definition and Gordon's (1962) critical assessment of it along with contributions from others working for a unified, common base (Bartlett, 1970; Boehmn, 1959) and acknowledging practice at various system levels and size (Pincus & Minahan, 1973; Schwartz, 1961; Siporin, 1975) helped lead the profession to a broader perspective on practice, as reflected in the generalist perspective. And a stage was set so that many scholars continue to search for a clearer definition/"problematic" and common ground: some arguing for a holistic theoretical approach while others applauding the heterogeneity of frameworks, for example, theory in practice and systematic electism.

PRIMACY OF THE METHODS TRIAD

Prior to the 1970s, fields of practice, child welfare, corrections, medical social work, as well as methods like casework, group work, and community organization, defined approaches to practice. These distinct fields of practice and methods, though viewed as initially useful, over time were assessed as having some limitations or deficits. One critique was that this orientation was not conceptually adequate to sufficiently address the person-in-situation mantra. Another critique was that the methods and settings orientations did not foster unity within the profession, rather, they contributed to the historical separation or division: cause versus function; individual versus environmental. Yet another critique was that the methods orientation, particularly casework and group work, did not sufficiently respond to the needs of poor folks (Hepworth, Rooney, & Larsen, 2002; Morris, 2000; Pinderhughes, 1995; Spetch & Courtney, 1994).

One result was that more imagination and leadership was demonstrated in the civil rights movement and subsequent structural change eventually led to poor peoples' campaigns in urban areas. Nonviolent civil disobedience, the major 1950s to 1960s civil rights' strategy, was challenged and lost ground when younger, harsher voices called for more aggressive social change. Civil unrest in many urban centers became a factor of national concern (Report of National Advisory Commission on Civil Disorders, 1968). Most social institutions were charged with ineffectiveness in serving disadvantaged people. The nation's largest organization of poor people, the National Welfare Rights Organization, led by chemist George Wiley, challenged social welfare institutions and their main professional arm, social work. There were suggestions that therapeutic approaches in use were not sufficiently identified with poor people's causes, life complexities, transitions, and adverse environmental contexts or meeting their needs, which required structural changes in the environment. Economic and political disparities, inequities, and deprivation in health care, education, and housing, were pressing and paramount in the lives of many clients, but personal empowerment (Solomon, 1976), social justice, and social capital development seemed lost as viable and vigorous parts of the profession's nomenclature or semantics. Pressures from the civil rights movement and the War on Poverty programs in the aftermath of civil unrest nudged the profession to also view problems from a social science perspective and to engage in a more generic stance (Garvin, 1981). The writing of Paulo Freire, *Pedagogy of the Oppressed* (1972) in which he implored the conditions of oppressed people worldwide and prescribed consciousness raising and educational strategies for praxis and liberation, became a source of dialogue in schools, agencies, and among advocates for the poor. Some social workers aided in the struggle to help the poor providing expertise in challenging insensitive welfare and other bureaucracies and facilitating grassroots organizing. This expanding thought led to change in practice.

Previously, professional groups began coalescing to better identify as a unified voice and demonstrate greater organizational clout. The shift from methods was preceded by structural/organizational changes in the profession. In 1955, NASW was created to bespeak a more robust and unifying force that incorporated several independent practice organizations (Goldstein & Beebe, 1995). The NASW's decision to move away from sections in 1962 also helped facilitate the demise of methods. A result, however, was the de-emphasis of two of the profession's major methods; group work and community organization (Morris, 2000).

THE METHODS PARADIGM

Social Casework

Casework, a term for work with an individual, became the predominant practice method that includes functional, problem solving, psychobehavioral, and crisis intervention approaches (Meyer, 1987; Perlman, 1957; Pinderhughes, 1995; Thomas, 1967). The old methods, paradigm and role identities (e.g., social casework, medical social work, child welfare work), as well as the organizational culture of the various associations, did not disappear or dissolve immediately. Over time, however, these interests paled and a new and broader lexicon, practice, emerged with its greater repertoire of skills, and gained saliency in both the academic curriculum and field. After Flexner (1915) delivered his challenge at the National Conference of Charities, there was momentum to respond to his critique that social work was not yet a profession. The rationale for this critique was the reported lack of a sufficiently unifying undergirding, with an internally consistent methodology. Prior to the

1915 conference, social workers had discussed the systematic organization of education and the promotion of social work as a profession (Austin, 2000). Mary Richmond became an effective scholarly respondent to Flexner as demonstrated in her treatise, *Social Diagnosis* (1917), which set forth a process for study and diagnosis of case problems. Thus, casework gained both status and momentum but not without struggle and contest from Jane Addams and other leaders in the settlement cause (Abramovitz, 1998).

Practice today is built on giant steps that the new twentieth-century profession took as it responded to this country's fast-paced growth and transition from an agrarian, to an industrial, then to a technological society. Early theoretical approaches relied heavily on psychodynamic casework, which was Freudian based, particularly for the decades of the 1920s through the 1950s. This orientation, dominant as it was, brought focus to internal factors that resulted in less emphasis on the environmental impact on behavior. Even now much of the clinical literature draws from early American Freudians (Falck, 1995). The following decade witnessed an expansion of new theories including ego-psychology, systems, family and family therapy, and ecological factors, which over time led to deeper concern about, and analysis of, the environment as well as the exchange between individual(s) and the environment. Systems theory (Hearn, 1969) was acknowledged for its utility in aiding development toward a holistic view of practice, calling attention to the need for simultaneous emphasis on people and their systems. By the last quarter of the past century, significant changes in the range of practice theories and multiple inventions could be seen. The need to fit theories into a framework to aid integration, including the holistic nature of practice, was pressing; the ecological systems model (aka, ecosystemic model) proved broad enough to facilitate this goal (Hepworth, Rooney, & Larsen, 2002). It posits that persons are involved in ongoing transactions with several environmental systems that include other individuals and institutions (Brofenbrenner, 1977; Germain & Gitterman, 1980; Meyer, 1983). There are reciprocal actions among systems that can be either open or closed. If they are to grow and develop, each system must be willing to receive input from others (Compton & Galaway, 1999). The ecosystems model has evolved with utility for serving disparate populations who have evidentiary need for intervention at micro, mezzo, and/or macro systems levels (Morales & Sheafor, 2002).

Several newer practice models have drawn from pluralism, egalitarian, and participatory themes, coupled with theoretical, cultural, and personal assumptions that help shape opinions about clients (Berlin, 2005). Theorists, according to Berlin, include Wilkin (2000, 2001) and Connolly (2003) and others, focused on the impact of clients' environment (Gutierrez & Lewis, 1999; Kemp, Whittaker, & Tracy, 1997) and social justice (Finn & Jacobson, 2003). An empowerment model was developed earlier in the 1970s by Solomon and elaborated on by Pinderhughes (1983). Devore and Schlesinger (1999) provided the leadership in developing an ethnically sensitive practice framework. An empirically driven justice-based model (Hopps, Pinderhughes, & Shankar, 1995) identified how macro environmental systems compromised otherwise effective clinical social work.

Social casework gained widespread acceptance and was supported by the major professional organizations. However, neither the effectiveness of this method nor the application to a wide range of problems and clients traditionally serviced by social workers could be established (Fischer, 1973, 1976; Reid, 1997; Segal, 1972; Wood, 1978). Consequently, casework has had to establish a solid foundation and fend off its critics. A number of methodologically convincing studies on social work practice have since been published (Gorey, 1996; Gorey, Thyer, & Powluck, 1999; Henggeler & Borduin, 1990; Hopps, Pinderhughes, & Shankar, 1995; Jensen, 1994).

Over time, what once was called *problem-solving casework* became known as *direct practice.* In 1974, with acceptance of the bachelor's degree as the first professional social work degree, the profession relegated generalist knowledge, skills, and practice to BSW level practitioners and advance knowledge, skills, and practice to MSW level practitioners; thus, establishing the practice continuum of generalist and advanced (i.e., clinical, community, and administrative) social work practitioners.

Generalist Practice

Growing concerns relative to the specialization and bifurcation of the profession into clinical/psychotherapy and macro/reform became a point of debate in the 1970s and 1980s. As a result of study and discussion, bachelor's level social work education was revisited and re-presented as generalist practice, which integrates practice, policy, and research. It was assumed that most generalist practice would be carried out at the micro level, however, practitioners would nonetheless be knowledgeable about and capable of applying macro methods when necessary. Generalist preparation is required for practice at the bachelor's level by the Council of Social Work Education (CSWE; Brueggemann, 2006; CSWE, 2001). Generalist practitioners work at all system levels: individuals, families, groups, organizations, and communities. They practice in various settings including family and children's agencies, schools, hospitals/clinics, communities, and a host of other settings. Effective generalist practice requires knowledge of an eclectic knowledge base, capacity to demonstrate a range of skills, assumption of several professional roles, and awareness and assimilation of professional values for application with various client system levels for problem-solving purposes. Systems theory is a major theoretical base for generalist practice that emphasizes the interaction, interdependence, and reciprocity among and between systems and subsystems. These practitioners must know what knowledge and skills repertoire are appropriate for specific problem sets and systems levels. Practitioners are expected to work within an organization/agency structure, initially under supervision (Brueggemann, 2006; Gelman & Mirabito, 2005; Kirst-Ashman & Hull, 1999).

Clinical Social Work

Reid (1997) suggests that four major interrelated long-term trends in clinical social work are: (1) increasing variety of interventions, (2) emergence of short-term modalities, (3) the development of action oriented approaches, and (4) the importance of research as a basis for practice. With the rise in interventive strategies, techniques, and approaches, eclecticism (or integrationism) has emerged as practitioners have attempted to best serve clients through mixing different schools of thought. This is evident through an effort that integrated cognitive-behavioral therapy and interpersonal psychotherapy to treat depression in women (Jensen, 1994). Trends toward short-term modalities have been driven by the concerns of reducing waiting lists, cost containment, service outcomes, and client-holding capacities in open-ended treatment (Dziegielwski, Shield, & Thyer, 1998; Reid, 1997). Among those, cost containment looms over the head of practitioners as human service budgets began to shrink and managed care practices were introduced by third-party reimbursement sources (i.e., insurance providers). By questioning the service necessity, controlling access, and capping expenditures, the behavior of practice was managed. In the end, cost containment established who will get services, what services will be provided, and how much of the service will be received. A stronger research basis for practice, clients, practitioners, government, and society-at-large will benefit through reducing the impact of problem(s), strengthening the profession's practice technology, reducing the cost and dependency on governmental and institutional funding and providing a tangible cost savings by enhancing social functioning and supporting productivity.

Group Work

The faculty of Western Reserve University initially used the term *group work* in 1927 to describe the method that is defined as "goal-directed activity with small groups of people directed at meeting socioemotional needs and accomplishing tasks" (Toseland & Rivas, 2001, p. 12). Units of attention are targeted for service to these systems, group members, the entire group, and/or the group as a vehicle for initiating changes in larger systems including the environment. These functions have been described in some detail by Hopps and Pindershughes, who discuss specific treatment groups (Tosland & Rivas, 2001), and how they help to empower overwhelmed people to transform their lives as well as improve their environment. Hopps and Pindersdughes (1999) state:

> Our findings suggest that there may be emerging a stronger role and place for professionally led groups in contemporary society as a moderating and hopeful force for addressing both personal and societal problems. . . .Groups represent a powerful and underutilized resource for the helping professions in repairing the disconnection and relationship starvation from which many suffer, providing the supports necessary for survival, empowerment, personal growth, and change. (p. 3)

Group services were initiated in the mid-nineteenth century at the YMCA and later the YWCA. This method was widely identified with the settlement houses during the late nineteenth and early twentieth centuries. Group practice methods were used in the progressive reform movement endorsed by settlement houses to improve neglected urban infrastructure and poor sanitary conditions, deplorable and unsafe housing, exploitative employment, poor educational opportunities, restrictive, if available recreation, police brutality, and malpractice, as well as other quality-of-life concerns for immigrants and other poor people who were often isolated owing to language, culture, and/or resource limitations. Jane Addams, founder of Hull House, as well as other women from that important organization, deplored the degrading, humiliating circumstances that many endured and thought that opportunities for informal pedagogy could be instrumental in helping individuals improve their own human capital and competencies as well as the social capital of their environment via the group approach. The reform activities carried out by Black women of that period are not widely known (Carlton-LeNay & Hodges, 2004).

Relief was not the focus of settlement houses—reform was the goal. Most employers were women. They were well educated and powerful. They went on to hold important roles in state and federal agencies. Settlement house workers, however, were excluded from professional social work as the casework method become dominant. These early female leaders set the stage for professional group work and community organization. For all the good work that settlement house women contributed, the targeted population was largely White. Although African Americans suffered the hardships of others in addition to unrelenting prejudice and hatred, they were overlooked by these intelligent, dynamic helpers. In time, Addams did attempt to involve and serve African Americans, but was confronted with such resistance that she was forced to establish a "separate" settlement house for services to this population (Carlton-LeNay & Hodges, 2004; Day, 2006). Many Black women embraced social reform and made names for themselves including Mary McLeod Bethune, who founded Bethune-Cookman College for Blacks and was later befriended by Eleanor Roosevelt.

By the early 1930s, group work leaders began efforts toward professionalism. Grace Coyle was instrumental in moving the initiative to social work, although she remained ambivalent about the affiliation for some time (Schwartz, 1983). Several theorists provided foundation thinking and influenced the field: Cooley on small group analysis and the social nature of individuals, and Baldwin, Dewey, and Kropatin and some years later, Mead and Lewin, who echoed these views versus the collective need dichotomization (Shwartz, 1983). John Dewey's influence on ideology during that period was undeniable: he promoted progressive education. Group work was a method noted for the application of these principles to small informal groups (Garvin, 1981). The Depression provided impetus to the growth of group work as a social work method because the utility, importance, and objectives of casework in the face of great human need were questioned:

> The Great Depression produced a devastating challenge to social work and its institutions. The base function of relieving poverty on a case-by-case basis had been the foundation for helping individuals grow out of their troubles. Mass unemployment meant that almost all citizens were in such great economic trouble that the slim charitable agencies could not cope. The emergency introduction of public welfare with federal funding and administration was based on entitlement (because of definable conditions) and organization on a mass scale to provide income and public work to all in need. . . .
>
> Large-scale organization, mass administration, and emergency improvisations became a new reality. . . the private social agency survived, but with shrunken influence in community life and with a casework staff primarily committed to understanding individual and family behaviors and how to help individuals cope with crises in their personal lives. (Morris, 2000, p. 48)

Although group work gained acceptance, some caseworkers remained wary about the importance, weightiness, and rigor of the method, questioning its significance. During the 1940s, a period of war, international conflict, and domestic fear, group workers were judicious in not allowing their cause to be scapegoated or identified as a non-American social element. They pulled back from social reform and activism and expended time and talent in expanding and refining group work practice theory. Demand increased for this method for services oriented toward treating World War II veterans. Although some services in traditional agencies and organizations continued, group workers pushed toward treatment. In effect, the goal of social reform via groups was reduced if not set aside and interest in groups for treating a collective of individuals gained prominence (Garvin, 1981).

TREATMENT AND THE JOINING OF CASEWORK AND GROUP WORK

The use of therapy in groups began in the early 1920s with the ascendancy of individual responsibility for problems as distinct from social accountability and responsibility. Not a subtle variation, as described by Falck (1995) was the turn to the dominant American value and preoccupation with individualism and methodological individualism. Casework and group joined "as clinically focused social work became even more dominant—nearly always conceived of as with or on behalf of individuals even when spoken in group terms—social group work lost a great deal of its preferential relevance" (p. 66). Falck went on to argue that group therapy and family therapy have been substituted for group courses in the nation's schools of social work. The study of task groups was substituted for group work in macro practice. Tropp (1978) also questioned the rationale for reducing group work content by schools of social work at a time when other professions were including it. Vinter related treatment goals for group members as individual diagnosis (Garvin, 1981). Several theorists including Coyle (1948), Knopka, (1949), and Redl and Wineman (1952; as cited in Davis, Schople, & Galinsky, 1995), for example, have espoused the treatment approach. An area of concern however, has been the debate of group work as distinct from casework in a group (Kurland & Salmon, 1991) and how to ensure that group process occurs. Others clarified how social group work could be used in a wide range of activities, thereby helping group work to hold on to some of its early goals. Examples of groups in family interventions as preventive, treatment, and tasks groups and the treatment of choice for work with selected populations are expounded in discussions of practice with American Indians and Alaskan Natives (Edwards & Edwards, 2002), overwhelmed clients (Hopps & Pinderhughes, 1999), and women (Kravetz, 2002).

From the mid to latter part of the twentieth century, much thought was directed to the development of models and, according to Galinsky and Schopler (1993) and Schopler and Galinsky (1995), included the reciprocal model (Schwartz, 1961; Shulman, 1992) also called the mediating model, interactionist model and the humanistic model, and the remedial model (Vinter, 1967), which was later referred to as the rehabilitative/preventive approach (Sundel, Glasser, Sarri, & Vinter, 1985). A number of theories are in place to undergird groups: problem solving, cognitive behavioral, family, systems, psychodynamic empowerment, social learning, communication, and more (Hopps & Pinderhughes, 1999). By the 1990s, an empowerment focus became more closely associated with groups to enable members in achieving both individual and environmental change (Berman-Rossi, 1992; Breton, 1992; Gatierrz & Orteg, 1991; Hopps & Pinderhughes, 1999; Kravetz, 2002; Schopler & Galinsky, 1995).

COMMUNITY ORGANIZATION

Efforts for community organization's (CO) inclusion in the profession started early but it was not until 1962 that a comprehensive report on the definition of this method was presented by NASW. At that time, CO was given parity with casework and group work. Gurin (1971) identified key aspects of CO as a method of social work, social welfare planning, and social action. The roots of CO grew from the philosophies and stances of the Charity Organization Societies (COSs) and settlement houses. COS activities were the predecessor of CO and social planning (Gilbert & Specht, 1977). Community Chests were established for the purpose of developing rational procedures for allocation of funding growing out of the relief efforts during World War I. Another activity was the development of criteria and standards for fiscal responsibility and programmatic goals that conformed to traditional perspectives (Brierland, 1995; Perlman, 1977).

Community organizing was also the method of choice in the profession's early venture into social reform in the late nineteenth and early twentieth centuries. Early "social workers—reformers" organized at the neighborhood level—house by house—identified problems, studied them, developed proposals and policies for corrective action, organized pressure groups, and engaged in activities to promote change (Gurin, 1971). Saul Alinsky used this method with success in the 1930s and 1940s and particularly behind the stockyards in Chicago. It was used just as effectively in the fight for civil rights in the 1950s and 1960s. The Economic Opportunity Act of 1964 mandated that Community Action Agencies (CAAs) be set up to govern and manage a variety of Community Action Programs (CAPs) that sprang up to assist and rebuild older urban neighborhoods that had become dilapidated after earlier civil unrest. The maximum feasible participation clause required that local poor residents be involved in decision making in CAPs. Neighborhoods, filled with organization and activity, challenged the status quo resulting in reaction that changed the legislation requiring representation to also include the "establishment." Over time, these neighborhood-based change organizations became more conservative and offered traditional social service programs. During the conservative wave of the 1980s, CO became less feasible due to major budget cuts and a national retreat from social welfare. Since the last decade, faith-based groups and grassroots organizations have found this method a useful tool (Alinsky, 1974; Brueggmann, 2006; Lowe, 2004).

Currently, CO remains a core method of social work. It was divided conceptually into three models including locality development, social planning, and social action (Rothman, 2001). This method is demonstrated in work with needful population groups and rural, suburban, urban communities, hamlets, and/or barrios, and in cyberspace. It has been used to support the concept of community in work with urban and reservation American Indians. Assessment of need and the active participation of members of the community in planning, implementation, and evaluation were requisites for successful CO initiatives (Edwards & Edwards, 2000). Another example is work with Mexican Americans where CO skills were used to mobilize key individuals and barrio residents at the grassroots level to develop strategies designed to reduce conflicts and improve relationships between the police and residents (Morales & Salcido, 2002).

In work with specific population groups—rural, reservation, barrio, urban communities, and others—important steps include defining the problem, mobilizing residents, identifying resources for resolution of need, fund raising, coalition building, and advocacy. Women are using the Internet to aid organization, networking, and advocacy in attempts to reduce oppression across the globe (Queiro-Tajalli & Campbell, 2002). In all initiatives, change follows a trajectory from consensus-based to contest-based to conflict-based strategies (Hick & McNutt, 2002; Rothman, 2001). Even with revolutionary technology, there are strong ties between online and traditional organizing (Hick & McNutt, 2002). Although the value of CO has been demonstrated as an effective approach to community problem resolution, it has been subordinate to micro systems (e.g., individual, family, and small groups) and macro systems (e.g., CO, planning, and administration) interventions. However, electronic advocacy, a strong tool for "collective action and communication" is bringing new practitioners and citizen groups as well as focus to community organization (Hick & McNutt, 2002, p. 12; Hillier, Wernecke, & McKelvey, 2005). In fact, studies have documented positive results from the use of the Internet for advocacy. Community organizing and policy practice are being revolutionized as the Internet, which includes web-based techniques, e-mail based tools, and other approaches (i.e., faxes, conference calls), becomes more widely used (Hick & McNutt, 2002).

OTHER FORMS OF MACRO PRACTICE

Several other macro practice methods have had impact on the field and expanded CO opportunities.

Community Development

Community development has been a pivotal part of rebuilding American communities for some time. It was particularly effective after the Depression; successful programs included the Civilian Conservation Corps (CCC), Works Progress Administration (WPA), and the Tennessee Valley Authority (TVA). These federally supported initiatives were welcomed sources of employment and improvement of neighborhood and regional facilities and infrastructure. Nearly 30 years later, community development again emerged when it became clear that market conditions in distressed neighborhoods did not present viable options for creating necessary housing and business development (Coulton, 2002). Community development become an effective method used by African American leaders after the period of civil unrest in the 1960s to aid in the restoration of both urban and rural communities. There was recognition that the focus of their struggle should embrace socioeconomics, moving away from individually oriented legal strategies. Community self-determination and local control of institutions and resources became the new mantra. Community development corporations (CDCs) grew out of the initiatives of African Americans across the country who wanted an improved quality of life and who understood that they would have to engage in community organization to make a difference in their own communities (Brueggemann, 2006).

Community boards govern these place-based organizations. It was recognized early on that, whereas conflict-organizing strategies helped in developing some CDCs, a different style was necessary to accomplish goals of developing financial support for community rebuilding goals. Early CDCs relied on financial institutions, philanthropic and government resources, and were influenced by these organizations, although community residents did serve on boards. CDCs influenced residents through activities including building management and tenant selection rather than through direct work with residents. CDCs have been particularly successful in the building and rehabilitation of low-income housing as well as in the management of buildings. Recognizing that housing single-handedly would not transform neighborhoods, attention was directed to developing a stronger opportunity structure and social ethos. Consequently, newer initiatives were fostered including community organization, social services, jobs, and economic development. Partnerships linking organizations with the community and the community to the larger metropolitan area have been instrumental in the success of CDCs (Coulton, 2000). In fact, CDCs provided a pattern for current approaches to the restoration of poor, struggling communities, that is, comprehensive community initiatives and community building. Community organizers, planners, and policy practitioners have played important roles in community development. Examples of successful CDCs abound across the country (Brueggemann, 2006; Coulton, 2000).

Social Planning

Planning has been, and remains, a significant component of community organization, although it is an important macro method on its own. It was utilized in Pittsburgh in the early twentieth century by the nation's first council of social agencies in response to the country's first comprehensive review of problems in a major industrial city. The Pittsburgh Council, and others, dealt with existing social problems and developed standards to assist agencies in delivering services in an effective manner. Since local councils seldom had influence over allocation of resources to agencies, there was little clout for carrying out planning ideas. After the Depression, the government became the central force for addressing social problems and major planning initiatives were needed and implemented. It would be the 1960s antipoverty programs before large-scale planning would again be directed to social problem resolution (Gummer, 1995). For roughly a decade, all new social policy efforts mandated that planning be a component of the proposed programmatic effort. Program initiatives in fields of practice required planning and a rational, goal-centered approach was used. Rational planning faced difficulties because social services were fraught with irrational systemwide goals and objectives. By the 1980s, the short-lived national interest in rational planning was attacked by the conservative movement and the wave of decentralization and devolution from national to state/local, and market-based processes (Gummer, 1995; Iatridis, 2000). By the late 1990s, the country witnessed the devolution of services from the federal to state level via block grants (Korr & Brieland, 2000). Currently, faith-based initiatives, a policy approach espoused by the Bush administration, are highly decentralized at local levels requiring even less planning (Lowe, 2004). Rational planning in social work has often been compromised by insufficient information systems. The emergence and growth in microcomputing and supercomputing systems and the increased availability of the Internet and other technology is having a significant impact, helping to improve this short fall (Hick & McNutt, 2004).

Policy Practice

Increasingly, policy is considered as a problem-solving process (Figuerira-McDonough, 1993; Iatridis, 1995; Jansson, 1990; Phillips & Straussner, 2002). As such, it is, like the other methods, based on a systematic body of knowledge, methods, and skills. Policy practice is directed toward change in large systems (e.g., institutions, neighborhood, and society) for the purpose of aiding individuals and families (Iatridis, 1995). Too often, practitioners forget that the implementation of the profession's social justice stance requires an understanding and commitment to policy practice.

> If the value of social justice is taken to mean a commitment to ensure equal access for all to basic social goods, then the typical roles of social workers as case management and therapists fall short of that goal. This is not to deny the merit of such roles, but rather to point out that their objective is not to ensure a more equitable distribution of opportunity. Progress toward social justice requires direct involvement in the formation and modification of social policy. (Figueira-McDonough, 1993, p. 180)

Policy planners are involved in analyzing policies and designing plans/programs to carry out policies; and organizing, monitoring, managing, and evaluating interventive strategies in organizations and communities (Iatridis, 1995).

Several stages have been identified as relevant to intervention beginning with referral and ending with termination. Iatridis indicates that the most critical stages are formulation (similar to treatment), and implementation planning, largely oriented to organization and administration. Key phases in formulation include analysis of the problem, formulation of recommendations, communication of recommendations, and well-written policy positions to clients and feedback (Iatriadis, 1994; Phillip & Straussner, 2003). Phases of implementation planning include implementation, evaluation, and feedback. Multiple roles and skills for professionals in this area of practice include that of policy analyst, policy developer, policy advocate, lobbyist, political coalition builder, expert witness, legislative aide/advisor, social worker, and politician (Phillip & Straussner, 2003, pp. 216–217). There is argument that the profession has not sufficiently engaged in or viewed policy practice as the political process that it is. To remedy this dilemma, Figueira-McDonough (1993) advocates reform through the legislative and judicial systems, which demonstrates formal policymaking procedures, and community and organizational change, which represents constituency-based influence.

A new area of policy practice is political social work, which requires knowledge of community organization, administration, social welfare, and human behavior (Lowe & Hopps, in press). At present, six social workers serve in Congress, two in the U.S. Senate (Maryland and Michigan), and four in the U.S. House (California [2], New York, and Texas; NASW, 2000). Some Schools of Social Work are developing policy practice field placements. One is developing teaching approaches that expose students to experiential policy practice in BSW policy courses (Anderson & Harris, 2005). These options expand opportunities for students, especially through the early exposure to hands-on policy practice.

SOCIAL ADMINISTRATION AND MANAGEMENT

Starting with the Charity Organization Societies and settlement houses, distinct approaches to administration were evident. The former relied on wealthy businessmen and women who were on boards to carry out a plethora of roles, including some administrative responsibilities. Settlement houses were directed by full-time workers, who founded the organizations and recruited their board members, usually wealthy college educated friends. The 1930s represented a major shift in the structure of social services nationwide with the passage of New Deal legislation, specifically the 1935 Social Security Act, following the Great Depression. Private agencies became less prominent and new; large public agencies gained prominence. These large agencies were mostly bureaucratic and hierarchical and provided employment to the masses as well as to social workers who staffed them (Austin, 2000; Morris, 2000). A seismic shift occurred in the 1960s when new community action agencies (CAAs) sponsored by government were the antithesis of bureaucratic organizations. Citizen participation was encouraged in President Lyndon Baines Johnson's War on Poverty programs and mandated in the 1964 Economic Opportunity Act (EOA). Social workers landed many jobs as executives and practiced a politically active, entrepreneurial style of leadership. They did not focus on traditional casework services (Austin, 1995).

Later, emphasis was placed on program evaluation and accountability and administrators were challenged with this new politically driven thrust in government-funded programs (Sze & Hopps, 1978). However, this concern paled with the drastic cuts and reentrenchment in human services in the Reagan and Bush years and the Republican Contract on America. Privatization, a means to reduce budgets and cut the size of bureaucracies, became the new nomenclature and force in social services delivery and administration. Employment opportunities for practitioners grew in private for-profit companies and services performed by government employees were contracted out. Public-private partnerships were encouraged and managed health care and social services grew exponentially. Private agencies marketed their services for profits. These phenomena changed social service administration and the role(s) of executives drastically (Hopps, Pinderhughes, & Shanker, 1995; Iatridis, 2000). In this context, a concern remains regarding the protection of clients' rights and whether they will be sacrificed for financial profit and bottom lines.

Today, as in yesteryear, the aim of social administration is to provide services through organizations for the purpose of improving the welfare of all client systems. Administrators bring leadership to agencies in the provision of services and program development and are usually experienced generalists rather than managerial specialists. Solid administrators are capable of using the assets and resources of the agency to create a healthy, nurturing environment for staff. Administrators are equally concerned about helping clients to realize their goals. They must be skillful in working with task groups for policy and program development and know how to position the agency in the community so that it is perceived as helpful in fulfilling its mission (Brueggemann, 2006). Concerns for ways and means to ensure that the agency environment is supportive of goal attainment and high morale of personnel is always a priority. Knowledge of power and influence in organizations, communities, and networks as well as that of organizational theory and behavior are prerequisites for effective leadership.

Those who are responsible for administering programs and agencies include: executive director, program administrator, manager, supervisor, program planner and developer, consultant, evaluator, researcher, data manager, policy analyst, advocate, and public relations expert (Phillips & Straussner, 2002). These roles coupled with skills in fund raising, recruitment and development of quality staff, and the capacity to work with a board of directors are essential for managing an agency. In all roles and functions, leadership, interpersonal skills, common sense, and integrity are critical. There is, as well, the responsibility to remain current regarding laws and regulations that affect governance (e.g., Sarbanes-Oxley, civil rights, nondiscrimination and workplace laws to cite a few) and new technologies that improve practice (e.g., computer and electronic technologies).

People of color and women are moving into executive and top managerial roles, breaking through the glass ceiling. In the future, a very diverse group of social workers and particularly women will provide leadership in both academia and practice with a diverse clientele in response to the cultural transformation that is challenging society (Austin, 2000). Greater emphasis will need to be devoted to race, gender, and sexual orientation in leadership and administration in the years ahead (Hopps, 2000). All practice domains are impacted by several fairly recent trends including ethnic-sensitive practice and research on practice.

Ethnic-Sensitive Practice

Based on an ethnocultural perspective, the ethnic-sensitive practice model suggests that certain core concepts, ethnicity, socioeconomic class and oppression, are integrated within an organizing schema of intervention principles (Anderson, 2003). A major assumption is that the cultural difference of an ethnic group produces idiosyncratic realities for members of the group. Knowledge of these differences provides greater understanding of the ethnic group's realities. Schlesinger and Devore (1995) proffer several assumptions relative to ethnic-sensitive practice: History affects both the genesis and resolution of problems; the "here and now" is more significant than the past or future; family functioning capacity is affected by nonconscious phenomena; ethnicity can be both a source of cohesion, identify, and strength and at the same time a source of discordance, strain, and strife (Hopps & Kilpatrick, 2006, p. 39).

Another component of ethnic-sensitive practice is a multicultural perspective, which mandates that social workers not only value, but also embrace attributes of culture that are different from that of their own. Yet another component of effective practice is understanding culture and power and the relationship between the two concepts (Hopps & Pinderhughes, 1999). The dual perspective is also both useful and instructive for ethnic-sensitive practice. This approach posits that clients are a part of and thus, must deal with, two systems: one is the dominant or sustaining system and the second is the nurturing system. The former is the source of power and economic resources and the latter incorporates the physical and social environment of the family and community (Norton, 1978 as cited in Anderson, 2005). Cultural-practice is demonstrated when it is an integrated part of your assessment and intervention repertoire at both the micro and macro levels (Tourse & Blythe, 2003).

Research in Practice

Major strides have been made in research, particularly over the past 2 to 3 decades. The government's retrenchment from its social welfare responsibility has been evident since the 1970s. Attitudes and interests of a relativity prosperous voting public changed and a message stating "good motives and good goals are not good enough for an increasingly critical electorate that is opposed to social reform and wants assurance that those programs it funds are working" (Hopps, 1985, p. 467). At that time, demands for demonstration of practice effectiveness outstripped definitions of effectiveness and reliable means of documenting it. Increasingly, as funders and stakeholders required evidence that social work interventions were effective, there was movement away from reflective practice (Schon, 1995) and authority-based practice, for example, tradition or practice wisdom (Gambrill, 2003; Rosen, 2003). This development should not lead you to infer that the profession did not express some resistance: There were suggestions that evidence-based practice was out of step with the profession's value base (Gibbs & Gambrill, 2002). Skeptics were perhaps mindful that the early systematic evaluation studies threw cold water on many claims regarding the success of interventions (Fisher, 1973, 1976; Mullen & Dumpson, 1972).

One way social workers, along with other health and human service professionals, responded was via evidence-based practice (Taylor & White, 2002). Efforts to integrate practice and research through single-case evaluations (Bloom & Fisher, 1982; Briar, 1979) gained some attention, but not sufficient momentum. Nonetheless, several more recent studies are noteworthy (Gambrill, 2004; Glisson & Hemmelgam, 1998; Henggeler, Pickel, Brondino, & Crouch, 1996; Thyer, 2004). Glisson and Hemmelgam (1998), for example, investigated the impact of intra- and inter-organizational mechanisms used for service coordination on service quality and their outcomes in an effort to improve human services to children. Most notable, they found that an agency's organizational climate has direct bearing on the effect of psychosocial functioning of such a needful and vulnerable population, whereas: (a) organizational climate positively affected service quality and outcomes; (b) improved service quality does not translate into more positive outcomes; (c) and although both intra- and inter-organizational characteristics affect service quality, increased service coordination decreases quality of service. Practice research findings such as this demonstrate that educators, practitioners, service planners, and administrators must keep abreast of the changing state of practice science.

Evidence- (or empirically) based practice (EBP) in the meantime has become the "gold standard" to judge social work practice, as it should (Fisher, 1973; O'Hare, Tran, & Collins, 2002; Thyer, 2004; Tran & Collins, 2002). This approach is believed to be the answer to the profession's challenges regarding "depth and breath" because EBP has been given a high priority in the profession and among stakeholders (Hopps & Collins, 1995; Sze & Hopps, 1978). These internal and external forces underscore how the profession's practices, boundaries, and responsibilities continue to mature and move toward the ranks of its more established contemporaries. Practice research in the form of outcomes and service evaluation will be the driving force.

FIELDS OF PRACTICE

The social work profession has traditionally served disenfranchised population groups. As waves of immigrants, urbanization, and industrialization of the late 1800s and early 1900s took hold in the United States, "friendly visitors," precursors of professional social workers, engaged individuals, families, groups, organizations, and communities in transformative efforts with different motivation, approaches, and degrees of success (Brieland, 1995). Although new immigrants, women and children, primarily of European descendents, were the focus of mainstream advocates, the concerns of people of color, Native Americans, and others were often left to self-help efforts that paralleled the mainstream community.

Professional social workers today are found in many fields serving many populations. It is impossible to discuss all fields of practice because many overlap. Data from the Department of Health and Human Services, for example, finds that professional social workers are the nation's most common providers of mental health services (DHHS, 1998).

In these fields, they serve diverse populations with many biopsychosocial and economic needs. Among the most common areas or fields:

- *Advocacy services:* Includes service for children, family, elderly, prisoners, victims of domestic violence, gay, lesbian and transgendered, homeless, immigrants, women, people of color, persons with disabilities, and many others who may require political and economic advocacy.
- *Behavioral health services:* Includes acute, ambulatory, and residential care and private practice that may be provided in mental health and substance abuse settings to clients and communities with identified needs.
- *Child welfare and youth services:* Includes child custody, adoption, abuse and neglect, kinship care, protection, delinquency/gangs, and family services that may be provided in public, private nonprofit, and/or profit organizations.
- *Communities and neighborhood services:* Includes organizing communities (geographic and nongeographic) and neighborhoods around common interests such as violence, education, and others.
- *Criminal justice services:* Includes diversion, forensic, juvenile justice, drug courts, parole, probation, and other related services.
- *Educational/school services:* Includes advocacy, after-school, delinquency, prevention, special education, and other services for at-risk populations.
- *Emergency/disaster services:* Includes direct and indirect services such as crisis intervention, resource development, and coordination of service for internally displaced and refugee populations that are provided by the American Red Cross and other relief agencies.
- *Environmental justice:* Includes engaging in community organizing, advocacy, mobilization, and other practices with communities and organizations committed to bringing justice to areas suffering from industrial pollution and exposure to unsafe levels of environmental contaminants.
- *Families, couples, singles services:* Includes a range of community-based, faith-based, and advocacy services designed to enhance, support, and develop the social functioning of partners, marriages, and families through agencies such as family service agencies, Planned Parenthood, Inc., and others.
- *Gerontology services:* Includes physical and psychiatric care, in-home, residential, and advocacy services for seniors.
- *Immigrant and refugee services:* Includes providing direct and indirect service to recent immigrants and refugees needing advocacy, resettlement, financial, and legal assistance.
- *International social work:* Includes the use of direct and indirect interventions in other host nations serving in practitioner, educator, and consultant roles.
- *Policy/legislative practice:* Includes a number of roles such as legislative aides, lobbyists, advocates, policy analysts, politicians, and others who may serve at the local, state, and national levels.
- *Medical/health services:* Includes a range of acute and ambulatory care that includes genetic, prenatal, psychosocial, HIV/AIDS, nutritional, and discharge planning services that may be provided in primary, institutional, and public health settings.

- *Military services:* Includes physical and behavioral health services provided to current and former soldiers and their families, such as crisis and support services.
- *Research/evaluation services:* Includes investigating social problems, documenting effectiveness of social work practice, policy, treatment, and service outcomes.
- *Occupational social work services:* Includes employee assistance, referral, and other services that maybe provided by public, private, or nonprofit organizations.
- *Vocational rehabilitation services:* Includes job readiness and rehabilitative care for individuals with disabilities.

THE FUTURE

Social work practice in the future will continue to be charged by forces that will forever influences its boundaries. Continuing struggles regarding enhancing social functioning and advancing social justice require that practitioners remain vigilant regarding the needs of both old and new vulnerable populations. The challenge of responding to such problems, however, must be considered in the context of the profession's core mission. By doing so, the profession can maintain and expand public trust that could enhance support of its goals. A major part in winning greater trust (and funding) is predicated on strong evidence relative to the effectiveness and usefulness of intervention strategies, theories of change, and policy approaches.

Major advances have been documented since the beginning of this twentieth-century profession. This chapter noted many successes as well as areas that need further development and consensus. Paramount among these is evidence-based knowledge among students, practitioners, and educators. Ongoing attention should be directed, not only toward culturally sensitive practices, but also to eradicate the "isms" (i.e., race, gender, age, sexuality, class, religion) and advancement of social and economic justice. The profession must continue to support refining its "problematic" or paradigm, and move on with advancing theory based on evidence if it expects cognate professions to use social work generated knowledge and to move up the hierarchy of professions. It is the responsibility of both academics and practitioners to advance the profession's knowledge. The time has come for the profession to define itself to the public through engaging in social marketing of its practice strengths and capabilities.

Finally, all should remain mindful of implications brought to practice by the changing demographics. Overarching questions remain: Is social work practice committed to addressing new as well as traditional groups of vulnerable populations and also educating a cadre of professionals willing to respond, in this country and abroad? Is the profession capable of acknowledging the need for flexibility and elasticity to anticipate and forecast future dilemmas where the profession's resources will be needed?

REFERENCES

Abramovitz, M. (1998). Social work and social reform: An arena of struggle. *Social Work*, *43*(6), 512–526.

Addams, J. (1910). *Twenty years at Hull House*. New York: Macmillan.

Anderson, D. K., & Harris, B. (2005). Teaching social work welfare policy: A comparison of two pedagogical approaches. *Journal of Social Work Education*, *1*(3), 511–526.

Anderson, J. (2003). Strengths perspective. In J. Anderson & R. W. Carter (Eds.), *Diversity perspectives for social work practice*. Boston: Allyn & Bacon.

Austin, D. (2000). Greeting the second century: A forward look for a historical perspective in social pedagogy in informal learning. In J. Hopps & R. Morris (Eds.), *Social work at the millennium: Critical reflections on the future of the profession* (pp. 18–41). New York: Free Press.

Bartlett, H. (1961). *Analyzing social work practice in the health field*. New York: National Association of Social Workers Press.

Berlin, S. B. (2005). The value of acceptance in social work direct practice: A historical and contemporary view. *Social Service Review*, *79*(3), 483–510.

Boehm, W. (1959). *Objective of the social work curriculum of the future*. New York: Council of Social Work Education.

Boland, K., Barton, J., & McNutt, J. (2002). Social work advocacy and the internet the knowledge base. In S. Hick & J. McNutt (Eds.), *Advocacy, activism and the internet: Community organization and social policy* (pp.19–31). Chicago: Lyceum Books.

Briar, S. (1979). Incorporating research into education for clinical practice in social work: Toward a clinical science in social work. In A. Ruben & A. Rosenblatt (Eds.), *Source on research utilization: A compilation of papers presented for discussion at the Conference on Research Utilization in Social Work Education, New Orleans, LA (Oct. 5–7, 1977)*. New York: Council of Social Work Education.

Brieland, D. (1995). Social work practice: History and evolution. In R. L. Edward (Ed.), *Encyclopedia of social work* (19th ed., Vol. 2, pp. 2247–2258). Washington, DC: National Association of Social Workers Press.

Brieland, D., & Korr, W. S. (2000). Social work: Conceptual frameworks revisited. In J. Hopps & R. Morris (Eds.), *Social work at the millennium: Critical reflections on the future of the profession* (pp. 123–137). New York: Free Press.

Brofenbrenner, U. (1977). Toward an experimental ecology of human development. *American Psychologist*, *32*, 513–555.

Brueggemann, W. (2006). *The practice of Marco Practice*. Belmont, CA: Brook/Cole.

Carlton-LeNay, I., & Hodges, V. (2004). African-America reformers' mission: Caring for our girls and women. *Affilia*, *3*(19), 257–172.

Compton, B., & Galaway, B. (1999). *Social work processes* (5th ed.). Pacific Grove, CA: Brooks/Cole.

Connolly, M. (2003). Cultural components of practice: Reflexive responses to diversity and difference. In T. Ward, D. R. Laws, & S. M. Hudson (Eds.), *Sexual deviance: Issues and controversies* (pp. 103–118). Thousand Oaks, CA: Sage.

Coulton, C. (2000). Restoring communities within the context of the metropolis. In J. Hopps & R. Morris (Eds.), *Social work at the millennium: Critical reflections on the future of the profession* (pp. 175–206). New York: Free Press.

Council on Social Work Education. (2001). *Educational policy and accreditation statement*. Alexandria, VA: Author.

Davis, L., Schopler, J., & Galinsky, M. (1995). RAP: A framework for leadership of multiracial group. *Social Work*, *40*(2), 155–165.

Day, P. J. (2006). *A new history of social welfare*. Boston: Allyn & Bacon.

Department of Health and Human Services. (1998). *Mental health, United States, 1998* (Publication No. 99-3285). Washington, DC: Substance Abuse and Mental Service Health Administration.

Devore, W., & Schlesinger, G. (1999). *Ethnic-sensitive social work practice* (5th ed.). Boston: Allyn & Bacon.

Dziegielwski, S. F., Shields, J. P., & Thyer, B. A. (1998). Short-term treatment: Models, method, and research. In J. B. W. Williams & K. Ell (Eds.), *Advances in mental health research implications for practice* (pp. 287–308). Washington, DC: National Association of Social Workers Press.

Edwards, E. D., & Edwards, M. E. (2002). Social work practice with American Indians and Alaskan natives. In A. Morales & B. Seafor (Eds.), *The many faces of social work clients*. Boston: Allyn & Bacon.

Falck, H. (1995). Central characteristic of social work with Groups—A socio-cultural analysis. In R. Kurland & R. Solomon (Eds.), *Group work practice in a troubled society: Problems and opportunities* (pp. 63–72). New York: Haworth Press.

Federal Interagency Forum on Aging-Related Statistics. (2004, November). *Older Americans 2004: Key indicators of well being*. Washington, DC: U.S. Governmental Printing Office.

Figueira-McDonough, J. (1993). Policy practice: The neglected side of social work intervention. *Social Work, 38*(2), 179–188.

Finn, J., & Jackson, M. (2003). *Justice practice: A social justice approach to social work*. Peosta, IA: Eddie Bowers.

Fischer, J. (1973). Is casework effective? A review. *Social Work, 18*, 5–20.

Fischer, J. (1976). *The effectiveness of social casework*. Springfield, IL: Charles C Thomas.

Gabboard, G. O. (1992). Psychodynamic psychiatry in the decade of the brain. *American Journal of Psychiatry, 149*, 991–998.

Galinsky, M., & Schopler, J. (1993). Group work competence: Our strengths and challenges. In R. Kurland & R. Solomon (Eds.), *Group work in a troubled world* (pp. 33–44). New York: Haworth Press.

Gambrill, E. (2003). Evidence-based practice: Implications for knowledge development and use in social works. In A. Rosen & E. Proctor (Eds.), *Developing practice guidelines for social work practice: Issues, methods and interventions* (pp. 37–58). New York: Columbia University Press.

Garvin, C. (1981). *Contemporary group work*. Englewood Cliff, NJ: Prentice-Hall.

Gelman, C. R., & Mirabito, D. M. (2005). Practicing what we teach: Using case studies from 9/11 to teach crisis intervention form a generalist perspective. *Journal of Social Work Education, 41*(3), 479–494.

Germain, C., & Gitterman, A. (1980). *The life model of social work practice*. New York: Columbia University Press.

Germain, C., & Gitterman, A. (1996). *The life model of social work practice* (2nd ed.). New York: Columbia University Press.

Gibbs, L., & Gambrill, E. (2002). Evidence-based practice: Counterarguments to objections. *Social Work Practice, 12*, 452–476.

Gilbert, N., & Specht, H. (1977). Social planning and community: Approaches. In J. B. Turner (Ed.), *Encyclopedia of social work* (17th, ed., Vol. 2, pp. 1412–1425). New York: National Association of Social Workers Press.

Glaser, G. (2001). Reflections of a social work practitioner: Bridging the 19th and 21st centuries. *Research on Social Work Practice, 11*(2), 190–200.

Glisson, C., & Hemmelgam, A. (1998). The effects of organizational climate and inter-organizational coordination on the quality and outcomes of children service systems. *Child Abuse and Neglect, 22*(5), 401–421.

Gorey, K. M. (1996). Effectiveness of social work intervention research: Internal versus external evaluation. *Social Work Research, 20*, 119–128.

Gorey, K. M., Thyer, B. A., & Powluck, D. E. (1999). Differential effectiveness of prevalent social work practice models. *Social Work, 43*(3), 269–278.

Gummer, B. (1995). Social planning. In R. Edward (Ed.), *Encyclopedia of social work* (19th ed.). Washington, DC: National Association of Social Workers Press.

Gurin, A. (1971). Social planning and community organization. *Encyclopedia of social work* (16th ed.). New York: National Association of Social Workers Press.

Gutierrez, L., & Lewis, E. (1999). *Empowering women of color*. New York: Columbia University Press.

Henggeler, S. W., & Borduin, C. M. (1990). *Family therapy and beyond: A multisystemic approach to treating the behavior problems of children and adolescents.* Pacific Grove, CA: Brooks/Cole.

Henggeler, S. W., Pickel, S. G., Brondino, M. J., & Crouch, J. L. (1996). Eliminating (almost) treatment dropout of substance abusing or dependent delinquents through home-based multisytemic therapy. *American Journal of Psychiatry, 153*(3), 427–428.

Hillier, A., Wernecke, M. L., & McKelvey, H. (2005). Removing barriers to the use of community information systems. *Journal of Community Practice, 13*(1), 121–139.

Hopps, J. (1985). Effectiveness and human worth. Editorial. *Social Work, 30*(6), 467.

Hopps, J. (2000). Social work: A contextual profession. In J. Hopps & R. Morris (Eds.), *Social work at the millennium: Critical reflections on the future of the profession.* New York: Free Press.

Hopps, J., & Collins, P. M. (1995). Social work profession overview. In R. L. Edward (Ed.), *Encyclopedia of social work* (19th ed.). Washington, DC: National Association of Social Workers Press.

Hopps, J., & Kilpatrick, A. with assistance of Nelson, J. (2006). Contexts of helping: Commonalities and human diversities. In A. Kilpatrick & T. Holland (Eds.), *Working with families: An integrated model by level of need.* Boston: Allyn & Bacon.

Hopps, J., & Pinderhughes, E. (1987). Social work in the United States: History, context, and issues. In M. Hokenstad, S. Khinduka, & J. Midgley (Eds.), *Profiles in international social work* (pp. 163–179). Washington, DC: National Association of Social Workers Press.

Hopps, J., & Pinderhughes, E. (1999). *Group work with overwhelmed clients.* New York: Free Press.

Hopps, J., Pinderhughes, E., & Shankar, R. (1995). *The power to care: Clinical practice effectiveness with overwhelmed clients.* New York: Free Press.

Iatridis, D. (1995). Policy practice. In R. Edward (Ed.), *Encyclopedia of social work* (19th ed., pp. 1855–1866). Washington, DC: National Association of Social Workers Press.

Iatridis, D. (2000). State social welfare: Global perspectives. In J. G. Hopps & R. Morris (Eds.), *Social work at the millennium.* New York: Free Press.

Jansson, B. (1990). *Social welfare policy: From theory to practice.* Belmont, CA: Wadsworth.

Kemp, S., Whittaker, T. E., & Tracy, E. (1997). *Person-environment practice: The social ecology of interpersonal helping.* New York: Aldine de Gruyter.

Korr, W., & Brieland, D. (2000). Social justice, human rights and welfare reform. In J. G. Hopps & R. Morris (Eds.), *Social work at the millennium.* New York: Free Press.

Kurland, R., & Salmon, R. (1998). Purpose: A misunderstood and misused keystone of group work practice. *Social Work in Groups, 21*(3), 5–17.

Lowe, T. B. (2004). *The Bush administration's faith-based and community initiative policy: Meaningful policy or smoke screen?* Invited paper presented at the University of Georgia's school of social work's annual field conference in Athens, GA.

Lowe, T. B., & Hopps, J. G. l. (in press). African American's response to their social environment: A macro perspective. In L. See (Ed.), *An African American perspectives in human behavior in the social environment* (2nd ed.). New York: Haworth Press.

Margolin, L. (1997). *Under the cover of kindness: The intervention of social work.* Charlottesville: University Press of Virginia.

Meenaghan, T. (2001). Exploring possible relations among social sciences, social work and health intervention. *Social Work in Health Care, 33*(1), 43–50.

Meyer, C. H. (1976). *Social work practice* (2nd ed.). New York: Free Press.

Meyer, C. H. (Ed.). (1983). *Clinical social work in the eco-systems perspective.* New York: Columbia University Press.

Meyer, C. H. (1987). Direct practice in social work: Overview. In A. Minahan (Ed.), *Encyclopedia of social work* (18th ed., Vol. 1, pp. 409–422). Silver Spring, MD: National Association of Social Workers Press.

Minahan, A., & Briar, S. (1977). Introduction to the special issues. *Social Work, 22*(5), 339.

Morales, A., & Sheafor, B. (2002). *The many faces of social work clients*. Boston: Allyn & Bacon.

Morales, A., & Salcido, R. (2002). Social work practice with Mexican Americans. In A. Morales & B. Sheafor (Eds.), *The many faces of social work clients* (pp.267–293). Boston: Allyn & Bacon.

National Association of Social Workers. (2000, November 9). *Social workers elected to congress*. Press Release. Retrieved January 24, 2006, from www.naswdc.org/pressroom/2000/110900/.

Norton, D. (Ed.). (1978). *The dual perspective: Inclusion of ethnic minority content in the social work curriculum*. New York: Council on Social Work Education.

O'Hare, T., Tran, T. V., & Collins, P. (2002). Validating the practice skills inventory: A confirmatory factor analysis. *Research on Social Work Practice, 12*, 653–668.

Perlman, H. H. (1957). *Social casework: A problem solving process*. Chicago: University of Chicago Press.

Perlman, R. (1977). Social planning and community organization. In J. Turner (Ed.), *Encyclopedia of social work* (17th ed.). New York: National Association of Social Workers Press.

Phillips, N. K., & Straussner, S. L. A. (2002). *Urban social work: Introduction to policy and practice in the cities*. Boston: Allyn & Bacon.

Pincus, A., & Minahan, A. (1977). Conceptual frameworks for social work practice. *Social Work, 22*, 347–352.

Pinderhughes, E. (1983). Empowerment: For our clients and for ourselves. *Social Casework, 64*, 312–314.

Pinderhughes, E. (1995). Direct practice overview. In R. L. Edward (Ed.), *Encyclopedia of social work* (19th ed., pp. 740–751). Washington, DC: National Association of Social Workers Press.

Queiro-Tajalli, I., & Campbell, C. (2002). Organizing women of color. In S. Hick & J. McNutt (Eds.), *Advocacy, activism and the internet: Community organization and social policy* (pp. 113–127). Chicago: Lyceum Books.

Reamer, R. G. (1994). The evolution of social work knowledge. In R. G. Reamer (Ed.), *The foundations of social work knowledge*. New York: Columbia University Press.

Redl, F., & Wineman, D. (1952). *Controls from within: Techniques for the treatment of the aggressive child*. New York: Free Press.

Reid, W. J. (1997). Long-term trends in clinical social work. *Social Service Review*, 200–213.

Report of the National Advisory Commission on Civil Disorders. (1968). *The Kerns Commission*. New York: Bantam Books.

Richmond, M. (1917). *Social diagnosis*. New York: Sage.

Richmond, M. (1920). *Some next steps in social treatment, proceeding of national conference of social work*. Chicago: University of Chicago Press.

Rosen, A. (2003). Evidence-based social work practice: Challenges and promise. *Social Work Research, 27*, 197–208.

Ross, H. (2000). *Growing older: Health issues for minorities—Closing the gap*. A newsletter of the Office of Minority Health, U.S. Department of Health and Human Services. Washington, DC: U.S. Government Printing Office.

Rothman, J. (2001). Approaches to community intervention in strategies for community intervention. In J. Rothman, J. L. Erlich, & J. E. Tropman (Eds.), *Strategies in community interventions* (pp. 27–64). Itasca, IL: Peacock.

Schlesinger, E., & Devore, W. (1995). Ethnic-sensitive practice. In R. Edwards (Ed.), *Encyclopedia of social work* (19th ed.). Washington, DC: National Association of Social Workers Press.

Schon, D. A. (1995). Reflective inquiry in social work practice. In P. M. Hess & E. J. Mullen (Eds.), *Practitioner-research partnerships: Building knowledge from in and for practice*. Washington, DC: National Association of Social Workers Press.

Schore, A. N. (1994). A century after Freud's project: Is a rapprochement between psychoanalysis and neurobiology at hand? *Journal of the American Psychoanalytic Association, 45*(3), 809–840.

Schwartz, W. (1961). *The social worker in the group. Social welfare forum.* New York: Columbia University Press.

Schwartz, W. (1983). The group work tradition in social work practice. *Social Work with Groups, 28*(3/4), 69–89.

Segal, S. P. (1972). Research on the outcome of social work therapeutic interventions: A review of the literature. *Journal of Health and Social Behavior, 13*, 3–17.

Shapiro, J. R., & Applegate, J. S. (2000). Cognitive neuroscience, neurobiology and affect regulation: Implication for clinical social work. *Clinical Social Work Journal, 28*(1), 9–21.

Siporin, M. (1975). *Introduction to social work practice*. New York: Macmillan.

Solomon, B. (1976). *Black empowerment*. New York: Columbia University Press.

Solomon, B. (2002). Social work practice with African Americans. In A. T. Morales & B. W. Sheafor (Eds.), *The many faces of social work clients* (pp. 295–315). Boston: Allyn & Bacon.

Spetch, H., & Courtney, M. (1994). *Unfaithful angels*. New York: Free Press.

Sundel, M., Glasser, P., Sarri, R., & Vinter, R. (Eds.). (1985). *Individual change through small groups* (2nd ed.). New York: Free Press.

Sze, W., & Hopps, J. (1973). *Program evaluation and accountability*. Cambridge, England: Schenkmane.

Taylor, C., & White, S. (2002). What works about what work? Fashion, fad and EBP. *Social Work and Social Science Review, 10*(1), 63–81.

Thomas, E. J. (Ed.). (1967). *The socio-behavioral approach and applications to social work*. New York: Council on Social Education.

Thyer, B. A. (2004). Science and evidence-based social work practice. In H. E. Briggs & T. L. Rzepnicki (Eds.), *Using evidence in social work practice: Behavioral perspectives* (pp. 54–65). Chicago: Lyceum Books.

Tropp, E. (1978). Whatever happened to group work? *Social Work with Groups, 1*(1) 85–94.

Toseland, R., & Rivas, R. (2001). *An introduction to group work practice* (3rd ed.). Boston: Allyn & Bacon.

Tourse, R., & Blythe, B. J. (2003). Promoting positive development in children, youth and families: A social work cultural practice perspective. In R. Lerner, D. Lide, & F. Jacobs (Eds.), *Handbook of applied developmental science: Promoting positive child, adolescences and family development through research policy and practice* (Vol. 4, pp. 337–352). Thousand Oaks, CA: Sage.

Wood, K. M. (1978). Casework effectiveness: A new look at research evidence. *Social Work, 23*, 437–458.

Chapter 4

PROFESSIONAL CREDENTIALS AND PROFESSIONAL REGULATIONS: SOCIAL WORK PROFESSIONAL DEVELOPMENT

Donna DeAngelis and Mary Jo Monahan

DEVELOPMENT OF SOCIAL WORK AS A PROFESSION

The American Heritage Dictionary defines profession as, "An occupation or vocation requiring training in the liberal arts or sciences and advanced study in a specialized field" (p. 989). *The Social Work Dictionary* defines profession as, "A group of people who use in common a system of values, skills, techniques, knowledge, and beliefs to meet a specific social need. The public comes to identify this group as being suited to fulfill the specific need and often gives it formal and legal recognition through licensing or other sanctions as the legitimate source for providing the relevant service" (Barker, 2003, p. 379).

In addition, *The Social Work Dictionary* defines a professional as "an individual who qualifies for membership in a specific profession and uses its practices, knowledge, and skills to provide services to a client system, and in so doing, always adheres to its values and code of ethics," (Barker, 2003, p. 379) which is a codified and accepted set of values and ethics guiding conduct in the practice of the profession.

Social work did not start as a profession. Reamer (2006) divides the evolution of social work values and ethics into four periods: the Morality Period, the Values Period, the Ethical Theory and Decision-Making Period, and the Ethical Standards and Risk Management Period. In the nineteenth century, social work was practiced by "friendly visitors" who would try to strengthen the morality of the poor. During the last quarter of the twentieth century, that moral focus was replaced with social work practitioners' attempts to establish "intervention strategies and techniques, training programs, and schools of thought" (Reamer, 2006). By the middle of the twentieth century, the social work profession articulated core values and developed formal ethical guidelines to guide the conduct of practitioners. The first Code of Ethics was adopted in 1947 by the Delegate Conference of the American Association of Social Workers. The National Association of Social Workers (NASW) adopted its first Code of Ethics in 1960, 5 years after the organization was formed from several professional social work organizations.

During the 1970s, the burgeoning interest in ethics in the social work profession coincided with a broader interest in applied and professional ethics among other professions. Ethics became a subject in and of itself, during this period, spurred on by the growing interest in bioethics. The most recent stage, the Ethical Standards and Risk Management Period, is characterized by the significant expansion of ethical standards to guide practitioners' conduct and by increased knowledge concerning professional negligence and liability (Reamer, 2006).

PROFESSIONAL CREDENTIALS

The First Social Work Certification—ACSW

Shortly after its Code of Ethics went into effect, NASW began to offer the first voluntary professional certification, the Academy of Certified Social Workers (ACSW). The ACSW credential was targeted to social workers with a masters degree and 2 years of supervised postgraduate social work experience. For the first 2 years, the certification was offered to social workers who made application, provided verification of degree and supervision, and provided professional references. During this time, NASW developed an examination that would be the final requirement for the ACSW. A job analysis was conducted, comprised of a survey that asked what social workers did, how important it was that they did it correctly, and how frequently they did it. From this survey research, an examination outline was constructed and test questions written. The first ACSW examination was given in 1962.

To certify that there was no discrimination built into the eligibility system for the ACSW, in the mid-1990s, the NASW decided that the overall passing score for the ACSW would be computed on three equally weighted factors: number of years of postgraduate experience, a score calculated from three numerically rated reference forms submitted by social work supervisors and colleagues, and the number of correct answers on the examination.

In the 1960s, 1970s, and into the 1980s, many states accepted the ACSW certification as verification of qualifications for social work licensure, in lieu of a national licensing examination.

Since that time, NASW has developed a number of voluntary certifications, including Qualified Clinical Social Worker (QCSW), for listing in the *NASW Register of Clinical Social Workers;* the Diplomate in Clinical Social Work; the Academy of Certified Baccalaureate Social Workers; the School Social Work Specialist, and others. The American Board of Examiners in Clinical Social Work (ABE) has offered a Board Certified Diplomate in Clinical Social Worker (BCD) since the late 1980s. Other organizations offer specialty certifications in drug and alcohol treatment, marriage and family therapy, case management, and so on.

Definition of Licensing Terms

Credential is often used to describe any document that verifies the qualifications of a social worker. It is the term most often used to refer to voluntary recognitions from professional associations such as those mentioned in the previous section. Credentialing programs are usually operated by private organizations and serve to promote the profession and the professional holding them as having demonstrated knowledge, abilities, and achievement beyond the minimum competency requirements to become licensed.

Certification, credentialing, licensure, and registration are terms that are applied to the regulation of social work in different jurisdictions. For purposes of regulation, there is no legal distinction between certification and licensure, although it is common for *certification* to describe a less rigorous regulatory structure than *licensure,* which usually refers to a more comprehensive system. These terms are further confused in their use as part of the title of a legally regulated social worker, such as "Licensed Social Worker" or "Certified Social Worker."

The real distinction in legal regulation is between a *practice act,* the legislation that defines and regulates practice and establishes who can call themselves a social worker, and *title protection* legislation, which regulates what social workers who have met the legal requirements can call themselves, such as "Licensed Social Worker." Practice acts define the professional activities that can be performed and require anyone engaging in these activities to hold a license. Title protection acts are less stringent and do not prevent others who do not meet the qualifications from practicing, only from calling themselves by the regulated title, such as "Licensed Social Worker."

The term *registration,* within the United States, is used to describe a system of voluntary registration with a governmental authority in order to use a prescribed restricted title. Michigan was the last state to have a system of registration, until it enacted its practice act licensing law in 2004. Some states, like Louisiana, have a system of registration for baccalaureate social workers.

In Canada, the legal regulation of social work is referred to as *registration.* Canadian provincial laws have enacted mandatory registration systems which operate in ways very similar to practice act/title protection models in the United States.

Social Work Licensing

Professions are legally regulated to protect the public through legislatively defining minimum competence and setting a code of conduct for professional behavior. Regulation enacted by statute sets the terms for who can practice a profession and call themselves a member of that profession by delineating the needed qualifications and competencies. Legal regulation also provides the public with an avenue of recourse should something go wrong in the delivery of services or professional behavior. A codified and uniform set of values and ethics must necessarily be in place before a profession can be legally regulated and held publicly accountable to not only an expectation of knowledge, skills, and abilities, but also to conduct according to an accepted code of ethics.

The first professions to be regulated were medicine and dentistry, followed by architecture and accountancy, all of which became regulated in the late nineteenth and early twentieth centuries. Social work was just being formed as a profession then. The social work profession became legally regulated through legislation first in Puerto Rico in 1934. In 1945, California was the second state to pass legislation to regulate social work, and the first state to license clinical social workers. It took until 1961 before the next state, Rhode Island, passed a bill to license social workers. During the 1960s, six more states began to license social workers: New York and Oklahoma in 1965; Virginia in 1966; Illinois in 1967; South Carolina in 1968; and Maine in 1969. Fourteen more states licensed social workers in the 1970s (Association of Social Work Boards, 2002).

The NASW developed a model social work licensing law in 1980 and disseminated it to its chapters. The NASW chapters took their policy practice assignment very seriously and went about proposing and advocating for social work licensure legislation. Twenty-six more states passed social work licensure during the 1980s and, by 1992, all states, the District of Columbia, Puerto Rico, and the Virgin Islands legally regulated social workers in some form. The last three states to license social workers were Indiana, New Jersey, and Wisconsin, in 1990, 1991, and 1992, respectively. As of 2005, the Association of Social Work Boards (ASWB) estimated that there are almost 400,000 licensed social workers practicing in the United States and Canada. (See Table 4.1)

For the most part, the only common thread among these jurisdictional efforts was the attempt to regulate: as early laws were enacted, a hodgepodge of different structures for regulating social work emerged. There were, and still are, many variations in how states and territories regulate the social work profession. Some states licensed social workers in a single category upon graduation with a master's degree, or in a single category for a master's degree and 2 years of postgraduate experience, or 2 years of specifically clinical social work experience. Other jurisdictions legally regulated baccalaureate social workers upon graduation, master's social workers upon graduation, and master's social workers with 2 years of postgraduate experience, some requiring specific clinical experience. There were variations in the supervision requirements, the qualifications required of the supervisor, and the examination required. There were also many jurisdictions with social workers employed in certain settings that were exempt from licensure, for example, federal, state, and local governmental agencies.

The model law developed and promulgated by NASW provided a three-tiered licensure structure: baccalaureate social workers (BSW) upon graduation, master's social workers (MSW) upon graduation, and an "advanced" licensure for master's social workers with 2 years of supervised experience. There was no distinction made for this category to be strictly for a license to practice clinical social work. The practicalities of parity with other mental health professions—including the need to qualify for third-party reimbursement—drove the pursuit of specific clinical social work licensure.

The Association of Social Work Boards

Sometime in the late 1970s, the NASW called a meeting of NASW staff and volunteers and social workers who were serving as members of the social work regulatory boards at the time to discuss working together on licensing examinations to offer to state boards of social work. Some of the attendees at that meeting felt that the regulatory boards needed their own organization and that licensing examinations should be independent of the professional organization.

The first meeting of what was to become the American Association of State Social Work Boards (AASSWB) was attended by 23 social work regulators from 12 states. The meeting was held September 24 through 26, 1978, in Louisville, Kentucky: by March 1979, AASSWB was incorporated in Virginia. Shortly thereafter, on March 23, 1979, the AASSWB constitutional convention was held in Denver, Colorado, with delegates from 18 of the 23 states that had some kind of social work regulation at that time.

The purpose of forming an organization specifically devoted to social work licensure was to promote networking among social work regulators to share information about the structure and issues involved in legal regulation. It soon became evident that another purpose was at the forefront of this organization's work—the development of a national social work licensing examination program. The founding members agreed to make this a priority and

Table 4.1 Social Work Law Enactment

By Date		By Jurisdiction	
1934	Puerto Rico	Alabama	1977
1945	California	Alaska	1988
1961	Rhode Island	Alberta	1969
1965	New York	Arizona	1988
	Oklahoma	Arkansas	1975
1966	Virginia	California	1945
1967	Illinois	Colorado	1975
1968	South Carolina	Connecticut	1985
1969	Maine	Delaware	1976
	Alberta	D. of Columbia	1986
1972	Louisiana	Florida	1981
	Michigan	Georgia	1984
	Utah	Hawaii	1989
1974	Kansas	Idaho	1976
	Kentucky	Illinois	1967
1975	Arkansas	Indiana	1990
	Colorado	Iowa	1984
	Maryland	Kansas	1974
	South Dakota	Kentucky	1974
1976	Delaware	Louisiana	1972
	Idaho	Maine	1969
1977	Alabama	Maryland	1975
	Massachusetts	Massachusetts	1977
1979	Oregon	Michigan	1972
1980	Tennessee	Minnesota	1987
1981	Florida	Mississippi	1987
	Texas	Missouri	1989
1983	Montana	Montana	1983
	New Hampshire	Nebraska	1986
	North Carolina	Nevada	1987
	North Dakota	N. Hampshire	1983
	Virgin Islands	New Jersey	1991
1984	Georgia	New Mexico	1989
	Iowa	New York	1965
	Ohio	N. Carolina	1983
	West Virginia	North Dakota	1983
1985	Connecticut	Ohio	1984
1986	D. of Columbia	Oklahoma	1965
	Nebraska	Oregon	1979
	Vermont	Pennsylvania	1987
	Wyoming	Puerto Rico	1934
1987	Minnesota	Rhode Island	1961
	Mississippi	S. Carolina	1968
	Nevada	South Dakota	1975
	Pennsylvania	Tennessee	1980
	Washington	Texas	1981

(continued)

Table 4.1 (*Continued*)

By Date		By Jurisdiction	
1988	Alaska	Utah	1972
	Arizona	Vermont	1986
1989	Hawaii	Virginia	1966
	Missouri	Virgin Islands	1983
	New Mexico	Washington	1987
1990	Indiana	West Virginia	1984
1991	New Jersey	Wisconsin	1992
1992	Wisconsin	Wyoming	1986

contracted with a psychometrician to obtain the expertise needed. In 1981, the first social work job analysis was conducted. A job analysis is a survey of social workers asking them to rate a series of tasks as to how often each task is performed, how important it is when the task is performed that it is done correctly, and whether they need to know how to do it at entry to the profession. The results from the survey are statistically analyzed, and reviewed by social work subject matter experts who use the data to construct examination blueprints, or content outlines. The 1981 job analysis resulted in three national examinations that paralleled the NASW Model Social Work Law: Level A for baccalaureate social workers (BSW) upon graduation, Level B for master's social workers (MSW) upon graduation, and, Level C for social workers with a master's degree and a minimum of 2 years of practice experience. AASSWB began to offer these examinations in 1983.

In order for examinations to remain valid, a job analysis must be conducted every 5 to 10 years to keep the content tested current with practice. The second job analysis was done in 1988, which resulted in four examinations that AASSWB began to give in 1990: Basic for BSW graduates, Intermediate for MSW graduates, Advanced for MSW graduates with 2 years of generalist experience, and Clinical for MSW graduates with 2 years of postgraduate clinical social work experience.

By 1991, all states that required an examination for social work licensing were using the AASSWB exams. Two more surveys, now called practice analyses, have been done since then. The one completed in 1997 resulted in examinations administered effective July 1998. The most recent practice analysis was finished in 2003 with examinations administered in May 2004. Although the categories of examinations target the same groups, again the names were changed to Bachelor's, Master's, Advanced Generalist, and Clinical. California stopped using the national AASSWB Clinical examination in April 1999 and currently administers its own state-specific examination. All other states, the District of Columbia, the Virgin Islands, and two Canadian provinces, Alberta and British Columbia, use the AASSWB examinations. These exams are given electronically at over 200 ACT Test Centers, most of which are open 5 or 6 days a week.

As membership in the original AASSWB grew, Canadian provinces began to express interest in membership. Alberta became the first provincial member in 1998. At the 20th anniversary Annual Meeting of the Delegate Assembly, AASSWB voted to officially change its name to the Association of Social Work Boards (ASWB). Today, its membership includes eight Canadian provinces: Alberta, British Columbia, Manitoba, New Brunswick, Nova Scotia, Quebec, Prince Edward Island, and Saskatchewan. The only full members of ASWB are social work regulatory boards. Each board has a delegate representative to the annual meeting and there is one vote per member jurisdiction. The delegate assembly votes on changes to the bylaws, sets the examination fee, and elects an eight-member board of directors that conducts the association's business.

Over the years, ASWB has offered more and more services to its member boards. In 1992, ASWB began to offer training for regulatory board members and this has grown to three new board member training sessions each year. ASWB also started and maintains the Disciplinary Action Reporting System (DARS) to which social work regulatory boards report final disciplinary actions taken against licensed social workers. Social work boards screen the names of licensing applicants against the DARS list. This system protects the public by preventing a social worker who is disciplined in one jurisdiction from going to another jurisdiction and getting a license without disclosing the disciplinary action.

In 1998, ASWB developed a new *Model Social Work Practice Act,* which is reviewed and updated annually in keeping with changes in the social work profession and within legal professional regulation. The *Act* has been used as a resource by a number of social work licensing boards to update and upgrade their laws.

ASWB also approves continuing education programs and individual courses through its Approved Continuing Education (ACE) program and the Social Work Registry operated by ASWB allows social workers to place their credentialing information, including examination test scores, academic transcripts, supervision, and continuing education documentation in a permanent location that each regulatory board may access to facilitate licensure within its jurisdiction.

Professional Regulation—Current Licensure Structure

Today, social work can include as many as four parts: BSW, usually upon graduation; MSW upon graduation; independent after 2 years of supervised general experience; and clinical after 2 years of specific supervised clinical experience. Most jurisdictions license social workers in two or more of these categories. According to ASWB, as of 2006 baccalaureate social workers were legally regulated in 35 states. The same number of states, 35, although not necessarily the same ones, regulated master's social workers. Social workers practicing independently, but not necessarily as clinical social workers, were licensed in 23 states, and clinical social workers were licensed in 45 states. In 2006, six states had a category of associate licensure for people who work in the social service field but who do not have a formal social work degree.

The picture is a bit different in Canada. All 10 provinces have registration for baccalaureate social workers, and eight provinces register master's social workers, unusually under the same registration act and title. Two provinces also license clinical social workers, and one province also registers social workers for independent practice.

The regulatory trends for social work in both the United States and Canada are to move from title protection to a practice act along with title protection, increase the categories of licensure, and remove exemptions from licensure so that all social workers, regardless of practice area or setting, must be licensed. This serves the regulatory boards' mission of public protection by ensuring that all of the public is served by social workers who meet minimum qualifications and standards and are accountable to a governmental body for their practice.

Licensure Requirements

Typically, the requirements for licensure are education, supervised experience, demonstration of knowledge—minimum competence—by passing an exam, references, good moral character, and fees. A BSW or MSW degree is required for the bachelor's and master's categories of licensure, and a few states also require postgraduate experience before qualifying for these licenses. An MSW and a minimum of 2 years of postgraduate supervised experience are required for the independent and clinical categories of licensure. Some states require more than 2 years of supervised clinical experience, and/or proof of a minimum number of hours in a clinical field placement, and/or proof of specific clinical coursework, most typically psychopathology.

Generally, after a licensure candidate has submitted documented proof of meeting the board's requirements, the candidate is approved to take a licensing examination. Those examinations developed and maintained by ASWB are almost universally used in the United States, except as mentioned before by California. There are four categories of examination, parallel to the categories of licensure. The bachelor's and master's examinations are constructed to test knowledge upon graduation with a BSW or MSW degree. The advanced generalist and clinical examinations are developed for social workers with an MSW and a minimum of 2 years postgraduate experience. For the clinical examination, this must be specific clinical social work experience.

The content of each of the four examinations is determined by a survey, conducted at regular intervals, usually every 5 to 10 years, to keep the knowledge tested current with practice. Social workers are asked to rate a series of tasks on how frequently they do each one, how important it is that when they do the task they do it competently and correctly, and whether it is important to know how to do it upon entry to practice. The survey is constructed by a group of social workers who are subject matter experts. This same group reviews the results and from these results and their expert opinions construct the content outlines for each examination.

Licensure can be complex and variable. It is strongly recommended that social workers become familiar with the licensing laws in the jurisdictions where they practice. Social work students should become knowledgeable about licensure as soon as possible so that they can plan their education, supervision, and experience to meet the requirements. Information on the licensure requirements in each state and province, along with direct links to the licensing board's web sites, can be found at www.aswb.org.

Functions of Regulatory Boards

Boards that regulate the practice of social work perform multiple functions, with the protection of the public as the cornerstone. Social work is a professional practice that affects the public health, safety, and welfare of the citizens of the jurisdiction, and the regulatory board has the statutory power to define and establish the credentials required for various levels of practice competency, the ability to issue or deny a professional license, and the power to investigate allegations of improper practice and impose disciplinary sanctions on a social worker who violates the statutes of the practice act within the jurisdiction.

Legislation in each jurisdiction in the United States and Canada defines the qualifications and educational requirements for social workers, and specifies the activities associated with social work practice at the bachelor's, master's, and clinical levels. The requirements for licensure are specified in each practice act. Exemptions from licensure, generally based on employment categories, are also delineated; exemptions are discouraged in the ASWB model law, but do continue to exist in some jurisdictions. The regulations extend to all social workers practicing in the jurisdiction regardless of the place of actual residency.

Regulatory boards define the scope of practice and standards for professional conduct for each category of social work license, thereby defining what unlawful practice and violation of the code of conduct is. In order to fulfill the responsibility of public protection, boards have the authority to discipline individuals who violate the act or its rules, including the ability to prohibit these individuals from threatening the public with harm. Disciplinary provisions state the grounds for disciplinary actions, the procedures for the filing and investigation of a complaint, deciding on the imposition of a disciplinary action, and application of penalties for the violation. Grounds for disciplinary procedures may include, but are not limited to, unprofessional conduct as determined by the board, practicing outside of the applicable scope of practice, unlicensed practice, conviction of a felony, or incapacity or impairment that prevents the licensee from engaging in the practice of social work with the reasonable competence required to protect the public.

Disciplinary regulations also contain the specific conditions for imposition of penalties, including consideration of mitigating or aggravating circumstances and establish the grounds for reinstatement of a license. Penalties may include the denial of a license, new or renewed, a monetary fine, restrictions on the license, imposition of supervised practice by a board-approved practice monitor, required continuing education, and/or suspension, probation, or revocation of the license.

A licensed social worker who is physically or mentally unable to practice safely because of mental illness or the use or addiction to drugs or alcohol is considered an impaired professional. Some jurisdictions have diversionary programs to provide treatment to these impaired social workers, under the supervision of the regulatory board, and usually restrict or supervise their practice during the time they are receiving treatment. In some states, the NASW chapter provides the helping program for impaired practitioners, but the social worker always remains ultimately accountable to the board.

Supervision

As the regulation of social work practice evolves, regulatory boards face the challenge of articulating the necessary components of supervision for specific levels of licensure. Supervision has always been addressed in social work education and practice, but regulatory boards increasingly are feeling the need to examine and define what constitutes adequate supervision for a candidate for licensure. Supervision for the purpose of qualifying for licensure is one of the last gates through which a candidate must pass to qualify for a license. The supervisor is accountable to the regulatory board for the supervision, practice, and evaluation of the licensure applicant, in addition to being accountable to the supervisee and the agency. Most regulatory boards have specific requirements, especially for clinical supervision, including number of hours required, qualifications of the supervisor, individual supervision requirements and group supervision limits, provisions for supervision by alternate mental health professions, and if allowed, how many of the required supervisory hours are permitted to be provided by other professionals. The trend is for regulatory boards to strengthen and more closely specify the qualifications for clinical supervisors. Some boards have a list of approved clinical supervisors, and most boards require the supervisor to possess a license of the same category for which the supervision is being provided and a minimum number of years of experience, which are increasing in many jurisdictions to five. More information about the specific supervision requirements in each jurisdiction can be found at www.aswb.org, and standards are available in the ASWB model law.

An additional challenge for regulatory boards is the appropriate use of supervision as a disciplinary measure. Many disciplinary actions involving social workers who violate practice regulations or standards include some form of supervision to assist the social worker in understanding and conforming to practice standards. The optimum use of supervision for this purpose continues to be an area of focus for regulatory boards.

Public Protection

Protection of the public remains the essential function of all social work regulation. Social work regulations, including certification and licensure, ensure that minimum standards for the practice of social work are established at the bachelor's, master's, and advanced clinical practice level, and that the requirements for competency are met. In addition, citizens who receive social work services have a mechanism to address poor practice by a social worker or the violation of practice ethics and standards, or practice by an unlicensed worker. As technology expands and the need for highly skilled and ethical practitioners grows to meet the increasing demands of complex social problems, regulatory boards will evolve with the profession and continue to serve the mission of public protection.

The recognition that a profession needs to be regulated to protect the public is a significant milestone in the development of a profession. That, in 2007, there is some form of legal regulation of social work in all the jurisdictions in the United States and Canada, and increasingly in other countries, is an indication that the profession has reached the point in its development where it is recognized and acknowledged for its importance and power. The responsibility of a profession to be regulated and to hold its members accountable for practicing competently and ethically is commensurate with this power and importance.

REFERENCES

American Heritage Dictionary of the English Language (4th ed.). (2006). Boston: MA: Houghton Mifflin.

Association of State Social Work Boards. (2002). *Social work laws and regulations online comparison guide*. Retrieved April 16, 2007, from www.aswbdata.powerlynxhosting.net.

Barker, R. L. (2003). *The social work dictionary* (5th ed.). Washington, DC: National Association of Social Workers.

Reamer, F. G. (2006). *Social work values and ethics* (3rd ed.). New York: Columbia University Press.

Chapter 5

SOCIAL WORK ORGANIZATIONS

Gary R. Lowe and Terry L. Singer

A clear theme throughout the development and evolution of social work as an occupation and a profession is one of structural and organizational diversity. The profession continues to engage in a national effort to forge an integration of several major entities all representing large constituencies of both practitioners as well as educators. The effort and struggle, perhaps even crisis, to establish a more unified voice for the profession reflects a century-long organizational history marked by constant forming and splintering of voices and forces never seeming to be able to coalesce around a single core. While the medical profession, the historical professional template for social work's founding mothers and fathers; and the discipline of psychology, maturing social work's emergent historical practice/clinical template, have both managed to create powerful and politically potent organizational bases via the American Medical Association (AMA) and the American Psychological Association (APA), social work is still struggling to find a similar coherent, overarching organizational structure that embraces the diversity of interests that can be subsumed under the notion of social work as an occupation and profession. The fields of medicine and psychology are very diverse with professional subgroupings reflecting this rich canvas; nevertheless, there is still the clear power of perceived unity when a position is declared under the brand of the AMA or the APA. Social work does not have such a powerful unified voice.

This chapter provides an historical overview and record of the professional and educational organizational evolution of social work in the United States. The history that belongs to social work and that is chronicled here reflects a constant motif of approach/avoidance as the profession began to emerge in the late 1800s and struggled to assert itself as a definable new profession through the first half of the twentieth century, equal to medicine, law, and other newly emerging occupational categories. Finally, the historical record will show that social work has been less than successful in its quest for professional integration and that as the profession entered the twenty-first century, its leaders were seeking, via a newly initiated national effort, to once again find a unified voice that would embrace a still splintered and somewhat troubled profession.

Professional organizational development must be understood in the context of history. That history frames motives and opportunities. This chapter chronicles events and significant legislation that helped to shape the growth of social work organizations.

This chapter relies extensively on the foundational work of Chauncey Alexander whose work is the gold standard for understanding the formative elements of the social work profession.

THE BEGINNING: 1600 TO 1900

The history of social work's development as a profession is one of an old religiously grounded ethos of offering aid and comfort growing into an activity based on a range of social sciences. This development would also reflect the social forces of capitalistic development, urbanization, immigration, and the related forces seeking to rationalize society and respond to these forces through the formation of organized occupational categories generally identified as professions. The historical record begins in England in the fifteenth and seventeenth century with both religious and societal structures coalescing and then being brought to the new colonies of North America.

The development of what would become social work begins prior to the revolutionary period, but the pace increased significantly during the nineteenth century due to such events as the American Civil War. The structures that would serve as the basis for modern social work and welfare would begin to take shape primarily in the growing urban centers of the country and these entities would become the foundation for an even more rapid and diverse development at the dawn of the twentieth century. The record begins in England at the opening of the seventeenth century with the promulgation of the Elizabethan Poor Laws of 1601.

Elizabethan Poor Laws

The roots of modern social work reach back into the early English and European churches and their role in providing aid and comfort to the poor and indigent. While the aid provided was often given with a posture of judgment and was not always bountiful, the impetus to help others did exist as one's pious duty. Also, the policy and structural foundation of social work and welfare is generally considered to have begun with the Elizabethan Poor Laws (EPL; 1601). These laws consolidated a number of other organized responses to the poor in England that stretched back to 1495. In effect, the Poor Laws established the first semblance of an organized, secular response to the challenge of increased dependency and social needs created by changing economic structures and the dislocation resulting from natural communal disasters such as poor harvests in rural England at the time. As an outcome of the social dislocation resulting from various social and communal forces, the Poor Laws created some control and order amidst the increased demands for both financial and dependent care by defining categories and ranking persons who were eligible for public aid as well as the nature and structure of the aid to be provided by the local authority. In addition, the laws designated the role of "overseer" of the poor, representing the first designated official role responsible for addressing and managing assistance to the poor and dependent. However, it is important to observe that the overseer was an appointed local citizen who served in basically a voluntary, unpaid role. The notion of the volunteer would become an important aspect of early American social work and would impact its organizational development throughout its historical development.

The original laws remained more or less intact until 1834 when parliament passed the Poor Law Amendment Act. This act was a reactionary measure designed to put a stop to the increasing belief that public relief provision had created a large class of indolent poor through the provision of "outdoor relief." The 1834 Act established the workhouse phenomena (indoor relief) so powerfully invoked in many of Charles Dickens' novels.

In terms of the ultimate development of organized social work in the United States, the official legislative acts and the accompanying attitudes informed the earliest responses to the poor in the American Colonies as well as into the nineteenth century when the first organized efforts to address poverty, dependence, and indigence were made.

Association for the Improvement of the Conditions of the Poor

The principles promulgated in Elizabethan England were transported to the American colonies and became the basis for early social welfare practices and policies. Prior to the Civil War, probably the first significant social welfare organization in the United States was the formation in 1843 of The Association for the Improvement of the Conditions of the Poor (AICP) in New York City.

The AICP utilized volunteers to conduct investigations of the poor and dependent and their living conditions. The volunteers were predominantly women who, as a result of their social position, had the time to engage in such unpaid community service. Though the role was fundamentally different from the English overseer, nevertheless, the central role of the volunteer was established within the AICP. Both the predominance of women and the defined roles being structured as volunteers would continue as a central ingredient within social work as a mixed blessing in terms of its organizational development, particularly in terms of the goal of seeking full professional standing. The AICP established the concept of the "friendly visitor" which would become the cornerstone of the Charity Organization Society (COS) that would emerge roughly 40 years later.

Mid-Century Developments

During the decade prior to the American Civil War, several important agencies and events unfolded in the United States that would have significance for ultimate development of social work. In 1850, the first school for "idiotic and feeble-minded" youth was incorporated in Massachusetts. In 1851, Traveler's Aid (now Traveler's Aid International) was founded by Bryan Mullanphy in St. Louis, Missouri. In 1853, the Children's Aid Society of New York, the first child placement agency separate from an institutional program, was established by the Reverend Charles Loring Brace. In 1855, the first Young Men's Hebrew Association (YMHA) was organized in Baltimore. In the same year, the first YMCA in the United States was started in Boston by retired sea captain, Thomas C. Sullivan (Alexander, 1995).

In 1859, *The Origin of Species* by Charles Darwin was published, setting forth his theory of evolution. The importance of such a book to the development of social work is that it served to begin to move the basis for understanding human problems toward a more objective, scientific basis and away from a predominantly religious morality based perspective. The long-term effect of works such as Darwin's controversial ruminations would be to promote a growing context of science over sentiment and thus promote the move toward scientifically based professional activity that would begin to take shape at century's end.

The Civil War

Clearly the Civil War represented a cataclysmic event for the still young country, the conflict itself as well as the aftermath. However, like many similar societal upheavals, there were important and ultimately positive outcomes, several of which would have significance for the development of social work and social welfare.

In the wake of the American Civil War, Congress established the Bureau of Refugees, Freedmen and Abandoned Lands generally referred to as the Freedmen's Bureau under the administrative supervision of the War Department. The Freedmen's Bureau was a controversial creation reflecting the turmoil of the time. It was established to provide a wide range of services to refugees displaced during the Civil War and operated within the states of the former confederacy. While the Bureau's record of positive achievement is mixed, it did provide a wide array of emergency food, housing, medical, and education services to former slaves and some poor Whites displaced by the conflict. The Bureau fully functioned between 1865 and 1868 and was finally abolished in 1872 when President Andrew Johnson succeeded in cutting its funding. The Freedmen's Bureau was the first social service entity created by the federal government to provide social services to an identified population via government employees. It would not be until the 1930s and the emergence of Roosevelt's New Deal in response to the Great Depression that a similar federal effort emerged.

Urbanization and Immigration: A National Orientation Begins

In the aftermath of the Civil War, the continuing growth of large urban centers, and the influx of new immigrant groups, there was a significant growth of voluntary charitable organizations and associations. These entities were rooted in the on-going presence of religious and benevolent motives stretching back to the earliest medieval roots of social welfare. Another primary impetus for these organizations was to gain some semblance of social control of the very real challenges, as well as fears, emanating from rapid urbanization. The growth of these organizations did not mean that they were effective in addressing the problems, but it did represent a growing attention to matters of societal poverty and dependence. As a result of the several serious economic crises during the mid- to late-1870s, the still young private charitable voluntary sector was significantly challenged.

One response to the recognition of the limitations of the voluntary charitable associations was the emergence of more rationalized formal agencies. The League for Social Services and the American Institute of Social Services were formed as initiatives to develop and provide more effective and organized responses to social welfare needs (Wenocur & Reisch, 1989).

These reform organizations began to lay the foundation for the newly defined profession of social work.

In 1874, the State Board of Charities of four states (Connecticut, Massachusetts, New York, and Wisconsin) organized the Conference of Boards of Public Charities as a unit in the American Social Sciences Association (ASSA). Five years later in 1879, the Conference became the National Conference on Charities and Corrections. During this same 5-year period, the first Charity Organization Society (COS) was established in Buffalo, New York. Alexander (1995, p. 2634) summarizes the four operating principles of the COS to be, "(1) detailed investigation of applicants, (2) A central system of registry to avoid service and aid duplication, (3) Cooperation between the various relief agencies, and (4) Extensive use of the volunteer in the role of 'friendly visitors.' "

As these organizational entities developed, several themes emerged as well in terms of forces that would be dimensions of social work's overall professional development: the role of the volunteer versus the trained paid professional; the role of women and men in the development of the profession, and the beginning of the social treatment/social justice continuum. This continuum would become a central internal struggle as social work became more and more rationalized as an organized, scientific endeavor and particularly as it sought to obtain recognition as a profession.

As the COS movement grew primarily as an urban, Eastern regional phenomenon with its increased emphasis on rational organizational principals, a counterforce emerged: There was a renewed growth in self-help organizations such as the Irish Emigrant Society, the Hebrew Benevolent Society, and the White Rose Home for Girls (Wenocur & Reisch, 1989). The primary source of services to new urban immigrants through the 1870s was sectarian self-help groups. A driving motivation for many of these services was an effort to provide concrete help to those in need without the moral "preaching" that informed much of the moral uplift orientation of the COS movement. Also, the self-help groups were primarily voluntary in nature while the staff model developing from the COS movement was more toward paid staff. These societies tended to undercut COS's influence in promoting social work as a profession.

During the 2 closing decades of the nineteenth century, important organizational developments provided a strong foundation for the new profession of social work that took shape in the twentieth century. The decade of the 1880s saw the establishment of several important organizations that would be significant in the development of the social work profession and the overall delivery of social services in the United States. In 1880, the Salvation Army began in the United States, imported from England, and in 1881 Clara Barton organized the American Association of the Red Cross. On a regional basis, an important development was Booker T Washington's founding of the Tuskegee Normal and Industrial Institute. As Alexander (1995, p. 2634) notes, the Tuskegee Institute was "a leading black educational institution that [emphasized] industrial training as a means to self-respect and economic independence for African Americans."

The Settlement House Movement: The Treatment versus Justice Paradigm Emerges

Along with the development of the COS movement, a parallel social service agency began to appear in American cities: settlement houses. This movement was another concept imported from England, with Toynbee Hall in London being one of the most notable examples. In contrast to the COS approach of organizational rationalization and service coordination with a centralized office, the settlement house approach involved locating a facility in the neighborhood where the work was to be focused and the staff, still mostly volunteers, lived either in the house or within the immediate community, working to deliver mostly material services. Whereas the COS movement was establishing a social treatment model base, settlement houses were the foundation for the social action community organizing/development emphasis; in short, the other end of the continuum of social treatment/social justice.

In 1886, the first settlement house, the Neighborhood Guild, was established on the Lower East Side of New York; in 1889, Jane Addams established Hull House in Chicago; and in 1893, Lillian Wald founded the Nurses' Settlement, which was relocated in 1895 when it became the Henry Street Settlement (Alexander, 1995). The development of the settlement house movement was seen as a potential threat to the field of social work. The COS orientation was toward addressing individual needs and betterment, perhaps expanding a perspective to incorporate family; the settlement house perspective, in contrast, was to address not only the individual needs but the contextual social and economic conditions that were seen as contributing to the individual troubles. In short, the settlement house movement was clearly more social action and social change oriented than the COS movement. While this contrast, when seen from the perspective of the current era, may not seem very different, within the context of the time there was clear tension between the two approaches. By the turn of the century, over one hundred settlement houses existed in the United States, with 32 in New York State alone (Wenocur & Reisch, 1989).

During the last decade of the nineteenth century, two important books were published that brought further focus on the plight of the urban poor as well as provided a description of the organizational and institutional response to these social and economic challenges. In 1890, *How the Other Half Lives,* by Jacob A. Riis, was published. Riis's important book was "a documentary and photographic account of housing conditions in New York City slums, and it [helped] initiated what would become the U.S. public housing movement" (Alexander, 1995, p. 2634). Following the appearance of Riis' book, *American Charities,* by Amos G. Warner, was published in 1894. Warner's book was the first book to provide a systematic description of charities in the United States as well as "to formulate the principles of relief" (Alexander, 1995, p. 2634). In keeping with the rapid development of social service agencies at the end of the century, the first Federation of Jewish Charities was established in Boston in 1895.

As the nineteenth century drew to a close, the development of a growing network of social service agencies and the growing body of focused study dedicated to understanding the nature of poverty and dependence created an awareness that special training was needed in order to effectively meet the challenges of the population's growing need and dependence. While the ideal of the volunteer, altruistic worker continued to be a central fixture of social service activity, it was becoming clearer that special knowledge and related training were essential to meet the challenge. In addition, as the new century began, the push by various occupational groups such as medical practitioners to achieve the status of professional became very clear. As a result, the field of diverse social work addressed the necessity of raising the level of knowledge and scientific competence of those who wish to be considered social workers. This resulted in the beginning of formal training and education for social work.

THE EDUCATIONAL AND ORGANIZATIONAL FOUNDATIONS FOR SOCIAL WORK

Not until late in the century did recognition emerge that the issues of solving matters of poverty required more than spare time and a good heart. According to Alexander (1995, p. 2634) in 1885 "the first course on social reform was initiated by Dr. Francis G. Peabody at Harvard University." Listed as Philosophy 11, it was described as "The Ethics of Social Reform: The Questions of Charity, Divorce, the Indians, Labor, Prisons, Temperance, Etc., as Problems of Practical Ethics-Lectures, Essays and Practical Observations" (Alexander, 1995, p. 2634). As the twentieth century dawned, the altruistic endeavor that would come to be called social work experienced a rapid pace of development of a conscious occupational identity as well as a broad range of organizational infrastructure, both educationally as well as in the realm of services.

1898 to 1917

The emergence of formal training and preparation is generally identified as having taken place in the summer of 1898 when the New York COS initiated the first social work training school. This program was an annual summer course for agency workers. Following the continued success of the New York effort, Graham Taylor found the Chicago School of Civics and Philanthropy in 1903, which eventually affiliated with the University of Chicago and became School of Social Service Administration. In 1904, the New York summer school program was formalized as the New York School of Philanthropy and the course of study was expanded into a 1-year program.

Also in New York, Florence Kelley initiated and organized the National Consumers League in 1899. The League previewed the beginning scientific awareness by promoting, as a basic approach to social action, the need to obtain factual data to guide action. Another emergent trend reflected in the philosophy of the League was to seek and establish coordination among charity organizations to address social conditions. This latter coordinating focus was clearly reflected in Josephine Shaw Lowell's New York City efforts to confront the conditions that existed in sweat shops by campaigning for better working conditions and establishing limits on hours of work for girls (Alexander, 1995).

As further proof of the efforts toward the rationalization of charity work and the establishment of an organizational foundation, *Friendly Visiting among the Poor* was published in 1899. This publication, authored by Mary E. Richmond, was promoted as "A Handbook of Charity Workers" (Alexander, 1995, p. 2635). Richmond's publication reflected the beginning recognition that there was a planful basis for altruistic charity work.

In keeping with the clear urban emphasis of charity work at the time, the final year of the nineteenth century saw the creation in New York City of The National Conference of Jewish Charities (NCJC). The NCJC reflected the emerging organizational theme of coalition and coordination. As Alexander (1995, p. 2635) points out, the NCJC's "aim was to coordinate the developing network of private Jewish social services emerging in cities."

Perhaps reflecting the clearly increased momentum toward charity work evolving into an explicit realm of occupational and policy activity, in 1904 the National Child Labor Committee came into being through the combined efforts of settlement house groups in New York and Chicago and together assumed the primary sponsors and organizers of the first White House Conference on Children held in 1909. Also in 1904, Robert Hunter published an in-depth study of poverty. Hunter's book *Poverty* provided a profile of the challenge of indigence by noting that one out of every eight Americans are poor, roughly totaling ten million individuals. As a reflection of a growing awareness of the ever-increasing need to coordinate services, as well as the still strong private orientation of agency/charity work, in 1908 the first community welfare council was organized in Pittsburgh, Pennsylvania. The Pittsburgh Associated Charities was a precursor to what would ultimately become urban planning councils affiliated with the United Way later in the century. In the same year, the Federal Council of Churches of Christ in America began to coordinate its network of social services (Alexander, 1995).

The first 2 decades of the new century witnessed a steady series of developments within the educational/training realm of charity work. All of these developments, following the initial efforts in New York and Chicago, provided the foundation for the identification of social work as an emerging occupation and shaped what would become viewed as formal social work. While there were various efforts to address urban and related immigrant poverty in the emerging urban centers, there were also important initiatives on behalf of the African American population.

The first social work training program specifically for African American workers was founded in 1910 by Dr. George Edmund Haynes at Fisk University in Nashville, Tennessee. The establishment of this important educational enterprise followed a series of other important organizational developments, some also involving Dr. Haynes, focusing on the African American population. In 1907, Haynes and Eugene Kinckle Jones founded the National League on Urban Conditions among Negroes (ULUCAN; that would ultimately become the National Urban League). ULUCAN was formed by the combining of the existing Committee for Improving the Industrial Conditions of Negroes in New York (originally formed in 1907), the National League for the Protection of Colored Women (formed in 1906), and the Committee on Urban Conditions among Negroes (formed in 1910). Haynes served as the executive director from 1911 until 1918 at which time ULUCAN became the National Urban League and Jones became the first executive director of the newly named organization (Alexander, 1995).

In the midst of these important organizational developments, another central event took place in 1915 at the meeting of the National Conference of Charities and Corrections. Abraham Flexner was invited to address the conference on the question, "Is Social Work a Profession?" Flexner was well known for his major study of American medical education that laid the foundation for what would become the university-based medical training model in the United States. Flexner's answer to this question was "no." Flexner presented a six-point attribute model required for a bona fide profession to exist. As summarized by Lowe (1987, p. 202), the six key points were: "(1) intellectual operations, (2) scientific learning base, (3) practical and definite ends, (4) educationally communicable technique, (5) self-organization, and (6) altruistic motivation." This event would influence the development of social work in fundamental ways for the remainder of the century. The impact would primarily be played out as social work sought to establish its practice/skill orientation. This task of defining the practice core and uniqueness of social work would influence both the organizational evolution of social work, but also the area of educational organization. In essence, many of developments prior to Flexner can be seen as addressing larger social issues related to poverty, accompanied by an unexamined assumption of moral correctness. That is, while organizational development described so far reflects efforts to provide structural and organizational order to the efforts to combat poverty and indigence, these efforts and their practitioners assumed that a sense of positive and unexamined morality would somehow rub off on those less fortunate than they whom they served. The Flexner event would provide some significant impetus for social work to begin to more consciously define what it really did that was unique and this would result in the profession beginning to more self-consciously examine itself. What would emerge over time would be a formal educational enterprise, a growth in scientific practice activities, and a large organizational environment to enhance and support these dimensions.

1917 to 1930

As Wenocur and Reisch (1989) observed, "The period between World War I and the onset of the Great Depression was one of great growth and consolidation for... professional social work" (p. 89). Prompted by the 1915 Flexner verdict that social work was not a profession, the field clearly sought to respond to prove him wrong. In addition, the aftermath of World War I where the country was forced to begin to realize external challenges and the continued influx of immigrants into urban areas as well as the spread of the populations across the country into the Midwest and West provided further impetus for social work to seek more formal organizational structures. Therefore, a significant core of organizations with a national perspective emerged between 1917 and 1930.

The publication in 1917 of *Social Diagnosis* by Mary Richmond was very significant because the book, as Leiby (1978, p. 122) observed, served "to transform (friendly visiting) into the notion of deliberate and constructive casework." While perhaps not in direct response to Flexner's assertions in 1915 that social work was not a profession, nevertheless, Richmond's book represented a significant contribution to the important task of social work in defining its unique particular skills. In addition, the foundation laid by this book would have a profound influence on the still emerging profession of social work as well as on the philosophy and development of education and training for the profession. Given the future developments and challenges between social work determining whether it was to be a public social welfare endeavor or a more clinical therapeutic oriented activity, it is somewhat ironic that in the same year as the publication of *Social Diagnosis,* the first state department of public welfare was established in Illinois (Alexander, 1995). Therefore, as noted in the introduction, some of the dimensions of the struggle for identity that were manifested in developmental and structural activities occurring in 1917 in hindsight previewed the struggle for the profession's identity that still resonates in the present.

Between 1917 and the beginning of the Great Depression, social work basically established its foundation organizationally and educationally, and for the remainder of the twentieth century the profession devoted significant energy toward integrating the various pieces. From 1917 until 1929 "social workers established legitimacy. . . through the formation of influential national organizations" (Wenocur & Reisch, 1989, p. 89). For example:

1917 The National Jewish Welfare Board (NJWB) was founded and the National Conference on Charities and Corrections changed its name to the National Conference of Social Work.

1918 The American Association of Hospital Social Workers, the National Association of Jewish Center Workers, and the Community Chests and Councils of America were founded.

1919 The beginning date for the American Association of Organizing Family Social Work and the Community Chests and Councils of America. The latter organization would eventually become the United Community Funds and Councils of America (UCFCA, 1956) and finally in 1970, the United Way.

1920s The formation of the National Conference of Catholic Charities and the Child Welfare League of America.

1921 The National Social Workers Exchange recast itself into the first national association for professional social workers and changed its name to the American Association of Social Workers (AASW).

> Related to the creation of the AASW was the founding of the Social Work Publicity Council "as the primary agency for interpreting social problems and social work . . . (and) . . . the council served as clearinghouse for ideas and materials on public relations and published Channels periodical and special bulletins" (Alexander, 1995, p. 2638).
>
> The Maternity and Infancy Hygiene Act was passed by the U.S. Congress providing "for the first national maternal and child health program, (and) . . . The Commonwealth Fund establishes demonstration clinics for child guidance, initiating the child guidance clinic movement and establishing the essential role of social workers" (Alexander, 1995, p. 2638).

In addition to the development of national organizations and associations, the same period saw the establishment of major professional practice-focused organizations. In 1918, the American Association of Medical Social Workers (AAMSW), and in 1919 the National Association of School Social Workers (NASSW), originally named the National Association of Visiting Teachers, was formed, and in 1921 perhaps the most significant organization appeared: the American Association of Social Workers (AASW) (Wenocur & Reisch, 1989). The AASW was the first national organizational entity to represent the still emerging activity of social work and it would become central to the process of determining the direction of practice, education, and the boundaries that would define professional social work. The formation of the AASW also was a very particular organizational response to Flexner's definition of what constituted a profession. AASW's purpose was stated as follows: "acting together, (members) shall endeavor through investigation and conferences to develop professional standards in social work" (Pumphrey & Pumphrey, 1961, p. 307). Another important dimension of the emergence of the first national professional organization was the clear emphasis on the method of casework as the central practice method.

With the increasing emphasis on national practice standards and conscious identity with a defined profession, it was only natural that attention would begin to increase toward the matter of professional training and education. In terms of the organization and formalizing of social work education, a significant development in 1919 was the formation of the Association of Training Schools for Professional Social Work (ATSPSW). This organization represented the initial effort to address the ever-emerging training and education issues confronting the rapidly developing profession. As Wenocur and Reisch (1989) note, "In 1919, . . . fifteen social work schools formed an embryonic accrediting body . . . . This coalition marked the formal commitment by social work leaders to university-based education; it soon insisted that new schools could not be admitted without being an integral part of an accredited university" (p. 130). The formalizing of social work training is significant in the evolution of social work because it marked the resolution of whether social work preparation was to be agency based or university based.

Also, in the same vein as the AASW, the creation of this first educational organization can be seen as yet another response to Flexner's 1915 verdict declaring that in order to be a profession there needed to be formalized methods of preparation. In 1920, the Chicago School of Civics and Philanthropy, noted earlier as having been founded in 1903, became the Graduate School of Social Service Administration housed at the University of Chicago.

In that same year, the Atlanta School of Social Service emerged from a collaboration of the Institutes of Social Service sponsored by the Neighborhood Union of Morehouse College. This school developed under the leadership of E. Franklin Frazier and in 1924 became the first school of social work for African Americans in the United States (Alexander, 1995). Today, this school is the Whitney M. Young Jr. School of Social Work at Clark Atlanta University.

The year 1923 is very important within the context of emerging social work education due to the completion and publication of the first major study of social work education titled "Education and Training for Social Work." This study and subsequent report was conducted by James H. Tufts, professor of philosophy at the University of Chicago. The Tufts study was the first of five efforts initiated to examine and reexamine social work's educational philosophy and structure. The process of educational studies initiated by the Tufts study became a major method by which social work continually defined and redefined its aim and purpose.

In 1926, a particularly significant event was the founding of the American Association of Psychiatric Social Workers as an independent professional organization, separate from its original home as a section of the American Association of Hospital Social Workers. In the following year, the first school of social work was professionally certified by the American Association of Schools of Social Work. In 1927 in Paris, social work asserted itself as a growing global activity marked by the founding of the International Conference of Social Work (ICSW) during the first international conference of philanthropists, charity organizers, social workers, government officials, and others. The ICSW would later became the International Council on Social Welfare (Alexander, 1995).

In 1925, the National Conference of Social Welfare appointed a study committee to investigate the question of the rapidly developing diversity in social work practice. The so-called Milford Conference report was submitted in 1928 and published in 1929. The Milford Conference Report basically defined generic social practice as casework. As Lowe (1987) observed, "The Milford Conference position did not stem the tide of specialist association formation, but it represented a symbolic statement asserting that casework was the base for future professional development regardless of the particular or specialized setting" (p. 192) and promulgated the principle that process in social casework and the equipment of the social worker basically should be the same for all fields of practice.

In 1929, two events were significant in confirming the success social work had achieved in its efforts to gain recognition as a profession: *The Social Work Year Book,* the predecessor of *The Encyclopedia of Social Work* was initiated under the auspices of the Russell Sage Foundation (Alexander, 1995), and most significantly, the national census underway at the time classified social workers as "professional" (Lowe, 1987, p. 203).

By the end of the 1920s, the stock market crashed and the Great Depression loomed and social work, according to Lowe (1987, p. 192–193) "had acquired many of the basic ingredients for professional legitimacy called for in the Flexner . . . perspective." One result of this process was the increasing definition of social work as treatment rather than an activity of social reform. As social work moved away from volunteer-based, altruistic motivated engagement and became increasingly identified with a more formalized salaried professional activity, there was also a philosophical shift captured by Porter Lee's presidential address to the 1929 National Conference of Social Work titled "Social Work as Cause and

Function." Wenocur and Reich (1989, p. 139) provide the following relevant excerpt from that address:

> Charity in its origin and in its finest expression represents a cause. The organized administration of relief, under whatever auspices, has become a function. The campaigns to obtain widow's pensions and workmen's compensation have many of the aspects of the cause. The administration of these benefits has become a function of organized community life in most American states.

As Lee declared the shift in social work from cause to function, within the context of the economic depression emerging in the United States as well as the world, there was still, the unexamined "conventional American belief that economic depressions were temporary and unemployment hardships were personal... social workers relied on the ideas and structures for dealing with social need that they had built around this belief system over the previous thirty years, ideas like the sanctity of well-organized private charity and its refinement through the application of professional social casework" (Wenocur & Reisch, 1989, p. 157).

That is, as the nation confronted the Depression, social work was still forming its organizational base that in many ways was totally unprepared for the challenges about to confront it. The 20-year period between 1930 and 1950 was certainly, as Wenocur and Reisch (1989, p. 151) observe, "one of the most painful in American history," and like the nation, social work was faced with major and difficult challenges.

1930 to 1950

The Depression of the 1930s clearly had a profound effect on all structures in the country. Wenocur and Reisch (1989) provide a useful discussion of the challenge posed by the shift toward governmental sponsorship of social relief and observe that "The social welfare system that emerged as a response to the Depression transformed social work. The public sector became the dominant force in social work rather than the private" (p. 156).

One organizational development that was propitious given the seemingly sudden emergence of a public welfare sector was the creation in 1930 of the American Public Welfare Association (APWA). This organization brought together a coalition of individuals who heretofore had been considered in the background of the organizational service environment previously dominated by private, casework-oriented individuals. The APWA became the leading advocate for social work's involvement and participation in the emerging public sector and by 1931 was in a position to assure social work's participation in the new public-sponsored world.

In 1932 (Alexander, 1995):

- President Herbert Hoover signed the Emergency Relief and Construction Act which was a relatively conservative piece of legislation, but it did have a provision enabling the Reconstruction Finance Corporation to lend money to states for relief purposes, moving federal government into the field of public relief (Alexander, 1995).
- The AASSW initiated formal accreditation of social work educational programs located in universities with the requirement that such programs should have a minimum curriculum requiring at least one academic year of professional education encompassing both classroom and field instruction (Alexander, 1995; Lowe, 1987). The significance of this was two-fold: (1) it represented the culmination of the effort to

establish high academic standards for professional membership; but (2) the model required the would-be social worker to be a college graduate and then attend school for a further year of study. That is, social work education had adopted a postgraduate model for entry into the profession. Given that 1932 was the worst year of the Depression and that the public welfare sector would begin to develop with even greater velocity, the organization of social work education had established a rather high educational threshold for professional acceptance.

- Two significant national social welfare organizations were established: Goodwill Industries of America and the Council of Jewish Federations and Welfare Funds.

With the inauguration of Franklin D. Roosevelt in 1933, the legendary period noted as the 100 days was initiated. With over roughly 13 million unemployed and the banking sector virtually shut down, Roosevelt began a process of governmental action establishing an entirely new level of public financing and service delivery. In March, the Civilian Conservation Corps Act was passed establishing a public funded program providing work and education programs for unemployed and unmarried young men ages 17 to 23 years (Alexander, 1995). In May, the Federal Emergency Relief Act was passed creating the Federal Emergency Relief Administration (FERA), authorized to provide matching and direct grants to states for public distribution for relief, and social worker Harry Hopkins became the first director. The quick establishment of these two federal initiatives characterized the pace of similar developments over the remainder of the decade.

In 1935, the Social Security Act was passed. Officially titled the Health, Education and Welfare Act, it provided old-age assistance benefits, a Social Security Board, grants to states for unemployment compensation administration, aid to dependent children, maternal and child welfare, public health work, and aid to blind people. A social worker, Jane M. Hoey, became the first director of the Federal Bureau of Public Assistance, which administers federal-state aid to aged people, blind people, and dependent children under the provisions of the act. Also, in 1935, FERA was replaced by the Works Projects Administration (WPA). The WPA's focus was to provide work relief rather than home relief and, within a month, the National Youth Administration was also created. Both initiatives were committed to provide work "for able-bodied but destitute workers . . . (and) . . . work and school aid (for youth)," (p. 2639) respectively. Continuing the pattern of social workers playing central roles in this important period of social welfare development, the National Youth Administration (NYA) was headed by social worker Aubrey Williams (Alexander, 1995).

As these very important governmental social relief agencies were established, there continued to be other organizational developments marked by the founding in 1935 of the National Foundation for Infantile Paralysis which was the precursor to the Annual March of Dimes whose support of research would ultimately lead to the cure for polio. Reflecting the continual development of the sophistication of social work practice, group work, an important function for social work, was included in the reorganization of the National Conference on Social Work. A year later (1936) these social work professionals organized the American Association for the Study of Group Work (AASGW; Alexander, 1995).

The decade of the 1930s closed with the passage (1937) of the Housing Act (Alexander, 1995) "to provide subsidies and credit to states and local governments . . . (and) is the first attempt to finance residential accommodations for tenants not exclusively federal employees" (p. 2639). In 1938, the previously created Works Projects Administration was renamed the Works Progress Administration and continued to provide very important work-based relief opportunities until 1943.

EDUCATION

Against the backdrop of the unfolding New Deal and the central role being played by social work, there was also a significant series of developments related to the organization of education and training for social work. As noted, as the Depression was deeply impacting the U.S. economy, social work's educational leadership was establishing policies that were promoting a clear path toward university and even postgraduate preparation being necessary for anyone wishing to become a member of the social work profession. As Wenocur and Reisch (1989) stated, "The evolution of the public welfare system was strongly influenced by the drive of the private charity workers . . . (and) . . . They succeeded in making the norms and methods of the more prestigious private agency the standard to be emulated by the public" (p. 156).

The rapid development of a public-sponsored public welfare structure, and the increasing demand for a range of trained workers, from entry level administrative tasks to more sophisticated caseworkers, mandated the development of a range of training and educational approaches. However, the educational leaders, as noted by Wenocur and Reisch (1989) were pushing and succeeding in establishing ever higher levels of required educational preparation. According to Lowe (1987), "throughout the 1930s in the context of the Depression and the growing public welfare sector, leadership moved social work toward the incorporation of a professional model that, in effect, defined as nonprofessional the fastest growing number of occupational roles available" (p. 197). By 1935, the AASSW had developed a minimum curriculum and made a policy "that only schools of social work affiliated with AAU member universities would receive formal accreditation" (p. 197). By the end of the decade, as a result of a decision taken by the AASSW, the education credential required in order to be considered fully professional for social work was comprised of a 4-year college degree followed by a 2-year postbaccalaureate master's degree (Lowe, 1987). In spite of this organizational direction, the need for a range of trained and educated professionals to administer the large public welfare structure was immediate and pressing. However, social work seemed to turn away from assuming these roles by considering them as merely administrative and/or clerical.

In response to this emphasis away from local public welfare, in 1942, a group of social work educational leaders allied with local public welfare officials formed the National Association of Schools of Social Administration (NASSA). NASSA's primary focus was to promote an undergraduate, entry-level degree for social work. The educational institutions affiliated with NASSA tended to be public and located outside of the traditional Eastern/Urban centers that had so dominated the profession previously.

During the 1930s, the social work profession experienced its peak of organizational influence, reflected in the roles played in the Roosevelt administration as the social programs of the New Deal were developed. Also, as noted previously, social workers were key players as both the shapers of the new social programs and the leaders of programs such as FERA, the Federal Bureau of Public Assistance, and the National Youth Foundation within the WPA. Many other social work leaders were at the policy development table during the decade.

However, the 1940s became a period of new challenges as the profession faced its diversity, both educationally as well as organizationally. In the organizational arena, the AASW was challenged in terms of issues of membership and the definition of who was a professional. A major cause of this particular issue was the field's rapid growth during the 1930s. This diversity within social work also impacted the organization of social work education.

Before focusing on the 1940s, it is important to make mention of the *rank and file movement* that emerged in 1931 and exerted an interesting counterforce within the profession throughout the decade. The rank and file movement traced its fundamental motivation back to the era of social reform and cause that Porter Lee had declared moribund in 1929 on the eve of the economic crisis of the Depression. Wenocur and Reisch (1989) summarize the rank and file movement in the following way,

> Between 1931 and 1942, rank and file social workers exerted a strong, politically progressive counterforce to the profession's attempts to control the emerging national social welfare industry . . . the Rank and File movement helped push social work to accept political action as a legitimate professional function to support a national system of public protections. At its peak in 1936, the Rank and File Movement numbered some 15,000 members, The majority of whom worked in public relief agencies and lacked professional social work credentials. (p. 182)

This summary previews the nature of the internal challenges that would confront professional social work for virtually the remainder of the century and influence major organizational decisions and resulting structures.

The profession entered the 1940s with a large public social welfare enterprise, with personnel who were viewed as social workers or welfare workers, but who were not considered to be "professional" social workers by the profession itself. Due to the decision made by the AASSW in 1937 for professional credentials to be only a 2-year postgraduate degree, thousands of public welfare employees were defined as being outside the organizational boundaries of the profession. The previously noted emergence of NASSA in 1942 was one direct response to this split in the social work profession.

It would take the country's entry into World War II for full economic recovery to occur, providing new opportunities for the profession. Alexander (1995, pp. 2639–2640) chronicled a series of new organizations that formed during the 1940s that were clearly in response to the country's entry into World War II:

1942 The United Service was incorporated to coordinate services provided to armed forces and defense workers by six voluntary agencies: (1) National Jewish Welfare Board, (2) National Catholic Community Service, (3) National Traveler's Aid Association, (4) Salvation Army, (5) YMCA, and (6) YWCA. Also the first U.S. day care for children of working mothers was initiated through the Lanham Act providing 50% matching grants to local communities for use in operation of day care centers and family day care homes. The United Seaman's Service was established in the National Maritime Union to provide medical, social work, and other services to merchant seamen; Bertha C. Reynolds was named the director. As noted earlier, NASSA was formed by 34 land grant college undergraduate social work programs.

1943 The United Nations Relief and Rehabilitation Administration was established by 44 nations for postwar relief and refugee settlement. The American Council of

Voluntary Agencies for Foreign Service was established to promote joint program planning and coordination of national voluntary agency activities on foreign relief and rehabilitation.

1945 National Social Welfare Assembly, formerly the National Social Work Council formed in 1923, was organized. The United Nations was chartered in April, including the Economic and Social Council, to provide "international machinery for the promotion and social advancement of all peoples" and coordinate agencies dealing with social welfare problems, such as the World Health Organization, United Nations International Children's Emergency Fund, International Labor Office, and International Refugee Organization, and the Girls Clubs of America was founded.

1946 The Big Brothers of America was founded. Three legislative bills were passed: the Hospital Survey and Construction Act, the National Mental Health Act, and the Full Employment Act.

All three of these legislative items had an influence on the organization and practice of social work. The expansion of inpatient hospitals provided an impetus for the promotion of hospital/medical social work. The National Mental Health Act contributed to the further development of social work as a clinical treatment oriented activity and enhanced the status of the profession while also exacerbating the still simmering tensions between the public versus private practice advocates within the field of social work. While not completely implemented, the Full Employment Act was certainly a statement of policy that asserted an economic service goal that would involve some sectors of the profession.

As the decade drew to a close and the profession faced mid-century, two entities were created that reflected the continuing maturation of the social work profession, but also provided additional proof of the diversity that was creating issues of unity within the profession: the Association for the Study of Community Organization was formed in 1946 and the previously created American Association originally created in 1936 became the American Association of Group Workers, and finally in 1949 the Social Work Research Group was organized (Alexander, 1995).

The social work profession entered the decade of the 1950s with major issues confronting its leadership in both the educational as well as organizational areas. Though not in the purview of this chapter, the emergence of group work and community organization focused associations represented the culmination of long-standing internal conflict over the nature of the breadth of social work. As a result, the profession entered the second half of the twentieth century facing fragmentation and the need to redefine its central identify. The profession addressed these issues and significant organizational decisions and structures emerged. The profession again experienced the beginning of a period of growth and expansion similar to the 1930s.

THE 1950s

At one level, the profession entered the 1950s on a high note. The Bureau of Labor Statistics published a survey canvassing 75,000 social workers and basing the report on 50,000 replies. In addition, the Social Security Act was amended to broaden programs to serve the permanently disabled, Aid to Dependent Children, and finally amendments expanding Old-Age and Survivor's Insurance (Alexander, 1995). Perhaps reflecting a growing awareness of the maturing of the nation's population, the National Council on Aging came into existence.

However, these actions forced the profession to get its house in order. On the educational front, the AASSW joined with NASSA and sponsored a major study of social work education resulting in what has become known as the Hollis-Taylor Report. Published in 1951, the report unified the educational enterprise and resulted in the creation, in 1952, of the Council on Social Work Education (CSWE) as the single organization with the responsibility and authority to accredit social work programs. With the creation of CSWE, the struggle between undergraduate and graduate advocates was at least neutralized for the moment, though undergraduate preparation was not fully endorsed as professional. As a result, this issue would reemerge at the end of the decade and would not be resolved, at least organizationally, until 1974.

The decade of the 1950s is often characterized as a quiet, conservative period in our nation's history symbolized by a society recovering from the hangover from the Depression and World War II and enjoying prosperity heretofore unknown in the country. Whether an accurate characterization or not, the decade in terms of social work and important developments was certainly not a time of inactivity.

Beginning in 1952 with special project funding provided by the U.S. Children's Bureau "to develop and coordinate statewide programs for medical and social services to unwed mothers" (Alexander, 1995, p. 2640), and the creation of the U.S. Committee of the International Conference on Social Welfare, a theme of expansion was clearly indicated.

At mid-decade, several events were significant to social work's organizational life and future. In 1953, the U.S. Department of Health, Education and Welfare was created bringing the central social welfare structures of the nation into a presidential cabinet level, representing a maturing of the nation's commitment to provide social welfare services reaching back to the New Deal of the Roosevelt era. On a local level, the establishment in 1954 of Rutland Corner House in Brookline, Massachusetts, "was the first urban transitional residence (halfway house) for mental patients" (Alexander, 1995, p. 2641). Such organizational service agencies became important as the increase in attention to mental health care grew well into the 1960s and 1970s.

The U.S. Supreme Court ruling in the *Brown v. Board of Education of Topeka, Shawnee County, Kansas*, eliminated the doctrine of "separate but equal" segregation in education. Although not implemented immediately, it certainly had a profound effect on the entire nation, and indeed on social work. The social shifts that evolved out of this decision influenced the focus of much of social work, particularly in terms of reinvigorating the social action aspects of the profession.

On a social work organizational level, perhaps the most significant event during the decade was the formation in 1955 of the National Association of Social Workers (NASW). On October 1, 1955, NASW began its operation as the newly created umbrella professional association representing the profession. NASW represented the consolidation of seven separate associations: the American Association of Social Workers (AASW), the American Association of Medical Social Workers (AAMSW), the American Association of Psychiatric Social Workers (AAPSW), the National Association of School Social Workers (NASSW), the American Association of Group Workers (AAGW), the Association for the

Study of Community Organization (ASCO), and the Social Work Research Group (SWRG) (Alexander, 1995; Leighninger, 1980; Wenocur & Reisch, 1989).

The formation of NASW was the result of several factors according to Wenocur and Reisch (1989):

> including the positive outcomes of joint action on professional issues during World War II, the push by various membership associations for inclusion in AASW, the formation of the Council on Social Work Education in 1952, and the apparent benefits of expanding organizational resources so as to influence local and state legislation and the postwar market for social work services. (p. 240)

In addition, the profession needed to establish some clarity in terms of its identity and perception from the public. Even though the profession saw itself as a casework oriented activity within the various sectors represented by the entities that came together to form NASW, "in the public's mind, social work was still strongly identified with public welfare work. About 40% of the nation's 75,000 social workers worked in public assistance, and few were professionally trained" (Wenocur & Reisch, 1989, p. 240). Further, as Wenocur and Reisch (1989) note, "The membership standards of NASW reinforced the accreditation requirements of the Council on Social Work Education, which had been formed a few years earlier, for retention of the graduate degree as the entry level to the profession" (p. 242).

In keeping with the trend of national organizations, and perhaps as a gesture toward asserting their unique place within the country's national composition, social workers in Puerto Rico founded the National Association of Puerto Rican Hispanic Social Workers (Alexander, 1995).

In 1957, 3 years after *Brown v. Board of Education*, Congress passed the Civil Rights Act (PL 85-315, 71 Stat 634), which established the Commission on Civil Rights. This Act was the first such legislation since 1875, and it served to strengthen federal enforcement authority and powers (Alexander, 1995). This Act was a precursor to the 1964 civil rights legislation. This Act would further promote a growing context of social activism that would become an important dimension of social work during the 1960s.

As the decade ended, the profession was engaged in some of the same organizational issues that had been faced at the beginning of the period. As the 1950s began, the processes leading to the creation of NASW and CSWE were underway. At the end of the decade, NASW published "A Working Definition of Social Work Practice" (1958) developed by the National Commission on Practice articulating the basic components of social work practice: values, purpose, sanction, knowledge, and method, and in 1959 CSWE published *The Social Work Curriculum Study*—a 13-volume study hailed as a "milestone in the development of effective educational programs for professions" (Alexander, 1995, p. 2641). The profession ended the decade still engaged in the fundamental process of defining itself.

1960 to 1980

The 20-year span from 1960 to 1980 represents for social work a journey reflecting the great social and economic turmoil in the country. As Wenocur and Reisch (1989) state, "The growth of professional social work accelerated rapidly between the mid-1950s and the mid-1980s with the continued expansion of government spending for social welfare" (p. 262). Both the public and the private sector increased their funding for social welfare programs: "Between 1960 and 1983, social welfare expenditures in the public sector, including education, rose from $52.3 billion to $641.7 billion, representing more than 55% of all government spending. The voluntary social welfare sector expanded as well . . . (with) allocations (increasing) from $4.03 billion to $28.5 billion" (p. 262).

Beginning in 1961 with the passage of the Juvenile Delinquency and Youth Offenses Control Act until 1983 and the passage of the Social Security Amendments the social welfare/public policy arena was represented as great activity and swings from the activism of the 1960s and through the social pullback of the Reagan years.

In keeping with its well-established emphasis on promoting standards for the profession, NASW established the Academy of Certified Social Workers (ACSW) "to promote standards for professional social work practice and the protection of social welfare clients. It requires a master of social work degree and two years of supervised practice by an Academy of Certified Social Workers member" (Alexander, 1995, p. 2641). This organizational reaffirmation of the master's level for professional social work practice provided some interesting challenges given the seemingly sudden focus on poverty that would take place in the 1960s with the War on Poverty.

An almost dizzying array of events beginning with the publication in 1962 of Michael Harrington's *The Other America*, marked this important decade for the profession. In the area of social legislation, virtually all of the governmental actions held relevance for social work practice.

The Manpower Development and Training Act (1961), the Mental Retardation Facilities and Community Mental Health Centers Construction Act (1963), and the very significant year of 1964 with the passage of the Civil Rights Act, the Food Stamp Act, and the Economic Opportunity Act were major events challenging social work to open itself up to working in a broad range of service areas while also serving to further enhance the traditional clinical areas of casework oriented practice.

In 1965, the U.S. Department of Health, Education and Welfare published "Closing the Gap in Social Work Manpower." The report was important to social work in two ways: It projected a clear need for social workers to address the range of populations being covered by the increase in governmental-sponsored social programs and therefore resulted in an increased demand for social workers, and second it pointed out that given the nature of the social work educational organization with its graduate-only requirement, social work needed to incorporate undergraduate education into its professional perspective.

The decade continued the trend already well established of increased governmental activism in the social welfare arena with the passage in 1966 of the Narcotic Addict Rehabilitation Act, the Comprehensive Health Planning and Public Health Services Amendments, and the Veteran's Readjustment Benefits Act.

In 1967, the Child Health Act was passed, greatly enhancing federal assistance to health care in the country. Perhaps reflecting this high level of attention directed to health care policy and services, in 1966 the Society for Hospital Social Work Directors was formed under the auspices of the American Hospital Association, changing its name in 1993 to the Society for Social Work Administrators in Health Care (Alexander, 1995).

In 1968, several new professional associations were formed further reflecting the continued process of change and struggles with diversity as well as "mirroring" the racial and ethnic tensions that existed in the larger society. They were the National Association of Black Social Workers, the National Association of Puerto Rican Social Service Workers, the

Asian American Social Workers, and the Association of American Indian Social Workers (Alexander, 1995).

In 1969, with the political terrain shifting with a Republican administration and the growing challenge of the Viet Nam War, President Nixon proposed the Family Assistance Plan that contained a proposed guaranteed annual income in place of the public welfare system that he all but claimed to have been a failure. The proposed plan ultimately failed to become policy. However, an opportunity may have been lost to profoundly reform public and family welfare assistance due to the political and ideological struggles.

In the professional organizational arena, a very important event occurred in 1969: The NASW recognized the undergraduate social work degree, culminating a struggle that had begun in the earliest days of the profession's existence. The decision to recognize the undergraduate degree resulted from an NASW national membership referendum. The decision was implemented in 1970 (Alexander, 1995). However, it was not until 1974 that CSWE began to accredit the baccalaureate degree.

As the 1970s began, a reaction to the rapid pace of social reform set in and the Republican administration began a process of neutralizing many of the initiatives started in the 1960s. The profession was experiencing new pressures from the greatly expanded human service field resulting from the increase in federal support for the wide range of programs initiated during the 1960s. During this same period, the social work profession experienced several important developments. In 1971, the NASW initiated the objective examination as a means of establishing national standards for social work knowledge and practice. This exam was the precursor to licensure and was attached to the already existing Academy of Certified Social Workers (ACSW) certification. Not unrelated to this action, but important was the establishment of the National Federation of Clinical Social Workers which later in 1976 became the National Federation of Societies for Clinical Social Work.

Reflecting the growing awareness and concern surrounding substance abuse, in 1972 the National Institute on Drug Abuse was established "to provide leadership, policies, and goals for the total federal effort to prevent, control, and treat narcotic addiction and drug abuse" (Alexander, 1995, p. 2643). In the same year, NASW intervened to have social workers included as part of the Professional Standards Review Organizations set up as part of the Social Security Amendments. By this action, social work asserted itself as a key player on the local and state organizational level in terms of providing services to beneficiaries of Medicare, Medicaid, and maternal and child health programs. In a similar fashion, in 1973, through NASW intervention, social service components and standards were included in the Health Maintenance Organization Act authorizing federal aid to support and stimulate group medical practice.

In 1974, as noted, CSWE began to accredit undergraduate social work programs. Wenocur and Reisch (1989) have stated that "Recognition of the BSW as the professional entry degree was probably the single most significant change in the internal structure of social work enterprise (since 1960)" (p. 267). The advocates of undergraduate professional education had finally managed to secure a firm place in the total organizational structure of social work. The decision to incorporate this level of preparation was controversial at that time and remains so today as the profession continues to unify itself.

Through the remainder of the decade, a variety of social legislation continued to appear to redefine the social welfare revolution that started in the 1930s. The Social Service

Amendments of 1974, known as Title XX of the Social Security Act, provided a 75% level of federal support for multiple levels of service delivery. NASW played a significant role in the policy process and the program and its funding match was an important resource that was used to enhance social work education, particularly at the undergraduate level.

The profession continued to have success in having social work services included in several pieces of national legislation, including the Education for All Handicapped Children Act (1975) and the Health Professional Educational Assistance (1976). Both pieces of legislation contained provisions for social work services. The Health Professional Assistance Act contained the first mention of schools of social work in national health legislation and authorized funding to train social workers in health care, including administration, policy analysis, and social work.

In 1976, NASW formed Political Action for Candidate Election (PACE), committing the social work profession to political action as a professional responsibility (Alexander, 1995). Symbolically, through this action, social work reestablished the aspect of "cause" that Porter Lee declared in 1929 to no longer have relevance to the profession. PACE endorsed "Carter and Mondale, the Democratic Party candidates for president and vice president, initiating the NASW Political Action for Candidate Election program to raise funds for political action, the first such political effort for a professional social work organization" (Alexander, 1995, p. 2644), and the Rural Social Work Caucus was initiated to aid rural social workers.

Another event of relevance in the anniversary year of the American Revolution was the adoption of the International Code of Ethics for Professional Social Workers. Written by Chauncey A. Alexander, then Executive Director of NASW, the Code was ratified during the Puerto Rico Assembly of the International Federation of Social Workers attended by 52 national professional social worker organizations.

During the last year of the decade, the NASW succeeded in forming the American Association of State Social Work Boards comprised of state boards and authorities. The Social Work Boards were "empowered to regulate the practice of social work within their own jurisdictions" (Alexander, 1995, p. 2644). This initiative was the major step toward the full regulation of the profession by the profession itself. It is not unreasonable to say that, by this action, social work as an organized profession had finally put the basic structures completely in place. The process had taken nearly 100 years from 1898 with the call for a training program for charity workers.

1980 to 2000

The final 2 decades of the twentieth century begin with a growing effort to reduce the role of the federal government in the broad social welfare sector. As Alexander (1995) notes,

> the 1981 passage of the Omnibus Budget Reconciliation Act initiates a federal policy reversal of general welfare responsibility for human services, reducing federal programs (including food stamps, child nutrition, comprehensive employment and training, mental health, and community development) by means of block grants under the guise of decentralization to states . . . (and) . . . The Social Service Block Grant Act (PL 97-35, 95 Stat. 357), passed by Congress on August 13, and part of the Omnibus Budget Reconciliation Act of 1981, amends Title XX of the Social Security Act to consolidate social services programs and to decentralize responsibility to the states. (p. 2644)

A very significant event in 1981 was the identification of HIV and AIDS and just as the nation and the world had begun to absorb the significance of the virulent epidemic, the profession was challenged and responded by actively informing itself about this health threat and ultimately assuming important leadership roles in both service delivery as well as research.

Continuing the cutbacks promulgated by the Reagan administration and continuing the trend started under the Nixon administration, in 1982 the Tax Equity and Fiscal Responsibility Act was passed initiating "severe reductions in service provisions of Medicare, Medicaid, Utilization and Quality Control Peer Review, Aid to Families with Dependent Children, child support enforcement, supplemental security income, and unemployment compensation" (Alexander, 1995, p. 2645).

In the midst of this challenging period of both programmatic and funding cutbacks, the National Network for Social Work Managers was formed in 1985 as "a professional society to advance knowledge, theory, and practice of management and administration in social services and the social work profession and to obtain recognition of social work managers, [and] NASW establishes the National Center for Social Policy and Practice to analyze practice data and make recommendations on social policy, including information, policy, and education services" (Alexander, 1995, p. 2645).

In 1988, "the NASW Communications Network is established by Suzanne Dworak-Peck as an affiliate group to encourage socially conscious media programming and accurate portrayal of social issues and professional social work. The network uses a computerized network of several hundred social workers for technical media assistance" (Alexander, 1995, p. 2646).

Also in 1988, The Civil Rights Restoration Act (PL 100-259) overturned the 1984 Supreme Court *Grove City College v. Bell* decision and clarifies that four major civil rights laws pertaining to gender, disability, age, and race must be interpreted to prohibit discrimination throughout entire organizations if any program received federal funds (Alexander, 1995).

The decade of the 1990s opened with the profession of social work being legally regulated in 50 states and jurisdictions, the NASW School Social Work Specialist Credential was created to provide objective testing and certification of school social workers, and NASW transformed its publications department into the NASW Press. These developments were followed in 1991 with the establishment of the NASW Academy of Certified Baccalaureate Social Workers to provide objective testing and certification of social workers with a bachelor of social work degree (Alexander, 1995, p. 2646). With this certification action, social work closed all historical loops and gaps that had been in the process of being sorted out since the Flexner verdict on the profession in 1915. The profession had basically established entities, policies, and practices that addressed all the points put forth by Flexner. Even so, the profession entered the twenty-first century with nagging issues and tensions related to fragmentation versus unity.

The preceding chronological time line identified various benchmark events and decisions; the following section provides some additional discussion of the still existing tensions that exist in the profession and that are primarily played out between and within the professional organizations and those that represent the interests of the social work educational enterprise.

FRAGMENTATION VERSUS UNITY: A REFLECTION ON A THEME BETWEEN PRACTICE AND EDUCATION

The profession of social work has struggled to find a single voice on matters of practice and public policy. With more than 100 formal organizations nationally that relate to social work themes, ranging from the Action Network for Social Work Education and Research to the Welfare Information Network, the profession often finds itself with unclear priorities and member identification that links more closely to specialized fields of practice and interests, separate from the larger social work identity.

In 1991, while Richard Edwards was president of the NASW, he initiated several actions to respond to the apparent fragmentation of the profession. He reinstituted a board committee of NASW that included representatives from the major social work organizations, the purpose being to engage issues of mutual concern and interest. In the same year, NASW organized a Conference on Conferences in Boston in an attempt to bring a number of organizations together, allowing time for individual organizations to meet—all in the context of forging a larger professional identity. Over 5,000 people participated in one of the largest gatherings of social work organizations in history. The Council on Social Work Education was not a participant in this effort. After Edwards' term of office with NASW was over, this synergy seemed to disperse back into organizational silos. During the next several years, greater fragmentation occurred, most specifically with social work education.

With regards to the social work education organizations, attendance at the Annual Program Meetings of the Council on Social Work Education began to drop off during the 1980s and 1990s with a proliferation of conference options for various social work educational interest groups. This trend closely mirrored that of the social work practice organizations.

Social work education affinity groups formally organized to attend to their constituent interests, often developing formal bylaws, structures, dues, and 501C3 status. In 1975, the Group for the Advancement of Doctoral Education (GADE) was organized to provide a venue for directors of doctoral social work programs to meet for shared ideas and interests. The group continues to meet each year to discuss matters of doctoral education. GADE was responsible for developing standards of excellence for doctoral programs. Although these programs are outside of the responsibility of the Commission on Accreditation of the CSWE, the standards became the gold standard for programs wishing to sustain doctoral programs.

In 1982, the Association of Baccalaureate Social Work Program Directors (BPD) was formed to provide a forum for directors of undergraduate social work programs to discuss common interests and foster support and excellence. The group later included field directors and faculty, growing to more than 500 programs. The annual meeting of this organization rivals that of the Council on Social Work Education in size and frequently is a source of conflict for the parent social work education organization in competing for program resources to support participation in annual conferences.

In 1984, the National Association of Deans and Directors of Social Work Programs (NADD) reorganized from the former National Conference of Deans and Directors of Graduate Schools. This organization was to represent the broad issues of social work education at the graduate level, with primary interest on masters programs. Some of the impetus for this restructuring came as a challenge to the Council on Social Work Education that was facing serious financial problems and possible dissolution. Deans and directors were preparing for contingencies should CSWE fall. The Council survived its difficult years, and NADD became a forum for discussing issues such as the rapid growth of social work programs, particularly of graduate programs that were no longer autonomous academic units, the role of research and advocacy in the profession, and even the future of the profession.

In 1994, the Society for Social Work and Research (SSWR) was founded to advance the interests of social work research. Its membership quickly grew to more than 1,000 members with representatives from almost every state and more than 15 countries. Some of this development came about as a reaction of research schools of social work wanting a larger forum to discuss research related to social work, distinct from the annual meeting of CSWE that often gave larger focus to matters of pedagogy and those directly related educational issues. Another competitive feature of this organization was that its scheduled meeting often predated that of CSWE, thus providing a better opportunity to become the principal venue for academic hiring.

With a greater focus on the place of research in social work education, the year 2000 found the St. Louis Group emerging from a small group of deans and directors from research extensive schools of social work who were looking for a forum to discuss the specialized needs of programs where research was emphasized. Its name arose from the location of the first meeting held at the George Warren Brown School of Social Work at Washington University in St. Louis. The organization grew to include more programs where there was experience and interest to develop infrastructures that would support greater research capacity. This organization also created some friction among colleagues because schools without the research emphasis saw this as a threat to create elitism among the programs.

These organizations all hold meetings at least annually, with several meeting more often than once a year. This created structural challenges for the educational entities that often shaped the vision for the profession. The divergent meetings required choices of how limited resources would be directed. There were member dues and travel costs necessitating choices for all but the most resourced programs. Political tensions often arose about the purpose and direction of professional education, including such issues as whether programs were proliferating at the expense of the profession; that undergraduate education was diluting the quality of graduate education; that research was usurping the importance and primacy of practice, and many more. These conflicts frequently emerged any time new accreditation standards for social work programs were being developed.

In addition collaborative efforts among all of these organizations, in addition to NASW, resulted in two new entities. The Institute for the Advancement of Social Work Research (IASWR) began in 1993 to provide technical assistance to social work programs regarding research funding. Much of its activity involved support to address the recruitment and retention of the social work workforce, particularly in relation to child welfare. Then in 1995, the Action Network for Social Work Education and Research (ANSWER) formed as a coalition of social work education and practice organizations to serve as a legislative and executive branch advocate on behalf of social work education, training, and research. A great deal of its energy continues to be for the creation of a National Center for Social Work Research.

The creation of NASW in 1955 may have been the largest and best attempt at professional unification because the principal social work organizations merged to create one large national body. Yet, even this effort failed to include social work education, one of the formative forces of the profession. The voice of professional unity is further threatened by declining and graying membership in NASW and nongrowth in CSWE membership. For these reasons, Kay Hoffman, president of CSWE and dean of the College of Social Work at the University of Kentucky, and Alberto Godenzi, dean of the Graduate School of Social Work at Boston College (2007, pp. 183–184) called for five specific reasons to unify:

1. *The value of branding* to create a critical mass an identity that would be recognized more widely from outside of the profession.
2. *The benefits of synergy* to increase influence and minimize internal competition for limited resources.
3. *The advantages of integration* in bringing science and practice closer together.
4. *The importance of both mission and market* toward strengthening university standing with the support of a large national organization and leveraging that influence.
5. *Supporting economies of scale* by minimizing the costs associated with multiple organization memberships.

In response to such calls as that from Hoffman and Godenzi, funding was secured from the Johnson Foundation to support a meeting of ten social work organizations, held in June 2007 at Johnson's Wingspread facility in Racine, Wisconsin, to discuss the future of the profession. This funding initiative was the result of years of conversation and the Leadership Roundtable comprised of the participating organizations, convened by CSWE over the previous decade. At this meeting, the participants unanimously signed a resolution to unify the profession with a super organization by 2012. Guided by the vision of several hundred social work educators and practitioners who met in 2005 at a Social Work Congress to consider the future of the profession, the Wingspread resolution charted the possibility of a unified voice for the profession. A transition team, with direction from the Leadership Roundtable team was tasked to bring this resolution to fruition during the following 5 years. The challenges of organizational identity, legal constitutions, varied governance structures, and broad-ranging professional interests all combine to create real obstacles to overcome: barriers that have, throughout the profession's existence, precluded the creation of a unified voice and vision of the social work profession.

CONCLUSION

The profession of social work is still searching for its unitary voice. The organizations that represent the vast interests of practice and education continue to explore possible venues that will lead to that voice. Throughout the history of social work, its many organizations have helped to shape public policy and practice, and that likely will continue. At the point at which unification ever occurs, there will be a great opportunity to leverage the capacity to promote positive social change and enhance the public profile of the profession.

REFERENCES

Alexander, C. A. (1995). Distinctive dates in social welfare history. In *Encyclopedia of social work*, 19th edition (pp. 2631–2659). Washington, DC: National Association of Social Workers Press.

Hoffman, K., & Godenzi, A. (2007). The requirement: Unification. *Journal of Social Work Education*, *43*(2), 81–185.

Leiby, J. (1978). *A history of social welfare and social work in the United States*. New York: Columbia University Press.

Leighninger, L. (1980). *The development of social work as a profession 1930–1960*. Doctoral dissertation. Berkley: University of California, School of Social Work.

Leighninger, L. (1987). *Social work: Search for identity*. Westport, CT: Greenwood Press.

Lowe, G. R. (1987, June). Social work's professional mistake: Confusing status for control and losing both. *Journal of Sociology and Social Welfare*, *14*(2), 187–206.

Pumphrey, R. E., & Pumphrey, M. W. (Eds.). (1961). *The heritage of American social work*. New York: Columbia University Press.

Wenocur, S., & Reisch, M. (1989). *From charity to enterprise: The development of American social work in a market economy*. Urbana: University of Illinois Press.

Chapter 6

VALUES AND ETHICS FOR PROFESSIONAL SOCIAL WORK PRACTICE

Kimberly Strom-Gottfried

Effective social work practice is guided by knowledge, skills, and values. The values of the profession reflect the historical foundation of the field and the ideological underpinnings of contemporary practice. They distinguish social work from other professions and, as operationalized through ethical standards, help guide social workers' decisions in practice. Ethical standards can also be used to hold social workers accountable for poor decisions, though malpractice suits, regulatory board sanctions, and other adjudication mechanisms. Regardless of their setting or role, social workers must be cognizant of professional and personal values and ethical standards. Further, they must be able to engage in problem solving to effectively resolve dilemmas when they arise.

UNDERSTANDING VALUES

Values are core beliefs about what is right, good, or preferable. The values held by each individual guide their choices and actions on a daily basis. Some values are broad or general, such as honesty, freedom, productivity, or accountability. Other values may be articulated more specifically, "I value human life, and therefore I am against the death penalty, abortion, and assisted suicide," or "I believe in protecting the environment, so I follow principles of sustainable development." In these explicit examples, personal beliefs are translated into the individual's actions and choices. For any given individual, some values are embraced more fully than others. For example, consider the person who believes in the humane treatment of animals but is comfortable eating beef and wearing leather shoes. In personal values, there may be limits in the extent to which a belief about what is right or preferable is conveyed into action.

Professional values refer to the core beliefs of a profession, to ideals reflecting the origins of the field and the hallmarks of contemporary practice. When professions express their values, they define themselves for the public and help those who might join the profession decide if the field is right for them. Professional values also form the basis for standards to guide the conduct of people within the profession. Six core values have been identified for the social work profession: service, social justice, dignity and worth of the person, importance of human relationships, integrity, and competence. Taken together, the values for social work say, "this is who we are," "this is what makes us unique," "this is what we think is important," and "this is how we live our professional lives."

The value of service refers to the expectation that social workers will "elevate service to others above self-interest" (National Association Social Workers [NASW], 1999, p. 5), bringing their skills and expertise to bear for all people, including those who cannot afford to pay for care. In embracing "helping others" as their primary goal, social workers explicitly make other goals (such as generating wealth or gaining fame) secondary.

In valuing social justice, social workers give a high priority to serving those who are particularly disadvantaged and marginalized, working on intractable systemic problems like poverty and unemployment and striving to change social systems that perpetuate oppression and disadvantage. The value of social justice also refers to an empowerment perspective, where all who are troubled by injustice work together to mutually bring about desired change.

The value placed on the dignity and worth of the individual is multifaceted. It refers to the importance of embracing all people, regardless of difference, and treating others respectfully. It upholds the rights of people to make autonomous life decisions and charges social workers with advocating for such empowerment. It acknowledges the prospect of cases where individuals' interests may clash with those of society, but commends social workers to address those cases in an ethical fashion.

In valuing human relationships, social workers identify relationships as the medium for personal and social change. The profession values relationships between practitioners and clients and fosters relationships among individuals to "promote, restore, maintain, and enhance the well-being of individuals, families, social groups, organizations, and communities" (NASW, 1999, p. 6). Here, too, the theme of empowerment is emphasized.

While some of these values distinguish social work from other fields, the values of integrity and competence are common across the helping professions. Integrity refers to the commitment to honesty and trustworthiness, to taking steps to assure ethical practice by individuals and organizations. Competence requires that social workers practice only within their domains of expertise, and take continuous measures to improve their capabilities as knowledge evolves and cases require.

OPPORTUNITIES FOR CONFLICT

In daily practice, social workers are confronted with an array of situations that may test these values. Particular conflicts arise when a person's personal values diverge from professional values and when societal values conflict with professional values. How can the well-intentioned professional reconcile the two?

While the social work profession embraces each person's dignity and worth, individual social workers may struggle to do so with clients who are cruel, self-destructive, or dishonest. While the profession advocates service to others, the individual social worker may feel that service to family is an equally important precept. Even when they embrace empowerment, social workers will encounter situations where institutions in society discourage enfranchisement of all people. For example, a social worker hired to advocate for humane work conditions in the agriculture industry may find that her efforts at bolstering worker rights are thwarted by local customs, insufficient oversight by workplace safety regulators, and indifference by citizens who are untroubled about the undocumented status of many farm workers.

Addressing Conflicts

While different steps may apply depending on the nature of the value conflict, reflection, education, consultation, and experience are generally effective methods for reconciling discrepant values. Self-awareness is an essential part of professional preparation. The professional social worker in training must critically examine his or her own history, beliefs, motivations, and expectations. Through this process of reflection, the social worker becomes aware of areas of conflict, where deeply held personal values may make adoption of the profession's values difficult. Once identified, education, consultation, and experience help the social worker move beyond ideas and preconceptions to addressing the values dilemmas (Hepworth, Rooney, Rooney, Strom-Gottfried, & Larsen, 2006).

Through education, the social worker may come to appreciate the history that leads a person to treat another abusively. Upon learning that history, the dilemma moves from the hypothetical to the actual and "the perpetrator" moves beyond a label to a multidimensional character whose behavior, however heinous, can be understood in a larger context. Education and supervision are also useful for exploring the implications of the individual's failure to embrace values such as those about acceptance and relationships. How can the social worker effectively carry out his or her responsibilities while simultaneously rejecting and distancing the client? Education and consultation help social workers develop the understanding and empathy to accept the individual, even when troubled by the person's actions. Experience and exposure also advance the cause of acceptance. Immersion in other cultures, broad experiences with diverse client and social groups, and opportunities to see professional values in action all help social workers bridge the personal and professional divide.

As noted earlier, value conflicts go beyond the individual social worker to reflect cultural schisms where the profession's values are at odds with those of the society in which it is situated. Since its inception, social work has been challenged to uphold its particular set of beliefs in a sometimes inhospitable environment. In fact, the values of the profession reflect that friction, otherwise social justice and service might not need to be accorded such priority for action. In part, the articulation of this particular set of values is intended to stake social work's claim as an agent of social, as well as individual, change.

Against this backdrop, we can find specific contemporary examples of professional/social values conflicts, for example in immigration policies, English-only legislation, and welfare reform. How can social workers uphold their dedication to family relationships, individual worth, and social justice when regulations separate families, punish non-English speakers, and make single mothers choose between work and child care? In part, the answers are the same as those offered for addressing individual value conflicts.

Reflection helps social workers identify the nature of conflicts and keep the profession's values in the forefront, even when the values are unpopular. Education helps professionals understand the genesis of each side's beliefs and the tactics that are effective for engaging in difficult dialogues. Consultation brings like-minded professionals together for change, and provides an outlet to effectively vent the frustrations of practice in unresponsive circumstances. Experience and education help social workers develop strategies for change and learn from their successes and failures. Exposure to the results of value conflicts helps workers articulate the toll of incompatible values on the profession and the people it serves.

Whether the dilemma is an individual adopting the profession's values or the profession integrating its values with those of society, a necessary first step is understanding the value positions of each party and the ways those function in practice.

ETHICS

Ethics are values in action. For the individual, personal values result in an individual code of conduct, which then translates into choices and behaviors. For the person as a professional, the values of the field are reflected in a code of ethics, which is translated into standards to guide practice. Social workers may subscribe to several codes of ethics.

The NASW's Code of Ethics is promulgated by the largest social work association in the United States, reflecting the broad range of activities, roles, and settings that characterize the profession. While attempts were made as early as the 1920s to create and disseminate a code for the profession, the NASW Code was not developed until 1960, 5 years after the organization was formed from the merger of other organizations (Reamer, 1998). The early Code consisted of 14 fairly general first-person proclamations such as "I respect the privacy of the people I serve." An additional statement was included in 1967 to avow nondiscrimination (Reamer, 1998). The landmark Code was found wanting, however, due to its level of ambiguity. Critics contended that the document was of limited utility as a guide to practitioners and as a tool to assure ethical practice through adjudication (McCann & Cutler, 1979). However, it took over 15 years to constitute a task force to revise the Code and seek approval through the professional association. The 1979 Code contains many of the same features as the one in use today, particularly in the structure and intent of the standards addressed. The Code underwent minor revisions over the next 15 years before a wholesale review took place in the mid-1990s. The resulting changes to the Code addressed greater sensitivity to the ethical dimensions of practice and vast changes in the way services are delivered, in light of technology, managed care, and other emerging issues. The revision was timely, in light of increased knowledge about ethics, available data on misconduct across the helping professions, and growing concerns about risk management (Reamer, 1998).

The current NASW Code of Ethics (1999) contains 155 standards reflecting social workers' responsibilities to clients, colleagues, and practice settings, in their professional roles, to the profession itself, as well as to society. Under this schema, principles such as integrity might appear in several areas because the concept applies to various types of worker responsibilities. The Code's structure is not intended to imply a decision-making hierarchy where one set of standards takes precedence over others that appear later in the Code. The Code is not intended to be an exhaustive catalog of standards or a list of mutually exclusive priorities. As the Code's authors acknowledge, conflicts will occur in the interpretation of principles and standards and in weighing them for decision making. Therefore, familiarity with the code and with ethical decision making is required for resolving conflicting obligations.

The NASW Code contains both aspirational and enforceable standards. The former represent ideals of the profession, standards that social workers are expected to uphold or advance, but for which they would not be called into account, as would be the case for enforceable standards. The Code does not identify which items are aspirations and which are enforceable, intending that all social workers act to uphold all of the profession's standards. The NASW Code is made up of both prescriptive and proscriptive standards. Prescriptive standards, such as "Social workers should promote and facilitate evaluation and research to contribute to the development of knowledge" (NASW, 1999, 5.02b), stipulate actions that social workers should take. Conversely, proscriptive standards indicate prohibited activities. For example, "Social workers should not engage in solicitation of testimonial endorsements (including solicitation of consent to use a client's prior statement as a testimonial endorsement) from current clients or from other people who, because of their particular circumstances, are vulnerable to undue influence" (NASW, 1999, 4.07b).

The breadth of the NASW Code means that it contains opportunities for errors of omission and errors of commission. Errors of omission occur when the social worker fails to do something the Code stipulates he or she should do, for example, "understand culture and its function in human behavior and society, recognizing the strengths that exist in all cultures" (NASW, 1999, 1.05a). Errors of commission occur when the worker does something the Code forbids. For example, "Social workers should not take unfair advantage of any professional relationship or exploit others to further their personal, religious, political, or business interests" (NASW, 1999, 1.06b). Thus, social workers must be familiar with the contents of the Code in order to understand both types of obligations.

The NASW Code is intended to be a guide for practice for all members of the profession, irrespective of their role or setting. While NASW may address allegations of unethical behavior by members (Strom-Gottfried, 2000, 2003), the Code itself is a much broader document, setting standards of practice for all social workers, serving as a resource for the public, and providing a guide for students who are considering entering the profession (NASW, 1999). "The NASW Code of Ethics is to be used by NASW and by individuals, agencies, organizations, and bodies (such as licensing and regulatory boards, professional liability insurance providers, courts of law, agency boards of directors, government agencies, and other professional groups) that choose to adopt it or use it as a frame of reference" (NASW, 1999, p. 4).

While the NASW Code of Ethics sets forth a comprehensive set of ethical standards, it is not the only code to which social workers may turn. Social workers may belong to multiple associations or specialty practice groups, each with their own code of ethics. Examples include the National Association of Black Social Workers (n.d.), the Clinical Social Work Federation (1997), and the International Federation of Social Workers (2004).

With some form of licensure or certification for social workers in all 50 of the United States, the boards that regulate social work practice have also issued codes for the social workers over whom they have jurisdiction. Because regulatory boards are primarily concerned with protecting the public from negligent or harmful practice, those codes are typically more narrowly drawn than the NASW Code, focusing on the professionals' responsibilities to clients, and on those areas where malpractice is most likely to occur, such as impairment, boundary violations, or confidentiality. In issuing the license to practice, regulatory boards wield a great deal of power for enforcing their standards, in that adverse findings in an investigation of misconduct could result in sanctions limiting or suspending the worker's license.

Beyond the codes associated with regulatory boards or professional associations, individual organizations are developing codes of conduct for their employees. For some agencies, the code is a long-standing articulation of its beliefs and culture. For others, the codes are a strategy to buffer or reduce liability in the event of worker malfeasance as well as a response to well-publicized scandals in the corporate sector. Given the different origins, intents, and sites of such codes, there is likely a good deal of variability in their contents and consequences. It is up to the individual social worker to explore and apply the agency's code and it is incumbent on the agency to assure that workers are assisted in fulfilling the spirit of ethical conduct as well as the letter of the law.

CORE AREAS IN SOCIAL WORK ETHICS

Across different types of codes and across the helping professions, seven areas of ethics are prominent and consistent. While the specific provisions may vary by setting and code, the essential concepts do not. This section describes each of these seven core areas of ethics and uses the NASW Code to exemplify key provisions in the area.

Self-Determination

The right to make the decisions that guide your life, and indeed "the right to be let alone" (Brandeis & Warren, 1890, p. 193) are the essence of self-determination. American society places a high value on the right of those most affected by a decision to be the decision makers (Lowenberg, Dolgoff, & Harrington, 2000) and restricts paternalistic interventions that impinge on that right. In social work, the standard balancing those tensions states, "Social workers respect and promote the right of clients to self-determination and assist clients in their efforts to identify and clarify their goals. Social workers may limit clients' right to self-determination when, in the social workers' professional judgment, clients' actions, or potential actions pose a serious, foreseeable, and imminent risk to themselves or others" (NASW, 1999, 1.02).

Some contend that self-determination is more ideal and that, in fact, in reality, clients' choices are constrained by an array of factors that effectively limit their autonomy (Perlman, 1965). Put another way, what good is a client's right to choose which type of cancer treatment he wants if the only service he can afford is 20 miles away and of limited efficacy? Without concomitant attention to the structural factors that reduce individual liberties, the celebration of personal autonomy may be misleading.

A further complication is in the application of the standard. Social workers are hard-pressed to stand on the sidelines and watch clients fail when they have the tools to be of service, even if the client has decided not to take advantage of their assistance. And, professionals struggle when clients make unhealthy or unwise decisions that fall short of the standards of risk to self or others. While it is not right to use coercion, deception, or manipulation to subvert a client's autonomy, being a party to a client's risks seems wrong as well. Paternalistic beneficence, or the desire to intervene on the client's behalf despite the client's objections (Murdach, 1996), may be acceptable when a client is young or incompetent, when an irreversible act such as suicide can be prevented, or when the interference with the client's decisions or actions ensures other freedoms or liberties, such as by preventing a serious crime (Abramson, 1985; Reamer, 1987). Beyond these circumscribed instances, how can social workers reconcile the tension between client autonomy and professional paternalism? Acknowledging the dignity inherent in the right to try and to fail and utilizing the helping relationship to encourage the client to anticipate and avoid negative outcomes can help reconcile the rights and risks of self-determination.

Informed Consent

The doctrine of informed consent requires that helping professionals disclose the nature of the services to be provided and the accompanying risks, benefits, and alternatives. Equipped with an understanding of their options, clients then have the right to consent to treatment or to refuse it. Similarly, researchers are expected to secure informed consent from study subjects. Whether for research or social services, informed consent should also address the consequences, if any, of the client's or subject's refusal to consent.

In discussing the origins of informed consent, Appelbaum, Lidz, and Meisel (1987) note that it is "a theory based on ethical principles, given effect by legal rulings and implemented by clinicians" (p. 3). Based on the principle of autonomy, informed consent implies that individuals should make their choices without coercion based on adequate and unbiased information. The right to informed consent is also imbedded in the nature of fiduciary relationships wherein one party has differential power, and thus that party has the inherent responsibility to share necessary information with the other (Kutchins, 1991; Morreim, 1988). This premise distinguishes informed consent from a contractual "let the buyer beware" model where a party is obliged to disclose no more information than the other party demands.

Today, informed consent generally encompasses three standards or preconditions: competence, the freedom from coercion (or "voluntariness"), and understanding (Reamer, 1995) and several "elements of disclosure," or the areas of information to be shared. The NASW Code of Ethics addresses both the standards and elements of disclosure, stating in part: "Social workers should use clear and understandable language to inform clients of the purpose of the services, risks related to the services, limits to services because of the requirements of a third party payer, relevant costs, reasonable alternatives, clients' right to refuse or withdraw consent, and the time frame covered by the consent. Social workers should provide clients with an opportunity to ask questions" (1999, 1.03a).

NASW standards describe the provisions that should be made for assuring informed consent from clients who are not literate, who may experience language barriers, whose capacity to give consent is impaired, or who are receiving services involuntarily. In all these instances, workers are compelled to make alternative means of communication available, to build in client choice wherever possible, and to assure that parties representing clients are informed and acting in the clients' best interests. Further, the Code requires that consent be obtained prior to taping a session or allowing observation by a third party, and that services delivered by media (such as TV, radio, or computers) be accompanied with information on the limits and risks attendant to those methods.

While clearly linked to the standard of self-determination, informed consent also relates to other principles such as competence, confidentiality, and conflicts of interest. Informed consent procedures set the stage for conversations about the worker's capacity to address client difficulties, the application of new or emerging treatment techniques, the limits of confidentiality and the conditions under which it may be breached, and the potential for conflicting roles and responsibilities (e.g., in rural practice or when providing family services; Strom-Gottfried, 2005). Following a forthright discussion of the issues, the clients involved have the opportunity to decide whether to proceed under those conditions, with full understanding of the consequences of their decisions. Thus, agreeing to receive a novel treatment may entail greater risk for the client and more intense supervision for the worker. Commencing with treatment under the constraints on confidentiality means that the client should not be surprised or betrayed if the worker must at some point disclose threats, child abuse, or other potential harms. By anticipating the complexities of receiving mental health care from an acquaintance or conjoint treatment with family members, the client can consider the risks and benefits before agreeing to proceed with services.

Although it is a crucial and seemingly straightforward concept, several factors can complicate the adherence to informed consent. Because consent is a process that evolves over the course of service and in the context of a helping relationship, providers must constantly be alert to the opportunities for consumer participation in decision making, shifts in the client's capacity to render consent, culturally variant views of autonomy, and pressure to curtail consent (Manning & Gaul, 1997). As such, paternalism, misunderstandings, and expediency can jeopardize informed consent in the same way that they endanger the principle of self-determination (Tower, 1994).

Professional Competence

Ethical standards addressing professional competence are intended to assure that practitioners have the requisite knowledge and skills to carry out their professional responsibilities. The standards for competence apply to the capacity for cross-cultural practice, for providing education and supervision, and for responding to emerging bodies of knowledge. For example, "Social workers who function as educators, field instructors for students, or trainers should provide instruction only within their areas of knowledge and competence and should provide instruction based on the most current information and knowledge available in the profession" (NASW, 1999, 3.02a). Further, "Social workers should strive to become and remain proficient in professional practice and the performance of professional functions. Social workers should critically examine and keep current with emerging knowledge relevant to social work. Social workers should routinely review the professional literature and participate in continuing education relevant to social work practice and social work ethics" (NASW, 1999, 4.01b). And, "Social workers should seek the advice and counsel of colleagues whenever such consultation is in the best interests of clients" (NASW, 1999, 2.05a).

The NASW Code does not prescribe how much training, experience, and consultation are necessary for competence, instead it makes social workers responsible for such self-awareness and self-control. The privilege of self-regulation is a defining feature of any profession. Thus, social workers and other professionals are expected to know their own abilities and limits, setting boundaries on activities that are outside their particular scope of practice, rather than depending on supervisors or superiors to set limits for them.

Beyond assuring capable practice, ethical standards also compel social workers to address personal problems that may interfere with effective service delivery. When colleagues demonstrate unethical or impaired practice, standards of competence stipulate the social workers must act to address these issues. Specifically, the NASW Code states, "Social workers who have direct knowledge of a social work colleague's impairment that is due to personal problems, psychosocial distress, substance abuse, or mental health difficulties and that interferes with practice effectiveness should consult with that colleague when feasible and assist the colleague in taking remedial action" (1999, 2.09a) and "Social workers who believe that a social work colleague's impairment interferes with practice effectiveness and that the colleague has not taken adequate steps to address the impairment should take action through appropriate channels established by employers, agencies, NASW, licensing and regulatory bodies, and other professional organizations" (1999, 2.09b). Similar provisions exist when the concern involves incompetent or unethical practices, beyond those that are the result of impairment.

Conflicts of Interest

While social workers are expected to give preeminence to clients' interests, a variety of situations can challenge this ideal. Conflicts of interest arise when the worker's own interests (personal, financial, occupational, sexual, and/or spiritual) interfere with attention to the client's needs or interests. Conflicts may also occur when workers are serving multiple individuals in a client system, as in family or conjoint therapy. In these cases, the tension is in upholding the rights of several parties to whom the worker owes loyalty, when those rights may be at odds. Conflicts of interest are not limited to clinical relationships. They can challenge supervisory relationships and complicate educational and administrative responsibilities.

The NASW Code contends that "Social workers should be alert to and avoid conflicts of interest that interfere with the exercise of professional discretion and impartial judgment. Social workers should inform clients when a real or potential conflict of interest arises and take reasonable steps to resolve the issue in a manner that makes the clients' interests primary and protects clients' interests to the greatest extent possible. In some cases, protecting clients' interests may require termination of the professional relationship with proper referral of the client" (NASW, 1999, 1.06a). Further, "When social workers provide services to two or more people who have a relationship with each other (e.g., couples, family members), social workers should clarify with all parties which individuals will be considered clients and the nature of social workers' professional obligations to the various individuals who are receiving services. Social workers who anticipate a conflict of interest among the individuals receiving services or who anticipate having to perform in potentially conflicting roles (e.g., when a social worker is asked to testify in a child custody dispute or divorce proceedings involving clients) should clarify their role with the parties involved and take appropriate action to minimize any conflict of interest" (NASW, 1999, 1.06d). And, "Social workers should not engage in dual or multiple relationships with clients or former clients in which there is a risk of exploitation or potential harm to the client. In instances when dual or multiple relationships are unavoidable, social workers should take steps to protect clients and are responsible for setting clear, appropriate, and culturally sensitive boundaries. (Dual or multiple relationships occur when social workers relate to clients in more than one relationship, whether professional, social, or business. Dual or multiple relationships can occur simultaneously or consecutively)" (NASW, 1999, 1.06c).

The violation of therapeutic boundaries—through sexual involvement, dual relationships, or other distorted roles—constitutes a particularly visible and distressing category of conflicts of interest. These forms of misconduct can lead to serious professional and legal consequences for the workers involved and can result in distrust, self-doubt and deterioration for the clients, students, or employees who are exploited in the process (Congress, 2001; Peterson, 1992; Stake & Oliver, 1991). Research on ethics complaints indicates that in NASW-adjudicated cases, boundary violations accounted for more than half of the cases in which there were violations (Strom-Gottfried, 1999). Similarly, in research on the frequency of malpractice claims against social workers for the period 1961 to 1990, Reamer (1995) found that sexual violations were the second most common type of case and the most costly in terms of claims paid. Sexual attraction to clients is a common and poorly managed clinical phenomenon (Pope, Sonne, & Holroyd, 1993). Crossing the line into sexual misconduct is often the culmination of a "slippery slope" of boundary problems that may include excessive self-disclosure on the part of the social worker, the exchange of personal gifts, socializing or meeting for meals outside the office, and arranging for the client to perform office and household chores or other favors (Borys & Pope, 1989; Epstein, Simon, & Kay, 1992; Gabbard, 1996; Gartrell, 1992).

How can social workers determine when activities such as accepting a gift from a client are benign and when they foreshadow deeper problems? To properly address conflicts of interest, social workers should be mindful of the power that accompanies their educational, clinical, managerial, and research roles. They must take steps to assure that they do not "take unfair advantage of any professional relationship or exploit others to further their personal, religious, political, or business interests" (NASW, 1999, 1.06b). Gaps in the social worker's own well-being, maturity, self-awareness, work-life balance, or openness to feedback can set the stage for conflicts of interest because personal strength is required to subjugate your needs to those of others (Peterson, 1992; Rowan, 2002).

In addition to working on self-improvement, social workers should anticipate situations in which conflicts of interest are likely to occur. Information obtained at intake; during the course of the professional relationship; through one's planning, supervision, or managerial roles; or even during termination may provide an opportunity for the social worker to foresee future complications. If, due to sensitivity and foresight, the social worker identifies a potential conflict of interest, he or she must then assess whether it is avoidable (Doyle, 1997). For example, if the social worker ascertains that accepting a client's gift would cloud his or her clinical judgment, then the best course of action is to decline the gift. Similarly, if accepting a friend as a client, student, or supervisee would compromise the social worker's ability to carry out the clinical, educational, or supervisory role, then one of the two parties should withdraw from the case to eliminate the possibility of a conflict of interest.

In being alert to potential conflicts of interest, social workers can also evaluate the context of the situation to determine the complications that might arise. Kitchener 1988 maintains that risk is increased when the expectations between roles are incompatible, when obligations diverge, and when there are greater differences in prestige and power. For example, serving as a client's therapist and employer suggests high risk on all variables because the demands of the roles are incompatible, the obligations of the roles may well lead to divided loyalties or decreased objectivity, and the power differential in both roles is quite vast. In contrast, developing a social relationship with a former employee represents low risk in that the power differential and role conflicts are minimal, in part because the dual relationships are not concurrent, but also because the power, role, and responsibility disparities are not as vast.

Even when a worker determines that an action, decision, or relationship will not create a conflict of interest, he or she must still institute precautionary measures to shield the less powerful party from harm. These steps include providing informed consent, discussing the ethical and practical implications of the intersecting interests, documenting such discussions, continually monitoring the relationship for conflicts or boundary threats, and seeking consultation or supervision for assistance with objective reflection and guidance on the case (Erickson, 2001). If any one of these activities raises a red flag about the worker's ability to carry out his or her role, it is incumbent on the social worker to resolve the issue in such a way that the client's best interests are protected.

Privacy and Confidentiality

The protection of clients' personal information is the foundation on which helping relationships are created. This admonition is reinforced in significant legal protections for patient privacy and privileged communications (Dickson, 1998) and in the Code, which urges restraint in soliciting patient information and caution in sharing it, even when the client is not expressly identified (NASW, 1999). While case information can be shared for compelling professional reasons such as supervision, client safety, or mandated reporting, clients should be informed in advance of these possibilities. Clients should also provide informed consent for the sharing of private information under other circumstances, such as for the submission of insurance claims, sharing case records, referrals, and so on. When sharing information, social workers should disclose as little information as necessary to achieve the intent of the disclosure. And, when feasible, clients should be notified before the actual disclosure is made.

Confidentiality transcends the helping relationship and the death of the social worker or the client. Therefore, social workers should consult state laws and organizational policies about the proper timing and disposal of client records. Private practitioners should take steps to assure the security and succession of case files in the event that the worker retires, dies, or is incapacitated. And, requests for case information post termination require the same vigilance and discretion as requests made during the course of treatment.

Social work standards also seek to assure client privacy through other measures. Tenets of the NASW Code state that "workers should not discuss confidential information in public or semipublic areas such as hallways, waiting rooms, elevators, and restaurants" (NASW, 1999, 1.07i). Social workers must be cautious in responding to requests for information from the media, disclosing data only with proper client consent. Workers should protect written and electronic documents containing sensitive information and assure that electronic transfers of information are secure. Client's identities should be obscured when their cases are used for training purposes or consultation, unless the client has consented to sharing the information.

While privacy protections are essential, there are limits on the client's right to confidentiality. As noted, case information may be shared for supervision, when mandated by law, as in cases of child or elder abuse, for client safety, and as needed for the social worker's defense when accusations of malpractice are filed. Confidentiality may also be restricted by courts of law. Social workers practicing in states that do not recognize privileged communication may be compelled by courts to reveal confidential information and to produce confidential records. "Privileged communication" refers to all communications made within a "legally protected relationship," which "cannot be introduced into court without the consent of the person making the communication," typically the patient or client (Dickson, 1998, p. 32).

However, determining the presence and applicability of privilege can be complicated. As Dickson notes, "Privilege laws can vary with the profession of the individual receiving the communication, the material communicated, the purpose of the communication, whether the proceeding is criminal or civil, and whether the professional is employed by the state or is in private practice, among other factors" (1998, p. 33). On the federal level, the U.S. Supreme Court in *Jaffee v. Redmond* upheld client communications as privileged and specifically extended that privilege to licensed social workers (Reamer, 1998). While this ruling helped clarify social workers' privilege in the federal courts, ambiguity and variability continue on the state level. As a result, social workers must understand their state laws and regulations and assure that clients are fully informed about the limits to confidentiality should their records be subpoenaed or testimony required.

Even with the protection of privileged communication, the client's right is not absolute (Levick, 1981). If, in a court's judgment, the disclosure of confidential information would produce benefits that outweigh the injury that might be incurred by revealing that information, the presiding judge may waive the privilege. In criminal investigations, for example, privilege is occasionally disregarded because the need for information is deemed more compelling than the need to protect privacy (Schwartz, 1989). Ultimately, then, courts make decisions on privilege on a case-by-case basis.

Subpoenas, whether for records or testimony, are orders of the court, and thus require the worker's response. However, subpoenas may be issued for irrelevant or immaterial information and in these instances social workers should be wary about submitting privileged materials. Careful review of the subpoena, consultation with the client, and with a supervisor and agency attorney can help staff determine how to respond. As NASW standards state, "Social workers should protect the confidentiality of clients during legal proceedings to the extent permitted by law. When a court of law or other legally authorized body orders social workers to disclose confidential or privileged information without a client's consent and such disclosure could cause harm to the client, social workers should request that the court withdraw the order or limit the order as narrowly as possible or maintain the records under seal, unavailable for public inspection" (NASW, 1999, 1.07j).

Complications in protecting confidentiality can arise when social workers are treating multiperson systems. While the worker may articulate and accept responsibility for maintaining privacy, he or she may be unable to promise that other members of the system will do the same. As the NASW Code states, "When social workers provide counseling services to families, couples, or groups, social workers should seek agreement among the parties involved concerning each individual's right to confidentiality and obligation to preserve the confidentiality of information shared by others. Social workers should inform participants in family, couples, or group counseling that social workers cannot guarantee that all participants will honor such agreements" (1999, 1.07f). A further complication involves the information that can acceptably be shared by the worker with other members of the system. As such, "Social workers should inform clients involved in family, couples, marital, or group counseling of the social worker's, employer's, and agency's policy concerning the social worker's disclosure of confidential information among the parties involved in the counseling" (NASW, 1999, 1.07g).

Beyond information directly received in service to clients, social workers are expected to protect "confidential information shared by colleagues in the course of their professional relationships and transactions" and ensure that they "understand social workers' obligation to respect confidentiality and any exceptions related to it" (NASW, 1999, 2.02). Social workers must protect subjects' privacy when conducting research. When reporting evaluating and research results, they "should protect participants' confidentiality by omitting identifying information unless proper consent has been obtained authorizing disclosure" (NASW, 1999, 5.02m).

In addition to ethical standards, laws and policies give weight to confidentiality protections. For example, the Health Insurance Portability and Accountability Act of 1996 (HIPAA) established federal standards to protect the privacy of personal health information. HIPAA regulations affect pharmacies, health care settings, and insurance plans as well as individual health and mental health providers. The rules cover identifiable client information in all forms, including paper records, psychotherapy notes, electronic data and communications, and verbal communications. HIPAA also requires patient access to records, procedures for correcting errors in records, and the provision of informed consent about the organization's privacy policies (HIPAA Medical Privacy Rule, 2003).

Nondiscrimination

A number of ethical standards specifically reflect the profession's commitment to fair and unbiased practices in relationships with clients, colleagues, employees and trainees. "Social workers should not practice, condone, facilitate, or collaborate with any form of discrimination on the basis of race, ethnicity, national origin, color, sex, sexual orientation, age, marital status, political belief, religion, or mental or physical disability" (NASW, 1999, 4.02). Beyond avoiding discriminatory behavior in their own actions, social workers "should act to prevent and eliminate domination of, exploitation of, and discrimination against any person, group, or class" (NASW, 1999, 6.04d).

Other provisions on equality relate to specific professional roles and responsibilities. In administration, "Social workers should advocate for resource allocation procedures that are open and fair. When not all clients' needs can be met, an allocation procedure should be developed that is nondiscriminatory and based on appropriate and consistently applied principles" (NASW, 1999, 3.07b). Further, "social workers should act to prevent and eliminate discrimination in the employing organization's work assignments and in its employment policies and practices" (NASW, 1999, 3.09e).

"Social workers should avoid unwarranted negative criticism of colleagues in communications with clients or with other professionals. Unwarranted negative criticism may include demeaning comments that refer to colleagues' level of competence or to individuals' attributes such as race, ethnicity, national origin, color, sex, sexual orientation, age, marital status, political belief, religion, and mental or physical disability" (NASW, 1999, 2.01b). While it is incumbent for social workers to speak up when colleagues are engaged in harmful or exploitive practices, practitioners must be mindful of the tone, direction, fairness, and basis for their complaints.

"Social workers who provide supervision should evaluate supervisees' performance in a manner that is fair and respectful" (NASW, 1999, 3.01d) and "Social workers who have responsibility for evaluating the performance of others should fulfill such responsibility in a fair and considerate manner and on the basis of clearly stated criteria" (NASW, 1999, 3.03). In addition to using fair personnel practices, social workers should discourage discrimination in the hiring, retention, compensation, and termination processes of their own organizations and those that serve at social work field sites (Reamer, 1998).

Professionalism

The final category of standards addresses an array of responsibilities for upholding personal and professional integrity. The NASW Code clearly states that "Social workers should not participate in, condone, or be associated with dishonesty, fraud, or deception" (NASW, 1999, 4.04). In upholding this standard, social workers are expected to accurately represent their education, expertise, and credentials, and seek corrections if others misconstrue those qualifications. Social workers are expected to accurately represent the views of their employing organizations and distinguish official positions from their personal opinions when providing public commentary. Integrity also demands that social workers take credit only for work they have actually performed and assure that the contributions of others are appropriately recognized.

In regard to clients, professionalism dictates that social workers should use "accurate and respectful language" in their communications "to and about clients" (NASW, 1999, 1.12). "Social workers should not exploit clients in disputes with colleagues or engage clients in any inappropriate discussion of conflicts between social workers and their colleagues" (NASW, 1999, 2.04b).

Standards around professionalism encourage social workers to go beyond their individual behaviors to take responsibility for improving their organizations' practices and assure that agencies' policies do not impinge in ethical practice. "Social workers should not allow an employing organization's policies, procedures, regulations, or administrative orders to interfere with their ethical practice of social work. Social workers should take reasonable steps to ensure that their employing organizations' practices are consistent with the NASW Code of Ethics" (1999, 3.09d). Standards of integrity also extend further than the social worker's actions in a professional capacity. Specifically, "social workers should not permit their private conduct to interfere with their ability to fulfill their professional responsibilities" (NASW, 1999, 4.03).

Ethical professional behavior demands that the individual worker take responsibility for his or her actions, work proactively to improve conditions where discontentment or conflicts exist, and engage in conduct that reflects positively on the field of social work. It relates to the principles of honesty and trustworthiness that are essential for effective service in the helping professions.

Ethical Dilemmas

The NASW Code of Ethics states "principles and standards must be applied by individuals of good character who discern moral questions and, in good faith, seek to make reliable ethical judgments" (NASW, 1999, p. 4). Embracing the values of the profession and internalizing its ethical standards are important elements of effective decision making. Social workers, however, are often confronted with situations that are not easily resolved by the application of ethical standards.

A number of situations can give rise to ethical dilemmas. Typically, these include incidents where the worker is uncertain about the application of a specific principle, those where principles or obligations are in conflict, and those in which no satisfactory solution seems attainable. Confusion about how ethical standards might apply may stem from the complexity of cases or from the nature of the standards themselves. For example, consider the case where a minor client divulges risky behavior to her social worker. The ethical dilemma may spring from the worker's uncertainty about parental rights in the minor's care, or it may stem from ambiguity in the Code's provisions. Would the youth's behavior constitute "serious, foreseeable, and imminent risk" (NASW, 1999, 1.02)? Would concern for the client's safety be considered a "compelling professional reason" to break confidentiality and notify the parents (NASW, 1999, 1.07c)?

In addition to dilemmas that arise in the interpretation of ethical standards, dilemmas also arise when responsibilities or obligations diverge. In the previous example, the social worker's responsibility to maintain the client's privacy is at odds with the client's status as a minor and the responsibility to protect clients from harm. Dilemmas also arise when professional standards conflict with legal responsibilities or organizational imperatives. For example, a law may prohibit the use of funding for services to undocumented immigrants, and an agency may compel workers to terminate services to clients who cannot demonstrate citizenship. The individual worker, however, may experience a dilemma in reconciling these directives with values around social justice and standards on termination that state "Social workers should terminate services to clients and professional relationships with them when such services and relationships are no longer required or no longer serve the clients' needs or interests" (NASW, 1999, 1.16a). Further, "social workers should take reasonable steps to avoid abandoning clients who are still in need of services. Social workers should withdraw services precipitously only under unusual circumstances, giving careful consideration to all factors in the situation and taking care to minimize possible adverse effects. Social workers should assist in making appropriate arrangements for continuation of services when necessary" (NASW, 1999, 1.16b).

The third category of dilemmas arises from situations where the direction is clear and uncompromised by competing pressures, but which still results in unsatisfactory options. For example, the Code and state laws require that social workers report suspected child abuse to local child protection agencies, yet social workers often struggle with the implications such disclosures have for the helping relationship and with doubts that overwhelmed and under-resourced child welfare services will effectively help in the matter.

The ability to detect and address ethical dilemmas is rooted in an understanding of the profession's values and familiarity with the tenets of the codes that govern practice. Being alert to the conditions under which dilemmas can arise furthers this understanding and enables the practitioner to methodically apply a resolution framework.

Ethical Decision Making

While some practitioners rely on intuitionism for ethical decision making, the complexity and stakes involved in ethical dilemmas demand more systematic processes (Gambrill & Pruger, 1997; Reamer, 2002). The effective resolution of ethical dilemmas requires consistent use of established protocols that encourage the examination of alternatives and employ written and consultative resources for weighing choices and selecting the proper direction. Several decision-making models are commonly utilized in social work practice (Congress, 1999; Lowenberg et al., 2000; Reamer, 1999). Reamer's seven-step model balances utility and thoroughness, requiring the user to:

1. Identify the ethical issues, including the social work values and duties that conflict.
2. Identify the individuals, groups, and organizations likely to be affected by the ethical decision.
3. Tentatively identify all viable courses of action and the participants involved in each, along with the potential risks and benefits for each.
4. Examine these choices and the reasons for and against each. How do they fit with ethics? Social work practice theory? Your principles? Any rules or laws that apply?
5. Consult with colleagues and appropriate experts.
6. Make the decision, and document the process that led to it.
7. Monitor, evaluate, and document the decision (Reamer, 1999, pp. 76–77).

As described in the preceding section, the first step in decision making requires an understanding of the nature of the conflict or the dilemma. Doing so enables the social worker to better articulate the concepts that are at odds and assure that it is not merely a situation of right over wrong, but rather a tension between competing rights or obligations. Knowing which concepts are in tension creates clarity and facilitates research and consultation about the matter.

In addition to determining that the dilemma is an ethical one, and analyzing the elements in conflict, the practitioner must identify the individuals and groups with a stake in the decision as well as the nature of their involvement. These parties may include the client's family and social network, other professionals working with the client, the social worker's employing agency, and the social worker himself or herself.

Clarity about the nature of the dilemma and the stakeholders provides the basis for generating viable alternatives for action. In this process, the social worker considers the short term and long-term consequences of each choice for the individuals involved. Each of the choices generated under step 3 will contain both advantages and disadvantages for the people involved. Step 4 in Reamer's model thus requires the worker to carefully evaluate the choices in light of codes of ethics and relevant laws, regulations, policies, and principles. This rather complex step is greatly facilitated by the worker's existing command of the ethical and practice principles. Social workers should also endeavor to understand the directives that regulate their particular fields of social work practice. This includes laws or statutes developed by legislative bodies at the federal, state, and local levels, and as a result of court decisions (case law), regulations and administrative codes which are typically issued by local, state, or federal agencies with financial or other rule-making authority (Dickson, 1998) and policies formulated on regional or organization levels. Sources of information about pertinent laws and regulations include texts (Madden, 1998; Saltzman & Furman, 1999), the *U.S. Code* for federal statutes and the *Code of Federal Regulations* for administrative law (Dickson, 1998). Some regulatory boards may also provide links to appropriate administrative codes and most organizations have policy handbooks and personnel with specialized expertise in the topic.

Ethical and clinical theories must also be used as a lens by which to evaluate ethical dilemmas and the related options. Two prominent theories of normative ethics are utilitarianism and deontology (Reamer, 2002). Utilitarian or ends-based theories evaluate the desirability of a particular action based on the outcomes or consequences of that choice. A familiar guide for decision making under this framework would be selecting the option that yields the greatest good for the greatest number, or the least harmful outcome (Bandman & Bandman, 2002). In contrast, deontological or rule-based theories contend that "certain actions are inherently right or wrong as a matter of fundamental principle" (Reamer, 2002, p. 67). If an action is stipulated or valued, that choice should be pursued, irrespective of the results.

While each of these prominent perspectives has critics and limitations, these shortcomings do not mean the theories themselves are irrelevant (Rachels, 2003). As decision makers become familiar with them and other ethical theories, they can be employed to understand biases for one action or another (Is the tendency to be ends-based or rule-based?) and to generate a broader array of choices. (What would a utilitarian position suggest?)

Beyond the two prominent ethical theories, six ethical principles are commonly utilized in the professions when evaluating desirable choices. The principle of *autonomy* refers to the individual's right to make his or her own life decisions without undue or unwarranted interference. *Beneficence* refers to the importance of doing good, enhancing another's well being. Its corollary, *nonmaleficence,* refers to the duty to cause no harm or prevent harm. *Fidelity* is the principle of behaving in a trustworthy manner, keeping one's promise or word. Related to fidelity is the principle of *veracity* or the commitment to truthfulness. *Justice* is the premise that individuals in similar circumstances will be treated equitably, distributing risks and benefits equally. The principle also refers to justice in its broadest form, referring to nondiscrimination and the fair distribution of scarce resources (Beauchamp & Childress, 2001; Corey, Corey, & Callanan, 2003).

These principles can be used to generate alternatives (What actions would meet the principle of beneficence, that is, would promote the client's interests? What decision would be just?). The principles can also be used to evaluate choices (Is this action truthful? Which of my choices results in the least harm for the stakeholders involved?). The principles provide professionals with a common language for discussing dilemmas and weighing options.

In addition to ethical theories and principles, step 4 in Reamer's model calls for social workers to utilize social work theories in order to better understand a dilemma, the impact of certain decisions, and the skills and strategies that might be employed in effectively implementing a decision. In particular, knowledge about human behavior, effective communication and change processes can help social workers to implement ethical decisions. When ethical action is stymied, social workers can look to the literature on moral courage, advocacy, and professional responsibility for support and guidance in doing the right thing (Jansson & Dodd, 2002; Kidder, 2005; Kritek, 2002; Strom-Gotttfried, 2004).

Consultation is a crucial element of ethical decision making. Supervisory and expert resources can be called on in understanding the dilemma, in generating and evaluating options and in selecting a course of action. Discussing the issue with appropriate others helps elicit information, obligations, or alternatives that might otherwise go unnoticed and provides opportunities to rehearse or prepare for the decision. Consultation may include ongoing collegial or supervisory relationships, which imply confidentiality, familiarity, and trust. It may also involve formal ethics committees, licensure boards, social work associations, other professionals involved in the case, and people with particular expertise, such as attorneys, ethicists, or specialists in a given field. In research dilemmas, it would involve consultation with an Institutional Review Board (IRB). In any consultation, the social worker should take precautions to protect client or subject identities and avoid revealing excessive personal information. Like ethical standards, theories, and principles, consultations may result in conflicting advice. As Reamer notes, "reasonable people may disagree," but clients and others involved have a right to expect "that the social workers involved in the decision will be thorough, thoughtful, sensitive and fair" (1999, p. 91). Even in the absence of convergence around a particular direction, research and appropriate conversation will acquaint the social worker with new options and new dimensions to consider about existing options. The decision that results will be strengthened if it results from a better informed, more thorough process.

Social workers should take care to document their decision-making process, including all of the outcomes and factors that were taken into account when choosing a course of action. The documentation can be placed in the client's record, in the social worker's personal files, or another appropriate document, depending on the setting and the nature of the decision. The information should preserve, for the social worker and any other concerned parties, a contemporaneous account of the decision-making process, specifying the people and documents consulted, the social worker's appraisal of the risks and benefits of certain options, and the bases for the final decision. Because responsible decision making requires evaluation of the decision's impact, and remedial actions, if appropriate, documentation should include those steps, too. Beyond the individual case, the social worker should evaluate the decision and the process to strengthen his or her capacity for responding to future dilemmas, scrutinizing the case to determine how it could have been handled more efficiently or more beneficially.

CONCLUSION

The profession's values define the field of social work and distinguish it from other disciplines. Over the past 50 years, those values have been translated into ethical standards, intended for social workers to utilize as they carry out a variety of roles within the profession. Further, ethical standards inform the public about the profession and provide laypeople and regulators guidance regarding proper professional conduct in social work.

Dilemmas arise as practitioners strive to uphold standards in complex case situations. Social workers must carefully examine their options when faced with competing standards, conflicting responsibilities, and ambiguities in applying ethical concepts. Effective decision making involves seeking appropriate input from supervisors, consultants, and experts and critically evaluating options in light of laws, policies, standards, and the implications for the stakeholders involved. Ethical practice goes beyond mere risk management to assure that social workers uphold the profession's values in their interactions with clients, students, employees, research subjects, and colleagues. Ethical standards also guide the conduct of individual social workers as representatives of the profession, as well as of their employing organizations. Professional competence requires that social workers continually improve and apply the knowledge, skills, and values that characterize the discipline.

REFERENCES

Abramson, M. (1985). The autonomy-paternalism dilemma in social work practice. *Social Casework, 66*, 387–393.

Appelbaum, P. S., Lidz, C. W., & Meisel, A. (1987). *Informed consent: Legal theory and clinical practice*. New York: Oxford University Press.

Bandman, E., & Bandman, B. (2002). *Nursing ethics through the life span* (4th ed.). Upper Saddle, NJ: Prentice-Hall.

Beauchamp, T. L., & Childress, J. F. (2001). *Principles of biomedical ethics* (5th ed.). New York: Oxford University Press.

Borys, D. S., & Pope, K. S. (1989). Dual relationships between therapist and client: A national study of psychologists, psychiatrists, and social workers. *Professional Psychology: Research and Practice, 20*, 283–293.

Brandeis, L. D., & Warren, S. D. (1890, December 15). The right to privacy. *Harvard Law Review, 4*(5), 193–220.

Clinical Social Work Federation. (1997). *Code of ethics*. Retrieved February 6, 2006, from www.cswf.org/www/CSWF%20Ethics%20Code%20Prtctd.pdf.

Congress, E. (1999). *Social work values and ethics: Identifying and resolving professional dilemmas*. Chicago: Nelson-Hall.

Congress, E. (2001). Dual relationships in social work education: Report on a national survey. *Journal of Social Work Education, 37*(2), 255–266.

Corey, G., Corey, M. S., & Callanan, P. (2003). *Issues and ethics in the helping professions* (6th ed.). Belmont, CA: Brooks/Cole.

Dickson, D. T. (1998). *Confidentiality and privacy in social work: A guide to the law for practitioners and students*. New York: Free Press.

Doyle, K. (1997). Substance abuse counselors in recovery: Implications for the ethical issue of dual relationships. *Journal of Counseling and Development, 75*, 428–432.

Epstein, R. S., Simon, R. I., & Kay, G. G. (1992). Assessing boundary violations in psychotherapy: Survey results with the Exploitation Index. *Bulletin of the Menninger Foundation, 56*(2), 150–166.

Erickson, S. H. (2001). Multiple relationships in rural counseling. *Family Journal: Counseling and Therapy for Couples and Families, 9*(3), 302–304.

Gabbard, G. O. (1996). Lessons to be learned from the study of sexual boundary violations. *American Journal of Psychotherapy, 50*(3), 311–322.

Gambrill, E., & Pruger, R. (Eds.). (1997). *Controversial issues in social work ethics, values, and obligations*. Boston: Allyn & Bacon.

Gartrell, N. K. (1992). Boundaries in lesbian therapy relationships. *Women and Therapy, 12*(3), 29–50.

Hepworth, D. H., Rooney, R. H., Rooney, G. D., Strom-Gottfried, K. J., & Larsen, J. (2006). *Direct social work practice: Theory and skills* (7th ed.). Belmont, CA: Brooks/Cole.

HIPAA Medical Privacy Rule. (2003, August). *Complete privacy, security, and enforcement (procedural) regulation text (45 CFR Parts 160 and 164)*. U.S. Department of Health and Human Services.

International Federation of Social Workers. (2004). *Ethics in social work: Statement of principles*. Retrieved January 28, 2006, from www.ifsw.org/en/p38000324.html.

Jansson, B. S., & Dodd, S. J. (2002). Ethical activism: Strategies for empowering medical social workers. *Social Work in Health Care, 36*(1), 11–28.

Kidder, R. M. (2005). *Moral courage: Taking action when your values are put to the test*. New York: Morrow.

Kitchener, K. S. (1988). Dual role relationships: What makes them so problematic? *Journal of Counseling and Development*, *67*, 217–221.

Kritek, P. B. (2002). *Negotiating at an uneven table: Developing moral courage in resolving our conflicts*. Hoboken, NJ: Wiley.

Kutchins, H. (1991). The fiduciary relationship: The legal basis for social workers' responsibilities to clients. *Social Work*, *36*(2), 106–113.

Levick, K. (1981). Privileged communication: Does it really exist? *Social Casework*, *62*, 235–239.

Lowenberg, F. M., Dolgoff, R., & Harrington, D. (2000). *Ethical decisions for social work practice* (6th ed.). Itasca, IL: Peacock.

Madden, R. G. (1998). *Legal issues in social work, counseling, and mental health: Guidelines for clinical practice in psychotherapy*. Thousand Oaks, CA: Sage.

Manning, S. S., & Gaul, C. E. (1997). The ethics of informed consent: A critical variable in the self-determination of health and mental health clients. *Social Work in Health Care*, *25*(3), 103–117.

McCann, C. W., & Cutler, J. P. (1979). Ethics and the alleged unethical. *Social Work*, *24*, 5–8.

Morreim, E. H. (1988). Cost containment: Challenging fidelity and justice. *Hastings Center Report*, *18*(6), 20–25.

Murdach, A. D. (1996). Beneficence re-examined: Protective intervention in mental health. *Social Work*, *41*, 26–32.

National Association of Black Social Workers. (n.d.). *Code of ethics*. Retrieved January 28, 2006, from www.nabsw.org/mserver/CodeofEthics.aspx? menuContext=720/.

National Association of Social Workers. (1999). *Code of ethics*. Washington, DC: Author.

Perlman, H. H. (1965). Self-determination: Reality or illusion? *Social Service Review*, *39*, 410–422.

Peterson, M. R. (1992). *At personal risk: Boundary violations in professional client relationships*. New York: Norton.

Pope, K. S., Sonne, J. L., & Holroyd, J. (1993). *Sexual feelings in psychotherapy: Explorations for therapists and therapists-in-training*. Washington, DC: American Psychological Association.

Rachels, J. (2003). *The elements of moral philosophy* (4th ed.). Boston: McGraw-Hill.

Reamer, F. G. (1987). Informed consent in social work. *Social Work*, *32*(5), 425–429.

Reamer, F. G. (1995). Malpractice claims against social workers: First facts. *Social Work*, *40*, 595–601.

Reamer, F. G. (1998). The evolution of social work ethics. *Social Work*, *43*, 488–500.

Reamer, F. G. (1999). *Social work values and ethics* (2nd ed.). New York: Columbia University Press.

Reamer, F. G. (2002). Ethical issues in social work. In A. R. Roberts & G. J. Greene (Eds.), *Social workers' desk reference* (pp. 65–69). New York: Oxford University Press.

Rowan, S. (2002). The slippery slope: Violating the ultimate therapeutic taboo. *Psychotherapy Networker*, *26*(2), 39–40, 73.

Saltzman, A., & Furman, D. M. (1999). Locating and using the law. In A. Saltzman & D. M. Furman (Eds.), *Law in social work practice* (pp. 77–116). Chicago: Nelson-Hall.

Schwartz, G. (1989). Confidentiality revisited. *Social Work*, *34*(3), 223–226.

Stake, J. E., & Oliver, J. (1991). Sexual contact and touching between therapist and client: A survey of psychologists' attitudes and behaviors. *Professional Psychology: Research and Practice*, *22*(4), 297–307.

Strom-Gottfried, K. J. (1999). Professional boundaries: An analysis of violations by social workers. *Families in Society: Journal of Contemporary Human Services*, *80*(5), 439–449.

Strom-Gottfried, K. J. (2000). Ensuring ethical practice: An examination of NASW Code violations, 1986–1997. *Social Work*, *45*(3), 251–261.

Strom-Gottfried, K. J. (2003). Understanding adjudication: The origins, targets and outcomes of ethics complaints. *Social Work*, *48*(1), 85–94.

Strom-Gottfried, K. J. (2004). *Ethics in social work and social welfare: A primer*. Boston: McGraw-Hill.

Strom-Gottfried, K. J. (2005). Ethical practice in rural environments. In L. Ginsberg (Ed.), *Social work in rural communities* (4th ed., pp. 141–155). Alexandria, VA: Council on Social Work Education.

Tower, K. (1994). Consumer-centered social work practice: Restoring client self-determination. *Social Work*, *39*(2), 191–196.

Chapter 7

THE STRENGTHS PERSPECTIVE: PUTTING POSSIBILITY AND HOPE TO WORK IN OUR PRACTICE

Dennis Saleebey

All humans possess the urge to be heroic; to transcend their condition, to develop their powers, to overcome adversity, to stand up and be counted, to be a part of something that surpasses the petty interests of self, to shape and realize vibrant hopes and dreams. This is a precious longing and it is often a fragile one. Liberation and empowerment—the heart of the work that we are privileged to do—have ripened as ideas and practices and are designed to unleash the heroic: human energy, critical thinking, possibility and purpose, challenges to the conventional wisdom, moral imagination, the humanitarian impulse, and the ability to survive and thrive in the face of taxing ordeals. This all may occur within the parameters of a person's daily life and may often be simple things like experimenting with new behaviors, entertaining new ideas and points of view, escaping the drudgery of oppressive work or throwing off the shackles of abusive relationships, developing a more generous fund of communal spirit, giving help to a stranger, volunteering in a community agency, withstanding and confronting a dreadful disease or challenging situation with dignity and resolve, or holding the hands and speaking out for those who are marginalized and mute.

Appreciating and stimulating the heroic in clients is to assist them not only in confronting their circumstances, but to make an alliance with the robust and resilient in them, to consort with their dreams and hopes, to connect them with significant outside resources, to collaborate with them on projects that ultimately deliver conviction, relevance, and meaning in their lives.

An old saying among Caucasus mountaineers is that "heroism is endurance for one moment more." Many of the people we seek to assist have often endured situations and conditions that stagger our minds and break our hearts. This is the starting point of connecting to the heroic. We must discover how people have managed to survive. How have they summoned the grit to overcome or, at least, face these ordeals? Tapping into the energy and imagination, the will and the promise of clients is to help them recover or command the power to change, using old skills and resources and/or discovering and developing new ones. We really don't know what people are capable of and sometimes they don't either. But some of the now conventional as well as newly emerging literature on capacity development, resilience, empowerment, liberation theology, health realization, positive psychology, solution-focused, and narrative approaches to practice offer some clues to the answer to the question: How do people endure for one moment more?

- People who confront harsh stress, even on a daily and unremitting basis, almost always develop some ideas, capacities, qualities, virtues, and defenses that may ultimately stand them in good stead as they confront life's challenges. Until recently, we have been nearly obsessed with calculating the injuries and impediments, the deficits and desolation rather than peoples' countervailing and transformative responses to the trials in their lives.
- In the most demanding, cruel, lean, and mean environments, there are always natural resources—individuals and families, institutions and organizations, associations and groups—available to individuals and families. While some are clearly more bountiful than others, all communities have the moral, instrumental, and interpersonal means for surmounting adversity.
- Even though some people may have labored under the blame and disapproving opinions of others, or under incessant self-criticism, and pessimism, or unfortunate life decisions, at some level, they almost always know what is the right thing to do.
- In rough evolutionary terms, as a species we surely have an innate capacity for health, self-righting, and survival—or we would not have survived thus far.
- Healing, transformation, regeneration, and resilience almost always occur within the good offices of a personal, friendly, supportive, encouraging, and dialogical relationship. Whether a friend, relative, social worker, teacher, coach, physician—it seems to make little difference—the more we actualize the power of a caring relationship with those we help and live with, the better for their future and well-being.
- Everybody has knowledge, talents, capacities, skills, and resources that can be used as building blocks toward their aspirations, the solution of their problems, the meeting of their needs, and the boosting of the quality of their lives.
- A positive orientation to the future, the alliance with hopes and possibilities is far more important, in the long run, for healing and helping than an obsession with a dark and disappointing past.
- Every maladaptive response or pattern of behavior may contain within it the hints and murmurs of resources for health and self-righting.

In your mind's eye, imagine an equilateral triangle. The left angle is preceded by the letter C, and the angle to the right is prededed by the letter R. The apex of the triangle is topped with the letter P—CPR, as it were. The letter C represents capacities, competencies, courage, and character. The letter R symbolizes resources, resourcefulness, reserves, resilience, and relationships. The letter P stands for promise, possibility, potential, purpose and positive expectations. This graphic signifies the dynamic core of the strengths-based approach to practice. All three angles must be a part of any kind of strengths-oriented framework for healing and helping. In the original sense of CPR, we breathe for someone who cannot breathe for themselves, until they can. In this CPR, we believe in someone until they can believe in themselves.

The interaction of these life elements represents the dynamic core of a strengths-based approach to practice. All three must be a part of any kind of holistic healing or helping. In a sense, the interaction of these elements in a person's life lead to a kind of everyday, prosaic heroism, unsung but effective in meeting many of life's challenges.

ORIGINS AND BACKGROUND OF STRENGTHS-BASED KNOWING AND DOING

In one form or another, in the profession and the culture, some of the root appreciations of a strengths approach have been evident and operative. Transcendentalism and the Social Gospel in the late nineteenth and early twentieth centuries are early examples. Knitted together with strands from pragmatism, naturalism, Puritanism, Quaker philosophy, and old-fashioned American idealism, one of the essential ideas of transcendentalism was that the self or soul is the spiritual center of the universe and self-realization, the expression of that self in the real world is a hallowed obligation. Self-realization requires the harmonizing of two discordant tones: the desire of the self to become one with the world, to identify fully with it, and, incongruously, to become a self-asserting, autonomous self (Boller, 1974; Reuben, 2000).

The Social Gospel arose around the same time in this country, principally as a reaction against the incursions of Social Darwinism, unrestrained industrial expansion, and the unbridled oppression of laborers, adults, and children. The principles of democratic socialism, among other ideals, contributed to the notion that human beings were innately good and that the applications of the teachings of the church—more specifically, Jesus—would be necessary to ensure the good and just society. It would be the obligation of good Christians to address the brutal conditions that workers typically faced, and that confrontation with the forces of domination would be carried out through bringing the teachings of Jesus to the working classes and masses. Some of these ideas eventually found their way into the New Deal legislation of the 1930s. So the basic tenets of the Social Gospel still abound in one form or another: the affirmation of the basic goodness and wisdom of the people, the application of Christian principles of justice and equity to social problems, and the perfectibility of humankind (Phillips, 1996; Social Gospel, 2000).

Social work traditionally has nodded to the idea of strengths, and building on the strengths of people, although rarely elucidating the means by which this can be accomplished. The writings of Jane Addams, Virginia Robinson, Bertha Capen Reynolds, and later Ruth Smalley and Herbert Bisno can all be mined to find allusions and hints of the importance of appreciating and fostering strengths. In 1902, Jane Addams wrote,

> We are gradually requiring of the educator that he (sic) shall free the powers of each man and connect him with the rest of life. We ask this . . . because we have become convinced that the social order cannot afford to get along without his special contribution. (p. 178)

Bertha Capen Reynolds (1951) asked 50 years later, "Shall we be content to give with one hand and withhold with the other, to build up or tear down at the same time the strength of a person's life" (p. 175).

Social group work also has had a long history of appreciation of the resources and strengths of group members and their neighbors:

> There is so much talk today about health and wellness. This is hardly a new or revolutionary concept. But it has been neglected for too long. However, good group work practice has been paying attention to people's strengths since the days of the original settlement houses over 100 years ago, mostly without fanfare. (Malekoff, 2001, p. 247)

The works of Paulo Freire, Barbara Simon, Barbara Solomon, Anthony Maluccio, and, more recently, Lorraine Gutierrez, Judith A. B. Lee, and the contributions of multicultural and feminist critiques of the conventional wisdom have all provided guidance for a nascent strengths perspective. Some of their key ideas include: (a) developing a critical consciousness or "conscientization" (Freire, 1996); an awareness of the rudiments and fundamentals of oppression, and the purposes and practices of oppressors; (b) developing a sense of agency, and self-efficacy through a person's struggles toward deliverance; (c) fostering dialogue between those who would be free and those who emancipate; (d) assuring equality, promoting collective responsibility and ties to social and cultural resources so that all have a chance of more significant activity as fully endowed citizens who contribute to the social good (Freire, 1996; Gutiérrez, 1990; Lee, 1994).

Strengths Model of Case Management

In 1982, the School of Social Welfare at the University of Kansas was awarded $10,000 by a local mental health facility to provide case management services to people with severe and persistent mental illness (principally one of the many forms of schizophrenia). With Ronna Chamberlain, Charles Rapp assessed the standard practices of case management with this population. He was confident that, with its emphasis on linking clients only with formal mental health and health services, standard practice could not achieve the outcomes that people wanted—living in the community, having an actual job, normalized leisure time, and so forth. Over time, they replaced the conventional approach with one that emphasized the employment of community strengths and resources in league with individual strengths and resources. A small practicum unit of four MSW students "field" tested the model and found that, at the end of the year, 19 of 22 indicators of positive outcomes had been achieved. By the mid-1980s, the strengths model was becoming the heart of community support programs in Kansas and was expanding to other states as well. In addition, the strengths model was being employed with a wider variety of fields of practice—juvenile justice, child welfare, AFDC recipients, and others. But it was the original work at the University of Kansas School of Social Welfare that provided the theoretical, methodological, and ethical tools for the launching of the model (Chamberlain, personal communication, 2004).

REACTION AGAINST THE MEDICAL/DEFICIT MODEL

In a way, much of the impetus for the subsequent spread of strengths-based approaches comes as a reaction to our culture's incessant captivation with pathology, disease, mental and moral aberrations, interpersonal conflict, and victimization. A mushrooming cartel of professions and businesses, institutions and agencies from medicine to pharmaceuticals, from the insurance industry to the mass media, reaps incredible financial spoils by assuring us that we are in the grip (or soon will be) of any number of emotional, cognitive, interpersonal, behavioral, and/or biological woes. Each of us, it is suggested, is a reservoir of possible susceptibility to weaknesses and fallibilities, usually born of toxic experiences in early life. The most visible testament to this is the *Diagnostic and Statistical Manual of Mental Disorders*, fourth edition, text revision (*DSM-IV-TR*, American Psychiatric Association, 2000). It is the primer for making psychiatric diagnoses. Widely used (not just in psychiatric settings but in child welfare, child protective services, juvenile justice, schools, etc.), most insurance companies now require, as a basis for reimbursement for the treatment of mental disorders, a diagnosis fashioned out of the *DSM* lexicon.

The first *DSM*s (*-I* and *-II*, published in the 1950s and 1960s) were modest documents of less than 100 pages each containing descriptions of mental disorders (signs, symptoms, causality, and sequelae) written by a handful of psychiatrists. They were crafted in psychodynamic/psychoanalytic argot. *DSM-III*, however, was another matter. Spearheaded by Robert Spitzer, MD, it sought to emulate the diagnostic precision and detail of Emile Kraepelin's work in the late nineteenth and early twentieth centuries (who, over time, published 11 editions of his classification system, each more detailed and comprehensive than the last). He was, by most accounts, a master clinician, researcher, teacher, and leader in the new field of psychiatry (Andreasen, 2001). He made the initial distinctions between the dementias that occur in later life (like Alzheimer's disease), dementia praecox (early occurring dementia—schizophrenia), and manic-depressive disorder—a differentiation that remains today. He was a master of observation and classification. For some psychiatrists, his observations remain as pertinent today as when they first were published (Andreasen, 2001). Like Kraepelin's texts, the *DSM-III, DSM-IV*, and *DSM-IV-TR* are essentially descriptive, and include increasing numbers of disorders with each passing edition. Whereas *DSM-III* had some 350 pages of text on disorders, the last edition had over 700 pages. Since the *DSM* appears to be on a 12-year cycle, the *DSM-V* should be out in 2006 and *DSM-V-TR* in 2012 (however, the latest word is that *DSM-V* will probably not be out until 2010 or later). Each edition will certainly have new disorders (not out of discoveries but out of discussions and dialogues in various groups, deliberations informed by clinical experience, primarily). Look at the back of the later editions under the heading *Criteria Sets and Axes Provided for Further Study* and you will see a list of disorders-in-waiting. Kenneth Gergen (1994) calls these developments a rapidly accelerating "cycle of progressive infirmity" (p. 155).

These observations are not meant to disregard the genuine anguish and struggles of individuals, families, and communities; neither is it meant to avert our gaze from the real tragedies of the abuse of children; nor the tenacity and thrall of addictions, for example. Rather it is to denounce the ascendancy of psychopathology, deficits, problems, and defects as a central moral and categorical imperative of society. Steven and Sybil Wolin (1997) say this about achieving balance between two paradigms (risk and resiliency/strength):

> [T]he resiliency paradigm is no match for the risk paradigm. Talking about the human capacity to repair from harm, inner strengths, and protective factors, professionals feel that they have entered alien territory. They grope for words and fear sounding unschooled and naïve when they replace pathology terminology with the more mundane vocabulary of resourcefulness, hope, creativity, competence, and the like. (p. 27)

Allegiance to a strengths-based approach does not call for you to unthinkingly ignore or turn away from the genuine pains and ordeals that confront children, groups, families, and communities. We all understand, for example, that poverty exists, child sexual abuse exists, violence exists, and cancer exists. The strengths perspective does not require you to discount the grip and thrall of addictions, or the humiliating and terrifying anguish of child abuse, or the unwelcome disorder and bewilderment of psychosis. But from a strengths standpoint, *it is as wrong to deny the possible as it is to deny the problem.* Practitioners of a strengths-based approach clearly believe that all people who have been traumatized *do not* inevitably become damaged goods. In fact, reviews of the evidence by the Wolins (1997) and later by Benard (2004), suggest that most individuals who have had a dreadful childhood turn out much better than anyone would have predicted on the basis of the torments of their early years. This is not to squelch the fact that these individuals have suffered and still do. But it is to call attention to the often unheralded and, in many cases, clearly remarkable fact that rebound from adversity is the rule and not the exception.

Old paradigms die hard. Our thinking about people who are beset with an array of troubles, hurts, and restrictions has been around for a while. As social workers, we are bound by our values to acknowledge and affirm the worth and dignity of all individuals, and I suspect we try hard to realize that ethical injunction, but the language of problems, deficits, and diseases, because of its power and cultural vigor, elbows its way into our lexicon in both subtle and conspicuous ways. Words create imagery, imagery creates orientations or expectations, orientations become a part of behavior, and behavior may become part of one's identity—ensconced in the marrow of one's being, professional and/or personal. In the clinical, helping professions, there are probably no words that strike terror in the heart of the clinician more than Borderline Personality Disorder. The supposed conglomeration of behaviors, emotions, and relationships that characterize this disorder can only be seen as daunting. The expectations of those with this diagnosis (no matter how unreliable it has proven to be) are unremittingly negative, creating the prospect of extremely difficult work with a high probability of failure, not to mention, frustration. Unchallenged (and unproven) these expectancies gradually become "theories" that govern what we do and, at some point, they may create confirmations in the identities of the people we are seeking to help.

Many other diagnoses or labels have a similar effect: schizophrenic, perpetrator, victim, cancer patient, co-dependent, for example. Too often our formal and personal premises obscure the complex and evanescent reality before us and conspire to make us ascribe traits, patterns, motives, and even experiences that really are not there or not in that form. Similarly, these also may hinder us from seeing the real possibilities and capacities that are inherent in every person, family, and community we assist. The longer the people we define as clients are in the system—child welfare, mental health, juvenile justice, and so on—the more difficult they may seem to help. It may well be that this is an artifact of the symbols, words, images, designations, and confirmatory experiences we expose them to.

Further, by not exposing ourselves to clients' views of their situation, their ideas about how it might change, by ignoring or slighting their capacities and interests, hopes and dreams, we lose not only much information, but the possibility for high levels of client and social worker motivation, collaboration, and some interesting and even innovative ways to do our work (this probably applies to some medical interventions as well; see Pelletier, 2000; Weil, 1995). A friend who has worked with people with this diagnosis for many years, and ended up at one point frustrated with and angry at her clients, eventually had an epiphany or change of heart, possibly occasioned by her self-questioning over a long period of time. She came to realize that she had fallen prey to what Duncan, Hubble, and Miller (1997) call "attribution creep" (p. 43):

> This means that no matter how committed a therapist is to seeing a client objectively, the client will eventually take on characteristics and qualities defined by the therapist's theory. (p. 43)

She recognized that she saw in these clients what the theory encouraged her to see—bedeviled, challenging, demanding, immature, ambivalent people with high maintenance needs. In thinking about it, it seemed to her that five things conspired to change her mind:

1. She began to think that the old saw "Keep'em alive 'til 35" might hold some meaning. Perhaps there *was* a fund of strengths or some sort of developmental process, a maturation factor at work that could be capitalized on and speeded up.
2. In spite of her frustration and occasional anger at clients, she really liked most of them, empathized with many of their difficulties, and saw that there often might be good reason for them to act the way that they did.
3. She was amazed at the complex, dramatic, interesting, and frightening tales that they told but only after a long time began to think that these stories might hold the seeds of a theory about what they wanted, what went wrong, and what they could do about it.
4. She had the insight that although she regarded herself as having a strong ability to form affirming and therapeutic relationships, she often stopped short with many of these women because of the widely advertised concerns about "boundary" problems. She vowed that she would work to open herself up to forming more complex, open, relaxed, respectful, and positive relationships with these individuals.
5. Finally, she found some literature that affirmed the fact that most of these individuals, perhaps because of the fundamental "wisdom of the ego" (Vaillant, 1993), no matter how terrifying their behavior at an early age (adolescence and early adulthood), turned out much better than one would have thought seeing them in the midst of their trials and self-inflicted tribulations.

In this story lie many of the appreciations of the strengths approach:

- Believe the client and believe in the client (until proven otherwise—but even then, such standards of proof have to be questioned thoroughly).
- Elicit and affirm the client's view of things. The narratives and stories of struggle and failure have relevance and are potential resources for understanding and change.
- Focus on change and movement toward client hopes and dreams. As Freire wrote (1996), "There is no change without the dream, as there is no dream without hope." (p. 91).
- Focus on clients' assets, capacities, abilities, and internal and external resources.
- Believe that somewhere within or around the client are forces for, if not healing, at least improving the quality of life.

CORE CONDITIONS OF CHANGE AND POSITIVE DEVELOPMENT

In their review of and statistical analyses of studies on positive outcomes in psychotherapy (and by extension, other methods of interpersonal helping), Asay and Lambert (1999) concluded that out of these studies you could derive four central components of change—statistically and conceptually. Each of these elements has varying degrees of influence on the process of successful psychotherapy.

The Client and the Environment

The most significant of these factors occur outside the arena of helping and are prior conditions; Asay and Lambert (1999) refer to them as "extratherapeutic" factors. These include: personal strengths and assets; resources in the environment (people and institutions) such as caring kin, and/or a supportive church and/or at least one person who is a steadfast champion or supporter. Significantly (though often overlooked), luck or contingent factors play a considerable role. Obviously, there are contextual and personal factors that may mitigate against a positive outcome—overwhelming stress, a persistent addiction, exposure to devastating violence, a serious physical illness—but even at that, it is unlikely that anyone can predict in a given case when these factors will inhibit a beneficial result.

The well-documented discovery that many clients improve spontaneously without therapeutic intervention is likely a testament to the environmental and experiential factors that promote growth, change, and maturation. It is also a demonstration of the fact that individuals, given a chance, are self-healers or as Roger Mills (1995) has demonstrated, that all people have within a kind of wisdom about who they are and can be, and a capacity for self-righting and health. If that is the case, then what the environment, other people, and/or a therapist actually do is foster or trigger this inherent capacity in individuals (and families and communities as well). As Tallman and Bohart (1999) affirm after reviewing the research: "Self-help approaches are as effective as professionally provided therapy, and no significant differences between different modalities for providing self-help have been identified" (p. 98). If this is the case then, as Prochaska, Norcross, and DiClemente (1994) claim, "it can be argued that all change is self-change, and that therapy is simply professionally coached self-change" (p. 17). According to Asay and Lambert (1999), these factors account for 40% of positive change.

Relationship Factors

In social work, the idea that the quality of the helping relationship is the key dynamic of change has become lore. Carl Rogers (1951) was among the first to give the relationship its due. He believed that a strong therapeutic relationship, one that fostered motivation and change, was based on the therapist's capacity for genuineness, accurate empathy, and a nonjudgmental stance, among others. More recently, the research on beneficial interaction, has shown that: (a) it is the client's view of the relationship that is most important; (b) that the relationship has to be created and experienced as a collaborative alliance; and (c) that the alliance must be played out in a project, a mutually crafted plan with tasks and goals specified and negotiable (Bachelor & Horvath, 1999).

Charles Rapp (1998), perhaps the most important figure in the development of the strengths model of case management, defines the effective helping relationship as purposeful, reciprocal, friendly, trusting, and empowering. Orlinski, Graw, and Parks (1994) in their appraisal of the relevant literature over the past nearly 50 years, say: "The quality of a patient's participation in therapy stands out as the most important determinant of outcome.... The therapist's contribution toward helping the patient achieve a favorable outcome is made mainly through empathic, affirmative, collaborative, and self-congruent engagement with the patient" (p. 361). Asay and Lambert assess this quality as accounting for 30% of positive change in therapy.

Theory and Technique

Theory and technique, in this scheme, are relegated to a somewhat lesser place in the pantheon of change. They remain important, but their effects probably are, in part an effect of the previous two factors. However, it does seem clear that there are specific theories and methods that are helpful for particular problems. It is clear that cognitive behavioral therapy, and interpersonal therapy both, often in conjunction with medication, are effective in the treatment of moderate to moderately severe depression. Recently there has been some research that casts this in some doubt (see expectancy, hope, and the placebo effect that follows). Ascendant now in the treatment of people with severe and persistent mental illness is the idea of recovery; that with a variety of encouragements, supports, vigorous strengths, and assets building, individuals can and do lead normal lives—independently, within a community, and working in a job.

These conceptual structures and technical operations sometimes provide a canvas for helpers and clients to rework some of their concerns and conundrums, hopes and hang-ups into a more evocative and appealing portrait. Certainly they give helpers something to hang their hats on. But the fact remains that, in the end, it is the clients who do the work, who make the changes, who challenge their beliefs and behaviors, and who confront the hassles and promises of daily living. Asay and Lambert (1999) calculate that these factors account for 15% of positive change.

Expectancy, Hope, and the Placebo Effect

The placebo effect is a commonly known, fairly well understood, but little used phenomenon in medical and psychosocial treatment. It is kin to expectancy and hope in that it trades on the power of our belief in a person or process to bring about usually beneficial change. It is funded by trust and longing. Examples abound about the power of the placebo. Some of these follow.

Michael Fisher (2000) reports that in the 1950s at the University of Kansas Medical Center, in order to test a new surgical procedure to relieve angina, surgeons performed real operations in the chest cavities of half of a sample of men randomly assigned to this group or to a control group. The control group, under anesthesia, received "fake" surgery—superficial incisions were made on their chests and then sewn up, but there was nothing done in the chest cavity. Appalling ethics aside, the results of this study are nothing short of amazing. Over 5 years, 70% of those who had the real operation reported significant improvement in their angina. Fine and good. But over the same time period, the entire placebo group did also.

It is not uncommon in clinical trials of psychoactive drugs for the placebo groups to show anywhere from 25% to 65% improvement (Arpala, 2000). The extent to which the actual drug is better than the placebo in its effects is thought to be the extent to which it is useful. But we cannot say, for example, just how much of the effect of the real medication is also a placebo effect. More recently, participants in clinical trials have been getting "active" placebos in which they get side effects (you have to wonder about the ethics of that as well). It seems that people are more likely to experience an abatement of symptoms on the active placebo. The experience of side effects may convince them they are getting the real thing. Joseph Arpala (2000) reports that, in a study by Greenberg and Fisher, the placebos were as effective as the drug in 30% to 40% of the studies they reviewed. But the most thorough and statistically adroit study was done by four physicians who, using the Freedom of Information Act, were able to get results of clinical trials over the past 15 years reported by drug companies to the Food and Drug Administration for the six most popular antidepressants (SSRIs); (Kirsch, Moore, Scoboria, & Nicholls, 2003). Up until now, no one has had access to the results of these trials so we have to take the drug companies' word about their efficacy. These researchers conducted several meta-analyses of these data and, no matter how generous or conservative their analysis, they found *no clinically significant differences* between the drugs and the placebos. "Whatever else this means it does, I think, bespeak the power of hope, possibility, positive expectations, and the belief in the healing power of the ministration" (Saleebey, 2006). Expectancy and the placebo effect account for 15% of desirable change (Asay & Lambert, 1999).

Related, I think, to the power of the placebo is the *plasticity of the brain*. Once thought to be as virtual monolith after adolescence, it is now known that the brain is changing constantly. It is something of a miracle that it, as Richard Restak (2003) observes, "never loses the power to transform itself on the basis of experience and the transformation can occur over short intervals . . . your brain is different today than it was yesterday" (p. 8). Most of these changes take place at the synapse (the space through which neurons "communicate" with each other) and are the result of experience and learning or simply one's current state of mind (emotions, e.g., have a profound ability to change the brain, both in the moment and occasionally, permanently; LeDoux, 2002). Therefore, we have a stunning capacity to alter, extend, and reshape behavior, feeling, motivation, and cognition. This is why talk therapies can be successful because, at one level when we interact with each other, we are talking to our brains. As we do so, we effect minute changes in the brain's (and, thus, the mind's) landscape. This is also why, individually and collectively, our brains will be different in future decades because they undergo these relentless minute alterations daily (Andreasen, 2001; LeDoux, 2002; Restak, 2003).

PRINCIPLES OF THE STRENGTHS PERSPECTIVE

A perspective is not a theory. A theory purports to explain some phenomenon or, at least, to parse it analytically. It is not a model. Models are meant to represent some aspect of the world logically and graphically. A perspective is a standpoint, a way of getting into experience and understanding it. It is a lens through which we perceive and appreciate. It creates a world built of images and words, phrases and metaphors. The principles that follow are guiding assumptions and are tentative, still evolving, and certainly subject to revision.

Every Individual, Group, Family, and Community Has Strengths and Resources

This tenet may be hard at times to conjure up but it is essential to the strengths approach. Every individual (family, community, group), no matter how dispirited, despised, disorganized, has strengths and capacities—most of which you know nothing about. It is incumbent on someone practicing from this vantage point to discern, elicit, and affirm those assets. It is also imperative to understand that these competencies and resources may have the potential for helping to reverse misfortune, easing pain, strengthening resolve, and reaching goals. To harvest strengths, the practitioner must be authentically interested in, and respectful of, clients' stories and narratives. The interpretive slants that people take on their experiences are "theories" that can help guide practice. The uncovering of clients' identities and perspectives comes not just from a recital of troubles, embarrassments, snares, and quandaries. Rather, individuals come more sharply into view when you suppose that they have valuable knowledge, they have taken lessons from their experiences, that they have hopes, interests, and that they can do some things masterfully. These may be buried by the stresses of the moment, smothered by the heavy hand of crisis, or oppression. But they endure.

Illness, Trauma, Abuse, and the Array of Life's Crises May Be Painful, Demoralizing, and Wearisome, but They Also Are Sources of Challenge and Opportunity

The Wolins (1993) have artfully illustrated and documented the fact that even though there may have been damage in childhood that has left its residue in adult life, children who live through such ordeals often develop capacities and understandings that fortify their ability to confront the tests that life inevitably brings. Some of the capacities they found include: insight, independence, the ability to form relationships, creativity and humor, and moral imagination. Any child may develop one or more of these and the capacities all undergo expansion toward complexity as children become adults. The vestiges and scars may remain and may still hurt, but the person clearly has developed some unique and useful traits and virtues for having undergone these ordeals. (Benard, 2004) There is dignity to be drawn from having prevailed over the trials thrown one's way; the Wolins call it "survivors' pride."

Individuals, families, groups, and communities are much more likely to become resilient and to continue their development when they are subsidized by the coin of their abilities, intelligence, and skills (Delgado, 2000). The strengths perspective also suggests to us that many people who struggle daily to secure a place to live, to get food in their belly, to find a job, are already, to varying degrees, resilient and enterprising—that is to say, they do have strengths. Individuals may not recognize them as such; or they may be in disuse; or they have forgotten them; or the fog of stress obscures them.

Assume That You Do Not Know the Upper Limits of the Capacity to Grow and Change

Sometimes we mistakenly believe that a diagnosis, a profile, or a tangle of problems constrain possibility and hope for our clients. In our own lives, if we look back and take stock, we may have traveled much further than we would have thought possible during an earlier period of our lives. But there are times when, because of a particular matrix of difficulties, it becomes difficult to imagine that our clients may be able to travel a distance we cannot fathom. We may let the assessments and diagnoses applied to them metamorphose into a verdict and a sentence. Our clients would be better served if we made an overt, binding pact with their promise and possibility.

Research increasingly shows that emotions have a profound effect on health and well being. Negative emotions, such as anger, anxiety, and depression, have direct and usually unhealthy effects on various systems of the body. Stress, for example, produces cortisol, a hormone that in the short run helps us adapt to stress. But if it lingers, it begins to disrupt the functioning of various systems in a variety of ways. For example, it may destroy part of the hippocampus in the brain, a system devoted largely to memory storage and retrieval. The reverse is also true. Positive emotions can activate the pharmacy within you, producing chemicals and hormones that relax, assist in fighting infections, and restore our energy and vigor. This does not mean that people do not get sick mentally and physically. It does mean that when they do, we can make an alliance with those forces for healing and rebounding (Damasio, 1994; LeDoux, 1996). Roger Mills' (1995) work, mentioned earlier, reflects the notion that everyone has the capacity for healing; a kind of innate wisdom about what is right and good for them. He says that his goals are "to reconnect people to the [physical and mental] health in themselves and then direct them in ways to bring forth the health of others in their community. The result is a change in people and communities which builds up from within rather than [being] imposed from without" (cited in Benard, 1999, p. 84).

We Best Serve Clients by Collaborating with Them

We make an egregious mistake when we suppress clients' wisdom, knowledge, viewpoints with the institutional weight of our own. There is something freeing about inviting clients' stories, narratives, and standpoints to the forefront and letting our own protocols and accounts recede into the background. We must, as Blundo (2006) says, start where the client is (a notable social work principle, right?), and not where the theory is (p. 39). Duncan et al. (1997) put it like this:

> We have learned to listen more, turn off the intervention spigot, stay still, and direct our attention to them [the clients], recalling as Ram Dass once said, "The quieter you become, the more you will hear." The greater success we have experienced in doing this, the more room clients have had to be themselves, use their own resources, discover possibilities, attribute self-enhancing meanings to their actions, and take responsibility. (p. 207)

In like manner, Kisthardt (2006) argues that, "Each person is responsible for their own recovery. The participant [client] is the director of the helping efforts. We serve as . . . consultants" (p. 177). Finally, a lengthy quote from Paulo Freire (2001) says it well, situating us in the larger context of cultural oppression, and liberation and freedom:

> We must never merely discourse on the present situation, must never provide people with programs that have little or nothing to do with their own preoccupations, doubts, hopes and fears—programs which at times in fact increase the fears of the oppressed consciousness. It is not our role to speak to the people about our own view of the world, nor to attempt to impose that view on them, but rather to dialogue with people about their view and ours. We must realize that their view of the world, manifested variously in their action, reflects their situation (author's emphasis) in the world. (p. 96)

Every Environment Is Full of Resources

The resources that may be found in a community are both formal and informal, naturally occurring and institutionalized. They include individuals, families, associations, organizations, agencies, and groups of all kinds. In inclusive and welcoming communities, there are many opportunities for individuals of all ages to be involved, to contribute to the moral and civic life and well-being of the community. A severe environment can test the spirit of its inhabitants, but it can also be understood as a potentially fertile landscape of people and resources. In every community and neighborhood, even those that seem to the outsider to be crumbling, there are individuals and groups who have something to give, something that others may want or urgently need: knowledge, experience, comfort, talents, wisdom, and time. These are outside the usual matrix of agencies and organizations. Melvin Delgado (2000), in discussing the capacity-enhancement approach to community-building lays out its five basic assumptions: "(1) The community has the will and the resources to help itself; (2) it knows what is best for itself; (3) ownership of the strategy rests within, rather than outside the community; (4) partnerships involving organizations and communities are the preferred route for initiatives; and (5) the use of strengths in one area will translate into strengths in other areas . . . a ripple effect" (p. 28).

Care, Caretaking, and Context

That care is vital to civil life, is an idea that doesn't always go down easy in a society with a long history and preference for rugged individualism. Deborah Stone (2000) contends that we have three rights to care. First, every family must be permitted and assisted in caring for their family members. Second, all caregivers must be able to give the level of care that is proportionate to their ideals and abilities without compromising their well-being. All people who need care (and there may be 30 to 50 million adults as well as the 38 million children under the age of 10 who do) get it. Stone argues that:

> Caring for each other is the most basic form of civic participation. We learn to care in families, and we enlarge our communities of concern as we mature. Caring is the essential democratic act, the prerequisite to voting, joining associations, attending meetings, holding office, and all the other ways we sustain democracy. (p. 15)

Like social caretaking and social work, the strengths perspective is about the radical possibility of hope: hope realized in the strengthened ligaments of social relationships at all levels in the community.

These, then, are some of the principles of the strengths perspective. They are not unique or exclusive to the approach. Rather, they come together in a more immediate and vigorous way here.

WHAT ARE STRENGTHS AND HOW DO YOU DISCOVER THEM?

There is a little irony here in that almost anything can be a strength under certain conditions, and anything that can be a strength might not be under certain other conditions. For example, while caring for a spouse with a lingering, terminal illness, patience might be a virtue but having patience with a brutalizing spouse may, in the end, bring on more pain and suffering and not be an asset. So, it may always be the case that you have to contextualize your assessment of an individual's, family's, or community's resources.

Some Common Classes of Strengths

People have learned about themselves and others as they have struggled, coped with, surmounted, or been overcome by their troubles. People do learn from their adversities, even those they seem to bring on themselves. They may find the energy to muster a kind of resolve to go on and make life better. A 16-year-old wrote this about her mother:

> I grew up when I realized this: my mother is not going to change because I want her to. She's only going to change when she wants to . . . . I don't want to have children at a young age to show my mother what a "real mother" is. I want to break the cycle. If I don't, I might end up doing the same thing my mother did. (Desetta & Wolin, 2000, p. 14)

People who have faced and surmounted adverse conditions in their lives often feel a sense of pride about having done that. Getting beyond the shame requires a real belief, hopefully buoyed by others, in the existence of self-respect and dignity that comes from coping with hardships. What follows is a short list of capacities and resources that people may develop and/or discover as they confront troubles and endure suffering:

- *Personal qualities, traits, and virtues that people possess.* These are sometimes forged in the fires of trauma but they can also be the gifts of temperament, products of living, and the fruits of experience. Whatever their origin, these attributes may become valuable resources in helping clients find the kind of life they want to lead.
- *What people know about the world around them.* These can be ideas, perspectives, reminiscences that have come to people intellectually and because of formal learning or they can be things that people have come to know through their life experiences. Perhaps, for example, because of personal tragedy, a person has learned to comfort and guide others through the grieving process.
- *The talents that people have.* These can be anything (and they may be gifts that have lain dormant over the years) from telling stories, to playing a musical instrument, to carpentry, to cooking. Who knows what they might be? These can be additional resources and tools for people as they work toward their immediate and distant goals.

They also can be shared and given to others to foster solidarity, to entertain and amuse, to strengthen relationships, and to cement friendships.

- *Cultural and personal stories and lore* are often rich source of guidance, inspiration, comfort, and transformation. For many minority groups, and for women, for example, such stories have been suppressed and often replaced with others' stories about them. These stories and narratives, the teachings and traditions within them, are wellsprings of strength and wisdom, hope and belief. These narratives and myths, these accounts of origins, stories of migration and settlement, narratives of trauma and survival may be potent sources of meaning and inspiration during times of strife or upheaval. Likewise cultural practices and approaches to helping—from the sweat lodge to *curanderismo*, from the medicine wheel to drumming—may be powerful tools for healing and rejuvenation.
- *The community* is often overlooked as a rich store of personal, familial, institutional, and organizational goods. The informal and natural environment is full of people and associations who, if asked, would provide their talents and knowledge in the service of making the neighborhood or community a better place to live. The work of community development and organizing is, in many ways, "dedicated to germinating the saplings of strength and resourcefulness in the community" (Saleebey, 2006, p. 84).
- *Spirituality* is a font of strength and meaning for many people. Ed Canda's (2006) work in this area is illuminating. He makes three core assertions. First, spirituality is a kind of meaning-making that is gathered from the essential, holistic sense of a given person. It transcends the biological, psychological, and social, but incorporates them all. In so doing it destroys the dubious dichotomies we make between mind and body, or spirit and substance. It does reveal our struggle to find meaning in this huge and overwhelming cosmos. Finally, it does refer to a self that breaks the chains of ego. This might be realized in meditation, visions, peak experiences, unconscious adaptation, even under severe stress. Spirituality, which is not the same as religion and, may be expressed and experienced in many different ways, is the grand rampart against stress, meaninglessness, oppression, and anomie.

Finding Out about Strengths

The discovery of strengths depends on some simple ideas. Look around you. Look to the client. Do you see evidence of client interests, talents, and dreams? Listen to client stories and narratives very closely instead of rushing through some prefabricated protocol. These accounts and anecdotes usually contain within them inklings and allusions of strengths, capacity, and hopes.

There are several sorts of questions you might ask in order to discover strengths and to help individuals begin thinking along strength dimensions. These include:

- *Survival questions:* Given all the challenges in your life that you have described, how have you managed to survive, even thrive? How have you been able to meet the tests that have been a part of your lot? What was your frame of mind as you faced these trials? What have you been able to learn about yourself and your world during these struggles? Which of these ordeals has given you special insight, resolve, or skill? What are the special abilities and traits do you now rely on?

- *Support questions:* What people have given you encouragement and assistance? Who are those special people upon whom you can depend? What is it that these individuals offer that is matchless? How did you find them or how did they come to you? What do you think they were responding to in you that made them what to be of assistance? What associations, institutions, and/or organizations have been especially supportive or comforting in the past?
- *Exception questions:* (from the practitioners of solution-focused therapy) When things are going well in life, what is different? Have you had times in your past when these problems and concerns were not a part of your life? If so, what was different? What moments, incidents, or people in your life have given you special insight, resilience, and/or courage? What elements of these special times do you want to recapture?
- *Possibility questions:* What do you now want out of life? What are your hopes, dreams, and visions? How far are you along in realizing these dreams? What people or personal qualities are giving you a boost toward your dreams? What do you like to do? What do you want to do? How would you like to see your life in a few months from now? How can I be of help in reaching your goals?
- *Esteem questions:* When people say nice things about you, what are they likely to say? What is it about your life, your situation, and your accomplishments that give you real self-respect? What gives you real satisfaction in your life? When did you begin to believe that you can accomplish some of the things that are important to you?
- *Perspective questions:* What are your theories and ideas about what's happening in your life; about what is causing you pain or trouble? How do you comprehend, and make sense of these? How would you explain your situation to someone else?
- *Change questions:* What are your ideas about how things in your life—thoughts, feelings, relationships, behavior, situations—might change? In the past, what has worked for you in making a better life for yourself, or in solving a problem? What do you think you should or could do now to bring about a positive change in your life? Can I help?
- *Meaning questions:* Do you have a set of beliefs or values that give you guidance, courage, and/or comfort? What are these? Can you strengthen or draw upon them?

There are many more possible questions. Again, these are not a protocol, but rather a set of suggestions about how to tap into people's stories and accounts to find the allusions to capacities, possibilities, and dreams.

Other Assessment Ideas

Charles Cowger, Kim Anderson, and Carol Snively (2006) have some sound ideas about a strengths assessment. I briefly review some of them here. They propose four quadrants of information that allow you to get a sense of strengths and capacities as well as deficits and obstacles. In one quadrant, they list social and political strengths; in another, they enumerate psychological and physiological strengths. In yet another, they list social and political obstacles, and in the last, they spell out psychological and physical obstacles. In assessing the capacities of an individual, they suggest, among others, these questions:

- Is there anything about you that you feel you were born with that has helped you in your life?
- Is there anything about the way you have coped that has helped you in your life?
- Are there any relationships that were helpful to you in you life? How were they helpful?
- Are there any turning points or critical moments in your life that have helped you? Are there spiritual or religious activities in your life that helped you in your life?

Robert Hutchins (2002, personal communication) has proposed that we call assessment documents the *DSM* "documents of identity." Because of their seriousness and effect on the fate of the individual, we have to balance diagnosis with gnosis (knowing the person or how the person understands his or herself—self-acquaintance). After Hutchins:

Gnosis	**Diagnosis (*DSM-IV-TR*)**
Axis I Goals or life dreams	Axis 1 Clinical disorders
Axis II Core gifts and abilities	Axis II Long term cognitive disorders/personality disorders
Axis III Physical gifts	Axis III General medical conditions
Axis IV Psychosocial supports	Axis IV Psychosocial problems
Axis V System gifts	Axis V Global assessment of function

At the least, restoring balance to a mental health system careening out of control within the deficit, disease, problem paradigm, is essential. In his updated *Limits to Medicine: Medical Nemesis* (1995, 2002), Ivan Illich argues that heavily medicalized health care is a threat to health in three ways. First, it encourages clinical iatrogenesis (an adverse effect or illness caused by the treatment itself; literally physician-caused illness). This replaces our natural capacity for health and healing. Second, social iatrogenesis steers families away from those natural supports and conditions that provide care and spur healing. Third, cultural iatrogenesis is a widespread condition in which the medical/psychiatric cartel erodes the will of the people to "suffer their reality.... Professionally organized medicine has come to function as a domineering moral enterprise that advertises industrial [and commercial] expansion as a war against all suffering" (p. 127).

The other side of the coin, the subject of this chapter, is that people have a native capacity for health and self-correction that can be drawn on. Positive beliefs about yourself and your world can have salubrious effects on health and wellness. Positive emotions stemming from these beliefs also have documented effects in maintaining and strengthening the immune system (LeDoux, 2002). It is understood, too, as Illich has written, that the community—the immediate environment—plays a major role in whether we thrive or wither. So what we end up with is a genuine biopsychosocial and spiritual understanding of human nature and the human condition.

Like disease, "health and wellness are the artifacts of a complex, reticulate relationship between body, mind and environment (the separation of mind and body here is a conceptual convenience not a reality). Natural or spontaneous healing is predicated on the mobilization of resources—hormonal, immunological, and neurochemical—within the body, psychological resources and perspectives, and environmental supports and encouragement" (Saleebey, 2005, p. 34).

CONCLUSION

At the very least, the strengths perspective and the resilience literature obligate us to understand that, however downtrodden, battered, sick, or disheartened and demoralized, individuals usually have managed to survive, sometimes even flourish. They have taken steps, summoned up nerve, coped, maybe just muddled through or raged at the darkness. We need to know what they have done, how they did it, and what resources provided ballast in the stormy seas of their lives. No matter how it may appear, at some level, people are always engaged in their situations, working on them, even if it turns out they merely decide to suffer them. Circumstances and experiences can debilitate. We know plenty about that. But calamitous circumstances can also bring a surge in resolve and resilience. We must know more about that. We must know more about making a pact with those forces for health and growth.

Of the strengths perspective, Stan Witkin (2002) has written: "Do not be fooled by the simplicity of the strengths perspective; it has transformational potential. Indeed, if all of its tenets were adopted and put into practice, we would be living in a different world . . . . The strengths perspective has been quietly fostering a small revolution in which the hegemony of deficit explanations is beginning to weaken, belief in resilience is rebounding, and collaborative practice is growing" (pp. xiv–xv).

On a larger canvas, historian Howard Zinn (1999) paints this picture: "To recall this [the rebellions] is to remind people of what the Establishment would like them to forget—the enormous capacity of apparently helpless people to resist, of apparently contented people to demand change. To uncover such history is to find a powerful human impulse to assert one's humanity. It is to hold, even in times of pessimism, the possibility of surprise" (p. 648).

Here's to that possibility.

REFERENCES

Addams, J. (1902). *Democracy and social ethics*. New York: Macmillan.

American Psychiatric Association. (2000). *Diagnostic and statistical manual of mental disorders* (4th ed., text rev.). Washington, DC: Author.

Andreasen, N. C. (2001). *Brave new brain: Conquering mental illness in the era of the genome*. New York: Oxford University Press.

Arpala, J. (2000, July–August). Sweet sabotage. *Psychology Today*, *32*, 66–67.

Asay, T. P., & Lambert, M. J. (1999). The empirical case for common factors in therapy: Quantitative findings. In M. A. Hubble, B. L. Duncan, & S. D. Miller (Eds.), *The heart and soul of change: What works in therapy* (pp. 33–55). Washington, DC: American Psychological Association.

Bachelor, A., & Horvath, A. (1999). The therapeutic relationship. In M. A. Hubble, B. L. Duncan, & S. D. Miller (Eds.), *The heart and soul of change: What works in therapy* (pp. 133–178). Washington, DC: American Psychological Association Press.

Benard, B. (1999). Fostering resiliency in communities: An inside out process. In N. Henderson, B. Benard, & N. Sharp-Light (Eds.), *Resiliency in action* (pp. 81–86). Gorham, ME: Resiliency in Action.

Benard, B. (2004). *Resiliency: What we have learned.* San Francisco: WestEd.

Blundo, R. (2006). Shifting our habits of mind: Learning to practice from a strengths perspective. In D. Saleebey (Ed.), *The strengths perspective in social work practice* (4th ed., pp. 25–45). Boston: Allyn & Bacon.

Boller, P. F. (1974). *American transcendentalism, 1830–1860: An intellectual inquiry.* New York: Putnam.

Cowger, C. D., Anderson, K. N., & Snively, C. A. (2006). Assessing strengths: The political context of individual, family, and community empowerment. In D. Saleebey (Ed.), *The strengths perspective in social work practice* (pp. 93–115). Boston: Allyn & Bacon.

Damasio, A. R. (1994). *Descartes' error: Emotion, reason, and the human brain.* New York: Grosset/Putnam.

Delgado, M. (2000). *Community social work practice in an urban context: The potential of a capacity-enhancement perspective.* New York: Oxford University Press.

Desetta, A., & Wolin, S. (2000). *The struggle to be strong.* Minneapolis: Free Spirit Publishing.

Duncan, B. L., Hubble, M. A., & Miller, S. D. (1997). *Psychotherapy with "impossible" cases: The efficient treatment of therapy veterans.* New York: Norton.

Fisher, M. J. (2000, October). Better living through the placebo effect. *Atlantic Monthly, 286,* 16–18.

Freire, P. (1996). *Pedagogy of hope: Reliving the pedagogy of the oppressed.* New York: Continuum.

Freire, P. (2001). *Pedagogy of the oppressed* (30th anniversary ed.). New York: Continuum.

Gergen, K. J. (1994). *Realities and relationships: Soundings in social construction.* Cambridge, MA: Harvard University Press.

Gutiérrez, L. M. (1990). Working with women of color: An empowerment perspective. *Social Work, 35,* 149–155.

Illich, I. (1995, 2002). *Limits to medicine. Medical nemesis: The expropriation of health.* London: Marion Boyars.

Kirsch, I., Moore, T. J., Scoboria, A., & Nicholls, S. (2003). The emperor's new drugs: An analysis of antidepressant medication data submitted to the U.S. Food and Drug Administration. Prevention and Treatment, *5,* 5–23. It is a now discontinued online journal http://journals.apa.org/prevention/volume5/preoo5oo23a.html.

Kisthardt, W. (2006). The opportunities and challenges of strengths-based, person-centered practice: Purpose, principles, and applications in a climate of systems' integration. In D. Saleebey (Ed.), *The strengths perspective in social work practice* (4th ed., pp. 171–196). Boston: Allyn & Bacon.

LeDoux, J. (1996). *The emotional brain: The mysterious underpinnings of emotional life.* New York: Touchstone Books.

LeDoux, J. (2002). *The synaptic self: How our brains become who we are.* New York: Viking.

Lee, J. A. B. (1994). *The empowerment approach to social work practice.* New York: Columbia University Press.

Malekoff, A. (2001). The power of group work with kids: A practitioner's reflection on strengths-based practice. *Families in Society, 82,* 243–250.

Mills, R. C. (1995). *Realizing mental health.* New York: Sulzburger & Graham.

Orlinski, D. E., Graw, K., & Parks, B. K. (1994). Process and outcome in psychotherapy: Noch Einmal. In A. E. Bergin & S. I. Garfield (Eds.), *Handbook of psychotherapy and behavior change* (4th ed., pp. 270–376). New York: Wiley.

Pelletier, K. R. (2000). *The best alternative medicine. What works? What does not?* New York: Simon & Schuster.

Phillips, P. T. (1996). *A kingdom on earth: Anglo-American social Christianity, 1880–1940.* State College, PA: Pennsylvania State University Press.

Prochaska, J. O., Norcross, J. C., & DiClemente, C. C. (1994). *Change for good.* New York: Morrow.

Rapp, C. A. (1998). *The strengths model: Case management with people suffering from severe and persistent mental illness.* New York: Oxford University Press.

Restak, R. (2003). *The new brain: How the modern age is rewiring your mind.* New York: Rodale.

Reuben, P. P. (2000, January 24). Early 19th century American transcendentalism: A brief introduction. (online) *Perspectives in American literature.* Available from www.csustan.edu/English/reuben/pal/chap4/4intro.html.

Reynolds, B. C. (1951). *Social work and social living: Explorations in policy and practice.* New York: Citadel Press.

Rogers, C. (1951). *Client-centered therapy: Its current practice, theory, and implications.* Chicago: Houghton Mifflin.

Saleebey, D. (2005). Balancing act: Assessing strengths in mental health practice. In S. A. Kirk (Ed.), *Mental disorders in the social environment: Critical perspectives* (pp. 23–44). New York: Columbia University Press.

Saleebey, D. (2006). The strengths approach to practice. In D. Saleebey (Ed.), *The strengths perspective in social work practice* (pp.77–92). Boston: Allyn & Bacon.

Social Gospel. (2000). *Columbia encyclopedia* (6th ed.). New York: Columbia University Press.

Stone, D. (2000). Why we need a care movement. *Nation, 270,* 13–15.

Tallman, K., & Bohart, A. C. (1999). The client as a common factor. In A. Hubble, B. L. Duncan, & S. D. Miller (Eds.), *The heart and soul of change: What works in therapy* (pp. 91–132). Washington, DC: American Psychological Association.

Vaillant, G. E. (1993). *Wisdom of the ego.* Cambridge, MA: Harvard University Press.

Weil, A. (1995). *Spontaneous healing: How to discover and enhance your body's natural ability to heal itself.* New York: Alfred A. Knopf.

Witkin, S. (2002). Foreword. In D. Saleebey (Ed.), *The strengths perspective in social work practice* (3rd ed., pp. xiii–xv). Boston: Allyn & Bacon.

Wolin, S., & Wolin, S. (1993). *The resilient self: How survivors of troubled families rise above adversity.* New York: Villard.

Wolin, S., & Wolin, S. (1997). Shifting paradigms: Taking a paradoxical approach. *Resiliency in Action, 2,* 23–28.

Zinn, H. (1999). *A people's history of the United States: 1492 to the present.* New York: HarperCollins.

Chapter 8

CHILD WELFARE: HISTORICAL TRENDS, PROFESSIONALIZATION, AND WORKFORCE ISSUES

Robin E. Perry and Alberta J. Ellett

Child welfare, as it is generally recognized and discussed in this chapter, includes child protective, foster care, and adoption services to children and their families. As a specialization, child welfare has a long and rich history within the profession of social work. The work in child welfare is perhaps more complex than any social work practice area due to the risk of serious injury to children in multiproblem families, public scrutiny, court and multiple oversight mechanisms, underfunding and high employee turnover. This important work needs the attention of professional social workers with the knowledge, skills, abilities, and values to work with clients affected by parental conditions such as substance abuse, mental illness, limitations, and involvement with the legal system. Unlike most areas of social work, child welfare workers regularly make home visits to work with their clients, transport children and parents (typically using their own vehicles), are expected to make perfect decisions about child safety, and spend considerable time in court with their cases. In addition, child welfare work is situated within a complex, external, sociopolitical environment that influences the size, minimum qualifications, and direction of the workforce, funding for employees and services to clients, constantly changing legal mandates and attendant practice issues, and ongoing public scrutiny. Thus, recruiting and retaining professional social workers to do this important work while remaining committed to child welfare is an ongoing challenge.

Pecora, Whitaker, Maluccio, Bart, and Plotnick (2000) cite the American Humane Association when reporting an estimated increase in reports of maltreatment from 669,000 in 1976 to 2,178,000 in 1987. By the 1990s, the rate of maltreatment in the United States was being referred to as an epidemic (U.S. Advisory Board on Child Abuse and Neglect, 1990). Three National Incidence Studies (the fourth study is currently in process) provide the best incidence data on maltreatment to date. Although there have been some modifications in procedures used, debate regarding the significance and meaning of findings and recommended modifications to future studies (Children's Bureau, 2000; King, Trocmé, & Thatte, 2003; Rogers, Gray, & Aitken, 1992; Sedlak, 2001), the National Incidence Studies conducted in 1979 to 1980 (NIS-1), 1986 to 1987 (NIS-2), and 1993 to 1995 (NIS-3) suggest an increase in the rate of maltreatment incidence (as a rate per 1,000) from 9.8 to 23.1 or from 625,000 to 1,553,800 incidents (Sedlak, 1988, 1991; Sedlak & Broadhurst, 1996). Reports of maltreatment by state officials may not capture the true incidence rates of maltreatment.

In 1995, data collected via the National Child Abuse and Neglect Data System (NCANDS) reported that approximately 1.1 million children were victims of abuse and neglect (a figure significantly less than NIS-3 estimates in 1993 to 1995) and a victimization rate of approximately 15 children per 1,000 (U.S. Department of Health and Human Services, 1997). This rate of victimization resulted from nearly two million reports of maltreatment related to three million estimated children. These same reports suggest a decrease in the victimization rate between 2001 and 2004 (U.S. Department of Health and Human Services, 2003, 2004, 2005, 2006) from 12.5 children per 1,000 to 11.9 children per 1,000. Regardless, the estimated 872,000 victims that came to the attention of child welfare agencies in 2004 is a significant amount. The observed decrease in victimization rate, however, is not realized in the rate of report of maltreatment. Between 2001 and 2004, the rate (and number) investigated from maltreatment has increased from 43.2 children per thousand children (3,136,000 children) to 47.8 children per thousand (3,503,000 children). The current NIS-4 study will help shed light on how representative reported cases of maltreatment are of a broader estimation of true incidence using additional data sources than state reports.

The Panel on Research on Child Abuse and Neglect (1988, p. 78) highlight:

> The alarming rise in the number of reported cases of child maltreatment since the 1970s is a significant development but the full dimensions of its meaning are not yet clear. A significant number of cases reported to child protective services (CPS) agencies are not substantiated. The results of the second National Incidence Study, for example, indicate that in 1986 the alleged maltreatment was unfounded for 47% of those children reported in CPS cases (NCCAN [National Center for Child Abuse and Neglect], 1988). However, the process of substantiating a reported case may be affected by a wide range of social and economic factors within the case investigation system (such as the number of caseworkers) as well as the characteristics of the case itself.

The purpose of this chapter is to provide information and timely discussion of historical trends, current issues, and future projections in child welfare as they relate to the development and continued professionalization of child welfare within the larger social work profession. The focus and scope begins with historical trends in child welfare and their interface with social work education and practice. Included in this chapter are: (a) an analysis of historical workforce trends and professional issues, (b) a discussion of the current professional status of child welfare, (c) child welfare research, and (d) future projections and recommendations about the continued professionalization of child welfare.

HISTORY OF SOCIAL WORK AND THE CHILD WELFARE PARTNERSHIP

Child Welfare Workforce and Professional Social Workers

Concern for the welfare of children within the U.S. social work community likely began with children being placed in orphanages rather than in almshouses. This practice was subsequently followed by the enlightened practice of placing over 200,000 children with Midwestern farming families via the orphan trains begun by Charles Loring Brice of the Children's Aide Society of New York beginning in 1852 and ending in 1929. When placed youth ran away and reported their mistreatment, Brice sent agents to do home studies to assess families before the orphan train arrived. Early efforts to meet the needs of dependent children were run by religious and private charity and aide societies until additional assistance was needed resulting in the public/private mix of child welfare services that continues to the present. Thus, the early evolution of child welfare is rooted in social work and the need for professionals to intervene in the lives of troubled children and their families.

Throughout most of the twentieth century, there had been debate (that ebbed and flowed at different times) regarding the defining features of social work and whether social work deserved professional status. In 1915, Abraham Flexner spoke at the Conference on Charities and Corrections to address the question of social work as a profession. He concluded that it was not, preferring to title it a semi-profession due to its lack of an educationally or intellectually transmissible skill or technique, and a knowledge base founded on scientific literature (Flexner, 1915). Flexner's speech was profound and had a mobilizing effect on social work at the time (Austin, 1978; Deardorff, 1930; Hodson, 1925). Indeed, the formation of the Association of Training Schools of Professional Social Work in 1919 (renamed the American Association of Schools of Social Work in 1933, hereafter referred to as AASSW) and the American Association of Social Workers (hereafter referred to as AASW) in 1921 represented structured efforts toward training and monitoring practice and providing a representative association for all social workers.

One of the main tasks of the AASSW and the AASW was to distinguish professional social work from the practice of the well intended (early charity work) and to convince society (and more particularly government authorities) that social workers were educated in "proven methods of service." These tasks, however, proved formidable in Flexner's opinion given the inability to pinpoint the time when charitable acts became professional activities (Flexner, 1915).

By the time the AASW was formed in 1921 (West, 1933), social work practice had diversified beyond providing relief to the poor into the fields of mental hygiene (Lee & Kenworthy, 1929; Lowrey, 1926; Macdonald, 1920), medicine (Bartlett, 1957; Cannon, 1913), education (Culbert, 1933; Meredith, 1933), child and family services (Pumphrey & Pumphrey, 1961; Walker, 1928) and criminal justice (Brown, 1920; Williamson, 1935). Consequently there were a variety of associations and organizations already formed (or in the process of forming) that social workers (professionally trained or not) could, and did, belong to. These included the Family Welfare Association of America (formed in 1911); the American Association of Hospital Social Workers (formed in 1918; Deardorff, 1930); the Child Welfare League of America (CWLA; in 1920); the American Association of Psychiatric Social Workers (formed in 1922 as a section of AAHSW, from which it separated in 1926); the National Association of School Social Workers (formed in 1919); the International Migration Service; the National Association of Traveler's Aid Societies; the National Committee on Visiting Teachers; and the National Probation Association. The diversity of settings in which self-ascribed social workers could be found led Walker (1928) to conclude: "It was suggested that social work was 'not so much a definite field, as an aspect of work in many fields,' and that social work has grown up to supply the shortcomings of the professions, whose development may not yet be completed" (pp. 88–89). These findings were reinforced by Conrad (1930) and Abbott (1933). Conrad notes that in a program review of 24 of the 29 accredited schools in 1928, 13 were graduate programs, of which nine would admit students who did not possess any undergraduate degree. Further, there were 42 different courses of study. Abbott described most school curricula in the 1930s as having a "frequently inadequate organization" (p. 145).

The first schools of social work (and year formed) included: the New York School of Philanthropy (1898), the Chicago School of Civics and Philanthropy (1901),[1] the Boston School of Social Work (1904), the Philadelphia Training School for Social Work (1908), and the Missouri School of Social Economy (1908). Interestingly, none of these early schools had a primary focus on child welfare issues or training despite the import child welfare issues had for early leaders in social work and identified links between child welfare and social work practice at that time.

These early schools were considered private institutions structured to: (a) train individuals to meet the service/administrative needs of Charity Organization Society (Richmond, 1897), (b) further the academic study (pragmatic study) of the effects of poverty and attempted solutions/charitable relief acts (Conrad, 1930), and (c) teach skills specific to the distribution of relief and personal and family rehabilitation (Devine, 1915). These curricula priorities were in response to the demands of agencies in the communities in which schools were formed, not necessarily to address the demands of all populations served by social workers throughout the United States. As a result, each school varied in form and focus. The philosophy guiding the structure of each school reflected the diversity of opinions regarding the role and mission of this newly developing profession. Hence the emphasis on medical social work in Boston, economics and rural poverty in Missouri, social reform and public aspects of social work and social research in Chicago, and the "intensive study of personality factors entering into problems of social maladjustment" (Abbott, 1933, p. 146) in the New York and Pennsylvania schools. This would change over time. By 1928, there were 29 accredited schools of social work in the United States of which 17 (58%) had courses (not necessarily a specialization) in child welfare (Conrad, 1930).

In its infancy, social work was closely aligned with child welfare issues and children's services (protection, placement, care, etc.). The influence and advocacy of Jane Addams (elected president of the National Conference of Charities and Corrections in 1909 and the only social worker to receive a Nobel Peace Prize in 1931) along with Lillian Wald (originally a nurse by trade) led to the first White House Conference on the Care of Dependent Children in 1909 and the subsequent formation of the U.S. Children's Bureau. The influence of Florence Kelley (another prominent social work leader) cannot be understated. She was also influential in creating the Children's Bureau, advocating the passage of early federal child welfare legislation (e.g., the 1921 Sheppard-Tower Act to reduce infant mortality), child labor reform and improving maternal and child health services throughout the United States (Goldmark, 1953; Sklar, 1995). Another prominent social work pioneer, Julia Lantrop, was appointed the first chief of the Children's Bureau in 1912, only to be succeeded by Edith and Grace Abbott, other social work leaders.

---

[1] Conrad (1930) suggests this school was formed in 1903 not 1901 (as AASSW documents suggest) as the Institute of Social Science. This school was formed as a result of the efforts of Graham Taylor of Chicago Commons and Julia Lathrop of Hull House. In 1907, its name would be changed to the Chicago School of Civics and Philanthropy. The Philadelphia Training School for Social Work became the Pennsylvania School for Social Service in 1916.

Despite the documented influence and early leadership of social workers in advocating for, organizing, and structuring a foundation for child welfare services in the United States, little is known about the number of social workers or social work graduates (from professional schools) that assumed positions within child welfare settings. It seems fair to conjecture that the early schools of social work were not necessary responsive to demands for social workers within an ever-increasing market (public and private) of child welfare services. Indeed, in their study of the curricula of the 38 member schools, the AASSW observed "marked difference in educational philosophy" (p. 39) along with course subjects and the manner in which they were taught between and among schools (AASSW, 1942). Attempts to find data that reported or projected a census of social workers stratified by field of practice (including child welfare) or employment settings prior to 1950 were futile, some information is available regarding the number of social work graduates, AASW membership information and the size of social work workforce using Census Bureau Data (AASW, 1936, 1938, 1945, 1946; Bureau of the Census, 1914, 1915, 1921, 1923, 1930, 1940, 1950; Culbert, 1933).

It is clear from a review of this data that the majority of self-identified "social workers" (from Census data) and members of the AASW were not necessarily graduates from accredited schools of social work. Many individuals who enrolled in social work programs in the 1930s and 1940s dropped out of studies to assume positions in an expanding public sector (where jobs were more plentiful than other service sectors during the Great Depression of the 1930s). Further, membership criteria of the AASW did not demand the possession of a degree or diploma in social work from an accredited school (as comparisons between the number of graduates and increases in AASW membership statistics for any given year will reveal). The estimates of social workers determined by the Census Bureau are based on self-reported data. Further, the Census Bureau has changed the definition or occupational titles of those classified as social workers across census years. These changes appear to have reflected general changes in titles or occupations recognized during each period. For example, in 1910 there was no occupational listing for "social worker" or "social welfare worker." The 15,970 individuals commonly thought of as early social workers in 1910 were referred to as "Religious and Charity Workers" (Bureau of the Census, 1914). This occupational classification was considered "semi-professional." In 1920, the Census Bureau revised the occupation title of "Religious and Charity Workers" to "Religious, Charity and Welfare Workers." The specific job titles that were contained in this occupational category included those considered in the 1910 census with the notable addition of "social worker (any)," "welfare worker," and "welfare supervisor" (Bureau of the Census, 1921). These occupations were classified as semi-professional pursuits by the Census Bureau (Bureau of the Census, 1923, p. 494). Partly in response to lobbying efforts of the AASW, the Census Bureau revised its classification system in 1930 to include as a "professional" occupation "social and welfare worker." The occupational title of "social and welfare worker" would apply for the 1930 through 1960 Census. Beginning in 1970, the occupational title was changed from "social and welfare worker" to simply "social worker." Unfortunately, there was no distinction or classification of social workers as child welfare workers. Information regarding the number of child welfare workers and those with social work education and training backgrounds would have to come from limited agency and Children's Bureau reports and select labor studies.

By 1939, 709 individuals were reportedly working in public child welfare units (Children's Bureau, 1940). However, the 1930s witnessed an expansion of public child welfare services. By 1938, the Children's Bureau had approved 44 states' child welfare programs (Children's Bureau, 1940.) In addition, the Children's Bureau perceived a social work degree as an important foundation for early child welfare practice. The Children's Bureau recommended at least 1 year of MSW education for direct service workers and the MSW degree for child welfare supervisors. The Children's Bureau funded educational leave to states to send their child welfare employees to graduate schools of social work and proudly reported that by 1939, 35 states and Hawaii had sent 256 individuals to work on their MSW degrees.

The formation of the Council on Social Work Education (CSWE) in 1952 and the National Association of Social Workers in 1955 brought about an intensification of efforts aimed at seeking professional recognition and social sanction for social work. NASW embraced the diversity of activities that represented social work practice, including child welfare practice. Although there is some reference to child welfare practice as a focus of interest within social work curricula in period publications, little was known about the numbers of social workers that practiced in public and private child welfare agencies (or within any other field of practice for that matter). Toward this end, two studies by the U.S. Bureau of Labor Statistics attempted to answer who social workers were, where they worked, and what they did. These findings provide a baseline for analyzing practice trends among social work graduates and for understanding the relative significance of child welfare settings as a labor market for social workers.

The 1950 and 1960 U.S. Bureau of Labor Statistics Studies

The U.S. Bureau of Labor Statistics (BLS), in conjunction with the Federal Security Agency (in 1950), and the U.S. Department of Health, Education, and Welfare (in 1960) engaged in the most comprehensive national study of salaries and working conditions in social work to date. The 1950 study was published in 1952 by the AASW and was partially sponsored by the National Social Welfare Assembly. It combined survey data solicited separately by the BLS and the Federal Security Agency in 1950. Both studies utilized representative (stratified random) sampling methods to survey social workers in state, county, and municipal agencies that administered child welfare and public assistance services in the United States. Weights were assigned to each case in accordance with its probability of selection (BLS, 1952, pp. 23–26; BLS, 1962, pp. 109–115). Subsequent population estimates were generated and tabulated as results of the study.[2]

---

[2]In this study, a "social worker" was considered anyone employed in a "social work" position or capacity within a multitude of agencies recognized (initially) by the National Advisory Committee of Social Workers as actual and potential employers of social workers. Thus, the BLS definition of a social worker conforms to Census Bureau definitions and unlike that of a "professional" social worker as defined by representative professional associations. Regardless, information regarding whether individuals participated in and achieved a graduate degree in social work was obtained. The 1950 study was replicated in 1960 by the BLS and the National Social Welfare Assembly. Utilizing the same sample plan and weighting procedures, population estimates for a universe of 115,799 social workers in the United States were obtained from 28,290 completed survey instruments. Like the 1950 study, this study utilized information solicited independently from three agencies within the Department of Health, Education, and Welfare via a survey of all (42,137) social workers employed by state and local governments.

Findings from these studies demonstrate that the public sector was the overwhelming employer of social workers in both 1950 and 1960. The ratio of the proportionate distribution of social workers in the public (at or about 65%) to the private sector (at or about 35%) remained relatively constant despite the increase in public sector services throughout the 1950s. The overall majority of social workers in the public sector were employed in public assistance. Yet, child welfare agencies were the second largest employer of social workers in the United States. In total, 17% of all public sector social workers ($N = 48{,}149$) worked in public child welfare agencies in 1950. This percentage represents approximately 8,185 social workers and seems in conflict with later estimates (by the Children's Bureau) in 1956 of 5,628 public child welfare workers (Low, 1958 as cited in Lindsey, 2004) employed in the United States. These contradictions highlight concern about select estimation procedures used or cited in publications of the time. The BLS study, however, attempted to maximize the external validity of their findings using more rigorous sampling and estimation procedures. Given such, the share of social workers employed in public settings represented by child welfare workers increased to 25.2% by 1960 (of 66,806). When public and private settings are considered, in total, 17% and 22.7% of all social workers in the United States were employed in child welfare (public and private) agencies in 1950 and 1960, respectively.

When level of graduate education experience is considered, in 1950, 54.3% of social workers employed in public child welfare, compared to 66% of those in private child welfare agencies, had graduate social work experience. When the proportion of workers with MSWs is considered, the rate increases slightly, from 23.8% in 1950 to 24.3% in 1960. Further, when the distribution of all MSWs in the workforce (both sectors combined) is considered, the child welfare agencies employed more MSWs than any other field, increasing from 25.5% in 1950 to 29.0% in 1960. Child welfare services had become a dominant market for MSW graduates throughout the United States by 1960, when employment in child welfare was a respected and prestigious area of social work practice.

Terpstra (1996) aptly reports a close, collaborative working relationship between schools of social work and child welfare agencies. Child welfare content was included in schools of social work curricula and agencies readily hired social work graduates between 1935 and the early 1970s. Information in the 1950 and 1960 BLS studies (when contrasted against CSWE statistics) suggests an imbalanced or disproportionate focus of interest in child welfare within accredited MSW programs. For example, psychiatric services employed 12.6% of all MSWs in 1950 compared to 18.6% of all MSWs in 1960. When the distribution of MSW students by field placement setting in 1960 is observed from CSWE documents (CSWE, 1960, 1962a), 25.6% of all students (assigned to field instruction) were placed in "psychiatric services" followed by 14.7% in family service agencies and 13.8% in child welfare settings. Given this information, it appears schools were disproportionately training more students for psychiatric services than the market could absorb. Although 29% of all employed MSWs were employed in child welfare services in 1960, only 13.8% of all graduate students were receiving field training in this area.[3] There would be no

---

Approximately 20% (8,358) of these were combined with 19,932 (of a possible 24,218) social workers who responded to the BLS survey to make up the study sample.

[3]These types of discrepancies between where MSW students receive their field placement versus where they are likely to be employed cast doubt on the usefulness of relying on field placement statistics as a means of monitoring market trends for social work services. It is conjectured that the demand for, and receptiveness to,

marked increase in the proportion of MSW students receiving field placements or training in child welfare within accredited MSW programs throughout the 1960s (CSWE, 1960, 1962a, 1962b, 1963, 1964; Dea, 1966; DeVera, 1966; Loewenberg, 1967, 1968, 1970) despite forecasted increased demand for more graduate educated child welfare workers (U.S. Department of Health, Education, and Welfare, 1965).

De-Professionalization of Child Welfare

Child welfare is often described as a professional area within social work practice. This perspective assumes that child welfare exhibits core characteristics that define a profession. As with medicine, law, and other professions, the extent to which child welfare conforms to these characteristics determines the extent to which child welfare can be considered a professional area within social work.

What are some of the more visible and accepted characteristics of a profession? Most would agree that the primary elements that are shared by and define professions in our society include:

- A knowledge base (protracted preparation program usually in a professional school within a college or university).
- A set of professional skills.
- Public sanction and recognition (such as professional license, organization membership).
- A code of ethics, set of values.
- Accountability within profession itself (rewards and sanctions).
- An essential social function performed.
- Reasonable autonomy in one's practice/work.
- Continuous professional development, generally through annual continuing education.

Social work seems to meet these criteria for defining a profession and child welfare is considered a professional practice area in social work.

Social work is the only profession to claim child welfare as its own and to prepare graduates for this important and complex work. Disciplines other than social work (e.g., psychology and medicine) conduct research on child maltreatment and/or provide treatment services. However, social work has from its inception addressed child welfare from a much larger perspective that includes concern for (a) professional education/preparation for child welfare work; (b) strength-based, family-centered practice; (c) advocacy for children and families; (d) access and allocation of resources; and (e) safety, permanency, and well-being

---

provide field training in any service sector or agency is shaped by influences separate from the market demands for these students once they graduate. Should this conjecture defy refutation, implications for social work education abound. Additional study is needed to determine whether training received in graduate school adequately prepares students for employment in varied service sectors that express differential demands for social workers. Further, it would be interesting to ascertain whether graduate students have a more or less accurate understanding of the demand for their services once they graduate than schools of social work.

of children and families. The argument is made that child welfare as a practice area in social work has historically gone through a period of de-professionalization and needs to regain its professional status.

There are a number of factors that historically contributed to the de-professionalization of public child welfare services in the United States. Influences include (but are not limited to) amendments to the Social Security Act in the 1960s, failure on the part of schools of social work to meet the assessed need for social workers (particularly MSWs) in child welfare in the 1960s and 1970s, the exponential growth of demands placed on child welfare systems following passage in 1974 of the Child Abuse Prevention and Treatment Act, and philosophical and practice priorities that redefined professional social work practice and a migration of social workers from public sector employment.

The Social Security Act (SSA) of 1935 included child welfare services under the Children's Bureau that emphasized professionalism with the goal of hiring trained social workers to address the "protection and care of homeless, dependent, neglected and children in danger of becoming delinquent" (Children's Bureau, 1940). Aid to Dependent Children (ADC) was established to enable deserving women who were widowed or abandoned to raise their children rather than become wards of the state with the ADC program administered by the Board of Public Assistance (A. J. Ellett & Leighninger, 2007). In 1962, amendments to the SSA changed the ADC program to Aid to Families with Dependent Children (AFDC) changing the purpose from preserving families to an anti-poverty program. Social workers and activists recruited families for the AFDC program that grew beyond the program's capacity. In response to the 1967 amendments to the SSA, child welfare programs were subsumed under the larger AFDC organization to provide their professional services to poor families. In so doing, child welfare caseworkers whose caseloads were growing even faster than the AFDC's lost their social work leadership and expertise as well as, their identity with, and connections to, social work education (A. J. Ellett & Leighninger, 2007; Terpstra, 1996). Regardless, prior to the 1967 SSA amendments, the assessed need for social workers (especially MSWs) for public child welfare practice was particularly high.

A few studies attempted to gauge where demand for social workers was greatest. Some studies (Social Security Bulletin, 1961, as cited in Barker & Briggs, 1968; U.S. Department of Health, Education, and Welfare, 1965; Witte, 1960) were more comprehensive and rigorous in design than others (American Public Welfare Association, 1958; Board of Social Work Examiners, 1950, 1959; Bureau of Research and Statistics, 1956; French, 1947; French & Rosen, 1958). In 1965, the U.S. Department of Health, Education, and Welfare conducted a manpower study concluding that, "for programs in which agencies in the Department of Health, Education, and Welfare are directly concerned, the gap between the available number of social workers with graduate social work education and those estimated as needed by 1970 approaches 100,000 persons" (p. 79). Among these 100,000 needed workers, 21,000 MSWs (21% of the forecasted need for all MSWs) were needed in public child welfare by 1970. The U.S. Department of Health, Education, and Welfare report (1965) served as a primary impetus for the expansion of social work programs, intensification of recruitment efforts (beginning in high school) and revisions of school curricula as a means of meeting the current and anticipated demand for social workers in an ever-expanding public social service market (Kendall, 1964; Pins, 1965; Wittman,

1965). As the role of the public service sector increased during the 1950s and 1960s,[4] concern was expressed about the extent to which schools of social work could meet the market demands for professional social workers (Board of Social Work Examiners, 1958; Cohen, 1970; Pins, 1965; Ross & Lictenberg, 1963; U.S. Department of Health, Education, and Welfare, 1965). It appears schools were unable to meet the demand for those seeking training in social work. In a CSWE (1964) report, 48 of 59 schools demonstrated that 962 qualified applicants were turned away from member schools because they could not be accommodated by existing resources. Although U.S. Department of Health, Education, and Welfare estimated a need for 100,000 new MSWs between 1965 and 1970, CSWE statistics list the enrollment of MSWs (in 2-year programs) ranging from a low of 8,186 in 1965 to a high of 13,008 in 1970 (Dea, 1966; DeVera, 1966; Eldredge, 1971; Loewenberg, 1967, 1968, 1970; Loewenberg & Shey, 1969) for which as little at 10% (in 1970) to as high of 14.1% (in 1965 and 1966) of students' primary field of practice was child welfare. Figures suggest a duplicate count of 64,105 MSW students enrolled in MSW programs in the United States between 1965 and 1970. Given that students may be counted twice in this aggregate sum, the number of graduates during this time would be significantly less (almost half) and tragically unresponsive to identify need in the public sector for 100,000 MSWs (21,000 for public child welfare) during this same period of time. Thus, although there was an expansion of public sector jobs and the number of Schools of Social Work (and their associated curricula), it was not a proportionate, measured response to the demand for social workers across various fields of practice, especially child welfare.

These demands prompted a re-evaluation of the importance of the BSW as a professional degree by CSWE and other leaders in social work (Chernin & Taylor, 1966; Western Interstate Commission for Higher Education, 1965; Winston, 1965; Witte, 1966). This occurred despite the fact that the U.S. Department of Education did not consider a bachelor degree a "first professional degree" during this time period (Ross & Lichtenberg, 1963). The generalist practice model would rise in prominence and direct the structure of many social work curriculums in the expansion of schools offering Bachelor of Social Work degrees (Western Interstate Commission for Higher Education, 1965). It was thought that the versatility of a generalist degree best suited an expanding and dynamic social service sector. These events led, in part, to a proportional de-emphasis and focus on child welfare practice in U.S. MSW programs throughout the 1970s, 1980s, and 1990s (Eldredge, 1971; Hidalgo & Spaulding, 1987; Lennon, 1992, 1993, 1994, 1995, 1996; Purvine, 1972; Ripple, 1974, 1975; Rubin, 1981, 1982, 1983, 1984, 1985; Rubin & Whitcomb, 1978, 1979; Sheehan, 1976; Shyne & Whitcomb, 1977; Spaulding, 1988, 1990, 1991) despite the fact that public child welfare agencies have long been perceived as key training and employment settings

[4]There were 78 additions to existing legislation, amendments or new legislation that expanded resources (public services) for social work manpower between 1956 and 1965 (U.S. Department of Health, Education, and Welfare, 1965). Aaron (1978) demonstrated how direct expenditures on human resources (social services) and in-kind benefits by the U.S. federal government as a percentage of full employment GNP increased from 6.3% in 1961 to 8.7% in 1969 to 13.4% in 1976. The reader should refer to the following resources for descriptions of the social welfare state in the United States and its growth and expanding functions through the 1960s (Aaron, 1978; Barr, 1987; Dobelstein, 1985; Ginsburg, 1979; Pigou, 1952; Wolf & Lebeaux, 1968). The direct effect of the expansion of the welfare state on social work manpower can be examined by the 42% increase in "social welfare" manpower between 1950 and 1960 (Bureau of Labor Statistics, 1962). Further, educational training support for various "social work" positions was provided for by the Vocational Education Act of 1963, the Manpower Development and Training Act of 1963, and the Economic Opportunity Act of 1964.

for professional social workers in the United States (Bureau of Labor Statistics, 1952, 1962, 2006; CSWE, 1952, 1960, 1963; Lennon, 1992, 1995, 1996; Loewenberg, 1970; Rubin, 1981, 1983, 1984, 1985; Sheehan, 1976; Spaulding, 1988, 1990). Regardless, following 1970 and throughout much of the 1990s, fewer than 10% of MSW students primary field of practice or social problem concentration was child welfare (although slightly higher percentages were placed in child welfare field settings between 1985 and 1995). Thus, the unresponsiveness of MSW programs and the minimization of the importance of the MSW as a preferred professional degree for public child welfare in combination with other policy and practice events helped contribute to the de-professionalization of public child welfare in the United States. These events would have a compounded effect as the service demands placed on child welfare agencies/systems would dramatically increase in the 1970s and 1980s.

Following the regular use of X-rays, radiologists drew the public's attention to nonaccidental injuries of children and the occurrence of child abuse and neglect. In the 1960s, every state in the country passed child abuse and neglect reporting laws and federal legislation was subsequently enacted in 1974 with the Child Abuse Prevention and Treatment Act, which required the states to set up a registry and response system to such reports. From 1976 to 1986, the number of reports tripled and continued to increase into the mid-1990s while funding for states to provide child protective services did not (CWLA, 1993; U.S. Department of Health and Human Services, 1996). More reporting led to more than 500,000 children in foster care by 1980. High caseloads spurred turnover and lost expertise of experienced child welfare professionals. In order to hire enough caseworkers, administrators dropped the minimum qualification for BSW and MSW degrees for child welfare employees and schools of social work dropped child welfare content in their curricula (Karger, 1982).

As these events unfolded, some writers perceived the movement of graduate educated social workers away from public sector employment (including child welfare) as an outgrowth of a view of professionalism that reinforced a preoccupation of social workers that wanted to work with economically affluent and highly motivated clients (Falck, 1984; Katz, 1982; O'Conner, Dalgleish, & Khan, 1984; Reeser & Epstein, 1987; Reisch & Wenocur, 1986; Rubin & Johnson, 1984; Specht & Courtney, 1994). The steady increase of NASW members engaged in private practice in the 1980s and 1990s (Gibelman & Schervish, 1993, 1997; Kelley & Alexander, 1985; NASW, 1983; Wallace, 1982), coupled with the prominence of psychotherapy/clinical methods as preferred modes of intervention taught in many graduate schools throughout the United States, helped fuel this debate. Irrespective of its origins, it is clear that over a 30-year period legitimate concern was expressed regarding the perceived de-professionalization of many public social service jobs, making a large portion of social work positions engaged in income support and public child welfare unappealing to the professionally educated (Aaron, 1978; Beck, 1969; Dobelstein, 1995; Dressel, Waters, Sweat, Clayton, & Chandler-Clayton, 1988; A. J. Ellett & Leighnigner, 2007; Frabricant, 1985; Getzel, 1983; Ginsberg, Shiffman, & Rogers, 1971; Groulx, 1983).

In addition to these influences, the change in purpose of public assistance and the trend of increased work/caseloads, there were other concomitant circumstances that perpetuated de-professionalization of child welfare. These included a focus on investigation over services to improve family functioning, rationing services, specialization within child welfare, class action lawsuits, and increasing oversight of the child welfare system beyond the courts by court Appointed Special Advocates, Citizen Review Panels, Governor's Child Advocates, none of whom require social work education or child welfare experience. The press for accountability further requires increased time spent on written documentation, preparation for state and federal audits, and media investigations, resulting in reduced time available to work with clients. De-professionalization of child welfare has also resulted in hiring untrained, nonsocial workers, increased worker turnover, loss of degreed social workers, reduced public confidence in child welfare staff and lost professional status (A. J. Ellett & Leighninger, 2007).

CURRENT STATUS OF CHILD WELFARE: ISSUES, PRACTICES, AND CONTROVERSIES

As described at the beginning of this chapter, child welfare work plays out in a taxing, complex environment embedded in a larger, and often times problematic, external environment. Most would agree that child welfare work is difficult and requires advanced social work knowledge and skills (elements of a profession) to be successful with clients. Though the work is difficult, and the history of child welfare documents considerable de-professionalization, there are a number of ongoing efforts that can move child welfare toward greater professionalization in the years ahead. Those considered most important from our perspectives are described in the sections that follow.

Accountability

During the past 3 decades, child welfare practice has been characterized by increased attention to accountability issues and concerns. It is possible to assert that increased accountability in child welfare may be the result of historical de-professionalization (e.g., a diminution in required credentials). Accountability in child welfare, as in all professions, is a necessary but insufficient condition for professional practice. In child welfare, however, the unwritten standards and expectations set by the general public and policymakers seem to reflect perfect casework practice with little margin for error. Child welfare agencies and staff are expected to make error-free assessments and decisions, unlike those in other professions (e.g., medicine and law). In child welfare, there is public outrage in child fatality and serious injury cases, and the assumption of error and subsequent blame for faulty practice typically follows. There is general acceptance that doctors sometimes make mistakes and cannot save the lives of all patients, so errors in their practice are overlooked and/or forgiven. Similarly, law enforcement officers cannot prevent the murder of a domestic violence victim after an investigation and are held blameless in these situations. The high standards for professional practice in child welfare, combined with historical de-professionalization, have resulted in multiple accountability systems not seen in other professions. These systems are briefly described in the following sections.

Court

To assure that parents' rights are protected from unlawful government intrusion into the sanctity of the family, the courts have heard cases since the Mary Ellen case in 1874. The first juvenile court was established in Cook County (Chicago) in 1899 and courts have had jurisdiction over the removal from and return of children to their parent(s) or custodian(s). Courts also have jurisdiction over adoption surrenders and termination of parental rights. The court's oversight of these judicial hearings assures parents' due process in these life-altering matters with regard to their children. Over the past 3 decades, federal legislation has increased the courts scrutiny and oversight of child welfare systems. Federal legislation now delineates specific limitations on and outcome expectations in child welfare cases (A. J. Ellett & Leighninger, 2007; A. J. Ellett & Steib, 2005).

Guardian Ad Litem and Court Appointed Special Advocate

The Child Abuse Prevention and Treatment Act of 1974 (CAPTA) requires that a Guardian ad Litem (GAL) be appointed by the court to act in the best interest of children in child abuse and neglect judicial proceedings (Blome & Steib, 2007). CAPTA was the first federal child maltreatment reporting law to protect what were considered a few children. Public child welfare agencies were quickly overwhelmed with the numbers of families reported, as were GAL attorneys to represent children in court. CAPTA provided limited funding to states that was insufficient to meet the far greater need.

The first Court Appointed Special Advocate (CASA) program was developed in Seattle, Washington, in 1977 out of frustration that overwhelmed caseworkers and GAL could not provide the details they believed necessary to rule in child abuse and neglect cases (Weisz & Thai, 2003). These volunteers have access to child records, children, caseworkers, and attorneys and can participate in meetings to understand both the case and the needs of the child necessary to make recommendations to the court (Welte, 2005). The federal Victims of Child Abuse Act of 1990 states that "court appointed special advocate shall be available to every victim of child abuse or neglect in the United States that needs such an advocate" (Youngclarke, Ramos, & Granger-Merkle, 2004, p. 110). There are now over 900 CASA programs (Weisz & Thai, 2003). Research on the effectiveness of CASA programs is inconclusive due in part to less stringent methodologies and studies have not generally compared child outcomes of CASA volunteers to outcomes of child welfare employees (Blome & Steib, 2007).

Foster Care Reviews

Since an increasing number of children placed in foster care (over 500,000) often remained in care for years, the Adoption Assistance and Child Welfare Act of 1980 was passed to bring additional oversight and accountability. This Act requires a case plan for every child in foster care in addition to a court, administrative, or citizen review every 6 months with at least one of these reviews held in court annually. The purpose of these reviews is to provide parental due process, reasonable efforts to prevent foster care and reunification services as well as to assess:

- The continued need for and appropriateness of the placement.
- Level of compliance with the case plan.
- Extent of progress made to alleviate the problems that necessitated placement in foster care.
- The projected date the child can be returned home or placed for adoption or legal guardianship (National Association of Foster Care Reviewers, n.d.).

Parents and children are invited to attend these reviews along with the caseworker and others involved with the family. In administrative or citizen reviews, the administrator or citizen has no line authority for management of the case. Citizen reviewers are volunteers who are provided varied training to explain the child welfare system, the review process, and types of required decisions. Recommendations from administrative and citizen reviews are sent to the court for judicial approval. It is incumbent on the agency and worker to adhere to administrative review recommendations even if resources for clients are not available (Blome & Steib, 2007).

Citizen Review Panels

The CAPTA legislation was amended in 1996 to require states to have Citizen Review Panels in their child protective service programs for the purpose of additional oversight at both the case and system level. These panels are to "examine existing information management system reports, conduct case record reviews, and interview workers, families and mandated reporters" (Blome & Steib, 2007) and then to make recommendations that are advisory to the agency. This legislation, which encourages panel composition to consist of members from other review processes, seems redundant. To date, a comprehensive evaluation of Citizen Review Panel processes and outcomes has not been completed.

Court Approval of Case Plans

Since reasonable efforts lacked a definition, some children reunified with parents were subsequently maltreated while others lingered in foster care for years to provide parents opportunities to regain custody of their children. The Adoption and Safe Families Act of 1997 (ASFA) amended PL 96-272 of 1980 to better the balance parents' rights with children's safety and to reduce time in foster care. The goals as delineated in the ASFA for child welfare cases are for safety, permanence and child and family well-being. Increased court oversight of child welfare now includes court approval of case plans that were previously the role and responsibility of child welfare professionals (A. J. Ellett & Steib, 2005). Many concerns have subsequently been raised by child welfare workers, attorneys, judges, and others about this legislation, including the possible creation of legal orphans since the law requires "termination of parental rights for children in foster care 15 of the last 22 months" when it is unlikely that the parents can fulfill their parental duties (Adoption and Safe Families Act of 1997).

The Press and Child Advocates

The press has the duty to accurately report and inform citizens of issues of concern in child welfare. When children are victims of preventable death and injuries, the community wants to know what happened and to hold parents and/or child welfare employees responsible. What is often missing in these tragic stories are the federal and state mandates that child welfare systems support families to care for their children and protect parents' rights to due process in child abuse and neglect cases. Unfortunately, sensationalized stories rather than success stories tend to capture the public's attention. More investigative reporting that goes beyond the tragedy to expose parental conditions leading to maltreatment, shortage of foster and adoptive homes for children with special needs, underfunded child welfare agencies, and on-call, overworked, and underpaid employees is needed. Professional organizations assume the role of advocates for abused and neglected children. Child Advocates look for solutions they believe will resolve problems and organize to promote legislation, investigation, funding, class action lawsuits, and so on. Class action lawsuits against child welfare state, county, and local systems have been filed in about half of the states with nearly all entering into consent decrees. These actions often move governors and legislatures to better fund and staff child welfare agencies, however, they also result in federal court oversight.

Child and Family Service Reviews

The Children's Bureau is the federal oversight agency for state child welfare systems and it makes decisions about the receipt of federal funding. Beginning in 2000, all states have now completed at least one Child and Family Service Review (CFSR) from the Children's Bureau and all states had deficiencies. The CFSR reviews have found that positive client outcomes are tied to frequent worker contact with parents and children (Blome & Steib, 2007).

From 1935 until the last decade, the majority of child welfare services were delivered by the public sector. With growing numbers of children in state custody and increased cost for their care, in the 1990s, states began making a decided philosophical shift to move many child welfare services to the private sector presuming that they would deliver better child welfare services at a substantial savings through managed care focused on outcomes. Evaluation research of privatized verses public child welfare services is inconclusive and lacking in rigor at this time (Quality Improvement Center on Privatization of Child Welfare, 2006).

Child welfare agency and employee accountability are essential to improve child welfare outcomes for children and families. Most agencies have internal reviews or quality assurance in place. Legislative committees and governors' task forces are still other means of child welfare system oversight and accountability. Child welfare employees report being overwhelmed trying to provide competent child welfare services, while at the same time, multiple oversight groups require information from these employees to point out what they have not been able to accomplish (A. J. Ellett, Ellett, & Rugutt, 2003). As previously described, multiple levels of oversight may have resulted from de-professionalization in child welfare and such oversight is not characteristic of other professions such as medicine and law. Has accountability reached a level in child welfare of diminishing returns for children, families, agencies, employees, and society as a whole? (Blome & Steib, 2007). With limited child welfare funding, would clients, employees, and systems benefit if funding for redundant oversight was instead used to better fund and staff child welfare systems and courts to improve services and raise salaries to attract and retain social work professionals and attorneys in the juvenile court system? (Blome & Steib, 2007).

Concomitant with the development and implementation of multiple child welfare accountability and oversight systems, there is much discussion about factors and conditions that can serve to enhance the professionalization of child welfare. Some of the more prominent of these are discussed in the sections that follow.

TOWARD RE-PROFESSIONALIZATION IN CHILD WELFARE: RECRUITMENT, RETENTION, AND AGENCY/UNIVERSITY TITLE IV-E PARTNERSHIPS

Public child welfare services are sanctioned to provide important protective, preventative, and preservative services for children and families with complex needs and across a myriad of contexts. These children and families deserve the highest level of professional expertise and competence. In the 1990s, there was an intensified effort to re-professionalize public child welfare. The social work profession has taken the lead in this effort, which involved advocating for better working conditions for child welfare workers, more resources for the training of child welfare workers, and for the development and maintenance of unique university-agency partnerships (using Title IV-E funds) to prepare social workers for careers in public child welfare settings (Briar-Lawson & Wiesen, 1999; E. J. Clark, 2003; Hopkins, Mudrick, & Rudolph, 1999; McDonald & McCarthy, 1999; NASW, 2004a, 2004b; Pecora, Briar, & Zlotnik, 1989; Risley-Curtiss, 2003; U.S. General Accounting Office [GAO], 2003; Zlotnik, 2002; 2003). It is the intensification and outgrowth (since the 1990s) of formal partnerships between schools of social work and state agencies overseeing the provision of child protection services that has received the most attention as an agent of re-professionalization (Briar, Hansen, & Harris, 1992; Briar-Lawson & Wiesen, 1999; Hopkins et al., 1999; McDonald & McCarthy, 1999; Risley-Curtiss, 2003; Zlotnik, 1993, 2003) although the measured impact—at a national level—is not entirely known. Zlotnik (2006) cites several sources (American Public Human Services Association, 2005; Cheung & Taylor, 2005; Zlotnik, DePanfilis, Daining, & Lane, 2005) when reporting that more than 40 states have some form of Title IV-E educational program with BSW and MSW programs.

Title IV-E funded educational and financial incentives were initially developed with the goal of increasing the numbers of MSWs seeking employment in public child welfare (Grossman, Laughlin, & Specht, 1992). Federal Title IV-E money was used for the provision of stipend and training support for social work students who dedicate 1 year of service to a public child welfare agency for each year of support received. These incentives may have stimulated new interest in public child welfare among social work students although it is unclear how much so. It is clear (at least in California) that there were a noteworthy amount of MSW students interested in child welfare practice, prior to and following the implementation of the Title IV-E stipend programs (Perry, 2001, 2004) and that several years of program operation contributed to the majority of child welfare workers and supervisors possessing a master's degree in California (Clark & Fulcher, 2005).

Perry (2001) found that the percentage of all entering MSW students throughout California (between 1992 and 1996) that had a distinct interest in public child welfare ranged from a low of 10.2% to a high of 15.6%. It appears the interest in child welfare practice remains strong but the longevity of interest may wane once individuals are employed and work environments fail to reinforce career ambitions. In this regard, the Title IV-E incentives may have served less as a recruitment tool than a source of support or additional reinforcement to prepare for a job or career in public child welfare among those already interested in the field. Perry (2004) found the most notable influences on MSW students' interest in public child welfare included the impact of past practice and practice training experiences. Findings from this study suggest that governments or schools of social work interested in re-professionalizing public child welfare services might best focus their time, energy, and money on those currently working in or those with past work experience in public child welfare.

In this context, re-professionalization can begin with those already employed in child welfare with a commitment to work with children and families in need, yet, lacking a professional degree/education. Those with past experience in public child welfare, and those exposed to and training within public child welfare agencies within graduate programs (regardless if participating in Title IV-E training programs) consider public child welfare as a viable and important sector for career MSWs. Regardless, as A. J. Ellett (2006) notes, most students of Title IV-E partnership programs (throughout the United States) generally take specific child welfare courses, fulfill their social work degree internships in public child welfare agencies and have a work obligation within a public child welfare agency on graduation. These experiences, it is assumed and some findings suggest, increase the likelihood that Title IV-E graduates are more likely to enter child welfare positions with the requisite knowledge, skills, and dispositions and a clear understanding of what child welfare work entails than are non-Title IV-E graduates (Gansle & Ellett, 2002). These graduates report a stronger professional commitment to child welfare than those without BSW or MSW degrees (A. J. Ellett et al., 2003).

The initial focus of many of these collaborative programs focused on MSW programs (Grossman et al., 1992) and represented a re-focus on the historical precedent and practice (pre-1965) that perceived the MSW as a desired/preferential professional degree for child welfare practice. However, their impact and influence quickly extended into BSW programs as well. The Title IV-E partnerships have received tremendous support from educational institutions (S. Clark, 2003; Grossman et al., 1992; Perry, 2004), the National Association of Social Workers (E. J. Clark, 2003; NASW, 2004a, 2004b), child welfare associations (CWLA, 1991; National Association of Public Child Welfare Administrators, 1987) as well as Federal and State agencies that have asserted social workers are better skilled and apt for engaging in competent practice within the child welfare field (GAO, 2003; Zlotnik, 2003). There are isolated findings that assert that MSW students attain better outcomes with clients than those with bachelor degrees, Title IV-E stipend recipients are more knowledgeable and skilled in child welfare practice than others, and that social work educated workers remain in public child welfare longer than others (Booz-Allen & Hamilton, Inc., 1987; Dhooper, Royse, & Wolfe, 1990; A. J. Ellett, 2000; A. J. Ellett et al., 2003; Fox, Miller, & Barbee, 2003; Gansle & Ellett, 2002; Hopkins et al., 1999; Jones & Okamura, 2000; Lewandowski, 1998; Lieberman, Hornby, & Russell, 1988; Olsen & Holmes, 1982; Rosenthal & Waters, 2004; Russell & Hornby, 1987; Scannapieco & Connell-Carrick, 2003; University of Southern Maine, 1987). Alternatively, there are isolated findings that suggest that participation in a Title IV-E program has no measurable impact on retention rates (Rosenthal, McDowell, & White, 1998) and that the performance of child welfare workers (primarily with undergraduate degrees) is not dependent on the educational background of workers (Perry, 2006). All of these studies have varied methodological rigor and limited external validity. More importantly, there are few studies that link or contrast the impact of re-professionalization efforts and the educational background and training of child welfare workers to child welfare outcomes while controlling for the varied contexts in which workers practice.

Despite an increase of social work graduates in public child welfare settings (brought about by these partnerships), concern still exists regarding the rate of burnout and job satisfaction among all child welfare workers, factors impacting on the poor retention rates of qualified staff, organization climates, the increase in complexity and seriousness of the types of cases workers are confronted with, and the administrative demands placed on workers that subsequently limit contact time and the attainment of desired outcomes with children and families (Cahalane & Sites, 2004; Cyphers, 2001; Dickinson & Perry, 2002; A. J. Ellett et al., 2003; Glisson & Durick, 1988; Henry, 1990; McNeely, 1992; NASW, 2004a, 2004c; Oktay, 1992; GAO, 2003; Weiner, 1991). As Perry (2006) notes: "Even the most competent worker's ability to maximize client outcomes will be strained at best, and eliminated at worst, when they have a high caseload of multiproblem families, little supervisory support, burdensome paperwork demands that limit client contact time, limited reinforcements (including poor pay), and work within a dysfunctional organizational climate" (p. 444). A more critical examination of the impact of professional training and workforce conditions on client outcomes in child welfare settings is needed in order to improve the efficiency and efficacy of service delivery in the public and private sector settings. More importantly, more detailed and rigorous studies are needed to determine if Title IV-E partnerships have a longitudinal effect on maximizing the likelihood of worker competence, obtaining desired outcomes for child welfare populations, increasing the quality of service, and improving retention rates of quality workers. There is general support within the literature for these initiatives (Dickinson, 2006; A. J. Ellett, 2006; Hughes & Baird, 2006; McCarthy, 2006; Perry, 2006).

Supervision and Mentorship[5]

Accountability has become a dominant issue framing current child welfare practice. As a result, agencies have typically responded by requiring supervisors to more directly focus on task supervision, rather than on the more traditional focus on mentoring and professional development to strengthen practice skills. Task supervision is primarily motivated by issues such as compliance, record keeping, and a cult of efficiency and accountability. For example, supervisors use information system reports to determine if workers are making first client contacts within the prescribed time frame, monthly contacts with parents and children, court reports submitted timely, and so on (Collins-Camargo, 2006).

Although advances in the use of automated systems, dynamic data bases, personal digital devices, voice dictation and other technologies have documented benefits for child welfare practice (Anderson, 2004; Barton Child Law and Policy Clinic, 2002; Computer Associates, 2004; Compuware Corporation, 2005; Kershaw, 2002; Microsoft, 2004a, 2004b; Miller, 2001; National Resource Center for Information Technology in Child Welfare, 2002, 2003; NPower New York, 2002), these benefits exist only if they enable the streamlining and minimization of burdensome administrative, bureaucratic functions that take away from client contact time, real casework (i.e., really working with cases) and professional practice aimed at the development of working relationships and goal attainment with client

[5]Because supervision is such an important element of child welfare employee retention and professional development, considerable text is devoted to the discussion of supervision and to findings from pertinent research studies that identify the quality of supervision as an important element of child welfare practice.

systems (Cyphers, 2001; A. J. Ellett et al., 2003; GAO, 2003; Malm, Bess, Leos-Urbel, Green, & Markowitz, 2001; NASW, 2004a; Samantrai, 1992; Vinokur-Kaplan & Hartman, 1986). Child and family services reviews conducted between 2001 through 2004 found that the frequency of contact and visits between caseworkers and children and parents is consistently associated with the attainment of desired outcomes associated with child safety, permanency and child well-being (Administration for Children and Families, 2004). Professional child welfare workers need the time with clients to practice their trade and, perhaps more importantly, they need quality supervision, mentorship, and a learning environment to advance their knowledge and applied skill set.

Child welfare practice is multifaceted, demanding and requires a foundation of knowledge in (but not limited to) social policy, state laws and protocols, child development, family dynamics, conflict/crisis management and resolution, case management, critical thinking, substance abuse, mental health issues and organizational functioning (Horejsi, Bertsche, Francetich, Collins, & Francetich, 1987; Rittner & Wodarski, 1999; Rothman, 1991). The pressures placed on child welfare workers and individuals and entities for which they are accountable to are enormous, well-documented and include (but are not limited to): maltreated children, children of clients, families, foster care providers, abusive parents/caregivers, the court system, agency administrators, the community and media, and so on (Crosson-Tower, 2002).

Salas (2004) and others (Beggs, 1996; GAO, 1995, 2003; NASW, 2004c; Perry & Houlious, 2006; Rycus & Hughes, 1994) have listed the multitude of performance expectations and responsibilities child welfare workers (protective investigators and service workers) are required to do. The above functions (if competently completed) require a foundation in knowledge and practice experience. These functions, however, may involve an additional series of interrelated tasks and an expanded skill set. Perry, Graham, Kerce, and Babcock (2004) found that child protective investigators in Florida are required, as part of their work requirements, to be competent in 141 separate essential tasks as a means of fulfilling performance expectations established by state laws and service protocols. In a similar task analysis of child and family service (not protective investigators) workers in central Florida, Perry and Houlious (2006) itemized a total of 115 separate essential tasks that workers may be called on each day in order to fulfill job expectations.

Findings from Pertinent Research Studies

The workload demands brought about by heavily mandated services and the associated stress with providing protective, preservative and prevention-based interventions with multiproblem families can have an aversive impact on the retention of quality social workers beginning their professional career. Within these contexts, quality/competent supervision and worker-supervisor relationships are paramount for the recruitment and retention of child welfare workers (Child Welfare Training Institute, 1997; Cyphers, 2001; Dickinson & Perry, 2002; Fleischer, 1985; McCarthy, 2004; Mor Barak, Nissly, & Levin, 2001; Smith, 2004). Workers require supervisors with experience, competency-based knowledge, and are perceived as being supportive of workers efforts to gain knowledge, experience, and increasing their competency. These are important considerations in evaluating the performance of supervisors (Drake & Washeck, 1998; Kadushin, 1992; McCarthy, 2004; Ruston & Nathan, 1996). Here, the quality of the supervisor-worker relationship is frequently cited as an important consideration in the professional development and/or learning of workers, the minimization of worker stress and burnout, and with the maximization of worker retention in a field beset with high turnover (Dickinson & Perry, 2002; A. J. Ellett et al., 2003; Gleeson, 1992; McCarthy, 2004).

There is an abundance of literature that highlights the skills and knowledge considered representative of quality supervision or management in the human service fields, including child welfare (Bunker & Wijnberg, 1988; Kadushin, 1985; Menefee, 1998; Menefee & Thompson, 1994; Middleman & Rhodes, 1985; Morton & Salas, 1994; Preston, 2004; Salas, 2004; Tropman, Faller, & Feldt, 2004). Social work educators and researchers typically endorse the MSW degree as preferred for those assuming supervisor and/or management positions in child welfare and social service agencies (CWLA, 1984; Edwards, 1987; Rittner & Wodarski, 1999). These endorsements seemed to be based on the historical role of social work in educating and training professionals to assume supervisory and administrative roles in social service agencies. Historically, the MSW degree has been the preferred degree for child welfare supervisors and is still endorsed as such by the NASW (2005), CWLA (1984), and the Council on Accreditation for Children and Family Services (2001). The endorsement of MSWs typically results from critical reviews of curricula in graduate schools of social work and the applicability and relevance of these curricula to on-the-job demands and competencies required of child welfare supervisors. Although it is clear social work (as a profession) and schools of social work have been leaders in developing specialized curricula and programs to prepare social workers for supervisory roles in child welfare, there is some disagreement as to the extent to which a social work degree enhances the skills of those that assume supervisor positions in contrast to those without a social work degree (Perry, 2006; Thyer, Williams, Love, & Sowers-Hoag, 1989). Regardless, select studies and writings have highlighted the need for child welfare supervision to become less of a regulatory exercise in favor of an opportunity for a quality, reflective, practice-oriented, and supportive exchange between worker and mentor.

Several large-scale research studies completed recently provide support for the importance of quality supervision in child welfare. Most of these studies have been completed using measures specifically developed for child welfare of personal (self-efficacy and human caring) and organizational (organizational culture, morale, evidence-based practice and quality supervision) variables related to organizational outcomes (intent to remain employed; A. J. Ellett, Collins-Camargo, & Ellett, 2006). C. D. Ellett (1995) found that the highest levels of satisfaction among a group of long-term employees' retention in child welfare was quality supervision. In a two-state study (Louisiana $n = 562$ and Arkansas $n = 357$), A. J. Ellett (2000) reported a statistically significant correlation (.27; $p < .0001$) between professional sharing and support (an element of quality supervision) and intent to remain employed. Using structural equation modeling ($n = 990$) of organizational/occupational commitment with intention to remain, Landsman (2001) found a positive relationship between supervisory support and job satisfaction ($r = .30$), which was positively linked to occupational and organizational commitment and intent to remain employed in child welfare.

A. J. Ellett et al. (2003) completed the largest known statewide study of retention and turnover in child welfare ($n = 1423$, survey; $n = 385$, 60 focus groups). This study documented a rather strong, positive correlation ($r = .63$; $p < .0001$) between intentions to remain employed in child welfare and *professional commitment* (a dimension of human caring). Workers' perceptions of professional support and the quality of supervision and administration were positively related to a measure of intention to remain employed in child welfare ($r = .36$, $r = .33$). Focus group participants identified supervisors' professional support and guidance as important to strengthening work-related self-efficacy beliefs and intentions to remain employed in child welfare (A. J. Ellett, Ellis, Westbrook, & Dews, 2007). Westbrook (2006) completed a statewide study in Georgia of 1,033 child welfare staff perceptions of multiple dimensions of organizational culture and relationships between these perceptions and their intentions to remain employed in child welfare. Her results showed a rather strong relationship between intent to remain employed in child welfare and supervisory support ($r = .45$) and administrative support ($r = .43$).

Collins-Camargo (2005) completed a study of linkages between supervision, organizational culture promoting evidence-based practice, self-efficacy and public child welfare outcomes with 876 child welfare workers and supervisors in a Midwestern state. She found that 53% of the culture variance promoting evidence-based practice was explained by the effectiveness of supervision measure. In addition, she found a significant difference in the level of self-efficacy expectations (the extent to which workers believed that work tasks were likely to result in desired outcomes such as the ability to effect positive change in clients) and the perceived effectiveness of supervision for workers regardless of years of service.

An interesting and quite timely finding from the Collins-Camargo (2005) study was that effective supervision and professional organizational culture were predictors of case outcome indicators at a level similar to the predictive strength of larger community indicators, such as poverty. Findings from her study highlight the need for a quality supervisor-worker relationship built on a strong knowledge base and commitment to competency-based practice. Considered collectively, findings from the research studies described above, as well as many others, show that quality supervision in child welfare makes important contributions to: (a) creating an organizational culture focused on achieving positive outcomes; (b) maintaining a sense of hope within staff that their efforts can make a difference in client outcomes; (c) strengthening the professional commitment of staff and subsequent employee retention; and (d) enhancing worker knowledge, critical thinking and self-reflective learning.

Best Practices, Social Work Research and Child Welfare

As circumstances and events accelerated (since the mid-1960s) the de-professionalization of child welfare practice, research in child welfare (most notably since the 1980s) thrived. There appeared to be an inverse relationship between the decrease in professional social workers entering and remaining in public child welfare settings and the exponential growth of child welfare knowledge brought about by social work leadership in research and the establishment of best practice standards. Social work and social work researchers made significant strides toward advancing child welfare knowledge on a number of fronts (Barth, Berrick, & Gilbert, 1994; Berrick, Barth, & Gilbert, 1996). This is not to suggest that social workers did not make significant contributions to social work knowledge prior to the 1980s, as they did (for select examples, see Fanshel, 1962; Fanshel & Maas, 1962; Fanshel & Shinn, 1978; Kadushin, 1965, 1970; Kadushin & Seidl, 1971; Maas & Engler, 1959; Norris & Wallace, 1965; Stein, Gambrill, & Wiltse, 1978). However, the past 25 years has been a particularly active period where social work leadership in child welfare research has been dominant and has made contributions of particular import to advancing knowledge, policy, and providing a foundation for evidence-based practice.

As a profession, social work has clearly established a standing of prominence within child welfare research. It would be difficult to highlight all of the accomplishments and significant outcomes generated from this active period of discovery. Several volumes would be needed to highlight, discuss and debate the significance of research conducted during the past quarter century. Regardless, notable contributions by social workers can be found across a myriad of fields of interest/study in child welfare including (for example) child protection and maltreatment (Daro & Mitchel, 1990), foster care (Lindsey, 1991a, 1991b; Webster, Barth, & Needell, 2000; Whitaker & Maluccio, 2002; Wulczyn, Harden, & George, 1998), foster care youth and independent living programs (Cook, 1992; Courtney & Barth, 1996), kinship care (Berrick, Barth, & Needell, 1994; Courtney & Needell, 1997; Hegar & Scannapieco, 1999), ethnic/racial disproportionality (Barth, 2005; Courtney & Skyles, 2003; Derezotes, Testa, & Poertner, 2005; Needell, Brookhart, & Lee, 2003), prevention (Daro & Donnelly, 2003; Daro & McCurdy, 2006); family preservation (Lindsey, Martin, & Doh, 2002; Pecora, Fraser, & Haapala, 1991) and permanency planning (Barth & Berry, 1987, 1994; Barth, Courtney, Berrick, & Albert, 1994; Maluccio, Fein, & Olmstead, 1986). Particular note is made of the contributions of select research institutes/organizations, their leaders and their associates (current and former), including but not limited to the Child Welfare Research Group affiliated with the Center for Social Services Research at the University of California at Berkeley, Chapin Hall at the University of Chicago, the Urban Institute, and Casey Family Programs.

The emphasis on accountable practice corresponded with an expansion of research initiatives and an interest in the development of best practice standards. Although the CWLA has been a leader in the establishment and refinement of practice standards for child welfare practice (CWLA, 1984, 1995, 1998, 1999a, 1999b, 2000), other initiatives have resulted in the establishment of training, knowledge, and curriculum standards for child welfare workers (Berrick, Needell, Shlonsky, Simmel, & Pedrucci, 1998; California Social Work Education Center, 2006; S. Clark, 2003; NASW, 2005; Rycus & Hughes, 1994, 1998; Stein & Gambrill, 1976; Stein & Rzepnicki, 1984). These standards have been generated, in some cases, from prevailing logic or opinion regarding the skills and knowledge needed to perform well as a front-line worker, consensus among experts or key stakeholders in academia and state agencies, and/or practice knowledge garnered from existing evaluation or cross-sectional research studies. These standards are an important foundation from which to build practice and knowledge. However, within the last decade, attention has focused on the need to critically appraise the validity of practice assumptions and findings generated from studies with noteworthy limitations (Dingwall, 1989; Lindsey et al., 2002; Perry, 2006; Rossi, 1994; Shlonsky & Gambrill, 2001) to move toward more evidence-based practice models, to emphasize critical thinking and to focus on more advanced longitudinal outcome studies that rigorously test the success or failure of different practice interventions and policy initiatives (Barth, Crea, Thoburn, & Quinton, 2005; California Social Work Education Center, 2006; Chaffin & Friedrich, 2004; Courtney, 2000; Dawson & Berry, 2002; Gambrill, 2003; Gibbs, 2003; Gibbs & Gambrill, 1999; National Association of Public Child Welfare Administrators, 2005; Roberts & Yaeger, 2006; Shlonsky & Gibbs, 2004; Shlonsky & Wagner, 2005; Thomlison 2003, 2005; Usher & Wildfire, 2003; Wulczyn, Barth, Yuan, Harden, & Landsverk, 2005).

These recent events/trends reflect an evolution in perspective and spirit that, when manifested, will build on knowledge already garnered from an active period of investigation and further advance knowledge about the efficacy of interventions meant to solve real problems encountered by children and families.

PROFESSIONALIZING AND IMPROVING CHILD WELFARE

Perhaps the most important alterable variable related to the future professionalization and improvement of child welfare is the quality of the workforce. A continued, integrated focus on workforce development that includes concern for personal, organizational and work context variables is needed to move toward a professional model of child welfare practice. The sections that follow briefly describe important elements of the child welfare workforce and attendant concepts, issues and concerns that need to be addressed if child welfare is to continue on the path of greater professionalization and improvement of services to children and families in need.

An Increased Societal Need for Child Welfare Services

It is apparent that the provision of social services for children and families in need will be necessary as the size and complexity of the general population continues to increase. Given the multiple and serious problems that abusing and neglecting families face, the work within child welfare will remain complex and challenging. Substance abuse, mental illness, mental deficits, teen parenthood and incarceration do not lend themselves to quick resolutions. Children in families with one or more of these problems often have developmental delays, behavioral and/or emotional disorders, and/or lack adequate problem-solving and social skills. These families typically need multiple social services. Therefore, accurate assessments and the ability to communicate with and actively engage family members in planning and implementing evidence-based interventions will remain critical elements of child welfare practice.

An Increased Need to Prepare Child Welfare Professionals

The U.S. Department of Labor and NASW projections identify an increasing future demand for social workers in a variety of practice areas, especially in child welfare (Bureau of Labor Statistics, U.S. Department of Labor, 2006; Center for Health Workforce Studies and Center for Workforce Studies, 2006). Thus, it will be important in the years ahead for those preparing social workers (colleges and universities) and for professional associations (e.g., CSWE, SSWR, NASW) to continue to support child welfare as an important identity in the social work profession. Colleges and universities preparing social workers will need to continue to develop and implement curricula that respond to the projected increase in the national need for child welfare workers. Currently, many students enter MSW programs with the belief that they desire careers as private, clinical practitioners. Changing market and work context factors (e.g., managed care) have diminished the likelihood that there will be a sufficient need for all social work graduates who desire full time jobs in private practice. Thus, colleges and universities that prepare social workers for the future will need to be keenly aware of societal changes and the increased need for child welfare workers and adjust their social work curricula accordingly.

Social Work Education Partnerships between University and Child Welfare

The Title IV-E child welfare education and training collaborations between universities and agencies have been wise investments and have been important to enhance professionalization of child welfare. These partnerships exist in nearly all states and have increased the number of child welfare workers with BSW and MSW degrees. The national Title IV-E effort includes:

- Preservice and continuing education for child welfare employees as well as for foster and adoptive parents.
- Stipends for employees and potential employees working to obtain BSW and MSW degrees.
- Support for expanding child welfare content in college/university curricula.
- Support for internships in child welfare agencies.
- Formal education and on-the-job experiences that engage students and/or child welfare employees in social work theory, research, and practice.

Multiple benefits have accrued to child welfare and social work education through these partnerships. Among these are (a) strengthening advocacy and developing a stronger voice for child welfare; (b) improving child welfare practice; (c) developing greater leadership capacity; and (d) increasing the number of child welfare employees obtaining doctoral degrees (many of whom take positions in higher education which increases the number of experienced child welfare faculty). Some social work educators also participate in the development of agency IV-B Plans and Program Improvement Plans in response to Child and Family Service Reviews. It is thought that all of these activities and others emanating from Title IV-E partnerships have contributed to and strengthened professionalization of the child welfare workforce in ways that better meet the needs of children and their families.

Employee Recruitment, Selection, and Retention

The Title IV-E social work education partnerships have, by design, included recruitment of BSW and MSW students (including child welfare employees) for the purpose of educating and preparing graduates for a career in child welfare. While degreed social workers have professional knowledge and some practice skills, many are not suited for the taxing work of child welfare and some self-select out. As these partnerships have evolved, more attention is being given to selecting students and employing workers that possess the personal characteristics identified through recent research that enhance employee retention and strengthen the child welfare workforce. Selection of Title IV-E students is a key component of the Title IV-E partnership in Georgia for example, where applicants are jointly interviewed and selected by an experienced panel of child welfare agency professionals and university faculty.

Currently, too little attention is being paid to the importance of employee selection as an important means of strengthening the child welfare workforce and improving the quality of services to children and families. Many applicants for child welfare positions are hired without regard to the requisite knowledge and skills needed to survive and to be successful in child welfare and many of these do not remain in child welfare practice for very long. While there has been recent discussion and debate about the value of the social work degree for successful and competent practice in child welfare (see Dickinson, 2006; Ellett, 2006; Hughes & Baird, 2006; Lieberman & Levy, 2006; McCarthy, 2006; Perry, 2006a, 2006b; Zlotnik, 2006) there are emerging lines of inquiry designed to improve employee selection with the goal of strengthening employee retention and reducing employee turnover.

In Georgia, for example, high turnover among newly hired child welfare workers is a major concern (28% within the first 90 days before being assigned cases). To address this concern, the University of Georgia is working in partnership with the Georgia Division of Family and Children Services to develop a new, comprehensive Employee Selection Protocol (ESP; A. J. Ellett, Ellett, Westbrook, & Lerner, 2006). The ESP is standardized across applicants and includes three major components: (1) Web-based text, realistic job preview video, and self-assessment for likely job fit; (2) written application materials that include cover letter, resume, writing sample, and references; and (3) onsite completion of an in-basket assessment exercise and a semi-structured interview by a panel of three experienced child welfare professionals. A brief screening interview via phone is also completed before the decision to invite an applicant to complete on-site assessment activities is made.

The ESP is being piloted during the spring and summer of 2007 and the current plan is to fully implement it as a required selection process for all new applicants for child welfare worker positions. One important element of the ESP is the Web-based self-assessment task. This task is completed after reading the Web text and viewing the realistic job preview. It is framed around assessment indicators known to be positively related to child welfare workers' intentions to remain employed in child welfare (A. J. Ellett et al., 2003; Ellis, Ellett & DeWeaver, 2007). It is expected that the results of the self-assessment task will encourage some applicants to discontinue the application process and self-select out of employment in child welfare. Many applicants for child welfare positions in Georgia (and in other states as well), particularly those without a social work degree, have little understanding of the complexities and expectations of the work, and after considerable investments of time and money in 12 weeks of on-the-job training/certification programs, leave child welfare for other employment. Hopefully, the new ESP in Georgia will better inform job applicants about the nature of child welfare work, encourage some applicants to self-select out, lead to the selection of better qualified candidates, save human and financial investments made in new workers, and reduce existing high employee turnover rates.

Credentialing, Career Concerns and a Vision for the Future of Child Welfare

Credentialing is an important component of any profession. Credentials communicate a level of professional competence, expertise, and accountability to the larger society. Credentialed professions also typically reap greater monetary investments and rewards, and generate greater public confidence, respect, and prestige than noncredentialed occupations.

Though not guaranteeing competence and expertise, credentials have strong symbolic value. One only needs to consider the strong symbolic value of credentials in high-paying professions such as medicine and law to understand their value, and the prestige and trust placed in highly credentialed doctors and lawyers. According to A. J. Ellett (2006):

> As with academic credentials in any profession, the social work degree has considerable symbolic value and it serves to signal the public that child welfare is a profession worthy of considerably increased, and hopefully continued investment. (p. 410)

As previously described in this chapter, the MSW was once considered the appropriate entering level credential for child welfare work. However, and perhaps largely because of increased demands for more workers to cover ever increasing caseloads, most states do not require a BSW as an entry level credential, though most require at least a bachelor degree in a related discipline (e.g., psychology, sociology, counseling, education; CWLA, 1999b; Lieberman et al., 1988; Perry, 2006).

As mentioned, there is ongoing debate and discussion about the value of the social work degree to competent practice. However, the lack of a professional degree requirement as an initial credential (BSW) in child welfare is problematic from several perspectives. First, the message is sent to the public that anyone with a bachelor degree can do this complex work. Second, the lack of a BSW requirement suggests that there is no body of specialized knowledge that is important to include in college/university curricula. Third, and perhaps most importantly, a signal is sent to the general public and to policymakers that child welfare work is not professional work (any one can do it) and is not worthy of increased monetary investments. Thus, those employed in child welfare are viewed as workers, not as professionals. These same issues apply and same arguments can be made about the lack of MSW degree requirement for child welfare supervisors.

Child welfare workers have few options for professional advancement within a child welfare organization. Lack of such options has been shown to contribute to child welfare employee turnover (A. J. Ellett et al., 2003; Westbrook, Ellis, & Ellett, 2006). Within the child welfare organization a job assignment might change (e.g., child protective services, foster care, adoptions), however, there are few opportunities for career advancement to higher-level positions. Therefore, the predominant model for increased compensation is a lateral model in which length of employment, sometimes indexed by education level (e.g., BA, BSW, MSW), rather than the nature of the work, is the predominant factor that determines salary increases. For most child welfare staff, there are few career choices beyond moving from front-line worker to supervisor. What seems needed to further professionalize child welfare is rethinking and redesigning child welfare in a way that:

- Is sensitive to career options and choices.
- Accommodates individual differences in employees' interests, knowledge, and skills.
- Provides differentiated pay for differentiated work.
- Includes opportunities for competency/performance-based rewards through merit-based and bonus-based pay.
- Values, encourages and rewards the attainment of appropriate advanced degrees (e.g., MSW rather than BSW).

- Designates clear qualification and designates different levels of renewable licensing and professional certification for work each child welfare position.
- Provides mentoring and close supervision and support for new employees.
- Is sensitive to reasonable case/workloads balanced with other job responsibilities.
- Implements a valid and reliable job performance evaluation system.

Each of these redesign elements would be included in a new plan for child welfare that targets better education, practice, credentialing, professional development, supervision, compensation, retention and ultimately, improved services and outcomes for children and families.

As indicated by attempts to redesign other professions (e.g., teaching, nursing) realizing this vision for child welfare will not be an easy task and it will require considerable resources and support from policymakers, the general public, and perhaps strategic champions who will advocate for the professionalization of child welfare as the means to achieve outcomes for children and families.

CONCLUSION

This chapter addresses the history of child welfare as a distinct practice area of social work and its early development as a profession and subsequent de-professionalization. As a result of de-professionalization, child welfare has become highly regulated with multiple levels of oversight not found in other professions. A discussion of the contributions of Title IV-E university/agency partnerships to the preparation of child welfare staff, the documented need for quality supervision and administration, and social work research identifying evidence-based practice to professionalize child welfare, is included. The final section describes the increasing societal need for child welfare services, social work education's important role in the preparation of child welfare staff and the need for continued higher education and child welfare agency partnerships and collaboration. A vision for employee selection, retention, and credentialing is discussed as the means to professionalize child welfare and to ultimately improve services and outcomes for children and their families.

REFERENCES

Aaron, H. J. (1978). *Politics and the professors: The great society in perspective*. Washington, DC: Brookings Institute Press.

Abbott, E. (1933). Education for social work. In F. S. Hall (Ed.), *Social work year book: 1933*. New York: Sage.

Administration for Children and Families. (2004). *General findings from the federal child and family services review*. Retrieved March 17, 2005, from www.acf.dhhs.gov/programs/cb/cwrp/results.htm.

American Association of Schools of Social Work. (1942). *Education for the public social services*. Chapel Hill: University of North Carolina Press.

American Association of Social Workers. (1936). We stand up to be counted. *Compass*, *17*(7), 1.

American Association of Social Workers. (1938). Report of special committee on structure and participation. *Compass*, *19*(9), 15–24.

American Association of Social Workers. (1945). School enrollment increases. *Compass, 26*(2), 8–12.

American Association of Social Workers. (1946). Students in schools of social work. *Compass, 27*(3), 25–28.

American Public Human Services Association. (2005). *Report from the 2004 child welfare workforce survey: State agency findings*. Washington, DC: Author.

American Public Welfare Association. (1958). *Planning, costs and procedures in public welfare administration*. Chicago: Author.

Anderson, R. (2004, January/February). The child welfare workforce gets wired. *Children's Voice*, 32–33.

Austin, D. M. (1978). Research and social work: Educational paradoxes and possibilities. *Journal of Social Service research, 2*(2), 159–176.

Barker, R. L., & Briggs, T. L. (1968). *Differential use of social work manpower: An analysis and demonstration study*. New York: National Association of Social Workers Press.

Barr, N. (1987). *The economics of the welfare state*. Stanford, CA: Stanford University Press.

Barth, R. P. (2005). Child welfare and race: Models of disproportionality. In D. Derezotes, J. Poertner, & M. Testa (Eds.), *Race matters in child welfare: The overrepresentation of African American children in the system* (pp. 25–46). Washington, DC: Child Welfare League of America.

Barth, R. P., Berrick, J. D., & Gilbert, N. (Eds.). (1994). *Child welfare research review* (Vol. I). New York: Columbia University Press.

Barth, R. P., & Berry, M. (1987). Outcomes of child welfare services under permanency planning. *Social Service Review, 61*, 71–90.

Barth, R. P., & Berry, M. (1994). Implications of research on the welfare of children under permanency planning. In R. P. Barth, J. D. Berrick, & N. Gilbert (Eds.), *Child welfare research review* (pp. 323–368). New York: Columbia University Press.

Barth, R. P., Courtney, M., Berrick, J. D., & Albert, V. (1994). *Pathways through child welfare services: From child abuse to permanency planning*. New York: Aldine de Gruyter.

Barth, R. P., Crea, T. M., John, K., Thoburn, J., & Quinton, D. (2005). Beyond attachment theory and therapy: Towards sensitive and evidence-based interventions with foster and adoptive families in distress. *Child and Family Social Work, 10*, 257–268.

Bartlett, H. M. (1957). *50 years of social work in the medical setting: Past significance/future outlook*. New York: National Association of Social Workers Press.

Barton Child Law and Policy Clinic. (2002). *Workplace supports to improve Georgia's Child Protective Services*. Atlanta, GA: Emory University.

Beck, B. M. (1969). Nonprofessional social work personnel. In C. Grosser, W. E. Henry, & J. G. Kelley (Eds.), *Nonprofessionals in the human services* (pp. 66–77). San Francisco: Jossey-Bass.

Beggs, M. (1996). *In a day's work: Four child welfare workers in California*. San Francisco: San Francisco Study Center.

Berrick, J., Barth, R. P., & Gilbert, N. (Eds.). (1996). *Child welfare research review* (Vol. 2). New York: Columbia University Press.

Berrick, J., Barth, R. P., & Needell, B. (1994). A comparison of kinship foster homes and foster family homes. *Children and Youth Service Review, 16*(1/2), 33–63.

Berrick, J., Needell, B., Shlonsky, A., Simmel, C., & Pedrucci, C. (1998). *Assessment, support, and training for kinship care and foster care: An empirically-based curriculum*. Berkeley, CA: University of California, Berkeley Child Welfare Research Center.

Blome, W. W., & Steib, S. (2007). An examination of oversight and review in the child welfare system: The many watch the few serve the many. *Journal of Public Child Welfare, 1*(3), 3–26.

Board of Social Work Examiners. (1950). *Report of survey of social workers registered in California*. San Francisco: Author.

Board of Social Work Examiners. (1958). *Sixth biennial report to the governor*. Sacramento, CA: Author.

Booz-Allen & Hamilton, Inc. (1987). *The Maryland social work services job analysis and personnel qualifications study*. Baltimore, MD: Maryland Department of Human Resources.

Briar, K., Hansen, V., & Harris, N. (Eds.). (1992). *New partnerships: Proceedings from the national public child welfare symposium*. Miami: Florida International University.

Briar-Lawson, K., & Wiesen, M. (1999). Effective partnership models between state agencies, the university, and community service providers. In *Child welfare training symposium: Changing paradigms of child welfare practice: Responding to opportunities and challenges* (pp. 73–86). Washington, DC: U.S. Children's Bureau.

Brown, C. L. (1920). Co-ordinating the work of public and private agencies in probation service. In *Proceedings of the national conference of social work at the forty-seventh annual session*. Chicago: University of Chicago Press.

Bunker, D., & Wijnberg, M. (1988). *Supervision and performance: Managing professional work in human service organizations*. San Francisco: Jossey-Bass.

Bureau of the Census. (1914). *Population 1910: Occupation statistics*. Washington, DC: U.S. Government Printing Office.

Bureau of the Census. (1915). *Index to occupations: Alphabetical and classified*. Washington, DC: U.S. Government Printing Office.

Bureau of the Census. (1921). *Classified index to occupations*. Washington, DC: U.S. Government Printing Office.

Bureau of the Census. (1923). *Abstract of the fourteenth census of the United States: 1920*. Washington, DC: U.S. Government Printing Office.

Bureau of the Census. (1930). *Alphabetical index of occupations: Fifteenth census of the United States*. Washington, DC: U.S. Government Printing Office.

Bureau of the Census. (1940). *Alphabetical index of occupations and industries: Sixteenth census of the United States*. Washington, DC: U.S. Government Printing Office.

Bureau of the Census. (1950). *1950 census of population: Alphabetical index of occupations and industries*. Washington, DC: U.S. Government Printing Office.

Bureau of Labor Statistics. (1952). *Social workers in 1950*. New York: American Association of Social Workers.

Bureau of Labor Statistics. (1962). *Salaries and working conditions of social welfare manpower in 1960*. New York: National Social Welfare Assembly.

Bureau of Labor Statistics. (2006). *Occupational outlook handbook, 2006–07 edition. Social workers*. Retrieved March 21, 2006, from www.bls.gov/oco/ocos060.htm.

Bureau of Research and Statistics. (1956). *Survey of interest in professional social work training*. Sacramento: State of California Department of Social Welfare.

Cahalane, H., & Sites, E. W. (2004). *Is it hot or cold? The climate of child welfare employee retention*. Unpublished manuscript, University of Pittsburgh.

California Social Work Education Center. (2006). *Critical thinking in child welfare assessment: Safety, risk and protective capacity: Trainer's guide*. Berkeley, CA: Author. Retrieved March 2, 2007, from calswec.berkeley.edu/CalSWEC/Assess_Trainer_Binder_v1_1.pdf.

Cannon, I. M. (1913). *Social work in hospitals: A contribution to progressive medicine*. New York: Sage.

Center for Health Workforce Studies & Center for Workforce Studies. (2006). *Licensed social workers in the U.S., 2004*. Washington, DC: National Association of Social Workers Press.

Chaffin, M., & Friedrich, W. (2004). Evidence-based treatments in child abuse and neglect. *Children and Youth Services Review*, *26*, 1097–1103.

Chernin, M., & Taylor, H. B. (1966). Principles of organization of undergraduate social service education programs: Content and supporting courses. In *Observations on undergraduate social welfare education*. New York: Council on Social Work Education.

Cheung, M., & Taylor, T. (2005). *National survey of IV-E stipends and paybacks*. Retrieved October 29, 2005, from www.uh.edu/ocp/CWEP/State%20Stipend%203–05.pdf.

Child Welfare League of America. (1984). *CWLA standards for organization and administration for all child welfare services*. Washington, DC: Author.

Child Welfare League of America. (1991). *A blueprint for fostering infants, children, and youths in the 1990s*. Washington, DC: Author.

Child Welfare League of America. (1993). *The child welfare state book*. Washington, DC: Author.

Child Welfare League of America. (1995). *CWLA standards of excellence for family foster care services*. Washington, DC: Author.

Child Welfare League of America. (1998). *CWLA standards of excellence for services for abused or neglected children and their families*. Washington, DC: Author.

Child Welfare League of America. (1999a). *CWLA standards of excellence for kinship care services*. Washington, DC: Author.

Child Welfare League of America. (1999b). Minimum education required by state child welfare agencies, percent, by degree type, state child welfare agency survey. Washington, DC: Author.

Child Welfare League of America. (2000). *CWLA standards of excellence for adoption services*. Washington, DC: Author.

Child Welfare Training Institute. (1997). *Retention of child welfare caseworkers*. Portland, ME: Muskie School of Southern Maine and Bureau of Child and Family Services, Department of Human Services.

Children's Bureau. (1940). *Child welfare services under the Social Security Act, Appendix: Text of the sections of the Social Security Act relating to grants to states for child welfare services* (Publication #257). Washington, DC: U.S. Department of Labor.

Children's Bureau. (2000). *Symposium on the third national incidence study of child abuse and neglect: A summary report on proceedings, February 24–25, 1997*. Washington, DC: U.S. Department of Health and Human Services.

Clark, E. J. (2003). *Written testimony of Elizabeth J. Clark, executive director national association of social workers for the human resources subcommittee U.S. committee on ways and means*. Retrieved January 5, 2005, from www.socialworkers.org/advocacy/issues/child_welfare.asp.

Clark, S. (2003). The California collaboration: A competency-based child welfare curriculum project for master's social workers. *Journal of Human Behavior in the Social Environment*, *7*(1/2), 135–157.

Clark, S., & Fulcher, G. (2005). *The 2004 California public child welfare workforce study*. Berkeley: University of California, California Social Work Education Center, Berkeley School of Social Welfare.

Cohen, N. (1970). The schools of social work within the university system. In C. W. McCann (Ed.), *Exploring the interfaces of social work education* (pp. 19–42). Boulder, CO: Western Interstate Commission for Higher Education.

Collins-Camargo, C. (2005). *A study of the relationship among effective supervision, organizational culture promoting evidence-based practice, worker self-efficacy, and outcomes in public child welfare*. Unpublished doctoral dissertation, University of Kentucky, Lexington.

Collins-Camargo, C. (2006). Clinical supervision in public child welfare themes from findings of a multistate study. Professional development. *International Journal of Continuing Social Work Education*, *9*(2/3), 100–110.

Computer Associates. (2004). *CA child welfare solutions: Technology to help improve lives*. Retrieved February 10, 2005, from www.ca.com/Files/Brochures/child_welfare_solutions.pdf.

Compuware Corporation. (2005). *Child welfare agency steps up service through automation with Compuware*. Retrieved February 10, 2005, from www.compuware.com/pressroom/customers/2249_eng_html.htm.

Conrad, I. F. (1930). Education for social work. In F. S. Hall (Ed.), *Social work year book: 1929* (pp. 148–154). New York: Sage.

Cook, R. (1992). *A national evaluation of Title IV-E foster care independent living programs for youth: Phase 2 final report*. Rockville, MD: Westat.

Council on Accreditation for Children and Family Services. (2001). *COA standards and self-study manual, private organizations* (7th ed.). New York: Author.

Council on Social Work Education. (Ed.). (1960). *Statistics on social work education: November 1, 1960 and academic year 1959–1960*. New York: Author.

Council on Social Work Education. (Ed.). (1962a). *Statistics on social work education: November 1, 1961 and academic year 1961–1962*. New York: Author.

Council on Social Work Education. (Ed.). (1962b). *Statistics on social work education: November 1, 1962 and academic year 1962–1963*. New York: Author.

Council on Social Work Education. (Ed.). (1963). *Statistics on social work education: November 1, 1963 and academic year 1962–1963*. New York: Author.

Council on Social Work Education. (Ed.). (1964). *Statistics on social work education: November 1, 1964 and academic year 1963–1964*. New York: Author.

Courtney, M. E. (2000). Research needed to improve the prospects for children in out-of-home placement. *Children and Youth Services Review*, *22*(9–10), 743–761.

Courtney, M. E., & Barth, R. P. (1996). Pathways of older adolescents out of foster care: Implications for independent living services. *Social Work*, *41*(1), 75–83.

Courtney, M. E., & Needell, B. (1997). Outcomes of kinship foster care: Lessons from California. In R. P. Barth, J. D. Berrick, & N. Gilbert (Eds.), *Child welfare research review* (Vol. 2, pp. 130–149). New York: Columbia University Press.

Courtney, M. E., & Skyles, A. (2003). Racial disproportionality in the child welfare system. *Children and Youth Services Review*, *25*, 355–358.

Crosson-Tower, C. (2002). *Understanding child abuse and neglect*. (5th ed.) Boston, MA: Allyn & Bacon.

Culbert, J. F. (1933). Visiting teachers. In F. S. Hall (Ed.), *Social work year book: 1933*. New York: Sage.

Cyphers, G. (2001). *Report from the child welfare workforce study: State and county data and findings*. Washington, DC: American Public Human Services Association.

Daro, D., & Donnelly, A. C. (2003). *Child abuse prevention: Accomplishments and challenges*. Retrieved March 10, 2007, from www.endabuse.org/programs/children/files/prevention/ChildAbusePrevention.pdf.

Daro, D., & McCurdy, K. (2006). Interventions to prevent child maltreatment. In L. S. Doll, S. E. Bonzo, J. A. Mercy, D. A. Sleet, & E. N. Haas (Eds.), *The handbook of injury and violence prevention*. New York: Springer.

Daro, D., & Mitchel, L. (1990). *Current trends in child abuse reporting and fatalities: The results of the 1989 annual 50 states survey*. Washington, DC: National Commission for the Prevention of Child Abuse.

Dawson, K., & Berry, M. (2002). Engaging families in child welfare services: An evidence-based approach to best practice. *Child Welfare*, *81*, 293–317.

Dea, K. L. (Ed.). (1966). *Statistics on social work education: November 1, 1965 and academic year 1964–1965*. New York: Council on Social Work Education.

Deardorff, N. R. (1930). Social work as a profession. In F. S. Hall (Ed.), *Social work year book: 1929*. New York: Sage.

Derezotes, D., Testa, M. F., & Poertner, J. (Eds.). (2005). *Race matters in child welfare: The overrepresentation of African American children in the system*. Washington, DC: Child Welfare League of America.

DeVera, R. (Ed.). (1966). *Statistics on social work education: November 1, 1966 and academic year 1965–1966*. New York: Council on Social Work Education.

Devine, E. T. (1915). Education for social work. In *National conference of charities and correction*. Baltimore, MD: Hildmann.

Dhooper, S. S., Royse, D. D., & Wolfe, L. C. (1990). Does social work education make a difference? *Social Work, 35*(1), 57–61.

Dickinson, N. (2006). Commentary on "Do social workers make better child welfare workers than non-social workers?" by Robin Perry [Special issue]. *Research on Social Work Practice, 16*, 431–433.

Dickinson, N., & Perry, R. (2002). Factors influencing the retention of specially educated public child welfare workers. *Journal of Health and Social Policy, 15*(3/4), 89–103.

Dingwall, R. (1989). Some problems about predicting child abuse and neglect. In O. Stevenson (Ed.), *Child abuse: Professional practice and public policy* (pp. 28–53). London: Havester Weatsheaf.

Dobelstein, A. W. (1985). The bifurcation of social work and social welfare: The political development of social services. *Urban and Social Change Review, 18*(2), 9–12.

Drake, B., & Washeck, J. (1998). A competency-based method for providing worker feedback to CPS supervisors. *Administration in Social Work, 22*(3), 55–74.

Dressel, P., Waters, M., Sweat, M., Clayton, O., & Chandler-Clayton, A. (1988). Deprofessionalization, proletarianization, and social welfare work. *Journal of Sociology and Social Welfare, 15*(2), 113–131.

Edwards, R. L. (1987). The competing values approach as an integrating framework for the management curriculum. *Administration in Social Work, 11*(1), 1–13.

Eldredge, J. F. (Ed.). (1971). *Statistics on social work education: November 1, 1971 and academic year 1970–1971*. New York: Council on Social Work Education.

Ellett, A. J. (2000). *Human caring, self-efficacy beliefs, and professional organizational culture correlates of employee retention in child welfare*. Unpublished doctoral dissertation, Louisiana State University, Baton Rouge.

Ellett, A. J. (2006). Broad study but narrow question: A friendly critique of Perry's article. *Research on Social Work Practice, 16*, 406–411.

Ellett, A. J. (2007). Linking self-efficacy beliefs to employee retention in child welfare: Implications for theory, research, and practice. *Journal of Evidence-Based Social Work, 4*(3/4), 39–68.

Ellett, A. J., Collins-Camargo, C., & Ellett, C. D. (2006). Personal and organizational correlates of outcomes in child welfare: Implications for supervision and continuing professional development. *Professional Development: International Journal of Continuing Social Work Education, 9*(2/3), 44–53.

Ellett, A. J., Ellett, C. D., & Rugutt, J. K. (2003). *A study of personal and organizational factors contributing to employee retention and turnover in child welfare in Georgia*. Athens: University of Georgia, School of Social Work.

Ellett, A. J., Ellett, C. D., Westbrook, T. M., & Lerner, B. (2006). Toward the development of a research-based employee selection protocol: Implications for child welfare supervision, administration, and professional development. *Professional Development: International Journal of Continuing Social Work Education, 9*(2/3), 111–120.

Ellett, A. J., Ellis, J., Westbrook, T., & Dews, D. G. (2007). A qualitative study of 369 child welfare professionals' perspectives about factors contributing to employee retention and turnover. *Children and Youth Services Review, 29*, 264–281.

Ellett, A. J., & Leighninger, L. (2007). What happened? An historical analysis of the deprofessionalization of child welfare with implications for policy and practice. *Journal of Public Child Welfare, 1*(1), 3–33.

Ellett, A. J., & Steib, S. D. (2005). Child welfare and the courts: A statewide study with implications for professional development, practice and change. *Research on Social Work Practice, 15*(5), 339–352.

Ellett, C. D. (1995). *A study of professional personnel needs* (Vol. 1). Baton Rouge: Louisiana State University, Office of Research and Economic Development.

Ellis, J. I., Ellett, A. J., & DeWeaver, K. (2007). Human caring in the social work context: Continued development and validation of a complex measure. *Research on Social Work Practice, 17,* 66–76.

Falck, H. S. (1984). A loud and shrill protest. *Journal of Education for Social Work, 20*(2), 3–4.

Fanshel, D. (1962). Research in child welfare: A critical analysis. *Child Welfare, 41*(10), 484–507.

Fanshel, D., & Maas, H. (1962). Factorial dimensions of the characteristics of children in placement and their families. *Child Development, 33,* 123–144.

Fanshel, D., & Shinn, E. (1978). *Children in foster care: A longitudinal investigation.* New York: Columbia University Press.

Fleischer, B. J. (1985). Identification and strategies to reduce turnover among child welfare case workers. *Child Care Quarterly, 14*(2), 130–139.

Flexner, A. (1915). Is social work a profession. In *National conference of charities and corrections.* Baltimore, MD: Hildmann.

Fox, S., Miller, V., & Barbee, A. P. (2003). Finding and keeping child welfare workers: Effective use of training and professional development. *Journal of Human Behavior in the Social Environment, 7*(1/2), 67–81.

Frabricant, M. (1985). The industrialization of social work practice. *Social Work, 30*(5), 389–395.

French, D. (1947). The schools report: Statistics on social work education. *Compass, 28*(3), 15–20.

French, D., & Rosen, A. (1958). Personnel entering social work employment from schools of social work, 1957. In *Recruitment for social work education and social work practice.* New York: Council on Social Work Education.

Gambrill, E. (2003). Evidence-based practice: Implications for knowledge development and use in social work. In A. Rosen & E. K. Proctor (Eds.), *Developing practice guidelines for social work intervention: Issues, methods, and research agenda* (pp. 37–58). New York: Columbia University Press.

Gansle, K., & Ellett, A. (2002). Child welfare knowledge transmission, practitioner retention, and university-community impact: A study of Title IV-E child welfare training. *Journal of Health and Social Policy, 15*(3/4), 69–88.

Getzel, G. S. (1983). Speculations on the crisis in social work recruitment: Some modest proposals. *Social Work, 28*(3), 235–237.

Gibbs, L. (2003). *Evidence-based practice for the helping professions: A practical guide with integrated media.* Monterey, CA: Brooks/Cole.

Gibbs, L., & Gambrill, E. (1999). *Critical thinking for social workers: Exercises for the helping professions* (2nd ed.). Thousand Oaks, CA: Pine Forge Press.

Gibelman, M., & Schervish, P. H. (1993). *Who we are: The social work labor force as reflected in the NASW membership.* Washington, DC: National Association of Social Workers Press.

Gibelman, M., & Schervish, P. H. (1997). *Who we are: A second look.* Washington, DC: National Association of Social Workers Press.

Ginsberg, M. I., Shiffman, B. M., & Rogers, M. (1971). Nonprofessionals in social work. In C. Grosser, W. E. Henry, & J. G. Kelley (Eds.), *Nonprofessionals in the human services* (pp. 193–202). San Francisco: Jossey-Bass.

Ginsburg, N. (1979). *Class, capital and social policy.* London: Macmillan.

Gleeson, J. P. (1992, Fall). How do child welfare caseworkers learn? *Adult Education Quarterly, 43,* 15–29.

Glisson, C., & Durick, M. (1988). Predictors of job satisfaction and organizational commitment in human service organizations. *Administrative Science Quarterly, 33*(1), 61–81.

Goldmark, J. (1953). *Impatient crusader.* Urbana: University of Illinois Press.

Grossman, B., Laughlin, S., & Specht, H. (1992). Building the commitment of social work education to publicly sponsored social services: The California model. In K. Briar, V. Hansen, & N. Harris (Eds.), *New partnerships: Proceedings from the national public welfare training symposium 1991* (pp. 55–72). Miami: Florida International University.

Groulx, L. (1983). Deprofessionalization of social services: Demands of democracy or pretensions to a new power? *International Social Work, 26*(3), 38–44.

Hegar, R. L., & Scannapieco, M. (Eds.). (1999). *Kinship foster care: Practice, policy, and research*. New York: Oxford University Press.

Henry, S. (1990). Non-salary retention incentives for social workers in public mental health. *Administration in Social Work, 14*(3), 1–15.

Hidalgo, J., & Spaulding, E. C. (1987). *Statistics on social work education in the United States: 1986*. Washington, DC: Council on Social Work Education.

Hodson, W. (1925). Is social work professional? A reexamination of the question. In *Proceedings of the national conference of social work at the fifty-second annual session*. Chicago: University of Chicago Press.

Hopkins, K. M., Mudrick, N. R., & Rudolph, C. S. (1999). Impact of university-agency partnerships in child welfare on organizations, workers, and work activities. *Child Welfare, 78*(6), 749–773.

Horejsi, C., Bertsche, J., Francetich, S., Collins, B., & Francetich, R. (1987). Protocols in child welfare: An example. *Child Welfare, 65*, 423–431.

Hughes, R. C., & Baird, C. (2006). B.A.s are B.S. in child welfare: Did anybody learn anything? *Research on Social Work Practice, 16*, 434–437.

Jones, L. P., & Okamura, A. (2000). Reprofessionalizing child welfare services: An evaluation of a Title IV-E training program. *Research on Social Work Practice, 10*, 607–621.

Kadushin, A. (1965). Introductions of new orientations in child welfare research. In M. Norris & B. Wallace (Eds.), *The known and unknown in child welfare research: An appraisal* (pp. 28–39). New York: Child Welfare League of America.

Kadushin, A. (1970). *Adopting older children*. New York: Columbia University Press.

Kadushin, A. (1985). *Supervision in social work* (2nd ed.). New York: Columbia University Press.

Kadushin, A. (1992). *Supervision in social work* (3rd ed.). New York: Columbia University Press.

Kadushin, A., & Seidl, F. W. (1971). Adoption failure: A social work postmortem. *Social Work, 16*, 32–38.

Karger, H. J. (1982). Reclassification: Is there a future in public welfare for the trained social worker? *Social Work, 28*(6), 427–433.

Katz, A. J. (1982). Social work education: The near future. *Administration in Social Work, 6*(2/3), 147–157.

Kelley, P., & Alexander, P. (1985). Part-time private practice: Practical and ethical considerations. *Social Work, 30*(3), 254–258.

Kendall, K. (1964). Expansion and improved quality. *Social Work Education, 12*(6), 1, 27–31.

Kershaw, S. (2002, September 3). Digital photos give the police a new edge in abuse cases [Electronic Version]. *New York Times*, p. A1.

King, G., Trocmé, N., & Thatte, N. (2003). Substantiation as a multitier process: The results of a NIS-3 analysis. *Child Maltreatment, 8*, 173–182.

Landsman, M. J. (2001). Commitment in public child welfare. *Social Services Review, 75*, 386–419.

Lee, P., & Kenworthy, M. (1929). *Mental hygiene and social work*. New York: Commonwealth Fund.

Lennon, T. M. (1992). *Statistics on social work education in the United States: 1991*. Alexandria, VA: Council on Social Work Education.

Lennon, T. M. (1993). *Statistics on social work education in the United States: 1992*. Alexandria, VA: Council on Social Work Education.

Lennon, T. M. (1994). *Statistics on social work education in the United States: 1993*. Alexandria, VA: Council on Social Work Education.

Lennon, T. M. (1995). *Statistics on social work education in the United States: 1994*. Alexandria, VA: Council on Social Work Education.

Lennon, T. M. (1996). *Statistics on social work education in the United States: 1995*. Alexandria, VA: Council on Social Work Education.

Lewandowski, C. A. (1998). Retention outcomes of a public child welfare long-term training program. *Professional Development: International Journal of Continuing Social Work Education, 1*, 38–46.

Lieberman, A., Hornby, H., & Russell, M. (1988). Analyzing the educational backgrounds and work experiences of child welfare personnel: A national study. *Social Work, 33*, 485–489.

Lieberman, A., & Levy, M. M. (2006). The (mis)measurement of job performance in child welfare using (non)experimental design. *Research on Social Work Practice, 16*, 417–418.

Lindsey, D. (1991a). Factors affecting the foster care placement decision: An analysis of national survey data. *American Journal of Orthopsychiatry, 61*, 272–281.

Lindsey, D. (1991b). Reliability of the foster care placement decision: A review. *Research in Social Work Practice, 2*, 65–80.

Lindsey, D. (2004). *The welfare of children*. New York: Oxford University Press.

Lindsey, D., Martin, S., & Doh, J. (2002). The failure of intensive casework services to reduce foster care placements: An examination of family preservation studies. *Children and Youth Services Review, 24*, 743–775.

Loewenberg, F. M. (Ed.). (1967). *Statistics on social work education: November 1, 1967 and academic year 1966–1967*. New York: Council on Social Work Education.

Loewenberg, F. M. (1968). *Statistics on social work education: November 1, 1968 and academic year 1967–1968*. New York: Council on Social Work Education.

Loewenberg, F. M. (Ed.). (1970). *Statistics on social work education: November 1, 1970 and academic year 1969–1970*. New York: Council on Social Work Education.

Loewenberg, F. M., & Shey, T. H. (Ed.). (1969). *Statistics on social work education: November 1, 1969 and academic year 1968–1969*. New York: Council on Social Work Education.

Lowrey, L. G. (1926). Some trends in the development of relationships between psychiatry and general social case work. *Mental Hygiene, 10*(2), 277–284.

Maas, H., & Engler, R. (1959). *Children in need of parents*. New York: Columbia University Press.

Macdonald, V. M. (1920). Social work and the national committee for mental hygiene. In *Proceedings of the national conference of social work at the forty-seventh annual session*. Chicago: University of Chicago Press.

Malm, K., Bess, R., Leos-Urbel, J., Green, R., & Markowitz, T. (2001). *Running to keep in place: The continuing evolution of our nation's child welfare system (Occasional Paper No. 54)*. Washington, DC: Urban Institute.

Maluccio, A., Fein, E., & Olmstead, K. (1986). *Permanency planning for children: Concepts and methods*. New York: Tavistock.

McCarthy, M. L. (2004). The relationship between supervision and casework retention in county based child welfare systems. *Dissertation Abstracts International: A. Humanities and Social Sciences, 65*(3), 1119A.

McCarthy, M. L. (2006). The context and process for performance evaluations: Necessary preconditions for the use of performance evaluations as a measure of performance—A critique of Perry. *Research on Social Work Practice, 16*, 419–423.

McDonald, J., & McCarthy, B. (1999). Effective partnership models between the state agencies, community, the university and community service providers. In *Child welfare training symposium: Changing paradigms of child welfare practice: Responding to opportunities and challenges* (pp. 43–72). Washington, DC: U.S. Children's Bureau.

McNeely, R. L. (1989). Gender, job satisfaction, earning and other characteristics of human service workers during and after midlife. *Administration in Social Work, 13*(2), 99–116.

Menefee, D. (1998). Identifying and comparing competencies for social work management: II. A replication study. *Administration in Social Work, 22*(4), 53–61.

Menefee, D., & Thompson, J. (1994). Identifying and comparing competencies for social work management: A practice driven approach. *Administration in Social Work, 18*(3), 1–25.

Meredith, L. A. (1933). Education and social work. In F. S. Hall (Ed.), *Social work year book: 1933* (pp. 137–142). New York: Sage.

Microsoft. (2004a). *Child care and welfare systems from Microsoft partners*. Retrieved February 10, 2005, from www.microsoft.com/Resources/Government/welfare.aspx?pf=true/.

Microsoft. (2004b). *Florida child welfare agency improves care for kids and use of resources*. Retrieved March 28, 2005, from www.microsoft.com/resources/casestudies/CaseStudy.asp?CaseStudyID=15543/.

Middleman, R. R., & Rhodes, G. B. (1985). *Competent supervision*. Englewood Cliffs, NJ: Prentice-Hall.

Miller, J. (2001). PDAs cut social workers' paper. *Government Computer News, 7*(12). Retrieved February 10, 2005, from www.gcn.com/state/7_12/tech-report/16783–1.html.

Mor Barak, M., Nissly, J., & Levin, A. (2001). Antecedents to retention and turnover among child welfare, social work, and other human service employees: What can we learn from past research? A review and meta-analysis. *Social Service Review, 75*, 625–661.

Morton, T. D., & Salas, M. K. (1994). *Supervising child protective services caseworkers*. Washington, DC: U.S. Department of Health and Human Services, Administration for Children and Families.

National Association of Foster Care Reviewers. (n.d.). *Foster care review: Past and present*. Retrieved March 2, 2006, from www.nafcr.org/docs/foster_cae_review/.

National Association of Public Child Welfare Administrators. (1987). *Guidelines for a model system of protective services for abused and neglected children and their families*. Washington, DC: American Public Welfare Association.

National Association of Public Child Welfare Administrators. (2005). *Guide for child welfare administrators on evidence-based practice*. Washington, DC: American Public Human Services Association. Available from www.aphsa.org/home/doc/Guide-for-Evidence-Based-Practice.pdf.

National Association of Social Workers. (1983). Membership survey shows practice shifts. *NASW News, 28*, 6–7.

National Association of Social Workers. (2004a). *The case for retaining the Title IV-E child welfare training program*. Retrieved March 1, 2005, from www.socialworkers.org/advocacy/updates/2003/081204b.asp.

National Association of Social Workers. (2004b). *Fact sheet: Title IV-E child welfare training program*. Retrieved January 20, 2005, from www.socialworkers.org/advocacy/updates/2003/081204a.asp.

National Association of Social Workers. (2004c). *If you're right for the job, it's the best job in the world*. Washington, DC: Author.

National Association of Social Workers. (2005). *NASW Standards for Social Work Practice in Child Welfare*. Washington, DC: Author.

National Center for Child Abuse and Neglect. (1988). *Study findings: Study of national incidence and prevalence of child abuse and neglect*. Washington, DC: U.S. Department of Health and Human Services.

National Resource Center for Information Technology in Child Welfare. (2002). Handheld devices and social work practice. *NRC-ITCW Tips, Tools and Trends, 3*. Retrieved March 24, 2005, from www.nrccwdt.org/docs/ttt_handheld.pdf.

National Resource Center for Information Technology in Child Welfare. (2003). Document imaging promising practice. *NRC-ITCW Tips, Tools and Trends, 7*. Retrieved March 24, 2005, from www.nrccwdt.org/docs/ttt_docimg.pdf.

Needell, B., Brookhart, A., & Lee, S. (2003). Black children and foster care placement in California. *Children and Youth Services Review, 25*(5/6), 393–408.

Norris, M., & Wallace, B. (Eds.). (1965). *The known and unknown in child welfare research: An appraisal*. New York: Child Welfare League of America.

NPower New York. (2002). *Mobile technology in the non-profit world*. Retrieved February 10, 2005, from www.npowerny.org/tools/mobilereport1.pdf.

O'Conner, I., Dalgleish, L., & Khan, J. (1984). A reflection of the rising spectre of conservatism: Motivational accounts of social work students. *British Journal of Social Work, 14*(3), 227–240.

Oktay, J. S. (1992). Burnout in hospital social workers who work with AIDS patients. *Social Work, 37*(5), 432–439.

Olsen, L., & Holmes, W. (1982). Educating child welfare workers: The effects of professional training on service delivery. *Journal of Education for Social Work, 18*(1), 94–102.

Quality Improvement Center on Privatization in Child Welfare. (2006). *Literature review on the privatization of child welfare services. Planning and learning*. Lexington: University of Kentucky, & Technologies, Inc.

Panel on Research on Child Abuse and Neglect, Commission. (1993). *Understanding child abuse and neglect* (Report of the Commission on Behavioral and Social Sciences and Education of the National Research Council). Washington, DC: National Academy Press.

Pecora, P., Briar, K., & Zlotnik, J. (1989). *Addressing the program and personnel crisis in child welfare: A social work response*. Silver Springs, MD: National Association of Social Workers Press.

Pecora, P., Fraser, M., & Haapala, D. (1991). Client outcomes and issues for program design. In K. Wells & D. Biegel (Eds.), *Family preservation services: Research and evaluation* (p. 3–32). Newbury Park, CA: Sage.

Pecora, P., Whitaker, J., Maluccio, A., Barth, R., & Plotnick, R. (2000). *The child welfare challenge: Policy, practice, and research*. New York: Aldine de Gruyter.

Perry, R. (2001). The classification, intercorrelation, and dynamic nature of MSW student practice preferences. *Journal of Social Work Education, 37*, 523–542.

Perry, R. (2004). Factors influencing MSW students' interest in public child welfare. *Journal of Human Behavior in the Social Environment, 10*(2), 1–31.

Perry, R. (2006a). Do social workers make better child welfare workers than non-social workers? *Research on Social Work Practice, 16*, 392–405.

Perry, R. (2006b). Education and child welfare supervisor performance: Does a social work degree matter? *Research on Social Work Practice, 16*, 591–604.

Perry, R., Graham, J., Kerce, K., & Babcock, P. (2004, August). *Determining workload standards for child protective services: Overview of an interactive web-based data collection instrument*. Paper presented at the 44th annual workshop of the national association for welfare research and statistics. Oklahoma City, Oklahoma.

Perry, R., & Houlious, C. (2006). *The partnership for strong families task analysis study*. Tallahassee, FL: Institute for Child and Family Services Research.

Pigou, A. C. (1952). *The economics of welfare* (4th ed.). London: Macmillan.

Pins, A. M. (1965). Development of social work recruitment: A historical review. *Social Service Review, 39*(1), 53–62.

Preston, M. S. (2004). Mandatory management training for newly hired child welfare supervisors: A divergence between management research and training practice? *Administration in Social Work, 28*(2), 81–97.

Pumphrey, R. E., & Pumphrey, M. W. (1961). *The heritage of American social work: Readings in its philosophical and institutional development*. New York: Columbia University Press.

Purvine, M. (Ed.). (1972). *Statistics on graduate social work education in the United States: 1972*. New York: Council on Social Work Education.

Reeser, L. C., & Epstein, I. (1990). *Professionalization and activism in social work: The sixties, the eighties, and the future*. New York: Columbia University Press.

Reisch, M., & Wenocur, S. (1986). The future of community organization in social work: Social activism and the politics of profession building. *Social Service Review*, *60*(1), 70–93.

Richmond, M. (1897). The need of a training school in applied philanthropy. In I. C. Barrows (Ed.), *Proceedings of the National Conference of Charities and Correction* (pp. 181–186). Toronto, Ontario, Canada: George H. Ellis.

Ripple, L. (Ed.). (1974). *Statistics on graduate social work education in the United States: 1973*. New York: Council on Social Work Education.

Ripple, L. (Ed.). (1975). *Statistics on social work education in the United States: 1974*. New York: Council on Social Work Education.

Risley-Curtiss, C. (2003). Current challenges and future directions for collaborative child welfare educational programs. *Journal of Human Behavior in the Social Environment*, *7*(1/2), 207–226.

Rittner, B., & Wodarski, J. S. (1999). Differential uses for, BSW and MSW educated social workers in child welfare services. *Children and Youth Services Review*, *21*, 217–238.

Roberts, A., & Yaeger, K. (Eds.). (2006). *Foundations of evidence based social work practice*. New York: Oxford University Press.

Rogers, C. M., Gray, E., & Aitken, S. (1992). *Final report: Summary proceedings and recommendations of the national incidence study expert conference*. Washington, DC: Consulting Services and Research.

Rosenthal, J. A., McDowell, E. C., & White, T. L. (1998). *Retention of child welfare workers in Oklahoma*. Norman: University of Oklahoma, School of Social Work.

Rosenthal, J. A., & Waters, E. (2004, July). *Retention and performance in public child welfare in Oklahoma: Focus on the child welfare professional enhancement program graduates*. Paper presented at the Weaving Resources for Better Child Welfare Outcomes Conference, Santa Fe, NM.

Ross, B., & Lichtenberg, P. (1963). *Enrollment in schools of social work*. New York: Council on Social Work Education.

Rossi, P. H. (1994). Review of "Families in crisis." *Children and Youth Services Review*, *16*, 461–465.

Rothman, J. (1991). A model of case management: Toward empirically based practice. *Social Work*, *36*, 520–528.

Rubin, A. (Ed.). (1981). *Statistics on social work education in the United States: 1980*. New York: Council on Social Work Education.

Rubin, A. (1982). *Statistics on social work education in the United States: 1981*. New York: Council on Social Work Education.

Rubin, A. (1983). *Statistics on social work education in the United States: 1982*. New York: Council on Social Work Education.

Rubin, A. (1984). *Statistics on social work education in the United States: 1983*. New York: Council on Social Work Education.

Rubin, A. (1985). *Statistics on social work education in the United States: 1984*. Washington, DC: Council on Social Work Education.

Rubin, A., & Johnson, P. J. (1984). Direct practice interests of entering MSW students. *Journal of Education for Social Work*, *20*(2), 5–16.

Rubin, A., & Whitcomb, G. R. (Eds.). (1978). *Statistics on social work education in the United States: 1977*. New York: Council on Social Work Education.

Rubin, A., & Whitcomb, G. R. (Eds.). (1979). *Statistics on social work education in the United States: 1978*. New York: Council on Social Work Education.

Russell, M., & Hornby, H. (1987). *1987 national study of public child welfare job requirements*. Portland: University of Southern Maine, National Child Welfare Resource Center for Management and Administration.

Ruston, A., & Nathan, J. (1996). The supervision of child protection work. *British Journal of Social Work, 26*, 357–374.

Rycus, J., & Hughes, R. (1994). *Child welfare competencies: Promoting family-centered, culturally relevant, and interdisciplinary child welfare practice and training*. Columbus, OH: Institute for Human Services.

Rycus, J., & Hughes, R. (1998). *Field guide to child welfare* (Vols. 1–4). Washington, DC: Child Welfare League of America.

Salas, M. (2004). *Supervising child protective services caseworkers*. Washington, DC: U.S. Department of Health and Human Services, Administration for Children and Families.

Samantrai, K. (1992). Factors in the decision to leave: Retaining social workers with MSWs in public child welfare. *Social Work, 37*(5), 454–458.

Scannapieco, M., & Connell-Carrick, K. (2003). Do collaborations with schools of social work make a difference for the field of child welfare? Practice, retention, and curriculum. *Journal of Human Behavior in the Social Environment, 7*(1/2), 35–51.

Sedlak, A. (1988). *Study of national incidence and prevalence of child abuse and neglect: Final report*. Washington, DC: U.S. Department of Health and Human Services.

Sedlak, A. (1991). *National incidence and prevalence of child abuse and neglect: 1988*. Rockville, MD: Westat.

Sedlak, A. (2001). *A history of the national incidence study of child abuse and neglect*. Rockville, MD: Westat.

Sedlak, A., & Broadhurst, D. D. (1996). *The third national incidence study of child abuse and neglect (NIS-3): Final report*. Washington, DC: U.S. Department of Health and Human Services, National Center on Child Abuse and Neglect.

Sheehan, J. C. (Ed.). (1976). *Statistics on social work education in the United States: 1975*. New York: Council on Social Work Education.

Shlonsky, A., & Gambrill, E. (2001). The need for comprehensive risk management systems in child welfare. *Children and Youth Services Review, 23*, 79–107.

Shlonsky, A., & Gibbs, L. (2004). Will the real evidence-based practice please stand up? Teaching the process of evidence-based practice to the helping professions. *Brief Treatment and Crisis Intervention, 4*, 137–152.

Shlonsky, A., & Wagner, D. (2005). The next step: Integrating actuarial risk assessment and clinical judgment into an evidence-based practice framework in CPS case management. *Children and Youth Services Review, 27*, 409–427.

Shyne, A. W., & Whitcomb, G. R. (Eds.). (1977). *Statistics on social work education in the United States: 1976*. New York: Council on Social Work Education.

Sklar, K. K. (1995). *Florence Kelley and the nation's work*. New Haven, CT: Yale University Press.

Smith, B. D. (2004). Job retention in child welfare: Effects of perceived organizational support, supervisor support, and intrinsic job value. *Children and Youth Services Review, 27*, 153–169.

Spaulding, E. C. (1988). *Statistics on social work education in the United States: 1987*. Washington, DC: Council on Social Work Education.

Spaulding, E. C. (1990). *Statistics on social work education in the United States: 1989*. Alexandria, VA: Council on Social Work Education.

Spaulding, E. C. (1991). *Statistics on social work education in the United States: 1990*. Alexandria, VA: Council on Social Work Education.

Specht, H., & Courtney, M. E. (1994). *Unfaithful angels: How social work has abandoned its mission*. New York: Free Press.

Stein, T., & Gambrill, E. (1976). *Decision making in foster care: A training manual*. Berkeley, CA: University Extension Publications.

Stein, T., Gambrill, E., & Wiltse, K. T. (1978). *Children in foster homes: Achieving continuity of care*. New York: Praegar Press.

Stein, T., & Rzepnicki, T. (1984). *Decision-making in child welfare services: Intake and planning*. Hingham, MA: Kluwer-Nijoff/Kluwer Academic.

Terpstra, J. (1996). *Child welfare, from there to where?* Unpublished manuscript, U.S. Children's Bureau, Washington, DC.

Thomlison, B. (2003). Characteristics of evidence-based child maltreatment interventions. *Child Welfare*, *82*, 541–569.

Thomlison, B. (2005, September). Using evidence-based knowledge to improve policies and practices in child welfare: Current thinking and continuing challenges. *Research on Social Work Practice*, *15*(5), 321–322.

Thyer, B. A., Williams, M., Love, J. P., & Sowers-Hoag, K. (1989). The MSW supervisory requirement in field instruction: Does it make a difference? *Clinical Supervisor*, *6*, 249–256.

Tropman, J., Faller, K., & Feldt, S. (2004). *Essentials of supervisory skills for child welfare managers*. Ann Arbor: University of Michigan, School of Social Work. Retrieved July 12, 2005, from www.umich.edu/tpcws/articles/EntireEditedManual_91404CE.pdf#search='child20welfare %20supervisors'/.

University of Southern Maine. (1987). *Professional social work practice in public child welfare: An agenda for action*. National Child Welfare Resource Center for Management Administration, Portland, ME: Author.

U.S. Advisory Board on Child Abuse and Neglect. (1990). *Child abuse and neglect: Critical first steps in response to a national emergency*. Washington, DC: U.S. Department of Health and Human Services.

U.S. Department of Health, Education, and Welfare. (1965). *Closing the gap in social work manpower: Report of the departmental task force on social work education and manpower*. Washington, DC: U.S. Government Printing Office.

U.S. Department of Health and Human Services. (1996). *National child abuse and neglect report*. Washington, DC: (Author).

U.S. Department of Health and Human Services, Administration on Children, Youth, and Families. (1997). *Child maltreatment, 1995*. Washington, DC: U.S. Government Printing Office.

U.S. Department of Health and Human Services, Administration on Children, Youth, and Families. (2001). *Child maltreatment, 1999*. Washington, DC: U.S. Government Printing Office.

U.S. Department of Health and Human Services, Administration on Children, Youth, and Families. (2003). *Child maltreatment, 2001*. Washington, DC: U.S. Government Printing Office.

U.S. Department of Health and Human Services, Administration on Children, Youth, and Families. (2004). *Child maltreatment, 2002*. Washington, DC: U.S. Government Printing Office.

U.S. Department of Health and Human Services, Administration on Children, Youth, and Families. (2005). *Child maltreatment, 2003*. Washington, DC: U.S. Government Printing Office.

U.S. Department of Health and Human Services, Administration on Children, Youth, and Families. (2006). *Child maltreatment, 2004*. Washington, DC: U.S. Government Printing Office.

U.S. General Accounting Office. (1995). *Child welfare: Complex needs strain capacity to provide services*. Washington, DC: Author.

U.S. General Accounting Office. (2003). *Child welfare: HHS could play a greater role in helping child welfare agencies recruit and retain staff*. Washington, DC: Author.

Usher, C. L., & Wildfire, J. B. (2003). Evidence-based practice in community-based child welfare systems. *Child Welfare*, *82*, 597–614.

Vinokur-Kaplan, D., & Hartman, A. (1986). A national profile of child welfare workers and supervisors. *Child Welfare, 65*(4), 323–335.

Walker, S. H. (1928). *Social work and the training of social workers*. Chapel Hill: University of North Carolina Press.

Wallace, M. E. (1982). Private practice: A nationwide study. *Social Work, 27*, 262–267.

Webster, D., Barth, R. P., & Needell, B. (2000). Placement stability for children in out-of-home care: A longitudinal analysis. *Child Welfare, 79*, 614–632.

Weiner, M. E. (1991). Motivating employees to achieve. In R. E. Edwards & J. A. Yankey (Eds.), *Skills for effective human services management* (pp. 302–316). Silver Spring, MD: National Association of Social Workers Press.

Weisz, V., & Thai, N. (2003). The court-appointed special advocate (CASA) program: Bringing information to child abuse and neglect cases. *Child Maltreatment, 9*, 204–210.

Welte, M. (2005). *Major federal child welfare laws*. Retrieved July 2, 2006, from www.casanet.org/reference/major-child -welfare-laws.htm.

West, W. M. (1933). Social work as a profession. In F. S. Hall (Ed.), *Social work year book: 1933* (492–496). New York: Sage.

Westbrook, T. M. (2006). *Initial development and validation of the Child Welfare Organizational Culture Inventory*. Unpublished doctoral dissertation, University of Georgia, Athens.

Westbrook, T. M., Ellis, J., & Ellett, A. J. (2006). Improving retention among public child welfare staff: What can we learn from the insight and experiences of committed survivors? *Administration in Social Work, 30*(4), 37–62.

Western Interstate Commission for Higher Education. (1965). *Report of the conferences on undergraduate education for the social services: An examination of the role of undergraduate education in the preparation of personnel for corrections and social welfare*. Inglewood: California State Colleges.

Whitaker, J., & Maluccio, A. (2002). Rethinking "Child Placement": A reflective essay. *Social Service Review, 76*, 108–134.

Williamson, M. (1935). *The social worker in the prevention and treatment of delinquency*. New York: Columbia University Press.

Winston, E. (1965). New dimensions in public welfare: Implications for social work education. In council on social work education social work. *Education and social welfare manpower: Present realities and future imperatives*. New York: Council on Social Work Education.

Witte, E. F. (1960). Developing professional leadership for social programs. *The Annals of the American Academy of Political and social Sciences, 329*(1), 123–136.

Witte, E. F. (1966). Articulation between graduate and undergraduate education for the social services. In *Observations on undergraduate social welfare education* (pp. 27–34). New York: Council on Social Work Education.

Wittman, M. (1965). Information on personnel needs and social work students: Implications for manpower planning and research and for programs of recruitment and education. In *Social work education and social welfare manpower: Present realities and future imperatives* (pp. 15–25). New York: Council on Social Work Education.

Wolf, E. P., & Lebeaux, C. N. (1968). Class and race in the changing city: Searching for new approaches to old problems. In L. F. Schmore (Ed.), *Social science and the city: A survey of urban research* (pp. 99–129). New York: Praeger.

Wulczyn, F. H., Barth, R. P., Yuan, Y. T., Harden, B. J., & Landsverk, J. (2005). *Beyond common sense: Child welfare, child well-being and the evidence for policy reform*. New Brunswick, NJ: Aldine.

Wulczyn, F. H., Harden, A. W., & George, R. M. (1998). *Foster care dynamics, 1983–1997: An update from the multistate foster care data archive*. Chicago: University of Chicago, Chapin Hall Center for Children.

Youngclarke, D., Ramos, K. & Granger-Merkle, L. (2004). A systematic review of the impact of court appointed special advocates. *Journal of the Center for Families, Children, and the Courts*, 109–126.

Zlotnik, K. (1993). *Social work education and public human services: Developing partnerships.* Alexandria, VA: Council on Social Work Education.

Zlotnik, J. (2002). Preparing social workers for child welfare practice: Lessons from an historical review of the literature. *Journal of Health and Social Policy, 15*, 5–21.

Zlotnik, J. (2003). The use of Title IV-E training funds for social work education: An historical perspective. *Journal of Human Behavior in the Social Environment, 7*, 5–20.

Zlotnik, J. (2006). No simple answers to a complex question: A response to Perry. *Research on Social Work Practice, 16*, 414–416.

Zlotnik, J., DePanfilis, D., Daining, C., & Lane, M. M. (2005). *Factors influencing retention of child welfare staff: A systematic review of research.* Washington, DC: Institute for the Advancement of Social Work Research.

Chapter 9

FAMILY CENTERED PRACTICE

Barbara Thomlison

In the past 2 decades, family-centered practice has shown a great deal of promise for preventing many child problem behaviors and demonstrating improvements in family functioning. Research in general suggests that when families are strong and parents are competent, there are significant decreases in the risk of child and youth problem behaviors, mental health problems, delinquency, criminal behavior, and other interrelated problems as the factors that mediate these risks (Fraser, Kirby, & Smokowksi, 2004; Kazdin & Weisz, 2003). Effective family-centered interventions are comprehensive in nature, and they conceptually employ an ecological-developmental approach, within a family system perspective, to understand family processes and continuity of problem behavior over time. This model captures the ongoing interactions among aspects of contexts and persons. From this approach, problem behaviors are viewed as having multiple determinants and there are multiple pathways to a specific problem behavior (Ferrer-Wreder, Stattin, Cass Lorente, Tubman, & Adamson, 2004). This model is based on the assumption that family-of-origin experiences impact, in a significant manner, children's relationships and developmental outcomes (Widom, 1989). Child and youth behavior problems serve a function within the family system and are initiated and maintained by maladaptive interpersonal processes (Liddle & Rowe, 2006). Interventions therefore target multiple risk factors to change destructive interactional patterns and enhance protective factors to reinforce positive ways of responding to establish more adaptive outcomes.

Family relationships are sources of the most intense emotions in people's lives; they are both the source of joy and happiness under positive circumstances (Baumeister & Leary, 1995; Scherer, Wallbott, & Summerfield, 1986) and great distress and sorrow when things go badly (Bowlby, 1982; Mira, 2007). Therefore, since family and family relationships are important to who we become as an individual, it is critical to think of approaching child and youth problem behaviors with a family-centered approach. Many different types of family-centered interventions exist that are as diverse as the families they serve. These interventions have been applied to numerous disorders among children, adolescents, and adults, and have demonstrated efficacy with each target population (Liddle & Rowe, 2006). Family-centered interventions generally demonstrate superior effects to no-treatment groups or alternative treatments (Shadish, Ragsdale, Glaser, & Montgomery, 1995). Engagement and retention rates of clients and their families are enhanced even with the most difficult problems. Family-centered interventions appear to be most effective with child behavior problems, substance use disorders, and marital and relationship stress (Dishion & Kavanagh, 2003; Kumpfer & Alvarado, 1998; Shadish et al., 1995; Szapocznik & Williams, 2000).

This chapter provides a summary to family-centered interventions for social workers, educators, and those practitioners interested in an effective intervention approach to selected child and youth problem behaviors. The chapter has two goals.

First, it provides background information on the theoretical context for family-centered practice. A summary of the ecological-developmental perspective is provided to aid in understanding the influences from transactions of multiple contexts on family behavior. Given that a number of risk and protective factors have been linked to different adjustment patterns among children and adolescents, a brief overview of risk and resiliency factors linked to outcomes is presented. This assists in understanding what is needed to overcome problems and which protective factors to focus on as the critical supports and opportunities for children and families.

Second, the chapter identifies exemplary family-centered interventions as preventing problems in childhood and promoting the advancement of positive youth development. Based on the number of effective family-focused strategies for targeted family needs and family types, only parenting and family strengthening programs are included here (Kumpfer & Alvarado, 1998). These evidence-based programs are classified within a framework developed by the Institute of Medicine into three categories: universal, selective, and indicated preventive interventions. Each of the interventions included here are based on published findings from studies which employed either a representative community sample or a clinical sample with an appropriate control group, clearly defined the problem targeted by the intervention and, described the intervention in adequate detail to permit replication. In some cases, a treatment manual is available (Thomlison & Craig, 2005). To the extent possible, the programs are organized by the guidelines proposed by the Institute of Medicine (Mrazek & Haggerty, 1994). The first category attempts to prevent problems and the second and third categories provide services to those at risk for or identified as having a problem:

- *Universal preventive interventions* target the general public or an entire population of interest such as schools or a group of classrooms without attempting to identify which particular children are at risk (e.g., childhood immunizations; media based parenting information campaign).
- *Selective preventive interventions* target subgroups of the general population who are at higher risk for developing a problem than other members of the broader population (e.g., folic acid for women of child-bearing age; information and advice for specific parenting or child behavior or development concerns).
- *Indicated preventive interventions* target individuals who have detectable signs or symptoms of difficulty but not long-standing serious problems or full-blown clinical disorders (e.g., parent education and skills training for children with multiple behavior problems or aggressive behavior or learning delays).

FAMILY-CENTERED APPROACH

Prior to family-centered practice, social workers approached problem solving by focusing on individual maladaptive behaviors, believing the solution was within the individual and attempting to deal with intrapsychic aspects of the personality. The influence of family-centered practice first appeared in the 1950s as researchers such as Scherz, Bateson, Jackson, Haley, and Satir (as cited in Janzen, Harris, Jordan, & Franklin, 2006) observed that the only way to understand or help the individual was within the interaction of family members and the various contextual influences that the family interacts with. The assumption is that the individual can only be understood within the context of the family, and the contributions of family dynamics to the individual's functioning. In this regard, the child or adolescent is part of the family and therefore cannot be understood or helped apart from the family if changes in behavior are to be maintained. By seeing members of the family, the practitioner then has information about family interaction, family difficulties, and family supports. Then the role of each member in the family structure and process is apparent. Attending to the family as a transactional system requires the practitioner to think in terms of two or more people interacting and influencing each other (Thomlison, 2007). Thus, a different perspective of problem formulation and problem solution is required because the family as a unit, and not the individual, requires the intervention. In particular, evidence-based or empirically supported family-centered interventions that are ecologically sound need to be used when making a clinical decision to offer service (Gambrill, 2006). Although outcomes of research differ by type of family intervention, overall, family-centered interventions tend to have more immediate and direct impact on improving family difficulties (Kumpfer & Alvarado, 1998) and family functioning (Liddle & Rowe, 2006).

Family-centered practice is not one method or model of practice but a way of thinking about practice or intervention. It is an ideology where families are a central and lasting element in children's lives (Hooper-Briar & Lawson, 1994). When children experience problems, services often place the child in the center as the main focus for change. However, if the family is not involved, then there are low expectations for the family to change and the family can continue to blame the child for difficulties (Dishion & Kavanagh, 2003; Szapocznik & Williams, 2000). More importantly, it is essential that families understand their role in their child's development and behavior difficulties. In this way, family-centered intervention provides information and skills necessary to raise healthy children and promote learning opportunities. The environment where the child and family develop informs us about their strengths, supports, emerging competencies, stresses, and needs (Thomlison, 2007, p. 14). This view of family-centered practice underscores the value of maintaining and enhancing family relationships.

PRINCIPLES OF EFFECTIVE FAMILY-CENTERED PRACTICE

Principles and assumptions underpinning family-centered practice are supported by the empirical research in family interventions. The principles of effective interventions are:

- The focus is the entire family. Families are unique systems of influence.
- The family is viewed as the expert and therefore the best source for solutions to their difficulties. Families need to be involved as full partners in the change process.
- Place emphasis on family strengths, assets, and their aspirations because this promotes resilience. Reframe the problem as a strength because this leads to finding more strengths.

- Be sensitive, nonjudgmental, and, above all, do not blame.
- Interventions need to have multicomponents that address critical domains and influence the development and perpetuation of the behaviors to be prevented. The context of interventions considers social and environmental factors, personal beliefs, and cultural values as influences on development and behavior.
- Environmental influences play a critical role in impacting various individual and family behaviors. Interventions need to fit the community and cultural norms of the family.
- Consider each family's personal beliefs and preferences. This affirms that the family's own solutions to problems are the ones that are most effective and long lasting.
- The goal is to instill hope in the family, provide realistic possibilities, and build positive experiences for family members and to look forward (Thomlison, 2007).

THEORETICAL FRAMEWORK FOR FAMILY-CENTERED PRACTICE

Frameworks provided for family-centered practice emerge from tested principles and concepts in evaluated practice programs. The principles were designed to target risk factors and enhance protective factors associated with problem behaviors. Although intervention programs vary among the developers, all programs are alike in that they begin with an understanding of factors that children and their families at risk, or protect them from a problem behavior (National Institute for Drug Abuse, 2003). Treatment outcomes and clinically relevant conclusions from process studies of family change mechanisms inform the theory and conceptual framework for practice. With respect to theory, this approach draws on both the structural (Minuchin, 1974) and strategic family systems theories (Haley, 1976; Szapocznik & Williams, 2000) and other empirically derived findings from developmental psychopathology prevention studies. This section summarizes the major conceptual elements to family-centered practice, including ecological-transaction model, family structural framework, social development model, and social learning systems, as well as the family risk and resiliency factors as the unifying descriptive and predictive framework for strengthening families. The emphasis on the family in these perspectives is consistent with application to most minority culturally defined values on the developmental trajectories of children and family interventions (Kumpfer, Alvarado, Smith, & Bellamy, 2002; Szapocznik & Williams, 2000).

Ecological-Transactional Overview

An ecological perspective focuses both on the individual and the context. Children and youth, and their families, are viewed as operating or influenced by interdependent parts or systems ranging from peers to schools, neighborhood and community contexts (Fraser, 2004). In social work, some individuals refer to this as the person-in-environment perspective first described by Tharp and Wetzel in 1969 (Gambrill, 1997, p. 212). This model captures the ongoing interactions among aspects of families, the multiple environments they experience, and their prior developmental history. All of these systems interact in an ongoing manner and they constantly influence each other. Development is influenced then by the social ecological transactions throughout childhood (Bronfenbrenner, 1986).

The family is a unique system, with particular responsibilities and functions. It is a special environment for socializing children and youth. Families interact and are interdependent with parts of itself and with other systems from the environment outside of the family. Families and the multiple systems interacting with them mutually influence each other's behavior. Any and all change affects all family members. The family needs to be able to create a balance between change and stability—adaptation or maladaptation. Understanding families and their social environments helps to locate the place for intervention. This model provides a rationale for intervention efforts that target multiple risk factors for a specific problem behavior outcome, and enhance protective factors predictive of more adaptive outcomes (Ferrer-Wreder et al., 2004). It does not tell us which interventions to use, but evidence-supported practice assists with that decision (Roberts & Yeager, 2004; Thomlison, 2007).

Within the systems influencing the family, the idea is to identify risk factors, or those influences leading to harm, and the strengths or protective factors and influences that will lead to resilience. By approaching a complicated family situation from the ecological perspective, the practitioner can be somewhat more objective about the family issues. Practitioners who see the family context as interactions of multiple systems—the family and its social environments—will be better able to build on strengths in families and promote family self-change, a notion critical to practice. The goal of many intervention programs is to change the family's attitudes, motivations, skills, knowledge, and behaviors. Families then can be linked to resources they need to be successful. When children have supportive connections between and across their social contexts, family, school, neighborhood and community, then prosocial outcomes and positive youth development occurs. Interventions may also be designed to address the child and family within a particular environment or in multiple contexts.

Family Structural Framework

The structural approach (Nichols & Schwartz, 2004) emphasizes the importance of family structure, family subsystems, boundaries, and the patterns of interactions as integral to understanding family functioning. Interactions between families and their environments determine how parents and children adapt to the stresses in their environments. Family interactions that elicit satisfactory responses in the family structure (patterns of interactions) meet individual and family demands and needs, and families flourish; and where there is difficulty responding effectively, disorganization and dysfunction results (Thomlison, 2007). Maladaptive family interactions are an important contributor to ongoing problem behaviors and to the maintenance of problem behaviors (Szapocznik & Williams, 2000). Lack of personal and familial skills and resources are the primary reasons families have difficulty responding positively to stress and demands in their environments. Other factors include family experiences and the presence of resilient factors (Rothery & Enns, 2001).

Family structure refers to the boundaries or "invisible demarcations or dividers between family members or among parts of the system, such as between parents and children (the parent-child subsystem), or between the family and the community" (Thomlison, 2007, p. 38). Families function through these boundary interactions and functions often define boundaries. The major subsystems defining boundaries that develop in the family structure over time include the couple subsystem, the parental subsystem, the sibling subsystem, and the parent-child subsystem (Janzen et al., 2006). Parental roles may be filled by other caregivers such as grandparents, aunts, or nonrelated individuals.

Structure develops around belief systems, ideas, or roles. Interactions then regulate contact between the individuals, children and parents and therefore determine the amount of contact with others outside of the family (Nichols & Schwartz, 2004). This interaction can be characterized as satisfactory or unsatisfactory responses from other family members. It organizes the ways in which family members interact and support autonomy and differentiation of its members. Repeated transactions result in interactional patterns between the family and its members and the community and establish healthy functioning or dysfunction. The greater the clarity and distinction of interactional patterns, the more effective the family functions. Boundaries and interaction patterns change across the life span. Healthy boundaries allow members to shift and change as needed (Thomlison, 2007).

Family interactions emerge also from family rules that are overt (articulated) or covert (implicit). Rules, either implicit or explicit, prescribe the agreed on relational patterns that organize and provide family management. Both rules and roles describe the characteristics and functioning of the family system. For example, the power hierarchy is influenced by the rules indicating the differential levels of authority between the parents and the children. Interventions should aim at changing family patterns of interaction between parents and children to help them achieve an improved style of communication and thereby change family relations that in turn changes family problems.

Social Development Model

The primary social contexts for child and youth development are the family, school, peer, and neighborhood, and these are interrelated influences. The social development model (SDM) developed by Catalano, Haggerty, Oesterle, Fleming, and Hawkins (2004) attempts to build attachment and commitment of individuals to these socializing units. It is through their impact on family members that interactions with these systems have an impact on children and youth (Hawkins et al., 1992). They may enrich or impoverish the individual's development (Szapocznik & Williams, 2000). Cultural patterns and acculturation and institutionalized policies also contribute in both positive and damaging ways to influence a child's development. "The stronger and more complementary the linkages within and between systems, the more powerful their influence on a child's development" (Perrino et al., as cited in Szapocznik & Williams, 2000, p. 127). Children directly participate and learn patterns of behavior whether prosocial or antisocial from these environments, through four processes:

1. Opportunities for involvement in activities and interactions with others.
2. Actual involvement.
3. Skill for involvement and interaction with others.
4. Perceived rewards from involvement and interaction.

Involvement is seen as part of the socialization process that leads to bonding, and the values and beliefs of the social unit acts as a mediator of the effect of bonding on behavior outcomes. Prosocial or antisocial behavior is impacted by social interactions. Children will form social bonds to significant others if the following conditions are met:

- The child thinks there is a viable change for a social interaction to take place.
- The child has to actually engage in a social encounter.
- Children and their partners must have adequate skills to successfully interact.
- The child expects that the social exchange will be a rewarding experience (Ferrer-Wreder et al., 2004, p. 160).

Through this additive and cyclical social learning process children, are able to develop lasting positive attachments.

Social Skills Training

A social skills approach describes the mechanisms by which individuals learn to behave in social contexts and influences both prosocial and antisocial patterns of behavior. It is based on the notion of competence, which suggests that behavior problems are the result of deficits in a child's or parent's response to a situation. Interactional patterns are often the basis for change in behavior. Teaching prosocial interactional skills and competencies enhances relationships and improves day-to-day functioning between children, their families, and others in their environment. These techniques attempt to change the stimuli and cues that reinforce negative behavior. Social skills training is effective in teaching parents more appropriate discipline methods which is helpful in strengthening families. For children and youth, effective techniques include: withholding attention, natural and logical consequences, time-out, assigning extra work, and taking away privileges (Janzen et al., 2006). Intervention components attempt to improve the parent-child relationship and then focus on family communication, parental monitoring, and discipline (Kumpfer & Alvarado, 1998). The programs are distinguished from parent education because they include a structured set of behavioral skills in parenting. Other skills training techniques include behavioral rehearsal to teach role performance and build confidence and contracting for changes in behavior. Learning new skills involves a four-step process:

1. The social worker models or demonstrates the skill.
2. The child and parent role-play and practice the skill in front of the social worker.
3. The parent and child are assigned to practice the skill in daily life.
4. The social worker provides feedback to the child and parent regarding the success in learning the new skill (Janzen et al., 2006, p. 161; Thomlison, 2007).

Teaching parents to increase monitoring and supervision of children and youth has been found to be a strong mediator of peer influence (Dishion, French, & Patterson, 1995; Kumpfer & Alvarado, 1998). Parenting skills training programs are effective in reducing coercive family interactions (Dishion & Kavanagh, 2003; Webster-Stratton, Kolpacoff, & Hollingsworth, 1988) and improving parental monitoring (Dishion & Kavanagh, 2003).

Risk Factors

Risk factors include characteristics or conditions such as biological, psychological, behavioral, social, and environment factors that, if present for a given child, make it more likely that this child rather than another child selected from the general population, will experience a specific problem (Fraser, 2004; Thomlison & Craig, 2005). Risk factors are present in every system the child interacts with. Risk factors often occur together or cluster to produce heightened susceptibility for a problem. As the number of risk factors increases, the cumulation exerts an increasingly strong influence on parent and child (Dishion & Kavanagh, 2003; Fraser et al., 2004). Examples of common risk factors at the neighborhood and community level include too few opportunities for education and employment, racial discrimination and injustice and poverty. Risk factors at the family level include child maltreatment, family history of behavioral problems, family conflict and marital discord, poor parent mental health, poor parent-child relationship, poor supervision of the child, and harsh parenting (Fraser, 2004; Thomlison, 2004).

The more risk factors a child experiences in interactions with various systems, the more likely that he or she will experience problems such as substance abuse, delinquency, school dropout, and other related problems (Dishion & Kavanagh, 2003). Not all risk factors are susceptible to change such as gender, race, or genetic susceptibility to substance use (National Institute for Drug Abuse, 2003). Research has found, however, that specific risks can be reduced, for example, by treating mental disorders, improving parent and family management skills, and family interactions (Dishion & Kavanagh, 2003; Janzen et al., 2006). Hawkins et al. (1992), Kumpfer and Alvarado (1998), and other researchers repeatedly identify the following 10 factors that increase vulnerability in youth:

1. Lack of bonding to family, school, or community.
2. Frequent, early antisocial behavior.
3. Family history of high-risk behaviors.
4. Poor family management.
5. High family conflict.
6. Social and economic deprivation.
7. Failure in school.
8. Low commitment to education.
9. Associating with delinquent peers.
10. Disorganization of community.

Risky Parenting Practices

Many childhood and adolescent behavior disorders are strongly and consistently linked to a number of poor or ineffective parenting practices that maintain antisocial behavior into and through adolescence (Liddle & Rowe, 2006). Two factors are related to these outcomes. First, antisocial behavior is learned at an early age in the home through negative reinforcement of coercive patterns, which then generalizes to school and peer group environments. When there is both coercive parenting and poor parental monitoring at age 4.5 there is the emergence of conduct problems among socioeconomically disadvantaged minority children by age 6 (Liddle & Rowe, 2006, p. 97). Second, family conditions such as child maltreatment, family violence, conflict between parents, and harsh or abusive parenting and child-rearing practices increase the risk factors for child and adolescent problem behaviors. In addition, parental conditions such as substance abuse and mental disorders are strongly related to family risk factors for behavior problems. Again, children who do not have positive parent-child interactions are twice as likely to have persistent behavioral problems than those who have positive interactions (Bry, Catalano, Kumpfer, Lochman, & Szapocznik, 1998; Dishion & Kavanagh, 2003; Liddle & Rowe, 2006). For example, poor parenting practices, such as inadequate supervision of children, inconsistent responses to children's behavior, and constant nagging, may increase the risk that a child will be noncompliant at home, school, and in other settings. Frequently, families are experiencing several of these risk factors simultaneously, thereby compounding the developmental issues facing the child.

"Research on parenting clarifies that it is what parents do, and not their history, that has the most influence on children's protection and risk. Parents who have insight about their own past, and who have acquired parenting skills to respond competently, are less likely to perpetuate pathology across generations" (Dishion & Kavanagh, 2003, p. 13). Research identifies the following ineffective parenting practices:

- *Child maltreatment and family violence:* Children and adolescents exposed to parental maltreatment and family violence tend to develop aggressive and violent coping styles in their interpersonal relationships and in their school and peer environments. This behavior places them at risk for delinquency, criminal behavior, and school dropout. Women who are exposed to intimate partner violence are less able to care for their children (Kumpfer, Molgaard, & Spoth, 1996; Thomlison, 2004).
- *Conflict between parents:* The presence of spousal discord, threats of separation, and conflict in the social support network are associated with distress and ability to parent (Dishion & Kavanagh, 2003; Webster-Stratton & Taylor, 2001). Children also learn aggression through observing aggression in their family (Hawkins et al., 1992).
- *Harsh discipline practices:* Parents who are low on warmth and nurturing qualities and high on criticism are likely to use harsh or excessive physical punishment in their problem-solving responses to child discipline situations (Kumpfer & Alvarado, 1998). Coercive parent-child interactions may emerge when children display aggressive and noncompliant behaviors toward a parent with distorted child-rearing knowledge (Dishion & Kavanagh, 2003). Webster-Stratton and Taylor (2001) found that children who are more impulsive and quick to anger tend to overwhelm parents and raise the risk of negative parental responses such as those characterized by high arousal, anger, and harsh discipline—all risk factors for ineffective parenting. For a more thorough review of risk factors for conduct disorders, see Dishion and Kavanagh (2003), Webster-Stratton and Taylor (2001), and Hawkins and colleagues (1992).
- *Poor family management:* Parents who lack involvement with, spend little time with their child, and who are unavailable to provide support in times of stress have poor family management skills. This includes low levels of supervision and poor monitoring child and adolescent behavior, and ineffective skills to manage child and youth behaviors (Hawkins et al., 1992; Olds, 2002). Children who experience nonnurturing

relationships show impairment in their ability to develop positive and reciprocal interpersonal relationships with others and are described by their parents as noncompliant compared with children who have strong bonds of attachment who develop a deep sense of belonging and security (Dishion & Kavanagh, 2003). A predictable, stable, and consistent parenting environment is central for attachments to develop.

Family Protective and Resilience Factors

At the heart of any given intervention is the aim of enhancing specific protective factors to permit functioning under adversity. Resilience allows the child or family to maintain a normative or high level of functioning when confronted with a time-limited stressor or a developmental challenge. Protective factors mediate or moderate the effect of the risk factors and result in reducing the risk that the problem will occur. Protective factors such as strong family bonds and success in school help safeguard children from many problems. Personal attributes and positive school, peer, and community conditions lower the chances of poor developmental outcomes in the presence of risk (Fraser, 2004; Pollard, Hawkins, & Arthur, 1999; Thomlison, 2004). Protective factors appear to buffer or balance the negative impact of risk factors. An example of a protective factor linked to positive adolescent development is a family's positive and promotive daily interactions (Kumpfer & Alvarado, 1998). Caring and support, positive experiences, and ongoing opportunities for participation in families and communities are powerful protective factors (Ferrer-Wreder et al., 2004).

One consistent finding in the resilience research is that positive parent-child interactions is the most influential factor in shaping child and youth behavior (Fraser et al., 2004; Kumpfer & Alvarado, 1998). So, how do these relationships develop? Positive parent-child interactions and relationships develop among parents with high self-esteem and self-efficacy and who function within normal boundaries of socially accepted behavior and social competence (Kinard, 1999; Rutter, 1987, 2000). Protective parent-child interactions include:

- Use of nonviolent methods of teaching and discipline.
- High levels of warmth and acceptance and low levels of criticism.
- Low levels of stress and aggression in the family, (d) high levels of monitoring and supervision of children.
- A positive and supportive parent-child relationship.
- The presence of a supportive spouse or partner.
- Socioeconomic stability, success at work and school.
- Sufficient social supports and positive adult role models in their life (Dishion & Kavanagh, 2003; Thomlison, 2004).

Research consistently emphasizes parenting skill and competence as one of the strongest protective factors regardless of child characteristics such as easy going temperament or other personal attributes (Guterman & Embry, 2004; Olds & Kitzman, 1993; Osofsky & Thompson, 2000; Veltman & Browne, 2001).

When problem behaviors emerge within the context of family risk factors then they are likely to continue in other settings or systems and through adolescence (Bernard, 2002;

Dishion & Kavanagh, 2003). Researchers and prevention specialists (Kumpfer, Alexander, McDonald, & Olds, 1989) suggest that the major strengths of a family-centered approach to many child and adolescent problems is improving the ways that parents care for and socialize their children so that family relationships improve. These interventions teach skills that are effective for improving family communication, discipline, and establishing firm and consistent rule making in parents of young children (Kumpfer et al., 1996, 1998; Spoth, Kavanagh, & Dishion, 2002; Webster-Stratton, 1998; Webster-Stratton & Taylor, 2001).

Bry et al. (1998) and other researchers identify the following five major types of family protective factors in promoting resilience to child and youth problems:

1. Supportive parent-child relationships.
2. Positive discipline methods.
3. Monitoring and supervision.
4. Families who advocate for their children.
5. Parents who seek information and support.

Kumpfer and Alvarado (1998) and Dunst and Trivett, (1994) found characteristics of strong, resilient African American families to be a strong economic base, a strong achievement orientation, adaptability of family roles, spirituality, strong kinship bonds, racial pride, display of respect and acceptance, resourcefulness, community involvement, and family unity characteristics. A strong family is the basis of positive family socialization processes and therefore, when strong family management functions are present in family systems, these processes act as a protective factor (Dishion & Kavanagh, 2003).

Positive parental attachment, relational competence, and parent-child interaction in particular afford children the opportunity to develop skills for positive social interaction and behavior (Bernard, 2006; Liddle & Rowe, 2006). Although many succeed regardless of their families, it is the effect of parenting that acts as a protective factor in the more extreme situations, such as in violent and unsafe homes (Blum et al., 2000; Masten et al., 1999).

EFFECTIVE FAMILY-CENTERED PROGRAMS

Selecting the best or most effective family-centered intervention must be done carefully with the target population in mind and knowledge of the developmental stage of the child and the types of risk factors in the family served. Be sure the interventions are of sufficient intensity and duration to address the large number of risk factors and inadequate number of protective factors that affect children and their families (National Institute for Drug Abuse, 2003). Many programs are too narrow in focus and do not attend to the fully range of child outcomes, such as cognitive, behavioral, emotional, physical, and social needs of the child, nor do they attend to the child's needs in all environments until positives developmental changes are demonstrated to have a long-term impact (Kumpfer & Alvarado, 1998). Family-centered types of programs effective in reducing risk factors and increasing protective factors are parent training, family therapy, and family skills training (also referred to as behavioral family therapy).

Parent Training

Behavioral parenting training programs are the most extensively evaluated programs available. Many research studies have demonstrated their effectiveness in reducing disruptive child behaviors, coercive child parent interactions, and improving parental monitoring (Kumpfer & Alvarado, 1998; Patterson, Reid, & Dishion, 1992). Essentially, parent management programs aim to develop and increase parental skills while correcting parental behaviors that contribute to negative behavior problems (Liddle & Rowe, 2006). Behavioral parent training consists of four components: (1) initial assessment of parenting issues, (2) teaching parents new skills, (3) application of the new skills by the parent with their children (homework or out-of-session practice), and (4) feedback by the facilitator or trainer (Taylor & Biglan, 1998). A minimum of 45 hours of training is necessary to modify risk factors for child and adolescent behavior problems (Kumpfer & Alvarado, 1998). Programs follow a treatment or intervention manual for session topics addressing information, skills and strategies for managing child behaviors. Many of the parent training programs evolved from the model developed by Gerald Patterson of the Oregon Social Learning Center (Patterson, Reid, & Dishion, 1992). An exemplary and comprehensive parent training program is *Incredible Years: Parents, Teachers and Children Training Series* (Webster-Stratton, Hollinsworth, & Kolpacoff, 1989 [BASIC]; Webster-Stratton, Kolpacoff, & Hollinsworth, 1988 [BASIC]), and *Treatment Foster Care* (Chamberlain, 1994; Chamberlain & Reid, 1991). For a summary of effective parent training programs (see the Appendix).

Family Therapy

Family therapy programs are well suited to preteens and adolescents who are experiencing problems. The aim is to determine the function that children's behavior problems serve within the family system and target change in the maladaptive interactional patters to establish more effective problem solving approaches in the family. Family communication improves, family control and management improves as well as family relationships. These programs are classified as comprehensive in nature and target indicated populations. This approach has demonstrated reductions in delinquency, antisocial behaviors and drug use in youth. Three well-researched and exemplary programs are structural family therapy (brief strategic family therapy; Szapocznik, Scopetta, & King, 1978), functional family therapy (Alexander & Parsons, 1982; Alexander, Robbins, & Sexton, 2000), and multisystemic therapy (Henggeler & Borduin, 1990; Henggeler, Schoenwald, Borduin, Rowland, & Cunningham, 1998). For a summary of the three effective family therapy interventions see Appendix.

Family Skills Training Programs

Family skills training provides children and families with several components combining family therapy and behavioral skill training targeted to selective populations. These comprehensive interventions include parent skill training, social skills training for children, and behavioral family therapy (parent-child activities, also called behavioral parent training or family skills training). These are comprehensive programs because they offer practical, social, and instrumental supports and at the same time use a high dose of role-playing with ample coaching included (Kumpfer & Alvarado, 1998). Kumpfer and Alvarado 1998 note that "family skills training affects the largest number of measured family and youth risk and protective factors" (p. 7). Through structured activities, the aim is to improve family unity and attachment, reduce conflict, and improve communication so that parent-child bonding and attachment is attained. The objectives are realized through activities such as coaching in therapeutic play, observation and videotape feedback, coaching and interactive practice of parent-child positive play. Exemplars of effective family skills training programs include the Nurturing Parenting Program (Bavolek, 1987; Bavolek, McLaughlin, & Comstock, 1983); Families and Schools Together (FAST; Conduct Problems Prevention Research Group, 2000; McDonald, Coe-Braddish, Billingham, Dibble, & Rice, 1991); and Strengthening Families Program (SFP; 14-session program; Kumpfer, DeMarsh, & Child, 1989) and Strengthening Families Program (SFP; 7-session program; Kumpfer et al., 1996; Molgaard & Kumpfer, 1994); and Family Effectiveness Training (FET for Hispanic adolescents; Szapocznik, Santisteban, Rio, Perez-Vidal, & Kurtines, 1989). See Table 9.1 for examples of family-centered programs.

See the other effective family-centered programs for a more extensive description of these programs (Kumpfer, 1999). We have presented some programs that are currently being disseminated. However, a final point needs to be made regarding the cost of delivering an effective family-centered intervention. According to the literature review of exemplary intervention programs, the following information about parenting programs emerged:

> Parent-training and family therapy intervention programs, particularly with young children who have shown aggressive behavior in school, were found to be relatively cost-effective over the long run at a cost of approximately $6,500 per serious felony prevented. However, the effects of this type of intervention usually does not show any significant consequences for at least 10 years because participating youths are usually in the 7- to 10-year age range. Delinquent supervision programs cost nearly $14,000 per serious crime prevented. (p. 33)

Parent support is another approach to complement these interventions.

CONCLUSION

Social workers have long recognized that when the family is viewed as the client rather than focusing only on the child, parents need to feel included and essential to aspects treatment. Child and youth problem behaviors serve a function with the family system and are initiated and maintained by maladaptive interpersonal processes (Liddle & Rowe, 2006). Children who are socially competent and prosocial in their behavior have parents who use exemplary parenting practices, such as offering regular amounts of praise, providing adequate supervision, maintaining a safe home environment, using nonviolent discipline techniques, and providing consistency through routines and supportive interactions with their children (Kazdin & Weisz, 2003; Thomlison, 2004). Children of effective parents experience family cohesion, warmth, harmony, and the absence of neglect in their families (Thomlison, 2004).

Table 9.1 Family-Centered Programs

Program Title	Developmental Period	Levels of Intervention	Cultural Relevance/Outcome Evaluations	Theoretical Basis	Implemented By
Parent Training Programs					
Incredible Years: Parents, Teachers, and Children Training Series	Childhood	Universal Selected Indicated (comprehensive)	Canada, United States, Great Britain, and Norway	Cognitive Social Learning Theory (Patterson's Social Learning Model)	Trained therapists and interventionists, parents, and teachers
Treatment Foster Care	11 to 18 years old	Indicted	United States and Canada	Behavioral skills training, social skills training, cognitive social learning theory	Trained therapists and interventionists, parents, teachers, and trained professional foster parents
Family Therapy Programs					
Functional Family Therapy	Late childhood or adolescence (11 to 18 years old)	Selected Indicated	United States and Sweden	Information processing, social cognitive, ecological-transactional, behavioral and social learning theories	Trained therapists and social workers
Multisystemic Family Therapy	Adolescence (11 to 18 years old)	Selected Indicated (comprehensive)	United States, Canada, and Norway	Social ecology (Bronfenbrenner)	Master's level therapists, PhDs, and clinical supervisors
Brief Strategic Family Therapy Structural Family Therapy	Late childhood or adolescence (11 to 18 years old)	Indicated	United States—bicultural and Hispanic populations	Information processing, social cognitive, ecological-transactional, behavioral and social learning theories	Trained therapists and social workers

Family Skills Training Programs					
Strengthening Families Program	Preschool Childhood Adolescence	Universal Selective Indicated	United States, Canada, Australia, Costa Rica, Spain, and Sweden	Resiliency model; social ecology of substance use	Trained staff
Nurse-Family Partnership	Prenatal Infancy Early childhood	Selective	United States—urban and rural	Social ecology (Bronfenbrenner), social learning, attachment theories	Nurses, trained nonprofessional home visitors
Incredible Years: Parents, Teachers, and Children Training Series	Childhood	Universal Selected Indicated (comprehensive)	Canada, United States, Great Britain, Norway	Cognitive Social Learning Theory (Patterson's Social Learning Model)	Trained therapists and interventionists, parents, and teachers
Families and Schools Together (FAST)	Childhood	Universal Indicated (comprehensive)	United States	Ecological-transactional, developmental theory based on risk and protective factors, cognitive social learning theory (Patterson's Social Learning Model)	Teachers, parents, low-risk classmates, paraprofessionals in education settings, and counselors
Nurturing Parent Program	0 to 18 years old	Selective	United States	Cognitive behavioral, social skills learning, attachment theory	Trained therapists and interventionists, and parents
Family Effectiveness Training	Adolescents	Selective Indicated	United States—(Miami), Hispanic youth	Information processing, social cognitive, ecological-transactional, behavioral and social learning theories	Trained therapists and interventionists, parents, and teachers

Note: Based on *The Strengthening Families Exemplary Parenting and Family Strategies*, by K. L. Kumpfer, 1999, Washington, DC: U.S. Department of Justice, Office of Justice Programs, Office of Juvenile Justice and Delinquency Prevention; and *Successful Prevention and Youth Development Programs across Borders*, by L. Ferrer-Wreder, H. Statin, C. Cass Lorente, J. G. Tubman, and L. Adamson, 2004, New York: Kluwer Academic/Plenum Press.

To have maximum effect in improving parenting, family communication, family relationships, and youth functioning, family-centered preventive interventions have the following characteristics:

- Comprehensive (targeting family, peers, and community) programs that more effective in modifying a broader range of risk or protective factors and processes in children.
- Are more effective than cold-focused or parent-focused only.
- Parenting and family interventions tailored to the developmental stage of the child or youth and the specific risk factors in the family served.
- Programs that provide sufficient intervention to produce the desired effects and provide follow-up to maintain effects.
- Tailor the parent or family intervention to the cultural traditions of the families involved to improve recruitment, retention, and outcome effectiveness (Martinez & Eddy, 2005).

Excellent programs are identified to improve practices and child, youth, and family functioning. Nevertheless, in order to continue to go forward, researchers and practitioners need to move away from treating problems and more toward preventing problems. To address problem behaviors, more attention needs to be paid to the lack of support in the environments of children and youth; specifically the lack of support in families, schools, communities, and in the sociopolitical context. Policies need to be directed to improving the environments of children and youth rather than on changing individual characteristics or behaviors. In this way, research can inform policy and the involvement of parents, policy makers, and politicians can demonstrate how essential it is to have a rationale for multiple problem prevention programs because children and youth are at risk for multiple negative outcomes because of their dysfunctional and stressed environments. There is now sufficient knowledge about the characteristics of effective programs for researchers and practitioners to support policies that encourage multicomponent, coordinated preventive interventions.

REFERENCES

Alexander, J. F., & Parsons, B. V. (1982). *Functional family therapy: Principles and procedures.* Carmel, CA: Brooks/Cole.

Alexander, J. F., Robbins, M., & Sexton, T. (2000). Family-based interventions with older, at-risk youth: From promise to proof to practice. *Journal of Primary Prevention, 21*(2), 185–205.

Baumeister, R. F., & Leary, M. R. (1995). The need to belong: Desire for interpersonal attachment as a fundamental human motivation. *Psychological Bulletin, 117*, 497–529.

Bavolek, S. J. (1987, Winter). *Validation of the nurturing program for parents and adolescents: Building nurturing interactions in families experiencing parent-adolescent conflict.* Research report. Retrieved March 15, 2007, from www.nurturingparenting.com/research_validation/a9_np_validation_studies.pdf.

Bavolek, S. J., McLaughlin, J. A., & Comstock, C. M. (1983). *The nurturing parenting programs: A validated approach for reducing dysfunctional family interactions.* Final report 1R01MH34862. Rockville, MD: National Institute of Mental Health.

Bernard, B. (2002). Turnaround people and places: Moving from risk to resilience. In D. Saleebey (Ed.), *The strengths perspective in social work practice* (3rd ed., pp. 213–227). Boston: Allyn & Bacon.

Bernard, B. (2006). Using strengths-based practice to tap the resilience of families. In D. Saleebey (Ed.), *The strengths perspective in social work practice* (4th ed., pp. 197–220). Boston, MA: Allyn & Bacon.

Blum, R., Beuhring, T., Shew, M., Bearinger, L., Sieving, R., & Resnick, M. (2000). The effects of race/ethnicity, income, and family structure on adolescent risk behaviors. *American Journal of Public Health, 90*, 1879–1884.

Bowlby, J. (1982). *Attachment and loss. Vol. 1: Attachment*. New York: Basic Books.

Bronfenbrenner, U. (1986). Ecology of the family as a context for human development: Research perspectives. *Developmental Psychology, 22*(6), 723–742.

Bry, B. H., Catalano, R. F., Kumpfer, K. L., Lochman, J. E., & Szapocznik, J. (1998). Scientific findings from family prevention intervention research. In R. Ashery & K. L., Kumpfer (Eds.), *Family-focused preventions of drug abuse: Research and interventions* (pp. 103–129). NIDA Research Monograph. Washington, DC: Superintendent of documents U.S. Government Printing Office. Retrieved March 14, 2007, from www.hawaii.edu/hivandaids/Scientific%20Findings%20From%20Family%20Prevention%20Intervention%20Research.pdf.

Catalano, R. F., Haggerty, K. P., Oesterle, S., Fleming, C. B., & Hawkins, J. D. (2004). The importance of bonding to school for healthy development: Findings from the social development research group. *Journal of School Health, 74*, 252–262.

Chamberlain, P. (1994). *Family connections*. Eugene, OR: Castalia.

Chamberlain, P., & Reid, J. B. (1991). Using a specialized foster care community treatment model for children and adolescents leaving a state mental hospital. *Journal of Community Psychology, 19*, 266–276.

Conduct Problems Prevention Research Group. (2000). Merging universal and indicated prevention programs: The fast track model. *Addictive Behaviors, 25*(6), 913–927.

Dishion, T. J., French, D. C., & Patterson, G. R. (1995). The development and ecology of antisocial behavior. In D. Cicchetti & D. J. Cohen (Eds.), *Developmental psychopathology. Vol. 2: Risk, disorder, and adaptation* (pp. 421–471). New York: Wiley.

Dishion, T. J., & Kavanagh, K. (2003). *Intervening in adolescent problem behavior. A family-centered approach*. New York: Guilford Press.

Dunst, C. J., & Trivett, C. M. (1994). Methodological considerations and strategies for studying the long-term follow-up of early intervention. In S. Friedman & H. C. Haywood (Eds.), *Developmental follow-up: Concepts, domains and methods* (pp. 277–313). San Diego, CA: Academic Press.

Ferrer-Wreder, L., Stattin, H., Cass Lorente, C., Tubman, J. G., & Adamson, L. (2004). *Successful prevention and youth development programs across borders*. New York: Kluwer Academic/Plenum Press.

Fraser, M. W. (Ed.). (2004). *Risk and resilience in childhood: An ecological perspective* (2nd ed.). Washington, DC: National Association of Social Workers Press.

Fraser, M. W., Kirby, L., & Smokowski, P. R. (2004). Risk and resilience in childhood. In M. W. Fraser (Ed.), *Risk and resilience in childhood. An ecological perspective* (2nd ed., pp. 13–67). Washington, DC: National Association of Social Workers Press.

Gambrill, E. (1997). *Social work practice. A critical thinker's guide*. New York: Oxford University Press.

Gambrill, E. (2006). Evidence-based practice and policy: Choices ahead. *Research on Social Work Practice, 16*(3), 338–357.

Guterman, N. B., & Embry, R. A. (2004). Prevention and treatment strategies targeting physical child abuse and neglect. In P. Allen-Meares & M. W. Fraser (Eds.), *Intervention with children and adolescents. An interdisciplinary perspective* (pp. 130–158). Boston: Allyn & Bacon.

Haley, J. (1976). *Problem solving therapy*. San Francisco: Jossey-Bass.

Hawkins, J. D., Catalano, R. F., Morrison, D. M., O'Donnell, J., Abbott, R. D., & Day, L. E. (1992). The Seattle social development project: Effects of the first four years on protective factors and problem behaviors. In J. McCord & R. Tremblay (Eds.), *Preventing antisocial behavior* (pp. 139–161). New York: Guilford Press.

Henggeler, S. W., & Borduin, C. M. (1990). *Family therapy and beyond: A multisystemic approach to treating the behavior problems of children and adolescents*. Pacific Grove, CA: Brooks/Cole.

Henggeler, S. W., Schoenwald, S. K., Borduin, C. M., Rowland, M. D., & Cunningham, P. B. (1998). *Multisystemic treatment of antisocial behavior in children and adolescents*. New York: Guilford Press.

Hooper-Briar, K., & Lawson, H. (1994). *Serving children, youth, and families through interprofessional collaboration and service integration: A framework for action*. Oxford, OH: Institute for Educational Renewal at Miami University and the Danforth Foundation.

Janzen, C., Harris, O., Jordan, C., & Franklin, C. (2006). *Family treatment: Evidence-based practice with populations at risk*. Belmont, CA: Brooks/Cole.

Kazdin, A. E., & Weisz, J. R. (2003). *Evidence-based psychotherapies for children and adolescents*. New York: Guilford Press.

Kinard, E. M. (1999). Psychosocial resources and academic performance in abused children. *Children and Youth Services, 21*, 351–376.

Kumpfer, K. L. (1999). *Strengthening America's families: Promising parent and family strategies for delinquency prevention*. (User's guide prepared for the U.S. Department of Justice under Grant No. 95-JN-FX-K010). Washington, DC: U.S. Department of Justice, Office of Justice Programs, Office of Juvenile Justice and Delinquency Prevention.

Kumpfer, K. L., Alexander, J. F., McDonald, L., & Olds, D. L. (1998). Family-focused substance abuse prevention: What has been learned from other fields. In R. Ashery, E. B. Robertson, & K. L. Kumpfer (Eds.), *Drug abuse prevention through family interventions (NIDA Research Monograph), 17*, 78–102. Retrieved February 25, 2007, from www.drugabuse.gov/pdf/monographs/Monograph177/078-102_Kumpfer.pdf.

Kumpfer, K. L., & Alvarado, R. (1998, November). Effective family strengthening interventions. *OJJDP Juvenile Justice Bulletin* [NCJ 171121]. Washington, DC: U.S. Department of Justice, Office of Justice Programs, Office of Juvenile Justice and Delinquency Prevention.

Kumpfer, K. L., Alvarado, R., Smith, P., & Bellamy, N. (2002). Cultural sensitivity and adaptation in family-based prevention interventions. *Prevention Science, 3*, 241–246.

Kumpfer, K. L., DeMarsh, J. P., & Child, W. (1989). *The strengthening families program: Parent training manual*. Salt Lake City: University of Utah, Department of Health Education, and Alta Institute.

Kumpfer, K. L., Molgaard, V., & Spoth, R. (1996). The strengthening families program for the prevention of delinquency and drug use. In R. D. Peters & R. J. McMahon (Eds.), *Preventing childhood disorders, substance abuse, and delinquency* (pp. 241–267). Thousand Oaks, CA: Sage.

Liddle, H. A., & Rowe, C. L. (2006). Advances in family therapy research. In M. P. Nichols, R. C. Schwartz, & S. Minuchin (Eds.), *Family therapy: Concepts and methods* (6th ed., pp. 395–436). Needham Heights, MA: Allyn & Bacon.

Martincz, C. R., Jr., & Eddy, J. M. (2005). Effects of culturally adapted parent management training on Latino youth behavioral health outcomes. *Journal of Consulting and Clinical Psychology, 73*(5), 841–851.

Masten, A. S., Hubbard, J. J., Gest, S. D., Tellegen, A., Garmezy, N., & Ramirez, M. (1999). Competence in the context of adversity: Pathways to resilience and maladaptation from childhood to late adolescence. *Development and Psychopathology, 11*(1), 143–169.

McDonald, L., Coe-Braddish, D., Billingham, S., Dibble, N., & Rice, C. (1991). Families and schools together: An innovative substance abuse prevention program. *Social Work in Education, 12*(2), 118–128.

Minuchin, S. (1974). *Families and family therapy*. Cambridge, MA: Harvard University Press.

Mira, S. (2007). *Maternal and paternal nurturance and involvement in intact and divorced families as a predictor of adult children's romantic relationship satisfaction.* Unpublished manuscript. Miami: Florida International University.

Molgaard, V., & Kumpfer, K. L. (1994). *Strengthening Families Program 2.* Ames, IA: Iowa State University, Social and Behavioral Research Center for Rural Health.

Mrazek, P. J., & Haggerty, R. J. (Eds.). (1994). *Reducing risks for mental disorders: Frontiers for preventive intervention research.* Washington, DC: National Academy Press.

National Institute for Drug Abuse. (2003). *Evidence-based prevention practices.* Retrieved January 8, 2007, from http://captus.samhsa.gov/southwest/documents/AppendixIEvidence-BasedPreventionPrac_000.doc.

Nichols, M. P., & Schwartz, R. C. (2004). *Family therapy: Concepts and methods* (6th ed.). Needham Heights, MA: Allyn & Bacon.

Olds, D., & Kitzman, H. (1993). Review of research on home visits for pregnant women and parents of young children. *Future of Children, 3*(3), 53–92.

Olds, D. L. (2002). Prenatal and infancy home visiting by nurses: From randomized trials to community replication. *Prevention Science, 31*(3), 153–172.

Osofsky, J. D., & Thompson, M. D. (2000). Adaptive and maladaptive parenting: Perspectives on risk and protective factors. In J. P. Shonkoff & S. J. Meisels (Eds.), *Handbook of early childhood intervention* (2nd ed., pp. 54–76). New York: Cambridge University Press.

Patterson, G. R., Reid, J. B., & Dishion, T. J. (1992). *Antisocial boys.* Eugene, OR: Castalia.

Pollard, J. A., Hawkins, J. D., & Arthur, M. W. (1999). Risk and protection: Are both necessary to understand diverse behavioral outcomes in adolescence? *Social Work Research, 23*(3), 145–158.

Roberts, A. R., & Yeager, K. R. (Eds.). (2004). *Evidence-based social work practice.* New York: Oxford University Press.

Rothery, M., & Enns, G. (2001). *Clinical practice with families. Supporting creativity and competence.* New York: Haworth Press.

Rutter, M. (1987). Psychosocial resilience and protective mechanism. *American Journal of Orthopsychiatry, 57,* 316–330.

Rutter, M. (2000). Resilience reconsidered: Conceptual considerations, empirical findings, and policy implications. In J. P. Shonkoff & S. J. Meisels (Eds.), *Handbook of early childhood intervention* (2nd ed., pp. 651–683). New York: Cambridge University Press.

Scherer, K. R., Wallbott, H. G., & Summerfield, A. B. (1986). *Experiencing emotion: A cross-cultural study.* Cambridge: Cambridge University Press.

Shadish, W. R., Ragsdale, K., Glaser, R. R., & Montgomery, L. M. (1995). The efficacy and effectiveness of marital and family therapy: A perspective from meta-analysis. *Journal of Marital and Family Therapy, 21,* 345–360.

Spoth, R. L., Kavanagh, K. A., & Dishion, T. J. (2002). Family-centered preventive intervention science: Toward benefits to larger populations of children, youth and families. *Prevention Science, 3*(3), 145–152.

Szapocznik, J., Santisteban, D., Rio, A., Perez-Vidal, A., & Kurtines, W. M. (1989). Family effectiveness training: An intervention to prevent drug abuse and problem behavior in Hispanic adolescents. *Hispanic Journal of Behavioral Sciences, 11,* 3–27.

Szapocznik, J., Scopetta, M. A., & King, O. E. (1978). Theory and practice in matching treatment to the special characteristics and problems of Cuban immigrants. *Journal of Community Psychology, 6,* 112–122.

Szapocznik, J., & Williams, R. A. (2000). Brief strategic family therapy: Twenty-five years of interplay among theory, research, and practice in adolescent behavior problems and drug abuse. *Clinical Child and Family Psychology Review, 3,* 117–134.

Taylor, T., & Biglan, A. (1998). Behavioral family interventions for improving child-rearing: A review of the literature for clinicians and policy makers. *Clinical Child and Family Psychology Review*, *1*(1), 41–60.

Thomlison, B. (2004). Child maltreatment: A risk and protective factor perspective. In M. W. Fraser (Ed.), *Risk and resilience in childhood: An ecological perspective* (2nd ed., pp. 89–133). Washington, DC: National Association of Social Workers Press.

Thomlison, B. (2007). *Family assessment handbook: An introduction and practical guide to family assessment and intervention* (2nd ed.). Belmont, CA: Brooks/Cole Wadsworth.

Thomlison, B., & Craig, S. (2005). Ineffective parenting. In C. Dulmus & L. Rapp-Paglicci (Eds.), *Handbook of preventive interventions for adults* (pp. 327–359). Hoboken, NJ: Wiley.

Veltman, M. W., & Browne, K. D. (2001). Three decades of child maltreatment research: Implications for the school years. *Trauma, Violence, and Abuse: A Review Journal*, *2*, 215–240.

Webster-Stratton, C. (1998). Preventing conduct problems in Head Start Children. Strengthening parenting competencies. *Journal of Consulting and Clinical Psychology*, *66*, 715–730.

Webster-Stratton, C., Hollinsworth, T., & Kolpacoff, M. (1989). The long term effectiveness and clinical significance of three cost-effective training programs for families with conduct-problem children. *Journal of Consulting and Clinical Psychology*, *57*(4), 550–553.

Webster-Stratton, C., Kolpacoff, M., & Hollinsworth, T. (1988). Self-administered videotape therapy for families with conduct-problem children: Comparison with two cost-effective treatments and a control group. *Journal of Consulting and Clinical Psychology*, *56*(4), 558–566.

Webster-Stratton, C., & Taylor, T. (2001). Nipping risk factors in the bud: Preventing substance abuse, delinquency and violence in adolescence through interventions targeted at young children (0–8 years). *Prevention Science*, *2*(3), 165–192.

Widom, C. S. (1989). Does violence beget violence? A critical examination of the literature. *Psychological Bulletin*, *106*, 3–28.

Chapter 10

SCHOOL SOCIAL WORK

Cynthia Franklin, Beth Gerlach, and Amy Chanmugam

School social work is a specific branch of the social work profession that works to support student learning and social and emotional adjustment through direct service, service coordination, and advocacy in an academic setting. Social workers have been providing school-based social services to children and families in the United States for over 100 years and have evolved into a unique profession within the United States. School social work is also an international profession practiced in many other countries. School social workers support the right of every child to receive an education successfully complete school (Huxtable & Blyth, 2002). School social workers believe that emotional and physical needs must be addressed in order for children to be able to fully benefit from the instruction provided at school. To enable the school to best meet its academic mission of educating students, school social workers provide a comprehensive approach to support the strengths of children and families.

This chapter defines the practice of school social work and provides an overview of the profession of school social work including its history and important contributions to school programs. It highlights the growth of school social workers as a unique profession and identifies the organizations and professional associations that support U.S. school social workers. It also highlights the role of social workers in providing school-based social and mental health services and describes current models of school social services delivery. It further discusses the adaptations that school social workers have made in the past to meet changing demands and offer suggestions for continuing to serve the complex needs of children in the schools. Finally, this chapter recognizes the invaluable role of school social workers in addressing the needs of children and families, and the expertise and skills of the school social worker in building programs that help remove obstacles to learning.

IMPORTANCE OF SCHOOL SOCIAL WORK PRACTICE

Schools are a particularly relevant setting for social work practice. Since schools are a reflection of the communities that they serve, students bring a wide array of social problems and needs into the schools. School social workers are often asked to attend to a wide range of physical health, mental health, and psychosocial concerns including crisis intervention, family and school violence, attendance issues, school dropouts, disability, abuse, substance use, relationship difficulties, delinquency, poverty, teen pregnancy, and homelessness.

In addition, based on the widespread challenges to children and families, it is inevitable that schools will need to respond in some way to the needs of its students. It is estimated that 12% to 22% of all children under the age of 18 are at some time in need of support for mental, emotional, or behavioral problems. In low-income schools affected by poverty, it is estimated that up to 50% of students have learning and emotional problems that are challenging their success in school and in life. As many as 3 million youth under 18 years old were considered to be at-risk for suicide in the year 2000 alone. A SAHMSHA study in 2003 estimated that 833,000 students aged 12 to 17 brought a gun to school in the previous school year. These statistics are particularly startling in light of the data that only 16% of children receive any mental health services, and of those that do receive support, 70% to 80% of them are provided care in a school setting (Center for Mental Health in Schools at UCLA, 2005).

DEFINITION OF SCHOOL SOCIAL WORK PRACTICE

As school social workers have evolved into a specialized profession with an important role in the schools, differing definitions and job descriptions have been provided for the important contributions of school social workers. Unique to these definitions have usually been a description of the role of the school social worker as a facilitator between school, home, and community relationships. The School Social Work Association of America (SSWAA), the largest U.S. school social work professional organization currently defines school social work in this way:

> School Social Work is a specialized area of practice within the broad field of the social work profession. School social workers bring unique knowledge and skills to the school system and the student services team. School Social Workers are instrumental in furthering the purpose of the schools: To provide a setting for teaching, learning, and for the attainment of competence and confidence. School social workers are hired by school districts to enhance the district's ability to meet its academic mission, especially where home, school and community collaboration is the key to achieving that mission. (www.sswaa.org)

HISTORY OF SCHOOL SOCIAL WORK

School social work practice emerged because schools were required to educate an increasing population of diverse children and needed to link with community services to be able to do so. The origins of school social work can be traced to New York City; Boston, Massachusetts; and New Haven, Connecticut in 1906. Social workers were already working in these areas with a community social welfare perspective and the schools became the next natural extension for their professional attention. During the early 1900s, schools were struggling to meet the multifaceted needs of their students. At that time, compulsory education laws introduced more children into public schools, while growing immigration and urbanization increased the diversity. Social workers were called on to help facilitate understanding between the public schools and the families of the children enrolled.

The first school social workers brought their knowledge of the varied effects of poverty into the schools to help school staff meet the new challenges in public education. In addition, the school social workers were able to connect families that had little experience with public education to important resources in the community and help them to participate more meaningfully in their children's education. School social workers' prominence grew throughout the first part of the 1900s and played a key role in helping schools and families through difficult times, like the Great Depression.

As the mid-century approached, the psychoanalytic movement in the mental health field was also growing. School social workers responded to the changing trends in mental health services and began to focus more on therapeutic interventions and clinical social work. At this time, public schools were also shifting toward a system that was more bureaucratic and isolated. Models of comprehensive schooling that embraced health and social services gave way to a more individualized view of education and mental health (Franklin & Streeter, 1995). In turn, school social workers enhanced their focus on a more clinical approach to social casework.

However, with the influence of the social changes like school desegregation and civil rights occurring in the 1960s, school social workers and education reformers incorporated more of the ideas from comprehensive schooling models from their past. Throughout the 1960s and 1970s, they combined their clinical skills with their systems perspective and re-energized the field's focus on the need for interventions that include attention to individuals, families, schools, and communities. In addition, debates and legislation about student rights, discipline, educational opportunity, civil rights, and gender equality sparked a renewed commitment to educational policy and social change.

During the last quarter of the twentieth century, there was an increased recognition that schools were often failing to meet the educational needs of its children. During this time, attention was focused on improving services and educational opportunities for children with learning and behavior problems, as well as children in poverty. School social workers were often included in the discussion of solutions for addressing the social and emotional problems that were adversely affecting learning. They have also been instrumental in the emphasis to prevent and intervene with the social issues that have permeated the public schools like substance abuse, teen parenting, and violence.

Throughout the changes in education, and whether working in schools by using more of a community practice approach or more of a clinical approach, school social workers seek solutions that make sense for the individual student in the context of the environment. By using the guiding principles of the ecological approach, school social workers know that educational opportunity and student well-being is best met when change occurs on an individual level, at home, in school, and with quality community supports. In order to do this effectively, school social workers must wear many hats.

PROFESSIONAL ORGANIZATIONS, CREDENTIALS, AND STANDARDS FOR SCHOOL SOCIAL WORKERS

In 1916, just 10 years after social workers began to formally work in schools, the National Conference of Visiting Teachers and Home and School Visitors was planned to support the work of school-based social services providers. Through the work of the conference, the National Association of Visiting Teachers was formed in 1919, later evolving into the National Association of School Social Workers (NASSW). In 1955, bringing together seven different social work professional organizations formed the National Association of Social Workers (NASW), including the NASSW. NASW is currently over 150,000 members strong and continues to dedicate specific attention to school social work.

In 1990, the International Network for School Social Work (INSSW) was formed to share information and provide resources to school social workers worldwide. The first international school social work conference was held in 1999 in Chicago and welcomed school social work professionals and educations from 20 different countries. Since then, the international school social community has met for two additional conferences in Sweden in 2003 and Korea in 2006.

School social work practitioners and educators are also supported by their own professional organization, the School Social Work Association of America (SSWAA). The mission of the SSWAA "is dedicated to promoting the profession of School Social Work and the professional development of School Social Workers in order to enhance the educational experience of students and their families" (www.sswaa.org). SSWAA also publishes a wide variety of resources and brochures to be used in the field and holds an annual national conference dedicated to school social work practice, education, research, and policy.

In addition, many states and regions have professional organizations for school social workers. Some of these organizations also hold annual conferences for school social workers. For example, the Midwest School Social Work Association was formed in 1968 and represents 11 Midwestern states and their professional school social work organizations. Additionally, they organize an annual Midwest School Social Work Conference every fall and created a leadership council to address important issues in the field (www.midwest-ssw.org/history.html). As a statewide example, Texas also holds an annual school social work conference each spring with close to 500 attendees (Nowicki, as cited in Franklin, 2006).

School social worker practitioners and educators can access support, resources, and share research in a number of excellent social work journals. Two journals in particular provide information specific to the field of school social work. *Children and Schools* is published quarterly by NASW and provides original articles pertaining to research, practice and policy in the school social work profession. The *School Social Work Journal* is sponsored by the Illinois Association of School Social Workers and is published twice a year. It also provides articles specific to social work practice in schools for social workers placed in schools, social work educators, and school social work policymakers.

CURRENT STATISTICS ABOUT NUMBERS OF SCHOOL SOCIAL WORKERS

The diverse roles, complex funding streams, and varied employment titles make it difficult to accurately estimate the number of school social workers in the United States. The School Social Workers Association of America (SSWAA) reports an estimate of 20,000 to 22,000 social workers working in the schools in the United States. They further report that the field of school social work is experiencing a slow, but steady growth in the labor market (Randy Fisher, personal communication, July 28, 2006). It is likely that the field will continue to grow, as the awareness of complex student needs increases with the attention to improving public education for vulnerable students.

PROFESSIONAL STANDARDS, LICENSING AND CREDENTIALS FOR SCHOOL SOCIAL WORKERS

Professional Standards

School social workers must have adequate training and maintain specific professional standards. NASW first developed a set of formal practice standards for school social work services in 1978. The standards are intended to serve as guidelines for best professional practice in the field of school social work. The standards were revised and updated in 1992 and in 2002 in order to reflect the current issues in the field and in changes in educational policy. The school social work standards first require adherence to the NASW Code of Ethics for social work practice. They further include expectations about filling multiple responsibilities, cultural competency, proper assessment techniques, interdisciplinary collaboration, and policy awareness, to name a few. Currently, NASW supports 42 specific standards for professional practice for school social work services that can be accessed through the NASW web site at www.socialworkers.org/practice/standards/NASW_SSWS.pdf.

Licensing and Credentials

Every school that employs a school social worker has expectations that he or she has been adequately trained and will function at a high professional standard. However, each state, and even district, might have different understanding about the necessary licensing and credentials for a school social worker. In fact, each state has its own educational jurisdiction that regulates the educational training, licensing, and credentials required to provide mental health services in a school. At this time, no state requires a specific school social work credential, although many do require licensing as a clinical social worker (Torres, 2006).

Some states, however, are moving toward credentialing and certification of school social work professionals as a way to ensure a more uniform quality of personnel. For example, Illinois requires school social workers to pass certification tests that demonstrate competence in both school social work and basic academic skills. NASW has also created a program for a Certified School Social Work Specialist that establishes a professional meets their explicit standards of school social work practice (Allen-Meares, 2004).

RESEARCH ON TASKS AND ROLES OF SCHOOL SOCIAL WORKERS

A substantial amount of research has examined the job responsibilities and tasks performed by school social workers in the past 40 years (Allen-Meares, 1994, 1994; Costin, 2002). In general, researchers have found a large number and wide range of tasks that school social workers are called on to perform including case management, agency referrals, advocacy, therapy, crisis intervention, and home visits. Although certainly not surprising to busy school social workers, in a survey in the early 1990s, Allen-Meares (1994) found 104 tasks performed by school social workers, 100 of which were deemed at least "very important."

In a landmark study in 1969, Costin conducted a national survey of masters-level school social workers to determine how they viewed their roles in the schools. She established that school social workers felt their key task was clinical casework that focused on individual emotion and personality. She also found that school social workers ranked leadership and policy advocacy last in their service delivery and often struggled to entrust tasks to other school professionals. Through a historical lens, these findings fit with the trends in education during this time. In 1994, Allen-Meares replicated the Costin study and found that school social workers continued to be expected to fill multiple tasks and a wide range of roles. However, she found a trend away from the role of a primary clinical caseworker to the role of a home-school-community liaison. Again, the evolving role of school social workers seems to correspond with the progressive education reform of the time and the educational mandates that are in vogue and how their jobs are funded. As public schools continue to change and evolve to meet the needs of students, school social work will likely respond in kind. However, the field will be challenged to balance the many expectations and to determine the roles and responsibilities best suited for school social work intervention.

The mass changes in education and the complexity in roles and tasks in the school social work field would indicate that there is real need for another national survey because the last survey undertaken by Allen-Meares is now over 10 years old. Recently, an effort to complete a new national survey has been led by Michael Kelly at Loyola University and his partners, Stephanie Berzin, Andy Frey, Michelle Alvarez, and Gary Shaeffer. These investigators are conducting the new survey with the help of a national advisory board (Kelly, Personal Communication, November 8, 2007). Since the new national survey is still forthcoming, however, it is instructive to look at the individual states that have replicated the national survey to look at the most recent roles and tasks of school social workers. Most recently, Kelly (2007) conducted a cross-sectional survey of school social workers presently employed in Illinois. This survey was delivered to a sample of 821 school social workers in Illinois contacted via e-mail to participate in an online survey. The survey instrument itself was an adaptation of the original survey instrument used Allen-Meares and the Educational Testing Service (ETS) for the national survey conducted in the early 1990s. Data obtained from this study ($n = 821$) found that an overwhelming majority of Illinois school social workers rate their job satisfaction as high, and their practice choices are largely unaffected by the mass school reforms that have taken place or the school climate issues around them. The majority of school social workers in Illinois report spending most of their time immersed in serving the demands of the special education/individualized education plan (IEP) process, and fewer report having time to do prevention work or deliver school social work services to a significant number of students in regular education. According to the findings in Kelly's survey, school social workers in Illinois appears to be specialized on the "core technology" of special education IEP mandates and individual and small group counseling, rather than participating in any of the recent practice innovations and community-based trends of the past 2 decades.

SCHOOL-BASED PRACTICES AND PROGRAM INNOVATIONS IMPACTING SCHOOL SOCIAL WORK

In the past 20 years, one trend in school social work has been the expansion of school-linked services and school-community collaborations in part due to necessity and in part due to effectiveness. Schools have become de facto mental health providers for a great number of children and families, especially low-income and at-risk students. It is becoming more and more evident that children are facing complex barriers to learning that schools alone cannot address. The primary mission of schools to educate students has been challenged by environmental effects like poverty, emotional stress, abuse, behavioral problems, and psychopathology (Adelman & Taylor, 1996; Anderson-Butcher & Ashton, 2004; Streeter & Franklin, 2002).

As educators battled with the many social and emotional problems that students brought to the classroom each day, school social workers (and other mental health professionals) and education reformers emphasized the need for schools and communities to collaborate with each other in order to enhance student learning. In many ways, it is a natural partnership since schools, families, and communities share a common goal of positive academic and social outcomes for children. Moreover, schools recognize the benefit of social services to address barriers to learning for students, and community agencies benefit from the access to vulnerable children and families (Taylor & Adleman, 2006). This can present a win-win situation for schools and community agencies when they successfully collaborate, and ultimately provide better services for children and families. School social workers may serve as the key facilitators of school-community collaborations, and sometimes are *the* link between the school and community. The trend, for community-based collaboration, however, has met some controversy within some states and has even been resisted by some school social workers because school districts have sought to replace school social workers with community-based, mental health workers in an attempt to save money in serving at-risk students (Franklin & Gerlach, 2006). The competition between services providers both within schools and within community-based mental health services providers is an on-going issue facing school social work in the twenty-first century. Community-based clinical and health practitioners from diverse disciplines have increasingly linked with schools and are delivering their services on school campuses. According to information cited in Franklin (2006), the movement toward increased community collaboration has been influenced by several factors including related services provisions and demands of the Individuals with Disabilities Education Act (IDEA), the vanishing autonomy of private practice, and the school-linked services movement. Community collaborations often lead to schools housing and/or linking closely with mental health, social services, and other youth development programs. There have been varied projects across the country aimed at increasing the schools involvement with community-based services, and "statewide initiatives were established in California, Florida, Kentucky, Iowa, Missouri, New Jersey, Ohio, and Oregon, among others" (Taylor & Adelman, 2006). Although, partly designed to address fragmentation and to produce more efficient and effective programs, community linkages with school-based services has not resolved these issues. In fact, co-locating services on school campuses may just move the services fragmentation problem from one level to another as practitioners continue to be as disconnected and the services as fragmented on school campuses as they were in the community. The UCLA Mental Health project has considerable data and information on the school and community-based services and how to practice effectively in these types of school-based services programs (http://smhp.psych.ucla.edu/). The long-term sustainment of collaboration, and the appropriate policies and infrastructure for practice appears to be significant for all successful, community collaborations with schools.

MULTIPLE RESPONSIBILITIES AND PROFESSIONAL ETHICS IN SCHOOL SOCIAL WORK PRACTICE

School social workers not only juggle numerous tasks and complex problems, they must also balance multiple professional responsibilities and the expectations of multiple stakeholders. School social workers often have to navigate multifaceted obligations that are sometimes in conflict. It is imperative for school social workers to understand the NASW Code of

Ethics, as well as legal mandates at the federal, state, and local level. In addition, school social workers must be aware of the expectations and rules of the local school board and the school staff at their specific school. Often all of these responsibilities and expectations are compatible, but sometimes school social workers have to make tough decisions in the best interest of the children and families that they work with. In order for school social workers to appropriately handle these ethical dilemmas, they must have full knowledge of their ethical standards and laws, as well as strong critical thinking and communication skills. School social workers also use clinical supervision and professional consultation to help them resolve ethical questions.

In addition to traversing complex ethical responsibilities, social workers in schools face competing agendas from school and community stakeholders. Any activity that occurs in public schools falls under public scrutiny. Parents, politicians, school board members, religious leaders, social activists, and the media all closely examine and discuss the many strengths and challenges they perceive in the public schools. Again, school social workers must be aware of these various pressures and use skill in determining when to build consensus and when to speak out as an advocate.

One of the most pressing ethical concerns for school social workers is client confidentiality. Although confidentiality is an unequivocal tenet of social work practice, a school can be one of the most difficult settings to interpret the rules of confidentiality (Kopels & Lindsey, 2006). School social workers must follow the guidelines for confidentially in the NASW Code of Ethics that requires client information to remain confidential unless there is a compelling professional reason, like issues of protection and harm. However, teachers, parents, and administrators all share a concern for student and school well-being and can have expectations that school social workers will disclose important information. School social workers often struggle with knowing when it is ethical to disclose client information while maintaining the trust of the child and family, and sustaining working relationships within the school. Ultimately, at the heart of the decision to keep client information confidential or to disclose information to concerned parties is the best interest of the child. However, the school social worker must be well informed of legal and ethical responsibilities and handle the situation with great sensitivity toward the child, family, and school personnel. In addition to the NASW Code of Ethics and clinical consultation, schools social workers can obtain assistance pertaining to issues of confidentiality from position statements from school social work professional organizations, like the SSWAA and the Illinois Association of School Social Workers (Kopels & Lindsey, 2006).

CURRENT SOCIAL WORK SETTINGS IN PUBLIC SCHOOLS

The work settings and employment configurations of school social workers vary. Most school social workers are either employed by a school district and work as part of the pupil services team, or they are employed by a community organization with a school-district contract (Franklin, 2006). In some cases, school social workers may be public sector employees (Lewis, 1998). For example, school-based services are provided by social workers with Community Youth Services in Houston, which is part of Harris County Children's Protective Services.

Regardless of the particular employment and practice configuration, all school social workers serve as members of interprofessional teams. Meeting the needs of students requires working with professionals and paraprofessionals serving in a variety of roles (Harris & Franklin, 2004). Interprofessional teams are inevitable in the school setting and offer the opportunity of a "collective voice advocating for the needs of children and youth" (p. 284).

Team members, including the school social worker, can work together to address individual student needs as well as working toward the common goals of the school. Serving together on a team enables members to learn the perspectives of the other professions involved in the school community. Close collaboration with school staff on behalf of students requires a trusting relationship. School social workers must be aware of the priorities of the other personnel in the school as well as the goals they share in common. When serving in a consultant role with teachers or administrators, school social workers are directly assisting in the resolution of a current concern, and indirectly developing the skills of the consultee to manage similar needs as they arise in the future, thus providing a cost-effective service (Albers & Kratochwill, 2006).

ADMINISTRATIVE AND FUNDING CONFIGURATIONS OF SCHOOL SOCIAL WORK SERVICE DELIVERY

In recent years, a variety of new organizational configurations and collaborations providing school-based services have emerged (Allen-Meares, 2006a). "At a time when a significant number of children are considered to be at risk for academic, behavioral, and social-emotional difficulties, schools are viewed as a location to address these issues through the provision of comprehensive intervention services" (Albers & Kratochwill, 2006, p. 971). Various school models have emerged in response to increased recognition that, because schools are central in the lives of children, they may serve as a primary conduit for delivery of services needed by the child or family. These models include School-based Health Centers, Expanded School Mental Health Centers, and Community Schools (Franklin & Gerlach, 2006). All these models provide different ways for schools to link health, mental health, and social services into the school setting and make these services more accessible to students that need them. These approaches can be differentiated from more traditional approaches of hiring a school social worker to work for a school district and serve as alternative ways to connect social work services to school campuses. Many social workers work within these various community-based, school-linked programs providing social work services to students.

The community schools movement in particular creates school programs that are similar to those envisioned by early school social work leaders and those that were in the settlement house movements in Chicago such as Jane Adams at Hull House in Chicago. Community-based schools act as central market locations for an array of integrated health, mental health social, and recreational services, usually brought into schools by community-based agencies, and financed through multiple funding channels. The school building is open before and after school, evenings, weekends, and summers and becomes a central gathering place for community life. Parents are provided with opportunities to participate in school projects, to attend educational classes, and to build skills to help their children with homework. Family resource centers are organized by parent volunteers and provide space for counseling, meetings, family dinners, and socializing. For a community school to be effective, each community defines its own needs, identifies its own assets, and creates its own vision of a community school and decides what is needed to help children in school. All kinds of services might be provided from nutrition services, transportation, to health and social services depending on the needs of the students and families (Dryfoos, 2002). The community school might also become active in resolving larger community issues like drug abuse, crime, and neighborhood violence that affect children and their schooling. The school offers a hub for family support, advocacy, and problem solving.

CURRENT PRACTICE MODELS AND INTERVENTIONS IN USE

According to Constable, Kuzmickaite, Harrison, and Volkmann (1999) even though the school social worker has many tasks and roles in job functioning four common factors or tasks are common to most school social work jobs:

1. Assessment as applied to both direct services and program development.
2. Consultations with people across the school system (i.e., teacher and administrators) and as a member of a transdiscipinary team.
3. Direct services to individuals, groups, and families.
4. Program development activities that assist the school in developing and sustaining programs.

School social workers perform these tasks using the ecological systems perspective as a framework and intervene with multiple systems at the different levels that impact the lives of children and adolescents. Services may target individual students, groups, parents, and families, or an entire classroom, school, district, neighborhood, or community (Allen-Meares, 2004; Dupper, 2003; Franklin, 2006). Teachers and administrators may also be seen as the focus for intervention and change (Broussard, 2003; Frey & Dupper, 2005; Dulmus & Sowers, 2004). Local needs and funding structures may determine the general focus of a school social worker's intervention (Harris & Franklin, 2004).

Individuals

Most children in the United States attend public schools; thus the range of experiences and problems that are present in our society occur in the lives of the students school social workers know. Many students live in poverty. Students, or someone in their family, may have a mental illness, may have been abused or neglected, or might be involved with the criminal justice system. Many students have learning needs that require an advocate for special education services. Some may be dealing with issues of grief, or loss or separation from loved ones. Families may have relocated often or experienced homelessness. Some students, or a family member, may be abusing alcohol or drugs. School social workers may be called on to intervene because of these concerns at all levels, from individual crisis intervention to community or schoolwide prevention or education initiatives.

When practice is focused at the individual student level, the school social worker uses assessment and counseling skills, consults with others as needed, and works to link the student with other resources and service systems to address concerns (Franklin, 2004). With intervention at the individual level, the school social worker is often directly providing the service, or the school social worker may be collaborating with a community agency to bring the needed service into the school, or may be linking the client with services outside the school.

Effective and ethical practice requires knowledge and application of interventions that have been empirically supported or have a significant known track record as clinical best practices. A substantial number of school-based intervention methods for individual students meet these standards (Molina, Bowie, Dulmus, & Sowers, 2004). Franklin, Harris, and Allen-Meares (2006) have compiled detailed information on effective interventions into a comprehensive sourcebook for school social workers. Intervention information for most mental health diagnoses and developmental disabilities are included, as well as for a wide range of other specific student issues, for example adolescent parents; sexual assault survivors; students who are experiencing grief and loss; and students who are gay, lesbian, bisexual, or transgender. A school social worker seeking information on effective practice to address a specific concern may turn to the sourcebook for an overview of empirically supported interventions. In the case of self-mutilating students, for example, information is provided on cognitive and behavioral intervention (Shepard, DeHay, & Hersh, 2006) as well as integrative, brief solution-oriented treatment (Selekman, 2006).

Online resources are also available to help school social workers access current information on empirically supported practices. The What Works Clearinghouse, for example, is provided by the U.S. Department of Education with the goal of disseminating evidenced-based reviews of practices in education (www.w-w-c.org). Having the knowledge of what type of intervention works for whom is a critical first step to providing ethical and effective services to individuals.

Parents and Families

School social workers may intervene with parents and families to address concerns related to an individual student, or they may target parents themselves for intervention. For a student who is often truant, for example, the social worker may visit the student's home to assess reasons for nonattendance and engage the parent in problem solving. The social worker may also encourage the parent's participation in school activities, such as teacher conferences and PTA meetings. Parents are the experts on their children, and schools and parents are interdependent in their efforts to attend to the child's learning needs (Franklin, 2004). A problem in the lives of the parents or family may be stressing the individual child. A strong research base supports the importance and benefits of parental involvement in their children's education (Chavkin, 2006).

Immigrant families and their school-age children may be experiencing additional stressors related to adjustment, cultural, and language issues (Franklin, 2004). The school social worker assists thru skilled assessment of the family's needs, as well as recognition of barriers in the school that may be limiting their involvement, and efforts to eliminate or diminish these barriers. School social workers can work to empower parents in their interactions with the school, including at the policy and decision-making level (Frey & Dupper, 2005).

In general, parents and schools can be encouraged and assisted to strengthen their partnership to the benefit of the children. Many avenues are open for the school social worker to contribute to the ongoing development of parent-school partnerships (Broussard, 2003; Chavkin, 2006; Dulmus & Sowers, 2004; Dupper, 2003; Franklin, 2004; Ward, Anderson-Butcher, & Kwiatkowski, 2006). A variety of specific strategies and successful practice examples are available for school social workers to draw on. Franklin (2004) identifies the objectives that guide school social work practice in addressing parent-school partnerships:

- Educating school personnel toward understanding the psychosocial strengths and needs of families and supporting school staff relationships with vulnerable families.
- Offering relevant program interventions for parents and families based on an ongoing and current needs assessment.
- Helping the interprofessional team, the PTA, and school staff develop avenues for parent involvement in the operations and programs of the school. (p. 288)

Groups and Classrooms

School social workers often provide group services to children and adolescents. Empirical support exists for a considerable number of individual and group interventions, as discussed next. In addition to the well-known clinical benefits, such as the reduction of isolation and improvement of socialization skills, groups may be considered an efficient way for school social workers to provide services (Franklin, 2004). Entire classrooms may also be the focus for school social work services. For example, a school social worker may collaborate with an elementary school teacher to assist with the development of rules for social behavior with peers in the classroom.

INTERVENTIONS WITH THE SCHOOL

Schoolwide practice might include services such as prevention initiatives, teacher training, and initiatives to improve the overall school climate (Broussard, 2003; Dupper, 2003). Schoolwide interventions may be used as a means to target individual student behavior or to change the school environment itself (Dupper, 2003; Frey & Dupper, 2005). The most successful prevention programs attempt to do both (Dupper, 2003). A large number of effective prevention programs are available for school social workers to learn about and replicate at their schools, including programs targeting violence, substance abuse, truancy, adolescent pregnancy, and transmission of sexually transmitted diseases. There are many ways school social workers can assist in making the school environment one that nurtures the development of children. Broussard (2003) describes several strategies that school social workers can use, for example, to address elements of the school culture that may be creating an environment that is unwelcoming of families of diverse cultures.

Frey and Dupper (2005) have developed a conceptual tool, the "clinical quadrant," to assist school social workers with envisioning and planning a broad, ecologically and empowerment-based orientation to their overall practice. They note the complexity of school social work services, especially given recent legislation and education reform efforts, and encourage initiation of multilevel interventions. The clinical quadrant provides a clear graphic illustration of potential intervention targets and levels of service delivery. The authors recommend that school social workers develop skills in providing services that go beyond microlevel interventions focusing on student change, and they emphasize that school social workers must be flexible in their ability to adapt services to the needs of their particular school, and at the multiple levels of service as needed.

CURRENT ASSESSMENT MODELS

School social workers must assess the effectiveness of the services they provide, whether it is an intervention with an individual student or a schoolwide prevention program. They need to assess which interventions are effective for ethical reasons, for their own planning purposes, and because they are accountable for their services to others and may need to report outcomes to multiple stakeholders. A variety of designs, methods, and measurement tools are available to assist school social workers in the evaluation of their practice at all levels (Cobb & Jordan, 2006; Dupper, 2003; Jayaratne, 2004; Lindsey & White, 2007; Powers, Bowen, & Rose, 2005).

Like school social workers, public schools must increasingly demonstrate that they are meeting outcome goals. Since enactment of the Goals 2000: Educate America Act, funding for individual schools is linked to their attainment of eight educational goals outlined in the legislation (Franke & Lynch, 2006). The No Child Left Behind Act of 2002 has further increased pressure on schools to demonstrate their effectiveness, primarily measured with the standardized testing results of their students. The outcome priorities of social work practice and the goals of the educational system may seem different on the surface, but areas of mutual concern underlie both sets of goals (Harris & Franklin, 2004). For example, while school personnel may be concerned with student substance abuse primarily as an obstacle influencing academic outcomes such as grades and test scores, the school social worker may define substance abuse as a problem in multiple areas of the student's life, such as in the development of healthy peer relationships and individual identity. Professionals in the educational system and in social work are in agreement that substance abuse is a concern, and addressing the problem will further the outcome priorities of both groups. The recognition that there is substantial overlap in what must be done to meet the goals of the educational system and the goals of social work practice will assist the school social worker with defining, measuring, and reporting information about social work services in a way that links them with the priorities of the educational system.

The quality and effectiveness of school social work services may be evaluated in a variety of ways. Dupper (2003) notes that research designs familiar to social work practitioners, such as single-system and comparison group designs, are often appropriate for assessing the effectiveness of student-focused interventions in school settings. Measurement methods include the use of objective reports, test data, direct observations, standardized scales, and self-reports (Jayaratne, 2004). Cobb and Jordan (2006) recommend using different types of assessment measures together to evaluate services. School records, such as attendance reports, may be helpful objective reports. Numerous standardized rapid assessment instruments, addressing a wide spectrum of issues, are available for use with children and families. Two in particular have a long record of use in school settings, with extensive data available on their psychometric properties: Achenbach's Child Behavior Checklist (1991, as cited in Cobb & Jordan, 2006) and the Conners Scales (1997, as cited in Cobb & Jordan, 2006). Several assessment instruments are available with software that can do the scoring for the measure (Lindsey & White, 2007).

The School Success Profile provides an ideal standardized and validated measurement instrument for planning and assessing school social work services informed by an ecological perspective, with attention to both risk and resilience factors. It captures information at the level of the individual student and across the contexts of the school, neighborhood, and community (Powers et al., 2005). The developers continue to refine the instrument and to provide Web-based resources for school social workers to use as a guide in their selection of appropriate empirically supported interventions.

School social work interventions at the level of systems, such as an entire school or neighborhood, must also be evaluated. While the unit of analysis is different, some of the basic designs and types of measurement tools are similar to those used in the evaluation of direct services to students (Dupper, 2003). For example, standardized instruments are available to assess classrooms and neighborhoods. School and district level data is collected on numerous variables that may be targets of social work intervention, such as free/reduced-cost lunch program participation and dropout and truancy rates. Examples of indicators that may be studied to evaluate service effectiveness might include community utilization rates or teacher perceptions and attitudes.

Because of the variety and number of demands on a school social worker's time, and the potential need to report program information to multiple stakeholders, efficient management of student and program data is critical. Computerized data management may save time while providing an excellent accountability tool, especially for school social workers with varied and dynamic caseloads and program responsibilities (Jonson-Reid, 2006). In addition, accessing and utilizing the school's database may save time for the social worker, and provide valuable information needed for evaluating student progress, such as attendance records, grades, and dropout data (Patterson, 2006). The use of spreadsheets provides an efficient means of organizing service-related information. Patterson describes the simple sequence needed to use spreadsheets to graphically display student or group change with single-system designs. These may serve as an easily produced and interpreted accountability tool.

TRENDS AND ISSUES IN PRACTICE

Accountability

Political trends at local and federal levels influence schools. The No Child Left Behind Act, as described earlier, has increased the need for public schools to be accountable for the educational outcomes of students. The stakes are high, with school funding tied to the school's ability to demonstrate student achievement. Standardized tests serve as a primary measure of student achievement, and are thus increasingly a focus of the educational system. The increasing emphasis on testing has been controversial, and the debate between both members of the public and professionals in the educational system is a prominent issue for school social workers and educators (Franklin, 2006). Front-line social workers are dealing with some of the fallout of the discussion, with increased stress on students, families and educators, as they adapt to the focus on testing. Issues included in the discussion are the nature of school responses to the legislation, the stress of the high-stakes testing for children, the inappropriateness of the focus on standardized tests as the accountability measure for schools, and concerns related to measurement issues with ethnic-minority students, students with learning disabilities, and students learning English as a second language. Overall, the climate for professionals working in public schools today is performance and outcome-driven.

The growing accountability emphasis for schools is also contributing to the need for social workers to be more accountable for the services they provide and to be able to demonstrate how their services support the educational mission of the school. As a result, school social workers must have (a) skills to evaluate their own services, (b) knowledge of measurement and evaluation tools, (c) the ability to link the interventions they provide to the outcomes that are important to the school, and (d) the means and skills to communicate or publicize their contribution to the welfare of students and the school to stakeholders (Franklin, 2006).

Evidence-Based Practice

School social workers, like health professionals, educators, and social workers in other practice settings, are increasingly encouraged to select and provide interventions that have been supported with empirical research (Dupper, 2007; Franklin, 2006; Frey & Dupper, 2005). This practice trend calls for school social workers to use the best available research evidence to guide their practice with clients (Franklin, 2006). In the absence of empirical evidence, best practices derived from research, and meeting certain standards, are encouraged in evidence-based practice. Dupper (2007) describes steps school social workers can take to provide evidenced-based services, including information on how to identify appropriate interventions and how to analyze effectiveness literature.

Service Trends

Children and youth considered to be at risk are increasingly receiving services through public schools (Franklin, 2006). This includes children with mental health needs, and especially impoverished and ethnic minority students with mental health needs. According to the Center for Health and Health Care in Schools (2001), more than 70% of children who receive mental health services are receiving those services in their schools. The overall level of unmet need for mental health services for children and adolescents is estimated to be even greater. It is likely that many children will not receive needed services unless they are provided through schools. Some groups are especially likely to encounter obstacles to receiving quality mental health services. African American and Latino children in particular may have difficulty accessing mental health services. These two groups show highest rates of need for mental health services, yet are the least likely to receive quality services when they are not provided by public schools (RAND Health Research Highlights, 2001). African American children are also overrepresented in special education services (Frey & Dupper, 2005). Other groups who are likely to receive needed services through schools are homeless children, immigrants, and adolescent parents.

The directors of the SAMHSA-funded National Child Traumatic Stress Network have recommended that policy makers direct efforts toward assisting parents and teachers who have been traumatized, as a means of providing better support to children (Pynoos & Fairbank, 2003). They also note that some of the effective treatments for trauma that have been identified involve schools. With high rates of childhood exposure to traumatic events, wide media coverage of school violence around the country, and citizens of all ages living with continuing terrorist threats in the aftermath of 9/11, trauma-related mental health services continue to be needed.

In addition to the growing number of children needing mental health services, the number of children and youth coming to school with significant barriers to their learning is also increasing (Frey & Dupper, 2005). The number of students who are living in poverty is growing, as well as the number of students who have severe behavior problems. These trends indicate a continuing and growing need for school social work services.

School experiences and students' feelings and attitudes about school also come into play in school social work practice. Students may have safety concerns about school, and may actually have been victimized on the school campus (Dulmus & Sowers, 2004; Franklin, 2006). School social workers may intervene to address school-related concerns, for example, by providing crisis intervention services in response to a distressing event or experience on campus. Gay, lesbian, bisexual, and transgender (GLBT) youth may be at special risk for victimization at school (Elze, 2006; Frey & Dupper, 2005). School social workers may be proactive in taking specific steps to develop a climate in the school that is safe, nonstigmatizing, and affirming for GLBT youth (Elze, 2006).

Technology

Technology is a large part of the daily lives of children and adolescents, and plays a growing role in the provision of school social work services (Lindsey & White, 2007). It is essential for school social workers to be cognizant of technological resources and advances because technology can assist with administrative duties and professional communications, be part of an intervention, or be encountered as a student or school issue of concern. Computer software programs can be valuable tools for collecting and reporting program information, as described previously. There are also interactive software programs available that have been created as part of interventions for children.

School social workers must stay current on how students are using technology, both at school and at home. For example, it is important to be aware of the growing use of Instant Messaging as a means for students to instantly communicate and socialize with peers (Lindsey & White, 2007). This is one example of how technology use might arise as a student issue of concern, if something is communicated rapidly among students that has repercussions during the school day. Another technology-related student issue that might be brought to the attention of the school social worker is Internet sexual solicitation of children and youth, or unwanted exposure to sexual material online, which was reported by 25% of youth (ages 10 to 17) in a nationwide survey (Mitchell, Finkelhor, & Wolak, 2003).

FUTURE ISSUES

The drive for schools and school social workers to be accountable for the services they provide by demonstrating measurable results is likely to continue. In addition, it will be increasingly important for school social workers to be able to clearly show how their services contribute to the school's educational mission. Furthermore, the practice trend calling for school social workers to provide evidence-based services is likely to continue.

It is expected that children and youth will continue to need and receive mental health services through public schools in increasing numbers, especially impoverished and ethnic minority children (Franklin, 2006). School social workers can expect to work with increasingly complex issues and an increasingly diverse student population.

Culturally competent practice skills, interventions, and assessment methods are essential for school social workers and other school personnel as the U.S. population becomes more culturally diverse (Broussard, 2003; Dupper, 2007; Franklin, 2006). Swick, Head-Reeves, and Barbarin (2006) describe the necessity of developing effective strategies for meeting the needs of these children and their families as "one of the most important challenges facing school personnel in the twenty-first century" (p. 793). As Dupper (2007) notes, "There is a growing mismatch between linguistically, culturally, economically and racially diverse children entering monolingual, white, Anglo, middle-class schools. Consequently, it is imperative that school social workers become sensitive to cultural differences and learn specific competencies that will increase the likelihood of interacting effectively with diverse children and their families" (p. 217). Clearly, school social workers will play a key role in this area.

Technology may bring both opportunities and challenges for school social workers in the future. Increased use of electronic technologies to communicate with others may require school social workers to be even more vigilant about client confidentiality (Franklin, 2006; Lindsey & White, 2007). Efforts to maintain confidentiality may need to be reviewed frequently as more communication takes place electronically, especially in the context of interprofessional collaboration in schools.

More rapid communication with other professionals involved with a child or family, however, provides obvious advantages for the ability of team members to work together to address issues. By facilitating the dissemination of information, electronic communication may also facilitate prevention. For example, one of the chapter authors was serving as a school social worker in September 2001. In the days after the 9/11 terrorist attacks, she was one of 30 or more school social workers to receive electronic mail from a school social worker in a neighboring school district informing them of incidents of harassment and threats toward Muslim students on that campus. The social worker receiving the electronic mail was able to instantly share the information with her principal. Together they developed a preventative strategy for their campus, which also entailed quick dissemination of information to teachers via electronic mail. Presumably, many of the 30 social workers receiving the original message took similar steps, and may also have forwarded the information to further school social workers not on the original mailing list.

Increased use of technology is linked with other issues that will continue to be prominent in the future, such as the need to demonstrate the results of services and the need to be current on best practice methods. Various strategies were described earlier to utilize software in school social work services, including the overall management of programs, record keeping, tracking of student progress, administration of rapid assessment instruments, reporting of results to stakeholders, and even the administration of some innovative interventions. School social workers who have Internet access can readily obtain information on empirically supported interventions through web sites such as the Campbell Collaboration Library (www.campbellcollaboration.org/index.asp) and the National Child Traumatic Stress Network (NCTSN, www.nctsnet.org/nccts/nav.do?pid=ctr_rsch_biblio_works/). NCTSN provides a "What Works?" bibliography for practitioners working with children and youth who have experienced trauma, with summaries of research articles that they may not obtain as quickly through other means. The Campbell Collaboration Library provides a large, searchable, frequently updated web site describing systematic reviews of the effectiveness of various interventions for a wide range of concerns.

The evidence-based practice movement is expected to continue in the future. In fact, Allen-Meares (2006b) notes that, "The future of school social work may very well rest on the emerging concept of evidence-based practices, theories, interventions, and treatments" (p. 1189). School social workers must therefore develop an understanding of the reasoning behind the movement toward evidence-based services, and the skills needed to access and evaluate the information that will assist them to utilize the most effective interventions in their own practices.

The increased focus on schools as a logical place to provide services for children and youth will lead to increasing development of collaborations between schools and community service providers (Allen-Meares, 2006b). The coming decades may bring "unusual and innovative" partnerships and collaborations (Allen-Meares, 2006b, p. 1191). School social workers may well play a lead role in the development of these new partnerships, given their skills and expertise (Franklin & Gerlach, 2006).

Frey and Dupper (2005) have highlighted the need for school social workers to move beyond providing services to individual students and families in order to increase system-focused interventions targeting the school ecology itself. School social workers must be skilled at providing services at the different possible levels of intervention and should not restrict their services to focus only on individuals.

CONCLUSION

This chapter defined the practice of school social work and provided an overview of the profession of school social work including its history and important contributions within school programs. School social workers have grown as a unique profession among social workers and currently have their own professional associations, credentials, and practice standards. This chapter highlighted the role of school social workers in mental health services and described some contemporary organizational configurations and models for school social services delivery. It further discussed the adaptations that school social workers have made to meet changing demands and offered suggestions for what types of skills might be needed to continue to serve the complex needs of children in the schools.

Educating children in the twenty-first century is clearly quite complex and the demands on schools to successfully educate increasingly challenging and diverse populations is making it more important for school social workers to be well versed with varied areas of knowledge and skills. Franklin (2004) recommends that those who are considering a career in school social work thoroughly assess themselves in terms of their general professional competency, cultural competency, professional values, ethics, and issues of transference and countertransference. Strong assessment skills are needed for all aspects of school social work, from determining student needs at an individual level, to evaluating the sociopolitical issues at play in the school or community. As described, skills are also needed in the areas of intervention, evaluation, communication, managing interprofessional groups and community partnerships, marketing, and connecting social work activities to the overall goals of the school (Franklin, 2006). In addition to these skills and areas of knowledge, personal flexibility and willingness to work with ambiguity is clearly a valuable asset that allows school social workers to manage the wide-ranging and complex areas they navigate on a daily basis.

Throughout their careers, school social workers use their personal assets and professional expertise to address student needs in the context of their environments of school, home, and community. Although there are many tasks that school social workers perform, four core tasks are assessments; systemwide consultations; direct intervention with individuals, families, and groups; and program development. School social work practice has adjusted to trends in the field and in education reform, however, the basic charge to help all students successfully receive an education and to help remove learning barriers for vulnerable students has largely remained the same. School social workers meet this charge though dedication, advocacy, flexibility, and creativity, and will surely continue to do so as their role continues to evolve.

REFERENCES

Adelman, H. S., & Taylor, L. (2006). Want to work with schools? What is involved with successful linkages. In C. Franklin, M. B. Harris, & P. Allen-Meares (Eds.), *The school services sourcebook: A guide for school-based professionals* (pp. 955–970). New York: Oxford University Press.

Albers, C. A., & Kratochwill, T. R. (2006). Teacher and principal consultations: Best practices. In C. Franklin, M. Harris, & P. Allen-Meares (Eds.), *The school services sourcebook: A guide for school-based professionals* (pp. 971–976). New York: Oxford University Press.

Allen-Meares, P. (1977). Analysis of tasks in school social work. *Social Work, 22*, 196–201.

Allen-Meares, P. (1994). Social work services in schools: A national study of entry-level tasks. *Social Work, 39*(5), 560–565.

Allen-Meares, P. (2004). *Social work services in schools*, 4th ed. Boston: Allyn & Bacon.

Allen-Meares, P. (2006a, Summer). One hundred years: A historical analysis of social work services in schools. *School Social Work Journal* [Special issue].

Allen-Meares, P. (2006b). Where do we go from here? Mental health workers and the implementation of an evidence-based practice. In C. Franklin, M. Harris, & P. Allen-Meares (Eds.), *The school services sourcebook: A guide for school-based professionals* (pp. 1189–1194). New York: Oxford University Press.

Anderson-Butcher, D., & Ashton, D. (2004). Innovative models of collaboration to serve children, youths, families and communities. *Children and Schools, 26*(1), 39–53.

Broussard, C. A. (2003). Facilitating home-school partnerships for multiethnic families: School social workers collaborating for success. *Children and Schools, 25*(4), 211–222.

Center for Health and Health Care in Schools. (2001). Children's mental health needs, disparities and school-based services: A fact sheet. Retrieved March 10, 2005, from www.healthinschools.org/cfk/mentfact.asp.

Center for Mental Health in Schools at UCLA. (2005). *Youngsters mental health and psychosocial problems: What are the data?* Los Angeles: Author.

Chavkin, N. F. (2006). Effective strategies for promoting parental involvement: An overview. In C. Franklin, M. Harris, & P. Allen-Meares (Eds.), *The school services sourcebook: A guide for school-based professionals* (pp. 629–640). New York: Oxford University Press.

Cobb, N. H., & Jordan, C. (2006). Identifying and using effective outcome measures. In C. Franklin, M. Harris, & P. Allen-Meares (Eds.), *The school services sourcebook: A guide for school-based professionals* (pp. 1043–1051). New York: Oxford University Press.

Constable, R., Kuzmickaite, D., Harrison, W. D., & Volkmann, L. (1999). The emergent role of the school social worker in Indiana. *School Social Work Journal, 24*(1), 1–14.

Costin, L. B. (1969). An analysis of the tasks in school social work. *Social Service Review, 43*, 274–285.

Dryfoos, J. G. (2002). Full-service community schools. *Phi Delta Kappan, 83*(5), 393–400.

Dulmus, C. N., & Sowers, K. M. (2004). *Kids and violence: The invisible school experience.* New York: Haworth Press.

Dupper, D. R. (2003). *School social work: Skills and Interventions for effective practice.* Hoboken, NJ: Wiley.

Dupper, D. R. (2007). Incorporating best practices. In L. Bye & M. Alvarez (Eds.), *School social work: Theory to practice* (pp. 212–222). Belmont, CA: Brooks/Cole.

Elze, D. E. (2006). Working with gay, lesbian, bisexual, and transgender students. In C. Franklin, M. Harris, & P. Allen-Meares (Eds.), *The school services sourcebook: A guide for school-based professionals* (pp. 861–872). New York: Oxford University Press.

Franke, T., & Lynch, S. (2006). Linking school social work interventions to educational outcomes for schools. In C. Franklin, M. Harris, & P. Allen-Meares (Eds.), *The school services sourcebook: A guide for school-based professionals* (pp. 1021–1030). New York: Oxford University Press.

Franklin, C. (2004). The delivery of school social work services. In P. Allen-Meares (Ed.), *Social work services in schools* (4th ed., pp. 295–326). Boston: Allyn & Bacon.

Franklin, C. (2006). The future of school social work practice: Current trends and opportunities. *Advances in Social Work, 6*(1), 167–181.

Franklin, C., & Gerlach, B. (2006, Summer). One hundred years of linking schools with communities: Current models and opportunities. *School Social Work Journal* [Special issue].

Franklin, C., Harris, M., & Allen-Meares, P. (2006). *The school services sourcebook: A guide for school-based professionals.* New York: Oxford University Press.

Franklin, C., & Streeter, C. (1995). School reform: Linking public schools with human services. *Social Work, 40*(6), 773–782.

Frey, A. J., & Dupper, D. R. (2005). A broader conceptual approach to clinical practice for the 21st century. *Children and Schools, 27*(1), 33–44.

Harris, M., & Franklin, C. (2004). The design of social work services. In P. Allen-Meares (Ed.), *Social work services in schools* (4th ed., pp. 277–294). Boston: Allyn & Bacon.

Huxtable, M., & Blyth, E. (2002). *School social work worldwide.* Washington, DC: National Association of Social Workers.

Jayaratne, S. D. (2004). Evaluating practice and programs. In P. Allen-Meares (Ed.), *Social work services in schools* (4th ed., pp. 327–358). Boston: Allyn & Bacon.

Jonson-Reid, M. (2006). Constructing data management systems for tracking accountability. In C. Franklin, M. Harris, & P. Allen-Meares (Eds.), *The school services sourcebook: A guide for school-based professionals* (pp. 1031–1042). New York: Oxford University Press.

Kelly, M. S. (2007). Illinois school social workers' use of practice interventions: Results from a statewide survey. Unpublished doctoral dissertation. Chicago: University of Chicago.

Kopels, S., & Lindsey, B. C. (2006, Summer). The complexity of confidentiality in schools today: The school social worker context. *School Social Work Journal* [Special issue].

Lewis, M. R. (1998). The many faces of school social work practice: Results from a research partnership. *Social Work in Education, 20*(3), 177–190.

Lindsey, B. C., & White, M. K. (2007). Technology and school social work. In L. Bye & M. Alvarez (Eds.), *School social work: Theory to practice* (pp. 288–296). Belmont, CA: Brooks/Cole.

Mitchell, K. J., Finkelhor, D., & Wolak, J. (2003). The exposure of youth to unwanted sexual material on the internet: A national survey of risk, impact, and prevention. *Youth and Society, 34*(3), 330–358.

Molina, I., Bowie, S. L., Dulmus, C. N., & Sowers, K. M. (2004). School-based violence prevention programs: A review of selected programs with empirical evidence. In C. N. Dulmus & K. M. Sowers (Eds.), *Kids and violence: The invisible school experience* (pp. 175–190). New York: Haworth Press.

Patterson, D. A. (2006). Using the school's database system to construct accountability tools. In C. Franklin, M. Harris, & P. Allen-Meares (Eds.), *The school services sourcebook: A guide for school-based professionals* (pp. 1053–1060). New York: Oxford University Press.

Powers, J., Bowen, G., & Rose, R. (2005). Using social environment assets to identify intervention strategies for promoting school success. *Children and Schools, 27*(3), 177–187.

Pynoos, R., & Fairbank, J. (2003). The state of trauma in America, two years out. *Brown University Child and Adolescent Behavior Letter, 19*(10), 1–6.

RAND Health Research Highlights. (2001). Mental health case for youth. Retrieved March 10, 2005, from http://www.rand.org/publications/RB/RB4541.

Selekman, M. D. (2006). Integrative, solution-oriented approaches with self-harming adolescents. In C. Franklin, M. Harris, & P. Allen-Meares (Eds.), *The school services sourcebook: A guide for school-based professionals* (pp. 321–328). New York: Oxford University Press.

Shepard, K., DeHay, T., & Hersh, B. (2006). Effective cognitive-behavioral interventions for self-mutilation. In C. Franklin, M. Harris, & P. Allen-Meares (Eds.), *The school services sourcebook: A guide for school-based professionals* (pp. 305–320). New York: Oxford University Press.

Streeter, C. L., & Franklin, C. (2002). Standards for school social work in the 21st century. In A. Roberts & G. Green (Eds.), *Social workers desk reference*. New York: Oxford University Press.

Swick, D. C., Head-Reeves, D. M., & Barbarin, O. A. (2006). Building relationships between diverse families and school personnel. In C. Franklin, M. Harris, & P. Allen-Meares (Eds.), *The school services sourcebook: A guide for school-based professionals* (pp. 793–802). New York: Oxford University Press.

Taylor, L., & Adelman, H. S. (2006). Want to work with schools? What is involved in successful linkages. In C. Franklin, M. B. Harris, & P. Allen-Meares (Eds.), *School services sourcebook: A guide for school-based professionals*. New York: Oxford University Press.

Torres, S., Jr. (2006). Licensing, certification, and credentialing of school social workers and other school mental health professionals. In C. Franklin, M. Harris, & P. Allen-Meares (Eds.), *The school services sourcebook: A guide for school-based professionals* (pp. 1121–1128). New York: Oxford University Press.

Ward, H., Anderson-Butcher, D., & Kwiatkowski, A. (2006). Effective strategies for involving parents in schools. In C. Franklin, M. Harris, & P. Allen-Meares (Eds.), *The school services sourcebook: A guide for school-based professionals* (pp. 641–650). New York: Oxford University Press.

Chapter 11

SUBSTANCE ABUSE

Lori K. Holleran Steiker and Samuel A. MacMaster

Social workers have empathically worked with and for addicts and alcoholics since the beginning of the profession's history (Straussner, 2001). Long before Alcoholics Anonymous (AA) was founded, social worker Mary Richmond (1917/1944) stated that "inebriety is a disease." Several decades later, the rest of the world caught up. In 1951, the World Health Organization came to the same conclusion, finally acknowledging alcoholism as a serious medical problem. In 1956, the American Medical Association declared alcoholism as a treatable illness, and in 1965 the American Psychiatric Association began to use the term *disease* to describe alcoholism. Richmond not only recognized alcoholism as a disease, she created an instrument to assess drinking patterns, family history of drinking, drug problems, concurrent mental illness, social contextual factors, and even an attention to gender differences with regard to alcohol use patterns. Richmond was not alone in this awareness and incorporation of addiction into practice, however, a significant number of social workers were vital members of the Yale Plan Clinics, the first outpatient facilities for the treatment of alcoholism (Straussner, 2001).

From the current head of the Substance Abuse and Mental Health Services Administration (SAMHSA), Charles Currie, to the first social worker to head the Association for Medical Educators and Researchers in Substance Abuse (AMERSA), Mary Ann Amodeo, social workers are being recognized for their leadership role in the field of substance abuse. Some social workers have made groundbreaking contributions to the field of substance abuse scholarship and research. Diana DiNitto and Aaron McNeece have written quintessential books on substance abuse dynamics and policies with a systems base. Flavio Marsiglia has developed nationally acclaimed culturally grounded substance abuse prevention interventions and theoretical frameworks. Other social work researchers are on the cutting edge of a variety of substance abuse related issues, including the following: Robert Schilling (HIV), Nabilia El Bassel (female condom), Carl Leukefeld (criminal justice interventions), Roger A. Roffman (marijuana treatment), James Hall (rural case management), and E. Michael Gorman (the methamphetamine epidemic). As noted by the founder and editor of *Social Work Practice in the Addictions,* Shulamith Lala Ashenberg Straussner (2004, p. 8), "It is time that the important role of social workers in addictions, both past and present, is more widely recognized and that social workers be encouraged to further contribute to this field in the future."

The authors would like to thank Mark Singer and David Pollio for sharing their expertise in the advancement of social work research in substance abuse.

Despite the significance of these trailblazers, not all social workers have involved themselves in, or understood the importance of, the field of addictions. Some studies examining alcohol dependence and adolescent treatment outcome have found social work's contribution lacking (Jenson, Howard, & Vaughn, 2004; Vaughn, Howard, & Jenson, 2004). For example, in the past decade, the highest percentage of substance abuse related studies of the total articles published in 13 core social work journals was 5.9% in 1994 (Vaughn et al., 2004, p. 44).

Regardless of the paucity of the social work presence in the realm of alcohol, tobacco, and other drug (ATOD) research, the mark of social workers is growing and strengthening. Social workers are an ideal match for the field of substance abuse because the skills, knowledge, and value bases are harmonic. The following sections illustrate this point.

HOLISTIC VIEW

Social work emphasizes a holistic view of the person in the context of his or her environment. The biopsychosocial view of human behavior emerges with the goal of understanding the contributions of biological, psychological, and socioenvironmental factors and their interactions with a person's behavior (Saleebey, 1992; Simon, McNeil, Franklin, & Cooperman, 1991). More recently, social work has augmented this model to include "spirituality" so as to include all aspects in the dynamic nature of human functioning (Leukefeld & Leukefeld, 1999). The biopsychosociospiritual model is an excellent guide for social work conceptualizations but key substance abuse experts note that too often, social workers neglect to address the biological aspects of the model (Flanzer, Gorman, & Spence, 2001). The biological aspects of an addict must not be overlooked, especially because this is an area of science that is definitive and can dispel the myths related to alcoholism as "moral weakness" or "lack of willpower." As noted by the National Institute on Drug Abuse (NIDA) official and social worker, Jerry Flanzer, "What is so exciting is that our—Mary Richmond's, Grace Coyle's, Bertha Reynolds'—understanding of the dynamic, reciprocal, influential effect of the environment, of personal relationships, psychological/ego processes and biology/'brain wiring' on the social human being is being substantiated by science daily" (Flanzer et al., 2001, p. 104).

According to the social work profession, individual strengths are as important as personal concerns (i.e., that which hinders optimal functioning). Strengths, such as coping skills, talents, positive self-concept, ethnic identity, and spiritual belief may assist the client in resolving existing difficulties. Resilience is a concept that epitomizes and can help operationalize the strengths perspective (Saleebey, 1997). Resiliency theory (Werner & Smith, 1992; Wolin & Wolin, 1993) is part of the social work backbone, supporting most practitioners' interventions. Regarding drug users, resilience has been defined as "the ability to tolerate, to adapt to, or to overcome life crises" (Beauvais & Oetting, 1999, p. 103).

Social workers, holding roles in micro, meso, and macro helping positions, are uniquely poised to have powerful perspective, resources, relationships, and skills with disadvantaged individuals, groups, and communities. The profession exists where the proverbial "rubber hits the road" in what Singer and Pollio (in press) call "real-world" settings.

While the social worker examines aspects of the individual's functioning, he or she is trained to keep the complex interplay between the various personal issues in mind. For example, a client's culture and ethnicity have profound implications throughout all aspects of the client's life experience. In general, social workers recognize that (a) there is normally an extensive history of life experiences that impact the clients presentation, (b) coping mechanisms are more solidified and complex, and often less mutable, and (c) there are numerous areas of inquiry based on individual, family, and community functioning and interactions.

In an article that outlines the findings of the Addictions Service Task Force, Singer, Pollio, and Stiffman (in press, p. 4) highlight that the profession of social work emphasizes the complex interactions of person and context, "The recognition of this complexity is especially important in research in the addictions and HIV to address such co-existing issues as poverty, addiction, health disparities, and polymorbidity, and how these issues are manifested intrapersonally, interpersonally and environmentally."

Two major conceptual perspectives set the stage for social work in the substance abuse arena: the ecological and the health disparities. The ecological perspective emphasizes person-in-environment and the ensuing dynamic interactions between biological, psychological, social, and cultural elements, rather than utilizing a focus on either individual or environmental factors alone (Germain & Bloom, 2000). This is contrary to other disciplines, such as medicine and psychology, which tend to view phenomena as primarily an internal process occurring on an individual basis.

The Social Work Addictions Task Force (Singer & Pollio, in press) also notes that the field of social work is unique in that it has customarily focused on underprivileged populations. In fact, the goal of which the National Association of Social Worker's Code of Ethics is to "help meet the basic human needs of all people, with particular attention to the needs and empowerment of people who are vulnerable, oppressed, and living in poverty" (National Association of Social Workers [NASW], 1999, p. 1).

Thus, another fundamental perspective that illuminates the natural marriage between the social work and substance abuse fields is a focus on the health disparities perspective. Health disparities occur within a larger context of historical and contemporary inequalities with respect to social and economic realities, and provide a more focused framework from which the ecological perspective is developed. The Institute of Medicine (Smedley, Stith, & Nelson, 2003) has developed a provider-level model describing the complex interactions between clients, health-care providers and system-level factors that lead to these disparities. These factors include social, economic, and cultural influences; stereotyping and prejudice by clinicians; and the interactions between clinicians and service recipients (that may be subject to ambiguity and misunderstanding). From this perspective, these factors lead to racially inequitable clinical decisions and resulting outcomes.

These perspectives provide the foundation for a comprehensive approach that seeks to integrate two more specific models of treatment engagement and access that focus specifically on the interaction of the individual and the service system. It is the underlying assumption in holistic social work intervention that these are dynamic interactions that exist between service users and service providers, and that the perspective of the client can be better understood by service provider; and this understanding will lead to the development and provision of more culturally congruent services.

Evidencing the recognition of the importance of social work perspective, the Department of Health and Human Services has recently developed the first National Institute of Health (NIH) "Road Map" Plan for Social Work Research (2003), which encourages each institute and center to include social workers in grants and provides supplements to pay for these individuals to become involved in individual research projects. The NIH Road Map initiative (2003) acknowledges the intricacy of health-related issues. Professional social workers strive to develop paradigms that capture the complexities of substance use/abuse related services. Further evidencing the growing interest and presence of social workers in the addictions field during the past decade or so is the formation and rapid growth of an Alcohol, Tobacco, and Other Drugs specialty section of the NASW.

According to the NASW Practice Research Network, about 1% of practicing social workers designate their primary area as addictions (www.naswdc.org/naswprn/surveyOne/area.pdf, accessed February 8, 2006). While this may seem small, the number is growing. In addition, social workers in mental health, employee assistance programs (EAPs), hospitals, schools, and other community settings are enhancing their awareness, knowledge, skills, and interventions for substance use/abuse related cases out of necessity (i.e., so many cases include substance related factors). In fact, many professionals feel that they would be remiss if they did not become competent in the area of drug and alcohol abuse due to the prominence of these problems.

Historically, many social service practitioners have had ambivalence about substance abusing clients as evidenced by failures to assess, minimization, poor data acquisition/retention and a tendency to pass substance-abusing clients on to other agencies (Amodeo & Fassler, 2001; Lightfoot & Orford, 1986). One hopeful finding is that while a study in the mid-1980s illuminated that agencies were more of a hindrance than a help to social workers with regard to working with substance abusing clients (Lightfoot & Orford, 1986), a more recent study found that a majority of social workers noted that their agencies were indeed helpful, especially in the areas of supervision, administration, substance abuse specific training, flexibility regarding client assignment to workers and opportunities to educate and supervise others on substance abuse related issues (Amodeo & Fassler, 2001). In addition, social work researchers have fortunately found that the following three pivotal experiences lead to positive therapeutic attitudes and behaviors of clinicians toward substance abusing clients: (1) specific clinical training in substance abuse, (2) opportunities to work with these clients, and (3) supervisory and staff support (Cartwright & Gorman, 1993).

Clearly, social work clients in virtually all settings present drug and alcohol related issues and therefore, assessment of these problems is critical (Kaplan, 2005). In fact, according to NASW (2001), 43% of the Practice Research Network surveyed reported that they screened clients for substance use disorders. However, while the presence of bachelor's level social workers in the addictions field is growing, research has also found a fairly low involvement of master's level social workers in this area (Sun, 2001).

Social workers tend to receive scant training in substance use and abuse (Amodeo & Fassler, 2001; Hall, Amodeo, Shaffer, & Vanderbilt, 2000; McVinney, 2004). Despite attempts to highlight the need for all social workers to be educated in drug and alcohol problems, most graduate schools still offer a smattering of electives and little mandatory education on the subject (McVinney, 2004; O'Neill, 2001; Straussner, 2004). For this reason, the following section provides a basic outline of substance abuse diagnostic and intervention related concerns.

OVERVIEW OF SUBSTANCE ABUSE PROBLEMS

Due to the fact that most social work education programs do not have mandatory substance abuse courses, it is the authors' contention that this chapter would be remiss if it did not contain an overview of fundamental, basic information concerning work with substance abusing clients. When assessing any individual, it is important for social workers to consider the possibility of substance-related disorders, which consist of substance use, abuse, and/or substance dependence. The *Diagnostic and Statistical Manual of Mental Disorders,* fourth edition, text revision (*DSM-IV-TR;* American Psychiatric Association, 2000) offers a detailed way to diagnose various drug dependencies, alcoholism, and polysubstance (at least 3 of the 11 classes of substances in a 12-month period) dependencies.

Fundamental features of substance-related disorders include (a) the taking of a drug, medication, drink, or substance in order to experience an altered state; and (b) a cluster of cognitive, behavioral, and physiological symptoms when the substance use is continued despite problems associated with its use. Substance-related disorders are divided into two primary groupings: substance use disorders (primarily dependence and abuse) and substance-induced disorders (i.e., intoxication, withdrawal, and mental health consequences of abuse).

There are 11 classes of substances, which are as follows: alcohol, amphetamines, caffeine, cannabinoids, cocaine, hallucinogens, inhalants, nicotine, opioids, phencyclidine, sedatives/hypnotics/anxiolytics, polysubstance use (use of three or more of the above noted), other (substances not included in the 11 classes), and unknown (when substance is not known, including medication overdose or reactions and toxins). The *DSM-IV-TR* provides the criteria for the diagnoses associated with each of the 11 classes of substances.

Substance dependence includes a maladaptive pattern of substance use leading to clinically significant impairment or distress, as manifested by three (or more) of the following, occurring at any time in the same 12-month period (American Psychiatric Association, 2000):

- Tolerance, as defined by either of the following: (a) a need for markedly increased amounts of the substance to achieve intoxication or desired effect or (b) markedly diminished effect with continued use of the same amount of the substance.
- Withdrawal, as manifested by either of the following: (a) the characteristic withdrawal syndrome for the substance or (b) the same (or a closely related) substance is taken to relieve or avoid withdrawal symptoms.
- The substance is taken in larger amounts or over a longer period than was intended.
- A persistent desire or unsuccessful efforts to cut down or control substance use.
- A great deal of time is spent in activities necessary to obtain the substance (e.g., visiting multiple doctors or driving long distances), use the substance (e.g., chain-smoking) or recover from its effects.

- Important social, occupational, or recreational activities are given up or reduced because of substance use.
- The substance use is continued despite knowledge of having a persistent or recurrent physical or psychological problem that is likely to have been caused or exacerbated by the substance (e.g., current cocaine use despite recognition of cocaine-induced depression, or continued drinking despite recognition that an ulcer was made worse by alcohol consumption).

The primary distinguishing characteristics between a person who uses substances and one who is dependent on the substance are as follows: (a) the phenomena of craving, which is a psychological and biological drive, experienced by addicts, to use more substances regardless of consequences; (b) the need for more and/or stronger substances for the same effect; (c) progression, or increasing problems and consequences of use over time; and (d) the eventual fatality of the illness if untreated. These aspects are the grounds for the characterization of substance abuse and dependence as a disease.

One of the most prominent substance-related disorders that social work clinicians encounter is alcohol abuse or dependence. As described by the *DSM-IV-TR* (American Psychiatric Association, 2000), 90% of American adults have tried alcohol at some time in their lives and approximately two-thirds of men and one-third of women have experienced adverse experiences related to alcohol. Alcoholism has been recognized for many years by professional medical organizations as a distinct, primary, chronic, progressive, and often fatal disease. More than 60% of adults drank alcohol in the past year, and 32% of current drinkers had five or more drinks on at least 1 day in the past year (Centers for Disease Control and Prevention, 2006). Currently, nearly 14 million Americans—1 in every 13 adults—abuse alcohol or are alcoholics, with 53% of men and women in the United States reporting that one or more of their close relatives have a drinking problem (National Institute on Alcohol Abuse and Alcoholism, 2004). Eleven percent of 8th graders, 22% of 10th graders, and 29% of 12th graders had engaged in heavy episodic, or binge drinking within the past 2 weeks (Johnston, O'Malley, Bachman, & Schulenberg, 2006). Of 3.1 million Americans, approximately 1.4% of the population ages 12 and older, received treatment for alcoholism and alcohol-related problems in 1997; treatment peaked among people between the ages 26 to 34 (SAMHSA, 2000).

The *DSM-IV-TR* (American Psychiatric Association, 2000) has two broad categories for alcohol-related disorders: alcohol-use disorders and alcohol-induced disorders. Alcohol-use disorders include alcohol dependence and alcohol abuse. There are 13 different diagnoses under alcohol-induced disorders including alcohol intoxication, alcohol withdrawal, alcohol-induced mood disorder, and alcohol-induced persisting dementia (American Psychiatric Association, 2000, p. 212).

Once alcoholism is suspected, a social worker must assess a client for physical withdrawal symptoms that can be life threatening. Many social workers are surprised to learn that alcohol withdrawal is one of the most potentially fatal detoxifications, while cocaine and even heroin withdrawal (although very uncomfortable) is generally physically harmless.

Diagnosing substance-related disorders is complicated because (a) it is hard to differentiate chemically induced symptoms from symptoms of mental illness, (b) many clients have dual diagnoses, and (c) a major presenting issue of substance abuse is denial (i.e., a mechanism for minimizing and avoiding an issue). The symptoms of substance use and abuse often mimic symptoms of other mental illnesses, and vice versa. For example, almost all addicts have mood swings between periods of elation and apparent depression (e.g., restlessness, irritability, and discontentment); however, only some addicts may actually be diagnosed as bipolar disordered.

Many adults with diagnoses other than addiction use substances as a mechanism of self-medication. Still others can be diagnosed with concurrent illnesses. Such comorbidity, historically referred to as "dual diagnosis," is also referred to as coexisting psychological and substance disorder (COPSD) and in 12-Step recovery realms, "double trouble." COPSD individuals have complicated, multiproblem presentations in treatment, and inpatient and longer-term services may need to be provided to such individuals.

The other major complicating factor in diagnosing substance problems is the tendency for the user to minimize and deny the problems. Chemically dependent individuals are often aware that their use and subsequent behaviors are socially unacceptable. Therefore, they often become adept at hiding their use, and manipulating and lying to cover up their actions. They also may try to minimize consequences, and find ways to deceive others, especially the people who care about them who, in turn, enable or perpetuate the problem through caretaking.

Substance abuse is a pattern of substance use that results in recurrent and significant adverse consequences associated with the frequent use of substances. This pattern can significantly impair all aspects of functioning. Substance dependence refers to a cluster of cognitive, behavioral, and physiological symptoms indicating the person continues to use the substance despite substantial substance-related problems (Munson, 2000). A repeated pattern of self-administration usually results in tolerance, withdrawal, and compulsive drug use. The criterion for abuse differs from dependence, which requires the client to meet three criteria in a 12-month period.

Substance abuse causes a wide variety of medical and psychiatric symptoms and diseases. Therefore, all patients presenting to the health-care system should be considered for the diagnosis. However, certain organ systems and problems have such a high prevalence of underlying substance abuse that they must be viewed with an even higher index of suspicion. Common medical symptoms of substance abuse include vitamin deficiency, malnutrition, dyspepsia, upper gastrointestinal problems, peptic ulcer, hepatitis, pancreatitis, hypertension, new onset arrhythmia, cardiomyopathy, seizures, peripheral neuropathy, and AIDS. Trauma of any kind should arouse suspicion during an interview, especially accidents at work, single car crashes, and domestic violence. Substance abuse also manifests in the following behavioral, emotional, and cognitive problems: stress, insomnia, anxiety, depression, suicidal ideation or attempt, acute psychotic states, impaired cognition, and violent behavior. Perhaps the most subtle aspects of substance abuse are the associated social problems. Substance abusers are at high risk for marital and family problems, legal difficulties, loss of employment, and financial deterioration. Special consideration should be given to patients who are homeless, involved in prostitution, and those in the criminal justice system.

Substance abusers are at particularly high risk for HIV/AIDS. During the course of an assessment, social workers must be alert to symptoms that may be related to HIV infection (Fisher & Harrison, 2000). According to Barthwell and Gilbert (1993), these signs and symptoms may include complaints of swollen lymph nodes, severe abdominal pain, diarrhea, visual changes, and severe dermatological conditions or rashes. In addition, a mental status exam may reveal AIDS-related cognitive impairments.

ASSESSMENT INSTRUMENTS

The most common evaluative tool for physical withdrawal symptoms is the Clinical Institute Withdrawal Assessment (CIWA). The CIWA for Alcohol/Drugs Based on *DSM-IV-R* (CIWA-AD) is an 8-item scale for clinical quantification of the severity of the alcohol withdrawal syndrome. It originates from the 15-item CIWA-A and the more recent, revised 10-item CIWA-AR (Sullivan, Sykora, Schneiderman, Naranjo, & Sellers, 1989). It is a reliable, brief, uncomplicated, and clinically useful scale that can also be used to monitor response to treatment. This scale offers an increase in efficiency over the original CIWA-A scale, while retaining clinical usefulness, validity, and reliability. It can be incorporated into the usual clinical care of patients undergoing alcohol withdrawal and into clinical drug trials of alcohol withdrawal.

There are a variety of assessment instruments that can be used to determine the presence, nature, and treatment directions with regard to clients with potential substance abuse problems. The most commonly utilized and widely accepted assessment tools are discussed briefly next.

CAGE

This screening test was developed by Dr. John Ewing, founding director of the Bowles Center for Alcohol Studies, University of North Carolina at Chapel Hill. CAGE (Mayfield, McLeod, & Hall, 1994) is an internationally used assessment instrument for identifying alcoholics and other substance abusers. It is particularly popular with primary caregivers. CAGE has been translated into several languages. The patient is asked four questions:

1. Have you ever felt you ought to **C**ut down your drinking (or drug use)?
2. Have people **A**nnoyed you by criticizing your drinking (or drug use)?
3. Have you ever felt bad or **G**uilty about your drinking (or drug use)?
4. Have you had a drink (or used drugs) upon wakening (**E**ye opener) to steady your nerves, get you going, or get rid of a hangover?

Affirmative answers to two or more questions are a positive screen and should prompt further history.

Michigan Alcohol Screening Test

The Michigan Alcohol Screening Test (MAST; Selzer, 1971) is a written, 25-item screening test that may be given to a patient initially or in follow-up to another screening test, such as the CAGE. Its brevity makes it useful as an outpatient screening tool. Cut-off scores correlate well with more extensive diagnostic tests for alcohol disorders. The MAST has been modified for drug abuse (i.e., DAST).

Problem Oriented Screening Instrument for Teenagers

The Problem Oriented Screening Instrument for Teenagers (POSIT) is one of the most widely used instruments for adolescent substance use/abuse. It was developed by National Institute on Drug Abuse (NIDA) to identify potential problems and service needs of adolescents ages 12 to 19 years (see Latimer, Winters, & Stinchfield, 1997). It is composed of 139 Yes/No questions under the following 10 subscales: Substance Use and Abuse; Physical Health Status; Mental Health Status; Family Relations; Peer Relations; Educational Status; Vocational Status; Social Skills; Leisure and Recreation; and Aggressive Behavior and Delinquency. It is a paper-and-pencil test, but a CD-Rom version is available. Social workers can administer this without training or additional qualifications.

Substance Abuse Subtle Screening Inventory

The Substance Abuse Subtle Screening Inventory (SASSI) is a single-page, paper-and-pencil questionnaire that takes approximately 15 minutes to complete. The test can be administered in individual or group settings and has an adult and adolescent version. In addition, it has a Spanish version.

The SASSI was developed 25 years ago and since has been empirically validated by numerous research studies attesting to its effectiveness as an assessment instrument to diagnose substance abuse disorders. The SASSI reportedly is accurate in its assessment of substance-dependent people in approximately 93% of all cases. The subscales of the SASSI inform the clinician about the client's attitude, defensiveness, emotional pain, insight into problems, and risk of unlawful behavior (The SASSI Institute, 2001).

Addiction Severity Index

The Addiction Severity Index (ASI), developed in 1980 by the Treatment Research Institute (TRI) (see www.tresearch.org/asi.htm or contact TRI, 600 Public Ledger Building, Philadelphia, PA 19106, (215) 399-0980) and collaborators from the University of Pennsylvania's Center for the Studies of Addiction, is an assessment for patients who present for substance abuse treatment. The semi-structured interview takes approximately an hour to administer. It is an ecologically based measure providing information about the following domains: medical, employment/support, drug and alcohol use, legal, family history, family/social relationships, and psychiatric problems. Using a Likert scale (10 intervals), interviewer severity ratings indicate the degree of patient problems in each of the seven domains. While some of the scales collect historical accounts, the ASI's composite scores are based entirely on current information, therefore indicating the present status of the client. These scores are particularly valuable in treatment outcome studies because successive composite scores can be used to demonstrate the changes in patient status over time.

ASAM PPC-2R

In April, 2001, the American Society of Addiction Medicine (ASAM) published the Second Edition—Revised of its Patient Placement Criteria (ASAM PPC-2R), the most widely used and comprehensive national guideline for placement, continued stay, and discharge of patients with alcohol and other drug problems. This instrument was designed to better assess the needs of patients with co-occurring mental and substance-related disorders (dual diagnosis), for revised adolescent criteria and for clarification of the residential levels of care.

The ASAM PPC-2R provides one set of guidelines for adults and one for adolescents, and five broad levels of care for each group (i.e., Early Intervention, Outpatient Treatment, Intensive Outpatient/Partial Hospitalization, Residential/Inpatient Treatment, and Medically-Managed Intensive Inpatient Treatment). The diagnostic terminology used in the ASAM PPC-2R is consistent with the most recent language of the American Psychiatric Association's *DSM-IV.* A strength of the measurement is that the type and intensity of treatment recommended are based on the patient's needs and not on limitations imposed by the treatment setting.

The ASAM PPC-2R is an excellent tool for use in treatment planning, as well as in navigating and coordinating with managed care organizations and public and private treatment providers.

INTERVENTION: THE TRANSTHEORETICAL MODEL AND MOTIVATIONAL INTERVIEWING

Through research and practice experiences, it has become clear that effective work with substance users/abusers is best accomplished using the motivational interviewing technique, which grew from the stages of change (or transtheoretical) model created by Prochaska and DiClemente (1982). The transtheoretical model helps explain how both self-initiated and professionally assisted changes occur in addictive behavior. Prochaska and DiClemente put forth a five-stage theory based on empirical research. The basic premise of their work is that stages of change are temporal dimensions that say when particular shifts in attitudes, intentions, and behaviors occur. Table 11.1 outlines the model's stages. In general, each stage represents a period of time as well as a set of tasks needed for movement to the next stage. Although the time an individual spends in each stage may vary, tasks to be accomplished are assumed to be uniform.

With regard to treatment implications, it is important to note that while the vast majority of addicted people are not in the action stage, most programs are action oriented. Studies indicate that only 10% to 15% are prepared for action; 30% to 40% in the contemplation stages, and 50% to 60% are in the precontemplation stages (Prochaska, DiClemente, & Norcross, 1992). Therefore, most programs will underserve, misserve, or not serve the majority of their target populations. The amount of progress clients make following intervention tends to be a function of their pretreatment stage of change. If clients progress from one stage to the next in the first month of treatment, they can double their chances of taking actions during the initial 6 months of the program. In summary, it is important for social workers to remember that action-oriented treatment may work with people who are in the preparation or action stages, but could be totally ineffective with individuals in the pre- or contemplation stages.

In precontemplative states, people process less information about their problems, devote less time and energy to reevaluating themselves, and experience fewer emotional reactions to the negative aspects of their problems. These clients tend to be less open

Table 11.1 The Transtheoretical Model

1. Precontemplation stage

No intention to change in the foreseeable future.

Unaware or under aware that there is even a problem.

Present to treatment because of outside influences.

May even demonstrate change while pressure is on.

Resistance to recognizing or modifying a problem is the hallmark, for example, "I don't have any problems."

2. Contemplation stage

Aware problem exists—seriously thinking about overcoming it, but have not yet made a commitment to take action.

May be stuck here for a long time, for example, smokers—2 years.

"Knowing where you want to go, but not quite ready yet."

Weigh pros and cons of problem and solution—struggle with positive evaluations of their addiction and the amount of energy, effort, and loss it will cost to overcome the problem.

3. Preparation stage

Combines intention and behavioral criteria, for example, individuals in this stage are intending to take action in the next month and have unsuccessfully taken action in the past year.

Typically will report some action such as a decrease in the addictive behavior—but have not yet reached a criterion for effective action such as abstinence.

They are, however, intending to take such action in the future.

4. Action stage

Individuals modify their behavior, experiences, or environment to overcome their problems.

Involves the most overt behavioral changes and requires considerable commitment of time and energy.

Modifications here tend to be the most visible and receive greatest external recognition.

Don't confuse this stage with change, which often happens when the requisite work is overlooked that prepares changers for action and important efforts necessary to maintain the changes following action.

They have successfully altered the addictive behavior for a period of 1 day to 6 months, e.g. reach a certain criterion—does not necessarily satisfy the field's criterion.

Modification of the target behavior to an acceptable criterion and significant overt efforts to change are the hallmarks of action.

5. Maintenance

People work to prevent relapse and consolidate the gains attained during action.

Maintenance is not static and is viewed as a continuation of change. In addiction, it extends from about 6 months to indeterminate period past the initial action. For some, it's a lifetime of change.

Being able to remain free of the addiction behavior and being able to consistently engage in new, incompatible behavior for more than 6 months are the criteria for this stage.

Stabilizing behavior change and avoiding relapse are the hallmarks of maintenance.

Since relapse is the rule rather than exception with addictions, this model cannot be conceptionalized as a linear model with people neatly going from one stage to another, rather the authors present it as a spiral pattern.

In relapse, some return to the stage before relapse. Others begin again somewhere in the middle, for example, 15% of smokers who relapsed regressed back to precontemplation stage. The majority recycle back to later stages, that is, they potentially learn from their mistakes.

In a cohort of individuals, the number of successes continues to increase gradually over time, but a large number stay in the pre- and contemplation stages.

Note: Based on "Transtheoretical Therapy: Toward a More Integrative Model of Change." by J. O. Prochaska and C. C. DiClemente, 1982, *Psychotherapy: Theory, Research and Practice, 19*(3), pp. 276–288.

with others about their problems, and do little to shift their attention or their environment in the direction of overcoming problems—they are the most resistant and least active patients. In contemplation stages, they are most open to consciousness-raising techniques—confrontations, educational processes, and so on. They re-evaluate themselves more and struggle with questions such as "how do I think and feel about living in a deteriorating environment that places my families or friends at increasing risk for disease, poverty, or imprisonment?" In preparation stages, people begin to take small steps toward action—this is where is it appropriate to use counterconditioning and stimulus control techniques to begin reducing their use and to help them control situations in which they rely on substances.

During the action stage, they endorse higher levels of self-liberation, believe they have the autonomy to change their lives, and rely increasingly on support and understanding from helping relationships. In the maintenance stage, clients rely on all the processes that came before it. This stage entails an assessment of the conditions under which a person is likely to relapse and develops alternative responses for coping with such conditions. These findings clearly suggest the need to assess the stage of a client's readiness for change and to tailor interventions accordingly. Ultimately, efficient self-change depends on doing the right things (processes) at the right time (stages).

The concept of motivational interviewing evolved from experience in the treatment of problem drinkers (Miller & Rollnick, 1991). Miller and Rollnick define motivational interviewing as a directive, client-centered counseling style for eliciting behavior change by helping clients to explore and resolve ambivalence. Compared with nondirective counseling, it is more focused and goal-oriented. The examination and resolution of ambivalence is its central purpose and the counselor is intentionally directive in pursuit of this goal. Rollnick and Miller (1995) describe the "spirit" of motivational interviewing as follows:

- Motivation to change is elicited from the client, and not imposed from without.
- It is the client's task, not the counselor's, to articulate and resolve his or her ambivalence.
- Direct persuasion is not an effective method for resolving ambivalence.
- The counseling style is generally a quiet and eliciting one.
- The counselor is directive in helping the client to examine and resolve ambivalence.
- Readiness to change is not a client trait, but a fluctuating product of interpersonal interaction.
- The therapeutic relationship is more like a partnership or companionship than expert/recipient roles.

This work is based in the collaboration between client and facilitator and is shaped by an understanding of what it takes for individuals to change a behavior that is not working for them.

The following are the motivational interviewing strategies (Miller, 1998) for social workers (which can be learned and practiced). The order is a general progression, but clinicians should follow the client's lead and utilize the most natural skill possible to allow for increasing trust and openness on the part of the client. Warmth, empathy, and reflective listening should be utilized in conjunction with each of these skills:

- Seek to understand the person's frame of reference, particularly via reflective, empathic listening.
- Express acceptance and affirmation.
- Question purposefully about clients feelings, ideas, concerns, and plans, affirming the client's freedom of choice and self-direction.
- Provide structured feedback to client, preferably tangible reports with screening scores, and so on.
- Elicit and selectively reinforce the client's own self-motivational statements, expressions of problem recognition, concern, desire and intention to change, and ability to change.
- Monitor the client's degree of readiness to change, and ensure that the client sets this pace, not the clinician.
- For work with adolescents, remember that it is best if the youth argues for change and elaborates about his or her ambivalence than if the therapist does this.
- Monitor and "roll with" resistance and try to keep it minimized, in essence, avoid argumentation.
- Summarize and reframe perceptions in a new light and reorganized forms. Motivate the client to acknowledge problems, consequences, and changes whenever possible.
- Shift, when ready, from reasons to change to a plan for change. Consider a change plan worksheet with such sections as: the changes I want to make, the most important reasons to make these changes, the steps I plan to take in changing, the ways others can help me, I will know the plan is working if . . . , and some things that could interfere with my plans.

According to Miller (1998), the term *addiction* implies some reduction in volitional control of a behavior. Besides diminished volitional control, what qualifies a behavior as addicting is that it persists despite harmful consequences. The goal of the collaboration between client and clinician is to find motivations that outweigh the motivations of the problematic behavior. The competing motivations may be multiple, and suffering associated with an addictive behavior tends to increase over time, shifting the weight of payoffs and downsides. The subsequent transformation is described as follows:

> For a brief time in motivational interviewing, we lend clients another perspective, a mirror, a chance to step safely outside of their own frame of reference and to see themselves with new eyes. This is not done by saying, "Listen to me. Here is how I see you," which places the person in the role of a passive listener. It is done by a temporary kind of merging. From the perspective of the therapist we call it empathy, seeking to see the world through the eyes of the client. In a metaphoric sense, we temporarily step inside the client, or better—become one with the client. Naturally, this improves the therapist's understanding of the client, but I think that it also changes the client's perspective. It is as if the client, too, can step into this empathic frame of reference and look back upon himself or herself. From the merged perspective of empathy, the person sees that something is possible, and the seeing begins to make it possible. It was Fritz

Perls' definition of teaching: to show a person that something is possible. We refer to it as supporting self-efficacy, but I think it's more than telling a client, "you can do it." It is somehow helping the client see that he or she can do it.

SOCIAL SUPPORT SYSTEMS

Family Intervention

An intervention is a deliberate process by which change is introduced into peoples' thoughts, feelings, and behaviors. A formal intervention usually involves several people (usually family members, employers/coworkers, clergy, friends, etc.) preparing themselves, approaching a person involved in some self-destructive behavior, and talking to the person in a clear and respectful way about the behavior in question with the immediate objectives being for the person to listen and to accept help. The overall objective of an intervention is to begin to relieve the suffering caused by self-destructive behavior—the suffering of the person engaged in it, as well as the suffering of family and friends.

To prepare for an intervention, family members and friends gather to discuss the details with an interventionist. They jointly decide what form the intervention will take (i.e., choosing locale, taking turns listing factual evidence of the person's addiction, sharing the consequence of noncompliance with intervention), identify who should be included in the intervention, develop education and treatment plans, develop an intervention plan and schedule and then execute the plans. Family and friends often enter this process with apprehension and frequently with a high level of frustration and anger. They often feel betrayed, confused, guilty and defensive. They sometimes blame each other, as well as themselves and the addicted person, for their difficulties. It is for these reasons that social workers are ideal for this role. They are often trained in group work and consider the needs of participants as important to the process as the needs of the identified problem substance user. Often, the intervention consists of the family and friends listing the factual events and incidents that illustrate the person's problem with substances and it is often helpful to have them presented without excessive emotional expression. This hones the focus on the substance abuser's consequences and undeniable behaviors rather than digressing into power struggles, pleas, and angry outbursts. Such intervention meetings have the power to transform the support system in ways necessary for lasting change to occur. When this cohesive group approaches the substance abuser, they offer something much better than an individual confrontation by a clinician.

Time for Social Skill Building

The most salient predictor of clients' positive changes in substance abuse treatment is retention (Singer, Pollio, & Stiffman, in press). By keeping clients engaged in treatment, substance abuse and other risky behaviors are also reduced. In addition, pro-social attitudes and behaviors can be cultivated and negative patterns addressed. Anecdotally, substance abuse counselors have noted that substance abusing clients tend to have social intimacy challenges, perhaps due to the lack of healthy social skills and coping mechanisms (often delayed, restricted, or replaced by addictive behaviors). Thus, it takes time and skill building for clients to learn to utilize helping networks, peers, support groups, and therapeutic settings.

Social workers can help enhance clients' social skills in order to maximize their time and connections in treatment, but another important way to engage and retain clients is to culturally ground interventions. Clients stay when they feel a sense of belonging and resonate with the culture of the treatment.

SOCIAL WORKERS AS PREVENTIONISTS

Prevention of substance abuse is a complicated task. While much progress has been made in slowing the increase of youth substance abuse, few school-based prevention approaches have proven effective in reducing substance use among adolescents and even fewer have been tested with youth of minority cultures (Forgey, Schinke, & Cole, 1997). Social work researchers have championed the need for prevention programs that are grounded with respect to the culture of the targeted students. Culture has been redefined to include aspects beyond ethnicity, such as language, clothing, body language, music, and so on.

Historically, social workers provided information and education with the assumption that adolescent *awareness* of the health hazards of substances would lead to anti-drug attitudes and subsequently the choice not to use. Research that questions the effectiveness of "information only" prevention programs (Botvin, 1995; Bukowski, 1985; Tobler, 1986) finds that not only does this form of intervention fail to produce reduction in drug use, but some programs led to a subsequent increase in the use of substances afterward (Falck & Craig, 1988). The best example is Drug Abuse Resistance Education (DARE), the most widespread drug prevention program in the United States with well over 3 million participants. Not only was DARE ineffective initially, but some researchers found an increase in students' substance use after receiving this intervention (Clayton, 1991; Harmon, 1993).

More recently, models consider the interplay of individual, social, and environmental factors (Falck & Craig, 1988). These models consider the complex, multilevel interaction of children with their environment and social systems. For example, the ecological model stresses the concept of multiple levels of influence on child development and the complex interaction of child and environment (Lorion, 1987; Tolan, Guerra, & Kendall, 1995). The focus is on social skills and general functioning rather than on substances alone.

Many social workers hold positions in schools. Thus far, the majority of school-based programs espousing the most successful social skills and ecological models have been implemented with majority culture youth (Wilson, Rodrigue, & Taylor, 1997). Though some programs have focused on minority youth, few have been designed to address culturally specific factors. Research efforts have focused superficially on cultural nuances (Forgey et al., 1997) and there is a need for cultural grounding and mechanisms to accurately ascertain such factors. Current research suggests that culturally grounded interventions are critically needed (Botvin, 1995; Gordon, 1994). Programs designed to serve the needs of minority youth have more impact when they reflect sensitivity to the unique cultural characteristics of the students (Botvin, 1995; Lee & Richardson, 1991).

In line with social work values and perspectives, Price and Lorion's (1989) important contribution to the field of prevention is the identification that successful prevention program designs do not necessarily lead to effective implementation. They make the crucial point that the intervention involves complex transactions among individuals and the context adds further complexity by virtue of a "variety of dynamic organizational and cultural forces that can act either to protect and strengthen the innovation or to undermine and distort it" (p. 102). Program success depends on the sites taking ownership of the intervention. Also, the program must resonate with the culture, language, and mores of the participants (Holleran Steiker, in press).

There are several modes of intervention that affect the cultural grounding of a program. First, the program design can be population-specific; for example, the culturally tailored intervention (CTI) specifically targeted substance abuse among inner-city African American and Hispanic youth (Forgey et al., 1997). Second, the implementers can adapt an external program to the specific population at hand. An example of this is the life skills training model (Botvin, 1995), which only makes modifications to the generalized program, where warranted, to maximize cultural sensitivity, relevance and acceptability to varied populations. Third, programs can be modified, maintaining the core of the curricula, to include aspects of the recipients culture. For example, Holleran Steiker and Hopson (2007) are studying the impact of adaptation of the Drug Resistance Strategies (DRS; NIDA, R01 DA05629) curriculum (see Hecht et al., 2003), having youth rewrite scenarios in the workbooks and remake the videos demonstrating the drug resistance strategies. Social workers recognize and can implement programs in which the adolescent perspective allows for access to accurate vernacular, customs, and styles of the target population. Language usage in particular changes over short time spans and provides unique opportunities to connect with and understand the ideas and values of each specific group of adolescents (Shapiro, 1985).

Regardless of the technique, the accuracy of the cultural aspects of a prevention program is crucial for program effectiveness. Many prevention models have been devised based on conjectures and intuitions and even stereotypes (Kim, Coletti, Williams, & Hepler, 1995). Cultural groundedness can only be achieved with input from the target population. While there is scant attention to the role of adolescents in planning, designing, and implementing substance abuse prevention programs, Wodarski and Feit (1995) state, "there is a need for youth to provide input regarding what they feel are their greatest stresses and programs needed to directly address these issues" (p. 9). In order to use adolescent input to adapt prevention programs to the culture of the target population, there must be an openness to change, a willingness to allow the adolescents to be the "experts," and a commitment to listening to their contributions.

CULTURAL CONSIDERATIONS: ETHNICITY

Ethnicity is a poignant factor with regard to drug experimentation, alcohol use and abuse, and substance-related behaviors. While a significant body of research exists noting the varied levels of drug involvement by ethnic group, the literature is flawed in that it often fails to consider contextual variables such as poverty, gender, and acculturation. The stressors of poverty, joblessness, homelessness, and mental illness often contribute to substance abuse disorders despite ethnic identity.

Research shows that youth of varied ethnic groups maintain a spectrum of attitudes and behaviors with regard to drugs and alcohol (Hecht, Trost, Bator, & MacKinnon, 1997; Korzenny, McClure, & Rzyttki, 1990; Marsiglia, Kulis, & Hecht, 2001; Moon, Hecht, Jackson, & Spellers, 1999). In addition, choices of substance vary by ethnic group (Bachman et al., 1991; Dryfoos, 1998; Kumpfer & Turner, 1991; Newcomb & Bentler, 1986; Pentz, Trebow, & Hansen, 1990).

Native Americans

Native Americans have twice the arrest rate than any other ethnic group for alcohol-related offenses while drug rates were lower than other groups (Greenfeld & Smith, 1999). While many erroneously blame "the victims," the oppression related to colonialization is more recently being examined as a precipitant in Native American substance abuse (Yellowbird, 2001). Promising effective treatments are being developed that are culturally sensitive and built on the Native American traditions, values, and beliefs (see Napoli, Marsiglia, & Kulis, 2003).

Latinos

As noted earlier, ethnic differences in drug use are not well understood by researchers. Few studies have effectively evaluated issues directly impacting Latinos/as regarding drug and alcohol use and abuse. Over the past 15 years or so, however, there has been a strong push toward comprehending the emergent problem of substance abuse among Latinos/as in the United States (De la Rosa, Holleran, & Ashenberg-Straussner, 2005).

When studies have utilized checklist models without more specific cultural determinants, findings have been misleading at best and damagingly stereotypical at worst. The assumption of homogeneity has pervaded the literature obscuring important differences between Mexicans, Cubans, Puerto Ricans, Central Americans, South Americans, Spanish people, and others who have been lumped into the generic "Hispanic" (Felix-Ortiz & Newcomb, 1995; McNeece & DiNitto, 2003). Latinos/as are diverse in areas of education, living environment, family composition, language, religion, traditions, and socioeconomic status.

Attitudes have been shown to inform behaviors. Alcohol and drug use among Hispanics are often seen as moral weaknesses caused by "bad spirits" to be removed only by God or divine intervention (Comas-Diaz, 1986). Though some believe Hispanics have a particularly strong resistance to services, others feel that this is a myth (Gonzalez-Ramos, 1990; McNeece & DiNitto, 2003).

Though *la familia* (the family) is of central importance to Latinos, and *confianza* (independence and trust), is a crucial value, systems-oriented prevention and interventions are important (McNeece & DiNitto, 2003). Latino/a cultural norms dictate a focus on concern with relational solidarity and family and the immediate circle of close friends (Collier, Ribeau, & Hecht, 1986). However, familial patterns differ from culture to culture. For example, among Mexicans and Cubans, mother son relationships are particularly close, maternal and sibling relationships are key in Puerto Rican families, and Peruvians and Bolivians feel a stronger commitment to family of origin than to their spouses and siblings (Comas-Diaz, 1986; Melus, 1980). The *verguenza* (shame) experienced by drug and alcohol users (particularly women) may isolate Latinos/as from their family.

La comunidad (the community) is a central force in Latino life. Despite the fact that ritual celebrations, or fiestas, typically involve the use of alcohol, attachment to the community should be explored as a potential mediator against drug use among Latino adolescents.

Other cultural practices such as the use of *curanderos/as,* folk healers, herbal medicine, and spirits to address alcohol and drug problems has received little attention by researchers.

Regarding overall incidence, the large-scale 1984 National Alcohol Study, with a probability sample of close to 1,500 Hispanic Americans, found that the rate of frequent heavy drinking by Latino males is approximately 17% for 29-year-olds, 26% for 39-year-olds, 11% for 49-year-olds, 12% for 59-year-olds, and 3% for people 60 years old and over. When the heaviest drinking categories were composite, 44% of Mexican American men fell into the category compared to 24% Puerto Ricans and 6% Cuban Americans. In general, single, college-educated Latino males making over $30,000 were found to drink more (Caetano, 1989). Caetano also reported that Mexican American men and women fall most frequently into categories of heavy drinkers and abstainers when compared to Puerto Rican and Cuban Americans. Data from the Hispanic Health and Nutrition Examination Survey obtained on nearly 5,000 Hispanic people is consistent with other studies in that 44% were lifetime abstainers or light drinkers, more males were drinkers than females, and drinking was most highly correlated with higher levels of education and income (Christian, Zobeck, Malin, & Hitchcock, 1989).

In a study by Hecht et al. (1997), Latinos/as reported receiving drug offers at a significantly higher rate than either European Americans or African Americans. Latinas (females), in particular, were significantly more likely to be offered drugs than other females. These findings are consistent with studies that indicate more drug use among Latino/a adolescents, in general: among inner city 12-year-olds, use rates are equal or higher for Latinos and African Americans, and use begins earlier (Caetano, 1989).

With regard to gender, male drinking may be an acceptable practice among Latino males, and even justified as part of *machismo* with the family provider having a "right to drink without criticism" (Caetano & Mora, 1988, p. 343). In contrast, there is a lack of empirical support for the belief that Hispanic drinking is more macho and aggressive than other ethnic groups (Neff, Prihoda, & Hoppe, 1991). Latinas have considerably higher proportions of abstainers and fewer alcohol problems than American women in general (Caetano, 1989). However, drug offers were found to be more frequent to Latinas than any other group (Hecht et al., 1997). A large percentage of women who drank heavily were in the 50- to 59-year-old group, perhaps because they are U.S. born and acculturated (Caetano, 1989).

Acculturation is a primary area of concern regarding risk for drug and alcohol use. Research supports that recent immigrants differ in drug use patterns from members of ethnic groups who have settled into U.S. culture (Felix-Ortiz & Newcomb, 1995). Evidence also suggests that with acculturation, more people, particularly women of Hispanic origin, may become drinkers (Caetano, 1989; Gilbert & Alcocer, 1988). Felix-Ortiz and Newcomb (1995) report that Latino adolescents who report stronger cultural identification are less likely to use drugs. The stress of acculturation has been linked to problem behaviors including delinquency, mental illness, and drug abuse (Oetting & Beauvais, 1990–1991; Pabon, 1998; Rogler, Cortez, & Malgady, 1991; Szapocznik & Williams, 2000).

Some serious methodological problems exist in the study of Latino/a drug and alcohol use. First, research problems stem from lack of documentation, replicability, and experimental testing when studying minority youth and lack of specific studies of minority youth. Second, most studies of youth rely on school samples, and Hispanic Americans and other minority groups have higher drop out rates than European Americans (Gilbert & Alcocer,

1988). Third, report levels can be effected by how drinking and drugging categories and problems are defined (Caetano, 1989). Fourth, and perhaps most importantly, "A unidimensional measure of cultural identity distilled into a single score cannot capture the complexity of these relationships (i.e., domains of cultural identity)" (Felix-Ortiz & Newcomb, 1995, p. 161).

Several studies have been specifically designed to consider the complexity of cultural identity factors among Latinos/as. Schinke et al. (1992), in a study comparing Hispanic and non-Hispanic adolescents from the southwest, reported that mothers' high school dropout status and students' low grades were better predictors of substance use than ethnicity, and they concluded that social factors must be emphasized as opposed to factors associated with ethnic racial group membership. A promising study at the Hispanic Research Center used folktales to improve children's self-esteem and prevent problem behaviors (Costantino, Malgady, & Rogler, 1985) and used a similar model for adolescents with Puerto Rican folk heroes and heroines as role models (Costantino et al., 1986). A group of researchers have developed a program revolving around bicultural effectiveness training, which targets intergenerational and intercultural family adolescent conflicts and encourages development of better family relationships by appreciating Hispanic cultural values and behaviors and those adopted from mainstream American culture (Szapocznik & Williams, 2000).

Felix-Ortiz and Newcomb's (1995) study measures cultural identity multidimensionally and across domains (i.e., language, values, behavior, types/patterns of use) and entailed cultural identity scales that used factors including "defensive Latino activism" (i.e., activism, affiliation and perceived discrimination) and "traditional family role expectations" (*respeto* and feminism). They found the following:

a. No significant effects for gender.
b. Those who reported greater familiarity with Latino culture reported significantly less marijuana use during past 6 months than those unfamiliar with the culture.
c. Marginal students (unfamiliar with either culture) used significantly more alcohol and more frequently, followed by biculturals.
d. No significant effect for English language proficiency, but significant main effect for Spanish language proficiency on all eight drug use scales; most at risk were those with limited English and Spanish language skills. In this study, good Spanish language skills were protective. Language variables were more powerful/consistent for girls.
e. Components of cultural identity associated with higher levels of drug use were: defensive Latino activism, external sociopolitical influences (i.e., perceived discrimination).
f. Components of cultural identity were associated with lower drug use: for Latinas, traditional family role expectations.
g. Feminism is associated with increased drug use among Latinas perhaps due to conflict with family and community values and pressure to conform to traditional sex roles, and a need for rebellion (Felix-Ortiz & Newcomb, 1995).

Thus, they conclude that cultural identity affects drug use depending on the type of use, gender and specific aspects of the individual's cultural identity.

African Americans and Substances

Racial disparities exist with regard to substance abuse and African Americans. African Americans experience substance dependence and abuse at rates slightly higher, but generally comparable to Caucasians, 9.5% versus 9.3%, respectively (National Survey on Drug Use and Health, 2004). Despite these comparable rates, African Americans enter treatment at disproportionately higher rates: African Americans account for 12% of the population, but 24% of treatment admissions (Treatment Data Episode Set, 2004). However, the rates for substance abuse treatment admissions for African Americans steadily declined between 1994 and 1999, while rates for admissions for the total population increased (Drug and Alcohol Service Information System [DASIS], 2002). This issue is skewed by higher rates of involvement in the criminal justice system, as criminal justice referrals were the most frequent referral source for African Americans, accounting for 37% of all admissions (DASIS, 2002). Therefore, disparities in treatment access are primarily among African Americans not involved in the criminal justice system.

Interventions, particularly prevention interventions, for African American youth and families should include "racial socialization" as a component in effective programs (Coard, Wallace, Stevenson, & Brotman, 2004). *Racial socialization* is defined as "the developmental processes by which children acquire the behaviors, perceptions, values and attitudes of an ethnic group, and come to see themselves and others as members of the group" (Rotherham & Phinney, 1987, p. 11 as cited in Coard et al., 2004).

BROADER CULTURAL CONSIDERATIONS

Ethnicity is only one component of cultural implications in a client's life. Culture can also be defined to include region, socioeconomic status, rural versus urban settings, agency milieus, and other factors. Culture consists of the distinguishing patterns of behavior and thinking that people living in social groups learn, create, and share (Bodley, 1994). Culture includes such aspects of living as beliefs, rules of behavior, language, and rituals. Groups of people who share a common culture and, in particular, common rules of behavior and a basic form of social organization, constitute a society. Thus, the terms *culture* and *society* are somewhat transposable. The people of a society collectively create and maintain culture. Culture has several distinguishing characteristics: (a) it is based on symbols and the ability to communicate using language, (b) people in the same society share common behaviors and ideology through culture, (c) it is learned or socially inherited, and (d) people use culture to quickly and flexibly adapt to changes in the world around them.

The "recovery" community (especially Alcoholics Anonymous and other 12-step programs) is a distinctive cultural community (Holleran & MacMaster, 2005; Matto, 2004). In light of the characteristics noted, 12-step programs demonstrate the construction of a shared reality through language, narrative, principals, actions, and values.

Cultural identity scales require more development and testing, as does measurement of distinct ethnic values, attitudes, and behaviors. It is clear that reliable and valid measures of ethnic identity are sorely needed (Trimble, 1995). Also, risk and protective factors may affect cultural identity factors (Felix-Ortiz & Newcomb, 1995).

Connections within the community might mediate drug use among minority populations. Reactive and defensive activism places the youth at risk and alienates them, as does perceived discrimination. Respect for others may counteract this alienation, offering a sense of attachment to the conventional order (Felix-Ortiz & Newcomb, 1995).

Misconceptions about minority drug and alcohol use and abuse are pervasive, primarily due to a lack of consideration of cultural and identity variables in past studies. Castro, Berrera, & Martinez (2004) emphasizes the need for rigorous studies of culturally adapted versions of curricula. He suggests the importance of such studies, recommending controlled research trials in which cultural adaptations of model prevention program are tested against their original versions.

One study that pursues the adaptation question was conducted by Holleran Steiker and Hopson (2007) who researched the value of culturally adapted versions of the Keepin' It REAL drug resistance curriculum (Hecht et al., 2003). Their findings suggested that having youth involved in the process of culturally adapting a program may be advantageous with regard to their own perceptions of drug dangers, possibly leading to positive changes in their own drug use behaviors.

Since treatment realms have had limited success with adolescents, it is critical that social workers champion prevention efforts to intervene before full-blown addiction or dependence occurs. It is critical that social workers not reinvent the wheel (i.e., they must utilize evidence-based programs). However, they must work toward building bridges between prevention interventions and the diverse cultures being served.

CONCLUSION

It is clear that social workers need to have a strong foundation of understanding with regard to drug and alcohol use, abuse, and implications in order to serve their clients effectively. Social workers in both the substance abuse and general practice fields can apply their uniquely holistic, ecological techniques based on empirically supported research to provide the best care for clients they serve.

Much more social work research is needed in the area of substance abuse. As powerfully noted by the Addictions Services Task Force:

> The social work profession is the largest allied health care profession in the United States. As such, social workers function in "real world" settings and provide care to individuals, groups, families and communities dealing with drug abuse and related problems. Social workers work in these settings in collaboration with members of numerous other disciplines. The breath and depth of service provision and rich interdisciplinary collaborations afford Social worker researchers the opportunity to design studies in an array of intervention sites and to maximize external validity through the use of "real-world" settings. (Singer & Polio, in press, p. 4)

Mary Richmond started the social workers' quest to serve substance users and abusers and to retain their dignity, grace, and worth. This challenging work requires sensitivity, tenacity, and empathy. It is imperative that social workers continue to learn about, study, and open hearts to clients with substance abuse problems. This complex work starts with listening carefully to the experiences of those who struggle with these difficult issues. There is no profession better suited for this work.

REFERENCES

American Psychiatric Association. (2000). *Diagnostic and statistical manual of mental disorders* (4th ed., text rev.). Washington, DC: Author.

Amodeo, M., & Fassler, I. (2001). Agency practices affecting social workers who treat substance-abusing clients. *Journal of Social Work Practice in the Addictions, 1*(2), 3–19.

Bachman, J. G., Wallace, J. M., O'Malley, P., Johnston, L., Kurth, C. L. & Neighbors, H. W. (1991). Racial/ethnic differences in smoking, drinking, and illicit drug use among American high school seniors, 1976–89. *American Journal of Public Health, 81*, 372–377.

Barthwell, A. G., & Gilbert, C. L. (1993). Screening for infectious diseases among substance abusers. *Treatment Improvement Protocol (TIP) Series, No. 6*. Rockville, MD: U.S. Department of Health and Human Services.

Beauvais, F., & Oetting, E. R. (1999). Drug use, resilience, and the myth of the golden child. In M. D. Glanz & J. L. Johnson (Eds.), *Resilience and development: Positive life adaptations* (pp. 101–106). New York: Kluwer Academic/Plenum Press.

Bodley, J. H. (1994). *Cultural anthropology: Tribes, states, and the global system*. Mountain View, CA: Mayfield.

Botvin, G. J. (1995). Drug abuse prevention in school settings. In G. J. Botvin, S. Schinke, & M. A. Orlandi (Eds.), *Drug abuse prevention with multiethnic youth* (pp. 169–192). Newbury Park, CA: Sage.

Bukowski, W. J. (1985). School-based substance abuse prevention: A review of program research. *Journal of Children in Contemporary Society, 18*(1/2), 95–115.

Caetano, R. (1989). Differences in alcohol use between Mexican Americans in Texas and California. *Hispanic Journal of Behavioral Sciences, 11*, 58–69.

Caetano, R., & Mora, M. E. (1988). Acculturation and drinking among people of Mexican descent in Mexico and the United States. *Journal of Studies on Alcohol, 49*(5), 462–471.

Cartwright, A. K. J., & Gorman, D. M. (1993). Processes involved in changing the therapeutic attitudes of clinicians toward working with drinking clients. *Psychotherapy Research, 3*, 95–104.

Castro, F. G., Barrera, M., & Martinez, C. R. (2004). The cultural adaptation of prevention interventions: Resolving tensions between fidelity and fit. *Prevention Science, 5*(1), 41–45.

Centers for Disease Control and Prevention. (2006). *Health, United States, 2006: With chartbook of trends in the health of Americans*. Washington, DC: U.S. Department of Health and Human Services.

Christian, C., Zobeck, T., Malin, H., & Hitchcock, D. (1989). Hispanic alcohol use: General description, methodological issues, and preliminary findings (NIAAA Research Monograph No. 18, DHHS Pub. No. [ADM] 87-1435). In D. Spiegler, D. Tate, S. Aitken, & C. Christian (Eds.), *Alcohol use among U.S. ethnic minorities*. Washington, DC: U.S. Government Printing Office.

Clayton, S. (1991). Gender differences in psychosocial determinants of adolescent smoking. *Journal of School Health, 61*, 115–120.

Coard, S. I., Wallace, S. A., Stevenson, Jr., H. C., & Brotman, L. M. (2004). Towards culturally relevant preventive interventions: The consideration of racial socialization in parent training with African American families. *Journal of Child and Family Studies, 13*(3), 277–293.

Collier, M. J., Ribeau, S., & Hecht, M. L. (1986). Intercultural communication rules and outcomes within three domestic cultural groups. *International Journal of Intercultural Relations, 10*, 439–457.

Comas-Diaz, L. (1986). Puerto Rican alcoholic women: Treatment considerations. *Alcoholism Treatment Quarterly, 3*(11), 47–58.

Costantino, G., Malgady, R. G., & Rogler, L. H. (1985). *Cuento therapy, folktales as a culturally sensitive psychotherapy for Puerto Rican children*. Maplewood, NJ: Waterfront Press.

Costantino, G., Malgady, R. G., & Rogler, L. H. (1986). Cuento therapy: A culturally sensitive modality for Puerto Rican children. *Journal of Consulting and Clinical Psychology, 54*, 639–645.

De la Rosa, M., Holleran, L. K., & Ashenberg-Straussner, S. L. (2005). *Substance abusing Latinos: Current research on epidemiology, prevention and treatment*. New York: Haworth Press.

Drug and Alcohol Service Information System (DASIS) Report. (2002). *Black admissions to substance abuse treatment: 1999*. Washington, DC: U.S. Department of Health and Human Services.

Dryfoos, J. G. (1998) Safe passage: making it through adolescence in a risky society. New York: Oxford University Press.

Falck, R., & Craig, R. (1988). Classroom oriented, primary prevention programming for drug abuse. *Journal of Psychoactive Drugs*, *20*(4), 403–408.

Felix-Ortiz, M., & Newcomb, M. D. (1995). Cultural identity and drug use among Latino and Latina adolescents. In G. J. Botvin, S. Schinke, & M. A. Orlandi (Eds.), *Drug abuse prevention with multiethnic youth* (pp. 147–165). Thousand Oaks, CA: Sage.

Fisher, G. L., & Harrison, T. C. (2000). *Substance abuse: Information for school counselors, social workers, therapists, and counselors*. Needham Heights, MA: Allyn & Bacon.

Flanzer, J., Gorman, E. M., & Spence, R. T. (2001). Fear of neuroscience: A dialogue about social work practice in the addictions. *Journal of Social Work Practice in the Addictions*, *1*(3), 103–112.

Forgey, M. A., Schinke, S., & Cole, K. (1997). School-based interventions to prevent substance use among inner-city minority adolescents. In D. K. Willson, J. R. Rodrigue, & W. C. Taylor (Eds.), *Health-promoting and health-compromising behaviors among minority adolescents*. Washington, DC: American Psychological Association.

Germain, C., & Bloom, M. (2000). *Human behavior in the social environment: An ecological view*. New York: Columbia University Press.

Gilbert, M. J., & Alcocer, A. M. (1988). Alcohol use and Hispanic youth: An overview. *Journal of Drug Issues*, *18*(1), 33.

Gonzalez-Ramos, G. (1990). Examining the myth of Hispanic families' resistance to treatment: Using the school as a site for services. *Social Work in Education*, *12*(4), 261–274.

Gordon, J. U. (1994). *Managing multiculturalism in substance abuse services*. Thousand Oaks, CA: Sage.

Greenfeld, L. A., & Smith, S. K. (1999). *American Indians and crime*. Washington, DC: U.S. Department of Justice, Office of Justice Programs, Bureau of Justice Statistics, NCJ 173386.

Hall, M. N., Amodeo, M., Shaffer, H. J., & Vanderbilt, J. (2000). Social workers employed in substance abuse treatment agencies: A training needs assessment. *Social Work*, *45*(2), 141–154.

Harmon, M. A. (1993). Reducing the risk of drug involvement among early adolescents: An evaluation of Drug Abuse Resistance Education (DARE). *Evaluation Review*, *17*, 221–239.

Hecht, M., Marsiglia, F. F., Elek-Fisk, E., Wagstaff, D. A., Kulis, S., Dustman, P., et al. (2003). Culturally-grounded substance use prevention: An evaluation of the keeping it REAL curriculum. *Prevention Science*, *4*, 233–248.

Hecht, M., Trost, M., Bator, R., & MacKinnon, D. (1997). Ethnicity and gender similarities and differences in drug resistance. *Journal of Applied Communication Research*, *25*, 1–23.

Holleran, L. K., & MacMaster, S. A. (2005). Applying a cultural competency framework to twelve step programs. *Alcoholism Treatment Quarterly*, *23*(4), 107–120.

Holleran Steiker, L. K. (in press). Making drug and alcohol prevention relevant: Adapting evidence-based curricula to unique adolescent cultures. *Family and Community Health*.

Holleran Steiker, L. K., & Hopson, L. M. (2007, February). *Evaluation of culturally adapted, evidence-based substance abuse prevention programs for older adolescents in diverse community settings*. Paper presented at the Advancing Adolescent Health Conference, University of Texas, Center for Health Promotion Research, Austin.

Jenson, J. M., Howard, M. O., & Vaughn, M. G. (2004). Assessing social work's contribution to controlled studies of adolescent substance abuse treatment. *Journal of Social Work Practice in the Addictions*, *4*(4), 51–65.

Johnston, L. D., O'Malley, P. M., Bachman, J. G., & Schulenberg, J. E. (2006). Teen drug use continues down in 2006, particularly among older teens; but use of prescription-type drugs remains high.

Ann Arbor, MI: University of Michigan, News and Information Services. Retrieved October 22, 2007, from www.monitoringthefuture.org.

Kaplan, L. E. (2005). Dual relationships: The challenges for social workers in recovery. *Journal of Social Work Practice in the Addictions*, *5*(3), 73–90.

Kim, S., Coletti, S. D., Williams, C., & Hepler, N. A. (1995). Substance abuse prevention involving Asian/Pacific Islander American communities. In G. J. Botvin, S. Schinke, & M. A. Orlandi (Eds.), *Drug abuse prevention with multiethnic youth* (pp. 295–326). Newbury Park, CA: Sage.

Korzenny, F., McClure, J. & Rzyttki, B. (1990). Ethnicity, communication, and drugs. *Journal of Drug Issues*, *20*, 87–98.

Kumpfer, K. L., & Turner, C. W. (1991) The social ecology model of adolescent substance abuse: Implications for prevention. *International Journal of the Addictions*, *25*(4A), 435–563.

Latimer, W. W., Winters, K. C., & Stinchfield, R. D. (1997). Screening for drug abuse among adolescents in clinical and correctional settings using the problem-oriented screening instrument for teenagers. *American Journal of Drug and Alcohol Abuse*, *23*(1), 79–98.

Lee, C. C., & Richardson, B. L. (Eds.). (1991). *Multicultural issues in counseling: New approaches to diversity*. Alexandria, VA: American Association for Counseling and Development.

Leukefeld, C. G., & Leukefeld, S. (1999). Primary socialization theory and a bio/psycho/social/spiritual practice model for substance use. *Substance Use and Misuse*, *34*(7), 983–991.

Lightfoot, P. J. C., & Orford, J. (1986) Helping agents attitudes towards alcohol related problems: situations vacant? A test and elaboration of a model, *British Journal of Addiction*, *81*, 749–756.

Lorion, R. (1987). Methodological challenges in prevention research. In J. A. Steinberg & M. M. Silverman (Eds.), *Preventing mental disorders: A research perspective* (DHHS Pub. No. [ADM] 87–1492). Washington, DC: U.S. Government Printing Office.

Marsiglia, F. F., Kulis, S., & Hecht, M. L. (2001). Ethnic labels and ethnic identity as predictors of drug use. *Journal of Research on Adolescence*, *11*(1), 21–48.

Matto, H. C. (2004). Applying an ecological framework to understanding drug addiction and recovery. *Journal of Social Work Practice in the Addictions*, *4*(3), pp. 5–22.

Mayfield, D., McLeod, G., & Hall, P. (1994). The CAGE questionnaire: Validation of a new measure. *American Journal of Psychiatry*, *131*, 1121–1123.

McNeece, C. A., & DiNitto, D. M. (2003). *Chemical dependency: A systems approach* (3rd ed.). Needham Heights, MA: Allyn & Bacon.

McVinney, L. D. (2004). Epistemology of the bottle: The social construction of alcoholism and alcoholics in social work literature in the United States between 1950 and 1959. *Journal of Social Work Practice in the Addictions*, *4*(4), 3–35.

Melus, A. (1980). Culture and language in the treatment of alcoholism: The Hispanic perspective. *Alcohol and Health Research World*, *4*(4), 19–20.

Miller, W. (1998). Toward a motivational definition and understanding of addiction. *Motivational Interviewing Newsletter for Trainers*, *5*(3), 2–6. Available from www.motivationalinterview.org/clinical/motmodel.html.

Miller, W. R., & Rollnick, S. (1991). *Motivational interviewing: Preparing people to change addictive behavior*. New York: Guilford Press.

Moon, D. G., Hecht, M. L., Jackson, K. M., & Spellers, R. E. (1999). Ethnic and gender differences and similarities in adolescent drug use and refusals of drug offers. *Substance Use and Misuse* *34*(8), 1059–1083.

Munson, C. E. (2000). *The Mental Health Diagnostic Desk Reference*. Binghamton, NY: Haworth Press.

Napoli M., Marsiglia, F. F., & Kulis, S. (2003). Sense of belonging in school as a protective factor against drug abuse among Native American urban adolescents in the Southwest. *Journal of Social Work Practice in the Addictions*, *3*(2), 25–41.

National Association of Social Workers. (1999). *Code of ethics*. Retrieved October 22, 2007, from www.socialworkers.org/pubs/code/code.asp.

National Association of Social Workers Practice Research Network. (2001). Substance abuse treatment activities. *PRN Datagram, 1*(4). Available from www.socialworkers.org/naswprn/surveyOne/substance.pdf.

National Institute on Alcohol Abuse and Alcoholism. (2004). *Alcohol abuse increases, dependence declines across decade: Young adult minorities emerge as high-risk subgroups*. Retrieved October 22, 2007, from www.niaaa.nih.gov/NewsEvents/NewsReleases/NESARCNews.htm.

National Institutes of Health. (2003). *NIH plan for social work research* [Report]. Washington, DC: Department of Health and Human Services. Retrieved October 22, 2007, from http://obssr.od.nih.gov/Documents/Publications/SWR_Report.pdf.

National Survey on Drug Use and Health. (2004). *2002: Latest national survey on drug use and health*. Washington, DC: U.S. Department of Health and Human Services.

Neff, J. A., Prihoda, T. J., & Hoppe, S. K. (1991). "Machismo," self-esteem, education and high maximum drinking among anglo, black, and Mexican-American male drinkers. *Journal of Studies on Alcohol, 52*(5), 458–463.

Newcomb, M. D., Bentler, P. M. (1986). Substance use and ethnicity: differential impact of peer and adult models. *Journal of Psychology, 120*(1), 83–95.

Oetting, E. R., & Beauvais, F. (1990–1991). Orthogonal cultural identification theory: The cultural acculturation status on delinquency for Mexican-American adolescents. *American Journal of Community Psychology, 27*(2), 189–211.

O'Neill, J. V. (2001). Expertise in addictions said crucial. *NASW News, 46*(1), 10.

Pabon, E. (1998). Hispanic adolescent delinquency and the family: A discussion of sociocultural influences. *Adolescence, 33*.

Pentz, M. A., Trebow, E. A., & Hansen, W. B. (1990). Effects of program implementation on adolescent drug use behavior: The Midwestern Prevention Program (MPP). *Evaluation Review, 14*(3), 264–389.

Price, R. H., & Lorion, R. P. (1989). Prevention programming as organizational reinvention: From research to implementation. In D. Shaffer, I. Philips, & N. B. Enzer (Eds.), *Prevention of mental health disorders, alcohol and other drug use in children and adolescents. OSAP Prevention Monograph-2*. (DHHS Pub. No. [ADM] 90–1646). Washington, DC: U.S. Government Printing Office.

Prochaska, J. O., & DiClemente, C. C. (1982). Transtheoretical therapy: Toward a more integrative model of change. *Psychotherapy: Theory, Research and Practice, 19*(3), 276–288.

Prochaska, J. O., DiClemente, C. C., & Norcross, J. C. (1992). In search of how people change: Applications to addictive behaviors. *American Psychologist, 47*(9), 1102–1114.

Richmond, M. E. (1944). *Social diagnosis*. New York: Free Press. (Original work published 1917)

Rogler, L. H., Cortes, D. E., & Malgady, R. G. (1991). Acculturation and mental health status among Hispanics: Convergence and new directions for research. *American Psychologist, 46*, 585–597.

Rollnick, S., & Miller, W. R. (1995). What is motivational interviewing? *Behavioural and Cognitive Psychotherapy, 23*, 325–334.

Saleebey, D. (1992). *The strengths perspective in social work practice* (2nd ed.). New York: Longman.

Schinke, S., Orlandi, M., Vaccaro, D., Espinoza, R., McAlister, A., & Botvin, G. (1992). Substance use among Hispanic and non-Hispanic adolescents. *Addictive Behaviors, 17*, 117–124.

Selzer, M. L. (1971). The Michigan Alcoholism Screening Test: The quest for a new diagnostic instrument. *American Journal of Psychiatry, 127*, 89–94.

Shapiro, T. (1985). Adolescent language: Its use for diagnosis, group identity, values, and treatment. *Adolescent Psychiatry, 12*, 297–311.

Simon, C., McNeil, J., Franklin, C., & Cooperman, A. (1991). Letters and comments: Author's respond. *Families in Society: Journal of Contemporary Human Services, 71*(9), 436–438.

Singer, M. I., Pollio, D. E., & Stiffman, A. (in press). Addictions services task force. *Journal of Social Service Research* [Special issue].

Smedley, B. D., Stith, A. Y., & Nelson, A. R. (Eds.). (2003). *Unequal treatment: confronting racial and ethnic disparities in health care*. Washington, DC: National Academies Press, Institute of Medicine, Board on Health Sciences Policy.

Straussner, S. L. (2001). The role of social workers in the treatment of addictions: A brief history. *Journal of Social Work Practice in the Addictions*, *1*(1), 3–9. Retrieved January 27, 2006, from http://alcoholstudies.rutgers.edu/history.html.

Straussner, S. L. (2004). Social work in addictions: A historical perspective. *Currents of the New York City Chapter, NASW*, *6*, 12.

Substance Abuse and Mental Health Services Administration. (2000, March). *National Household Survey on Drug Abuse: Main findings, 1998*. Available from www.samhsa.gov/OAS/OASftp.html.

Substance Abuse Subtle Screening Inventory Institute. (2001). *Substance Abuse Subtle Screening Inventory general information*. Available from www.sassi.com/5–29-01/.

Sullivan, J. T., Sykora, K., Schneiderman, J., Naranjo, C. A., & Sellers, E. M. (1989). Assessment of alcohol withdrawal: The revised Clinical Institute Withdrawal Assessment for Alcohol Scale (CIWA-AR). *British Journal of Addiction*, *84*, 1353–1357.

Sun, A. (2001). Systematic barriers to the employment of social workers in alcohol and other drug agencies: A statewide survey. *Journal of Social Work Practice in the Addictions*, *1*(1), 11–24.

Szapocznik, J., & Williams, R. A. (2000). Brief strategic family therapy: Twenty-five years of interplay among theory, research and practice in adolescent behavior problems and drug abuse. *Clinical Child and Family Psychology Review*, *3*(2), 117–134.

Tobler, N. S. (1986). Meta-analysis of 143 adolescent drug prevention programs: Quantitative outcome results of program participants compared to a control comparison group. *Journal of Drug Issues*, *4*, 537–567.

Tolan, P. H., Guerra, N. G., & Kendall, P. C. (1995). A developmental ecological perspective on antisocial behavior in children and adolescents: Toward a unified risk and intervention framework. *Journal of Consulting and Clinical Psychology*, *63*, 579–584.

Treatment Data Episode Set (TEDS). (2004). Treatment Data Episode Set (TEDS) 1992–2001. Washington, DC: DHHS.

Trimble, J. E. (1995). Toward an understanding of ethnicity and ethnic identity, and their relationship with drug use research. In G. J. Botvin, S. Schinke, & M. A. Orlandi (Eds.), *Drug abuse prevention with multiethnic youth* (pp. 28–45). Thousand Oaks, CA: Sage.

Vaughn, M. G., Howard, M. O., & Jenson, J. M. (2004). Assessing social work's contribution to controlled outcome studies in the alcohol dependence treatment literature. *Journal of Social Work Practice in the Addictions*, *4*(4), 37–49.

Werner, E., & Smith, R. (1992). *Overcoming the odds: High risk children from birth to adulthood*. New York: Cornell University Press.

Wilson, D. K., Rodrigue, J. R., & Taylor, W. C. (Eds.). (1997). *Health-promoting and health-compromising behaviors among minority adolescents*. Washington, DC: American Psychological Association.

Wodarski, J. S., & Feit, M. D. (1995). *Adolescent substance abuse: An empirical-based group preventive health paradigm*. New York & London: Haworth Press.

Wolin, S., & Wolin, S. (1993). *The resilient self: How survivors of troubled families rise above adversity*. New York: Villard.

Yellowbird, M. (2001). Critical values and first nations people. In R. A. Fong & S. Furoto (Eds.), *Culturally competent practice: Skills, interventions, and evaluations* (pp. 61–74). Needham Heights, MA: Allyn & Bacon.

Chapter 12

THE MENTAL HEALTH FIELD OF PRACTICE

King Davis

What are the features of the mental health field in the middle of the first decade of the twenty-first century that make it attractive to social workers? The answer to this important question reflects the magnitude, complexity, and extensiveness of changes in mental health funding, people served, organizations, and required practice approaches in just over a decade. The changes in mental health are so substantive that it is easy to conclude that the dimensions of the system today do not resemble those found prior to 1991. For example, between 1990 to 2001, utilization of mental health services of all kinds increased by 65% and the proportion of the population using services increased from 12% to 20% (Wang et al., 2006). These increases in utilization, however, were not distributed evenly across all potential service providers. As early as the 1990s, 43% of mental health episodes were treated in the general medical settings, while 40% were treated in the mental health specialty field, and close to 20% by the "human services" professions (Wang et al., 2006). Between 1990 to 2001, the general medical setting showed the greatest increase (179%), with a corresponding increase for psychiatry of 117% and other mental health specialty a 59% increase (Wang et al., 2006). Treatment of mental disorders, mild and severe, now occurs more frequently in general medicine than in other sectors (Unutzer, Schoenbaum, & Druss, 2006; Wang et al., 2006).

In the 1990s, the preferred mode of treatment for mental disorders were varying forms of individual psychotherapy. By 2001, traditional psychotherapy had declined considerably under the restrictions placed by managed health care on number and types of services covered by various plans (Davis, 2001; Wang et al., 2005, 2006).

Another key example of the extensive changes is in the financing of mental health care in 2001 compared to the 1990s. In 2001, (Mark, Coffey, Vandivort-Warren, Harwood, & King, 2005) United States expended $104 billion for mental health services, an amount equivalent to 7.6% of all health care expenditures. In 1991, however, total mental health expenditures were close to $60 billion. (Mark et al., 2005). Mental health spending grew at a rate of 5.6% over the past decade, although the rate of growth was lower than that in other sectors of health care.

Medicaid has rapidly become the major source of funding for mental health care in the United States, while the overall federal share of mental health spending has increased to 28% (Mark et al., 2005). Although there has been a substantive increase in the federal share, state general fund spending on mental health (37%) remains the primary source. States continue to shoulder the financial burden of mental health care but the federal government's contributions should equal or surpass the states' before the end of the decade. The majority of state and federal spending (28%) pays for mental health services delivered in hospitals—mostly general hospitals. This, too, is a major shift in the locus of mental health services away from specialty hospitals (Wang et al., 2006). Overall, community mental health programs accounted for the least amount (16%) of mental health expenditures over the past decade.

Also of interest is the amount (17%) of all mental health funding used to defray the cost of pharmaceuticals. When the distribution of dollars is compared to providers, physicians garnered the largest share (12%) with social workers and other professions sharing close to 8% of the balance (Mark et al., 2005).

The field of mental health is a traditional source of interest, identity, status, and career opportunities for social workers. Social workers provide over 40% of the total clinical services in mental health settings (Williams & Ell, 1998) and close to 63% within managed care settings. Within the mental health field, there are more (28.4) social work clinicians per 100,000 population than any other professions (Manderscheid & Henderson, 2001). Historically, a significant number (39.8%) of social workers found careers in public and private psychiatric hospitals, community mental health centers, general hospitals with psychiatric units, outpatient clinics and inpatient units in university settings, and in individual private practice (Gibelman, 2000; Gibelman & Schervish, 1993; Manderscheid & Henderson, 2001). Involvement in these traditional mental health settings allowed social workers to practice within psychiatric teams, become intimately engaged in offering psychotherapy, and focus on mild to moderate mental disorders. Social workers in mental health also are involved in policy, planning, and administration of agencies (U.S. Department of Labor, 2006). In all states, social workers in clinical practice are required to be licensed, certified, or registered.

Nearly 116,000 (20%) of 562,000 social workers are employed in mental health and substance abuse settings. The overall number of social workers is predicted to increase faster than other professions during the next 10 years as the population ages and as the problem of substance use increases. The entry credentials over the next decade will continue to be the master's in social work but with a clear requirement that the individual be licensed or licensed eligible. The median income ($33,900) for social workers in mental health tends to be lower than in schools, general hospitals, local government, and nursing home care. The highest median income ($36,000) for social workers in mental health was found for those employed in psychiatric hospitals. The allure of private social work practice will remain high over the next 10 years, although the demand for social workers in private practice has declined with the rise of managed heath care policy and its cost containment policies (U.S. Department of Labor, 2006).

However, newer epidemiological studies, reports (governmental and nonprofit), and federal policies identify three related developments in mental health that are redefining and transforming all aspects of this important field of practice. Because these developments occurred in an uneven and unpredictable pattern over a 30-year span, the impact on social work appears diffuse but is felt acutely in the shift from inpatient services to outpatient and from long-term care to brief intervention.

These three developments include:

1. Federal efforts to transform public mental health (services, systems, and policies).
2. Epidemiological estimates/updates on the prevalence of mental disorders (access, service utilization, and quality of care).
3. Continuation of managed health care as de facto national policy.

Each of these three related developments portend important challenges and opportunities that are redefining and shaping social work practice, education, and research in the broad field of mental health. The contemporary challenge is to determine how the social work profession repositions itself to remain current and viable in a transformed mental health field, driven by federal and business sector interests, in controlling costs. The transformation effort is redefining the problem of mental illness, introducing such new concepts as recovery, shifting the goals of services, mandating evidenced-based practice, linking mental disorders to economics, and reducing the role of traditional state mental health authorities (New Freedom Commission on Mental Health, 2003; U.S. Department of Health and Human Services, 1999).

One of the primary causalities of these three developments is the former acceptance by both the government and the private sector of theoretical and authoritative-based approaches to mental health practice (Gambrill, 1999; Wang et al., 2006). Starting in 1994, the mental health specialty became subsumed under the broad rubric of behavioral health—due in part to the elevation of managed health care as a national policy. Clearly, the intent of these developments is to require evidence-based practices as the means to drive/undergird services, control costs, and determine the most desirable characteristics of the workforce allowed to join managed care networks and bill for services in the field.

FEDERAL EFFORTS TO TRANSFORM THE PUBLIC MENTAL HEALTH FIELD

In 2003, President George W. Bush appointed a 15-member commission (New Freedom Commission on Mental Health, 2006) to assess the mental health system in the United States and make recommendations to both him and the U.S. Congress for improvements in services, structure, funding, and policy. In his charge to the commission, the president voiced a desire to create a national system in which there would be parity in the nation's treatment of health and mental health problems, services, and consumers (Bush, 2006). Bush's interest in mental health follows almost 6 years of relative inactivity, or focus, on mental health during the Clinton administration.

Bush's executive order, establishing the commission, cited three obstacles to reaching the desired level of parity and raising the quality of care: stigma, fragmentation, and unequal coverage of mental health in health insurance plans (Bush, 2006). Bush reinforced a long-term federal intent expressed by several presidents (Carter, 2006; Eisenhower, 2006; Grob, 2005; Kennedy, 2006a, 2006b, 2006c; Truman, 1945) to modify the structure and functioning of the mental health service delivery system. Many of the early presidential and congressional efforts focused on resolving long-term treatment and human rights problems within state and county mental hospitals (Carter, 2006; Eisenhower, 2006; Kennedy, 2006b; Truman, 1945). Subsequent to key studies, Presidents John F. Kennedy and Jimmy Carter supported legislation to shift mental health care to local communities and nonprofit organizations (Carter, 2006; Grob, 2005; Kennedy, 2006a).

Although several other former presidents expressed interest in this issue, Bush's commission was only the second presidential mental health study commission in U.S. history. President Carter's commission in 1978 was the first such commission (Grob, 2005) but Bush's commission shared several parallel concerns and findings with Carter's. It is important to note that Carter's efforts to transform the mental health field were undermined by the Reagan administration (Stoesz & Karger, 1993; Thomas, 2006).

Two additional efforts made use of commission studies to bring about change in mental health in the United States. The 1945 and 1955 study commissions, established by Congress, examined the mental health system (Mental Health Study Act, 1955; National Mental Health Act, 1946) and made the first major recommendations by a federal body for changes in structure, quality, services, funding, and relationships between the federal and state governments. Each of the previous commissions (presidential and congressional) identified critical fault lines in the structure of mental health care and offered broad recommendations for change in the mental health field. However, the majority of the congressional commission recommendations were for substantive changes in the operation of state mental hospitals, the locus of care for lower income populations, but also the major source of jobs for many of their constituents.

Federal efforts to change conditions in state mental hospitals, whether by the president or congress, is problematic given that state governments control these services and their operating policies. Efforts by the federal government to exact structural or operational changes raises numerous historical questions about the extent to which the federal government can intervene in state matters and policy (Althouse, 2001; Baker & Young, 2001; Drake, 1999; Marshall, 2006; Pinkney, 1818). Historically, the states' authority has rested on their interpretation of the balance of powers addressed in the U.S. Constitution (Drake, 1999). Recent judicial rulings (Bazelon Center for Mental Health Law, 2006; Center for an Accessible Society, 2006; U.S. Supreme Court, 2006) have provided greater clarity about the extent of federal power to protect the rights of persons with mental disorders to receive services outside of traditional state institutions. The federal government has used its powers of legislation to create laws that have brought fundamental change to the field (Americans with Disabilities Act, 2005; Civil Rights of Institutionalized Persons Act, 1980; Community Mental Health Centers Amendments, 1970; Mental Health Systems Act, 1980; Mental Retardation Facilities and Community Mental Health Centers Construction Act, 1963). Nevertheless, considerable tension remains evident between the federal and state governments over who has the power to change the structure and functioning of mental health systems.

The New Freedom Commission agreed with President Bush that the mental health field of practice was severely fragmented, unnecessarily complex, and financially wasteful. These conclusions formed the basis of their recommendation for an extensive overhaul of the structure and functioning of the mental health field, essentially state and local mental health services. The commission viewed the long-term structural faults in the mental health system as the major sources of poor quality services, barriers to access, and escalating costs. In its final report, the commission put forth a comprehensive vision and established principles for guiding transformation of the entire system—public and private.

The commission envisioned a future mental health system in which "everyone with a mental illness will recover"(New Freedom Commission on Mental Health, 2003). The commission's emphasis on recovery reflects a fundamental belief that mental illness can be prevented, cured, and detected early, leading to recovery. The recovery vision included a set of core values, consistent with the *Olmstead* decision (U.S. Supreme Court, 2006) that persons with mental illness must be able to live in their communities and participate in work, education, and family life. The commission's final report also identified a number of principles that support their goal of transformation. These principles include the creation of services centered on the consumer and family and provide meaningful choices, build resilience, and finally, facilitate recovery.

The commission built its report around six goals that, once achieved, create a transformed mental health system (New Freedom Commission on Mental Health, 2003). These goals included:

1. Americans understand that mental health is essential to overall health.
2. Mental health care is consumer and family driven.
3. Disparities in mental health are eliminated.
4. Early mental health screening, assessment, and referral to services are common practice.
5. Excellent mental health care is delivered and research is accelerated.
6. Technology is used to access mental health care and information.

To achieve these six goals, the commission proposed that each person served (including both adults and children) receive an individual treatment plan. This expectation by the commission is congruent with the standards established in *Wyatt v Stickney* and reinforced in the *Olmstead* decision (Johnson, 1972; U.S. Supreme Court, 2006). The commission also identified disparities by race, culture, ethnicity, and rural residence as continued impediments to quality services for the mentally ill. In response, the commission proposed cultural competence as a core approach to service design and delivery.

Full implementation of the recommendations made by the commission depends on the extent to which states are able to abandon their traditional mental health systems and operational processes and plan for new processes that include coordination and collaboration between federal, state, local, and private organizations. Transformation at the state level is underway (Power, 2004; Substance Abuse and Mental Health Services Administration, 2006).

EPIDEMIOLOGICAL ESTIMATES/UPDATES ON THE PREVALENCE OF MENTAL DISORDERS

For quite some time, information on the incidence and prevalence of mental disorders in the United States was based almost exclusively on descriptive epidemiological research (Kessler, Abelson, & Zhao, 1998). A number of these descriptive studies focused on the distribution of illness, number of inpatient admissions, and utilization of services within specific populations as the basis of inference and generalization (Malzberg, 1959; Malzberg & Lee, 1956; Manderscheid & Sonnenschein, 1985; Pasamanick, 1959, 1963; Pasamanick, Lemkau, Robers, & Kruger, 1960; U.S. Department of Health and Human Services, 2001). As a result, many policy conclusions and recommendations reflected inaccurate estimates of mental disorder by race, gender, class, immigration status, and level of disability. Without analytic studies linking rates of illness and outcomes to specific correlates, such data reinforced existing stigma, policy, systems, and status quo approaches to services (Davis & Bent-Goodley, 2004; Kessler et al., 1998).

Three substantive research efforts have introduced new perspectives and findings on the prevalence of mental disorders and their impact on the individual and the society. The National Comorbidity Study was completed in 1980 (Kramer, Von Korff, & Kessler, 1980) and recently updated (Kessler et al., 2005; Wang et al., 2005). The second major effort to identify mental disorders in the population was the summary provided by the Surgeon General in 1999 (U.S. Department of Health and Human Services, 1999). The third major effort was completed by the World Health Organization (2001), and focused on a comparison of the burden associated with mental disorder and those associated with physical disorders. Each of these estimates clarifies the prospective "demand" for mental health services in the United States and provides an epidemiological basis for changes in the mental health field.

Kessler et al. recently replicated the National Co-Morbidity Study that was originally conducted in 1980 (Kramer et al., 1980). Generalizing from a national sample of 4,000 persons, Kessler et al. (2005) noted that over a 6-month time span close to 25% of the adult population of the United States, and 21% of children, experiences a *Diagnostic and Statistical Manual-IV* mental disorder. Over a lifetime, however, the prevalence of mental disorders in the adult U.S. population approaches 50%. The prevalence of mental disorders in the United States is very similar to the rates reported in Canada and Europe, but significantly higher than in less economically prosperous nations. It is important to recognize, however, that Kessler's study does not include prevalence rates for severe mental illnesses such as schizophrenia. The rates of this mental disorder appear to remain stable at 0.5–3.0% of the population.

Twelve-month use of mental health services was studied by Wang et al. (2005). Notably, close to 42% of the individuals in the survey obtained treatment during the preceding 12-month period. The majority (22.8%) of those served were treated in the general health care sector rather than the specialty sector. Of importance, those individuals served in the health care sector were 85% of all persons receiving care during the 12-month study period. The proportion of persons with mental illness obtaining treatment is substantially improved over the findings from the Ecological Catchment Area study of the 1980s. That study showed that only 19% obtained care within the 12 months prior to the survey (Kramer et al., 1980). Three of the findings from this study were particularly disturbing. The median number of visits was only 2.9 for the year and the authors note that less than one-third of the patients obtained "minimally adequate treatment" (Wang et al., 2005). Patients of color and the poor were less likely to obtain treatment at all and more likely to obtain poorer care in the specialty care sector.

In a second study, Wang et al. (2006) explored the extent to which services for persons with mental illness are shared across six service sectors and how these patterns changed from the 1990s. This information is important since the mental health specialty sector (psychiatric hospitals, psychiatrists, and other mental health specialists) historically monopolized the provision of psychiatric care episodes prior to 1990. As early as 1980, close to 40% of all mental health episodes were treated in general medicine settings and 40% by the mental health specialty sector. However, over the past decade, the provision of mental health services within general medical settings has become the dominant approach. The use of general medicine settings for psychiatric problems increased 150% during the decade while utilization of psychiatry increased by 29% and a combination of psychiatry with general medicine increased by 72% (Wang et al., 2006). There were significant declines in utilization of other mental health specialists (–73%) and from alternative health care (–132%). It is likely that managed health care policies and practices are driving the dramatic shift toward general medicine (Unutzer et al., 2006).

Prior to the Surgeon General's "Report on Mental Disorders," estimates of mental illness in the population were inconsistent. Many earlier studies were hampered by inconsistent and inadequately applied definitions of key concepts. As a result, the prevalence of mental disorders in the population was widely exaggerated—sometimes approximating 80% in some communities (U.S. Department of Health and Human Services, 1999). More modest estimates of prevalence were first associated with the Carter Commission (Carter, 2006). It estimated that mental disorders occurred in close to 15% of the U.S. population in 1978. The Surgeon General estimated that the prevalence rate of mental disorders for adults in the United States was 20% of the population. The estimates were based on the Ecological Catchment Area Study (Regier et al., 1993) and the National Comorbidity Survey (Kessler et al., 1994; Kramer et al., 1980). These studies provided a "best estimate" of the prevalence of specific mental disorders in the population. The highest estimates (16.4%) were for any anxiety disorders, 7.1% for any mood disorder, and 1.3% for schizophrenia (U.S. Department of Health and Human Services, 1999).

The Surgeon General's report was less clear about the prevalence of mental disorders in children and adolescents. The best estimate was that close to 20% of this population has at least a "mild" level of disorder and 5% to 9% has a more severe form of emotional disorder.

Mental disorders accounted for close to 15% of the disease burden worldwide (World Health Organization, 2001). Prevalence rates for children in the United States were close to 21%. Innovative reports from the Surgeon General (U.S. Department of Health and Human Services, 1999, 2001) helped to clarify that race or ethnicity does not increase the risk of developing a mental illness but may negatively influence access to services.

The continued prevalence of mental disorders in adults and children in the United States establishes a clear epidemiological base for the mental health field of practice. The current demand, however, is insufficient to offset the multiple dilemmas in policy and practice that have brought significant challenges to the mental health field and shifted services toward the general health care sector (New Freedom Commission on Mental Health, 2003; Unutzer et al., 2006; Wang et al., 2005, 2006).

MANAGED HEALTH CARE AS NATIONAL POLICY

The most significant of the trilogy of developments that have affected social work's involvement in the mental health field is the continuation of managed health care as national policy (Davis, 1998a). By the end of 2005, 90% of Americans with health insurance belonged to some form of managed health care plan or received their health care through such a plan. Although the U.S. Congress rejected the revolutionary health care plan developed by the Clintons in 1992, the entire health care industry has undergone extensive changes based on the principles, expectations, emphases, strategies, and control exerted by managed health care. American businesses adopted these plans as a promised means of reducing their annual costs for employee health care. The impact of managed health care, however, has revolutionized the health care industry in ways unpredicted by the Clinton plan.

Managed health care is essentially an extensive set of standard insurance procedures and principles for assessing, pricing, and redistributing the economic risk associated with illness (Davis, 1997, 1998b, 2001). It is not health care or mental health care that is managed per se, it is the risk (costs, dollars, fees, reimbursements, losses, and/or payments) associated with them that is managed and controlled tightly to ensure maximum return-on-investment. This effort to redistribute and manage risk in health care is based on the same procedures and principles as the effort to manage the economic risk associated with driving, owning a car, or home ownership. Managed care uses a variety of insurance procedures to redistribute the potential risk of economic loss. Some of these procedures include co-payments, capitated funding, caps on services, fixed payments, limitations on service, preauthorization requirements, restricted formularies, and service reviews. Networks and credentialing are two concepts that are unique to managed health care. These two procedures are designed to lower costs by restricting access of insured patients to providers who have agreed to fixed payments, as well as standards of care inclusive of evidence-based practices and guidelines. The essence of these provider agreements means the provider has agreed to share the risk with the insurer, something rarely done in fee-for-service health care.

Five things have occurred following implementation of de facto managed care policy. Two of these outcomes were planned, while three were not:

1. For a number of years, total societal costs of health care declined to a level less than inflation; and the proportion of the gross domestic product (GDP) consumed by health care declined considerably.
2. Demand for services was reduced substantially; and risk was redistributed to providers, consumers, and facilities.
3. Unplanned conflict developed between providers, consumers, facilities, and insurers over quality, choice, autonomy, costs, and procedures.
4. The cost of premiums increased by 10% to 20%.
5. The quality of care declined as shown in some high profile cases in which death or serious neglect occurred.

Managed care organizations allege that it is unregulated pharmacy costs that are driving up the cost of premiums. They propose that if government were to more adequately control the cost of drugs, as is done in most other nations, the cost of health care would remain more in line with projections. This latter outcome may push the overall cost of health care to a level that business and government will reconsider whether managed health care has successfully redistributed risk and lowered their costs. In addition, managed care alleges that quality remains high, despite some controversial cases where medical judgment, eligible benefits, alternative services, and costs were at odds.

The current de facto managed health care policy has major implications for the identity of social work and some propose that managed care is the greatest challenge in the history of this profession, Flexner notwithstanding, there are four reasons for this concern. The shift in policy toward managed care has:

1. Decreased the demand for traditional social work jobs and skills in health and mental health settings while expanding social work involvement in brief care;
2. Decreased the integral role of social work supervision in practice and education;
3. Reduced the allure of private practice and long-term services; and
4. Challenged social work education to incorporate more managed care principles and services approaches in the curriculum.

The most fundamental concept in understanding the status of health care in the United States is risk. Risk is a concept and principle found prominently in all types of insurance. It is defined simply as the chance that a cost will be incurred or that a monetary loss will occur. Associated with this fundamental concept is the recognition that with risk (i.e., cost or loss), someone must assume responsibility for payment. In the past, that was government and private business.

The public policy decisions by government and business to assume the risk of health care have had a number of outcomes:

- It helped convert health care into a commodity that could be offered, priced, bought, and sold in the laissez faire American economy like other goods and services.
- It helped change the field of medicine and related professions into businesses that saw health services as profit centers.
- Removed regulatory controls over pricing and quality of health care and drugs.
- Absolved consumers of responsibility for overseeing their care; and reduced their financial share of health care from 14% to 3%.
- Treated the risk of physical and mental health services in distinctly different ways as far as reimbursement.
- Tied access to health care to work and welfare.
- Made few provisions for the uninsured and under insured.
- Stimulated nonprofit HMOs to become profit oriented.

These policy byproducts increased the overall cost of providing health and mental health care without a substantial increase in the quality of services or beneficial outcomes. For businesses and government who had assumed responsibility for the economic risk of health care, the annual increases in costs stimulated a need to either get rid of the risk entirely or find ways of redistributing the risk to providers, consumers, and health care facilities. These combined circumstances brought about the Clinton proposal for managed competition and development of managed health care as the nation's current de facto public health policy.

A number of incongruities flow from the health care policy direction chosen in the United States. The number of Americans unable to access health care is evidenced by their lack of insurance, which continues to climb each year, reaching close to 45 million people today. A significant proportion of the uninsured are children in border states in families that cannot afford health insurance and men of color in urban areas who are either out of work entirely or who work in low wage jobs that do not provide health care insurance for them. Neither group qualifies for Medicaid or Medicare under current eligibility rules. In the past 25 years, health status in the United States has been marked by major disparities by race, ethnicity, language, income, education, and social class.

The United States continues to spend far more of its GDP for health care than other comparable nations. From 1940 to 1960, only 4% to 5% of the GDP went toward health care (Weisbrod, 1961). However, since the passage of Medicare and Medicaid in 1963, the percentage of the GDP going toward health care has approached 15%, with earlier forecasts of up to 22% by 2010. No other industrial nation comes close to these figures, but no other industrial nation fails to insure its population or allows health care and pharmacy costs to go unregulated. By the end of this year, the United States will spend $1.7 trillion or close to 14% of its GDP for health care. If all of the indirect costs associated with health care were included, the United States would be spending close to $3 trillion or close to 22% of the GDP.

Another incongruity is the major shift in the government's role in financing health care. Prior to 1960, the federal government paid less than 30% of all health care costs. However, when all direct payments by the federal government are added to the tax subsidies given to business for their contributions to health care, the federal share exceeds 56%. Private business pays the majority of the remaining 44% of the health care costs. These incongruities also existed under the fee-for-service reimbursement policy that characterized American health care for decades.

SOCIAL WORK PRACTICE IN A TRANSFORMED MENTAL HEALTH FIELD

The mental health field of practice circa 2006 is not the same system from 10, 20, or 30 years ago. Numerous changes have occurred in all facets of the field that have important implications for social workers entering the field as well as those who have practiced for several years. These changes actually started with the passage of the HMO Act of 1973 during the Nixon administration (Ambrose, 1991; Nixon, 1972) and continued with Carter's recommendation to expand the federal community mental health center's program in 1978 (Grob, 2005). However, the end of federal support for community mental health services in the first years of the Reagan presidency (Thomas, 2006) appears to have introduced the most significant alterations in the traditional mental health field. The transformation of the field has major implications for social work practice.

The demand for mental health care in combination with substance abuse treatment has increased greatly over the past decade; and predictions are that this rate of growth will increase (Wang et al., 2005) well into the next decade. Corresponding predictions are that social work will remain integral to this overall expansion in demand resulting in increased job opportunities (U.S. Department of Labor, 2006). The nature of social work practice expected in mental health and substance abuse services has changed, however, along with the rest of the professional groups. Increasingly, practice must conform to the strict demands of managed health care. Essentially, this means that social work practice must become increasingly evidence-based (Gambrill, 1999; McNeill, 2006), short-term, and cost-efficient. In addition, social work will be expected to offer services to an increasingly older population, baby boomers, and retirees.

The field of mental health has undergone a major upheaval in the past decade that has improved some areas of functioning. Even with managed health care, however, the field has not solved the lingering problem of mental health disparities. Disparities are differences in access, quality, and outcomes based on race and lower income. In Wang's (Wang et al., 2005) replication study, populations of color under consumed mental health services, received lesser quality of care, and were more dependent on publicly supported care. These are problems of long standing for which the field has not identified or implemented effective strategies. Although the New Freedom Commission proposed the adoption of cultural competence as the vehicle for reducing disparities minimal efforts have been made to adapt evidence-based protocols for these populations (Whaley & Davis, 2007). The long involvement of social work in developing culturally relevant services (Brisbane, 1998; Brisbane & Womble, 1992; Pinderhughes, 1989; Solomon, 1976) provides the profession with an opportunity to use its unique research knowledge and experiences to further the goals of transformation.

REFERENCES

Althouse, A. (2001). Why talking about "States' Rights" cannot avoid the need for normative federalism analysis. *Duke Law Journal*, *51*, 363–376.

Ambrose, S. E. (1991). *Nixon: Ruin and recovery 1973–1990*. (Vol. 3). New York: Simon & Schuster.

Americans with Disabilities Act, Pub. L. No. 101-336, 42 U.S.C. Sec. 2. Vol. 42. 12101–12213 (2005).

Baker, L. A., & Young, E. A. (2001). Federalism and the double standard of judicial review. *Duke Law Journal*, *51*, 143–149.

Bazelon Center for Mental Health Law. (2006). Olmstead v. L. C. Bazelon Center. Available from www.bazelon.org/issues/disabilityrights/incourt/olmstead/index.htm.

Brisbane, F. L. (1998). *Cultural competence for health care professionals working with African American communities: Theory and practice*. (Vol. 7). Rockville, MD: Center for Substance Abuse Prevention.

Brisbane, F. L., & Womble, M. (1992). *Working with African Americans: The professional's handbook*. Chicago: HRDI International Press.

Bush, G. W. (2006). *New Freedom Commission Executive Order*. The American Presidency Project. Available from www.whitehouse.gov/news/releases/2002/04/200020429-2.html.

Carter, J. (2006). *Presidents Carter's Commission on Mental Health*. The American Presidency Project. Available from www.presidency.ucsb.edu/ws/print.php?pid=6643/.

Center for an Accessible Society. (2006). *Supreme Court Upholds ADA "Integration Mandate" in Olmstead decision*. The Center for an Accessible Society. Available from www.accessiblesociety.org/topics/ada/olmsteadoverview.htm.

Civil Rights of Institutionalized Persons Act, Pub. L. No. 96-247, 42 U.S.C. Chapter 21, Vol. 42 (1980).

Community Mental Health Centers Amendments of 1970, Pub. L. No. 91-211, 42 U.S.C. Sec. 2661 (b) (3) 84. Stat. 1238 (1970).

Davis, K. (1997). Managed care, mental illness and African Americans: A prospective analysis of managed care policy in the United States. *Smith College Studies in Social Work*, *67*, 623–641.

Davis, K. (1998a). Managed health care: Forcing social work to make choices and changes. In G. Schamess & A. Lightburn (Eds.), *Humane managed care?* (pp. 409–424). Washington, DC: National Association of Social Workers Press.

Davis, K. (1998b). Race, health status and managed health care. In F. L. Brisbane (Ed.), *Special collaborative edition CSAP Cultural Competence Series* (pp. 145–163). Rockville, MD: Center for Substance Abuse Prevention.

Davis, K. (2001). The intersection of fee for service, managed health care and cultural competence: Implications for national health care policy and services to people of color. In N. Veeder & W. Peebles-Wilkins (Eds.), *Managed care services: Policies, programs and research* (pp. 50–73). London: Oxford University Press.

Davis, K., & Bent-Goodley, T. (2004). *The color of social policy*. Alexandria, VA: Council on Social Work Education Press.

Drake, F. D. (1999). *States' rights and American federalism: A documentary history*. Westport, CT: Greenwood Press.

Eisenhower, D. D. (2006). *Special message to the congress on the nation's health program. The American Presidency Project*. Available from www.presidency.ucsb.edu/ws/print.php?pid=10605/.

Gambrill, E. (1999). Evidence-based practice: An alternative to authority-based practice. *Families in Society*, *80*, 341–350.

Gibelman, M. (2000). Say it ain't so, Norm! Reflections on who we are. *Social Work*, *45*, 463–466.

Gibelman, M., & Schervish, P. H. (1993). *The social work labor force as reflected in the NASW membership*. Washington, DC: National Association of Social Workers Press.

Grob, G. N. (2005). Public policy and mental illnesses: Jimmy Carter's Presidential Commission on Mental Health. *Milbank Quarterly*, *83*, 425–456.

Johnson, M. (1972). Wyatt v. Stickney. [344 F. Supp. 373]. Alabama Court of Appeals, 1974.

Kennedy, J. F. (2006a). *Kennedy's remarks on proposed measures to combat mental illness and mental retardation: The American Presidency Project*. Available from www.presidency.ucsb.edu/ws/pring.php?pid=9547/.

Kennedy, J. F. (2006b). *Letter to the board of commissioners of the District of Columbia: The American Presidency Project*. Available from www.presidency.ucsb.edu/ws/print.php?pid=9563/.

Kennedy, J. F. (2006c). *Letter to Secretary Ribicoff concerning the role of the federal government in the field of mental health: The American Presidency Project*. Available from www.presidency.ucsb.edu/ws/print.php?pid=8469/.

Kessler, R. C., Abelson, J., & Zhao, S. (1998). The epidemiology of mental disorders. In J. Williams & K. Ell (Eds.), *Advances in mental health research: Implications for practice* (pp. 3–24). Washington, DC: National Association of Social Workers Press.

Kessler, R. C., Berglund, P., Demler, O., Jin, R., Merikangas, L. R., & Walters, E. E. (2005). Lifetime prevalence and age-of-onset distributions of DSM IV disorders in the national comorbidity survey replication. *Archives of General Psychiatry*, *62*, 593–602.

Kessler, R. C., McGonagle, K. A., Zhao, S., Nelson, C. B., Hughes, M., Eshleman, S., et al. (1994). Lifetime and 12-month prevalence of DSM-III-R disorders in the United States. *Archives of General Psychiatry*, *51*, 8–19.

Kramer, M., Von Korff, M., & Kessler, L. (1980). The lifetime prevalence of mental disorders: Estimation, uses and limitations. *Psychological Medicine*, *10*, 429–436.

Malzberg, B. (1959). Mental disease among negroes: An analysis of first admissions in New York State, 1949–1951. *Mental Hygiene*, *43*, 422–459.

Malzberg, B., & Lee, E. S. (1956). *Migration and mental disease: A study of first admissions to hospitals for mental disease, New York 1939–1941*. New York: Social Science Research Council.

Manderscheid, R. W., & Henderson, M. J. (2001). *Mental health, United States, 2000*. Washington, DC: Center for Mental Health Services.

Manderscheid, R. W., & Sonnenschein, M. A. (1985). *Mental Health United States, 1985*. Rockville, MD: National Institute of Mental Health.

Mark, T. L., Coffey, R. M., Vandivort-Warren, R., Harwood, H. J., & King, E. C. (2005). U.S. Spending for Mental Health and Substance Abuse Treatment, 1991–2001. *Health Affairs*, 133–142.

Marshall, J. (2006). The Marshall cases: McCulloch v. Maryland (1819). Groninger University. Available from www.let.rug.nl/~usa/D/1801-1825/marshallcases/mar05.htm.

McNeill, T. (2006). Evidence-based practice in an age of relativism: Toward a model for practice. *Social Work, 51*, 147–156.

The Mental Health Study Act of 1955, Pub. L. No. 84-182, 42 U.S.C. Vol. 42, Chapter 417, 301–305 (1955).

Mental Health Systems Act, Pub. L. No. 96-398, 42 U.S.C. 201, Chapter 102, Sec. 2, 94 Stat. 1564, 9401–9522 (1980).

Mental Retardation Facilities and Community Mental Health Centers Construction Act of 1963, Pub. L. No. 88-164, 42 U.S. C. Vol. 42, 77 Stat. 282, 309–329 (1963).

National Mental Health Act, Pub. L. No. 79-487, 42 U.S.C. Sec. 2, Chapter 6a, 20, 406–411 (1946).

New Freedom Commission on Mental Health. (2003). *Achieving the promise: Transforming mental health care in America*. Final Report (SMA Report No. 03-3832). Rockville, MD: DHHS.

New Freedom Commission on Mental Health. (2006). New Freedom Commission Members. New Freedom Commission. Available from www.mentalhealthcommission.gov/minutes/Hune02.htm.

Nixon, R. M. (1972). *Health care: Request for action on 3 programs* (Message to Congress on health care; PL 93-222). Committee on Labor and Public Welfare.

Pasamanick, B. A. (1959). *The epidemiology of mental disorder*. Washington, DC: American Association for the Advancement of Science.

Pasamanick, B. A. (1963). Mental disease among negroes. In M. M. Grossack (Ed.), *Mental health and segregation* (pp. 150–157). New York: Springer.

Pasamanick, B. A., Lemkau, P. V., Robers, D., & Kruger, D. E. (1960). *A survey of mental disease in an urban population: III. Prevalence and demographic distribution of some "psychosomatic" disorders*. Washington, DC: American Psychiatric Association.

Pinderhughes, E. (1989). *Understanding race, ethnicity, and power: The key to efficacy in clinical practice*. New York: Free Press.

Pinkney, W. (1818). John James McCulloch v. The State of Maryland, 17 U.S. 316 (1819).

Power, A. K. (2004). *Mental health system transformation bridging science and service*. Bethesda, MD: National Institutes of Mental Health.

Regier, D. A., Farmer, M. E., Rae, D. S., Meyers, J. K., Kramer, M., Robins, L. N., et al. (1993). One-month prevalence of mental disorders in the United States and sociodemographic characteristics: The epidemiologic catchment area study. *Acta Psychiatrica Scandinavica, 88*, 35–47.

Solomon, B. B. (1976). *Black empowerment: Social work in oppressed communities*. New York: Columbia University Press.

Stoesz, D., & Karger, H. J. (1993). Deconstructuring welfare: The Reagan legacy and the welfare state. *Social Work, 38*, 619–628.

Substance Abuse and Mental Health Services Administration. (2006). *Mental Health Transformation State Incentives Grant Program*. Available from www.samhsa.gov/matrix/mhst_ta.aspx.

Supreme Court of the United States. (2006). Olmstead, Commissioner, Georgia Department of Human Resources, et al. v. L. C., by Zimring, Guardian. Cornell University Law School. Available from http://supct.law.cornell.edu/supct/html/98-536.ZS.html.

Thomas, A. R. (2006). Ronald Reagan and the commitment of the mentally ill: Capital, interest groups, and the eclipse of social policy. *Electronic Journal of Sociology 1998*. Available from www.sociolkogy.org/content/vol003.004/thomas.html.

Truman, H. S. (1945). *Special message to the congress recommending a comprehensive health program*. Joint meeting of the House and Senate, November 19, 1945.

Unutzer, J., Schoenbaum, M., & Druss, B. (2006). Transforming mental health care at the interface with general medicine: Report for the President's New Freedom Commission for Mental Health. *Psychiatric Services, 57*, 37–47.

U.S. Department of Health and Human Services. (1999). *Mental Health: A report of the Surgeon General*. Rockville, MD: U.S. Department of Health and Human Services, SAMHSA and NIMH.

U.S. Department of Health and Human Services. (2001). *Mental Health: Culture, Race, and Ethnicity: A Supplement to Mental Health: A report of the Surgeon General*. Rockville, MD: U.S. Department of Health and Human Services, Substance Abuse and Mental Health Services Administration, Center for Mental Health Services.

U.S. Department of Labor. (2006). *Occupational Outlook Handbook 2006–2007*. Bureau of Labor Statistics. Available from www.bls.gov/oco/ocos060.htm.

Wang, P. S., Demler, O., Olfson, M., Pincus, H. A., Wells, K. B., & Kessler, R. C. (2006). Changing profiles of service sectors used for mental health care in the United States. *American Journal of Psychiatry, 163*, 1187–1198.

Wang, P. S., Lane, M., Olfson, M., Pincus, H. A., Wells, K. B., & Kessler, R. C. (2005). Twelve-month use of mental health services in the United States. *Archives of General Psychiatry, 62*, 629–640.

Weisbrod, B. (1961, September). Anticipating the health needs of Americans: Some economic projections. *Annals of the American Academy of Political and Social Sciences, 337*, 137–145.

Whaley, A. L., & Davis, K. (2007, September). Cultural competence and evidence-based practice in mental health services: Complementary not contradictory paradigms. *American Psychologist, 62*(6), 563–574.

Williams, J. B. W., & Ell, K. (1998). *Advances in mental health research*. Alexandria, VA: National Association of Social Workers Press.

World Health Organization. (2001). *The world health report 2001: Mental health—New understanding, new hope*. Geneva, Switzerland: Author.

Chapter 13

HEALING THE DISJUNCTURE: SOCIAL WORK DISABILITY PRACTICE

Elizabeth DePoy, and Stephen Gilson

Until late in the twentieth century, disability was conceptualized primarily as an embodied deficit, creating and perpetuating disability as the object of medicalized professional intervention and in many cases exclusion and segregation. This view, while still a dominant explanatory theme for disability, is limiting to social workers who seek to advance the commitment of social work to celebrate diversity and promote social justice for all people. Fortunately, rich theory and research developments in disability studies, humanities, and social sciences have been instrumental in simultaneously broadening and deepening descriptive, explanatory, contextual, and axiological analyses of disability necessary to guide responsive, holistic social work in the twenty-first century. The aim of this chapter is to foster discussion by informing social work knowledge and practice and by analyzing disability as an important and omnipotent element of human diversity and body-environment fit. This analysis is framed through two contemporary theoretical lenses, explanatory legitimacy theory, which unpacks and foregrounds the value and contextual dimensions of human categorization, and disjuncture theory, which provides explanatory guidance for informed social action relevant to disability in a global era.

To set the contextual stage for understanding and responding to disability as human diversity, we open with a discussion of the conceptual and chronological perimeters of human classification and an analysis of the emergence of contemporary conceptualizations of diversity as equivalent to marginalized population categories. Then two contemporary theories, explanatory legitimacy and disjuncture theory, are presented. Explanatory legitimacy theory is a contemporary theoretical framework that analyzes population categories through three intersecting dimensions, description, explanation, and legitimacy. Disjuncture theory is located within the explanatory dimension of explanatory legitimacy, and provides an interactive explanation for human action and participation. In the last section, the synthesis of these foundational sections are applied to disability practice in social work. This chapter concludes with guidelines for social workers to advance social justice and celebration of diversity.

In this chapter, the term *body* refers not only to a person's organic anatomy and physiology but to the range of human phenomena that derive from bodies in action, thought, belief, and experience (Baudrillard, 1995; DePoy & Gilson, 2007). This definition is potent in integrating the multiple elements of "embodied" human experience and thus in conceptualizing diversity beyond observed characteristics of the organic body. Thus, the body and its function includes, but is not limited to, its physiology and anatomy, and is also comprised of the sensory body, the emotional body, the spiritual body, the economic body, the productive body, the body of ideas and meanings, and the body in multiple garb and spaces.

INTERSECTION OF HUMAN CATEGORIZATION AND DIVERSITY

In the United States and other Western countries, diversity in the late twentieth and early twenty-first centuries generally has come to refer to ideas and principles that define and examine relationships between dominant and monitory, nondominant groups (Healy, 2004), with the element of diversity ascribed to and owned, voluntarily or nonvoluntarily, by members of nondominant population segments (Basson, 2004; Patterson, 1997). How diversity arrived at this point has been examined from numerous humanities and social science perspectives including, but not limited to, rhetorical and cultural research (Lange, 2005; Wilson & Wilson, 2001); population research (Kertzer & Arel, 2002); historical analyses of slavery, war, internment, and holocaust; early twentieth-century immigration patterns (Basson, 2004); exploitation; important intellectual and expressive shifts from monism to pluralism; the political-economic context in which the concepts of diversity were developed in large part by the advancement of images, symbols, and interactivity; through technology and media.

Wilson and Wilson (2001) suggest that bodies, while substantively present, acquire meaning, social worth, and political response through language and symbol. How these meaning emerge, in what contexts, and how symbols are interpreted are determined by the cultures with which bodies interact, consume, and contribute. Within this larger rubric of meaning, one critically important approach to explaining the evolution of the meaning and assignment of diversity to specific categories is the theory that holds the interaction of population segments as explanatory of human difference. Both Steinberg (2001) and Healy (2004) identified the foundation of current conceptualizations of diversity as power differentials, contentious and negative intergroup relations and marginalization of immigrant, enslaved, interned, exploited, and conquered populations. They assert that unfortunate historical trends set the symbolic stage for equating negative implications of being marginalized and oppressed with the concept of diversity.

Looking to census data as explanatory of diversity meanings, Kertzer and Arel (2002) suggest that the continued practices in the United States of defining and then counting the numbers of subpopulation groups members both constructs nomothetic diversity categories as well as tautologically reifies and perpetuates them. Looking at a similar data source, epidemiological data, Armstrong (2002) indicted the concept and measurement of the "normal body" over the past several centuries and suggested that large-scale screening and surveillance of the body resulted in identifying the most commonly occurring characteristics that were then given the meaning of "desirability." Building on this concept, medicalizing bodies through surveillance of frequency, and then substantiating norms through tautological frequency measures further serves to validate and ensconce meanings of "reality" within the concepts of normalcy and deviation (DePoy & Gilson, 2007; Rosenfeld & Faircloth, 2006).

A second school of thought that has been influential in delimiting diversity to "others" is classical developmental theory, a seminal body of work that often forms the substance of the Human Behavior in the Social Environment curriculum in social work education. A critical review of theorists such as Freud, Piaget, Erikson, and their contemporaries reveals these theories did not differentiate among groups on the basis of the ethnic, racial, and cultural diversity characteristics that are common parlance in today's theoretical diversity world. Social scientists who sought to verify and build on these classical theories used methods of inquiry that fell within the positivist tradition of research, which is founded on the heuristic of a single truth, knowable only through experimental-type methods of inquiry (DePoy & Gilson, 2007; Thomas, 2001).

Epistemologically, positivism leaves no conceptual room for interrogating and characterizing human diversity from an idiographic perspective (DePoy & Gitlin, 2005). Thus, through these developmental lenses, those whose physical, social, psychological, emotional, spiritual, and behavioral bodies did not fit within two standard deviations from the mean on the normal curve were therefore located outside of normal, in groups of the abnormal, marginal, and to a large extent, undesirable (DePoy & Gilson, 2004). (See Figure 13.1.)

But with the important shifts in the social, political, and intellectual contexts in the twenty-first century, "theoretical marginalia" was not useful in explaining the full range of contemporary, heterogeneous human experience in a global, multicultural, technologically advanced context, and thus postpositive and ultimately postmodern thinking has gained in hegemony (DePoy & Gilson, 2007). With postpositivism and postmodernism as tools to frame thinking about human diversity, groups who in traditional positivist theories were considered marginal, or outside of the monistic norm, could be characterized as valued and worthy of theoretical attention rather than simply portrayed as "different and unlike the desirables."

Thomas (2001) supported the importance of ontological and epistemological trends in explaining critical influences on meanings of diversity. He suggested that postpositivist ideas that moved beyond the acceptance of a single, discoverable truth, eschewed not only monism, but to a greater or lesser degree the construct of reality. The postmodernist emphasis on symbols (primarily language) as the mediators and even the creators of experience and interaction challenged a single "truth" as correct, prescriptive, and desirable and thus the theoretical opportunity for equality of acknowledgment of all people was born.

Clearly supporting Thomas's notion of symbolic pluralism and context-embeddedness are the multiple dictionary definitions of the term *diversity* within the past 100 years. In the 1913 edition of *Webster's Dictionary,* diversity is defined as "dissimilitude; multiplicity of

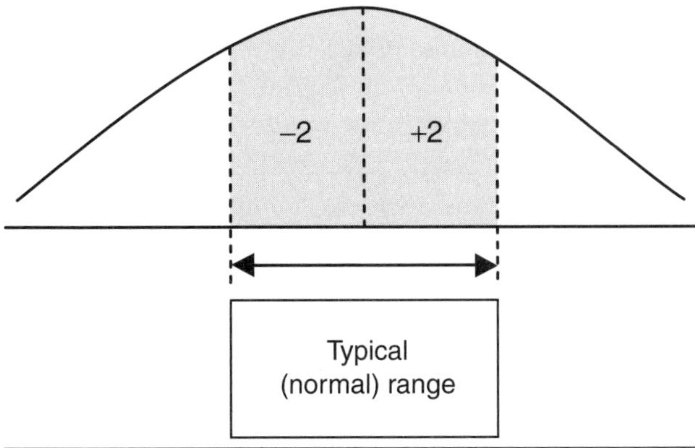

Figure 13.1 Normal Curve

differences; variety." Some prevailing and representative examples of contemporary definitions of diversity are biological difference (Wilson, 1999), racial difference (Shiao, 2004), noticeable heterogeneity (www.hyperdictionary.com, 2005), and minority group membership (Basson, 2004; Healy, 2004). These definitions are typical of current perspectives in which diversity is viewed as the nomothetic characteristic that both delineates predefined groups and identifies membership.

Moreover, in much of contemporary social work literature, policy, and practice discourse, the term diversity has been further delimited to a characteristic that belongs to groups perceived as nondominant and nonprivileged such as ethnic and racial minorities (or what is now referred to as human genome variation; Graves, 2005), women, nonheterosexual groups (Anderson & Middleton, 2005; Healy, 2004), and more recently, disabled groups (DePoy & Gilson, 2004; Mackelprang & Salsgiver, 1999).

While the numerous influential factors discussed here have been posited for the important shift in the meanings attributed to the concept of diversity, (DePoy & Gilson, 2007; Healy, 2004; Parillo, 2005; Tomlinson, 1999), multiculturalism and the failure of multicultural thought to reach the goals of equivalence and symmetry among population groups has been impugned. An understanding of the evolution of multicultural thinking (Shiao, 2004) is therefore key in explaining how diversity came to be equated with "otherness" and to suggest guidance for uncoupling the two (McClintock, 1995). This next section contains an analysis of this evolution.

MULTICULTURALISM, CATEGORY IDENTITY, AND DIVERSITY

According to Goldberg (1995), multicultural thought moved from an assimilationist to an integrationist and then to an incorporationist approach. Table 13.1 presents the distinction among the three perspectives. Both assimilationist and integrationist schools of thought begin with the heuristic that there is a dominant and desirable group of which marginal groups want to be members. The difference between assimilationist and integrationist thinking lies in the degree to which the marginal group, the "others" (McClintock, 1995), must acquire characteristics of the dominant group. However, both assimilationists and integrationists locate power within the dominant group that sits in judgment to determine the boundaries beyond which groups are marginal, and of those who are, which are acceptable

Table 13.1 Comparison of Multicultural Perspectives

Multicultural School of Thought	Viewpoints
Assimilationist	You can join us. You should join us. To join us, you need to be like us.
Integrationist	We can all live together in our world. Come and join us—We will help you ("others") come into the mainstream, but you do not have to be like us.
Incorporationist	We will transform each other for the betterment of all.

for membership, how the "other" must act, and the extent to which the "other" will be allowed to participate in, and share resources of, the dominant culture.

The incorporationist approach differs significantly from its predecessors in that it asserts equivalent worth, or what is referred to as group symmetry, among groups as the basis for cultural change. That is to say, all groups are seen as equal in their potential to collaboratively transform multicultural societies for the betterment of all. Thus, difference does not mean the maintenance of separate and distinct, or the imposition of dominant values and behaviors, as the basis for belonging. Rather, in this model all individuals and groups have the potential to both teach and learn, to value and be valued, and to select group or synthetic characteristics.

Consider a simple example of this model. Disabled individuals have typically been excluded from sports activities such as skiing. More recently, specialized volunteer programs have been developed for those who qualify as legitimate members of certain disability categories. In these groups, volunteers who ski with typical equipment and methods teach "disabled" individuals how to ski. Thus, the disabled skier is segregated, identifiable on the basis of his or her "special equipment" and often restricted to these specialized programs for instruction. Yet, what might be learned by everyone from atypical skiers? For the typical beginner or even the advanced skier, some of the equipment that is often prescribed only for mobility impaired skiers such as additional skis, seated skiing devices, and ski tip retention devices might advance the sport of skiing for all. Theoretically, the principles of incorporation and group symmetry adhere in the practices of inclusive schooling in which disabled students are physically located in regular education classrooms. That is to say, disabled and nondisabled students are expected to benefit and learn from one another (Ryan, 2005).

Despite the theoretical and rhetorical support for group symmetry (Kukathas, 2003), multicultural efforts in social work theory, research, education, and practice seem to be stalled primarily at the integrationist level of practice (DePoy & Gilson, 2004; Goldberg, 1995; McClintock, 1995; Shiao, 2004), and thus, diversity theory and application in large part have reflected approaches to the promotion of civil rights for predefined population groups that have been labeled as "diverse." While there are immediate, essential, and warranted benefits to restricting diversity theory and related responses to selected subgroups who have experienced discrimination, there are many limitations as well.

Equating diversity with oppression and marginalization has been, and to some extent continues to be, an important intellectual and policy impetus for promoting social action that advances equal opportunity. Although it is beyond the scope of this chapter to identify all of the advances anchored on theoretical views of diversity as minority, oppression, discrimination, and marginalization, some primary examples include Women's Suffrage, the Civil Rights Act of 1964, the Americans with Disabilities Act of 1990, the Violence Against Women's Act, legislation prohibiting hate crimes, affirmative action, and so forth.

However, restricting diversity theory to marginalized and oppressed categorical conceptualizations has long-term consequences and limitations (Badinter, 2006). First, viewing diversity as a characteristic of "otherness" sets and perpetuates the theoretical foundation for separation and scrutiny of marginalized groups by those who are in the position to marginalize. This phenomenon is particularly potent in experimental-type research, in which theory is taken as true until falsified.

Paradoxically, population-specific conceptualizations of diversity may unintentionally maintain stereotyping (Bonilla-Silva, 2003; Moller-Okin, Cohen, Howard, & Nussbaum, 1999; Rodriguez, 2002; Schneider, 2004), ghettoizing (DePoy & Gilson, 2004), and victimizing (Badinter, 2006) by positing homogeneity and the need for special treatment within the very groups that are defined as diverse and reifying the value of separation. Assuming group homogeneity on the basis of a single membership characteristic such as disability has the potential to promote essentialist thinking and identity politics and to restrict theory application and social work responses to assumed nomothetic need. Moreover, to continue to justify "specialized responses," a group must continue to assert its victim status, miring groups who want equality in the quicksand that they are trying to escape.

A final point to note about equating diversity with that which is comparatively infrequent is that doing so only ascribes diversity to those who lie at the extremes of the normal curve. As discussed later in this chapter, "flattening the curve" is an inclusive and socially just social work response (DePoy & Gilson, 2007). Expanding the theoretical paradigm of diversity to include and extend beyond minority group membership to include the uniqueness of all people provides many opportunities not only to maintain the important theoretical and applied gains that have occurred from civil rights concepts and movements, affirmative action, and other population specific responses, but to advance equal opportunity and justice through two important mechanisms, group symmetry and inclusion.

Group symmetry does not naively posit that all groups have equal opportunity and access to resources. Rather it is an ideal that refers to the equal value and contribution of disparate groups, and their subsequent reciprocal positive transformation of multicultural environments (Goldberg, 1994; Kukathas, 2003). Since group symmetry has yet to be broadly actualized in theory and its application, group specific affirmative thinking and strategies are still critically needed (Bonilla-Silva, 2003; Jacobs, 2004). However, group symmetry, if adopted as a social work ideal, has the potential of moving social work practice and related social action beyond group specific conceptualizations to inclusion. The previous example of inclusive education illuminates this point.

Inclusion, although used to denote multiple meanings in varied domains in the model of social work thinking and action proposed next, means the relocation of diversity beyond category membership based on difference away from the norm to individual ownership. Thus, varied beliefs, ideas, and experiences that are part of every human's existence reposition diversity as the foundation for tolerance (Kukathas, 2003), transformation, and incorporation. Explanatory legitimacy theory provides an important framework for social work action and thinking to meet these two professional challenges.

EXPLANATORY LEGITIMACY

Although explanatory legitimacy is an original theory (DePoy & Gilson, 2004), it synthesizes, builds on and advances conceptual clarity of classical and contemporary diversity theory, research and practice (Jost & Major, 2002). The concept of legitimacy is crucial to understanding the theoretical framework and its application to social work thinking and action. Legitimacy refers to the value-based establishment of "legitimate" criteria for role acquisition or group membership, the degree to which these criteria are met by potential individuals or groups, and the desirable and acceptable social work responses to those who qualify for social work attention (Jost & Major, 2002). Applying legitimacy to categorical thinking about humans, explanatory legitimacy theory (ELT) is a tripartite framework of intergroup and interpersonal judgment that posits three elements of diversity: description, explanation, and legitimacy (DePoy, 2002; DePoy & Gilson, 2004). These three elements are pivotal aspects to the category of disability.

Within the explanatory legitimacy framework, disability is defined as a contextually embedded, dynamic grand category of human diversity. Who belongs, and what social work responses are afforded to, category members is based on differential, changing and sometimes conflicting judgments about the value of explanations for diverse human phenomena (DePoy & Gilson, 2004).

Description encompasses the full range of human activity (what people do and do not do and how they do what they do), appearance, and experience. Of particular importance to description is the statistical concept of the "norm" briefly discussed earlier and illustrated in Figure 13.1. Developed by Quetelet in the late 1800s, "the normal man," was both *physically and morally normal*. Quetelet's statistical creation resulted in the application of numbers to bodies, among a range of other human phenomena (Davis, 1997) and further served to reify the binary concepts of normal and abnormal despite their operationalization as the most and least frequently occurring phenomena, respectively (Davis, 1997; DePoy & Gilson, 2004). Observation and measurement therefore turned to prescription and anyone exhibiting difference in activity, appearance, and/or experience was considered abnormal (DePoy & Gilson, 2004).

Since normal is a value statement, use of terms such as normal and abnormal does not provide the conceptual clarity sufficient for distinguishing description from axiology. Thus, in applying explanatory legitimacy to disability, the terms typical and atypical are used. They refer to magnitude rather than desirables (DePoy & Gilson, 2004).

Description contains two intersecting dimensions (typical/atypical and observable/reportable). Typical involves activity, appearance, and experience as most frequently occurring and expected in a specified context. Atypical refers to activity, appearance, and experience outside of what is considered to be typical. On the typical/atypical axis, disability potential is situated on the atypical end but this location by itself is not sufficient for disability status (DePoy & Gilson, 2004).

Consider the example of mobility. Typical adults walk without the use of wheeled mobility. Thus, those who use devices with wheels to move through physical space are atypical.

Observable phenomena are activities and appearances that fall under the rubric of those that can be sensed and agreed on. Reportable phenomena are experiences that can be known through inference only. This distinction is important in that descriptors that are observable provide more clarity and less room for disagreement than those that are inferred (reportable).

For example, mobility is observable but intelligence is not. Intelligence must be inferred by indicators such as performance on an IQ test, verbal interchange, and so forth. Or consider the constructs of physical and mental illness, which bifurcate health and illness into observable (physical) phenomena or reportable (mental) phenomena.

Looking backward in time, before disability was used as a proxy for some atypical human phenomena, descriptors such as cripple, blind, deaf, handicapped, and so forth were often articulated (DePoy & MacDuffie, 2004). These terms differentiated the disabled individual from the typical individual on the basis of a physical, sensory, cognitive, or mental "atypicality" a term Depoy and Gilson, (2004) coined to describe something that was not common or ordinary to a specified population.

In an effort to create a publicly respectful and politically correct language the term "disability" was redefined to refer to the undesirable, embodied atypical (DePoy & Gilson, 2004). However, amalgamating diverse observations of the atypical has created a definitional and theoretical quagmire. Under this conceptual rubric are people with many embodied atypicalities, both observable and reportable and who may or may not have any commonalities beyond their common classification. For example, people who cannot see, hear, think in typical ways, communicate typically, learn typically, or move through space are all considered members of the disability category and are often met with a singular response such as the Americans with Disabilities Act of 1990.

As implied in the theory title, the second element of explanatory legitimacy is explanation. Applied to disability, explanation is the set of reasons for atypical doing, appearance and experience. However, while creating the platform for membership in the disability category, explanation of the atypical by itself is still insufficient to define disability status.

Looking back in history at civilizations that predated the emergence of industrialization, medical knowledge, and technological sophistication, the grand category of disability, and thus its explanations, did not exist (Longmore & Umansky, 2001). However, in the 20th and 21st centuries, numerous contextual factors including economic productivity, medical knowledge, technology, professional authority, globalism, immigration and juxtaposition of diverse appearances, activities and beliefs, and postmodern intellectual thought have coalesced to produce two overarching and hotly debated explanations for the atypical: embodied and constructed (Gilson & DePoy, 2002).

Embodied definitions locate disability within humans and define it as an anomalous medical condition of long-term or permanent duration (Linton, 1998). Thus, within this conceptualization, the domains of disability definition, explanation, and response remain within the professional community.

In opposition, however, to what was perceived as a pejorative, the constructed explanatory school of disability emerged in the late 1980s and early 1990s. Within this broad theoretical category, disability was defined and explained as a set of limitations imposed on individuals (with or even without diagnosed medical conditions) from external factors such as social, cultural, and other environmental influences (Barnes, Mercer, & Shakespeare, 1999).

Within the constructed approaches, there are many different emphases, each which has been posited as a model of disability in itself. For example, looking at the political construction of disability, one barrier creating the disabling condition would be disempowerment due to unequal earning opportunity for individuals with undesirable conditions (Wehman, McLaughlin, & Wehman, 2005).

The cultural approach suggests that all individuals who define themselves as disabled belong to a unique group and share a common cultural disability identity (Wilson & Wilson, 2001). Hahn (Snyder & Mitchell, 1997) has suggested that the disability culture even has a shared food, fast food that can be accessed at drive-thru windows. Theoretically, membership in the culture is not attributed to diagnostic condition, since diagnosis is irrelevant in this approach to determining who is disabled. Those individuals who perceive their conditions to be treated unfairly and constructed as undesirable by dominant social institutions can claim to be members of the culture of disability in that they share disadvantage and curtailment of civil rights (Linton, 1998).

In an effort to join the civil rights movement that has been successfully used by minorities, another constructed explanation of disability is the "minority model" (Mackelprang & Salsgiver, 1999). In this view, oppression and discrimination are the causes of disability despite the majority prevalence of diagnosed disability throughout the globe.

While both major explanatory categories (embodied and constructed) continue to provide a forum for rich debate and intellectual dialogue, this explanatory binary may be limited in its use for social work professionals who seek to implement the social work commitment to diversity and social justice. Therefore, a third explanatory scheme is posited: disjuncture theory. Disjuncture, is broadly defined as the ill fit of the body with the environment. Current built, virtual and abstract (social, cultural, economic, and so forth) environments are explicitly or implicitly based on standards that harken back to the enlightenment and in large part continue to be a function of nomothetic thinking. That is to say, what is theoretically typical and average forms the basis for architectural, social, virtual, and functional design of environments, products, and other resources. The recent inquiry into the rationale for and derivation of architectural standards for door sizes, counter heights, and so forth, revealed the continued hegemony of DaVinci's Vitruvian man as both the foundational ideal and basis for estimating average adult body sizes. This male-centric, adult image forms the basis for mass-produced and standardized building and product design practices. Similarly, assumptions about typical bodies such as the ability to use both hands for manipulation, to walk with a typical gait, to hear, to see, and so forth provide the prevailing data on which design is anchored. Bodies that do not conform to prescriptive averages therefore are challenged to participate in environments in which they do not fit, setting up an environmental binary of juncture and disjuncture (see Figure 13.2).

The disjunctures between atypical bodies and their contexts in and of themselves, however, are not the explanatory locus of disability. Rather, the intersection of bodies and diverse environments (including but not limited to built, natural, virtual, social, and expressive contexts) explains what ability is and is not. Note, disability still has not been determined at the explanatory stage. Legitimate determination and responses occur in the next stage, legitimacy.

But before leaving explanation, a final point about this element is critical in guiding legitimate social work response. The reasons that are accepted as viable and accurate in explaining why the atypical is or has occurred not only is the bedrock of value determination,

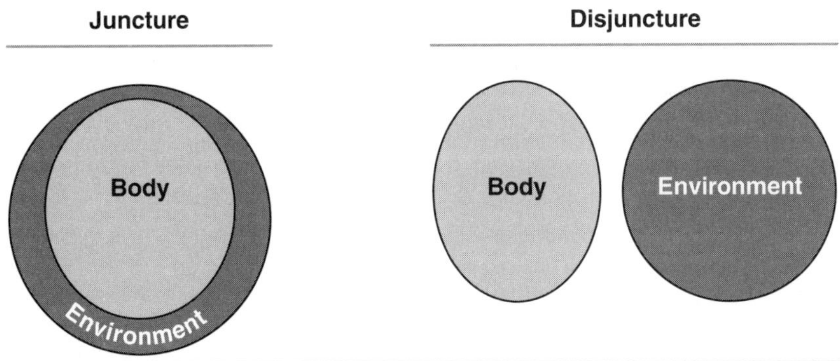

Figure 13.2 Disjuncture Theory

Table 13.2 Comparative Legitimacy

		Legitimacy	
Description	Explanation	Legitimate Disability Status	Response Examples
Unable to read social work textbook	Embodied: Medical diagnosis—blindness	Yes	Special services for blind students
Unable to read social work textbook	Constructed: Print format is not accessible	Yes	Make textbook available in CD and electronic formats
Unable to read social work textbook	Disjuncture: Information acquisition style does not fit with format presented	Yes	Create and deliver materials in multiple formats that can be translated into multiple languages for all qualified social work students

but is fundamental and essential in shaping and framing a legitimate social work response (Table 13.2).

Legitimacy, the third and most important definitional element of explanatory legitimacy, is comprised of two subelements: judgment and response. Judgment refers to value assessments of competing groups on whether what a person does throughout life (and thus what a person does not do), how a person looks, and the degree to which a person's experiences fit within what is typical and have valid and acceptable explanations that are consistent with an all-too-often unspoken value set. Responses are the actions (both negative and positive) that are deemed appropriate by those rendering the value judgments.

The term *legitimacy* has been selected to explicate the primacy of judgment about acceptability and worth in shaping differential definitions of disability and in determining legitimate social work responses at the individual, community, social group, and policy levels to those who fit within diverse disability classifications. As noted, while values shape the boundaries of typical and atypical and how these descriptors are both identified and verified, legitimacy determination and response are made on the worth of the explanation. Thus, two individuals may possess identical atypical descriptions, but on the basis of different explanations, one may qualify as legitimately disabled and the other may not.

SOCIAL WORK PRACTICE: HEALING THE DISJUNCTURE BETWEEN BODIES AND ENVIRONMENTS

To illustrate the application of explanatory legitimacy to social work practice, two scenarios are introduced.

Scenario 1

On the first day of their Human Behavior in the Social Environment class, John and Jane both bring audiorecorders for note taking. Dr. Joseph asks Bill and Crystal to turn off the recorders, letting them both know that she does not allow students to record her lectures.

After class, Bill talks with Dr. Joseph indicating that he uses the recorder as an assistive device for a learning disability as recommended by disabled student services. Crystal, however, records the lectures because she lives over an hour from the university and has a new infant who distracts her from reading at home. By listening to the recorded lectures, she is able to study in the car. In both cases, the observable atypical activity is audiorecording a lecture when all other students are taking notes either written or typed on the computer. Bill has a medical-diagnostic explanation and Crystal has a constructed explanation for the atypical activity. For Dr. Joseph, only Bill's explanation legitimates him as a disability category member worthy of special response.

Senario 2

Two women present in the emergency room with broken noses and bruises (description). Because Sue was injured in a fall after tripping on her husband's shoes left on the floor (explanation), she is not considered to be a victim (illegitimacy as a victim). Heidi, who was assaulted by her partner (explanation), qualifies for legitimate victim status and is afforded the services and supports of the domestic violence system (legitimacy response). Knowing that Sue has very poor balance due to a brain injury (explanation), her husband left the shoes on the floor with intent to harm. On the basis of disability membership (disability legitimacy determination), Sue is tacitly and perhaps unintentionally denied credibility as a victim (victim illegitimacy determination), and thus is not met with access responses to social work services that may prevent further injury or even death (illegitimacy response).

Both examples highlight the link between the explanatory legitimacy theory, inclusion, exclusion, and the disjuncture between individual and environment. However, the explanatory set for each scenario, despite identical descriptive need differences, creates differential platforms on which to render value judgments about category legitimacy and subsequently to guide a social work response. Consider Scenario 1. Both students had equivalent descriptive need. However, because Bill was legitimately a member of the "disabled students group" on the basis of a verified diagnostic circumstance, he qualified for an accommodative response, whereas Crystal did not. Inherent in Dr. Joseph's decision to allow Bill to audiorecord the lecture are assumptions and beliefs about the diagnostic efficacy and embodied limitations of people who are classified as learning disabled. The operative explanatory comparisons made by Dr. Joseph privilege Bill over Crystal at least in this situation. Furthermore, to heal the disjuncture between Bill's environment and his assumed bodily limitations, special accommodation was afforded to him that no other student, unless also a legitimate member of the disability group, would be able to use.

If responses to both students had been considered in terms of need rather than disability category membership, one possible option to equalize social work learning opportunity is the extension of audiorecorded note-taking to all students. The elements of the typical (as in Crystal's motherhood role), the atypical (diagnosed learning disability), and the degree of assumed ability to control one's limitation, in this context, are important tacit scripts in ascribing social work responses and thus they establish a binary in which Bill's embodied status, not the environment, is the locus of change. This approach to inclusion, referred to as reasonable accommodation, is condition specific and seeks to fit atypical individuals and groups into a standardized situation. Eligibility for response relies on the legitimation of a "valued" explanation for atypical experience and thus is only available to those who display a priori professionally documented, embodied, acceptable excuses for incapacity.

Implicit in the response is the notion that without it, the student's deficits would impede his progress and successful completion of the course. Thus, he is treated as impaired with his success dependent on the approval, willingness, and generosity of the social work faculty.

Similarly, the descriptive need for both Heidi and Sue are identical because both were harmed and in need of medical intervention. However, in this case, the explanation of brain injury, Sue's legitimate disability status, met with exclusion from another important category, victim status. On the basis of potentially essentialist assumptions and attitudes about the illegitimacy of disabled women as intimate partners and thus potential victims of domestic violence, the domestic violence social work service, criminal justice, and social work support responses that are afforded to those whose harm is explained in typical ways were not available to Sue.

Applied to social work's concern with the larger arena of diversity in which disability is only one element, explanatory legitimacy expands diversity conceptualizations and responses in several ways. First, building on contemporary theory, the following definition of diversity that includes but moves beyond embodied categorical diversity is proposed:

1. Varied viewpoints, ideas, and experiences.
2. The multiple "whats" and "whys" about humans.
3. Body-environment juncture.

The first element of the definition places population categorical definitions of diversity, including disability, into a larger context of the full range of human activity, appearance, and experience. By expanding the focus to the realm of thoughts, beliefs, and experiences, population specific and embodied phenomena are included but not the sole domain of diversity.

Second, specific to disability, the binary debate of disability as medical or constructed needs should be expanded and broadened to multiple whats and whys. And third, viewing diversity as an interactive rather than singular phenomenon enlarges the scope and nature of diversity and thus the potential social work responses to it.

Applied to disability, disability is a complex element of human diversity that should be viewed by social workers through pluralistic rather than essentialist lenses. Disjuncture explanations serve this end. If disability is viewed as an ill-fit between embodied phenomena and the environments in which one acts, the opportunities for social workers to expand the range of legitimacy as well as their professional responses increases exponentially. Consider Bill and Crystal as example. Both students had a descriptive need to have access to Dr. Joseph's lecture repeatedly after its initial delivery. From the lens of disjuncture theory, both students, had they been met at the level of descriptive need rather than value judgment levied at unacceptable explanations, might benefit. If the category necessary for a positive response to student need were reconceputalized away from population category to social work student enrollees, all students in the class would be included in equal learning opportunity responses.

Given that disjuncture theory guides responses to move beyond singularly targeting bodies or environments, the interaction of the two becomes the analytic unit as well as the broadened opportunity for responsive change. As suggested by Scenario 1, in the absence of purposive course objectives that require immediate verbatim recall of lecture materials,

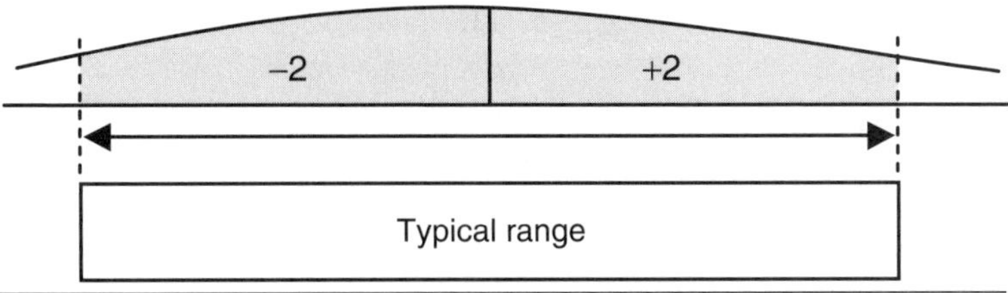

Figure 13.3 Flattened Curve

the social work education environment would have been an important locus for change such that all enrolled social work students with a full range of diverse learning styles and needs would be fully included and afforded the equivalent opportunity for mastering the material and entering the social work profession.

The danger of asserting special treatment or advantage as the only reason for Bill's success would be eliminated if Dr. Joseph had used disjuncture principles to frame the problem and her response. This point can be illustrated in Scenario 2 as well. Equality of social work responses to descriptive harm and reported cause would provide equivalent social work resources to both Sue and Heidi.

Reconceptualizing disability and all diversity categories as continua rather than binary constructs has great potential to flatten the curve. What is meant by flattening the curve is the widening and ultimate elimination of the binary dimensions of the normal curve discussed above.

Informed by current categorical diversity theory, an individual either belongs to the normal or not normal category. Those lying beyond + or –2 standard deviations away from the mean, would not fit within environments designed for assumed averages and thus would not legitimately qualify for social work responses that are built for and afforded to the typical person. Flattening the curve (Figure 13.3) would expand the range of acceptable human difference and variation and move standardized environments to respond to a wider range of acceptable diversity that is characteristic of and necessary for inclusion and group symmetry in a global environment.

Flattening the curve fits centrally within the social work mission. The metaphor does not refer to homogenization but rather acceptance and equality of response to diversity. Flattening the curve calls not only for rethinking diversity definitions but for retooling our thinking and action strategies about the essence, recognition, documentation, and responses to diversity.

CONCLUSION

The chapter concludes with an example that comparatively applies and analyzes the implementation of explanatory legitimacy and disjuncture theory in social work disability practice.

Consider Felicia, a 32-year-old woman who has sought clinical social work help for depression. Felicia uses a wheelchair for mobility, and although she would like to get married and have a family, she currently lives with her sister, brother-in-law, and two school-age nieces, in a one-story wheelchair accessible house. Felicia is currently employed as a full-time clerk at a bookstore in a northeastern U.S. city. Recently, her work environment has become contentious because a new management team has created a merit system that engenders competition among the employees. Table 13.3 presents two social work responses on the basis of embodied and constructed explanations. Note that a new group for membership, legitimacy as a social work client has been chosen.

As depicted in Table 13.3, using explanatory legitimacy, we can analyze how each explanation guides the social worker's direction. The social worker who proceeds from an embodied explanation of depression focuses his effort on "healing" the body. Note that considering wheeled mobility as a medical disability provokes a referral to rehabilitation, not an uncommon response for professionals who do not "specialize" in working with the disabled population. The desired outcome of this social work intervention would be alleviation of the depression.

The constructed explanation draws attention away from embodied phenomena to the assumed environmental exclusion. Proceeding on the explanation that Felicia is socially isolated, the social worker seeks and finds a therapeutic support group with those who are assumed to face similar issues related to a disabling condition. It is curious to note here that although the legitimate response addresses factors external to the body, the body is still the locus of difference and thus disability. In this scenario, the desired outcome would be alleviation of the depression because of new social contacts and support.

Now look at a third approach in which the social worker proceeds from a disjuncture explanation. From this explanatory perspective, both the embodied and environmental elements would be considered. The fit between Felicia and her home, social, and work environments would be the holistic focus. Possible social work responses would seek to flatten the curve by working to advance environments in which a full range of individuals could fit and be welcome. For example, if competition on the basis of merit was not a comfortable working environment for Felicia, the social worker might assist her in finding alternative work or to return to higher education where she could also engage in a new social milieu. Or the social worker might work with Felicia's family to improve the home

Table 13.3 Social Work Responses

		Social Work Legitimacy	
Description	Explanation	Eligibility for Clinical Social Work Response	Legitimate Social Work Response
Reportable depression Wheelchair user	Embodied: Diagnosed clinical depression due to disability	Yes	Referral to rehabilitation social worker; Referral for antidepressant medication
Reportable depression Wheelchair user	Constructed: Exclusion from typical social activity and intimacy; Competition in the workplace	Yes	Assists client to find disability social support group and provides problem-solving guidance for work related issues

environment. If that goal could not be achieved, the social worker might assist Felicia in identifying and seeking alternative living options.

While working with Felicia individually, the social worker proceeding through the lens of disjuncture theory would be obliged to engage in professional activity at the environmental and policy levels of practice as well. For example, the social worker might work in the community to expand the range of housing options for all types of mobility as well as other elements of diversity, might attend to the promotion of educational programs for displaced and transitional workers, might advocate for policy changes related to improving poor work climates, or work on efforts to organize inclusive recreation and social opportunity for all community members. In this scenario, Felicia's wheeled mobility is an important element of her experience and is not eschewed, but considered as only one among many factors that have contributed to the body-environment disjuncture. Healing the disjuncture requires rethinking assessments, strategies, and expected outcomes not only for Felicia but for the communities in which she works, loves, and lives.

REFERENCES

Anderson, S. K., & Middleton, V. A. (2005). *Explorations in privilege, oppression and diversity.* Belmont, CA: Wadsworth.

Armstrong, D. (2002). *A new history of identity: A sociology of medical knowledge.* New York: Palgrave.

Badinter, E. (2006). *Dead end feminism.* Cambridge, England: Polity Press.

Barnes, C., Mercer, G., & Shakespeare, T. (1999). *Exploring disability: A sociological introduction.* Cambridge, England: Polity Press.

Basson, L. (2004). *Blurring the boundaries of diversity: Racial mixture, ethnic ambiguity and indigenous citizenship in settler states.* Paper presented at the Fourth International Conference on Diversity in Organizations, Communities and Nations, University of California, Los Angeles.

Baudrillard, J. (1995). *Simulacra and simulation: The body in theory: Histories of cultural materialism* (S. F. Glaser, Trans.). Ann Arbor: University of Michigan Press.

Bonilla-Silva, E. (2003). *Racism without racists.* New York: Roman-Littlefield.

Davis, L. (1997). *Enforcing normalcy.* London: Verso.

DePoy, E. (2002). Will the real definition of disability please stand up. *Psychosocial Process, 15*(1), 50–54.

DePoy, E., & Gilson, S. F. (2004). *Rethinking disability: Principles for professional and social change.* Pacific Grove, CA: Brooks/Cole.

DePoy, E., & Gilson, S. F. (2007). *The human experience: Description, explanation and judgment.* Lanham, MD: Roman-Littlefield.

DePoy, E., & Gitlin, L. (2005). *Introduction to research: Understanding and applying multiple strategies.* St. Louis, MO: Elsevier.

DePoy, E., & MacDuffie, H. (2004). *History of long-term care.* Available from http://www.ume.maine.edu/cci/hrsaltc/.

Gilson, S. F., & DePoy, E. (2002). Multiculturalism and disability: A critical perspective. *Disability and Society*, 15207–15218.

Goldberg, D. T. (1994). *Multiculturalism: A critical reader.* Cambridge, MA: Blackwell.

Graves, J. (2005). *The race myth: Why we pretend race exists in America.* Los Angeles: Plume.

Healy, J. (2004). *Diversity and society.* Thousand Oaks, CA: Pine Forge Press.

Jacobs, L. (2004). *Pursuing equal opportunities.* New York: Cambridge University Press.

Jost, T., & Major, B. (2002). *The psychology of legitimacy: Emerging perspectives on ideology, justice, and intergroup relations*. Cambridge: Cambridge University Press.

Kertzer, D., & Arel, D. (2002). *Census and identity: The politics of race. Ethnicity and language in national censuses*. Cambridge: Cambridge University Press.

Kukathas, C. (2003). *The liberal archipelago*. New York: Oxford University Press.

Lange, S. (2005, January). *Diversity, ethnography, and technology*. Paper presented at the Technology, Knowledge and Society, Berkeley, CA.

Linton, S. (1998). *Claiming disability: Knowledge and identity*. New York: New York University Press.

Longmore, P. K., & Umansky, L. (Eds.). (2001). *The new disability history: American perspectives (History of disability)*. New York: New York University Press.

Mackelprang, R., & Salsgiver, R. (1999). *Disability: A diversity model approach in human service practice*. Pacific Grove, CA: Brooks/Cole.

McClintock, A. (1995). *Imperial leather: Race, gender, and sexuality in the colonial context*. New York: Routledge.

Moller-Okin, S., Cohen, J., Howard, M., & Nussbaum, M. (Eds.). (1999). *Is multiculturalism bad for women?* Princeton, NJ: Princeton University Press.

Parillo, V. (2005). *Diversity in America* (2nd ed.). Thousand Oaks, CA: Pine Forge Press.

Patterson, C. J. (1997). Children of lesbian and gay parents. In T. Ollendick & R. Prinz (Eds.), *Advances in clinical child psychology* (Vol. 19, pp. 235–282). New York: Plenum Press.

Rodriguez, R. (2002). *Brown: The last discovery of America*. New York: Viking.

Rosenfeld, D., & Faircloth, C. (2006). *Medicalized masculinities: The missing link?* Philadelphia: Temple University Press.

Ryan, J. (2005). *Inclusive leadership*. Hoboken, NJ: Jossey-Bass.

Schneider, D. (2004). *The psychology of stereotyping*. New York: Guilford Press.

Shiao, J. L. (2004). *Identifying talent, institutionalizing diversity*. Durham, NC: Duke University Press.

Snyder, S., & Mitchell, D. (1997). *Vital signs: Crip culture talks back*. Marquette, MI: Brace Yourselves Productions.

Steinberg, S. (2001). *The ethnic myth* (3rd ed.). Boston: Beacon Press.

Thomas, R. M. (2001). *Recent theories of human development*. Thousand Oaks, CA: Sage.

Tomlinson, J. (1999). *Globalization and culture*. Chicago: University of Chicago Press.

Wehman, P., McLaughlin, P., & Wehman, T. (2005). *Intellectual and developmental disabilities: Toward full community inclusion*. Austin, TX: ProEd.

Wilson, E. O. (1999). *The diversity of life*. New York: Norton.

Wilson, J. C., & Wilson, C. L. (2001). *Embodied rhetorics: Disability in language and culture*. Carbondale: Southern Illinois University Press.

Chapter 14

GERONTOLOGY: A FIELD OF PRACTICE

Roberta R. Greene and Namkee Choi

Geriatric social work practice is client-centered, focusing on clients' biopsychsocial and spiritual functioning. Practitioners engage in activities designed to obtain resources, such as housing, or help clients negotiate the sometimes complex health, mental health, community, and family systems (Gonyea, Hudson, & Curley, 2004). Geriatric social work practice encompasses a broad spectrum of roles and functions and addresses a variety of client needs ranging from acute health care to supportive social care (Gonyea et al., 2004). Social workers may act in a variety of roles: they may serve as part of health-care teams, provide private care managers, or act as legislative aides. Social workers who specialize in assisting older adults and their families are employed in an array of settings, including senior centers, nursing homes, mental health and home health-care agencies, and hospitals. Geriatric social workers may also be found in government agencies, corporations, and research and advocacy organizations.

Geriatric social workers may be engaged in direct service, assessing clients, and intervening to provide services; in program planning and evaluation, identifying needs and designing programs; in education and training, creating professional curriculum and training for paraprofessionals; in administration and policy, planning organizational structures and activities, implementing them, and analyzing their effects; and in research, extending the knowledge base of aging processes and program interventions (Hooyman & Kiyak, 2005). Chronic health conditions, frailty, and cognitive decline can lead to a decline in an older adult's functional capacity, making him or her unable to live in the community. In these instances, social workers are mandated by law to attend to their psychosocial care or a constellation of social, mental health, and emotional needs (Vourlekis, Zlotnik, Simons, & Toni, 2005).

Gonyea et al. (2004) have argued that while the broad scope of the social work mission in the field of aging is daunting, "this practice breadth affords social work the ability to make manifold contributions to the well-being of older people" (p. 2). This chapter provides an overview of that practice spectrum. Given the wide range of settings in which geriatric social work is conducted, practice is understood within the broader attitudinal, political, social, economic, and demographic context in which it occurs. Practice trends are also inseparable from and closely linked to the sources of funding and modes of delivery of public services (Rose, 1992). Therefore, policy implications and the demographics of care delivery are also presented.

PRACTICE CHALLENGES

Social workers have been specializing in practice with older adults and their families for more than a century. However, during the past few decades, there have been dramatic changes in how social work services to the elderly have been defined and delivered. To understand the current nature of social work practice in the field of aging, it is important to take into account the major attitudinal, economic, and social forces that have been shaping it (Greene, 2005b). Among these are changes in family form and structure, modifications in help-seeking behaviors, and transformations in social services and health-care delivery systems. Furthermore, recent research on how people age "has drastically altered the very foundations of existing paradigms regarding the elderly" (Scharlach & Kaye, 1997, p. xii). This challenge to existing paradigms is the result of decades of research examining the likelihood that people will experience a healthy and engaged old age (Holstein & Minkler, 2003). These forces have been so far-reaching that Berkman, Gardner, Zodikoff, and Harootyan (2005) have called for changes in social work practice that entail "engagement with intersecting biological, psychological, socioenvironmental, cultural, political, and economic contexts that are intertwined with aging in U.S. society" (p. 329).

Demographic Imperative

A comprehensive picture of geriatric social work practice must include the fact that advances in health care and technology have contributed to a "longevity revolution." Life expectancy at birth in the United States is now 75.2 years for men and 80.4 years for women (National Center for Health Statistics), and life expectancy for both men and women is expected to continue to increase, creating a demographic imperative to attend to the very old, who may be frail and or suffer from chronic health and cognitive impairments. By 2011, the baby boomers (those born between 1946 and 1964) will begin to cross the age 65 threshold, and both the number and proportion of elderly people in the U.S. population will grow rapidly. By 2030, the older population is projected to be twice as large as in 2000, growing from 35 million to 71.5 million representing nearly 20% of the total U.S. population (U.S. Decennial Census and Projections, 2000; see Figure 14.1).

The elderly population is also becoming increasingly ethnically diverse, adding to the complexity of service needs (Takamura, 2001; Torres-Gil & Moga, 2001). By the year 2050, the Caucasian population 65 years of age and older will have grown by 116.7%; African Americans by 262.1%; Asians by 720.3%; and Hispanics by 553.4% (U.S. Department of Health and Human Services [DHHS], 1999; Min, 2005). That is, the non-Hispanic Caucasian population 65 years of age and over, which accounted for 83% of the total U.S. population in 2003 is projected to account for only 61% by 2050 (U.S. Census Bureau, 2004).

Most analysts agree that the dramatic growth in the numbers and proportion of older adults in the U.S. population portends an increased need for health and social services (Johnson, Tooley, & Wiener, 2007). These dramatic demographic changes have prompted a growing dispute among policymakers about the economic and social implications of the aging of U.S. society. Much of the debate centers on whether U.S. taxpayers can afford to continue to pay for escalating health-care costs and the present range of aging programs and entitlements. Policy makers increasingly express concerns about how those who need

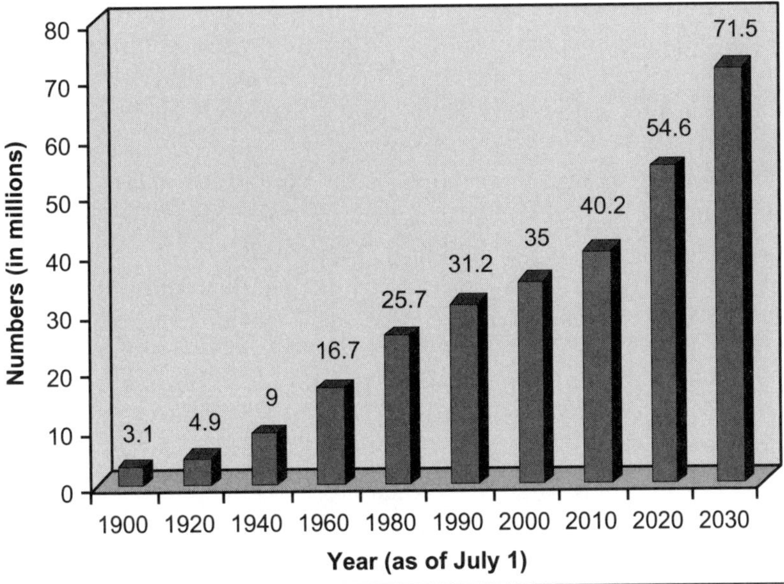

Figure 14.1 The growth of the U.S. population 65 years of age and older, 1900–2030. ***Notes:*** **Increments in years are uneven. Projections of the population by age are taken from the January 2004 Census Internet Release. Historical data are taken from "65+ in the United States," Current Population Reports, Special Studies, P23–P190; data for 2000 are from the 2000 Census; and 2003 data are taken from the Census estimates for 2003.**

health and social services will be served (Greene, 2005a). There is also a debate about the viability of formal caregiving systems and the proportion of the elderly population that will have a healthy aging experience. These emerging trends suggest the challenges and opportunities ahead for the direction of geriatric social work.

The future patterns of use of health, social services, and long-term care are still unclear. The baby-boomer generation may be more aggressive and educated consumers, considering themselves directors of their own care (Silverstone, 1996), while racial and ethnic minorities might underutilize services due to barriers such as language, lack of economic resources, and cultural care preferences (Min, 2005). Nonetheless, it is clear that major shifts in the financing and delivery of health and human services are likely to strongly influence the lives of older adults and their families and, in turn, social work practice.

GERIATRIC SOCIAL WORKERS

Social workers perform multiple functions for older adults and their families at multiple system levels. However, one of the most serious challenges the profession has been facing is the shortage of social workers who are willing to be trained to work effectively in the field of gerontological social work. A comparison of National Association of Social Workers (NASW) data from 1988, 1991, 1995, and 2000 reveals that the percentage of members who identify aging as their primary practice area has remained below 5% throughout the

12-year period. In addition, the *NASW News* reported that only 25% of their membership had caseloads with 50% over 50 years of age (Gonyea, Hudson, & Curley, 2003).

The National Institute on Aging and the Bureau of Labor Statistics have consistently indicated that more social workers will be needed to serve the increase in older adults (Lennon, 2004). Social work educators have also reiterated the need to educate social workers for an aging society (Greene, 1989; Scharlach, Damron Rodriguez, Robinson, & Feldman, 2000). The relative lack of emphasis on the late life span in social work curricula and the lack of enriched gerontological field practicum sites may have contributed to the shortage of gerontological social workers. Moreover, social workers who chose the aging field tended to leave it because the marketplace did not provide sufficient incentives to stay (*NASW News*, 2005).

Without significant investment in workforce development, a serious shortage of social workers that can work with, and for, the growing aging population is inevitable. The NASW, the Council on Social Work Education (CSWE), and other social work organizations are making a concerted effort to develop a trained and skilled gerontological social work workforce. Funding from the John Hartford Foundation for training and research grants that began in 1998 has been an important impetus for development of the geriatric social workforce.

Gerontology: A Biopsychosocial Discipline

Gerontology, the scientific and systematic study of aging, is a multidisciplinary field, addressing the biopsychosocial functioning of older adults (Greene, 1986, 2000b; Hooyman & Kiyak, 2005). The intellectual roots of gerontology can be traced to the historical traditions of its constitutive disciplines. Professionals in many fields, in addition to social work, including nursing, medicine, dentistry, occupational and physical therapy, and architecture, specialize in gerontology, applying biopsychosocial principles as appropriate to their mission. Clinical social workers in the field of aging usually conduct assessments of older adults' *functional age*, involving an understanding of the biopsychosocial-spiritual behaviors that affect a person's ability/competence to perform tasks that are central to everyday life. *Biological factors* related to functional capacity include health, physical capacity, or vital life limiting organ systems; psychological *factors* encompass an individual's affect state or mood, cognitive or mental status, and their behavioral dimensions; *sociocultural aspects* to consider involve the cultural, political, and economic aspects of life events (Greene, 2000b). *Spiritual factors* may include a person's relationship with his or her faith/religious community, and/or inner system of beliefs.

Definitions of Aging

Aging can be considered in three dimensions beyond chronological age: biological, psychological, and social. Chronological age marks the passage of time or the number of years that have passed since an individual's birth and has been the most commonly used definition of aging. Early in the twentieth century, however, researchers became increasingly interested in using scientific methods to explain the aging process, particularly differences in individual longevity (Birren & Schroots, 1995; Sprott & Austad, 1995). Birren (1969), a pioneer in gerontological research, distinguished normal from pathological aspects of aging in three spheres: (1) biological age, encompassing the study of changes in various bodily systems and how these changes affect the physical, psychological, and social functioning of older adults; (2) psychological age, the person's ability to adapt to and modify familiar and unfamiliar environments, including an individual's sensory and mental capacities as well as his or her adaptive capacity and personality; and (3) social age, a person's position or role in a given social structure, where age-based assigned roles specify an individual's rights and responsibilities, as well as his or her ability to relate to and connect with others, and accounts for the older adults' functionality in a social context. Birren's popular conceptualization has been translated into social work practice models (Greene, 1986, 2000b; see following section), and continues to guide the structure of gerontological social work (Hooyman & Kiyak, 2005; McInnis-Dittrich, 2002).

Contemporary Challenges

During the next 3 or 4 decades, there will be a very significant increase in the numbers of some very vulnerable groups of the elderly, including the oldest-old (those over 85 years of age), those living alone (especially unmarried or widowed women and racial/ethnic minorities, and with no living children and/or siblings), and very low-income older persons. The oldest-old are expected to have the greatest service needs, especially those living alone and the elderly poor (Siegel, 1999).

Living Alone

As age increases and their spouses die, the percentage of the population that lives alone increases. In 2003, half of women 75 years of age and older lived alone (U.S. Census Bureau, 2003). About 12% of the elderly residing alone had no living children nor siblings (U.S. DHHS, 1998).

Poverty

The income situation of the elderly, on average, is relatively favorable; and the extent of poverty is lower than for the population as a whole (U.S. Bureau of the Census, 2004–2005). There is, however, a wide disparity in the distribution of income and assets in the elderly population, which is more dramatic among subgroups: the income of many of the elderly falls below the poverty level or below 200% of the poverty level. Women, African Americans and Hispanics, people living alone, elderly people, those living in rural areas, and especially individuals with a combination of these characteristics, live in poverty to a disproportionate degree. In brief, a disproportionate number of racial/ethnic minority older persons will enter old age with few assets and low incomes (Torres-Gil & Moga, 2001). In recognition that racial/ethnic minority senior citizens often are at greater risk of poor health, social isolation, and poverty, the Administration on Aging (AoA) has created a special web site containing information on aging, diversity, and poverty (www.aoa.gov/prof/addiv/addiv.asp).

Access to Care and Economic Inequities

There are persistent disparities by race/ethnicity, gender, and income in access to health care, in family caregiving patterns, and in the use of long-term supportive services. Future generations of minority elders will consist of two groups: the current cohort of older people, those 65 years of age and older, and the present middle-aged population, who will be entering the 65 and older age bracket. Min (2005) predicts that, because of differences in acculturation and life experiences including educational attainment, career paths, and retirement plans, these two groups "will be very divergent, distinct, and complex, presenting enormous challenges to social work and testing our ability to respond to their needs" (p. 351). However, he concludes that because social workers have a longstanding commitment to helping those who are oppressed or marginalized, they are well positioned to assist minority elders.

The Changing Family

Geriatric social workers need to understand the consequences of demographic change on intergenerational family relationships (Bengtson, Giarrusso, Silverstein, & Wang, 2000). Major modifications in family structure and form have been underway and will continue. Multigenerational families are becoming increasingly common but family pyramids are becoming taller and narrower. Families used to have an elderly grandparent at the top and a broad base of children and grandchildren, but now the pyramid is likely to be higher, with great-grandparents still living, but with a narrower base because families have fewer children, grandchildren, and great-grandchildren. Families are also changing along the following lines, and in some racially/ethnically specific ways:

- Divorces are resulting in an intricate set of intergenerational relationships, including biological children and grandchildren, stepchildren, and step-grandchildren.
- Grandparents are more frequently raising grandchildren.
- The population of older adults is more heterogeneous in terms of race/ethnicity and gender.
- The larger and modified extended families of African American and Hispanic families exhibit cultural differences in family reciprocity or mutual care (Greene, 2005a).

For centuries, the informal support of the family has been critical in the care of older adults (Brody, 1985). Although filling a crucial need, formal social services played a lesser role. With the longevity revolution and changes in the structure and form of the family, gerontologists are concerned about what the future holds for the family of later years—if there will there be a continuation of high solidarity and intergenerational support among family members and whether the family will continue to be the main source of support for its older members.

CURRENT AND FUTURE DIRECTIONS

"Wellness philosophy" is an umbrella term embracing positive approaches to individual well-being that is gaining broader acceptance among gerontologists (Greene, 2000a, 2000b, 2005a). This involves a shift in practice paradigms to a "new gerontology." This shift suggests that practitioners develop more positive programs that promote health and psychosocial well-being and use assertive rehabilitation strategies. There are a number of such positive approaches to aging, for example, Antonovsky's (1998) *salutogenesis orientation* refers to the study of how people naturally use their inner resources to strive for health. Similarly, Atchley (1999) proposed the positive idea of life continuity in which older adults strive to maintain their thinking patterns, activities, living arrangements, and social relationships despite changes in health. Successful aging, according to Rowe and Kahn (1998), consists of three major factors: (1) avoiding disease by adopting a prevention orientation, (2) engaging in life by continuing social involvement, and (3) maintaining high cognitive and physical functioning through ongoing activity.

Some theorists have questioned how realistic this new gerontology or successful-aging paradigm will be in addressing the health needs of older adults (Strawbridge, Wallhagen, & Cohen, 2002). Some have argued that a focus on well-being and participation does not take into account the large numbers of individuals who do not have the power to achieve this "normative vision" (Holstein & Minkler, 2003, p. 787). They believe that the successful aging model may actually do harm to older people who are already marginalized, such as the poor and people of color.

On the other hand, Greene (2005a) has pointed out that social workers in the field of aging have often been tardy in adopting new theoretical concepts and practice strategies, lagging behind other fields of practice. While there is a need for health promotion and disease prevention, she suggests that practitioners should assess where an older adult falls on the continuum of functional capacity, from those with the most "abilities" to those with the least capacity, assessing a client's capacity against the full continuum of services and care. She goes on to state that this practice approach challenges clients to use their inner resources, continue their social involvement, and maintain their physical functioning (Vourlekis & Greene, 1992; see Table 14.1).

Problems and Major Issues Facing Older Adults

With the extraordinary growth of the population 65 years of age and older, it is critical for geriatric social workers to be more aware of those most in need of care. For example, here are three sets of concerns that should guide policy practice:

1. *Race:* Rates of disability are higher for African Americans over 65 than for Caucasians. A much higher share of African Americans with severe disabilities are likely to live with adults other than their spouses.
2. *Gender:* Rates of disability are higher among women in all age groups 65 and older, and disability rates are decreasing more for men than for women. Women 65 and older are more likely than men to live with adults other than a spouse and are much more likely to be residents of nursing homes.
3. *Income:* Persons 65 and older in the lowest income quartile are three times more likely to experience disability as those in the highest income quartile.

ASSESSMENT AND INTERVENTION

Geriatric social work practice has adopted traditional human behavior concepts and social work methods, while adapting techniques to form its own practice and knowledge base. For example, social work's dual concern for the person and the environment is central

Table 14.1 Five Continua for the Elderly

1. Continuum of Need

Independent (Little or no need)	Moderately dependent	Dependent (Multiple needs)

2. Continuum of Services

Health promotion/disease prevention	Screening and early detection	Diagnosis and pretreatment	Treatment Rehabilitation: evaluation services	Continuing care skilled nursing and hospice

3. Continuum of Service Settings

Own home, apartment, etc.	Friend or relative's home, apartment, etc.	Congregate living situation	Subacute (e.g., day hospital)	Acute-care care facility (hospital)	Skilled facility (e.g., long-term and hospice care facility)	Continuing care (e.g., nursing home)

4. Continuum of Service Providers

Nonservice	Self-care	Family friends	Paraprofessionals (support network)	Professionals

5. Continuum of Professional Collaboration

Single discipline	Multidisciplinary	Interdisciplinary

Source: "The Role of Gerontological Social Work in Interdisciplinary Care" by N. Hooyman, G. Hooyman, and A. Kethley, 1981, March, Paper presented at the annual program meeting of the Council on Social Work Education, Louisville, KY. Reprinted with permission.

to practice. History taking, or understanding a client's critical past events, is another frequently used technique in working with older adults, and the three core conditions of interviewing—empathy, warmth, and genuineness—are essential. This section discusses the major methodological differences that distinguish geriatric from general practice.

Special Assessment Issues

Geriatric assessment is differentiated by its particular attention to the nature of the aging population. Lichtenberg (2000) outlined four assessment principles for evaluating an older adult. The first is that age measured in years and age measured in functioning are not linearly related. Chronological age alone does not provide an appreciation of functional age or of a person's capacity to live effectively in his or her environment. An older adult's ability to live competently in his or her environment is central to the geriatric assessment process (Greene, 1986, 2000a). This person-environment perspective allows for a dynamic picture of the older adult's functioning as she or he continually adjusts to surrounding conditions (Hooyman & Kiyak, 2005). It offers information about how an individual responds to the social and physical demands in the areas of health, social behavior, and cognition that influence his or her functioning (Lawton, 1989; Lawton & Nahemow, 1973; Parmelee & Lawton, 1990).

Lichtenberg's (2000) second principle is that clinical gerontologists should emphasize brief assessment instruments, pointing to research that demonstrates the reliability and validity of many of them. Specialized assessment instruments such as depression scales or mental status exams can reduce the time it takes to evaluate older adults.

The third principle is that assessment must result in a delineation of strengths and weaknesses. The knowledge of a client's unique characteristics and capacities can inform the care planning process as well as treatment recommendations.

Finally, his fourth principle is that clinicians should use multiple assessment methods to improve the quality of information. Since assessment instruments have rarely been validated with minority populations, social workers may want to use caution when adopting such instruments (Tran, Ngo, & Conway, 2003).

Geriatric Interdisciplinary Teams

Not all elderly clients need a geriatric assessment team. However, when an assessment involves a very frail older adult with multiple, complex needs, it is ideally conducted by an interdisciplinary team. Team members from various disciplines such as medicine, nursing, occupational therapy, nutritional counseling, and social work collectively set goals and share responsibilities and resources (Merck, 2005). The client and caregivers should also be part of the team and included in team meetings. Meetings to evaluate outcomes should also involve the client.

Functional Assessment

The process of assessment of older adults has a similar function and purpose to that of other populations—to gain an understanding of a client's problems, needs, and strengths to develop an intervention plan (Naleppa & Reid, 2003), and to determine the resources needed to improve interpersonal functioning (Greene, 1989). Unfortunately, scientists and physicians have historically been concerned with what has gone wrong with older adults rather than with instituting preventive programs to promote health and well-being (Butler, Lewis, & Sunderland, 1998). Similarly, social changes that occur in later years that can bring about a sense of loss or isolation may go unnoticed.

It is not surprising, therefore, that most clients come to the attention of social workers when there is a problematic change in mental or physical status. Nonetheless, regardless of the service setting or client's difficulty, geriatric social work practice is generally based on a philosophy of providing psychosocial care to support optimal functioning (Greene & Sullivan, 2004). It is equally important for the social worker to learn the extent to which a person is able to live independently (should he or she so desire) as it is to learn if he or she can benefit from health-promotion and disease-prevention programs. Being able to live at home is of extraordinary importance to many older people (Butler et al., 1998). To determine whether this is feasible, social workers conduct a functional assessment of a client's everyday competence, or an older person's ability to care for him- or herself, manage his or her affairs, and live an independent, quality life in his or her community (Willis, 1991).

Social work assessments involve getting to know the whole person, including his or her motivations, interests, and capacity to change. Through this process, the social worker is better able to help an older client (and his or her family) plan for the future and make decisions about what kind of care may be needed. Assessment then goes beyond diagnosis "to a broader appraisal of the interrelationships between the physiological, emotional, and sociocultural factors and the external environmental conditions that influence well-being" (Northen, 1995, p. 12).

Cross-Cultural Assessment

As discussed, aging is not an equal process for people in poverty or those who are members of minority groups. The consequences of diversity, such as a person's cultural, ethnic, or gender differences, can be barriers to clients of any age accessing and receiving services (Green, 2002; Pinderhughes, 1989). It is therefore important for social workers to become culturally self-aware. Practitioners who are more self-aware are less likely to impose their values and beliefs on a client (Poulin, 2005). The process of identifying practitioner biases may also allow power differentials in the helping process to be addressed. A collaborative approach that promotes client participation in telling their own story is often best. In addition, clients who seek professional help may wish to define and resolve their own situations based on their experiences and perceptions (see Table 14.2).

Disabilities and Health Status

In a reference group of Medicare enrollees, the proportion of older Americans with chronic disabilities seems to be declining, but the absolute number is increasing (6.2 million to

Table 14.2 Ethnic-Sensitive Inventory

In working with ethnic minority clients, I:
Realize that my own ethnic and class background may influence my effectiveness.
Make an effort to assure privacy and/or anonymity.
Am aware of the systematic sources (racism, poverty, and prejudice) of their problems.
Assist them to understand whether the problem is of an individual or a collective nature.
Consider it an obligation to familiarize myself with their culture, history, and other ethnically related responses to the problems.
Am able to understand and "tune in" to the meaning of their ethnic dispositions, behaviors, and experiences.
Can identify the links between systematic problems and individual concerns.
Am sensitive to their fears of racism or prejudiced orientations.
Consider the implications of what is being suggested in relation to each client's ethnic reality (unique dispositions, behaviors, and experiences).
Clearly delineate agency functions and respectfully inform clients of my professional expectations of them.
Am able to understand that the worker-client relationship may last a long time.
Am able to explain clearly the nature of the interview.
Am respectful of their definition of the problem to be solved.
Am able to specify the problem in practical concrete terms.
Am sensitive to treatment goals consonant to their culture.
Am able to mobilize social and extend family networks.

From "Use of Ethnic-Sensitive Inventory (ESI) to Enhance Practitioner Skills with Minority Clients," by Ho, 1991, *Journal of Multicultural Social Work, 1*(1), pp. 60–61. Adapted with permission.

6.8 million) because of the rapid increase in the overall elderly population. Disability is often measured by assessing limitations on an older adult's activities in daily living (ADLs) or basic self-care tasks and instrumental activities in daily living (IADLs) or household/independent-living tasks. Practitioners often use six measures to assess a person's ADL: whether the person is able to (1) feed himself or herself, (2) use the toilet by himself or herself, (3) take a bath or shower without assistance, (4) get dressed, (5) get in and out of a bed or chair, and (6) get around inside the home. Older women generally report more problems with physical functioning than older men. In 2002, 31% of women over 65 years of age reported that they were unable to perform at least one of the six activities, compared to 18% of men. By 85 years of age, the proportions were 58% for women and 35% for men. The IADL are often assessed by a person's ability to do the following six tasks: (1) use the telephone, (2) take medications, (3) manage money, (4) do light housework, (5) prepare meals, and (6) shop for groceries (Kaiser Family Foundation, 2002).

Respondent Assessed Health Status

Practitioners will gain a somewhat different picture of an older adult's functional capacity if clients are asked to rate their own physical, emotional, and social health and well-being. Self-ratings of fair, poor, good, very good, and excellent are sound indications of well-being, since research has found these self-ratings of health to correlate with lower risks of mortality. During 2000 to 2002, 73% of people age 65 and over rated their health as good or better. Regardless of age, older non-Hispanic Caucasian men and women were more likely to report good health than their non-Hispanic African American and Hispanic counterparts (National Center for Health Statistics, 2004).

Mental Health and Psychosocial Problems Practitioners need to be on the alert for the most common mental health problems that can arise in old age. According to the U.S. Surgeon General's report on mental health one of every five persons age 55 and older experiences mental health concerns that are not part of the normal aging process (DHHS, 1999). In addition, the suicide rate for persons age 65 years of age and older is higher than for any age group (Gonyea et al., 2004). Therefore, practitioners should screen for mental health issues. At the core of the assessment is a person's psychosocial functioning—the capacity to make reasonable decisions and carry them out, as well as have the functional ability to live in their environment (Greene, 1986, 2000b).

Depression

The most common mental health problem in later life is depression (DHHS, 2004–2005). However, depression is frequently underdiagnosed and undertreated despite the fact that it is easily treatable by a combination of psychotherapy and medication. Since depression can be debilitating and often leads to other health problems, even suicide, geriatric social workers should become familiar with its everyday symptoms, including prolonged sadness, tiredness, loss of energy, eating and sleeping problems, weight gain or weight loss, difficulties in focusing, and thoughts of death and suicide (Lebowitz et al., 1997; American Psychiatric Association, 1994). If an older person makes suicidal statements, the practitioner should make a risk assessment that probes for the elderly client's intent. This includes the following questions (Philadelphia Corporation for Aging, 1995): Have you really thought of hurting yourself? Have you thought of killing yourself? Have you planned how you would do it? Do you have the means, such as pills?

Dementia

Alzheimer's disease (AD) is the most common cause of dementia in older people. An estimated four million Americans currently suffer from AD or related forms of cognitive impairment. AD is characterized by cognitive and physical decline and may last over a period of 20 years. As the disease progresses, at first a person may not remember simple things like the names of objects. The late stages are characterized by a complete inability to feed or care for him- or herself. Individuals with AD live an average of 8 years after initial diagnosis. Although psychosocial techniques have been shown to provide some symptomatic relief, there is at present no therapy that can reverse the progressive cognitive decline (Small et al., 1997).

Until the final stage of the disease, most AD patients live at home and are cared for by a family member (most often a spouse). The burden of caring for an AD patient until the advanced stage of the disease can be a tremendous strain on family caregivers, who often experience fatigue, anxiety, irritability, anger, depression, social withdrawal, or various health problems. Social workers assisting clients with AD may need to assist the caregivers in dealing with their feelings of fatigue, frustration, and inadequacy, and by helping them find additional caregiver resources and support (American Association for Geriatric Psychiatry, 2005).

Elder Abuse

Unfortunately, caregiving sometimes results in elder abuse. Abuse may take several forms. Neglect, the most common form of abuse, involves failure to provide essential physical or mental care for an older person. This may be unintentional or intentional (withholding food, medication, or water). Physical neglect includes withholding food or water; failure to provide proper hygiene or failure to offer physical aids or safety precautions. Physical violence involves inflicting pain, injury, or impairment. These acts may be pushing, striking, slapping, pinching, force-feeding, or improper use of physical restraints or medications. Psychological abuse is any action by the caregiver that causes fear, isolation, confusion, or disorientation. These acts are intended to harm and may include verbal aggression that humiliates and infantilizes. Financial exploitation is the misuse of an older person's income or resources for personal gain of another. Violation of rights is an abuse that involves depriving the older adult of legal rights and personal liberty. Another distinction is *domestic abuse,* referring to several forms of maltreatment of an older person by someone who has a special relationship (often the caregiver) with the elder in the home and *self-neglect,* involving cognitively impaired older adults unable to care for themselves (Sijuwade, 1995). Social workers should not be reluctant to ask the elderly client about care difficulties, safety issues, and general satisfaction with care (Lachs, Williams, O'Brien, Pillemer, & Charlson, 1998).

Anxiety Disorders

Anxiety disorders can range from simple nervousness before an important event to panic attacks. One of the most common behaviors is avoidance of what is perceived as a difficult situation. For example, older adults may avoid various activities because they are afraid of falling. However, practitioners can help an older adult clarify the source of this tension (Butler et al., 1998).

Addiction

Practitioners should ask direct questions about drug and alcohol use (Poulin, 2005). Although the extent of alcohol and drug abuse among people 65 years of age and older is difficult to measure, estimates range from 5% to 10% of the population (Pennsylvania Care Management Institute, 1990). Addiction may involve alcohol, prescription, and nonprescription drugs. When taken in combination, these addictions may have deadly consequences.

Intervention

Individual

Research has documented that older adults may benefit from advances in (treatment) interventions including crisis intervention, cognitive-behavioral therapy, and grief counseling (Butler et al., 1998; Greene, 2000b; McInnis-Dittrich, 2002). At the same time, many in the current cohort of older adults are reluctant to seek help from health and human services professionals because of perceived stigmas. Valided therapy interventions for clients suffering from dementia include:

- Allowing the client to ignore reality and retreat to a "safe" place;
- Accepting behavior as the person's attempt to communicate a need;
- Accommodating the person's feelings however difficult this may be; and
- Maintaining communication through various means (Feil, 1993).

Family

Geriatric social workers base their family interventions on a number of conceptual frameworks. Family-centered practice models are based on an understanding of systems theory, the family life cycle, and issues of interdependence versus dependence.

Auxiliary Function Model

One of the earliest family centered practice models was the auxiliary function model (Silverstone & Burack-Weiss, 1983). The authors/clinicians proposed that the major problems facing frail, impaired older adults were not disease or old age per se, but rather the effects these conditions might have on their mental or physical functioning. The proponents of this model contended that therapy should be based on a supportive relationship and designed to counter the factors associated with depletion or loss. Therefore, the social worker's major goal in intervention should be to combat the family's feelings of helplessness in the face of its multiple losses, that is, to convey a sense of hope.

Functional-Age Model of Intergenerational Family Treatment

Greene, (2000b) provided another resource to assess and intervene with older adults and their families in caregiving situations. This model suggests that the social worker understand the "family as a mutually dependent unit with interdependent pasts and futures" (p. 20).

In family crisis situations, the practitioner takes into account the developmental issues and the changing biopsychosocial needs of family members. To make an assessment, the social worker explores the functional capacity of the person needing care. The family is assessed as a social system, referring to how a group of people interact and influence each other; a set of reciprocal roles, involving the behavioral expectations members have for each other; and as a developmental unit, encompassing how the family faces life transitions.

Family-focused practice involves:

- Engaging the client system in treatment, involving connecting with significant members of the client system.
- Making an assessment, encompassing an evaluation of the functional capacity of the person receiving care and his or her family system.
- Working with other professionals to assess medical conditions, including medical and mental health diagnoses and factors associated with illness or disease.
- Reframing, learning together how illness may affect all family members.
- Formulating a mutually developed intervention plan, encompassing setting goals, establishing family responsibilities, and accessing resources.
- Implementing the plan, including mobilization of and stress reduction in the family system.
- Terminating or encompassing the evaluation of treatment and the sustainability of hope (Greene, 2000b, pp. 100–150).

Family or Informal Case Management

The vast majority of older adults who need assistance are cared for by a family member (American Association of Retired Persons [AARP], 2005). Tasks may undertake involve direct personal care, such as bathing or grooming and indirect care, such as cooking, cleaning, or running errands. Providing care for an older adult has become so widespread that Brody (1985) called this phase of the life course a "normative family stress" (p. 25). Therefore, social workers ought to consider the family the focus of case management services (see Table 14.3).

When an older adult has an acute or chronic illness, caregivng tasks may become so time consuming that it affects the caregiver's ability to balance their work and family obligations. In fact, an increasing percentage of the workforce is actively involved in caring for a relative or friend over 50 years of age (eldercare). According to a survey by the National Alliance for Caregiving and AARP, nearly one-quarter of U.S. households—22.4 million—include a family caregiver for someone over age 50. Nearly half of the U.S workforce has eldercare and/or childcare responsibilities, and many struggle with the competing demands of work and family responsibilities. According to a MetLife report in 1999, 62% of caregivers surveyed reported asking someone at work—supervisors, coworkers, or management—for support or help in coping with their caregiving responsibilities.

Task-Centered Model

Naleppa and Reid's (2003) task-centered approach consists of three phases: (1) in the initial phase, in which the social worker conducts intake and assessment, selects the problems that

Table 14.3 Key features of family-focused social work case management

Family-focused social work requires that the case manager:
Identify the family as the unit of attention.
Assess the frail or impaired person's biopsychosocial and spiritual functioning within a culturally sound family context.
Create a mutually agreed on family care plan.
Refer client systems to services and entitlements not available within the natural support system.
Implement and coordinate the work that is done with the family.
Determine what services need to be coordinated on behalf of the family.
Intervene clinically to ameliorate family emotional problems and stress accompanying illness or loss of functioning.
Identify resilience factors that contribute to family success.
Determine how the impaired person and family will interact with formal care providers.
Integrate formal and informal services provided by the family and other primary groups.
Offer or advocate for particular services that the informal support network is not able to offer.
Contact client networks and service providers to determine the quality of service provision.
Mediate conflicts between family and service providers to empower the family when it is not successful.
Collect information and data to augment the advocacy and evaluation efforts to ensure quality of care.

From *Social Work Case Management* (p. 12), by B. Vourlekis and R. R. Greene, 1992, Hawthorne, NY: Aldine De Gruyter. Adapted with permission.

require attention, and sets intervention goals; (2) the middle phase, in which the practitioner emphasizes the development of tasks that address the client's problems. Tasks are put forth, carried out, and reviewed; and (3) the final stage, involving the end of the intervention process including termination, reinforcing accomplishments, and making future plans.

The task-centered model stresses empirically tested methods and theories, is grounded in case data, and underscores client-defined problems. Time limits are built into the intervention plans—usually 4 to 12 sessions—and completed tasks are viewed as vehicles for change. This is intended to encourage client motivation and the successful completion of service activities and attainment of goals.

Group

Although social group work with the aged has a common philosophy and therefore may use similar techniques used with other age groups, one of the major purposes of group work with older adults is to provide connections to others in their own age group (Lowry, 1992). Social group work with older adults may be recreational or psychoeducational. Practitioners may also provide group members with an opportunity to reminisce (Greene, 1982, 2000b). Group methods are also used to educate, train, and support caregivers. Educational groups provide information about community services and resources. Psychoeducational and training groups offer short-term structured groups that reach specific problem-solving and coping skills; while support groups focus on mutual sharing of information, encouraging reciprocal exchanges, and self-help (Toseland & Smith, 2001; see Table 14.4).

Table 14.4 Summary of Forums for Educating and Training Caregivers

Forums	Summary
Community workshops and forums	Provides information about community services, may be single sessions lasting an hour to a day; can be sponsored by health and human services organizations.
Lecture series and discussion	Lectures are given by clinical experts on topics of interest to specific groups of caregivers.
Support groups	Offers mutual sharing of information, are usually unstructured and encourage reciprocal and self-help among group members.
Psychoeducational and skills building groups	Educates members usually in short-term, structured groups; teaches specific problem solving and coping skills and shares information about caregiving resources.
Individual counseling and training	Focuses on the individual caregivers' needs; Helps caregivers deal with the emotional and coping skills needed to be effective in the role and to handle stress and identify rewards.
Family counseling	Helps the family system deal with issues related to caregiving. Supports and sustains the care recipient and maintains family balance and cohesiveness. Connects the family with other resources in the community.
Care coordination and management	Educates caregivers on how to perform caregiving roles more effectively and on how to connect with formal caregivers.
Technology-based interventions	Uses telephone-mediated groups, computer-mediated groups, and videoconferencing to educate and train caregivers.

From *Supporting Caregivers through Education and Training* (pp. 10–12), by R. Toseland and T. Smith, 2001, prepared for the U.S. Administration on Aging, National Family Caregiver Support Program (NFCSP): Selected Issue Briefs, Washington, DC: U.S. Department of Health and Human Services. Adapted with permission.

Formal Case Management: Community-Based Care

Case management is a traditional, integral part of social work practice. Because the care an individual may need often involves multiple sources, effective coordination and monitoring of care are essential. The case management process is designed to assist individuals and families with multiple service needs. It is used in various fields of practice including mental health, HIV/AIDS treatment as well as services for older adults.

The focus of a long-term care system is the person (and his or her family) whose decreased functional capacity places him or her in a position to need assistance with activities of daily living, such as housekeeping, finances, transportation, meal preparations and/or administering medication. The case manager is the person who facilitates the client's movement through the service delivery system and, according to Intagliata (1992), is the human service provider who is the sole person responsible for ensuring that a client's needs are met.

Case management is also conducted at a social systems macro level, with geriatric social workers serving as planners and administrators. Weil and Karls (1985) have outlined eight major case management functions:

1. Client identification and outreach, determining the target population and eligibility.
2. Client assessment and diagnosis, evaluating a client's level of functioning and service needs.
3. Service planning and resource identification with clients and members of service networks, describing the steps and issues in service delivery, monitoring and evaluation.
4. Linking clients to needed services, connecting or securing client services.
5. Service implementation and coordination, service assessment and trouble-shooting, getting the work done or putting all the plan's pieces in place.
6. Monitoring service delivery, overseeing and supervising client services.
7. Advocacy for and with client in service network, pressing for client needs.
8. Evaluation of service delivery and case management, determining the progress of the service plan that may result in continued service with the same or revised service plan, termination, or basic follow-up.

MEZZO AND MACRO PRACTICE FOR AND WITH OLDER PERSONS

Aging is a complex process during which many older persons experience aggravation of existing physical, functional, and mental health problems as well as financial issues, while others experience onset of new health and economic problems. To help older persons cope with these problems of aging effectively but also to continue developing their potential in the later stage of their life course, social workers have always worked in and/or with many mezzo and macro systems, encompassing community-based consumer coalitions and interest groups; advocacy groups; family caregiver groups; service provider groups; academic institutions and research centers; local, state, and federal governments, legislatures, and legal systems. Practice that that takes place in a variety of settings with a variety of client systems that deal with micro- and macro-level interventions may be thought of as generalist social work. It requires a range of practice skills, the ability to function on an interdisciplinary team, and a recognition of cultural, historical, and other client differences that may influence the helping process (Poulin, 2005).

In recent years, social work policy practice in mezzo and macro systems has become more urgent:

- With the surge of baby boomers beginning to cross the age 65 threshold in 2011, macro-level adjustments and interventions required to support an aging population have become national concerns.
- The fundamental principle of public responsibility for dependent older persons is being questioned in a political environment where principles of taking responsibility for one's own future are emphasized.

- Budgets for core income maintenance, health-care, and social service programs for older persons and their families are under pressure in the face of mounting national deficits due in part to tax cuts and defense spending.

The 1935 Social Security Act established the most significant foundation for income security for retired workers and their dependents (as well as public assistance for low-income older or disabled persons along with families and children, and later, income security for survivors and disabled workers and their families). The addition of Medicare as Title XVIII, and Medicaid as Title XIX of the Social Security Act in 1965, expanded public responsibilities for health care for older, disabled, and low-income persons. The national focus of attention on the needs and potential of older persons was greatly expanded at the federal level with the 1961 White House Conference on Aging (WHCoA) and the passage of the 1965 Older Americans Act (OAA).

White House Conferences on Aging

At the 1961 WHCoA numerous interest groups advocating for older persons, including the National Council of Senior Citizens and AARP formed a coalition. The 1961 WHCoA also supported the passage of amendments to the Social Security Act that provided additional support to beneficiaries; amendment of the Housing Act of 1961 and the Community Health Facilities Act of 1961 that made special provisions for the aged; enactment of Medicare and Medicaid as titles XVIII and XIX of the Social Security Act in 1965; and enactment of the 1965 OAA, establishing the Federal Administration on Aging (U.S. AoA), an administrative structure to carry out the goals and services stipulated by the OAA. Subsequent WHCoAs were held in 1971, 1981, 1995, and in December 2005. Issues related to income maintenance, health care, and other issues were discussed at these conferences, and existing and new programs were supported by thousands of national delegates selected to represent a diversity of interests in aging and the aged.

Many social workers have served as delegates to the WHCoA and contributed to the resulting improvements in the policies and programs for seniors. The 2005 WHCoA passed 50 resolutions reflecting issues that the NASW advocated for through press releases and congressional testimony (NASW, 2003, 2005). The most important 15 resolutions of the 2005 WHCoA were to:

1. Reauthorize the OAA.
2. Develop a coordinated, comprehensive long-term care strategy.
3. Ensure transportation options.
4. Strengthen and improve Medicaid.
5. Strengthen and improve Medicare.
6. Support geriatric education and training for the entire health-care workforce.
7. Promote innovative models of noninstitutional long-term care.
8. Improve recognition, assessment, and treatment of mental illness and depression among older Americans.
9. Attain adequate numbers of health-care personnel in all professions who are skilled, culturally competent, and specialized in geriatrics.

10. Improve state- and local-based integrated delivery systems to meet the twenty-first-century needs of seniors.
11. Establish principles to strengthen Social Security.
12. Promote incentives for older workers to continue working, and improve employment training and retraining programs to better serve older workers.
13. Develop a national strategy for supporting informal caregivers of seniors with the goal of developing adequate quality and supply of services.
14. Remove barriers to the retention and hiring of older workers, including age discrimination.
15. Create a national strategy for promoting elder justice through the prevention and prosecution of elder abuse (www.whcoa.gov).

The Older Americans Act

Social workers who work with older Americans and their families should be intimately familiar with the OAA. It is one of the primary pieces of legislation that guide the protection and preservation of dignity, rights, and equal opportunities of Americans aged 60 and older. It facilitates the identification, planning and coordination, and provision of health, housing, and long-term care, and social services on federal, state, tribal, and local levels. Congress reauthorizes the OAA every 7 years, with the most recent reauthorization in 2000. Six core services are funded through the OAA and administered through its aging services networks, the National Network on Aging, which consists of 56 state units on aging; 655 area agencies on aging; 233 tribal and native organizations; two organizations that serve Native Hawaiians; 29,000 service providers; and thousands of volunteers (U.S. AoA, 2005). The core services are:

- *Supportive services:* Supplies rides to medical appointments and grocery and drugstores; handyman, chore, and personal care services; adult day care; and information, referral, and assistance systems linking consumers to resources and services that enable older persons to remain safe in their homes and communities.
- *Nutrition services:* Congregate nutrition services in senior centers, home-delivered meals, and nutrition screening and education.
- *Preventive health services:* Health promotion and disease prevention services.
- *The National Family Caregiver Support Program (NFCSP; a new addition since 2000):* Provision of information to informal caregivers (including grandparents caring for grandchildren, caregivers of those aged 18 and younger with mental retardation or developmental difficulties, and Native American caregivers; U.S. AoA, 2003).
- *Services that protect the rights of vulnerable older persons:* Detection and prevention of elder abuse, neglect, and consumer fraud; pension, health-care, and insurance benefits counseling programs; long-term care ombudsman programs that investigate and resolve complaints made by or for residents of nursing, board and care, and similar adult homes; and training of senior volunteers on how to educate older Americans to take a more active role in monitoring and understanding their health care.

- *Services to Native Americans:* Nutrition and supportive services designed to meet the unique cultural and social traditions of tribal and native organizations and organizations serving Native Hawaiians.

The OAA is based on the universal availability of services to all those aged 60 and older, but it also targets vulnerable older adults including Native Americans and other racial/ethnic minority groups, low-income persons, and persons living in rural areas with limited resources. Services funded by the OAA of fundamental importance for the well-being of older persons have been proven cost effective (e.g., Meals on Wheels programs; see Ponza, Ohls, & Millen, 1996). However, the federal funding level for grants to state and local aging service networks (fiscal year 2006 requested budget for the AoA: $1.37 billion) has been too low to provide services to all seniors in need or to meet the comprehensive and ambitious goals of the OAA programs. To assure the provision of services to enable all older adults to remain active, healthy, and independent, social workers need to continue to support higher appropriations for the OAA programs.

Social Work Policy Practice and Advocacy

As affirmed by the delegates of the WHCoAs, adequate retirement income, affordable and accessible acute and subacute health care, coordinated long-term care, and supportive housing and community services for independent living are essential ingredients in the provision of dignified aging for all. With the "graying" of the society and the increasing costs of income maintenance and health care, heated national debates are occurring on the subjects of fiscal sustainability and the future courses of Social Security, Medicare, and Medicaid. Both institutional and home- and community-based long-term care systems are also being tested as a variety of fiscal and programmatic issues have resulted in the shortage, and poor quality, of such services.

The need for more active involvement of social workers as advocates in these national debates and future policymaking resulted in the establishment, for the first time, of the Specialty Practice Section on Aging in the NASW in 1998. Since then, NASW has been actively involved in policy practice and advocacy related to aging issues and older persons, especially those with low incomes and/or are members of racial/ethnic minorities (Keigher, Fortune, & Witkin, 2000).

Social Security

Social Security is the public insurance program that is the primary source of retirement income for low-income minority older persons, especially minority women, and dependents of retired, disabled, or deceased workers. NASW, through its Government Relations and Political Action Unit and state chapters' legislative activities and rallies, has opposed the privatization of Social Security and emphasized the ideological and practical mandates of preserving the integrity of Social Security's public insurance function (NASW, 2005).

Since the mid-1990s, the biggest debate on the future of Social Security has been on the topic of private, individual accounts, which the current administration has promoted. According to AARP projections, Social Security's financial health will worsen as the worker-beneficiary ratio decreases as the baby boomers retire (Concord Coalition, 2004).

Despite the acknowledgment of the grave future fiscal problems of the Social Security program from all sides of the debate, recommended courses of necessary action by political parties, interest groups, and current and future beneficiaries of Social Security have differed drastically, depending on the ideological stance of the concerned parties.

Medicare

In addition to the ongoing, albeit slow, changes from the traditional fee-for-service system to managed care plans, since January 2005 the new Prescription Drug Benefit program (Part D of the Medicare program), has offered a sometimes confusing array of covered and noncovered drugs from numerous private risk-bearing entities under contract with the DHHS. Although enrollment in Medicare Part D is voluntary for most Medicare beneficiaries, low-income persons who are eligible for both Medicare and Medicaid will no longer receive their Medicaid drug coverage and with some exceptions will be automatically transitioned to the Part D program (Kaiser Family Foundation, 2003; Nemore, 2005; Steinberg & VanTuinen, 2005, July).

Through its letters to all members of the House and Senate and the administrator of the Centers for Medicare and Medicaid Services, NASW opposed the Prescription Drug Benefit program because of its concerns about the program's potential for transforming Medicare into a competitive, market-driven system. Other issues relate to affordability of premiums and deductibles, adequacy of drug coverage, and the Medicare-Medicaid dual eligibility. Now, with the reality of Part D implementation, NASW continues its involvement with the national Medicare Education Coordinating Committee, an alliance dedicated to educating consumers and providers about quality low-cost health care for older adults and those with disabilities.

Another issue that social workers have been concerned about is disparity in mental health-care coverage under Medicare. Medicare Part A covers a significantly shorter period of inpatient care for mental illness, and Part B covers only 50% of approved mental health outpatient care cost (as opposed to 80% of the approved physical health outpatient care cost). Moreover, social workers are excluded from billing Medicare directly for psychotherapy services rendered in skilled nursing facilities (SNFs), and as a result, nursing home residents are not getting the mental health services they need. The NASW, through its long-standing involvement with the National Coalition on Mental Health and Aging, has spoken out about the disparities in mental health care. The NASW has also provided written comments to the National Institute of Mental Health on the role of the social work profession in research on the mental health needs of older adults (NASW, 2005).

Medicaid

Although Medicaid is an essential federal-state health-care program for 50 million low-income vulnerable Americans, including 4.1 million low-income seniors, 7 million blind and disabled persons, and 36 million low-income families with children. In 2006, congress scaled back the Medicaid funding to states allowing them to redesign benefit packages. This will undoubtedly result in cutting coverage for certain health-care services for low-income older persons, disabled persons, and families with children (Park, Parrott, & Greenstein, 2005). More health-care providers will join those that have already rejected Medicaid patients. As a means to reduce long-term care expenses paid by Medicaid, lawmakers are also tightening rules and increasing oversight related to Medicaid estate planning or transfer of assets (by Medicaid applicants to their children or other relatives in order to artificially impoverish themselves). Although lawmakers have assumed that many older adults with private resources engage in such practices as a way of qualifying for Medicaid in case they may need nursing home care, research findings show little evidence of a large number actually doing so (O'Brien, 2005).

INSTITUTIONAL AND HOME- AND COMMUNITY-BASED LONG-TERM CARE SERVICES

Every older adult is at risk of needing long-term care; however, long-term care services in the United States are riddled with problems of inadequate funding, fragmentation, and lack of coordination between acute/subacute care and among different types of services provided by different agencies. The U.S. long-term care policy has traditionally emphasized institutionalized skilled nursing care of frail older adults and the disabled, based on an acute medical care model largely provided by proprietary nursing homes (Chen, 2005; Kane et al., 2003; Lidz & Arnold, 1995). In 2003, nearly half of all nursing home care expenses (46% of $111 billion) were paid by Medicaid and only a little over a quarter (27.9%) were paid out of pocket (Georgetown University, 2003, 2004). Because of the high cost of institutional care, many private-pay nursing home residents deplete their resources, becoming unable to pay for the expensive institutional care they require and thus becoming eligible for Medicaid assistance (Spillman & Kemper, 1995).

Because of the rising institutional care costs in states' Medicaid expenses, all states except Arizona have implemented, through Section 1915c, Medicaid home- and community-based waivers from the federal Centers for Medicare and Medicaid Services (CMS), some forms of home- and community-based long-term care service (HCBS) programs that would reduce institutionalization among frail older persons and the disabled who were nursing home eligible. Most HCBS wavier programs offer a mix of case management, homemaker, home health aide, personal care, adult day care, respite care and habilitation in an effort to prevent or delay institutionalization of the target population. There is evidence that a large-scale operation of HCBS programs reduces overall long-term care costs in the long run by preventing or delaying institutional care and improves quality of life among consumers (Kane, Kane, & Ladd, 1998; Weissert & Hedrich, 1994). In large part, however, long-term home- and community-based care is an expensive venture whose cost is likely to go up in the coming years because of increasing demand from growing numbers of frail and disabled older adults over 85 years of age.

In addition to the growth of HCBS programs, public demand for alternative models of long-term care services that are less medically oriented has resulted in the growth of assisted living facilities, personal care homes, and other forms of group-living programs. These alternatives to nursing homes, which have begun to multiply since the 1990s, serve seniors who are a little younger and less functionally impaired than those in need of skilled nursing care, as well as those who need specialized care for early stages of cognitive impairment. These facilities are largely owned and operated by private entities that cater to private pay older adults who are not covered by Medicare and Medicaid. Thus, they are not subject to the same federal and state regulations and oversight as Medicare/Medicaid-certified SNFs.

One of the greatest ongoing challenges in long-term care services is limited availability and restricted access to a variety of publicly funded HCBS programs for those who are not impoverished, and are functionally frail, yet are not eligible for immediate institutionalization. Moreover, even those who are eligible for publicly funded HCBS programs in many parts of the country, including depressed urban neighborhoods and resource- and provider-poor rural areas, cannot access the services because of the lack of programs and service providers. Frail and disabled older adults are often put on a waiting list for homemaker and home health aide services, adult day care services, and meal services.

Another challenge for the current and future long-term care policies and programs is the care needs of an increasing number of older persons with Alzheimer's disease, dementias and other forms of organic brain disorders. With the progression of the disease of their afflicted relative, informal caregivers find it hard to care for them. A significant proportion of residents in SNFs have varying degrees of cognitive impairment, but those in advanced stage of Alzheimer's disease or other forms of dementia require specialized care settings that tend to be very cost and labor intensive. Despite the additional human and other resources required for the care of cognitively impaired residents, Medicare's and state Medicaid's prospective payments to SNFs are heavily weighted toward residents' functional impairments. (The prospective payment system is based on the case mix classification using a resident classification system—Resource Utilization Groups III—based on data from resident assessments—Minimum Data Set 2.0—and relative weights developed from staff time data [CMS, 2005a].) Thus, SNFs are wary of admitting and caring for persons with primarily cognition and/or behavioral problems, which are often the consequences of severe cognitive impairments. With the increasing number of older and cognitively impaired persons who require specialized care settings, the Medicaid reimbursement policies need to be updated to facilitate provision of more acceptable environments for these dependent older adults.

The NASW has long-standing policy statements on long-term care services that emphasize, among other things (a) eligibility for and accessibility to a variety of health and support services, based on individual functional needs and not solely as a medical necessity, that would "enable individuals to maintain their maximum level of independence in the least restrictive environment"; (b) availability of services within a continuum that links all levels of long-term care and addresses the physical, mental, cultural, and psychosocial health needs of the individual, family, and caregivers; and (c) development of an adequate financing system for long-term care that preserves, increases, and redistributes revenue to increase access and provide universal coverage, relieving individuals and families of burdensome out-of-pocket costs (NASW, 2003, p. 243).

Unfortunately, roles of social workers in institutional long-term care settings have not been well-articulated, nor has the profession's interest in long-term care services (Vourlekis & Simons, 2005). By advocating for the holistic approach to long-term care services, NASW is also trying to emphasize the contributions that social workers can make to those who require such services as well as the need for expansion of education, training and continuing education programs for all levels of social workers employed in long-term care settings (NASW, 2003).

DEVELOPMENT OF INNOVATIVE LONG-TERM CARE SERVICE DELIVERY MODELS

Consumer-Directed Care

One of the most significant developments in long-term care service delivery since the late 1990s is consumer-directed care, in which consumers who qualify for public HCBS benefits are allowed to choose their preferred services and/or hire, train, supervise, pay their own workers (including professionals, friends, neighbors, and family members) and, if necessary, to fire them (Heumann, 2003). One of the consumer-directed care models, the cash and counseling demonstration project, was initiated and directed by a social work faculty in the mid-1990s. Medicaid-eligible consumers were given a flexible monthly allowance along with the freedom to direct and manage their personal assistance needs, including hiring and paying (with counseling and financial management assistance from the project) their personal assistance providers. The findings from the three-state (Arkansas, Florida, and New Jersey) pilot project showed significant reduction in unmet needs and improvement in the participants' physical and functional health outcomes as well as their quality-of-life indicators (Phillips et al., 2003). As a result, in October 2004, 11 states were awarded 3-year grants of up to $250,000 from the Robert Wood Johnson Foundation and the DHHS to implement the cash and counseling model and collect information to monitor the effectiveness of these programs (Cash & Counseling, 2005).

A key impetus for consumer direction was the U.S. Supreme Court's Olmstead decision in 1999, which ruled that, under the Americans with Disabilities Act, states are required to place persons with disabilities in the most integrated setting appropriate to them, typically their own homes and communities rather than in institutions. The state determines that community placement is appropriate when it learns that the transfer from institutional care to a less restrictive setting is not opposed by the affected individual, and that the placement can be reasonably accommodated (Rosenbaum, 2001). NASW is advocating for consumer self-determination when decision making affects their long-term care services. Thus, it supports not only the cash and counseling program, but many other federal initiatives (e.g., programs under the Real Choice Systems Change demonstration grants) designed to deemphasize the traditional, medically oriented institutional care model and diversify it into more consumer-oriented service delivery models. Important future tasks for social workers in keeping up with consumer self-determination and decision making in long-term care services are to (a) continue to work with consumers to bring forth culture change in the entire long-term care systems, and (b) monitor quality of the long-term care services, including consumer-directed care, primarily according to consumer-derived measures of quality (Geron, 2000).

Program for All-Inclusive Care for the Elderly

The need for cost control of long-term care and provision of integrated acute and long-term care services in the community was the impetus behind the creation of the Program for All-Inclusive Care for the Elderly (PACE), a capitated benefit for Medicare-Medicaid dual eligibility authorized by the Balanced Budget Act of 1997 (BBA). PACE, modeled on the system of acute and long-term care services developed by On Lok Senior Health Services in

San Francisco's Chinatown in the early 1970s, is a comprehensive service delivery system intended to help older adults continue receiving services, while living at home rather than being institutionalized. Capitated financing allows providers to deliver any Medicare- and Medicaid-covered services participants need rather than being limited to those reimbursable under the Medicare and Medicaid fee-for-service systems (CMS, 2005b). Although social workers are integral to the PACE interdisciplinary team, only limited attention has been paid to understanding and promoting the roles of social workers in PACE programs, as in other long-term care settings.

Housing and Supportive Services

For frail and functionally impaired older persons, living independently in their own communities and aging in place require an array of coordinated supportive services, including low-income subsidized housing appropriate to the frail and/or disabled, home modifications, energy and weatherization assistance, and property tax relief and/or deferral for homeowners. Other essential services include senior centers and activity programs, adult day-care services, transportation programs and home-delivered meal programs. Low-income housing programs have been financed largely by the federal Department of Housing and Urban Development (HUD), but like many other federal programs, could shrink with budget retrenchment.

The planning and delivery of most supportive services have been placed under the local governments' jurisdiction, although they are partially financed by the OAA, Social Services Block Grant (Title XX of the Social Security Act) as well as by other federal block grants to states (e.g., low-income home energy assistance funding to states) and localities (e.g., the community development block grant). The federal funding level has been too low for many states and localities to provide services for all who need these essential services, and future budget cuts will further limit these services (Horney, 2005). Some localities have been successful in raising private funds to cover the costs of some community-based services, while others have not, resulting in significant disparities in the availability and accessibility of many of these services.

SOCIETAL CONTRIBUTION OF OLDER PERSONS

A substantial proportion of older adults delay their retirement and continue to work or engage in part-time employment following their retirement. Labor force participation rates showed that 33% of men and 23% of women aged 65 through 69 were in the labor force in 2003 (Federal Interagency Forum on Aging, 2004). Others volunteer their time in formal organizations or provide informal caregiving to their family, relatives, friends, and neighbors. According to the Bureau of Labor Statistics' (BLS) annual study on volunteer rates in the United States, based on data from a supplement to the September 2004 Current Population Survey, a little over 30% of those between ages 55 and 64, and almost 25% of those aged 65 and older, volunteered for formal organizations in 2004 (BLS, 2005). The study also showed that older adults are more likely than younger age groups to volunteer through or for religious organizations. In 2004, 45% of volunteers aged 65 and older performed volunteer activities mainly through or for a religious organization.

When informal volunteering is included, the volunteer rates among older adults are higher than the BLS figure. According to an Urban Institute study based on data from the 2002 Health and Retirement Study (a large, nationally representative sample survey of older adults), about 74% of adults aged 55 and older volunteered their time or provided unpaid care to their family members. The value of this unpaid care was estimated at $100 billion, and the value of both formal volunteering and unpaid care for family members was estimated at $162 billion (Johnson & Schaner, 2005).

A majority of those who are well educated and healthy are likely to find meaningful retirement activities through engagement in paid work, volunteering, and advocacy and interest groups such as AARP, the Gray Panthers, and the Silver Haired Legislature. However, some older adults have limited opportunities to find meaningful activities because they may live in areas without such opportunities for formal volunteering. They may lack transportation or may not possess specific skills needed for meaningful volunteering activities. Older adults who are less well educated or suffer from chronic health problems also participate less. In addition, a lower proportion of racial/ethnic minorities (African Americans, Asian Americans, and Hispanics) than non-Hispanic Whites volunteer (BLS, 2005). Developing and extending opportunities for meaningful activities for these disadvantaged groups of older adults constitutes an important program planning and advocacy area for gerontological social workers.

Current Federal Volunteer Programs

The three Senior Corps programs: the Foster Grandparent Program, the Senior Companion Program, and the RSVP are the best-known public programs that promote volunteering of older adults and provide guidance, training, and connection to individuals, groups, and organizations that would benefit from the seniors' unique talents and expertise. The Senior Corps programs began in the 1960s, but were brought under the umbrella of the newly created Corporation for National and Community Service in 1994, along with the other domestic community service programs, AmeriCorps and Learn and Serve America. The Senior Corps currently links more than 500,000 Americans to service opportunities (Senior Corps, 2005).

Although these Senior Corps programs provide opportunities for volunteering among older adults, they are limited because: (a) they are not available in some geographic areas and are not advertised widely; (b) state and local governments lack resources, such as transportation, to facilitate volunteering by disadvantaged older adults; and (c) the programs lack of flexibility in income eligibility, age eligibility, service scope, and time commitment requirements (O'Neill & Lindberg, 2005). Moreover, these programs were conceived and designed in the 1960s and have not gone through many changes in fundamental structures since then, and their scope of service and training have not kept up with the increasing demand for technologically savvy volunteers from both public and private sectors.

Civic Engagement

Civic engagement can take many forms, from individual voluntarism to organizational involvement to electoral participation. It can include efforts to address an issue directly, work with others in a community to solve a problem, or interact with the institutions of representative democracy. Civic engagement encompasses a range of activities from working in a soup kitchen to serving on a neighborhood association board, to writing a letter to an elected official or simply voting. Many other public and private organizations, including the Corporation for National and Community Service, the National Council on the Aging, Civic Ventures, and AARP, are working on finding innovative volunteer outreach and recruitment strategies and models for low-income older adults.

The policy practice and advocacy roles of social workers in the efforts to recruit and retain the maximum number of older adults in civic engagements should include:

- Increasing awareness the public, policy makers, professionals and older adults of significant societal and personal benefits and values of volunteerism;
- Continuing outreach, recruitment, training and compensation of older adults who have low incomes, are members of racial/ethnic minorities, and are otherwise disadvantaged to encourage them to become volunteers;
- Continuing to advocate for volunteer (and paid work) programs that are meaningful and rewarding for these older adults;
- Lobbying at all levels of government to increase resources to enable volunteering by older adults;
- Developing strategies to match community needs with resources and skills that older adult volunteers can offer; and
- Collaborating with social service agencies in testing innovative volunteer programs and establishing a database for evidence-based program models.

Social workers can play an important role in encouraging and assisting older adults to continue to be productive members of their communities and society at large. Because older people have a lifetime of knowledge and skills and a willingness to share their experience, they should be thought of as assets, not burdens, to our society. Their continuing engagement in meaningful and productive activities, such as volunteering, can provide significant economic benefits. In addition, productive activities in later life should result in positive physical, functional, and psychological outcomes for the older adults themselves (Harlow & Cantor, 1996; Herzog, Franks, Markus, & Holmberg, 1998; Lum & Lightfoot, 2005; Musick, Herzog, & House, 1999; Van Willigen, 2000; Wheeler, Gorey, & Greenblatt, 1998).

REFERENCES

American Association for Geriatric Psychiatry. (2005). *Patients and caregivers: Alzheimer's and related dementias fact sheet*. Retrieved October 1, 2005, from www.aagponline.org/p_c/dementia.asp.

American Association of Retired Persons. (2005). *Reimagining America: AARP's blueprint for the future*. Washington, DC: Author.

American Psychiatric Association. (1994). *Diagnostic and statistical manual of mental disorders* (4th ed.). Washington, DC: Author.

Antonovsky, A. (1998). The sense of coherence: An historical and future perspective. In H. I. McCubbin, E. A. Thompson, A. I. Thompson, & J. E. Fromer (Eds.), *Stress, coping, and health in families* (pp. 3–20). Boston: Allyn & Bacon.

Atchley, R. C. (1999). *Continuity and adaptation in aging*. Baltimore: Johns Hopkins University.

Bengtson, V. L., Giarrusso, R., Silverstein, M., & Wang, H. (2000). Families and intergenerational relationships in aging societies. *Hallym International Journal of Aging*, *2*(1), 3–10.

Berkman, B. J., Gardner, D. S., Zodikoff, B. D., & Harootyan, L. K. (2005). Social work in health care with older adults: Future challenges. *Families in Society*, *86*(3), 329–337.

Birren, J. E. (1969). Principles of research on aging. In J. E. Birren (Ed.), *The handbook of aging and the individual*. Chicago: University of Chicago Press.

Birren, J. E., & Schroots, J. J. F. (1995). History, concepts, and theory in the psychology of aging. In J. E. Birren & K. W. Schaie (Eds.), *Handbook of the psychology of aging* (pp. 3–23). San Diego: Academic Press.

Brody, E. (1985). Parent care as normative family stress. *Gerontologist*, *25*, 19–29.

Butler, R. N., Lewis, M. I., & Sunderland, T. (1998). *Aging and mental health*. Boston: Allyn & Bacon.

Cash and Counseling. (2005). *Program overview*. Retrieved January 1, 2006, from www.cashandcounseling.org/about/index.html.

Centers for Medicare and Medicaid Services. (2005a). *Case mix prospective payment for SNFs: Balance Budget Act of 1997*. Retrieved January 2, 2006, from http://new.cms.hhs.gov/SNFPPS/.

Centers for Medicare and Medicaid Services. (2005b). *Program of All-Inclusive Care for Elderly (PACE) overview*. Retrieved December 26, 2005, from www.cms.hhs.gov/pace/.

Chen, L.-M. (2005). Policies affecting long-term care and long-term care institutions. In B. Berkman (Ed.), *Handbook of health and aging* (pp. 867–876). New York: Oxford University Press.

Concord Coalition. (2004). *Social Security reform: Facing up to the real trade-off*. Retrieved January 1, 2006, from www.concordcoalition.org/facing-facts.

Federal Interagency Forum on Aging. (2004). *Older Americans 2004: Key indicators of well-being*. Washington, DC: U.S. Government Printing Office.

Feil, N. (1993). *The validation breakthrough*. Baltimore: Health Professions Press.

Georgetown University Long-Term Care Financing Program. (2003). *Who needs long-term care?* Retrieved December 20, 2005, from http://ltc.georgetown.edu.

Georgetown University Long-Term Care Financing Program. (2004). *Who pays for long-term care?* Retrieved December 15, 2005, from http://ltc.georgetown.edu.

Geron, S. M. (2000). The quality of consumer-directed care: What do consumers mean by quality? *Generations*, *24*(3), 66–73. Retrieved December 15, 2005, from www.asaging.org/generations/gen-24–3/qualitycons.html.

Gonyea, J. G., Hudson, R. B., & Curley, A. (2004, Spring). The geriatric social work labor force: Challenges and opportunities in responding to an aging society. In *Institute for geriatric social work issue brief* (pp. 1–7). Boston: Boston University School of Social Work.

Green, J. (2002). *Cultural awareness in the human services*. Englewood Cliffs, NJ: Prentice-Hall.

Greene, R. R. (1982). Life review: A technique for clarifying family roles in adulthood. *Clinical Gerontologist*, *2*, 59–67.

Greene, R. R. (1986). *Social work with the aged and their families*. Hawthorne, New York: Aldine de Gruyter.

Greene, R. R. (1989). The growing need for social work services for the aged in 2020. In B. S. Vourlekis & C. G. Leukefeld (Eds.), *Making our case* (pp. 11–20). Silver Spring, MD: National Association of Social Workers Press.

Greene, R. R. (2000a). Serving the aged and their families in the 21st century: Using a revised practice model. *Journal of Gerontological Social Work*, *34*(1), 41–62.

Greene, R. R. (2000b). *Social work with the aged and their families* (2nd ed.). Hawthorne, New York: Aldine de Gruyter.

Greene, R. R. (2005a). The changing family of later years and social work practice. In L. Kaye (Ed.), *Productive aging* (pp. 107–122). Washington, DC: National Association of Social Workers Press.

Greene, R. R. (2005b). Redefining social work for the new millennium: Setting a context. *Journal of Human Behavior and the Social Environment, 10*(4), 37–54.

Greene, R. R., & Sullivan, W. P. (2004). Putting social work values into action: Use of the ecological perspective with older adults in the managed care arena. *Journal of Gerontological Social Work, 42*(3/4), 131–150.

Harlow, R. E., & Cantor, N. (1996). Still participating after all these years: A study of life task participation in later life. *Journal of Personality and Social Psychology, 71*, 1235–1249.

Herzog, A. R., Franks, M. M., Markus, H. R., & Holmberg, D. (1998). Activities and well-being in older age: Effects of self-concept and educational attainment. *Psychology and Aging, 13*, 179–185.

Heumann, J. E. (2003, October). *Consumer-directed personal care services for older people in the U.S. AARP Public Policy Institute Issue Brief.* Retrieved December 10, 2005, from www.AARP.org.

Holstein, M. B., & Minkler, M. (2003). Self, society, and the "new" gerontology. *Gerontologist, 43*(6), 787–796.

Hooyman, N., & Kiyak, H. (2005). *Social gerontology*. Boston: Allyn & Bacon.

Horney, J. (2005). *Senate cuts LIHEAP funding: Despite claims, there is no legitimate connection between ANWR and LIHEAP*. Retrieved December 28, 2005, from www.cbpp.org/12–22-05bud.htm.

Hudson, R. B., Gonyea, J. G., & Curley, A. (2003, Spring). The geriatric social work labor force: Challenges and opportunities. *Public Policy 7 Aging Report, 13*(2), 12–16.

Intagliata, J. (1992). Improving the quality of community care for the chronically mentally disabled: The role of the case manager. In S. M. Rose (Ed.), *Case management and social work practice* (pp. 25–55). New York: Longman.

Johnson, R. W., & Schaner, S. G. (2005, September). *Value of unpaid activities by older Americans tops $160 billion per year*. Washington, DC: Urban Institute Retirement Project. Retrieved December 15, 2005, from www.urban.org.

Johnson, R. W., Tooley, D, & Wiener, J. (2007). Meeting the long-term needs of the baby boomers: How changing families will affect paid helpers and institutions (Discussion paper 07-04 in the Retirement Project Series). Washington, DC: Urban Institute. Available from www.urban.org/publications/311451.html.

Kaiser Family Foundation. (2002, June). *Key findings from a national survey: Long-term care from the caregiver's perspective*. Retrieved December 15, 2005, from www.kff.org/kcmu.

Kane, R. A., Kane, R. L., & Ladd, R. C. (1998). *The heart of long-term care*. New York: Oxford University Press.

Kane, R. A., Kling, K. C., Bershadsky, B., Kane, R. L., Degenholtz, H. H., Liu, J., et al. (2003). Quality of life measures for nursing home residents. *Journal of Gerontology: Medical Sciences, 58A*(3), 240–248.

Keigher, S. M., Fortune, A. E. & Witkin, S. L. (2000). *Aging and social work: The changing landscapes*. Washington, DC: The National Association of Social Workers Press.

Lachs, M. S., Williams, C. S., O'Brien, S., Pillemer, K., & Charlson, M. E. (1998). The mortality of elder mistreatment. *Journal of the American Medical Association, 208*, 428–432.

Lawton, M. P. (1989). Behavior relevant ecological factors. In K. W. Schaie & C. Scholar (Eds.), *Social structure and aging: Psychological processes* (pp. 57–78). Hillsdale, NJ: Erlbaum.

Lawton, M. P., & Nahemow, L. (1973). Ecology and the aging process. In C. Eisdorfer & M. P. Lawton (Eds.), *Psychology of adult development and aging* (pp. 619–674). Washington, DC: American Psychological Association.

Lebowitz, B. D., Pearson, J. L., Schneider, L. S., Reynolds, C. F., Alexopoulos, G. S., Bruce, M. L., et al. (1997). Diagnosis and treatment of depression in late life: Consensus statement update. *Journal of the American Medical Association, 278*, 1186–1190.

Lennon, T. (2004). *Statistics on social work education in the United States: 2002*. Alexandria, VA: Council on Social Work Education.

Lichtenberg, P. A. (Ed.). (2000). *Handbook of assessment in clinical gerontology*. New York: Wiley.

Lidz, C. W., & Arnold, R. P. (1995). The medical model and its effect on autonomy: A comparison of two long-term care settings. In L. Gamroth, J. Semradek, & E. M. Tornquist (Eds.), *Enhancing autonomy in long-term care: Concepts and strategies* (pp. 87–108). New York: Springer.

Lowry, L. (1992). Social group work with the elderly: Linkages and intergenerational relationships. *Social Work with Groups*, *15*(2/3), 109–127.

Lum, T. Y., & Lightfoot, E. (2005). The effects of volunteering on the physical and mental health of older people. *Research on Aging*, *27*, 31–55.

McInnis-Dittrich, K. (2002). *Social work with elders: A biopsychosocial approach to assessment and intervention*. Boston: Allyn & Bacon.

Merck. (2005). *Manual of geriatrics*. Retrieved October 1, 2005, from www.merck.com/mrkshared/mmg/sec1/ch7/ch7a.jsp/.

Min, J. W. (2005). Cultural competency: A key to effective future social work with racially and ethnically diverse elders. *Families in Society*, *86*(3), 347–357.

Musick, M. A., Herzog, A. R., & House, J. S. (1999). Volunteering and mortality among older adults: Findings from a national sample. *Journal of Gerontology*, *54B*, S173–S180.

Naleppa, M., & Reid, W. J. (2003). *Gerontological social work: A task centered approach*. New York: Columbia University Press.

National Association of Social Workers. (2003). *Social work speaks: National Association of Social Workers Policy Statements, 2003–2006* (6th ed.). Washington, DC: Author.

National Association of Social Workers. (2005). *NASW Advocacy: Aging*. Retrieved December 12, 2005, from www.naswdc.org/practice/aging/default.asp.

National Association of Social Workers News. (2005, November). *Much of social work workforce also aging, retiring: Challenge of aging population nearing* (p. 4). Washington, DC: Author.

National Center for Health Statistics. (2004). *Chart book on trends in the health of America*. Hyattsville, MD: Author.

Nemore, P. B. (2005, November). *Medicare Part B: Issues for dual eligibles on the eve of implementation*. Retrieved December 12, 2005, from www.kff.org.

Northen, H. (1995). *Clinical social work knowledge and skills*. New York: Columbia University Press.

O'Brien, E. (2005, May). Medicaid's coverage of nursing home costs: Asset shelter for the wealthy or essential safety net? Georgetown University long-term care financing project issue brief. Retrieved December 12, 2005, from www.ltc.georgetown.edu.

O'Neill, G., & Lindberg, B. (2005). Civic engagement in an older America. Washington, DC: Gerontological Society of America.

Park, E., Parrott, S., & Greenstein, R. (2005). Budget conference agreement contains substantial cuts aimed at low-income families and individuals. Retrieved January 2, 2006, from www.cbpp.org/12–18-05bud3.htm.

Parmelee, P. A., & Lawton, M. P. (1990). The design of special environments for the aged. In J. E. Birren & K. W. Schaie (Eds.), *Handbook of the psychology of aging* (pp. 464–488). San Diego: Academic Press.

Pennsylvania Care Management Institute. (1990). *Care management orientation manual*. Philadelphia: Author.

Philadelphia Corporation for Aging. (1995). *Clinical protocol series for care managers in community based long-term care* (Grant #90-AM-0688). Washington, DC: Administration on Aging, Department of Health and Human Services.

Phillips, B., Mahoney, K., Simon-Rusinowitz, L., Schore, J., Barrett, S., Ditto, W., et al. (2003). *Lessons from the implementation of cash and counseling in Arkansas, Florida, and New Jersey*. Final Report. Princeton, NJ: Mathematica Policy Research, Inc. Retrieved December 12, 2005, from www.cashandcounseling.org/downloads/grl/state_report.pdf.

Pinderhughes, E. B. (1989). *Understanding race, ethnicity, and power: The key to efficacy in clinical practice*. New York: Free Press.

Ponza, M., Ohls, J. C., & Millen, B. E. (1996). *Serving elders at risk: The Older Americans Act nutrition programs: National evaluation of the elderly nutrition program, 1993–1995*. Prepared by Mathematica Policy Research, Inc. for the U.S. Department of Health and Human Services.

Poulin, J. (2005). *Strengths-based generalist practice*. Belmont, CA: Brooks/Cole.

Rose, S. (1992). *Case management and social work practice*. New York: Longman.

Rosenbaum, S. (2001). *Olmstead v. LC: Implications for family caregivers. Executive Summary No. 6 for who will provide care? Emerging issues for state policymakers*. San Francisco: Family Caregiver Alliance.

Rowe, J. W., & Kahn, R. L. (1998). *Successful aging*. New York: Pantheon.

Scharlach, A. E., Damron Rodriguez, J., Robinson, B., & Feldman, R. (2000). Educating social workers for an aging society: A vision for the 21st century. *Journal of Social Work Education, 36*(3), 521–538.

Scharlach, A. E., & Kaye, L. W. (Eds.). (1997). *Controversial issues in aging*. Boston: Allyn & Bacon.

Senior Corps. (2005). *Senior corps fact sheet*. Retrieved December 15, 2005, from www.seniorcorps.org/about/media_kt/factsheet_seniorcorps.pdf.

Siegel, J. S. (1999). Demographic introduction to racial/ethnic elderly populations. In T. P. Miles (Ed.), *Full color aging: Facts, goals, and recommendations for America's diverse elders* (pp. 1–19). Washington, DC: Gerontological Society of America.

Sijuwade, P. O. (1995). Cross-cultural perspectives on elder abuse as a family dilemma. *Social Behavior and Personality, 23*(3), 247–251.

Silverstone, B. (1996). Older people of tomorrow: A psychosocial profile. *Gerontologist, 36*(1), 27–32.

Silverstone, B., & Burack-Weiss, A. (1983). *Social work practice with the frail elderly and their families*. Springfield, IL: Charles C Thomas.

Small, G. W., Ravins, P. V., Barry, P. P., Buchholtz, N. S., Dekosky, S. T., Ferris, S. H., et al. (1997). Diagnosis and treatment of Alzheimer disease and related disorders. *Journal of the American Medical Association, 278*, 1363–1371.

Spillman, B., & Kemper, P. (1995). Lifetime patterns of payment for nursing home care. *Medicare Care, 33*(3), 280–296.

Sprott, R. L., & Austad, S. N. (1995). Animal models for aging research. In E. L. Schneider & J. W. Rowe (Eds.), *Handbook of the biology of aging* (pp. 3–20). San Diego: Academic Press.

Steinberg, M., & VanTuinen, I. (2005, July). The holes in Part D: Gaps in new Medicare drug benefit. *Families USA*. Retrieved December 1, 2005, from www.familiesusa.org.

Strawbridge, W. J., Wallhagen, M. I., & Cohen, R. D. (2002). Successful aging and well being: Self Rated compared with Rowe and Kahn. *Gerontologists, 42*(6), 727–733.

Takamura, J. C. (2001). Towards a new era in aging and social work. *Journal of Gerontological Social Work, 36*, 1–11.

Torres-Gil, F., & Moga, K. B. (2001). Multiculturalism, social policy, and the new aging. *Journal of Gerontological Social Work, 36*, 13–22.

Toseland, R., & Smith, T. (2001). *Supporting caregivers through education and training*. (Prepared for U.S. Administration on Aging, National Family Caregiver Support Program [NFCSP]: Selected Issue Briefs) Washington, DC: U.S. Department of Health and Human Services.

Tran, T. V., Ngo, D., & Conway, K. (2003). A cross cultural measure of depressive symptoms among Vietnamese Americans. *Social Work Research, 27*, 56–55.

U.S. Census Bureau. (2003). *Current population survey: Annual social and economic supplement*. Available from www.census.gov/hhes/www/poverty/poverty04/pov04hi.html.

U.S. Census Bureau. (2004). *Population estimates and projections*. Available from www.census.gov/ipc/wwwusinterimproj/.

U.S. Department of Health and Human Services. (1999). *Mental Health: A report of the Surgeon General*. Rockville, MD: U.S. Department of Health and Human Services.

U.S. Department of Health and Human Services Administration on Aging. (2003, September). *The Older Americans Act National Family Caregiver Support Program (Title III-E and Title VI-C): Compassion in action* (Executive summary). Retrieved April 28, 2004, from www.aoa.gov/prof/aoaprog/caregiver/overview/exec_summary.asp.

U.S. Department of Health and Human Services, Administration on Aging. (2003) *Promoting healthy lifestyles*. Retrieved October 1, 2005, from www.aoa.gov/eldfam/Healthy_lifestyles/Mental_Health/Mental_Health.asp.

U.S. Department of Health and Human Services Administration on Aging. (2005). *The Older Americans Act: Layman's guide*. Retrieved May 29, 2004, from www.aoa.gov/about/legbudg/oaa/laymans_guide/laymans_guide.asp.

U.S. Department of Health and Human Services National Center for Health Statistics. (1998). *The National Health Interview Survey, 1994: Second supplement on aging* (SOA II). Hyattsville, MD: U.S. Department of Health and Human Services, National Center for Health Statistics.

U.S. Department of Labor Bureau of Labor Statistics. (2004–2005). *Occupational outlook handbook*. Washington, DC: Author. Retrieved October 1, 2005, from www.bls.gov.

U.S. Department of Labor Bureau of Labor Statistics. (2005). *Volunteering in the United States, 2005*. Retrieved December 15, 2005, from www.bls.gov.news.releaase/volun.nr0.htm.

Van Willigen, M. (2000). Differential benefits of volunteering across the life course. *Journal of Gerontology, 55B*, S308–S318.

Vourlekis, B., & Greene, R. R. (1992). *Social work case management*. Hawthorne, NY: Aldine de Gruyter.

Vourlekis, B., & Simons, K. (2005). Social work practice in nursing homes. In B. Berkman & S. D'Ambruoso (Eds.), *The Oxford handbook of social work in aging* (pp. 601–614). New York: Oxford University Press.

Vourlekis, B., Zlotnik, J., Simons, K., & Toni, R. (2005). Blueprint for measuring social work's contribution to psychosocial care in nursing homes: Results from a national conference. In *Institute for geriatric social work issue brief* (pp. 1–4). Boston: Boston University School of Social Work.

Weil, M., & Karls, J. (1985). *Case management in human service practice*. San Francisco: Jossey-Bass.

Weissert, W., & Hedrich, S. (1994). Lessons learned from research on efforts of community-based long-term care. *Journal of the American Geriatrics Society, 42*, 348–353.

Wheeler, J. A., Gorey, K. M., & Greenblatt, B. (1998). The beneficial effects of volunteering for older volunteers and the people they serve: A meta-analysis. *International Journal of Aging and Human Development, 47*, 69–79.

Willis, S. L. (1991). Cognition and everyday competence. In K. W. Schaie (Ed.), *Annual review of gerontology and geriatrics* (Vol. 11, pp. 80–109). New York: Springer.

Chapter 15

FORENSIC SOCIAL WORK: CURRENT AND EMERGING DEVELOPMENTS

Katherine van Wormer, Albert Roberts, David W. Springer, and Patricia Brownell

Social work assessment and treatment with crime victims, juvenile offenders, and convicted felons have been viewed by some as the weakest link of social work practice, but by others as an area of boundless possibility as the field of criminal justice expands into new directions, many of them compatible with the values of social work (Roberts, Springer, & Brownell, 2007). Moreover, consistent with the social work focus on social justice and the mission to provide services to the most vulnerable and socially neglected (even despised) members of the community, the profession can be expected to provide leadership here. While social workers have worked in corrections since the earliest days of the profession, recent innovations in the criminal justice arena have opened up new opportunities for social workers in drug and mental health court systems, in helping prisoners who lack personal resources make a successful re-entry into the community, and in prevention work connected to victim assistance programming.

These opportunities are widely known by social work graduates who learn of field placements and job openings in the field of corrections, whose interpersonal skills and knowledge of mental health diagnosis and substance abuse treatment are in considerable demand for work with juvenile offenders, persons on probation and parole, and with methamphetamine (meth) addicts charged with criminal offenses and also brought before juvenile court for child neglect or abuse. Many specialty courts have developed innovative programs in recent years that provide ideal opportunities for employment of social workers. Some police departments use social workers to provide services to victims (Orzech, 2006). The social work profession is today beginning to take notice and return to its roots in this area, and slowly but surely, social work educators are beginning to offer the courses relevant to forensic social work.

Forensic social work is defined in the *Dictionary of Social Work* (Barker, 2003) as:

> The practice specialty in social work that focuses on the law, legal issues, and litigation, both criminal and civil, including issues in child welfare, custody of children, divorce, juvenile delinquency, nonsupport, relatives' responsibility, welfare rights, mandated treatment, and legal competency. Forensic social work helps social workers in expert witness preparation. It also seeks to educate law professionals about social welfare issues and social workers about the law. Many social workers in this field belong to the National Organization of Forensic Social Workers. Its web site address is www.nofsw.org. (p. 166)

This definition reveals how the practice of social work is integrated within courtroom and correctional settings, in situations of family violence, child neglect, and adult crime. This definition is at the intersection of social work and the law. Building on this definition, we operationally define forensic social work as policies, practices, legal issues and remedies, and social work roles with juvenile and adult offenders as well as victims of crimes. This definition describes the content of this chapter as well.

As students of social work find their way, often inadvertently, into jobs working with offenders and former offenders, working with persons who are court ordered into treatment, social work education is beginning to take notice. Let the students lead, we might say, and the educators will follow.

Consider the following examples of typical forensic work roles:

- Ann works for the Lincoln (Nebraska) Area Agency on Aging which is notified by the Corrections Department when an elderly inmate faces release and needs help in getting housing and other assistance.
- Laura, who is employed by the Crime Prevention Institute, helps organize a program of prison visits between mothers and daughters.
- Ted, as a victim assistance worker, helps crime victims secure the aid and protection they need and conducts victim offender conferencing at the victim's request.
- Mary did crisis intervention in immigrant families where droves of Mexican workers were arrested for their immigration status and use of forged documents in a raid at a meatpacking plant; foster families had to quickly be found for some of the children.
- Ron is a substance abuse counselor who connects with probation services and drug court to provide court-ordered treatment; he also gets referrals from drug court.
- Joe works in supported housing in Seattle; his organization provides apartments for homeless people with serious mental and substance disorders, thereby removing them from the streets and from encounters with the police and courts.

As these real-life vignettes show, social workers in every domain of the field—geriatrics, child welfare, substance abuse counseling, and so on—are connecting with the criminal justice system on a regular basis. Additionally, many social workers are hired directly by probation departments, correctional institutions, and juvenile services. Largely because of the war on drugs, with the arrests and sentencing of so many drug users, much of treatment undoubtedly will continue to be provided under the auspices of department of correction.

The Council on Social Work Education (CSWE) gives recognition to criminal justice as a major area of social work practice in their popular brochure, *Choices: Careers in Social Work*. The section on justice/corrections describes this burgeoning field as follows.

Case Example

Justice/Corrections

Joan, a woman in her mid-20s, has a history of drug addiction and writing bad checks. During a 4-year stay in prison, social work services including therapy and workshops on drug abuse and depression help her handle her addiction and make significant progress. But her children are in foster care, and she has lost touch with her mother and sisters.

As the time for her release approaches, Joan needs a job, housing, a continuing addiction recovery program, and reunification with her family. She meets with a prison social worker who arranges for placement in a halfway house and helps her find a job and transportation. After 8 months drug-free and holding her job, the halfway house social worker helps Joan find an apartment, arranges for the return of her children, locates her family, and helps her reunite with them.

In courts, rape crisis centers, police departments, and correctional facilities, you'll find social workers. In correctional facilities, the focus is on rehabilitation. Social workers may plan and provide drug and alcohol addiction treatment, life skills and basic competency training, and therapy to help offenders function once released into the community.

Social workers can be probation and parole officers, arranging for services after an offender is released, as in Joan's case, finding a group home residence, remedial classes, job training, addiction treatment, counseling, child care, and transportation. These activities generally help raise a client's independence and self-esteem.

Social workers may also be involved in restitution programs, or victim assistance services. They may serve the court as expert witnesses or work in partnership with attorneys. In police departments, social workers may help with domestic disputes or provide trauma and critical incident services to enforcement officers.

Social work activities in corrections are diverse, as are the clients, affording the chance to develop and use a broad range of skills. Corrections and justice is a field where a social worker can focus on rehabilitation and the constructive use of authority:

Related Areas

- Corrections.
- Probation.
- Forensics.
- Youth services.
- Parole.

Employers

- Prisons.
- Courts.
- Police departments.
- Victim services programs.

WHAT THE STATISTICS SHOW

According to the Bureau of Justice Statistics (2005) at the end of 2004, more than seven million adult offenders were under some form of correctional supervision including adult correctional institutions, juvenile correctional facilities, jails, detention centers, probation and parole agencies, or community diversion programs. The largest group of almost five million persons (4,916,480) were under the supervision of probation or parole agencies.

More than 600,000 people are released from prison in the United States each year (Stoesen, 2006b). Recidivism rates are a major concern; these rates are high due to difficulty getting jobs, lack of support systems, and histories of mental illness and substance abuse. At least one-third of incarcerated women have mental disorders and most have backgrounds of personal trauma.

Due to drug convictions and conspiracy sentencing laws, the number of women sent to prison is increasing at a rapid pace. Since 1995, the annual rate of growth in the number of female inmates has averaged 4.7%, higher than the 3% average increase of male inmates (Bureau of Justice Statistics, 2006). About 70% of these women leave children behind; many of these children will become known to social workers in one capacity or another, and many require child welfare services (Gumz, 2004; van Wormer & Bartollas, 2007).

Victim assistance is another area in which counseling of victims plays a major role. According to the federal Office for Victims of Crime (OVC; 2005), in 2004 there were 24 million youths and adults ages 12 and over who were victims of crimes. In this same year, over 16 million services were provided through federal and state funded victim service and victim-witness assistance agencies, and almost half (47.3%) of these victims were domestic violence victims.

What is the profession of social work doing to prepare social workers in light of this well documented need for services? Recent statistics from the Council on Social Work Education (CSWE, 2007) show that in 2004, only 2.4% of students at the bachelor's level are in field placements in corrections and criminal justice, but that in the related field of substance abuse there are another 2% and in family services another 6% are placed in these fields. Since 35% are not in the field for that year at all, these figures, are underestimates. More accurate figures, based on the students who actually are in the field would be 3.6% placed in corrections and criminal justice, 3% in a substance abuse agency, and 9% in family services. These numbers are still small in consideration of the possibilities. Still, we need to keep in mind, despite the recent date of publication, this survey was done 3 years before.

At the master's level, about one-third in the survey did not at that time have a placement. Taking that into account, and adjusting the figures provided by CSWE accordingly, we find that 3.2% are placed in corrections and criminal justice, around 3.8% in substance abuse settings, and almost 12% in family services. The potential again is probably a great deal more than this.

If we conceptualized and reframed social work in corrections and probation, forensic mental health, substance abuse, family and criminal courts, domestic violence and child abuse/neglect, juvenile justice, crime victims including the elderly, and police social work, it would become clear that many in our profession are engaged in forensic social work. However, the profession does not acknowledge the large number of MSW field placements with social work clients who have been either victims of violent crimes or juvenile or adult offenders is not widely acknowledged (Gibelman, 1995). That social work is still not yet doing all it can to tap into the opportunities in this burgeoning field, to reclaim the territory of criminal justice is a major argument of this chapter. There are historic reasons why this is so. Let us take a brief overview social work history as it pertains to correctional involvement.

HISTORY OF SOCIAL WORK AND CORRECTIONS

A brief historical overview of social welfare and social work demonstrates how much professional social work was identified with corrections and what we now define as forensic social work from its inception. For this overview, the authors use a modified version of the existing historical framework developed by (Day, 2006). Roberts and Brownell (1999) offer a more extensive overview of the evolution of forensic social work in American social welfare history for those with special interest in this topic.

Post-Civil War and Recovery, and Progressive Era (1865 to 1925)

During colonial times and up to the first part of the 1800s, youths labeled as rowdy and out-of-control were either sent home for a court-observed whipping, assigned tasks as farmer's helpers, or placed in deplorable rat-infested prisons with hardened adult offenders. The turning point was 1825 with the opening of a separate institution for juvenile offenders in New York City—"the New York House of Refuge. . . . Similar juvenile facilities opened in1826 and 1828 in Boston, and Philadelphia respectively" (Roberts, 2004b, pp. 130–131). By the mid-1800s, social work had become identified with corrections and other forms of social welfare institutions, including the "child-saving movement" whereby juvenile institutions and making juvenile delinquents indentured servants and apprentices for farmers and shop owners, also referred to as "parent surrogates" took place (Roberts, 2004b). By the late 1800s, many social reformers were involved with prisons, juvenile delinquency, and reformatories (Gibelman, 1995; Gumz, 2004). Before social work became a profession, it was identified with corrections to the extent that the National Conference of Charities and Corrections was founded in 1879. Jane Addams, founder of Hull House, served as its first woman president (Solomon, 1994).

In 1898, the first social work training school was established as an annual summer course for agency workers by the New York Charity Organization Society (Alexander, 1995). Social workers of that time, whether associated with the charity organization movement or the settlement house movement, were viewed as social reformers whose primary concerns were with serving the poor, beggars and disadvantaged, and social outcasts.

While social Darwinism was embraced as the dominant social philosophy of the charity organization movement, other social trends—including the settlement house movement—promoted progressive change (Day, 2006). The first juvenile court in the United States started in 1899 in Illinois as part of the circuit court of Chicago, through efforts initiated by the Chicago Women's Club (Popple & Leighninger, 2005). The Juvenile Psychopathic Institute was founded by William Healy, through the advocacy efforts of Hull House resident Julia Lathrop, to diagnose offenders brought before the Juvenile Court. The Institute began the practice of delinquency research and psychosocial assessment of children by a professional team (Popple & Leighninger, 2005).

Between 1915 and 1920, Women's Bureaus within police departments were established. All of the policewomen served in social work advocacy roles (particularly with juveniles). By 1919, Chicago had 29 police social workers; by 1920, there were police social workers in all the major urban areas (Roberts, 1997a).

Great Depression and Social Security for Americans (1925 to 1949)

While the 1929 stock market crash did not bring immediate and widespread devastation to the American economy, it damaged public confidence and brought to the surface a concern about the role of government in ensuring the social welfare of citizens (Day, 2006). While the charity organization and settlement house workers had successfully advocated for widow's pensions and old age assistance at the state and county levels, the federal government was not seen as responsible for social insurance and assistance. Private charity and local government was seen as the primary means of addressing poverty and deprivation until the widespread economic dislocations of the 1930s brought a realization that systems and not individual failings can cause poverty on a wide scale.

The Great Depression and the New Deal brought an influx of social workers into public life and government work. Harry Hopkins, a prominent New York social worker associated with the Charity Organization Movement, was appointed first by President Hoover and then by President F. D. Roosevelt to implement a program of emergency assistance and public works programs, including the WPA Youth Forestry Camps and the Civilian Conservation Corps, forerunners of modern day youth delinquency prevention programs. One of the earliest wilderness programs for juvenile offenders was established in the early 1930s in the Los Angeles County Forestry Department (Roberts, 2004b).

According to Roberts (2004b), "by the 1930s and 1940s, large numbers of psychiatric social workers had been hired to work in teams with psychiatrists to treat emotionally disturbed children, predelinquents and delinquents," p. 131. This represented the beginning of interagency collaboration between the juvenile courts and child guidance clinics management. In addition, individualized treatment programs were started in Corrections. Casework with offenders, especially youthful offenders, drew social workers into forensic work as treatment specialists.

Civil and Welfare Rights in the New Reform Era (1945 to 1970)

The emerging critical need for social workers to work in the field of corrections was underscored by University of Pennsylvania social work dean Kenneth Pray (1945). Police social work expanded as interest in juvenile delinquency increased due to the widespread proliferation of youth gangs. By the late 1950s, the number of child guidance clinics had grown to over 600 nationally: these included social workers who served as court liaisons (Roberts, 1998b).

In 1959, a set of 13 volumes on the social work curriculum was published by the Council on Social Work Education (CSWE). Among them was *Volume V: Curriculum for Teaching Correctional Social Work* by Studt (1959). This led to the development of correctional social work courses at major schools of social work.

During the 1940s, 1950s, and early 1960s, great strides were made in developing community-based councils and programs for delinquency prevention. Model programs such as NYC Mobilization for Youth, developed by social work professor Richard Cloward, the Midcity Program (Boston), and youth service bureaus proliferated (Roberts, 1998a). The continued concern about juvenile delinquency spurred innovative program initiatives such as juvenile diversion, youth service bureaus, detached street workers (social workers doing group work and community organizing). President Johnson's Task Force Report on

Juvenile Delinquency and Youth Crime in 1967 recommended dramatic policy innovations (such as decriminalization) of status offenders, the diversion of juveniles from official court processing (McNeece & Jackson, 2004). In 1967, *In re Gault* decision by the U.S. Supreme Court ruled that due process must be observed in juvenile delinquency proceedings. This landmark legal decision solidified due process protection for juveniles at the adjudication stage (Alexander, 1995).

The role of social workers in probation increased dramatically by the mid-1960s. Probation departments were established in all 50 states and over 2,300 counties nationwide. Social worker Milton Rector, executive director of the National Council on Crime and Delinquency (NCCD), directed a national study of probation and recommended that all new probation officers and supervisors should be required to have an MSW and 2 years of casework experience (Roberts, 2004a).

Retreat from the Welfare State and the New Federalism (1970 to 1992)

Social welfare programs shrank during the 1970s and 1980s, as the country experienced a conservative retrenchment, especially during the Reagan era (Day, 2006). However, there continued to be advancements in services and programs for juvenile offenders as well as victim services. In 1972, community-based alternatives (e.g., a network of group homes) and education programs for juvenile delinquents were established by the Massachusetts Youth Services Department after it closed several juvenile reformatories (Alexander, 1995). By 1980, the closing of juvenile correctional institutions and the expansion of community-based group homes had extended to other states, such as Pennsylvania, Illinois, and Utah.

The Juvenile Justice and Delinquency Prevention Act of 1974 was the first major policy legislation with a major funding appropriation that resulted in a new federal office—the Office of Juvenile Justice and Delinquency Prevention (OJJDP). The first director of OJJDP was social worker Ira Schwartz (now provost, Temple University in Philadelphia). Schwartz and his staff implemented the far-reaching legislation that provided federal funding to many states to deinstitutionalize status offenders, remove juveniles from adult jails and lock-ups, establish runaway youth shelters and counseling programs, and improve delinquency prevention programs. Social workers through their respective state governors' juvenile justice commissions and/or state criminal justice planning agencies were able to advocate for important system changes, particularly the deinstitutionalizing of runaways, truants, and incorrigible youths.

The Child Abuse Prevention and Treatment Act of 1974 provided funding for demonstration programs to test prevention, intervention, and treatment strategies for child abuse and neglect, and resulted in the establishment of the National Center on Child Abuse and Neglect (Alexander, 1995). In 1978, the Act was extended and funded new adoption initiatives. This child abuse federal funding initiative resulted in the development of interdisciplinary hospital-based child abuse assessment and treatment teams, usually with medical social workers as the coordinators or team leaders.

To this point, the social work profession had made significant advances since what could be defined as the beginning of forensic social work—the opening of the first juvenile court in 1899 in Cook County, Illinois, and the first organization to assist abused women—the Chicago Protective Agency (for women and children) established in 1885. (Roberts, 1996). Jane Addams and Julia Lathrop, founders of the settlement movement and strong advocates for the legislation that led to the first juvenile court, were leaders among the Progressive era reformers who built a foundation for the significant reforms in juvenile justice, domestic violence, and victim assistance programs and services during the past 106 years.

But there have also been setbacks. During these years and the key historical periods they represent, there were declines, and flourishing periods for major policy shifts in social workers' involvement and responsiveness to both criminal offenders and their innocent victims.

In the mid-1970s, a crushing indictment of all correctional treatment program appeared in the form of a review of 231 studies of rehabilitative programs in existence at that time. Robert Martinson (1974) conducted the review. His conclusion that "nothing works" has been bandied about ever since. For conservative politicians and cynical liberals alike, Martinson's denunciation was an answer to their prayers. So even when Martinson later refuted his own findings, acknowledging that he had disregarded the positive outcomes in many of the reports, the damage could not be undone (van Wormer, 2001). Rehabilitation essentially was dead. Social workers and other counselors exited the field or were driven out by lack of funding. At the same time, as the clash between social work values and the conservative ideology espoused by the American corrections system, social work simply abandoned the field (Gumz, 2004). This abandonment, no doubt, by a profession that put clients first, further accelerated the increasing punitive nature of corrections and the lack of forceful advocacy to reverse this trend.

The women's movement focused attention on domestic violence and victims' rights issues and programs. The Law Enforcement Assistance Act (LEAA), which passed in 1974, provided state block grants for local funding of police social work, as well as domestic violence and victim assistance programs. Model demonstration projects included the first shelter for battered women, which opened in St. Paul, Minnesota, and the first two police-based victim assistance programs, which were in Ft. Lauderdale and Indianapolis (Roberts, 1996). The civil rights movement and concerns about links between racism and imprisonment gave rise to a renewed focus on prison conditions and reform. In 1976, in a class action suit, the U.S. District court of Alabama ruled that conditions of confinement in the Alabama penal system constituted cruel and unusual punishment when they bore "no reasonable relationship to legitimate institutional goals" (Alexander, 1995, p. 2644).

By the mid-1980s, a major policy shift resulted in provision of woefully needed social services and crisis intervention for crime victims and less rehabilitation programs for convicted felons. The crime victims movement was bolstered significantly with the passage of the landmark Victims Of Crime Act (VOCA) of 1984 in which the many millions of dollars in funding came from federal criminal penalties and fines.

Decade of the 1990s to Today

Between 1984 and 1997, 2 billion dollars were allocated throughout the nation to aid domestic violence, rape, child sexual assault, and other violent crime victims. There are currently close to 10,000 victim/witness assistance, victim service, domestic violence, and sexual assault treatment programs nationwide. These programs have a total average staff of seven full time workers, of which 32% or approximately 22,400 are professional social workers (Roberts, 1997b). We predicted that the growth phase for forensic social workers would continue during the 1990s in victim assistance and domestic violence programs, and they did as a result of the $3.3 billion of funds through Violence against Women Act II. As the prison census escalates (Ginsberg, 1995), social work in community corrections continues to expand. Community-based courts, such as the Midtown Manhattan Community Court, which began in New York City in the early 1990s (Brownell, 1997), incorporate social work services into the overall program design. The specialized domestic violence courts which started to emerge in 1999 and 2000 in major cities throughout the United States also bodes well for the growing number of social workers working with domestic violence victims, batterers, and probationers (Keilitz, 2002).

Alternatives to incarceration programs for misdemeanor level crimes, as well as nonviolent felony level crimes related to IV drug use—highly associated with contemporary public health crises such as HIV and AIDS, and hepatitis C include social workers as case managers, addiction treatment specialists, crisis counselors, and family service specialists.

Today, fortunately, due to swings in the political pendulum, a public that wants offenders to change and believes they can, and evidence-based research proving the effectiveness of community-based programming such as drug courts and addiction treatment in general, rehabilitation is back.

A RICH TRADITION IN THE SOCIAL WORK CORRECTIONAL LITERATURE

According to Reamer (2004), "Relatively little serious scholarship on criminal justice issues is authored by social workers" (p. 213). We beg to differ with that assessment; we state our case in this section with a plethora of references provided from a sample of the voluminous body of research conducted by social work scholars. First, we will describe some basic textbooks that summarize empirical work done relevant to crime and delinquency; then we will consider some of the empirical research itself.

The late Professor Margaret Gibelman (1995) was one of a group of social work scholars who understood the need for greater attention by the profession to providing an active presence in the fields of crime and justice. She devoted an entire chapter to social work and the criminal justice system in the first edition of *What Social Workers Do,* published by NASW Press. H. Wayne Johnson (1998), similarly, emphasized practice in the criminal justice field in a widely used social services textbook which saw five editions. In *Social Work Almanac* (Ginsberg, 1995), substantial space is given to a discussion of corrections and juvenile delinquency. Among the social issues of increasing concern in the United States, noted by Ginsberg, "are crime and delinquency and the societal approaches for dealing with them" (p. 90). Van Wormer's (2006) introductory text, *Introduction to Social Welfare and Social Work: The U.S. in Global Perspective* contains an extensive chapter on human rights and criminal justice issues. Popple and Leighninger's (2005), *Social Work, Social Welfare, and American Society* also contains a chapter devoted to crime and criminal justice. Consider also Oxford's *Social Workers Desk Reference* (Roberts & Greene, 2002) that contains 12 original chapters in the forensic social work section by 16 experts in the field.

In recent years, four comprehensive volumes were published in which the latest social policies, social services, and social work practice roles with crime victims and offenders are documented. These books include original chapters by the leading forensic social workers in the United States. They are:

Juvenile Justice Sourcebook: Past, Present and Future (Roberts, 2004b), which includes chapters by 10 leading forensic social workers;

Substance Abuse Treatment for Criminal Offenders: An Evidence-Based guide for Practitioners (Springer, McNeece, & Arnold, 2003), a more specialized text;

Social Work in Juvenile and Criminal Justice Settings (Roberts & Springer, 2007); and

Handbook of Forensic Mental Health with Victims and Offenders: Assessment, Treatment, and Research (Springer & Roberts, 2007).

There are many other contributions on more specialized topics made by social work, including:

Children with Parents in Prison (Seymour & Hairston, 2001);

Counseling Female Offenders and Victims (van Wormer, 2001);

Understanding Legal Concepts that Influence Social Welfare Policy and Practice (Alexander, 2002);

Criminal Lessons: Case Studies and Commentary on Crime and Justice (Reamer, 2003);

Social Work and Human Rights (Reichert, 2003);

Confronting Oppression, Restoring Justice (van Wormer, 2004);

Women and the Criminal Justice System (van Wormer & Bartollas, 2007);

Battered Women and Their Families: Intervention Strategies and Treatment Programs (Roberts, Ed., 2007), and

Correctional Counseling and Treatment (Roberts, Ed., 2007).

The profession can take pride in the appointment of two social work professionals as editors of criminal justice journals. Albert Roberts is the founding editor of the international journal, *Victims & Offenders: Journal of Evidence-Based Policies and Practices* that began publication in 2006. Creasie Hairston, dean of the Jane Addams School of Social Work was appointed as editor of the interdisciplinary *Journal of Offender Rehabilitation* beginning in 2007.

A comprehensive survey of the social work literature conducted by Roberts and Springer (2007) identified 38 articles in *Social Work* during the 12-year period (1993 to 2005) that are germane to the growing field of forensic social work. Among the specific topics represented were: the plight of mothers in prison; pregnancy outcome during imprisonment; court-ordered treatment; the relationship between social work values and the corrections environment; therapeutic jurisprudence; issues involved in working with forensic clients; and multidisciplinary mitigation teams.

In addition, in *Social Work* during this period, seven articles were identified on various aspects of juvenile delinquency and youth violence. One article was published on sexual harassment law as well as one prison memoir. Six articles were published on domestic violence. An additional five articles were published on violence and victims. Prostitution and childhood sexual abuse were other topics covered.

Applying our definition of forensic social work, Roberts and Springer identified 29 articles in the prestigious *Research on Social Work Practice* during the 6-year period (1999 to 2005). Of these, there were several that coalesced around social work with troubled youth and juvenile delinquents, including school violence, anti-social behavior in a runaway shelter, reintegration services for adjudicated delinquents, mental health and substance abuse problems for detained youth, risk prediction among juvenile offenders, short-term outcomes for runaway youth, and delinquency prevention programs.

Other related topics represented in this social work research journal were victim-offender mediation and re-offense, posttraumatic stress disorder among inmates, and batterer intervention programs, child abuse issues, and sexual offender risk.

Under the able leadership of Associate Editor Rosemary Sarri, the latest edition of the *Encyclopedia of Social Work* (Edwards, 1995) was significantly expanded to include many articles related to forensic social work with victims and offenders. The 19th edition of the *Encyclopedia of Social Work* included 31 articles on a number of forensic related topics, specifically courts, criminality, incarceration, domestic violence, and correctional counseling.

The *Encyclopedia of Social Work Supplement* (Edwards, 1995) included three updates on forensic social work-related topics as well. The 20th edition of the encyclopedia, which is now in press, undoubtedly will contain as many or more articles on varied facets of correctional social work; it will include for the first time one entry on restorative justice.

It is certainly evident based on this content analysis of *Social Work* and other publications that the National Association of Social Workers (NASW) recognizes the importance of social work involvement with forensic-related issues. This is in spite of the acknowledgment that forensic social work has not yet received the attention it deserves within the profession.

PROMISING EDUCATION TRENDS

There has been a slow, but steady growth in the number of forensic social work courses and continuing education workshops. The focus and content areas of these workshops and courses include the following:

- Child custody evaluations and assessments to determine whether parental rights of persons who are mentally ill, convicted felons, and/or abusive parents should be terminated.
- Risk assessments of offenders who are mentally ill and substance-abusing (i.e., MICA-mentally ill chemically addicted, also known as dual disorders), with special attention to their risk of future violence and repeat criminality.
- Assessment and treatment of juvenile and adult mentally ill offenders in the criminal justice system and forensic mental health units to help in treatment planning as well as planning for a safe discharge or parole date.
- Preparation of presentence reports for juvenile court and criminal court judges
- Assessment of dangerousness and likelihood of recidivism among convicted sex offenders.
- Crisis assessment, crisis intervention, and trauma treatment protocols and strategies with victims of violent crimes.

- Domestic violence policies and intervention strategies with battered women and their children.
- Batterers psycho-educational and group treatment protocols and intervention strategies.
- Assessment and treatment with suicide-prone juvenile and adult offenders.
- Motivational interviewing and other strengths-based treatment strategies with substance abusers.
- Restorative justice policies and practices.
- Treatment Engagement and retention among substance-abusing offenders.
- Applying the stages-of-change and transtheoretical models to clinical treatment with criminal offenders.

The NASW received a $25,000 grant from the U.S. Department of Human Services to produce a conference for providers of services to prisoners reentering communities (Stoesen, 2006a). This grant was an expression of support by the federal government following President George W. Bush's announcement in his State of the Union address to fund a 4-year Prisoner Reentry Initiative to help inmates find work when they return to their communities. An article in *NASW News* (Stoesen, 2006b) highlighted these developments.

EVIDENCE-BASED RESEARCH

A major challenge facing the future of forensic social workers is treatment engagement and retention of juvenile and criminal offenders receiving clinical treatment. Concern regarding challenges in attracting and retaining substance-abusing clients in treatment, for example, has led researchers to focus on motivation as a construct that may contribute to an enhanced understanding of treatment engagement and retention (Battjes, Gordon, O'Grady, Kinlock, & Carswell, 2003; Battjes, Onken, & Delany, 1999). A growing body of research suggests that drug courts are effective in retaining a significant number of clients in substance abuse treatment and in reducing criminality thereby (Mueser, Noordsy, Drake, & Fox, 2003). Secondary analyses of two large national effectiveness studies found a positive relationship between adolescents' length of substance abuse treatment and their outcome (Hubbard, Cavanaugh, Craddock, & Rachel, 1985; Sells & Simpson, 1979). Hubbard et al. (1985) also found that client motivation is a major factor in determining length of treatment involvement and, thereby, treatment success. Battjes et al. (2003) investigated factors that predict motivation among youth admitted to an adolescent outpatient substance abuse treatment program; findings revealed that factors involving various negative consequences of substance use emerged as important predictors of motivation, whereas severity of substance use did not.

Despite these advances, new research is needed to identify factors that impact retention and therapeutic engagement, with the need especially for research that examines the relationship between patient outcomes and elements of the therapeutic process—namely, the treatment environment, patient needs, and delivery of services (Battjes et al., 2003; Simpson, Joe, Rowan-Szal, & Greener, 1997). Additional concepts, such as those representing a client's stage of change and motivation (DeLeon, Melnick, Kressel, & Jainchill, 1994;

Simpson & Joe, 1993) should also be integrated into a more comprehensive analytic model (Simpson et al., 1997). The importance of motivation and retention is underscored by the findings of a study by Lawendowski (1998) at the University of Mexico's Center on Alcoholism, Substance Abuse, and Addiction, which found that 50% of adolescent clients did not return after initial treatment and 70% terminated treatment prematurely. Additionally, Simpson et al. (1997) found that pretreatment motivation was a significant predictor of session attendance during early treatment among adult opioid addicts.

One theoretical framework relevant to motivation for engagement and retention in substance abuse treatment is the transtheoretical model (TTM). This model grew in response to dissatisfaction with simple behavioral models and the search for a more comprehensive approach to describe complex processes of human behavior change. Since its development, this model has been used extensively with practitioners, clinicians and researchers in the field of addictions and drug use. The stages-of-change model is the most frequently applied construct of the TTM model, and it offers the most research concerning the validity of TTM constructs (cf. Prochaska, Norcross, Fowler, Follick, & Abrams, 1992; Prochaska et al., 1994; Velicer, Norman, Fava, & Prochaska, 1999).

This model conceptualizes five stages-of-change that integrate processes and principles of change from a number of major theories (Prochaska & Norcross, 1999). The first stage is Precontemplation, in which there is no intention or motivation to change. People in this stage generally have no awareness of the problem or have greatly underestimated the seriousness of the problem. The second stage is Contemplation, in which there is awareness of a problem and a desire to overcome it, but no commitment to take the actions necessary to accomplish change. The third stage, Preparation, involves a decision to take action sometime in the near future, but a specific plan for accomplishing this goal is not present or has not yet been implemented. The fourth stage is Action, in which the individual makes changes in behavior and/or lifestyle and sustains those from 1 day to 6 months. The final stage, Maintenance, involves those activities necessary to maintain change and avoid relapse.

Progression through these stages is not expected to be linear and reversion to earlier stages is expected. Most clients move through the stages of change in a spiral pattern. Indeed, in one study (Prochaska & DiClemente, 1984), approximately 15% of smokers who relapsed went back to the Precontemplation stage, and 85% went back to the Precontemplation or Contemplation stage. Preliminary data suggest that this framework is useful in providing services to minority clients (Longshore, Grills, & Annon, 1999), preventing alcohol-exposed pregnancy after a jail term (Mullen, Velasquez, von Sternberg, Cummins, & Green, 2005), and guiding treatment with substance-abusing juvenile offenders (Springer, Rivaux, Bohman, & Yeung, 2006), to name just a few.

A major challenge is the successful treatment and retention of persons with co-occurring disorders (persons with both a mental disorder and substance-related problems). Programs that are tailored to individuals' readiness for change and that do not force clients to abstain from all drug use but that engage clients in a collaborative effort to reduce the harm to themselves are more successful than other approaches with this population. In their review of the literature on treatment effectiveness with dually and multiply diagnosed populations, Mueser et al. (2003) found that the best outcomes were with integrated, long-term dual diagnosis treatment geared toward the client's level of motivation.

Springer et al. (2006) examined factors that predict, and interventions that maximize, substance abuse treatment retention in three modalities among high-risk Anglo, Mexican

American and African American juvenile offenders. The study sample includes youth ($N = 211$) who were discharged from probation supervision and who received substance abuse services through a CSAT-funded federal demonstration project. Among the juveniles in this sample, 56 (18%) were female and 255 (82%) were male. Approximately half ($n = 163$, 52.4%) were Mexican American, one-quarter ($n = 88$, 28.3%) were African American, and the remainder were Caucasian ($n = 50$, 28.3%). The key predictors examined included the stage-of-change (i.e., precontemplation, contemplation, preparation) in which a juvenile fell, various dimensions captured by the Comprehensive Addiction Severity Index for Adolescents, and other intervention status (probation, case management, and mental health treatment). The research questions were addressed using survival analysis statistical models that treated time from entry into substance abuse treatment to exit from substance abuse treatment as the outcomes. Among key findings were that females were 73% more likely to leave day treatment relative to males; for each additional family problem ever experienced, Mexican American adolescents were 15% more likely to leave residential treatment compared to African American adolescents; and African American and Mexican American adolescents in the contemplation stage-of-change were 50% less likely to leave day treatment compared to Caucasian adolescents.

While studies such as this speak to the progress that has been made in recent years, little research has been conducted that examines factors that predict treatment retention and engagement for substance-abusing female and minority offenders (Longshore, Grills, Annon, & Grady, 1998). The results from the Springer et al. (2006) study suggest that continued research is needed to explore the extent to which various treatment components—such as family therapy or motivational interviewing—contribute to substance abuse treatment engagement and retention among African American and Mexican American clients across the stages-of-change continuum.

NODE-LINK MAPPING

One other innovative intervention that has been used to enhance treatment readiness is called *node-link mapping* (Pitre, Dansereau, Newbern, & Simpson, 1998; Simpson, Chatham, & Joe, 1993; Simpson, Dansereau, & Joe, 1997). Simpson and colleagues have developed a series of treatment readiness interventions as part of the NIDA-supported Cognitive Enhancements for the Treatment of Probationers (CETOP) Project. These interventions are designed specifically for use with offenders early in the treatment process (Precontemplation or Contemplation), and can be used in groups of up to 35 participants.

Essentially, node-link mapping is a visualization tool, in which elements of ideas, feelings, actions, or knowledge contained within "nodes" (circles, squares) are connected to each other by "links" (lines) that are named to specify relationships between the nodes (Dees, Dansereau, & Simpson, 1997; Pitre, Dansereau, & Simpson, 1997). These maps are usually drawn by practitioners in collaboration with their clients during group or individual sessions.

Node-link mapping has produced modest positive effects across studies. Mapping appears to increase counseling efficiency, help clients focus their attention, facilitate the development of the therapeutic relationship, and increase counseling efficiency (cf. Czuchry, Dansereau, Dees, & Simpson, 1995; Dansereau, Joe, & Simpson, 1995; Pitre et al., 1997).

Mapping has been found effective in outpatient methadone clinics (Dansereau, Joe, & Simpson, 1993) and in a residential criminal justice treatment setting that uses a modified therapeutic community approach with large-group sessions (Pitre et al., 1998). More specifically, an examination by client subgroups indicates that the following types of individuals benefit the most strongly from mapping-enhanced counseling: clients with attention difficulties (Czuchry et al., 1995; Dansereau et al., 1995); cocaine-using opioid addicts (Joe, Dansereau, & Simpson, 1994); African American and Mexican American clients (Dansereau, Joe, Dees, & Simpson, 1996); and clients who do not have a high school degree or GED certificate (Pitre, Dansereau, & Joe, 1996 as cited in Pitre et al., 1997).

Treatment readiness manuals are available through Lighthouse Institute, which is a part of the Chestnut Health Systems (see more information at www.chestnut.org). The manuals are also available for downloading from the web site of the Institute of Behavioral Research (IBR) of the Texas Christian University (TCU; www.ibr.tcu.edu), where Simpson and his colleagues are based.

Using the stages-of-change model to proactively apply stage-matched interventions (such as motivational interviewing and node-link mapping) with criminal offenders brings with it the potential to increase treatment engagement, retention, and outcomes. Exploring this in research, and subsequently applying it in practice, is important to the future of forensic social work if we are to enhance the effectiveness of clinical interventions with offenders.

Because of the work of social workers, substance abuse counselors, and other mental health practitioners familiar with the social psychological principles of motivational enhancement, the motivational model is making inroads in the criminal justice system.

A STRENGTHS PERSPECTIVE

In social work, the idea of building on people's strengths has become an overriding theme associated with an emphasis on empowerment. There is nothing very new about this theoretical concept; the parallels with the self-fulfilling prophecy concept, labeling theory, and "the-power-of-positive-thinking" conceptualizations are obvious. As a framework for treatment intervention, the strengths approach can offer a mental map, as Norman Polansky (1986) eloquently suggested several decades ago. Such a mental map can operate as a reminder when we as therapists get off course (get too caught up in the use of formal diagnosis, for example). Within the correctional system, viewing clients solely through the lens of the crimes they have committed can obscure our vision and impede treatment progress.

More recently, the strengths perspective has been catapulted to prominence by such writers as Dennis Saleebey and others of the University of Kansas School of Social Work. Saleebey (2006) describes the essence of this approach in these words: "Practicing from a strengths orientation means this—*everything* you do as a social worker will be predicated, in some way, on helping to discover and embellish, explore and exploit clients' strengths and resources in the service of assisting them to achieve their goals, realize their dreams, and shed the irons of their own inhibitions and misgivings, and society's domination" (p. 1). The title of Saleebey's introductory chapter is "Power in the People." Within the justice context, the challenge consists of promoting personal power in people whose lives have become circumscribed to varying degrees and whose very existence has been devalued and even criminalized.

More than any other population, correctional clients are the failures of the failures. Not only have they publicly been labeled through some kind of court action, but their encounter with professional counselors usually relates to some kind of punishment. Work in the correctional realm, then, with all the negatives stacked against it, is an excellent testing ground for a framework of strengths. In contrast to a diagnostic, pathology-based therapy, direct practice from this multidimensional framework looks beyond a client's diagnosis or offense—for example, borderline personality or drug possession—to positive attributes that can serve as an important resource even in the most desperate of circumstances.

A second major challenge to correctional social work is the challenge of viewing causality reciprocally. With criminal behavior, the locus of the problem is not the individual alone but the individual and society in interaction. To study the person-in-the-environment is not enough; one also needs to study the environment-in-the-person. If we conceive of the environment as the prison, we can view the new recruits as bringing into this milieu all of what Irwin (1980) calls the "cultural baggage" from their social background. And then we can view aspects of prison life—the social control, the convict norms—as internalized within the prison inmate. Both the person and the environment can be seen to be in continuous and dynamic interaction in this way. If we come to frame the inmates' confinement in a political sense, then we have moved toward a linking of the personal and political levels of existence.

As we hear from correctional social worker, Michael Clark:

> Embracing a strengths perspective in a criminal justice world has been fraught with frustration. Criminal justice is a field that is unbalanced as it entertains only problems, failures and flaws. Compliance is king while behavior change is often left wanting—viewed as something best left to others ("treatment"). I began to find inroads for using a strengths-based approach with my probation caseload and soon published articles detailing the application within juvenile delinquency. . . . I found a small group of like-minded practitioners and increased my skills. After a full year of advocacy, I was able to convince our court management to change a deficit-based family history form to one that was balanced between both problems and strengths.
>
> The old form was so bad; I often have groups review the old deficits form in my trainings as a good example of "what not to do." To gain more experience, I moved into a child welfare position and spent 5 years performing abuse and neglect casework. I was eventually appointed a Senior Juvenile Court Officer, which included the duties of Judicial Referee (Magistrate), holding preliminary hearings for our judges in both delinquency and child welfare cases. My publications led to conducting workshops and that spiraled into a complete career change. . . . I left the court and formed the Center for Strength-Based Strategies, a research and technical assistance organization that seeks to import strength-based and outcome-informed practices for work with mandated clients. Our Center champions direct practice and is actively engaged in training staffing groups in the "how to's" for one-on-one efforts with challenging clients.

(Clark goes on to explain how reading Miller and Rollnick's *Motivational Interviewing* further enhanced his strengths approach.)

> I found formal training in this approach and then moved my practice to another level, completing a train-the-trainer session to be named a "MINT" member (Motivational Interviewing Network of Trainers). I now am engaged in training probation officers in motivational Interviewing across the country. Several states are engaged in training all (!) of their supervising probation and parole officers in motivational approaches. (as cited in Roberts & Springer, 2007, pp. 9–10)

Initiatives such as these lend an enthusiasm to forensic social work that becomes altogether contagious.

CURRENT STATUS OF FORENSIC SOCIAL WORK

According to Diane Young, who was quoted as an expert on prison reentry by *NASW News* reporter, Stoesen (2006b), more departments of social work should offer a concentration in criminal justice. "The need is really great for social work involvement" (p. 4). Her recommendation is that social work get more actively involved in reentry work where the need is so urgent. As Jeffrey Draine, also interviewed in the article, observed, "People who might have been interested in going into social work went into criminal justice, which has a different set of professional standards. . . . Social workers need to reclaim this. We need to take initiative, propose innovation, (move beyond) the principle of surveillance and control as the primary organizing concept" (p. 4).

Correctional social workers ideally are trained in knowledge and skills on diagnostic and risk assessments, the nature of human development and behavioral dysfunctions, juvenile and adult laws, juvenile and criminal court procedures and structure, crisis intervention and trauma treatment protocols, the strengths perspective and solution-focused therapy, and mental health treatments for criminal offenders as well as violent crime victims.

Opportunities exist for professional social workers at the Legal Aid Society and work in family courts with abused and neglected children, as well as juvenile offenders with mental health and addictions problems. Victim service programs for crime victims and domestic violence survivors employ professional social workers to work with victims as well as perpetrators of family crimes.

The emergence of specialized courts, such as drug courts and domestic violence courts, has resulted in an increasing presence of social workers in the courts. Schools of Social Work have developed interdisciplinary programs with law schools, as well as joint degree programs in social work and the law.

The increase of women in prison due to some states' "get-tough" drug laws, and increased recognition of the plight of the forensic mentally ill, require the services of professional social workers for counseling and to serve as the link between child welfare, substance abuse, health and mental health systems on one hand, and the correctional system on the other. Other social and pubic health problems with which forensic social workers are engaged include the alarming surge of hepatitis C, HIV and AIDS, cancer, cardiovascular diseases, diabetes, as well as tuberculosis, among the county and city jail and state prison populations, and the increasing recognition of a forensic MICA and developmentally disabled inmate population.

CONTRASTING VALUES—CRIMINAL JUSTICE AND SOCIAL WORK

Contrast the terminology of criminal justice—punishment, zero tolerance, criminal personality—with that of social work—empowerment, strengths perspective, social justice, cultural competence—and the fields come across as worlds apart. For these two fields to come together would take a paradigm shift.

Social workers in the criminal justice field will note that the empirically-based cognitive approach is the dominant approach to counseling sessions. Counselors trained from this perspective focus on taking a very directive role in exposing the client's irrational thoughts, the "musts" and "shoulds" and the tendency to catastrophize in a crisis (model borrowed from Ellis, 2001). Social workers often use this model to help clients reframe their negative, self-defeating thoughts into positive statements. Correctional workers (and addictions counselors), however, typically draw on a format that is anything but positive. They utilize exercises derived from the theoretical framework of criminal psychologist Stanton Samenow (1984), which focuses on his understanding of "the criminal personality." Samenow's theory and techniques, which are geared to criminal thinking and manipulation, are commonly used in correctional addictions programming with both male and female offenders. His best-selling book, *Inside the Criminal Mind* was based on work with psychopathic males in confinement at St. Elizabeth's Hospital for the "criminally insane" in Washington, DC. In programming that Samenow developed and teaches through nationwide workshops, offenders are required to focus on their wrongdoings, with the goal of instilling "self-disgust" and a desire to reform their errant ways (van Wormer, 2007).

The strengths perspective, this is not. Many offenders, more victimized than victimizers, suffer from low self-esteem and shame due to their troubles with the law, pain inflicted on their families, and so on and a focus on the errors of their ways is counterproductive.

A competing philosophy that is now coming into its own within the criminal justice system is a cognitively based formulation that focuses on client motivation. *Motivational Interviewing,* developed by William Miller and Rollnick (1996), combines aspects of a laid-back, client-centered approach with a focus on reinforcement of positive, self-motivational statements. Collaboration and choice are guiding precepts. Instead of confrontation, counselors are advised to "roll with resistance." Instead of telling clients what is wrong with their lives or thinking, therapists are taught to focus on the positive and elicit statements of intended change efforts from the clients themselves, then to reinforce such statements. A theme of this approach is a focus on the client's self-efficacy, similar to the strengths perspective tapping into the client's own inner resources. Motivational interviewing is evidence-based; every precept of this model is derived from proven findings from social psychology concerning how people change (for a breakdown of these statements, see van Wormer & Davis, 2008). Motivational enhancement strategies are of demonstrated effectiveness with clients who are mandated to treatment and who are inclined to be angry (Wallace, 2005).

Correctional practice is very rarely social justice as endorsed in the social work code. "Strategies must be found for promoting social work values within the environmental contexts of offenders' lives," as Young and LoMonaco (2001, p. 479) note. Within total institutions and without, individuals need help in negotiating the system, however dehumanizing, so that ultimately they can be free from the shackles of the correctional system and maybe even reclaim their lives.

Social work, as a profession, is steeped in a history of advocacy for social justice and prevention work, especially with juveniles. Experience in family counseling and interdisciplinary teamwork are further relevant attributes of the profession that lend themselves to success in this work with people in trouble with the law. Significant numbers of social workers earn their living, as Reamer (2004) acknowledges, as probation and parole officers, caseworkers in public defender offices, counselors in correctional institutions and halfway houses, and so on. But as a profession, he indicates, social work no longer has a major presence in the criminal justice field. Social work, we might add, no longer has a major role in shaping legislation pertain to juvenile justice and adult corrections.

At the policy level, advocacy to change the system is vital. In order to curb crime and victimization, drug addiction must be viewed as a health problem, a disease that can be treated, rather than as a criminal justice problem. As social workers and students of social work visit their state legislators, as on lobby day, or testify at state legislative forums, the opportunity is provided to show legislators how they can be progressive and save the state money at the same time. A focus on the cost-effectiveness of prevention programming and diversionary programs such as drug courts that keep people with addiction problems in the community and out of the prison revolving door can be especially persuasive in times of budget tightening. Money saved in prison construction can be spent on treatment and prevention, and in the child welfare system, instead.

Rehabilitation, happily, is no longer a dirty word. The general public and politicians alike are speaking of the importance of offender treatment and rehabilitation. One sign that such a shift may be occurring is the proliferation of programming that is associated with a seemingly new movement that actually harks back to ancient times. This movement is known in its present reincarnation as restorative justice.

RESTORATIVE JUSTICE: A BRIDGE BETWEEN CRIMINAL JUSTICE AND SOCIAL WORK

The adversary system will not be replaced; prisons will not be razed and correctional officers won't be throwing away their uniforms just yet, but, according to the National Institute of Corrections, "a revolution is occurring in criminal justice" (Barajas, 1995). Rarely noted until recently in the social work literature in the United States (but widely emphasized in the social work literature of Canada, Britain, and New Zealand), restorative justice involves a reorientation of how we think about crime and justice. As a set of values, restorative justice offers great promise in regard to promoting healing and strengthening community bonds by addressing the criminal harm done to victims and communities.

Restorative justice is a collective term that loosely refers to a number of initiatives that hold offenders directly accountable to victims and the community. Although the term restorative justice has become popular only since the 1990s, this form of dispensing justice is rooted in the rituals of indigenous populations as tribal members settled disputes in sentencing circles. Its modern beginnings are in Canada in the 1970s. Canadian Mennonites, noted for their emphasis on pacifism and communal decision making, began to experiment with meetings between victims and offenders to establish restitution. From these simple beginnings, the victim-offender reconciliation movement was born; it continued to be used widely in Canada and came to the United States (Zehr, 2000). Feminist-inspired victim rights activists played a role in raising consciousness regarding the need for victims to be heard in the criminal justice process.

Restorative justice is the growing movement that aims to change the direction of criminal law by focusing it on the needs of victims and on repairing communities. Unlike retributive justice, which focuses on punishment of the guilty offender, restorative justice takes a more caring approach. Proponents of this nonadversarial model adopt a different lens for viewing crime and rectifying the harm done by the crime. Restorative justice entails active involvement by members of the community operating with official sanction of the local court. Just as calls for retribution often bring out the baser instincts in people, a focus on restoration and empowerment also tends to bring out the best in human nature.

Victim-offender conferencing is probably the most common restorative justice program in the United States; restitution and community service are widely used sanctions. There are now thousands of victim-offender programs in the United States (Orzech, 2006), and many more are operating around the world. New Zealand and Canada make extensive use of family group conferencing and healing circles for work with juveniles.

This focus is relevant to the field of social work, first and foremost because social workers may have caseloads containing persons who have been victimized by crime or who are court-ordered into treatment because of offending behavior. Such clients may or may not be entangled with the criminal justice system. Social workers may be directly or indirectly involved in court proceedings; they may even be in a position to influence legislation pertaining to correctional treatment.

To learn how the process works, consider the Canadian healing circle facilitated by social worker Angel Yuen, as reported in the *Toronto Star* (Healing circle shows offenders their human toll, 2001). "All the people touched by an offense have an opportunity to speak about how they were affected," according to the article. "That means an offender sees and hears, firsthand, the human impact of his or her actions. It means the victim hears why the offense occurred. And it means the offender hears his or her own voice, often apologizing through tears, offering to make amends. At the close, a contract is drawn up detailing what took place and how the offender will repair the harm" (p. NE04). The impact of such a community encounter can be positive, eliciting sincere apologies, reconciling neighbors who may then lose their fear of each other. In contrast to court adjudication, the conferencing encourages truth-telling and creative ways of making amends.

In 1991, Vermont decided to overhaul its system, setting up reparative boards statewide to focus on repairing the damage to the victim and community (van Wormer, 2004). Composed of volunteers, the reparative group is charged with ensuring that low-risk, nonviolent offenders are made aware of the impact of their behavior on members of the community. Vermont, in fact, is the first state to implement such conferencing on a statewide basis and the first to institutionalize the restorative justice philosophy. Minnesota followed and instituted restorative initiatives throughout the criminal justice system. Hawaii, as well, has made major strides in adopting this approach, a variety adapted from Native Hawaiian rituals that precede colonization.

The mission of social work is rooted in a set of core values. According to the NASW *Code of Ethics,* the core values of social work are as follows: social justice, dignity and worth of the person, importance of human relationships, integrity, and competence (1996).

Restorative justice relates closely to *social justice* or fairness in that the victims and offenders each have their interests represented in the proceedings. Social justice is provided to the victim in that effort is made to restore what the victim has lost, while at the same time requiring the offender to face the consequences of his or her acts and the personal pain caused to the victim, the victim's family, the offender's family, and the community. These strategies can be combined with those of community-based corrections to create multifaceted programs of benefit to all involved. Rehabilitation, rather than retribution, is the thrust of this approach.

Through embracing members of the extended family, restorative justice also has been found to be highly effective in minority communities. These minority communities—including Native American, African American, and Latino traditions are collectively, rather than individually, focused. The Circle Sentencing approach, as used in the Yukon of Canada, utilizes traditional justice processes of tribal communities to view crime holistically. Tapping into the strengths of community resources, the process develops sanctions based on consensus of community members. Often a strong, spiritual component is part of such sentencing and healing circles.

On a global scale, the most amazing example of truth-telling and catharsis for crime has taken place in South Africa before the Truth and Reconciliation Commission. In intensely emotional sessions, former officials of the apartheid regime were brought face-to-face with their victims, many of whom they had tortured. Healing was centered on the communication process itself rather than on retribution for the pain that was inflicted.

Dignity and worth of the person is the second core value of social work. Through restorative justice, the dignity of both the offender and victim are maintained through a process that is the opposite of customary criminal justice proceedings—the orange suit, publicity attached to the arrest and trial, the indignities and accusations heaped on witnesses by lawyers on the opposing side. The focus of restorative justice is on the offender's whole personality, not only on the acts that have caused the harm.

Importance of human relationships is another theme of the restorative justice movement. Through community service projects and psychologically through the contrition and remorse shown toward persons who are injured by the wrongdoing, offenders help compensate for what they have done.

The core social work value of *integrity* is evidenced in a format built on truth and frank disclosure. In contrast to conventional forms of justice, in which the accused remains silent while his or her lawyer fights against disclosures of guilt being admitted into evidence and challenges the integrity of prosecution witnesses, restorative justice encourages open sharing of information among involved parties.

As far as competence is concerned, we can look to the empirical evidence. What does research say about the effectiveness of victim offender conferencing, for example? Follow-up surveys show that victims consistently rate the process positively, according to Mark Umbreit (1993), director of the Center for Restorative Justice and Peacemaking, School of Social Work, University of Minnesota, St. Paul. The most extensive research to date shows that while the possibility of receiving restitution appeared to motivate victims to enter the mediation process, they reported that meeting the offender and being able to talk about what happened was more satisfying than receiving restitution (Umbreit, Vos, Coates, & Brown, 2003). In closely monitored meetings between inmates and former victims in British Columbia, victims reported they could see the offender as a person rather than a monster. This view helped them feel less fear and more peace. Offenders, in turn, felt more empathy for their victims, feelings and provided evidence of increasing self-awareness.

Restorative justice principles very neatly bridge the gap between the formality of conventional criminal justice processes and the social work ethos. In its incorporation of activities related to personal and community empowerment, spirituality, conflict resolution, healing of relationships through dialogue, and learning techniques of decision making inspired by indigenous people's traditions, restorative justice effectively links practice with policy. Because restorative justice is about uniting rather than dividing people on opposite sides of the law, and whole communities, it also offers common ground between theoretically diverse disciplines, one of which, in the simplest terms, seeks to protect the individual from the society, and the other which serves to protect society from the individual (at least, certain individuals). The field of criminal justice deserves credit for the leadership it has provided in bringing much needed innovations that have taken place in prisons and courtrooms and churches across the land. References to restorative justice are ubiquitous in the criminal justice literature. If you type in restorative justice on the *Criminal Justice Abstracts* search engine, for example (as of March 2007), you will find over 450 listings compared to a mere 10 at *Social Work Abstracts,* most of which are recent. Social work, therefore, has some catching up to do.

CHALLENGES FOR THE FUTURE

Schooled in strength-based interventions, social workers, at the present time, are striving to shift from a deficit, pathology-based model to one that builds on the untapped resources of people and communities. Criminal justice initiatives at the state and local levels are steadily moving in a more humanistic and pragmatic direction as well. The realization that massive numbers of released prisoners will be returning to in their communities is the impetus for serious concern about the need for expanded social services at all government levels (Orzech, 2006; Stoesen, 2006b).

There has been a growing concern also in recent years regarding the increasing number of offenders and victims in urgent need of mental health treatment and social services; some of whom are at high risk of future violence if they do not receive the evidence-based interventions they urgently need. Our vision for the future is that all vulnerable and at-risk clients will have the opportunity to be helped by especially trained social work advocates, clinicians, and policymakers. Forensic work is complex and involves an understanding of systems: intrapsychic, interpersonal, familial, and societal. Case management is an important model with the highly vulnerable offender populations, one of the many services in which social workers excel. The primary functions of case management include intake assessment, formulating personal objectives and service goals, treatment planning, linking with informal and formal support groups, resource identification, matching clients to agencies and concrete services, monitoring, outcome evaluation, and termination. Forensic social workers often focus on providing the full range and continuum of concrete services and clinical interventions to their clients.

One of the major opportunities for forensic social workers and educators is to orient and inform legislators, juvenile and adult correctional administrators, corrections professionals, and students about the latest model offender treatment and prevention programs as well as the latest research documenting the effectiveness of these programs in reducing recidivism (Roberts, 2004b). At the present time, too many legislators, correctional administrators, and practitioners are unaware of the latest research documenting the most effective interventions. As indicated by McNeece and Jackson (2004), the current emphasis in a number of states on punitive treatment and contracting out to private correctional companies who only care about making money by providing the lowest costing services are unjust, ineffective, and inhumane. A number of promising, humane, and effective rehabilitation programs are available in different parts of the United States.

Roberts (2004b) and Springer (2004) documented over 10 different evidence-based offender treatment models that are effective based on longitudinal research. These evidence-based interventions include: Probation monitored restitution and work placement, establishing offender treatment goals and targets for change, motivational interviewing and solution-focused treatment, structured wilderness education programs, occupational trades training and job placement, multisystemic therapy, problem-solving skills training, brief strategic family therapy, cognitive-behavioral approaches such as anger management and behavioral contracting, community day treatment and aftercare by case managers, and graduated community-based sanctions.

The tension between social control and social support is an ongoing and necessary one with which the profession must continue to struggle. Issues of poverty, gender, race, ethnicity, disabilities, domestic violence, mental illness, and pregnant and parenting substance abusers intersect with forensic social work. For decades there has been a debate among social workers as to whether we should help involuntary clients. A growing group of dedicated forensic social workers have navigated, advocated for, and overcome obstacles for their clients in the criminal justice system. Social workers in forensic settings do their best to adjust to the constraints of courts and correctional settings, while advocating for offenders and victims to realize their full potential.

The social work profession, with its long history of advocating for community-based treatment, believing that most human beings are redeemable, and stressing interdisciplinary teamwork can expect to play an increasingly active role in facilitating such nonadversarial forms of justice as restorative justice. The challenge to members of social work, "the policy based profession" (Popple & Leighninger, 2007), is to discover ways of making correctional strategies more consistent with the ethic of social justice and to participate in the planning and implementation of restorative community justice and other progressive initiatives. Several trends in criminal justice complement social workers' values and perspectives (Reamer, 2004). Chief among these, as Reamer indicates is the growth of interest in mediation and restorative programming. In this chapter, we viewed how strategies built on a strengths perspective, stages of change, motivational enhancement, at the micro level, and principles of restorative justice at the macro level can do much to reduce the punitive ethos of the present system and move the system forward toward a focus on rehabilitation rather than retribution.

Effective strategies for restorative justice advocacy are as follows: to embark on cost-effective analyses of ongoing programs; engage in special outreach efforts to victim/witness assistance groups to dispel any initial skepticism; unite with progressives in the field of criminal justice as well as natural allies at the grassroots level for educational efforts; lobby legislators for funding of state and local pilot projects for certain designated categories of offenders; and, finally, build community support with outreach to minority groups, especially native populations, to promote a restorative framework. If we can begin to repair the harm that has been done to the offender while helping the offender take responsibility for his or her actions, the offender will begin to repair the harm he or she has done to the community. At the same time, paying attention to the victim's emotional and physical needs can promote recovery of personal losses and a sense of satisfaction through active involvement in the resolution and reconciliation process.

We wrote this chapter in recognition of the social work profession's past century of dedication to serving oppressed, vulnerable, at-risk, and devalued groups. During this time, the most neglected and devalued groups have been victims of violent crimes and criminal offenders. In the past 2 decades, professional social workers have made significant progress in advocating for and obtaining critically needed social services for juvenile offenders, adult offenders and victims of violent crimes and in placing student in the correctional field. We look to the support of our professional organizations—Society of Social Work and Research (SSWR), the National Association of Forensic Social Work (NAFSW), the Council on Social Work Education (CSWE), the National Association of Social Workers (NASW) in recognizing the far-reaching potential of forensic social work. Our expectation is that the profession of social work to provide critically needed leadership in the correctional field and to reconnect and reclaim, as a profession, with the critically important domains of juvenile and criminal justice. This chapter is dedicated to that end.

REFERENCES

Alexander, C. (1995). Distinctive dates in social welfare history. In R. Edwards, & G. J. Hopps (Eds.), *Encyclopedia of social work* (19th ed., pp. 2631–2647). Washington, DC: National Association of Social Workers Press.

Alexander, R. (2002). *Understanding legal concepts that influence social welfare policy and practice*. Belmont, CA: Wadsworth.

Barajas, E., Jr. (1995). *Moving toward community justice. Topics in community corrections*. Washington, DC: U.S. Department of Justice.

Barker, R. L. (2003). *The social work dictionary* (5th ed.). Washington, DC: National Association of Social Workers Press.

Battjes, R. J., Gordon, M. S., O'Grady, K. E., Kinlock, T. W., & Carswell, M. A. (2003). Factors that predict adolescent motivation for substance abuse treatment. *Journal of Substance Abuse Treatment, 24*(3), 221–232.

Battjes, R. J., Onken, L. S., & Delany, P. J. (1999). Drug abuse treatment entry and engagement: Report of a meeting on treatment readiness. *Journal of Clinical Psychology, 55*, 643–657.

Brownell, P. (1997). *Female offenders in the criminal justice system: Policy and program development*. In A. R. Roberts (Ed.), *Social work in juvenile and criminal justice settings* (2nd ed., pp. 325–349). Springfield, IL: Charles C Thomas.

Bureau of Justice Statistics. (2005). *Probation and parole in the United States, 2004* (NCJ 210676). Washington, DC: U.S. Department of Justice, U.S. Government Printing Office.

Bureau of Justice Statistics. (2006, May). *Prison and jail inmates at midyear 2005*. Washington, DC: U.S. Department of Justice.

Council on Social Work Education. (2007). *Statistics on social work education in the United States: 2004*. Alexandria, VA: Author.

Czuchry, M., Dansereau, D. F., Dees, S. M., & Simpson, D. D. (1995). The use of node-link mapping in drug abuse counseling: The role of attentional factors. *Journal of Psychoactive Drugs, 27*, 161–166.

Dansereau, D. F., Joe, G. W., Dees, S. M., & Simpson, D. D. (1996). Ethnicity and the effects of mapping-enhanced drug abuse counseling. *Addictive Behaviors, 21*, 363–376.

Dansereau, D. F., Joe, G. W., & Simpson, D. D. (1993). Node-link mapping: A visual representation strategy for enhancing drug abuse counseling. *Journal of Counseling Psychology, 40*, 385–395.

Dansereau, D. F., Joe, G. W., & Simpson, D. D. (1995). Attentional difficulties and the effectiveness of a visual representation strategy for counseling drug-addicted clients. *International Journal of the Addictions, 30*, 371–386.

Day, P. J. (2006). *A new history of social welfare* (5th ed.). Boston: Allyn & Bacon.

Dees, S. M., Dansereau, D. F., & Simpson, D. D. (1997). Mapping-enhanced drug abuse counseling:

Urinalysis results in the first year of methadone treatment. *Journal of Substance Abuse Treatment, 14*, 45–54.

DeLeon, G., Melnick, G., Kressel, D., & Jainchill, N. (1994). Circumstances, Motivation, Readiness, and Suitability (the CMRS Scales): Predicting retention in therapeutic community treatment. *American Journal of Drug and Alcohol Abuse, 20*, 495–515.

Edwards, R. L. (Ed.). (1995). *Encyclopedia of social work* (19th ed.). Washington, DC: National Association of Social Workers Press.

Ellis, A. (2001). *Overcoming destructive beliefs, feelings, and behaviors: New directions for national emotive behavior therapy*. Essex, United Kingdom: Prometheus Book.

Gibelman, M. (1995). *What social workers do*. Washington, DC: National Association of Social Workers Press.

Ginsberg, L. (1995). *The social work almanac*. Washington, DC: National Association of Social Workers Press.

Gumz, E. (2004). American social work, corrections and restorative justice: An appraisal. *International Journal of Offender Therapy and Comparative Criminology, 48*, 449–460.

Healing circle shows offenders their human toll. (2001). *Toronto Star*. p. NE04.

Hubbard, R. L., Cavanaugh, E. R., Craddock, S. G., & Rachel, J. V. (1985). Characteristics, behaviors and outcomes for youth in the TOPS. In G. M. Beschner & A. S Friedman (Eds.), *Treatment services for adolescent substance abusers* (Treatment Research Monograph Series, DHHS Publication No. ADM 84-1286). Rockville, MD: National Institute on Drug Abuse.

Irwin, J. (1980). *Prisons in turmoil*. New York: Little, Brown.

Joe, G. W., Dansereau, D. F., & Simpson, D. D. (1994). Node-link mapping for counseling cocaine users in methadone treatment. *Journal of Substance Abuse, 6*, 393–406.

Johnson, H. W. (1998). *The social services: An introduction* (5th ed.). Belmont, CA: Wadsworth.

Keilitz, S. (2002). Specialized domestic violence courts. In A. R. Roberts (Ed.), *Handbook of domestic violence intervention strategies* (pp. 147–172). New York: Oxford University Press.

Lawendowski, L. A. (1998). A motivational intervention for adolescent smokers. *Preventive Medicine, 27*, A39–A46.

Longshore, D., Grills, C., & Annon, K. (1999). Effects of a culturally congruent intervention on cognitive factors related to drug-use recovery. *Substance Use and Misuse, 34*(9), 1223–1241.

Longshore, D., Grills, C., Annon, K., & Grady, R. (1998). Promoting recovery from drug abuse: An africentric intervention. *Journal of Black Studies, 28*, 319–333.

Martinson, R. (1974). What works? Questions and answers about prison reform. *Public Interest, 35*, 22–54.

McNeece, C. A., & Jackson, S. (2004). Juvenile justice policy: Current trends and 21st century issues. In A. R. Roberts (Ed.), *Juvenile justice sourcebook: Past, present and future* (pp. 41–68). New York: Oxford University Press.

Miller, W., & Rollnick, S. (1996). Motivational interviewing: Preparing people to change addictive behavior. New York: Guilford Press.

Mueser, K., Noordsy, D., Drake, R., & Fox, L. (2003). *Integrated treatment for dual disorders: A guide to effective practice*. New York: Guilford Press.

Mullen, P. D., Velasquez, M. M., von Sternberg, K., Cummins, A. G., & Green, C. (2005, April). *Efficacy of a dual behavior focus, transtheoretical model-based motivational intervention with transition assistance to present an alcohol-exposed pregnancy (AEP) after a jail term.* Poster presented at the 26th annual meeting and Scientific Sessions for the Society of Behavioral Medicine, Boston.

National Association of Social Workers. (1996). *Code of ethics*. Washington, DC: Author.

Office for Victims of Crime. (2005). *Report to the Nation 2005*. Washington, DC: Author.

Orzech, D. (2006). Criminal justice social work—New models, new opportunities. *Social Work Today, 6*(6), 34–37.

Pitre, U., Dansereau, D. F., Newbern, D., & Simpson, D. D. (1998). Residential drug abuse treatment for probationers: Use of node-link mapping to enhance participation and progress. *Journal of Substance Abuse Treatment, 15*(6), 535–543.

Pitre, U., Dansereau, D. F., & Simpson, D. D. (1997). The role of node-link maps in enhancing counseling efficiency. *Journal of Addictive Diseases, 16*, 39–49.

Polansky, N. (1986). There is nothing so practical as a good theory. *Child Welfare, 65*(1), 3–15.

Popple, P. R., & Leighninger, L. L. (2005). *Social work, social welfare, and American society* (6th ed.). Needham Heights, MA: Allyn & Bacon.

Popple, P. R., & Leighninger, L. L. (2007). *The policy based profession: An introduction to social welfare policy analysis* (4th ed.). Boston: Allyn & Bacon.

Pray, K. (1945). The place of social casework in the treatment of delinquency. *Social Service Review, 19*, 244.

Prochaska, J. O., & DiClemente, C. C. (1984). *The transtheoretical approach: Crossing the traditional boundaries of therapy*. Homewood, IL: Dow Jones-Irwin.

Prochaska, J. O., & Norcross, J. C. (1999). *Systems of psychotherapy: A transtheoretical analysis* (4th ed.). Pacific Grove, CA: Brooks/Cole.

Prochaska, J. O., Norcross, J. C., Fowler, J. L., Follick, M. J., & Abrams, D. B. (1992). Attendance and outcome in a work site weight control program: Processes and stages of change as process and predictor variables. *Addictive Behaviors, 17*(1), 35–45.

Prochaska, J. O., Velicer, W. F., Rossi, J. S., Goldstein, M. G., Marcus, B. H., Rakowski, W., et al. (1994). Stages of change and decisional balance for twelve problem behaviors. *Health Psychology, 13*, 39–46.

Reamer, F. G. (2003). *Criminal lessons: Case studies and commentary on crime and justice*. New York: Columbia University Press.

Reamer, F. G. (2004). Social work and criminal justice: The uneasy alliance. In E. Judah & M. Bryant (Eds.), *Criminal justice: Retribution vs. Restoration* (pp. 213–231). Binghampton, NY: Haworth.

Reichert, E. (2003). *Social work and human rights: A foundation for policy and practice*. New York: Columbia University Press.

Roberts, A. R. (1996). *Helping battered women: New perspectives and remedies*. New York: Oxford University Press.

Roberts, A. R. (1997a). The history and role of social work in law enforcement. In A. R. Roberts (Ed.), *Social work in juvenile and criminal justice settings* (2nd ed., pp. 105–115). Springfield, IL: Charles C Thomas.

Roberts, A. R. (1997b). The role of the social worker in victims/witness assistance programs. In A. R. Roberts (Ed.), *Social work in juvenile and criminal justice settings* (2nd ed., pp. 150–159). Springfield, IL: Charles C Thomas.

Roberts, A. R. (1998a). Community strategies with juvenile offenders. In A. R. Roberts (Ed.), *Juvenile justice: Policies, programs and services* (2nd ed., pp. 126–134). Chicago: Nelson-Hall.

Roberts, A. R. (1998b). *Juvenile justice: Policies, programs, and services* (2nd ed.). Chicago: Nelson-Hall.

Roberts, A. R. (2004a). The emergence of the juvenile court and probation services. In A. R. Roberts (Ed.), *Juvenile justice sourcebook: Past, present and future* (pp. 163–182). New York: Oxford University Press.

Roberts, A. R. (Ed.). (2004b). *Juvenile justice sourcebook: Past, present and future*. New York: Oxford University Press.

Roberts, A. R. (Ed.). (2007). *Correctional counseling and treatment*. Upper Saddle River, NJ: Prentice-Hall.

Roberts, A. R., & Brownell, P. (1999). A century of forensic social work. *Social Work, 44*(4), 359–369.

Roberts, A. R., & Greene, G. (Eds.). (2002). *Social workers' desk reference*. New York: Oxford University Press.

Roberts, A. R., & Springer, D. W. (2007). *Social work in juvenile and criminal justice settings*. Springfield, IL: Charles C Thomas.

Roberts, A. R., Springer, D. W., & Brownell, P. (2007). The emergence and current developments in forensic social work. In A.R. Roberts & D. W. Springer (Eds.), *Social work in juvenile and criminal justice settings* (pp. 5–24). Springfield, IL: Charles C Thomas.

Saleebey, D. (2006). Power in the people: Introduction. In D. Saleebey (Ed.), *The strengths perspective in social work practice* (4th ed., pp. 1–24). Boston: Allyn & Bacon.

Samenow, S. (1984). *Inside the criminal mind*. New York: Times Books.

Sells, S. B., & Simpson, D. D. (1979). Evaluation of treatment outcome for youths in the Drug Abuse Reporting Program (DARP): A follow-up study. In G. M. Beschner (Ed.), *Youth drug abuse: Problems, issues and treatments* (pp. 571–628). Lexington, MA: Lexington Books.

Seymour, C. B., & Hairston, C. F. (2001). *Children with parents in prison: Child welfare policy, program, and practice issues*. Piscataway, NJ: Transaction.

Simpson, D. D., Chatham, L. R., & Joe, G. W. (1993). Cognitive enhancements to treatment in DATAR: Drug abuse treatment for AIDS risk-reduction. In J. Inciardi, F. Tims, & B. Fletcher (Eds.), *Innovative approaches to the treatment of drug abuse: Program models and strategies* (pp. 161–177). Westport, CT: Greenwood Press.

Simpson, D. D., Dansereau, D. F., & Joe, G. W. (1997). The DATAR project: Cognitive and behavioral enhancements to community-based treatments. In F. M. Tims, J. A. Inciardi, B. W. Fletcher, & A. M. Horton, Jr. (Eds.), *The effectiveness of innovative approaches in the treatment of drug abuse* (pp. 182–203). Westport, CT: Greenwood Press.

Simpson, D. D., & Joe, G. W. (1993). Motivation as a predictor of early dropout from drug abuse treatment. *Psychotherapy, 30*, 357–367.

Simpson, D. D., Joe, G. W., Rowan-Szal, G., & Greener, J. (1997). Client engagement and change during drug abuse treatment. *Journal of Substance Abuse, 7*, 117–134.

Solomon, B. (1994). *The empowerment tradition in American social work: A history*. New York: Columbia University Press.

Springer, D. W. (2004). Evidence-based treatment of juvenile delinquents with externalizing disorders. In A. R. Roberts. (Ed.), *Juvenile justice sourcebook: Past, present and future* (pp. 365–380). New York: Oxford University Press.

Springer, D. W., McNeece, C. A., & Arnold, E. M. (2003). *Substance abuse treatment for criminal offenders: An evidence-based guide for practitioners*. Washington, DC: American Psychological Association.

Springer, D. W., Rivaux, S. L., Bohman, T., & Yeung, A. (2006). Predicting retention in three substance abuse treatment modalities among Anglo, African American and Mexican American juvenile offenders. *Journal of Social Service Research, 32*(4), 135–155.

Springer, D. W., & Roberts, A. R. (Eds.). (2007). *Handbook of forensic mental health with victims and offenders: Assessment, treatment, and research*. New York: Springer.

Stoesen, L. (2006a, November). Grant supports conference on reentry. *NASW News*, p. 8.

Stoesen, L. (2006b). Prisoner reentry: Reclaiming the challenge: Professionals often have criminal justice backgrounds. *NASW News*, p. 4.

Studt, E. (Ed.). (1959). *Education for social workers in the correctional field: Social Work Education Study* (Vol. 5). New York: Council on Social Work Education.

Umbreit, M. (1993). Crime victims and offenders in mediation: An emerging area of social work practice. *Social Work, 38*, 69–73.

Umbreit, M., Vos, B., Coates, R. B., & Brown, K. A. (2003). *Facing violence: The path of restorative justice and dialogue*. Monsey, NY: Criminal Justice Press.

van Wormer, K. (2001). *Counseling female offenders and victims: A strengths-restorative approach.* New York: Springer.

van Wormer, K. (2004). *Confronting oppression, restoring justice: From policy analysis for restorative justice.* Alexandria, VA: Council on Social Work Education Press.

van Wormer, K. (2006). *Introduction to social welfare and social work: The U.S. in global perspective.* Belmont, CA: Thomsons.

van Wormer, K. (2007). *Human behavior and the social environment, micro level: Individuals and families.* New York: Oxford University Press.

van Wormer, K., & Bartollas, C. (2007). *Women and the criminal justice system.* Boston: Allyn & Bacon.

van Wormer, K., & Davis, D. R. (2008). *Addiction treatment: A strengths perspective.* Belmont, CA: Brooks/Cole.

Velicer, W. F., Norman, G. J., Fava, J. L., & Prochaska, J. O. (1999). Testing 40 predictions from the transtheoretical model. *Addictive Behaviors, 24*(4), 455–469.

Wallace, B. C. (2005). *Making mandated addiction treatment work.* Lanham, MD: Aronson.

Young, D. S., & LoMonaco, S. W. (2001). Incorporating content on offenders and corrections into social work curricula. *Journal of Social Work Education, 37*(3), 475–489.

Zehr, H. (2000). *The little book of restorative justice.* Intercourse, PA: Good Books.

Chapter 16

INTERNATIONAL SOCIAL WORK

Doreen Elliott and Uma A. Segal

In discussing the term *international social work,* three groups of professional social worker responses can be considered. For ease of recognition, the first group may be referred to as the cynics, the second pragmatic converts, and the third progressive idealist internationalists. For many social workers in the first group, the cynics, international social work raises a number of questions such as: What is international social work? Is international social work inevitably oppressive of indigenous cultures? How can social work be international when it is socially constructed, that is, when it is dependent on local culture, values, laws, norms, and service delivery systems? Why should social work be practiced in other countries when the need is so great at home? How is international social work relevant to an individual's practice at home? These questions are legitimate and need to be considered.

For a second group of social workers, the pragmatic converts, the term *international social work* involves recognition that post 9/11 world perspectives are irrevocably changed; that professional perspectives, like their broader political, economic, and cultural counterparts, acknowledge that the profession must address more thoroughly the consequences of economic and cultural globalization, human migration, disaster, human rights abuses, poverty, and HIV/AIDS, and so on. Increasing globalization, with heightened international communication, commerce, migration, and a variety of cross-national exchanges, they argue, must influence the social work profession in the United States extending its understanding of the implications of international interdependence across and beyond its borders. Increasingly, schools of social work are calling on their students to recognize that international issues touch the practice of all social workers, and it is essential that they be cognizant of, and responsive to, the effects of globalization. Such a sentiment is encapsulated in a leading school of social work's web site:

> The realities of an ever-increasing globalized world and inequities between the rich and poor across the globe demand that Social Workers be at the forefront of international practice. Cultural, economic, social welfare, environmental, and security interdependence between all countries makes it essential for social workers to consider the global implications of practice, advocacy, and exchange of knowledge. It is critical for social workers to understand that globalization is not only a matter of economics and trade, but a social welfare, human rights, and social justice issue as well. (University of Washington, 2006)

In some of the quotations included in this chapter the non-American spelling is evident, for example, behaviour, utilising, indigenisation, moulding. These have been included as originally published where there are direct quotes from non-American authors. Otherwise American English spelling conventions are followed.

The third group, the progressive idealist internationalist social workers, believe Westernized post-industrial nations may learn from other countries, even from the so called "developing nations," and that international exchange should be a truly reciprocal exercise in which both parties give and receive benefits. Hockenstad and Midgley (2004), in their book *Lessons from Abroad,* include chapters that explore, among other topics, what may be learned from social security reform in Chile, Singapore, and Britain, as well as child welfare initiatives and mental health programs around the world. Since early international social work initiatives were set against the backdrop of colonialism, the interaction inevitably was patriarchal and unidirectional with ideas being exported from Western nations. Midgley (1990) gives examples from the developing world of community cooperatives in working with disabled people, of disaster preparedness and responses, and working with people in poverty as areas where the developed nations have much to learn. Toors (1992) makes similar arguments for reciprocity in international professional relations. Mayadas and Elliott (1997), in discussing the history of social work, present four phases, the last phase being an ideal situation where there are multiple learning networks and professional information exchange across the globe. This last phase is in contrast to earlier phases marked by the unidirectional export of professional ideas from the Western world, and later, the reaction of the developing world against this unidirectional approach.

Elliott and Mayadas (2000) also offer a social development model of social work practice that encompasses an international approach. In their compendium of models of international collaboration in social work, Healy, Asamoah, and Hockenstad (2003) state that "mutuality is a cornerstone of collaboration" (p. 20). They selected the models for publication using mutuality as one of the main criteria for acceptance. Ferguson (2005) reviews the limitations of four existing models of social work exchange and posits an alternative model of technology transfer demonstrating "global dissemination of initiatives originating in developing countries that are successfully applied in the developed world." Cox and Pawar (2006) also reiterate the importance of the developed world's needs to learn from innovations in the developing world. Thus, the progressive idealists represent a strong element in current international social work thinking and practice.

A caveat, however, should be noted about the categories presented here. In reality, these three categories are not necessarily discrete, and at times progressive idealists may be cynics, and all may be pragmatists to some extent. The division of social workers into these categories is more of a literary device to illustrate these three significant trends in current social work thinking about international issues. An example of this is that the radical idealists also have their feet on the ground. Healy (2003) concludes an introduction to the models of international collaboration compendium by recognizing that, given the history of unequal exchange, the profession needs to work hard to ensure that all international collaborations are based on mutuality. It should be further noted that knowledge of the history of internationalism in social work becomes important in ensuring that this goal of mutuality and equality in international exchange is carried out, lest ignorant, but well-intentioned interventions take the profession back to the colonial past. For this reason, a later section of this chapter is dedicated to the history of international social work.

This present section is focused on the concerns of the cynics, the position of the pragmatists, and the optimism of the progressive idealists. The concerns of the cynics are addressed through discussion of definitions of international social work, the pros and cons of international social work, and the relevance of a global dimension in local practice. The position of the pragmatists is more fully explored by considering the implications for the profession of globalization and the international political context of social work practice. The optimism of the progressive idealists is further examined and evaluated through consideration of history and of examples where social workers can and have already learned from the developing world. In doing so, it is possible that this piece may contribute some new dimensions to discussions on international social work. A new definition of international social work is offered as well as a new representation of activities. A new discussion of professional imperialism is presented in a recent context in social work education. In addition, the discussion of a previously presented model of international social work history has been significantly expanded and a summary of the most recent debate on indigenization and universalism is discussed. This chapter presents no easy solutions to some of the dilemmas presented, it would be reductionist to do so. This piece was designed to signal ways forward for further discussion and development and to provide both motivation and resources to pursue these issues in greater detail.

DEFINITIONS

In reviewing the literature for definitions of international social work, it was noted that, surprisingly, the *Encyclopedia of Social Work* (19th ed.) has no entry on international social work. It does, however, have related entries on international and comparative social welfare, international social welfare organizations and activities, and international social work education. This may accurately reflect the fact that international social work, though not new, is still a growing field, though there already exists a fairly substantial interest in international social policy and social welfare. It also reflects a pre-9/11 world where there was less emphasis on the need for global understanding and where a small minority of social workers and social work educators in the United States and abroad were interested in international social work (for reasons that will become clearer in the section of this chapter that reviews a historical perspective on international social work). It was only later, with the publication of the *Educational Policy and Accreditation Standards* (EPAS) in 2001, that the Council on Social Work Education (CSWE) recommended, but did not require, inclusion of a global perspective.

Implementation of the recommendation has been patchy at best, with many other curriculum requirements to consider. Post-9/11, the pattern has changed considerably: there are many more presentations at professional meetings with international content, and new active international committees have been formed in the Baccalaureate Program Directors' Group (BPD), and the National Association of Deans and Directors of Social Work (NADD). The Directors of Field Education have established a group to recommend standards for international field placements; CSWE has replaced the International Commission with two councils and a Global Commission as well as establishing the Katherine A. Kendall Institute for International Social Work Education. Thus, there is evidence of much revived interest and activity in international social work. This is a good time to review current views and definitions of international social work.

Watts (1999) reviews a number of definitions of international social work, including that of Barker (1999) in the *Dictionary of Social Work* who defines international social work as:

> A term loosely applied to 1) international organizations using social work methods or personnel, 2) social work cooperation between countries, and 3) transfer between countries of methods or knowledge about social work. (p. 250)

Another definition is offered by Healy (2001):

> [I]nternational social work is defined as international professional action and the capacity for international action by the social work profession and its members. International action has four dimensions: internationally related domestic practice and advocacy, professional exchange, international practice and international policy development and advocacy. (p. 7)

This definition makes a useful distinction between international practice, which some commentators have called "social work across borders" and the use of global knowledge to aid practice locally, which has elsewhere been called "think globally, act locally" or "the local is global." This notion of "the local is global" in international social work represents increasing recognition of the importance of global knowledge in multicultural practice and with migrant populations. Dominelli's (2005) definition emphasizes this view: "to consider international social work as a form of practice that localizes the global and globalizes the local."

Healy's definition also includes the importance of social workers' potential in using global knowledge to assist in domestic policy developments. Both Barker's and Healy's definitions separate professional intervention (action) and knowledge transfer.

Cox and Pawar (2006) develop the definition even further demonstrating how thinking is constantly developing in the field of international social work:

> International social work is the promotion of social work education and practice globally and locally, with the purpose of building a truly integrated international profession that reflects social work's capacity to respond appropriately and effectively, in education and practice terms, to the various global challenges that are having a significant impact on the well-being of large sections of the world's population. This global and local promotion of social work education and practice is based on an integrated perspectives approach that synthesizes global, human rights, ecological, and social development perspectives of international situations and responses to them. (p. 20)

Cox and Pawar's definition gives significance to the idea of a global profession, and separates out the functions of social work education and social work practice while focusing on a conceptual framework for international practice, which they call an integrated perspectives approach. This definition includes a much-needed theoretical and conceptual perspective.

Since international social work is so varied, and is still developing, more than one definition is inevitable and healthy. Hence, we expand the debate by offering a new definition on the basis that multiple definitions give a broader range of perspectives:

> International social work is concerned with the development, administration, implementation, research and evaluation, in and through global social institutions and organizations, of policies and programs that promote human rights, human diversity, the well being and empowerment of people worldwide, and global and social and economic justice. In the post-modern era, international social work values difference and diversity in human experience and seeks to engage with and to learn and adapt from people creating indigenous solutions to socio-economic problems around the world. International social work subscribes to ideologies, value systems and theoretical approaches that support these directions.

Included in this definition is research (of international problems and issues) and evaluation of international programs and practice. A range of practice methods is also specified, including administration, development, and with the use of the word *promote* an implication of advocacy. In this way, this definition can be considered more specific than previous ones. Perhaps the most significant addition in this definition is the recognition of the indigenization movements around the world and the need for Western social workers and social work educators to work cooperatively and learn from these efforts. Thus, the reciprocal nature of international social work is emphasized in this new definition. This definition does not cover all issues, however, and there is certainly a need for continuing debate and development.

Table 16.1 expands our definition by outlining examples of the activities that can be considered international social work. Indeed, it is a broad field and the table gives examples in each category, although is not a comprehensive survey of all that may be considered to be international social work.

The definition developed by the International Association of Schools of Social Work and the International Federation of Social Workers (IASSW/IFSW) in 2001 is, however,

Table 16.1 Defining International Social Work

Category	Activities
Students	Study abroad Student exchange programs International field placements Comparative research, projects, theses, dissertations Peace corps and other international volunteer agency work
Social work educators	Faculty exchanges to foreign universities Hosting overseas faculty at home university Government and NGO consultancies Conducting comparative social research Disseminating knowledge through writing and teaching
United Nations and its associated agencies	Disseminating information Disaster response Providing direct services, e.g., UNICEF, UNHCR Research and inquiry, e.g., UNDP Research Unit Developing measures for intervention effectiveness, e.g., Human development index, gender development index
Service delivery in International NGOs *"social work across borders"*	Developmental work with communities Programs targeted at specific problems, e.g., AIDS, poverty, hunger, health, child labor, child sexual exploitation, e.g., Oxfam, Save the Children, World Vision, Amnesty International, Human Rights Watch, http://www.un.org/esa/socdev/iyop/iyopac04.htm#INPEA
International professional organizations	Disseminate knowledge and research through conferences and journals Facilitate international professional networking International policy and practice advocacy, e.g., IFSW, IASSW, ICSD, ICSW
International practice at home *"global is local; local is global"*	Working with refugees International adoptions Social work on American military bases overseas

an international definition of social work, not a definition of international social work. This means that the definition is the consequence of extended discussions and a joint agreement reached by IASSW and IFSW representatives:

> The social work profession promotes social change, problem solving in human relationships and the empowerment and liberation of people to enhance well-being. Utilising theories of human behaviour and social systems, social work intervenes at the points where people interact with their environments. Principles of human rights and social justice are fundamental to social work. (IASSW/IFSW, 2001)

This definition represents an attempt to identify the universals in the profession of social work worldwide. Human rights, empowerment, social change, and problem solving are central. (In a later section of this chapter, some of the problems associated with attempting to find universals in a profession that is socially constructed are discussed further.) The danger is that such a definition, or in fact any of the previous definitions of international social work, may be representative of a Western neo-liberal perspective, and not representative of the many indigenous approaches that place less emphasis on the organized, professional aspects of the profession. The following section, which gives a brief history of international social work, further explains the development of indigenous approaches.

HISTORY

Internationalism has been a part of social work since the beginnings of the profession in the nineteenth century. In this section, the role and nature of internationalism in the history of the social work profession is outlined in the four phases first proposed by Mayadas and Elliott (1997). Table 16.2 summarizes these phases: the first column shows the dates of the four phases, the second column indicates the direction of the exchange, the third column shows the predominant professional values of the period, and the fourth column shows model of service delivery.

Phase One: Early Pioneers, 1880s to 1930s

Two organizations, the settlement movement and the Charity Organization Society (COS) are generally considered to mark the beginnings of the profession in establishing the major modes of service delivery: casework and individual and family solutions to social problems and community practice and social reform.

The COS (1869) and the settlement movement (1884) both began in England and the models were exported to the United States. There is well-documented evidence of much interaction and across the Atlantic after the establishment of Toynbee Hall Settlement House in the East End of London in 1884 (Estes, 1997; Kendall, 2000; Reinders, 1982). It is interesting to note that, at a time when transportation across the Atlantic was much slower and more difficult, there seemed to be more international cooperation and exchange in terms of practice and service delivery than there is now. The COS was established in London in 1869 and its influence spread quickly to the United States, where Charles Gordon Ames, who was said to be impressed with the London organization, founded the Philadelphia COS in 1873 (Rauch, 1976). The COS organizations spread and the Rev. Stephen Gurteen founded the Boston COS in 1877.

Table 16.2 Phases in International Social Work Exchange

Time Period	Predominant Direction of Exchange	Values	Model of Services
Phase I— 1880s–1930s Early pioneers The COS, Settlement movement The influence of Freud The influence of the Fabian movement	Mostly Europe to America Largely unidirectional America builds the basis of professional hegemony in social work	Paternalistic Ethnocentric	Social Control Charity Philanthropy
Phase II— 1930s–1970s Professional Imperialism	America to rest of world Centrifugal	Paternalistic Ethnocentric Colonialism Universalism	Remedial Medical Crisis-oriented
Phase III— 1970s–1990s Reconceptualization and indigenization	Within regions Worldwide Centripeta	Regionalization Polarization Separation Localization	Developmental in developing countries Remedial in Western industrial nations
Phase IV— 21st Century International social development	International networking	Globalization Transcultural/ Multicultural Democratic Social, Cultural, and Ethnic Interchange	Developmental in rural and urban areas worldwide

The beginning of the American settlement movement had similar transatlantic influences: visitors from the United States to Toynbee Hall included Jane Addams and Stanton Coit. The establishment of Hull House in Chicago in 1889 was influenced by these visits and the friendship between Jane Addams and Henrietta Barnett, wife of Canon Samuel Barnett, founder of Toynbee Hall. Jane Addams was inspired by Toynbee Hall and The People's Palace during her visit there in 1888 and the Barnetts subsequently had much admiration for Jane Addams and her work at Hull House (Besant, 1887; Kendall, 2000). Stanton Coit founded the neighborhood guild in New York in 1886, which later became known as the University Settlement (Trattner, 2007). This period of the export of an idea from one country, followed by the rapid expansion of COS organizations and settlement houses across the United States, is probably an unparalleled period of internationalism in the history of the profession. Books were translated into other languages and there were regular conferences and meetings (e.g., the International Congress of Charities, Corrections and Philanthropy in 1893). Beatrice and Sidney Webb, leaders in the British Fabian movement, influenced Edith Abbott and the School of Social Service Administration in Chicago. The ideas of Charles Booth founder of the Salvation Army and social reformer were also influential across the Atlantic (Kendall 2000; Pumphrey & Pumphrey, 1967).

Kendall (2000) documents that additionally at this time, both Britain and America were influenced by the Elberfeld movement in Germany, where a volunteer system based on districts dispensed social welfare assistance without the questions and terms associated with the more social control model of the COS. Another influence from Europe around this time which shaped social work in the years to come were the ideas of Sigmund Freud and others in the psychoanalytic movement (Freud, 1914). An area where the European influence was also strong was the founding of schools of social work for education and training in the social services. Following the establishment of the first school in Amsterdam in 1899 and the London School of Sociology in 1903, schools were established in quick succession in New York (1904), Boston (1904), Chicago (1904), and in Santiago, Chile, in 1925 (Kendall, 2000).

Hence this first phase is characterized by a transmission of knowledge and service delivery methods from Western Europe to the Americas. The traditional charity/philanthropy approach and its accompanying social control function dating back to the Poor Laws was the focal point of services. It can be argued that the settlement movement was founded as much as an antidote to concerns and fears of a beginning labor movement and to address social unrest in the crowded and violent urban industrial areas as it was to idealistic altruism for the poor. It was during this period, however, that American knowledge and practice of social services and social work was consolidated, strengthened, and developed to position America to become a world leader in the next phase.

Phase Two: Professional Imperialism, 1930s to 1970s

This phase represents the United States's role in global leadership in social work and social services. During the previous period, the emphasis in the United States on training, especially on a scientific approach to training, the location of social work education in the university, and the building of the major models of service delivery for the new profession: casework, groupwork, and community work, all contributed to the United States's position as leader in the profession. Schools of social work, or social work training courses, were established in Bombay (Mumbai), India, in 1936; Sao Paulo, Brazil, in 1936; Cairo, Egypt, in 1936; Uruguay in 1937; Sydney, Australia, in 1940; Costa Rica in 1942; Delhi, India, in 1946; Hong Kong in 1950; Lahore in 1954; University of Ghana in 1956; Indonesia in 1957; Teheran, Iran, in 1958; Makere, Uganda, in 1960; Ethiopia in 1961; the Philippines in 1965; and Khartoum in 1969 (Abo El Nasr, 1997; Cornely & Bruno, 1997; Ife, 1997; Midgley, 1981). These independent schools or programs, typically conducted within a department of social administration or sociology, were funded from a variety of public and private sources, and staffed largely by Westerners—British, French, Americans—in the colonial style. Curricula were based on Western models of social work practice and libraries and reading lists built from Western, predominantly American social work literature became the primary source of knowledge (Guzetta, 1996). Indigenous literature was sparse and frequently not consistent with colonial practices. In 1950, the United Nations sent teams of advisors to assist in setting up schools in many regions, and also conducted a study on the status of social work training around the world. Western faculty were encouraged to teach in the programs and Stein (1964, as cited in Aronoff, 2003) reports a quotation from Ford Foundation literature as follows:

> The faculty member who has taught abroad is likely to be a better teacher for having gained a broader view of his subject. Because he has faced new kinds of teaching problems, his ability to impart this knowledge to students will be improved. New courses and new ways of teaching old courses may result from the

> insights he acquires. Both inside and outside the classroom, the teacher with experience abroad can have a significant impact on the world outlook students. His courses lose some of their cultural bias; he gives his students perspective on their own society and culture. He becomes more effective in preparing students for study abroad and in teaching foreign students, since he understands some of the problems they face. And finally, whether or not he was engaged in research, new ideas for research projects often develop. (Ford Foundation, 1964, pp. 15–16)

While this statement seems to us as rather self-serving, Stein (1964, as cited in Aronoff, 2003), lamenting the difficulties of obtaining sufficient faculty, and of selecting good faculty for service abroad also points out the beginnings of questioning the export model of social work. He quotes Professor Livingstone of Liverpool University as saying that the West has had an undesirable influence on the development of social work training overseas and in developing countries in particular. Livingstone "deprecates the use of the individual premise in social work, the influence of Freud and western social policy as having any relevance for developing countries across the globe" (Stein, 1964, p. 240, as cited in Aronoff, 2003). During this phase, values remained predominantly paternalistic and social work was seen in the Western tradition as being individually based with the medical and remedial model of service delivery. This involved more focus on reaction to social problems than prevention and offering as little help as possible for as short a time as possible. This was in contrast to the fact that societies in developing countries were more family-oriented and that large-scale prevention programs were needed in areas such as health care.

In reviewing the colonial period of social work history, some interpreters have deemed Midgley's coining of the term *professional imperialism* inflammatory, and yet others have depicted, with rose spectacled hindsight, that the technology transfer was not colonialist, but a gift relationship in the Titmus sense (Healy et al., 2003; Titmus, 1971; Wagner, 1992). Still others have taken a more pragmatic view, recognizing that this transfer will be a one-way street at least at times and Billups and Julià (1996) have suggested that given the inevitability of the one-way street, it is essential that we implement mechanisms for a more careful review of the materials for transfer to ensure they are appropriate. It is hard to see this period, given the political, socioeconomic context and present-day understanding of the effects of the colonial period, as other than colonial. The analysis, in hindsight, may be comparable to the missionary movement in religion, and of course missionary movements influenced many schools of social work, as well as social work and social welfare service delivery systems. This view is not to denigrate the work of individuals who are products of socialization and who thought it was a "good thing" to share the "superior knowledge" of the West with developing countries. Many were inspired by noble individual motives and did good work, contributing to the building of institutions, for example. Many, at the same time they provided their services, were the first to raise questions about their efficacy. In the larger scheme of things, Midgley's (1981) critique was timely: he was reared and schooled under the colonial system and his experience as a student in an oppressive apartheid regime gave his message a clarity that many in the developed world could not see so clearly at the time.

This message has more recent relevance as well. After the fall of the Soviet Union, social work educators from Europe and America were invited to the newly independent states to advise on the setting up of social services. Many of these transactions are not recorded, but the question of whether the profession learned the message of professional imperialism, or was it repeated again in the 1990s and later, largely through ignorance of the profession's international history? A more recent debate among the CSWE's board also reflects this history, a question of whether the CSWE should offer an international accreditation was raised. A working party, appointed by the executive director, to write a background report for the board reported strong differences of opinion in the working group in relation to an overseas request for CSWE accreditation. Arguments for and against are summarized in Table 16.3, where the shadows of this phase of American dominance in social work education, and indeed also of the third phase, reconceptulization and indigenization can be seen.

Phase Three: Reconceptualization and Indigenization, 1970s to 1990s

The lack of goodness of fit of the exported model of Western social work led to a questioning of the appropriateness of importing technology on the part of developing countries. Also newly independent states, especially in Africa, free from colonial ties, wanted to divest themselves of systems that reflected their oppressive past. The reconceptulization movement in South America, and the indigenization movement in Africa, the Middle East, and India, all had the goals of shaking off the dependence on American and European models of social work and fostering a more culturally appropriate model for each country. This period is thus marked by a retreat to regionalism and separatism.

In South America, the strong influences were liberation theology, social development, and the ideas of Paulo Freire such as "conscientization," which made people more aware of their dependency on developed nations. Quiero-Tajalli (1997) reports Alayón's (1988) model of the four stages of social work development in Argentina: the first stage was marked by *asistencialismo* (assistance) and corresponded to the charity model that perpetuated, rather than solved, the poverty problem. The second stage was *cientificismo* (scientificism). This focused on community development and was not adequately resourced. The third stage was *reconcepualización* (reconceptualization or transformation). This stage was different in each Latin American country, but it began at a conference held in 1965 at the Federal University of Rio Grande do Sul in Porto Alegre, Brazil, and its aim was to change the methodological influences of the exported American and European models of social work to a more indigenous model. Political participation was encouraged in social workers with the goal of eradicating oppressive social conditions, along with the mobilization and conscientization of the population (Cornely & Bruno, 1997). Many conferences were held under the auspices of the Latin American Center of Social Work (CELATS) and Latin American Schools of Social Work (ALEATS) toward the development of an indigenous progressive radical model of social work. Quiero-Tajalli (1997) reports that the last and fourth phase of Alayón's model is *post-reconceptualization,* beginning in the early 1980s. This phase involved reconciling what could be salvaged from the more progressive period after the neo-conservative military regime placed stringent limits on social work. Privatization, the move from universal benefits to targeted benefits, all affected the profession and those they served.

In Africa, the Middle East, and India, there was more focus on a developmental approach to social problems and especially to poverty and survival. Nanavatty (1997) argues that in India, casework, usually carried out by trained social workers, predominated in the urban areas and a more developmental, community-based approach in the rural areas was carried out by local volunteers, teachers, and community workers. In Africa, it was inevitable that there was a search for a local model of social work, since the origin of almost all schools of

Table 16.3 International Accreditation of Social Work Education Programs

Against	For
Social work is socially constructed. Social work reflects the linguistic, social, legal, economic, cultural, health, and educational perspective of a particular country. It is a sufficiently complex task as it is for the commission on accreditation to be fully aware and sensitive to all the diversity within the United States.	**A strength of the current accreditation standards** as represented by EPAS is that they are nonprescriptive and flexible and therefore lend themselves to enabling site teams to judge whether a program is fulfilling its own standards on its own terms. This would apply equally to overseas programs.
Ethnocentricity. The assumption that social work educators are qualified to judge foreign programs for accreditation is based on an ethnocentric view of the world.	**Competence of site visitors**. The qualifications of existing site visitors are sufficient guarantees of competence. In fact, it is predicted that there will be no shortage of volunteers for international site visitors.
Role of the international organizations. It was noted that IASSW had reviewed and decided against international accreditation and had settled for producing some international guidelines for social work. It was felt that even those draft guidelines were sufficiently controversial, albeit having been made with international input.	**International Association of School of Social Work (IASSW)**. There is nothing in the IASSW guidelines that conflicts with the CSWE accreditation standards. The CSWE possesses the world's largest quality accreditation system for social work; there is little reason for IASSW to object as they are not seeking to accredit. Why should not overseas programs seek voluntary accreditation if this will attract students and faculty?
Representation in the accreditation process. While US educators would be represented on various commissions and boards of the CSWE, there is no current provision for extending this representation to overseas educators. Even if that were to be the case, how would the many countries involved be represented? Therefore overseas participation in the process for international accreditation would be severely limited.	**Deans, directors, and faculty of accredited programs** are eligible for election and nomination to various boards and committees. This would apply to overseas accredited programs also.
Influence of American foreign policy. This proposal was considered in 2003, and there was heightened awareness of the post 9/11 treatment of foreigners and the beginning of the war in Iraq. There was heightened awareness of American socioeconomic and political hegemony. For the social work profession to ignore the broader political context was not acceptable to many of the working parties' inquiry respondents.	**American hegemony**. If this were a serious concern, then CSWE would not give equivalent status to Canadian social work education programs.

(continued)

Table 16.3 *(Continued)*

Against	For
Cost benefit analysis. The argument that international accreditation would be a new source of income for CSWE would perpetuate the historic economic exploitation of the global south. Additionally, accreditation is already costly and labor intensive and the costs would seem to outweigh the benefits.	**Costs**. If the accreditation process imposes a burden on an overseas program, this would be similar to the situation in the United States. The overseas program has the choice to participate or not. This is not an imposed requirement. Furthermore, some overseas programs would be located in some affluent areas without concurrency conversion problems. CSWE might gain financially because more people would enroll for the APM.
	Impact of CSWE accreditation on nonaccredited programs. This situation exists currently in the United States where nonaccredited programs exist side by side with accredited programs. Eventually, if the impact of accreditation is to raise standards then all programs will seek accreditation.
	CHEA accreditation of CSWE. CSWE itself is accredited by the council for Higher Education Accreditation (CHEA). There would have to be special arrangements made or this criterion would need to be waived as irrelevant to foreign programs.
	Brain drain. It would be easier for both foreign and U.S. faculty to work in each other's programs. It would encourage more faculty and student exchange and would support the trend for portability of qualifications in the international job arena.

From a figure first published in "Lessons from International Social Work: Policies and Practices" (p. 176), by N. S. Mayadas and D. Elliott, in *Social Work in the 21st Century,* 1997, M. Reisch and E. Gambrill (Eds.), 1997, Thousand Oaks, CA: Pine Forge Press. Adapted with permission.

social work in Africa was from overseas. A focus for the indigenization movement in Africa was a meeting of ministers of social welfare in 1968, where a developmental orientation was proposed to counteract the remedial model of existing services (Asamoah, 1997). This was followed by subsequent meetings and the creation of ministries of social development so that this approach became well-established in countries such as South Africa and Zimbabwe. As well as the developmental perspective, and the challenge of merging the remedial and developmental models, Asamoah also argues that the indigenization of social work in Africa was influenced by three main theoretical strains: *agology,* a Dutch model meaning the science of guiding or leading; the German model of *social pedagogy,* an educational approach to social work; and *conscientization,* the South American empowerment model that raises consciousness of the masses in order to create social change from the grass roots (Asamoah, 1997, p. 314). With respect to indigenization in Egypt, indigenization was encouraged by a United Nations' international survey of social work training in 1971 in which the term indigenization was used. Abo El Nasr (1997) suggests a distinction between indigenization as the process by which a country accommodates the Western model of social work to local conditions, and authentization, which is the creation of a model originating from local philosophy, culture, norms, and practices. There are few truly authentic models in existence around the world, but this is an important distinction to remember when the term indigenization is so freely used.

This phase is clearly still not finished and merges with the fourth phase discussed next. Many areas of the world including, most notably, South Africa and China, are still searching for or developing an indigenized or truly authentic model of social work practice at the present time (Gray, 2006; Midgley, 2001; Yuen-Tsang & Wang, 2002). Recognizing the importance of this search for indigenization, Western authors have raised the question as to whether the idea of international social work is inevitably oppressive and whether it is possible to identify any kind of true universalism within the profession because of its social constructionist nature (Ahmadi, 2003; Dominelli, 2005; Gray, 2005; Gray & Fook, 2004; Nagy & Falk, 2000). This debate is discussed in detail after the fourth phase is analyzed.

Phase Four: International Social Development in the Twenty-First Century

Where developing countries have succeeded in making a paradigm shift from a Western-based service delivery model to an indigenous, and most often, social development model of social work, there is potential to move from a reactivist, remedial model of social work and social welfare to a new kind of international cooperation. This new kind of international cooperation includes equality, mutuality, reciprocal benefits, and a true exchange of ideas around the globe. International networking is the key to this phase, not bi-national relations. The values of social development are consistent with those of social work: social justice, cooperation, planning, prevention, participation, democracy, human dignity and worth, institutional change, and empowerment (Midgley, 1995). Social development emphasizes a multicausal view of both assessment and intervention in social problems, and thus moves away from the individual pathology perspective of the medical model. Social development sees diversity as a central principle because the context of practice is multicultural (Mayadas & Elliott, 1997). Social development is not inconsistent with clinical practice, but rather adds a new dimension to clinical practice.

Elliott and Mayadas (1996) report how considering the economics of clinical practice according to social development principles, for example, increases the awareness in clinical practice of the multibillion dollar health insurance industry behind the *Diagnostic and Statistical Manual.* Another example of the social development approach, which has had worldwide applications from its beginnings, is the *Grameen* Bank, meaning village bank. An organization begun by a professor of economics, Muhammud Yunus, the Grameen Bank pioneered an approach to poverty reduction based on micro-credit. This approach emphasizes the use of social capital in repaying loans and in the development of centers and groups through which loans are organized and has the highest loan repayment rate of any banking system (Yunus, 2006). Today, the organization has global applications of micro-credit in 58 countries and lends to over 5 million people, 96% of whom are women, for the purpose of investing in small entrepreneurial projects (Yunus, 2003). The

Grameen Foundation USA supports initiatives in 22 countries including the United States. An example of a successful U.S. project is the PLAN project in Dallas, Texas:

> The PLAN Fund was established in 1999 by the Grameen Foundation USA and Dallas City Homes, a local nonprofit organization, to provide small amounts of credit and other financial services to enable low-income individuals to start or expand "micro-businesses."
>
> . . . The *Dallas Morning News* recently highlighted its impact on low-income, and predominantly African-American and Hispanic communities in the Dallas metropolitan area, noting that its results "in Dallas, as elsewhere, have been superb." (Grameen Foundation USA, 2006)

Examples of diverse businesses begun by participants in the PLAN Fund are: property development; art pieces from natural products, creative gifts and designs, catering services, and Heelz & Deelz, shoes and accessories (Grameen Foundation USA, 2006). "Give Us Credit" by Counts (1996), a project in Chicago, Illinois, is another account of how the Grameen Bank micro-credit idea was adapted in the United States.

The activities of the Grameen Bank epitomize the characteristics of the fourth phase under analysis and also clearly meet the goals of the progressive idealist group of internationalists mentioned earlier in this chapter. International networking, transculturalism, globalization, democracy, social cultural and ethnic interchanges, irrespective of where in the world the idea originates, and as indicated in phase four, are all represented in this successful global project. Imagine if this degree of success could be applied to address universal health care, day-care provision, nursing homes, disaster readiness, response and recovery, and other pressing social problems in the United States through a genuine exploration of international ideas and best practices. If this were made possible, then this fourth phase would have become a reality.

Among Western social work educators with experience in international programs and research, there is a large measure of agreement that in order for international social work to progress there must be mutual respect, equality, and reciprocity in exchange. Conditions similar to the ones described in phase four of the model discussed previously. Healy et al., (2003) in their *Models of International Collaboration in Social Work Education,* make very clear that criteria for a successful collaboration are: (1) sustainability; (2) mutuality, with each partner contributing and benefiting in a meaningful way; and (3) the ripple effect that comes from institutional commitment and involvement that goes beyond that of a few individual faculty members. Healy et al. explore the nature of collaboration and recognize that while all exchanges cannot be exactly equal in benefits, "the outcomes are achieved through a type of sharing that encourages diversity, not homogenization. Cross-fertilization is replacing export as the dominant concept in international collaboration" (p. 20).

GLOBAL STANDARDS FOR SOCIAL WORK EDUCATION AND A GLOBAL DEFINITION OF SOCIAL WORK

There have been views, however, that suggest that even this fourth phase may now become outdated: Dominelli (2005) quotes the view of IASSW President Tassé Abye that powerful elites in the globalized mega cities of the world are already internationalized and quite probably trained in the West. Internationalizing or globalizing social work, he argues, is therefore, a Western pre-occupation, while the developing world is much more concerned with indigenization and developing new models of practice. Nevertheless, while recognizing some of the shortcomings of an approach that searches for a universal definition and global standards, the joint IASSW/IFSW task force remarkably secured broad agreement on the global definition quoted earlier in this chapter. They also were able to outline global standards for social work education worldwide. This represented a historic achievement for social work and a step toward its recognition as a global profession.

The task force's global standards for education and training in the social work profession identify 13 core purposes for the profession from which one may distil several principles such as: working to include and protect "marginalized, excluded, dispossessed, vulnerable and at risk" populations; working towards politicosocioeconomic structural change to enhance people's life situations; encourage advocacy at all levels, global, national, regional, organizational, and interpersonal. A significant area of discussion is the principle that "promotes respect for traditions, cultures, ideologies, beliefs, and religions among different ethnic groups and societies, *insofar as these do not conflict with the fundamental human rights of people*." The italicized phrase raises the question of who defines the fundamental human rights of people? Is this standard based on a Western notion of human rights? Is Western democracy and its concomitant values the only acceptable political solution for human rights? Clearly the debate will continue, but the global standards have carried forward this debate significantly. The document also sets out standards for program objectives and outcomes, field and core curricula, and also identifies eight paradigms, or value sets, which it is argued are the basis of the social work profession worldwide. In fact, in setting global standards for social work education, inevitably, the standards have moved forward the concept of a universal, global definition of social work.

The preparation, numerous consultations, discussion forums, and publications behind the final document "Global Standards for Social Work Practice Around the World?" prompted a discussion in the literature about the very nature of international social work (Ahmadi, 2003; Dominelli, 2005; Gray, 2005; Gray & Fook, 2004; Nagy & Falk, 2000). Gray (2005) has argued, in summarizing the arguments of other authors on the topic, that social work is struggling with the contradictory and competing issues of universalism and indigenization against a background of imperialism. The challenge that is raised is how can social work be authentic and socially constructed yet also seek global commonalities? These are not mutually exclusive. International social work must recognize postmodern developments and their adverse effects, as well as the advantages of globalization, and support directions that strengthen indigenous approaches as outlined in this chapter.

Rationale for International Social Work

Globalization as an economic and social phenomenon is an accepted fact in the early twenty-first century. This can be seen in the following ways: multinational corporations with transnational employees, the globalization of food, the Internet has facilitated international communications from the personal to governmental levels; popular culture and the media. These phenomena have all contributed to, or are a result of, globalization. Globalization has brought with it increasing recognition of the interdependence of nations and at the same time, that of their social and economic problems. The boundaries between nations have become porous and in some cases in the European community have become non-existent. The profession of social work cannot be unaffected by this context. Here are the views of one commentator on the impact of globalization on social work:

> International migration makes poverty, political and religious oppression, and the lack of civil rights in one society the concern of other societies. Woman trafficking and sex tourism make the sexual exploitation of women and children in one part of the world the moral, legal and public health concern of other parts. Low wages, harsh work conditions and the exploitation of underage work force in one country affect national employment policies and labour markets in other countries. (Ahmadi, 2003, p. 15)

There are other areas of practice that bring global problems into domestic practice here in the United States. Dominelli (2005) has used the phrase "globalize the local and localize the global" for this process of internationalizing in social work practice. Increasingly common in the caseload of social workers in the United States are issues involving international adoptions, child abductions across national boundaries, social work with asylees, migrant workers, immigrant populations, and undocumented immigrants. Another newer group of individuals are transnationals, who unlike traditional immigrants, may be professionals who work for a global corporation or other institution or may be unskilled workers who come across the Mexican-U.S. border daily for seasonal work. Link and Healy (2005) demonstrate the impact of changing demographics from the U.S. Bureau of the Census 2003 "approximately 11% of the U.S. population are foreign born, . . . one in five Americans speaks a language other than English at home, . . . 11.9 million people live in linguistically isolated homes, that is, no one 14 or older in the home knew English very well" (p. v). Social workers' caseloads in all settings, schools, hospitals, and child welfare agencies are therefore increasing in diversity, not only with domestic diverse populations, but with populations that are foreign born. This requires a new kind of knowledge of international social issues (because they are likely to be met in domestic practice) to be incorporated into the curriculum for the training and education of social workers. After the fall of the USSR, and the dropping of political barriers in the European community, many more social workers train in one country and practice in another. In these circumstances, to have a developed and commonly accepted sense of international standards, values, knowledge, and skills that make up the social work profession, would greatly enhance the portability and prestige of the profession.

A global perspective in social work offers " multiple dimensions of analysis and provides new ways of analyzing problems from a multicultural and pluralistic viewpoint" (Elliott & Mayadas, 1999, p. 53). It offers a new perspective on social problems, because they may be "writ large" or experienced at a more intense level than in the United States. For example, a study of poverty in different countries gives new insights into the experience of poverty at home. A comparative study, such as the World Bank ethnographic study, "Voices of the Poor" provides insight into the universality of the problems associated with poverty and a better understanding of poverty at home (Narayan, Chambers, Shah, & Petesch, 2000). Similarly, a study of social justice in which the dynamics of injustice and oppression are understood from an international perspective can enhance appreciation at home of social justice and oppression. Use of international materials, such as the U.N. Declaration of Human Rights, the U.N. Convention on the Rights of the Child, the U.N. Declaration on the Elimination of All Forms of Racial Discrimination or the Convention on the Elimination of

Discrimination against Women, can also enhance an appreciation of social justice at home (United Nations, 1963, 2006; van Wormer, 2004, 2006).

Elliott and Mayadas (1996, 1999, 2000) have proposed that strengthening the international connections of social work and, thus, incorporating a stronger global perspective and a greater shared identity into the profession can enhance the somewhat uncertain and fragile identity of the profession at home.

Broadening the perspective of social work practice with an international appreciation of the human condition challenges ethnocentrism and paternalism in social work practice. Overseas experiences, such as studying abroad, can help social workers recognize that different is not necessarily "weird" and thus improve their responses to diverse populations at home. Ultimately, relationships formed, knowledge gained and attitudes changed in an experience such as this can assist in international understanding and contribute ultimately to world peace.

A comparative perspective is needed to increase knowledge about social issues and problems. Recognizing that no one country can have all the answers for every social problem, then surely there must be something to be learned from global practice, but maybe also rejection, with efforts to seek further alternatives. There is a need for more comparative studies in all areas of social problems to consider what is most effective across the globe, as well as research and comparative analysis of social policies. The comparative studies lend insight for those who care to read them. There is a need for more and for their inception into mainstream social work education in order to achieve maximum future benefit.

So far, the rationales mentioned consider the majority of social workers working within the United States and the benefits bestowed by an international perspective and experience for domestic practice. The focus of an international perspective is in making their service at home more effective, especially when involving international populations or bringing new ideas for more effective service delivery from overseas. There are a minority of social workers who wish to work across borders in international agencies, such as Save the Children, Oxfam, or agencies of the United Nations such as UNICEF, UNHCR, and UNDP. These require a different kind of training and perspective (Hockenstad & Kendall, 1995). The focus in specialized training for international service should be on the knowledge and skill needed to function effectively across borders. Knowledge and skills in social development practice, as well as comparative social research and comparative policy analysis are required.

BARRIERS TO SUCCESS IN INTERNATIONAL SOCIAL WORK

A major barrier to success in international social work can be seen in the difference in models of practice in different countries. Many countries have adopted a community development or social development model of practice with less emphasis on individual work. In social work at home, generally the medical model still prevails, albeit with the addition of a few new approaches, such as the strengths and empowerment perspectives. It is difficult for individually trained practitioners to grasp a more group-oriented community approach, as in international social work (Elliott & Mayadas, 1996; Mayadas & Elliott, 1995). Another barrier is seen in the difference in service delivery systems: the privatization of welfare services, the role of government and the functions of nongovernment organizations (NGOs; sometimes called voluntary agencies, sometimes nonprofit agencies) differ to a great extent around the world (Elliott, 1997; Mayadas, Watts, & Elliott, 1997).

With regard to social work education, the established curriculum is already crowded with requirements for accreditation both at the professional level and the university level. Many programs are reluctant to add more content and more hours to the program. Resources in social work education are limited and international social work requires funding of exchanges for students and faculty. Outside funding is limited and is often difficult for nonresearch-based smaller schools and departments to obtain. Additionally, the difficulty in determining where multicultural social work ends and where international social work begins acts as a barrier to implementation of curricula and practice. Is working with immigrant populations in the United States multicultural social work or is it international social work?

The general modus operandi in the United States is that of protectionism and isolationism as a principle of foreign policy. This is a large obstacle to overcome in social work schools and departments. Local television news programs have little international content and it is difficult for students and practitioners to identify the relevance of, or generate interest in, international social work. An example of this is the reaction within the United States to Hurricane Katrina. The media focused intensely on the problem for many days. Individual stories of hardship were told and public sympathy was aroused. On the other hand, the devastating monsoon floods in Bangladesh or the Calcutta Basin may be reported sparsely, if at all, and with little or no inclusion of personal stories to make the problem more empathetic.

On the other side of the coin, maybe international social work has not sufficiently defined what it is and why it is relevant. An example of this is that the majority of social work textbooks do not generally include an international perspective. It is hard, therefore, for some programs where faculty have no international experience or links to implement the recommendations of the CSWE in its Educational Policy and Accreditation Standards (EPAS).

Another problem is that practical obstacles such as language differences, value differences, commitment to a nationalistic identity, and absence of universally accepted arrangements for equivalency determination of social work qualifications, are sometimes difficult to overcome (Harris, 1997; Midgley, 1997). While practitioners and social work students may have idealism in adherence to the ideas of social justice, oppression and human rights, these have not been sufficiently operationalized at the concrete practice level (Elliott & Mayadas, 1999).

International Social Welfare Organizations

Healy (1999, 2001) has identified major international organizations and their activities while recognizing that several domestic organizations have substantial international components. She categorizes those that specialize in international issues into three groups: United Nations (U.N.) structures, U.S. government agencies, and NGOs. Furthermore, international social work can be identified in the activities not only of social welfare organizations, but also in the programs delivered through organizations in other disciplines, such as health and economics.

The United Nations is charged with maintaining international peace as well as achieving international cooperation in promoting human rights by addressing economic and social problems. The United Nation's five significant areas of focus are (1) peace and security, (2) economic and social development, (3) human rights, (4) humanitarian affairs, and (5) international law. It is important to note that at least four are consistent with the mission of social welfare. Significant international social welfare services are provided through the following agencies: the Economic and Social Council, the Department of Policy Coordination and Sustainable Development, the U.N. Children's Fund, the U.N. Development Program, the World Health Organization, the U.N. Fund for population Activities, and the U.N. High Commission for Refugees (Healy, 1999). Initially composed of four organizations and 51 member states, the United Nations is now composed of 28 member organizations (see CEB, U.N. Chief Executive Board for Coordination membership list at http://ceb.unsystem.org/membership.htm (accessed July 18, 2006) and 191 nations (see www.un.org).

U.S. governmental agencies, in addition to being involved in U.N. programs, often participate in international collaborations and multilateral relationships, many that address social work issues. The U.S. Department of Health and Human Services (www.hhs.gov), the primary governmental social welfare agency in the United States, has several components with significant international emphases including, for example, programs for children, women, and families in international context. The Centers for Disease Control tackle both national and international health concerns, including prevention, mental health intervention, and services for trauma and violence. The Office of Global Health Affairs (www.hhs.gov/ogha) connects with other nations around health-care policy and programs. The U.S. Social Security Administration (www.ssa.gov), in addition to conducting research on social security programs worldwide, is engaged as the domestic link with the International Social Security Association. The U.S. Department of Homeland Security, which now houses U.S. Citizenship and Immigration and Services (www.usic.gov/graphics/index.htm), is responsible for immigration flows into the country as well as refugee resettlement. Other programs, also deliver a multitude of international social welfare services, including the Peace Corps, established in 1961, which contributes to social and economic development in several countries, and the U.S. AID (www.usaid.gov/about_usaid) that among its other goals, supports global health, conflict prevention, and humanitarian assistance.

The third category of organizations engaged in international social welfare is that of the NGOs, also known as private voluntary organizations (PVOs). These serve a variety of international functions including, (a) relief and development, (b) advocacy, (c) education and exchange, (d) networking of social and youth agencies, and (e) cross-national work in family issues such as adoptions, custody, and resettlement (Healy, 2001). While the missions of most are not necessarily international in focus, many have international leanings, collaborating with agencies across borders, providing consultation to the United Nations and its associated departments, and receiving and providing grants and contracts from both international and U.S. governmental sources.

Global interdependence has been recognized by segments of the social work profession in several nations and professional organizations in social welfare have been in existence for several decades. The IASSW (www.iassw-aiets.org) was founded in 1928 with 51 schools, and though it was based primarily in Europe, it now has members in all regions of the world. The IASSW promotes the development of social work education and standards to enhance its quality, encourages and provides forums for international exchanges, and engages in advocacy activities. In addition, it has a consultative role and participates as an NGO with the United Nations. The IFSW (www.ifsw.org) is a global organization committed to the improvement of the human condition through the development of social work and international cooperation between professionals. The International Council on Social Welfare (ICSW; www.icsw.org) and the International Consortium for Social Development (ICSD; www.iucisd.org) both committed to social development and the empowerment of individuals and groups, serve as consultants to the United Nations, the World Bank, and other international organizations.

Although lesser known, the National Association of Social Workers (NASW) and the CSWE have also long been internationally involved respectively through the International Activities Committee and the International Commission. In 2004, CSWE, in recognition of the need to increase global social work education, established the Katherine Kendall Institute for Social Work Education (www.cswe.org/about/kakinstitute.org). This new initiative, inspired by the life work of Katherine A. Kendall, a legendary, inspirational, and longtime leader in international social work, aims to foster the mainstreaming of international social work in social work education curricula in the United States, as well as to facilitate the development of resources to support educators and practitioners in achieving this goal. Also in 2004, CSWE re-structured the International Commission, which became known as the Global Commission, and consistent with other changes within the organization, two councils of the Global Commission were established: the Council on Global Research and Practice and the Council on External Relations. The Global Commission is charged by the CSWE Board with furthering the global agenda of CSWE, supporting the growth and development of the Katherine A. Kendall International Institute, encouraging the integration of global social work in the social work curriculum, providing leadership in research on global social work issues, and collaborating with international organizations to aid in these efforts. These efforts strengthened the role of international social work in the U.S. social work education agenda.

With increasing globalization, including trends in communication, trade, and migration, international social welfare organizations may be called on with growing regularity. The field of international social welfare has long been cognizant of international interdependence, as is reflected by the numerous organizations engaged in international social welfare activities, and it is time that the mainstream profession integrates it into its normal structure.

THE GLOBAL DIMENSION IN LOCAL PRACTICE: LOCAL IS GLOBAL AND GLOBAL IS LOCAL

An increasingly important aspect of international social work is the recognition that international issues and information are no longer a separate part of social work, but influence the everyday interactions of social workers with their clients. The first example of this issue relates to immigration from a direct practice perspective, and shows how work with immigrant individuals and their families within the United States can be influenced by both knowledge of human migration and knowledge about the prior experiences and culture of immigrants in their own countries. The second example relates to family violence around the world and how a global perspective can influence the way in which we understand the problem at home.

Global Awareness in Social Work with Immigrants

For all immigrants, whether they are in the United States legally, or without the proper documentation, this is an anxious and turbulent time. It is also a time of special concern for those who hire undocumented workers and those who provide services to them. On May 25, 2006, the U.S. Senate passed the New Immigration Bill that would provide a path to citizenship for illegal immigrants and permit a guest worker program. The U.S. House opposed both the path to legalization as well as the worker program, which would bring approximately 200,000 foreigners into the country annually on a temporary basis. This bill has six components, and regardless of whether a particular component is supported by either the House or the Senate, details of what each favors do differ (see Table 16.4).

Note that the terms *illegal, undocumented,* and *unauthorized* are used interchangeably in referring to immigrants who do not have the requisite legal papers to be in the United States.

The House and Senate must now come to a compromise about what they will forward to President George W. Bush for his final approval. Currently, undocumented workers worry that they belong in the group that will be forcibly repatriated and that they will not have the opportunity to return to this country once they have left. American employers who, either knowingly or not, hire undocumented workers are concerned about their workforces, and the implications of their deportation. Those who assist immigrants who are in the country illegally wonder if they will be exempt from penalties if they can prove they are providing "humanitarian" rather than "exploitative" assistance. Finally, those who immigrated legally, or are awaiting a decision regarding their applications for immigration, may evidence distress that the path to legal entry may be smoother for those who are here without the proper documentation than it is for those who attempt to enter through established institutional channels. Regardless of when a clearer picture of the bill emerges, in all likelihood, establishment of an infrastructure, implementation and enforcement will be slow and arduous processes, and the public will continue to debate the issue heatedly.

The last year has seen major movements among the U.S. population, both in support and in opposition to, this bill. Though this piece of legislation embodies the greatest changes in the immigration law in the last 20 years, mixed opinions about the presence of undocumented workers, particularly from Mexico, have historically been intrinsic to U.S. immigration policy since the late nineteenth century (Bernstein, 2006). The liberalized immigration law of 1965, which was designed to eliminate discriminatory practices against Europeans and to end the "remnants" of the exclusionary practices against Asians was, in fact, "coupled with measures explicitly designed to minimize 'brown' immigration from

Table 16.4 Components of Immigration Reform Bill

Component	House Position	Senate Position
1. Creation of a temporary worker program	Opposed	Passed
2. Legalization of undocumented immigrants	Opposed	Passed
3. Work site enforcement	Passed	Passed
4. Criminal penalties for illegal immigrants already in the United States	Passed	Passed
5. Border security—focusing on fencing	Passed	Passed
6. Border security—addressing the need for more personnel	Passed	Passed

Mexico and 'black' from the Caribbean" (Zohlberg, 2006, p. 8). However, since at least the turn of the twentieth century, perhaps in response to pressures from the agricultural industry and its need for plentiful and cheap labor, "legislators resisted closing the country's 'back door' despite their explicit commitment to preserving the 'original American stock' from contamination by Mexicans" (Zohlberg, 2006, p. 9). Clearly, a debate continues, at the very least, regarding the presence of workers who have entered, or remained in the United States illegally.

Individuals and families from around the globe form a continuous stream of immigrants to the United States. The backlog of new visa applications and waiting lists to enter the United States stretches to several years. Undocumented immigrants, both those who enter without legal papers and those who overstay their visits, abound. Refugees and asylees continue to enter in record numbers from countries in political turmoil. Disproportionately large numbers of entrants into the United States in recent years have been people of color from Asia, Africa, and Central and South America, and despite encountering a series of barriers, an overwhelming majority remain, making this nation their permanent residence.

Immigrants' adaptation in a new country reflects the interplay of the reasons for departure from the homeland, the experience of migration, their tangible and intangible resources for functioning in unfamiliar environments, and the effects of the receptiveness of the host country (both politically and socially) to their presence (Segal, 2002). Furthermore, regardless of the length of time immigrants are in the United States, they are invariably faced with a duality of cultures and must learn to function within norms and expectations that frequently conflict.

The U.S. Bureau of the Census indicates that in 2004, of the approximately 288 million residents of the country, 34 million (11.9%) were foreign born and another 30 million (10.6%) were children of those who had migrated from other countries (Table 16.5). These two groups, taken together, have been termed the "New Americans" and constitute 22.5% of the U.S. population. Table 16.6 presents immigrants between 1981 and 2004 by region of birth, while Table 16.7 identifies the region of birth of those refugees who became permanent residents (immigrants) between 1991 and 2004 (Office of Immigration Statistics, 2006; U.S. Census Bureau, 2006).

With increasing globalization and the ease of transnational migration, social workers are increasingly recognizing that "international" social work now occurs within this country. Immigrants bring with them their range of cultures and experiences, many of which may be useful in adapting to the U.S. society, environment, and economy, while many may conflict with dominant values (Segal, 2004). As immigrants learn to negotiate the U.S. system, they may struggle to understand the laws, programs, services and opportunities and may turn to social workers in the process. Some may find adaptation relatively easy, if they arrive with the requisite skills and language capabilities, but may learn later that their children have difficulty reconciling their own bicultural identities. Refugees, who arrive in the country after fleeing horrific experiences in their own homelands and being divested of all that is familiar to them, can suffer a number of serious psychosocial difficulties that require extensive social work intervention, both immediately and after they have established themselves. Social workers need to be cognizant of both immigrants' and refugees' experience prior to entering the country in order to better understand the problems they present to social services on entry as well as after (Mayadas & Lasan, 1984; Pine & Drachman, 2005; Segal, 2002; Segal, Mayadas, & Elliott, 2006; Sherraden & Martin, 1994). Undocumented workers may come to the attention of the social services, and social workers

Table 16.5 U.S. Population by Sex, Age, and Generation: 2004

			Generation					
	Total		First		Second		Third and Higher	
Gender and Age	Number	Percent	Number	Percent	Number	Percent	Number	Percent
Total Male and Female	288,280	100.0	34,244	100.0	30,430	100.0	223,606	100.0
Under 16 years	64,859	22.5	2,421	7.1	12,515	41.1	49,923	22.3
16 – 65 years	188,762	65.5	27,116	82.1	12,798	42.1	147,838	66.1
65 years and over	34,659	12.0	3,697	10.8	5,117	16.8	25,845	11.6
Median age (years)	35.9	(NA)	38.4	(NA)	21.4	(NA)	36.6	(NA)
Total Male	141,227	100.0	17,221	100.0	15,180	100.0	108,826	100.0
Under 16 years	33,173	23.5	1,210	7.0	6,521	43.0	25,442	23.4
16 – 65 years	93,257	66.0	14,480	84.1	6,377	42.0	82,399	66.5
65 years and over	14,797	10.5	1,531	8.9	2,282	15.0	10,984	10.1
Median age (years)	34.7	(NA)	37.3	(NA)	19.9	(NA)	35.6	(NA)
Total Female	147,053	100.0	17,023	100.0	15,250	100.0	114,780	100.0
Under 16 years	31,686	21.5	1,211	7.1	5,994	39.3	24,481	21.3
16 – 65 years	95,505	65.0	13,646	80.2	6,421	42.1	75,438	65.8
65 years and over	19,862	13.5	2,166	12.7	2,835	18.6	14,861	12.9
Median age (years)	37.0	(NA)	39.5	(NA)	23.0	(NA)	37.7	(NA)

Note: Numbers in thousands.
Source: Annual Social and Economic Supplement, 2004, Washington, DC: U.S. Census Bureau, Current Population Survey.

Table 16.6 Immigrants by Region of Birth: 1981 to 2004

	Totals			
Region of Birth	1981–1990	1991–2000	2001–2003	2004
All countries	7,338.1	9,095.4	2,833.9	946.1
Europe	705.6	1,311.4	450.3	127.7
Asia	2,817.4	2,892.2	936.6	330.0
Africa	192.3	383.0	163.0	66.3
Oceania	(NA)	48.0	16.0	6.0
North America	3,125.0	3,917.4	1,063.1	341.2
Canada	119.2	137.6	52.9	15.6
Mexico	1,653.3	2,251.4	541.7	175.4
Caribbean	892.7	996.1	268.9	88.9
Central America	458.7	531.8	199.5	61.3
South America	455.9	539.9	198.6	71.8

Note: Numbers in thousands. See also http://uscis.gov/graphics/shared/statistics/yearbook/index.htm.
Source: Yearbook of Immigration Statistics, 2004, Washington, DC: U.S. Department of Homeland Security, Office of Immigration Statistics.

must balance their ethical responsibilities to those in need with their responsibility to the nation and its laws.

Relatively little attention in the literature is devoted to temporary migrants (on short-term work visas) to the United States and business people and their families. While many may not be eligible for social services, they may require social work intervention if they are hospitalized, their children have difficulties in school, or if there are domestic violence or substance abuse issues present in their lives.

Table 16.7 Immigrants Admitted as Permanent Residents under Refugee Acts by Region of Birth: 1991 to 2004

	Totals			
Region and Country of Birth	1991–2000	2001–2002	2003	2004
Total	1,021,266	234,590	44,927	71,230
Europe	426,565	118,736	17,290	24,854
Asia	351,347	41,406	9,885	14,335
Africa	51,649	20,360	7,723	12,443
Oceania	291	52	18	28
North America	185,333	51,503	8,454	18,323
Cuba	144,612	47,580	7,047	16,678
Haiti	9,364	1,504	472	536
El Salvador	4,073	382	194	263
Guatemala	2,033	809	294	387
Nicaragua	22,486	631	169	137
South America	5,857	2,158	1,518	1,150

See also http://uscis.gov/graphics/shared/statistics/yearbook/index.htm.
Source: Yearbook of Immigration Statistics, 2004, Washington, DC: U.S. Department of Homeland Security, Office of Immigration Statistics.

A little recognized group of entrants into the United States, who may well arrive legally as immigrants but who often suffer from culture shock and isolation, are the mail-order brides. Many have difficulty adapting to the new lifestyle they encounter, have no knowledge of the men they will marry, and usually leave their families of origin permanently. Nevertheless, this business is a booming one that has yet to be regulated by the United States. A Google search for the term "mail order brides" yields over 10 million web sites in less than 10 seconds, attesting to the popularity of (a) getting a wife, and (b) of women, who may not qualify to enter the United States, receiving immigration. Social workers in the United States are gradually learning of new and unanticipated issues such as these.

Thus, social workers clearly may engage in international social work without ever having left the United States. They must draw on their diversity training, their knowledge of multiculturalism and their openness to new worldviews in order to adequately work with the increasingly international group of clients they are likely to encounter (Segal & Mayadas, 2005; Segal, Segal, & Diwakaran, 2006). It is essential that, in the process of being culturally sensitive and competent, social workers be mindful of extreme cultural relativism and carefully evaluate varying cultural norms that may conflict with fundamental social work values.

Example Two: Global Awareness in Working with Family Violence

A second example shows how viewing family violence internationally from a human behavior perspective deepens our understanding of the issue at home. Awareness of family violence in the United States, coupled with less awareness and less openness about this issue in other countries, has often led people to assume that maltreatment in the family is more common in the United States than elsewhere. This may merely be because many other nations continue to view relationships within families as private matters. Focus in many developing countries, such as those of Africa, Asia, and South America, has traditionally been on the health, education, and welfare needs of families, or on the societal (institutionalized) or extra familial abuse of individuals. The family has been sacrosanct and has been protected from inspection of its internal relations by outsides, while the society has claimed that no intrafamilial violence exists.

Although still in its infancy, awareness of family violence is beginning to burgeon in other countries. In 1983, as recently as 2 decades ago, Gelles and Cornell reported that literature claimed that child abuse in countries such as India and Japan was low. Yet, in 1988, India held its First National Seminar on Child Abuse and Neglect. In 1996, Japan established the Japan Society for the Prevention of Child Abuse and Neglect (JaSPCAN) and, in 2000, the Japan Diet passed the Child Abuse Prevention Act. In 1983, Kumagai and Strauss published findings that conjugal violence was low in India and Japan, with discussion suggesting that these are pacifist nations. However, Koithara (1996) indicated that violence against women in India is widespread, but not discussed, and Yoshihama and Sorenson (1994) found that 58.7% of 796 women, who responded to a nation survey in Japan, indicated that they were victims of marital violence. Clearly, family violence may well be as much a problem in those countries that do not acknowledge or study it as it is in those that do. In fact, even if the legal system recognizes family violence as a problem, the general public may be unaware of it. In 2001, the Japanese government passed the nation's domestic violence law, but as recently as April 15, 2006, the *Mainichi Daily News* ("Most

Japanese Unaware") reported that a nationwide survey conducted by the Japanese Cabinet revealed that of the 2,888 (64.2%) respondents, 66.2% were unaware of the contents of the law and 13.3% were even unaware of its existence, but in 2005, the reported cases of domestic violence jumped by 17.5% to 16,888 occurrences.

The Inter-American Commission on Women lists 30 countries of the Americas that have established family violence laws (www.oas.org/cim/English/LawsViolence.htm, retrieved May 12, 2006) and Harvard University's School of Law provides an up-to-date listing of domestic violence laws around the world with connecting web sites (http://annualreview.law.harvard.edu/population/domesticviolence/domesticviolence.htm, retrieved May 13, 2006) indicating that at least 46 countries, besides the United States, passed laws against family violence between 1992 and 2003. The International Network for the Prevention of Elder Abuse (INPEA), established in 1997, is launching the World Elder Abuse Prevention Day on June 15, 2006 (www.inpea.net/downloads/world_awareness_day_2006.pdf, retrieved May 14, 2006). Societies are torn between cultural norms that protect families from inspection and increasing recognition of the need for society to intervene to protect human rights violations. Increasingly, resources are being established around the world, and information about them is readily accessible to service users and providers through a variety of Internet search engines. Andrew Vachss, an attorney well-known for his work with child abuse and neglect, maintains a web site that includes a list of international resources that address family violence (www.vachss.com/help_text/domestic_violence_intl.html, retrieved May 14, 2006), and the Hot Peaches Pages, is a global inventory of hotlines, shelters, refuges, crisis centers and women's organizations; this can be searched by country and in more than 70 languages (www.hotpeachpages.net, retrieved May 10, 2006).

Violence may be defined as any act of commission or omission that results in physical, sexual, or emotional injury to another. Although there are a number of theories of family violence, many of which focus on individual psychological problems of perpetrators, victim characteristics, and environmental circumstances, another set of theories suggest that the cause of family violence lies in the structure of society (Connors, 1989) which is both a product, and a reinforcement, of the unequal distribution of power between men and women, between adult and child, and between provider and dependent. Patriarchal values support female inferiority, and are transmitted to younger generations with family violence tolerated as a male right to control those who are dependent (Carrillo, 1992; Heise, Pitanguy, & Germain, 1994). Most theories on the structure of family violence tend to agree that when society tolerates physical violence as a mechanism for conflict resolution, and when it accepts male authority and superiority in decision making within the home, it provides the ideal blueprint for family violence (Connors, 1989; Kantor, 1996).

In 2002, the World Health Organization (WHO) released its *World Report on Violence and Health* (Krug, Dahlberg, Mercy, Zwi, & Lozano, 2002) and prominent in it is information on child abuse, intimate partner violence, and elder abuse. The report assumes an ecological model for the understanding of violence, suggesting that a variety of factors influence violence including the biological, social, economic, political and cultural. The report identifies a relatively universal definition of child abuse that was developed in 1999 through a review of definitions from 58 countries and with the cooperation of the International Society for the Prevention of Child Abuse and Neglect (Krug et al., 2002). A 48 population-based study from around the world revealed high levels of intimate partner violence (Krug et al., 2002). In industrialized nations, violence appeared to result from either high levels of possessiveness on the part of the (usually) male partner or chronic frustration and anger that erupted into violence, while in more traditional societies, wife beating was considered the right of the male to elicit obedience and was considered acceptable to the women, who felt much was justified. However, in both industrialized and developing countries, the triggers for intimate partner violence appear to be similar, with most revolving around the female not attending to the perceived rights of the male. The WHO report, further indicates that elder abuse is prevalent in all nations of the world, and that since the 1975 "granny battering" described by British scientific journals, industrialized as well as developing countries have reported the prevalence of elder maltreatment (Krug et al., 2002).

While it appears that most societies recognize that there are both psycho-social and structural components to family violence, prevention, and intervention programs seem to indicate that cultures differ in extent to which they credit one component over another. It appears, further, that cultures and communities that are more allocentric (those with a group orientation) tend to focus on societal and environmental interventions, and those that are idiocentric (more individual-focused) are more likely to take the psycho-social and family intervention models. Three articles in Volume 49 of the journal *International Social Work* reported studies of domestic violence in Medan, Indonesia (Rowe, FakihSutan, & Dulka, 2006), an Australian indigenous community (Cheers et al., 2006), and Chinese families (Chan, 2006) and appear to provide explanation of domestic violence in cultural and structural terms. In Medan, the professional women's general tolerance of marital violence reflects acceptance of patriarchal values; in the Australian Aboriginal community, a new perspective of family violence places it "in the historical context of colonization, oppression, dispossession, disempowerment, dislocation and poverty" (p. 51), and in China, the higher the level of "face saving" concerns of males, the greater the likelihood of violence against a significant female.

A review of articles in journals such as the *Journal of Child Abuse and Neglect,* the *Journal of Elder Abuse,* and several journals on family studies indicates that studies in many western, industrialized countries tend to focus more on perpetrator/victim characteristics and experiences to provide explanation of behavior, and tend to suggest interventions that are focused on altering individuals' behavior. Based on cultural perceptions of the cause, or correlates, of violent behavior, recommendations for intervention target either the perpetrator/victim or public awareness and societal education. The focus in idiocentric (Hofstede, 1980) cultures appears to be on dealing with the psychosocial health of victims, while in allocentric (Hofstede, 1980) countries, focus is on community development (i.e., Cheers et al., 2006) or on helping women develop independent economic stability. In either case, one underlying aim is to provide victims with the resources, both psychological and practical, to strengthen coping abilities. In reviewing family violence from this global perspective, U.S. social work practice is seen as falling into the idiocentric category of responses worldwide. By reviewing new developments worldwide, new programs and policies can be considered for more structural approaches to the problem.

THEORETICAL FRAMEWORKS AND INTERNATIONAL SOCIAL WORK RESEARCH

A review of the international social work literature shows that there is limited discussion and no consensus relating to practice models or theoretical frameworks. The IASSW/IFSW global standards discussed earlier are largely atheoretical. Thus far, theoretical approaches such as these are very much at the beginning stages of formulation and much greater debate and interaction is needed to develop fully fledged theoretical and evidence based knowledge to take international social work into the next phase. Asamoah, Healy, and Mayadas (1997) review some theoretical approaches and in discussing unifying frameworks, they consider social work as a human rights profession, social work as social development, and "cross cultural competence as a core social work skill and focus" (p. 397). Healy (2001) discusses globally relevant conceptual frameworks including social development; human rights, multiculturalism, social exclusion/inclusion, security and sustainability. Guzetta (1998) addresses finding unity in diversity and argues that all religions require their followers to practice some form of assisting those in need. He proposes that distributive mechanisms, personal obligation, state responsibility family organization may be components of a unifying theme. Link (1999) discussed the role of international professional ethics and values and the IFSW international code of ethics, and Ramanathan and Link (1999) propose two framework's: one to assess engagement in global and social work learning, and the second, seven steps to global orientation van Wormer's (1997, 2004, 2006) approach to international social work includes a consideration of values, economic oppression, social oppression, and human rights and restorative justice. Midgley (1997), Billups (1990, 1994), Estes, (1995, 1997), Elliott (1993), Elliott and Mayadas (2000), Mayadas and Elliott (1997), all see potential in the social development framework for international social work practice.

The social development approach offers a framework that encompasses many of the approaches mentioned above: empowerment, institution building, prevention and development, sustainability and ecological issues, investment in human and social capital, human rights and social justice, diversity, multisystem and interdisciplinary focused, universal programs and optimal benefits for the fulfillment of human potential. Elliott (1993) and Elliott and Mayadas (2000), offer practice models that include both domestic and transnational social work practice. Cox and Pawar (2006) propose an integrated perspectives approach to international social work and incorporate this into their definition of international social work, quoted earlier. This approach includes the following guiding perspectives: globalization; ecological; human rights; and social development (Cox & Pawar, 2006). This approach provides a very clear framework for their text on international social work and represents significant progress in the direction of a theoretical framework for international social work.

Tripodi and Potocky-Tripodi (2007) advance a much-needed model for international social work research. While there has been consistent comparative research over the years in the field of social welfare, theoretical frameworks for international social work research have been largely neglected in the literature. Tripodi & Potocky-Tripodi have made a significant development in extending the definition of international social work research, "international social work research can be considered social work research that is relevant to international social work" (p. 18). They also offer a typology on international social work research, which includes supranational, intranational, and transnational research. According to the definitions proposed by Tripodi & Potocky-Tripodi, supranational social work research or research beyond borders, includes research with native born populations within one country, research where the research problem and the implications drawn from it are framed from the literature of more than one country. Intranational social work research, or research within borders, includes research with international migrants within a country, and literature from both countries is used. Transnational social work research, or research across borders, is comparative research. In this way the remit of international social work research is extended and it is argued through the Internet research tools, it is possible for a scholar to do international research while sitting at home. Through this definition and typology, Tripodi & Potocky-Tripodi hope that more people will be encouraged to undertake international social work research.

CONCLUSION

In this chapter, a new definition, the history, and some of the main issues and applications of international social work were discussed. Though these elements were addressed in detail, many issues were left unconsidered. To conclude, a way to move progressively forward in order to strengthen the position of international social work is offered.

To build an effective body of knowledge for international social work, the following three steps are necessary:

1. Agreement on common values, practices, skills, models. This has been largely achieved by the IASSW/IFSW Global Standards document. However, dissenting voices and conflicting issues around oppression and indigenous models need to be understood and incorporated.
2. Applying what Cox and Pawar (2006) have called *guiding perspectives,* these have been expanded to include recognition of:
   - The worldwide social construction of social work;
   - All human rights;
   - Global social work professional ethics and values;
   - The centrality of, respect for, and knowledge of, human diversity and indigenous approaches;
   - The role of economics in global, local, and personal economies;
   - The importance of social and economic justice, including issues of restoration, power, and politics;
   - The need to build a verifiable and testable knowledge base in a postmodern intellectual climate, including both quantitative and qualitative to international social work research;
   - Approaches to facilitating the empowerment of individuals, communities, and people;
   - Incorporating technology such as Internet use into international practice;
   - Research and evidence-based approaches to social work practice;
   - Application of "globalcentric" paradigms and way of thinking; and
   - The need for many approaches to advance thinking and practice.
3. The development of practice-based models to guide international practice at a more detailed and tested level.

Each of these stages has been addressed to some extent by the international scholars quoted in this chapter, as well as by many others whose ideas we did not have space to include. The enormous task before social workers and social work educators is to build on this base and extend and frame the context for international social work.

Indeed, the profession still has "miles to go."

REFERENCES

Abo El Nasr, M. M. (1997). Egypt. In N. S. Mayadas, T. D. Watts, & D. Elliott (Eds.), *International handbook on social work theory and practice* (Vol. 1). Westport, CN. Greenwood Press.

Ahmadi, N. (2003). Globalisation of consciousness and new challenges for international social work. *International Journal of Social Welfare*, *12*, 14–23.

Aronoff, N. L. (2003). *Challenge and change in social work education: Toward a world view—Selected papers by Herman D. Stein*. Alexandria, VA: Council on Social Work Education.

Asamoah, Y. (1997). Africa. In N. S. Mayadas, T. D. Watts, & D. Elliott (Eds.), *International handbook on social work theory and practice*. Westport, CN: Greenwood Press.

Asamoah, Y. (2003). International collaboration in social work education: Overview. In L. Healy, Y. Asamoah, & M. C. Hockenstad (Eds.), *Models of international collaboration in social work*. Alexandria, VA: Council on Social Work Education.

Asamoah, Y., Healy, L. M., & Mayadas, N. S. (1997). Ending the international domestic dichotomy: New approaches to a global curriculum for the millennium. *Journal of Social Work Education*, *33*(2), 389–401.

Barker, R. L. (1999). *Dictionary of social work*. Washington, DC: National Association of Social Workers Press.

Bernstein, N. (2006, May 21). 100 years in the back door, out the front. *New York Times*, *4*, 4.

Besant, W. (1887). "The People's Palace," *Contemporary Review, 51*, 226–233. (Available from University of Illinois, Chicago Department of Architecture and the Arts, Janes Addams Hull House Museum, http://tigger.uic.edu/htbin/cgiwrap/bin/urbanexp/main.cgi?file=new/show_doc.ptt&doc=462&chap=6/.

Billups, J. O. (1990). Towards social development as an organizing concept for social work and related social professions and movements. *Social Development Issues*, *12*(3), 14–26.

Billups, J. O. (1994). The social development model as an organizing framework for social work practice. In R. G. Meinert, J. T. Pardeck, & W. P. Sullivan (Eds.), *Issues in social work: A critical analysis*. Westport, CT: Auburn House.

Billups, J. O., & Julià, M. C. (1996). Technology transfer and integrated social development: International issues and possibilities for social work. *Journal of Sociology and Social Welfare*, *23*, 175–188.

Carrillo, R. (1992). *Battered dreams*. New York: UNIFEM.

Chan, K. L. (2006). The Chinese concept of face and violence against women. *International Social Work*, *49*, 65–73.

Cheers, B., Binell, M., Coleman, H., Gentle, I., Miller, G., Taylor, J., et al. (2006). Family violence: An Australian Indigenous community tells its story. *International Social Work*, *49*, 51–63.

Connors, J. F. (1989). *Violence against women in the family*. New York: United Nations.

Cornely, S. A., & Bruno, D. (1997). *Brazil*. In N. S. Mayadas, T. D. Watts, & D. Elliott (Eds.), *International handbook on social work theory and practice*, Westport, CN: Greenwood Press.

Counts, A. (1996). *Give us credit*. New York: Crown.

Cox, D., & Pawar, M. (2006). *International social work: Issues strategies, and programs*. Thousand Oaks, CA: Sage.

Dominelli, L. (2005). International social work: Themes and issues for the 21st century. *International Social Work*, *48*(4), 504–507.

Edwards, R., & Hopps, G. J. (Eds.). (1995). *Encyclopedia of social work* (19th ed.). Washington, DC: National Association of Social Workers Press.

Elliott, D. (1993). Social work and social development: Towards an integrative model for social work practice. *International Social Work, 36*, 21–36.

Elliott, D. (1997). *Conclusion.* In N. S. Mayadas, T. D. Watts, & D. Elliott (Eds.), *International handbook on social work practice and theory* (pp. 441–449). Westport, CT: Greenwood.

Elliott, D., & Mayadas, N. S. (1996). Social development and clinical practice in social work. *Journal of Applied Social Sciences, 21*(1), 61–68.

Elliott, D., & Mayadas, N. S. (1999). Infusing global perspectives into social work practice. In C. S. Ramanatham & R. Link (Eds.), *All our futures: Principles and resources for social work practice in a global era* (pp. 52–68). Belmont, CA: Wadsworth.

Elliott, D., & Mayadas, N. S. (2000). International perspectives on social work practice. In P. A. Meares & C. Garvin (Eds.), *The handbook of social work direct practice.* Thousand Oaks, CA: Sage.

Estes, R. (1995). Education for social development: Curricular issues and models. *Social Development Issues, 16*(3), 68–90.

Estes, R. (1997). Social work, social development and community welfare centers in international perspective. *International Social Work, 40*, 43–55.

Ferguson, K. M. (2005). Beyond indigenization and reconceptualization: Towards a global multidirectional model of technology transfer. *International Social Work, 48*(5), 519–535.

Freud, S. (1914). The history of the psychoanalytic movement. *Jahrbuch der Psychoanalyse, 4*. Available from York University, Toronto Ontario, Canada, http://psychclassics.yorku.ca/Freud/History/.

Gelles, R. J., & Cornell, C. P. (1983). Introduction: An international perspective on family violence. In R. J. Gelles & C. P. Cornell (Eds.), *International perspectives on family violence* (pp. 1–22). Lexington, MA: Heath.

Grameen Bank. (2006). Retrieved May 14, 2006, from www.grameen-info.org.

Grameen Foundation USA. (2006). The PLAN Fund Dallas Texas. Available from www.grameenfoundation.org/programs/partners/plan_fund/.

Gray, M. (2005). Dilemmas of international social work: Paradoxical processes in indigenization, universalism and imperialism. *International Journal of Social Welfare, 14*, 231–238.

Gray, M. (2006). The progress of social development in South Africa. *International Journal of Social Welfare, 15*(1), S53–S64.

Gray, M., & Fook, J. (2004). The quest for a universal social work: Some issues and implications. *Social Work Education, 23*(5), 625–644.

Guzetta, C. (1996). The decline of the North American model of social work education. *International Social Work, 39*, 301–315.

Guzetta, C. (1998). Our economy's global: Can our social work education be global? *Journal of International and Comparative Social Welfare, 14*, 23–33.

Harris, R. (1997). Internationalizing social work: Some themes and issues. In N. S. Mayadas, T. D. Watts, & D. Elliott (Eds.), *International handbook on social work theory and practice.* Westport, CN: Greenwood Press.

Healy, L. M. (1999). International social welfare: Organizations and activities. In R. Edwards (Ed.), *Encyclopedia of social work* (19th ed., pp. 1499–1510). Washington, DC: National Association of Social Workers Press.

Healy, L. M. (2001). *International social work.* New York: Oxford University Press.

Healy, L. M. (2003). A theory of international collaboration: Lessons for social work education. In L. Healy, Y. Asamoah, & M. C. Hockenstad (Eds.), *Models of international collaboration in social work.* Alexandria, VA: Council on Social Work Education.

Healy, L. M., Asamoah, Y., & Hockenstad, M. C. (2003). *Models of international collaboration in social work.* Alexandria, VA: Council on Social Work Education.

Heise, L., Pitanguy, J., & Germain, A. (1994). *Violence against women: The hidden health burden* (World Bank Discussion Paper 255). Washington, DC: World Bank.

Hockenstad, M. C., & Kendall, K. A. (1995). International Social Work Education. In *Encyclopedia of social work* (19th ed.). Washington, DC: National Association of Social Workers Press.

Hockenstad, M. C., & Midgley, J. (2004). *Lessons from abroad: Adapting international social welfare innovations*. Washington, DC: National Association of Social Workers Press.

Hofstede, G. (1980). *Culture's consequences*. Beverly Hills, CA: Sage.

Ife, J. (1997). *Australia*. In N. S. Mayadas, T. D. Watts, & D. Elliott (Eds.), *International handbook on social work theory and practice*. Westport, CN: Greenwood Press.

International Association of Schools of Social Work & International Federation of Social Workers. (2001). International definition of social work. Retrieved August 18, 2006, from www.iassw-aiets.org.

International Association of Schools of Social Work & International Federation of Social Workers. (2004). *Global standards for the education and training of the social work profession*. Final document adopted at the general assemblies of IASSW and IFSW, Adelaide, Australia in 2004 by Vishanthie Sewpaul (IASSW Chair) and David Jones (IFSW Co-Chair). Retrieved August 21, 2006, from www.iassw-aiets.org.

Kantor, P. (1996). *Domestic violence against women: A global issue*. Unpublished manuscript. University of North Carolina, Chapel Hill, Department of City and Regional Planning.

Kendall, K. A. (2000). *Social work education: Its origins in Europe*. Washington, DC: Council on Social Work Education Press.

Koithara, I. (Director). (1996, February 6). *Social workers and the challenge of violence worldwide* [Closed circuit national telecast]. Chapel Hill, NC.

Krug, E. G., Dahlberg, L. L., Mercy, J. A., Zwi, A. B., & Lozano, R. (2002). *World report on violence and health*. Geneva, Switzerland: World Health Organization. Retrieved May 14, 2006, from www.who.int/violence_injury_prevention/violence/world_report/en/full_en.pdf.

Kumagai, F., & Strauss, M. (1983). Conflict resolution tactics in Japan, India, and the USA. *Journal of Comparative Family Studies, 14*, 377–387.

Link, R. (1999). Infusing global perspectives into social work values and ethics. In C. S. Ramanathan & R. J. Link (Eds.), *All our futures: Principles and resources for social work practice in a global era*. Belmont, CA: Brooks/Cole.

Link, R., & Healy, L. M. (2005). Introduction to the collection. In R. J. Link & L. M. Healy (Eds.), *Teaching international content: Curriculum resources for social work education*. Alexandria, VA: Council on Social Work Education.

Mayadas, N. S., & Elliott, D. (1995). Developing professional identity through social groupwork: A social development model for education. In M. D. Feit, J. H. Ramey, J. S. Wodarski, & A. R. Mann (Eds.), *Capturing the power of diversity* (pp. 89–107). New York: Haworth.

Mayadas, N. S., & Elliott, D. (1997). Lessons from international social work: Policies and practices. In M. Reisch & E. Gambrill (Eds.), *Social work in the 21st century* (pp. 175–185). Thousand Oaks, CA: Pine Forge Press.

Mayadas, N. S., & Lasan, D. B. (1984). Integrating refugees into alien cultures. In C. Guzzetta, A. J. Katz, & R. A. English (Eds.), *Education for social work practice: Selected international models*. New York: IASSW/Council on Social Work Education Press.

Mayadas, N. S., Watts, T. D., & Elliott, D. (Eds.). (1997). *International handbook on social work practice and theory* (pp. 441–449). Westport, CT: Greenwood Press.

Midgley, J. (1981). *Professional imperialism*. London: Heinemann Educational Books.

Midgley, J. (1990). International social work: Learning from the third world. *Social Work, 35*(4), 295–301.

Midgley, J. (1995). *Social development: The developmental perspective in social welfare*. Thousand Oaks, CA: Sage.

Midgley, J. (1997). *Social welfare in global context*. Thousand Oaks, CA: Sage.

Midgley, J. (2001). South Africa: The challenge of social development. *International Journal of Social Welfare, 10*, 267–275.

Midgley, J., & Livermore, M. (1997). The developmental perspective in social work: Educational implications for a new century. *Journal of Social Work Education, 33*(3), 573–586.

Most Japanese unaware of domestic violence law, counseling facilities. (2006, April 15). *Mainichi Daily News*. Retrieved May 11, 2006, from http://mdn.mainichi-msn.co.jp/national/news/20060415p2a00m0na023000c.html.

Nagy, G., & Falk, D. (2000). Dilemmas in international and cross-cultural education. *International Social Work, 43*(1), 49–60.

Nanavatty, M. (1997). *India*. In N. S. Mayadas, T. D. Watts, & D. Elliott (Eds.), *International handbook on social work theory and practice*. Westport, CN: Greenwood Press.

Narayan, D., Chambers, R., Shah, M. K., & Petesch, P. (2000). *Voices of the poor: Crying out for change*. New York: Oxford University Press.

Office of Immigration Statistics. (2006). *2004 Yearbook of Immigration Statistics*. Washington, DC: Office of Homeland Security.

Pine, B. A., & Drachman, D. (2005). Effective child welfare practice with immigrant and refugee children and their families. *Child Welfare, 84*(5), 537–562.

Pumphrey, R. E., & Pumphrey, M. W. (1967). *The heritage of American social work: Readings in its philosophical and institutional development*. New York: Columbia University Press.

Quiero-Tajalli, I. (1997). *Argentina*. In N. S. Mayadas, T. D. Watts, & D. Elliott (Eds.), *International handbook on social work theory and practice*. Westport, CN: Greenwood Press.

Ramanathan, C. S., & Link, R. J. (1999). Future visions for global studies in social work. In C. S. Ramanathan & R. J. Link (Eds.), *All our futures: Principles and resources for social work practice in a global era*. Belmont, CA: Brooks/Cole.

Rauch, J. (1976). The charity organization movement in Philadelphia. *Social Work, 21*(1), 55–62.

Reinders, R. (1982). Toynbee Hall and the American settlement movement. *Social Service Review, 56*, 39–54.

Rowe, W. S., FakihSutan, N., & Dulka, I. M. (2006). A study of domestic violence against academic working wives in Medan. *International Social Work, 49*, 41–50.

Segal, U. A. (2002). *A framework for immigration*. New York: Columbia University Press.

Segal, U. A. (2004). Practicing with immigrants and refugees. In D. Lum (Ed.), *Cultural competence, practice stages, and client systems* (pp. 230–286). New York: Brooks/Cole.

Segal, U. A., & Ashtekar, A. (1994). Evidence of parental child abuse among children admitted to a children's observation home in India. *Child Abuse and Neglect, 18*(11), 957–967.

Segal, U. A., & Mayadas, N. S. (2005). Assessment of issues facing refugee and immigrant families. *Child Welfare, 84*(5), 563–584.

Segal, U. A., Mayadas, N. S., & Elliott, D. (2006). A framework for immigration. *Journal of Immigrant and Refugee Studies, 4*(1), 3–24.

Segal, U. A., Segal, Z. N., & Diwakaran, A. R. (2006). Immigrant children in poverty. In B. A. Arrighi & D. J. Maume (Eds.), *Child poverty in America today: Children and the state*.

Sherraden, M. S., & Martin, J. J. (1994). Social work with immigrants: International issues in service delivery. *International Social Work, 37*, 369–384.

Taylor, Z. (1999). Values, theories and methods in social work education: A culturally transferable core? *International Social Work, 42*(3), 309–318.

Titmus, R. M. (1971). *The gift relationship*. London: Allen & Unwin.

Toors, M. (1992). Is international social work a one way transfer of ideas and practice methods from the United States to other countries? No. In E. Gambrill & R. Pruger (Eds.), *Controversial issues in social work* (pp. 98–104). Boston: Allyn & Bacon.

Trattner, W. I. (1994). *From poor law to welfare state a history of social welfare in America.* New York: Free Press.

Tripodi, T., & Potocky-Tripodi, M. (2007). *International social work research: Issues and prospects.* New York: Oxford University Press.

United Nations. (1963). *United Nations declaration on the elimination of all forms of racial discrimination.* Retrieved August 29, 2006, from www.unhchr.ch/html/menu3/b/9.htm.

United Nations. (2006). A summary of United Nations agreements on human rights, Retrieved August 28, 2006 from www.hrweb.org/legal/undocs.html#UDHR/.

University of Washington. (2006). *What is international social work and why is it important.* Seattle, WA: School of Social Work. Retrieved March 23, 2006, from http://depts.washington.edu/sswweb/isw/.

U.S. Census Bureau. (2004). Current population survey. *Annual Social and Economic Supplement.*

U.S. Census Bureau. (2006). Statistical Abstract of the United States: 2006. *The National Data Book* (125th ed.). Washington, DC: U.S. Department of Commerce, Economics, and Statistics Administration.

U.S. Department of Homeland Security. (2004). *2004 Yearbook of Immigration Statistics.* Washington, DC: Office of Immigration Statistics.

van Wormer, K. S. (1997). *Social welfare: A world view.* Chicago: Nelson-Hall.

van Wormer, K. S. (2004). *Confronting oppression, restoring justice: From policy analysis to social action.* Alexandria, VA: Council on Social Work Education.

van Wormer, K. S. (2006). *Introduction to social welfare and social work: The U.S. in global perspective.* Belmont, CA: Brooks/Cole.

Wagner, A. (1992). Social work education in an integrated Europe: Plea for a global perspective. *Journal of Teaching in Social Work, 6*(2), 115–130.

Watts, T. D. (1997). An introduction to the world of social work. In N. Mayadas, T. D. Watts, & D. Elliott (Eds.), *International handbook on social work practice and theory.* Westport, CT: Greenwood Press.

Yoshihama, M., & Sorenson, S. B. (1994). Physical, sexual, and emotional abuse by male intimates: Experiences of women in Japan. *Violence and Victims, 9*(1), 63–78.

Yuen-Tsang, A. W. K., & Wang, S. (2002). Tensions confronting the development of social work education in China: Challenges and opportunities. *International Social Work, 45*(3), 375–388.

Yunus, M. (2003). *Banker to the poor: Micro-lending and the battle against world poverty.* New York: Public Affairs.

Yunus, M. (2006). *What is micro credit?* Retrieved May 14, 2006, from www.grameen-info.org/bank/WhatisMicrocredit.htm.

Zohlberg, A. R. (2006). *A nation by design: Immigration policy in the fashioning of America.* Cambridge, MA: Harvard University Press.

Chapter 17

IMMIGRANT AND INDIGENOUS POPULATIONS: SPECIAL POPULATIONS IN SOCIAL WORK

Jon Matsuoka and Hamilton I. McCubbin

Special populations have been defined as select clusters of individuals, families, or communities who were designated by a majority of members in society or the community to become the focus of stigmatization, prejudice, and discrimination. For whatever reason, such as skin color, ancestry, behaviors, or socially defined labels, these special populations are identified as unique, that is distinguishable in contrast to the majority adopted and imposed social norms, values, and expectations. Consequently, they are ostracized and treated as subordinate, if not less than human, in the eyes of the majority. Thus, they are scorned and treated with disrespect and humiliation.

These special populations emerge in the course of history, much as lepers, immigrants, and slaves, and have become constant reference points for ridicule and at times, inhuman subordination. At another extreme, but also stigmatizing, are subpopulations who fail to possess the *expected* characteristics of the time, such as beauty, physical health, fitness, slimness, and glamour. Clearly, the subject of special populations can be so broad as to defy meaningful analysis, particularly in the context of the social work profession. Consequently, the sifting and winnowing process of focusing this chapter has been both a challenge and an opportunity. The invitation to address the complex and vast subject of special populations became an opportunity to frame a social work issue that is ancient and at the same time emergent and pressing as a current issue. The focus of choice in this chapter begins with emersion in the struggles of special immigrant and indigenous populations, largely created through the historic processes of immigrations as well as colonization, but whose voices as a collective whole are coming to the forefront of social work concerns accompanied by frontal challenges to social work theory, research, and practice (Kim & Berry, 1993).

SPECIAL POPULATIONS—ROOTS OF DIVERSITY AND TENSION

What makes a special population special is that they provide diversity in society. The value of diversity varies according to social sector. There are large sectors of society that frown on diversity and hold firm to the beliefs that immigration and colonized groups have a responsibility to subordinate or eliminate their cultural heritage and assimilate into the mainstream of the majority population. However, those groups that represent the diversity tend to hold fast to their unique cultural identities and properties while striving toward a bicultural existence.

As a society becomes increasingly diverse, there are competing forces that ultimately determine the form and ideology underlying institutional design (Freire, 2002). Under a dominant design, all subsequent cultural entries are subjugated and modified. In American society, whose multicultural formation is driven by economics, the cultural base has been primarily Euro-American. Thus, as new cultures enter society with immigrants seeking economic opportunities, the base of imported cultures eventually erode and are replaced by Euro-American values. Immigrants are a self-selected population comprised of cohorts who leave their homelands in search of more promising economic or political opportunities to benefit their families. After generations of acculturation and miscegenation, ancestral traits have become disenfranchised.

This social process stands in stark contrast to indigenous people and groups who were involuntarily marginalized and subordinated in their ancestral homelands. American Indians, Alaskan Natives, Native Hawaiians, and other Pacific Islanders have a qualitatively different cultural contract experience than that of immigrants from other countries. First Nation people of North America, Native Hawaiians, and other Pacific Islanders had developed thriving and sovereign societies when Europeans and Euro-Americans arrived on the scene. The subsequent subjugation and genocide of these indigenous populations is well documented (Benham & Heck, 1998; Stannard, 1992). Resistance to the imposing forces of the West, especially when protecting their valued resources, accelerated the decline of the indigenous people.

Indigenous experiences of imposition and genocide, and their resulting worldviews and behaviors, diverge from that of immigrants. This is not to minimize the overt racism and struggles faced by immigrant groups, however, especially the first generations who came from abroad. The mentality of immigrants reflects a "push-pull" dynamic that includes a decision to move to what is conceived of as a better place with new and better opportunities, and choices made in relation to acculturation as a means to improve socioeconomic standing. This worldview is in sharp contrast with that of indigenous people whose identities, strengths, resources, beliefs, and values were trivialized or eliminated, leaving them with a loss of self-governance accompanied by diminished hopes and aspirations.

Thus, the experiences and social outcomes of immigrants and indigenous peoples depend in large part on where they find themselves on the continuum of assimilation and acculturation. Those that willfully immigrate are predisposed to acculturate to American cultural norms. Those who were invaded or taken against their will may be less motivated to adopt a new culture. Ethnic minorities who resist American culture are chastised for being unpatriotic or ungrateful. These notions turn into a collective sentiment of "blaming the victim." Perhaps this sentiment is most prominently directed toward immigrants who came to this country seeking a better life and entered into open competition with the majority stakeholders for resources and status.

Disparities in educational achievement and socioeconomic mobility are reflected in differential group histories. Asian Americans have been deemed the "model minority" and are often compared to other minority groups who have struggled to "make it" in American society. Attributions for differential success include higher intelligence, strong work ethic, and cultural affinity. Pervasive notions exist that Asians are predisposed to success because they possess inherent qualities of discipline and aspirations. In contrast, indigenous populations such as the case of Native Hawaiians are characterized as being unmotivated and with minimal aspirations. Thus, they are overrepresented in vocational and special education programs (Benham & Heck, 1998; Kamehameha Schools/Bishop Estate, 1983).These contrasting depictions of immigrants and indigenous people should not detract from the salience of their strengths and capabilities that are often masked by stereotypes and overgeneralizations. Equally important is the emergent voices of these special populations that render clarity as to how they see themselves, their culture, and their futures. The remainder of this chapter is dedicated to their unique characteristics, and delineating their expectations of themselves and of the social work profession in aiding them to survive, develop, and thrive.

Special Intelligence

Special populations in America are often confined to living within segregated communities that are removed from society's socioeconomic mainstream. Within these enclaves, people are socialized according to unique behavioral and cognitive norms. Insular and often materially deprived environs can serve to repress healthy human development but such circumstances can also breed creativity and innovation. A unique intelligence emerges that reflects a blend of cultural elements and oppressive circumstances. Innovations in terms of music and the arts, fashion, and idiomatic language have emerged from ethnic subcultures and crossed over into mainstream popular culture. Trends emerging from Native Hawaiian and American Indian youth culture have become the cultural standard in our society.

Intelligence is very much determined by situation and context. In resource deprived environments, intelligence is measured by people's ability to survive by developing skill sets that enable them to function while tending to constant and immediate threats from their surroundings. Those living in safe environments are not required to expend energies to guard against such threats and can focus on personal educational and career goals as well as family needs. In other words, attending to personal safety issues and basic survival needs are not primary issues of concern for privileged sectors of society, however, these issues can be major detractors from the achievements of the less advantaged.

Although there are great variations in social environs and associated intelligences within society, in society's effort to promote homogeneity, notions of intelligence are narrowly defined by standardized measures. Such measures are the means to assess if persons have the requisite intellectual capacity to warrant opportunities to further advance their education and careers.

Special populations raised in insulated environs that choose to venture out to pursue new opportunities are required to adopt broader behavioral, cognitive, and linguistic sets in order to function effectively. Except in rare circumstances, Euro-Americans are not required to venture out in the same way and acquire new cultural skill sets. "Making it" occurs within a cultural context that they are familiar with. Special groups who succeed in the larger society are required to be multicultural by the very nature of such success. That is, they must possess a repertoire of behaviors that allows them to move readily between sociocultural spheres and manage parallel and sometimes contradictory realities. Thus, in the process of becoming multicultural, special populations must develop a high level of social intelligence. This type of intelligence is manifested in the following examples:

- The acquisition of dual and sometimes conflicting behavioral and cognitive sets.
- Highly refined observational and sensory skills in order to accurately read and respond effectively to cues across sociocultural spheres.
- Mastery over the sociopolitics of culture and race while pursuing educational and career interests.
- Negotiating value conflicts shaped by ancestry and cultural differences.
- Balancing demands and social expectations and priorities of different groups.
- Recalibration of competing priorities to fulfill cultural and achievement goals.

Historical Trauma and Ancestral Memory

Notions of posttraumatic stress disorder as defined in the *DSM-V* suggest that symptoms associated with this disorder occur as a direct result of discrete and relatively recent life events. It is surmised that exposure to violent events such as military combat or rape predispose individuals to exhibit uncontrolled rage, nightmares, and isolationism. Etiological conceptions generally do not consider the cumulative effects of historical trauma and a long-term process of reconciling pain that extends across generations. Trauma alters human behavior and associated thinking.

Populations subjected to collective trauma have modified their strategies of socialization and survival as a way to protect themselves from external threats. Immigrants to the United States settled into ethnic enclaves not only as a way to recreate a familiar sociocultural environment with higher levels of predictability, but also as a way to guard against vigilant majority who blamed them for their economic woes. Native people in America experienced holocausts that culminated in their near extermination.

The first Western voyagers to Hawaii estimated a native population of approximately 400,000. Subsequent estimates based on more scientific data place the number of Hawaiians at the point of Western contact closer to 800,000 to 1 million. Hawaii is one of the most isolated landmasses in the world. It lies in the middle of the world's largest body of water. Because of its remoteness, anthropologists theorize that Hawaii was one of the last places on earth to be inhabited by humans, and that occurred about 1,000 A.D. The first Europeans, led by British sea captain James Cook, arrived in Hawaii in 1778. Missionaries arrived from New England in 1820. By 1831, through a mixture of both choice by the Hawaiian people and the pressing influence of missionaries, the indigenous spiritual and cultural system had been abolished and 1,000 Christian schools had been built. The second generation of missionaries abandoned their religious pursuits and embraced self-serving opportunities for wealth once they realized the vast economic opportunities in Hawaii.

In 1848, businessmen were the major force behind changing the traditional system of land ownership. The *Mahele,* as it is referred to in the Hawaiian language, allowed nonnative people to own Hawaiian land for the first time. From that point on, Americans hoarded lands through purchase, quit title, and adverse possession. By the turn of the century, a mere 50 years later, Whites owned 4 acres of land for every 1 acre owned by a Hawaiian. They used their vast land holdings to cultivate sugar and pineapple. Once firmly situated in the

Hawaiian economic and political system, a group of American sugar barons, whose lineage could be tied directly to the original missionaries, staged an overthrow, with the backing of the U.S. Marines, that ousted the last reigning monarch of Hawaii, Queen Lili'uokalani in 1893.

By this time, the native Hawaiian population was decimated. Captain Cook's maiden voyage to Hawaii brought sexually transmitted diseases. Missionaries, whalers, and other foreigners brought a host of other diseases that Hawaiians had no immunity to. By some estimates, the Hawaiian population diminished by 90% of its original pre-Western contact level. Hawaiians today continue to suffer severe health and social problems.

Native Hawaiians have some of the highest per capita rates of heart disease and cancer, diabetes, severe problems related to drug and alcohol abuse and consequent domestic violence problems, disproportionately high levels of mental health problems and suicide, the lowest educational achievement and employment levels, the highest number of teen pregnancies, and the highest rates of criminal convictions and incarceration (Office of Hawaiian Affairs, 2002).

In Hawaii, there is the highest number of residents in public housing and the highest percentage of homeless in the United States. Demographers predict that the population of pure Native Hawaiians will be extinct by the year 2040. The contemporary status of Hawaiians is obviously the result of their history of culture contact and dispossession. This storyline of overthrow and colonization has been played out multiple times throughout North America and the Pacific region and the social consequences are strikingly similar. Trauma is incurred from the loss of culture, traditional lands and resources, family members, and leaders; violent encounters and witnessing the physical and emotional suffering of your people; being rendered a minority in one's homeland; being required to live by the strictures of an alien society; and a deep inner sense of social injustice.

On a collective scale, symptoms of posttraumatic stress disorder are manifested in various ways including anger turned outward into violence or inward in the form of substance abuse and helplessness, refusal to conform to Western strictures or an obsessive adherence to tradition, high rates of fertility and teenage pregnancies, and political radicalism. Not all of these manifestations are negative if placed in a certain context. Being steadfast in protecting traditions is critical in perpetuating culture. High fertility can be viewed as a form of sociobiological compensation for decimated populations, and political activism is a healthy expression of social discontent.

The attitudes and dispositions of oppressed and traumatized populations do not necessarily follow a predictable schema but are a part of a larger and highly complex intaglio. As mentioned, strategies to avoid conflict and violence served to alter settlement and socialization patterns. Interpretations of direct experience and oral knowledge handed down by predecessors are mixed into a cognitive brew that influences political orientation and behavioral expression.

In cases where traditions and associated behaviors have been severed, efforts to restore culture have been met with competing notions of originality and authenticity. While such efforts are noble in the sense that entities are committed to cultural revival, they also serve to fracture cultural and political movements. In short, attitudes and behaviors that are borne out of collective trauma are not always decipherable and the unaccountability is especially perplexing to those not living the experience. Historical legacies can be used to understand posttraumatic reactions that extend well beyond our current conceptions.

Two hundred years of oppression and trauma are not remedied through job opportunities and new economies. Ancestral memory leads special populations to not trust or conform, especially when conformity means buying into a system that eradicated their stabilizing foundation through colonization.

FAMILY SYSTEM AS A SUPERORGANIC STRUCTURE

Families are generally conceptualized as nuclear systems comprised of one or two parents and children. More progressive notions of family include single-parent households and gay and lesbian parents raising natural or adopted children. In the many cultures that exist in the United States, the concept of family extends well beyond the notion of nuclear or even extended family systems. Those that pay homage to their ancestors through rituals or other practices view themselves as one segment in a highly protracted genealogical order. They are members of a family system that is connected to a superorganic structure existing across past, present, and future generations.

The families of today are current manifestations, linking ancestors to future generations. In cultures with oral traditions, knowledge of family progenity is passed between generations through stories, chants, and other customary practices. Often, these processes of passing information between generations have been interrupted by migration, language replacement, and genocide. Thus, families have lost their connection to their genealogical past. Stories and tales of ancestors' (whether accurate or exaggerated) character and virtues, roles and statuses, deeds and misfortunes, have ceased to exist. The displacement and diaspora of peoples have rendered meaningless the skill sets and technological knowledge that once defined the social status of ancestors.

Next, two personal family stories from each of the authors are shared with the intention of giving voice to immigration and indigenous oral family histories passed on across generations and to give meaning to the concept of the superorganic family.

The Matsuoka Family

My grandfather brought to America the *katana* or sword of the famous samurai Saigo Takamori. Saigo Takamori was the figure portrayed in the story of the *Last Samurai*. One day before the turn of the nineteenth century, my greatgrandfather was walking in his village in southern Japan when a dog began to follow him. This dog followed him all the way home. Once he arrived home, his neighbor informed him that that was the favorite dog of Saigo Takamori. Feeling an obligation to return the pet to its esteemed owner, my great grandfather took the dog to the temple where Saigo Takamori resided. On seeing his favorite dog, Saigo Takamori was extremely grateful and presented my greatgrandfather with his sword as a gift in return.

On the eve that my grandfather left Japan, his father presented him with the precious samurai sword. He wished him well and told him to never forget his homeland. When my father was growing up, the sword sat prominently on the mantle in the family home until the war broke out. Fearing that the FBI would confiscate the sword after the Japanese bombed Pearl Harbor, the family buried the sword underneath their house. Soon thereafter they were forced to leave their home and possessions and were relocated away from the West Coast. After the war was over, they returned to their house in Los Angeles' Little Tokyo area and found that the house had been razed and converted into a parking lot. According to my uncle who shared this story, the most painful part about losing the family house was losing the sword. The sword had symbolized a connection to family genealogy and the legacy of a revered figure who held fast to cultural tradition in the face of modernity and Westernization. The sword was a conduit for conveying stories with embedded cultural values regarding character, honorable behavior, and continuity across time and place. The loss of the sword and the war experience as a whole changed the mentality surrounding my father's family's approach to living in the United States. For survival purposes, they made a concerted effort to detach themselves from their homeland and blend in behaviorally to American society. Now all that remains is the story of the sword itself.

The McCubbin Family

This family, it is told, had two members who were diagnosed with leprosy or Hansen's disease, which at that time was a diagnosis of isolation and death. The diagnosis was confirmed when my uncles were in their early teens and they were transported to Kalaupapa, Molokai, the Hawaiian leper colony. Being unaware of this family history, I joined a team of mental health specialists who spent a week on Kalaupapa to gain first-hand knowledge and experience in working and talking with the residents of this highly stigmatized and isolated community. On arrival, a resident greeted me as I left the aircraft. His arms were wide open, inviting a physical hug and personal greeting. In spite of our host's lost fingers all the way to the knuckles and a face with a missing nose, the embrace was warm, genuine, and reciprocated. I felt at home. Following the exchange of names, my host shouted: "McCubbin? Mmmmm. . . . Did you have relatives here?" Taken back by the surprising inquiry, I paused to think, then responded, "I don't think so." He replied, "Your last name is unusual. . . . I wonder. There were two McCubbins here you know. Follow me to the graveyard then to the records office where anyone who resided here can be identified. I do recall that Hamilton, the youngest, died here and Willy, well, he is buried on Oahu. See we keep track of everyone who ever lived here." The burial site was confirmed and the records revealed my past, my history, and my geneology.

My mother anticipated my self-discovery and anxiously awaited my return from Kalaupapa. The matriarch, my mother, carried family secrets and told the story of my uncles with care, respect, and appreciation. Leprosy and Kalaupapa were not spoken of in public for fear of social stigma. In the family, however, although I was too young at the time to remember, both subjects were discussed openly and passed on from one generation to another. The story was not about the trials and tribulations but about the family's commitment to care for their own no matter where they lived and no matter under what condition. On relocation, the McCubbin family worked together to find ways to keep the family intact and together with weekly trips to Molokai to do what they could so Hammy and Willy could see them. My mother,

(*continued*)

a nurse, was able to connect with them directly. My father served as cook when he visited. This story was told over and over as a reminder of this organic family unity, united spiritually but torn apart physically. It was the strength of the family that became folklore in storytelling. Importantly, the family history gave meaning to a dismal situation but one graced with respect, pride, and appreciation for my uncles. The story kept us connected, spiritually and emotionally. Leprosy, the scourge and bane of our existence, became part of our past, a meaningful past, as well as a part of genealogy, identity, and future.

All too often support is defined as the exchange of tangible goods and interpersonal contact. The oral histories of the Matsuoka and McCubbin families reveal the strength of symbols, the sword and the isolated island, and the meaning attached to them, which unifies family and hope. Through storytelling, people are able to pass on a rich past, the meaning of adversity, and the value of cultural symbols, and in doing so, they capture and reaffirm the spiritual strength or *mana* underlying the story.

The loss of family history parallels the loss of culture. Where once there were thriving indigenous systems of knowledge transmission and continuity tied inherently to economic survival, there now exists a postmodern colonial system that is generally intolerant of cultural separation and distinctiveness within its national boundaries. The sociopolitical processes that have systematically and effectively severed people from their past have deposed many to a state of confused cultural identity.

Families who have studied their genealogy are able to connect themselves to ancestors who lived hundreds or even thousands of years ago. In the process of exploring genealogy, knowledge emerges that reunites extended families that evolved along different lines. Knowledge also provides information regarding the community role or specialization of ancestors and mends the fractured cultural identity by connecting people to their histories.

A strong sense of familial connectedness and obligation takes on a different meaning when we subscribe to a superorganic family conception. Many ethnic minority and indigenous people have been instilled with the responsibility of maintaining the beliefs and practices tied to their lineage. They have been assigned to be the proprietors of traditions.

Faculty of the School of Social Work at the University of Hawaii were contacted by the U.S. Department of Energy to conduct an ethnographic study of the sociocultural impacts of geothermal development of Hawaii's Kilauea volcano. Native Hawaiian subsistence practitioners living around the perimeter of the volcano were interviewed in depth. Economic change and infiltration had bypassed those residing in the remote corridor between the great mountain and the sea. Many residents shared their belief in and worship of Pele, the Hawaiian goddess of fire. She was believed to be the animate manifestation of the volcano.

Pele and her progeny are the core of an ancient religious system that was essentially eradicated by the introduction of Christianity to Hawaii. Over the centuries, a thin stream of practitioners managed to promulgate religious practices associated with Pele. To these practitioners, Kilauea volcano was not merely a geologic anomaly, it was a living deity not to be desecrated by tapping it for energy. They felt an absolute commitment to protecting the volcano from energy exploitation and honoring their ancestral beliefs. Drawing energy from the volcano was construed as a threat to the spiritual vitality of Pele. The goddess and all she represents would not die on their generation's watch. A political action group was formed called the Pele Defense Fund and they succeeded in staving off the geothermal development.

COLLECTIVITY AND CULTURE

Collective cultures, or those oriented toward group behaviors, exist because group members rely heavily on each other for livelihood and survival. Many cultures that originated from agricultural and subsistence-based economies continue to espouse collective values emphasizing social cohesiveness. Collective people through their socialization are inherently sensitive to their social ecology—its dynamic forces and the ramifications of change within a social milieu. A critical objective is to maintain balance and harmony in the social economy in their milieu.

Collective peoples have developed highly sophisticated social economies that are essentially safety nets for families and communities. Extended family and communal networks are relied on for support in raising children and caring for the aged, assisting in times of crisis, organizing special events, and engaging in work projects that benefit the community at large. With the exception of the aged and infirmed, participation in providing support is requisite. Prescriptive and proscriptive norms guide a stringent system of reciprocity that provides order and assigns roles to the group.

For both immigrant and indigenous people in the United States, settlement patterns and the formation of enclaves served to further affirm cultural values related to collectivity. A collective orientation was the basis for the development of community-based practices leading to economic self-reliance. Cultural and political associations, rotating loan and banking systems, and other informal services that aided the socioeconomic mobility of fellow ethnics emanated from community-based institutions that offered greater reliability and trust to the communities they served.

Resistance to change could be attributed to self-protective mechanisms. Cultural conservatism is reinforced by undesirable changes individuals observe in other domains. Through this orientation, they have created novel ways to protect their esteem and mental health.

Early research indicated that culturally divergent child-rearing practices resulted in differential personality traits in people. In some cultures, attachment and emotional bonding with parent and child, especially mothers, was observed through continuous physical attachment and tactile stimulation. The outcome of these behaviors, along with brevity of speech and verbal exchange, was developing children who were less verbally expressive. Children were also observed to be more attentive to other people and to their environment.

What emerges from differential child-rearing practices is an intelligence that is influenced by cultural values. In the West, intelligence is often equated to the ability to express ideas in words and through articulation of thought. In the Eastern and Pacific regions, intelligence is often equated to an ability to read social situations and to act in accordance with socially prescribed roles and protocols. A heightened sensitivity to social situations, as well as a self-consciousness regarding how people engage others socially, has also been explained as a basis for highly developed appraisal skills and social intelligence. This heightened sensitivity is also an explanation for the development of neurotic behavior when it goes awry. A strong collective sense is inversely related to individualism. Those who possess a collective identity generally consider the sentiment of the group before taking action.

RESEARCH ON SPECIAL POPULATIONS

Current theoretical formats and paradigms are remiss when it comes to understanding phenomenology of special populations (Kahuakalau, 2004). Traditional approaches relying on inferential statistics can only remotely capture the everyday social realms of those societies. Unfortunately, alternative methods, including grounded theoretical approaches that serve to provide holistic impressions of phenomenon, are deemed "soft" and lacking in credibility (Denzin & Lincoln, 1998). The tension generated from conflicting perspectives have stretched the boundaries of traditional research and led to new sensibilities that emphasize multimethod research approaches.

Bolland and Atherton (2000) described a heuristic paradigm that accepts all research methodologies, not privileging any ontology, epistemology, or method. They propose a relativistic approach that suggests there are no universal standards of right or wrong and that all knowledge is dependent on the subjective knower. The acceptance of broader conceptualizations of scientific inquiry lead to the evolution of paradigms and techniques that enable social scientists and policy makers to hold a clearer and deeper understanding of alternative life ways and issues.

The traditional period of positivism and associated methods and paradigms has done much to damage the reputation of social science in communities. This period has also challenged subsequent generations of researchers, both nonindigenous and indigenous, to erase the perceptions of anthropologists, sociologists, and others who exploited their trust and goodwill. Moreover, it has been difficult to convince indigenous leaders of the utility of empirical data in terms of protecting their rights, resources, and traditional and customary practices. As Smith (1999) stated, indigenous people are on an important quest to recover their languages and epistemological foundations. Research is a critical means to reclaim their histories.

Gaining Trust

Many communities, especially indigenous ones, have an inherent mistrust of government and university researchers. Overcoming the barrier of mistrust is the first major challenge in conducting community-based research. The mistrust is drawn from a history of exploitation from outsiders and a general community impression that study results unilaterally benefit the academic careers of researchers. Communities have acquired a political sensitivity and savvy that requires researchers to explain how the study will benefit residents. A researcher may possess an immense amount of technical and methodological knowledge and have the right motives for engaging in community-based research, yet still be denied entry into a community. Those bent on preserving their cultures and communities are not impressed by credentials and technical know-how.

In locales where communities are tightly linked through cultural or political affiliation, there is a high level of exchange between civic leaders. Researchers acquire reputations based on who they typically are contracted by (state, private developer, community), the rigor of their work, quality of the product, applications of the study results, sensitivity to community protocol, and the extent to which they make long-term commitments to a community. In many situations, the reputation of the researcher precedes him or her, and this determines their level of acceptance. For example, research consultants in Hawaii who are frequently contracted by developers for environmental impact assessments have at times been systematically locked-out of communities opposed to development projects. However, research consultants who traditionally work in communities and have applied a participatory action approach leading to tangible benefits are often sought after and embraced by communities. Level of compensation can be considered a determinant of motivation. Some residents may question the motivations and commitment to community well-being by high-paid research consultants, while those consultants working on a pro bono basis will not be accused of having ulterior motives.

Access and Protocol

There is an array of culturally based protocols that must be applied when initiating a research project. Contacting and gaining endorsements from the "right" persons, who are often respected elders or *kupuna* will determine the degree to which a researcher is able to access other critical informants. Indigenous communities are fraught with dynamics related to family affiliation and length of stay, history of personal contact, political orientation, socioeconomic status, and race/ethnic relations. It is requisite for researchers, through a reconnaissance, to explore and gain an awareness of these dynamics. Negotiating ties with one sector, however, may inadvertently close the door with competing sectors in the community and obviate a cross-sectional analysis.

Engaging a community in research requires many of the same strategies as community organizing including exhibiting culturally appropriate mannerisms and a nonintrusive style. In communities, maintaining objectivity through social distance is counterintuitive to gaining the trust of residents through a process of social immersion.

Social distancing does not permit a researcher to embrace the culture and its intricacies and subtleties, let alone gain access to residents who are inherently suspicious of strangers. Abiding by cultural protocol, such as asking permission rather than imposing oneself, sensitivity to nonverbal situations, sharing family background and genealogies especially if they are tied to the geographic area, speaking the dialect and using idiomatic language, and generally building a base of commonality are all means of establishing rapport and trust.

Thrusting uninvited researchers onto the community scene with a research agenda is a form of "carpet-bagging." This seemingly standard approach in earlier years has generated widespread skepticism in communities and subsequently created barriers for well-intentioned researchers who are committed to gathering critically needed data. Under such conditions, researchers must lay the groundwork for research by convincing community leaders that empirical data can be vital ammunition for promoting policies and planning decisions aimed at community preservation and social development.

In Pacific cultures, social reciprocity is a critical aspect of interpersonal relations. From an indigenous perspective, the economy of speech between negotiating parties is a good predictor of balance and parity in a working relationship. The role of the researcher is to listen, acknowledge the intelligence and wisdom of the residents, incorporate indigenous perspectives into the research methodology, and involve a working team of residents at every phase of the research process. "Politically enlightened" communities strive to develop true partnerships with researchers by providing critical information that guides the research process.

In many Pacific societies, strangers greet each other by reciting their family genealogy. This protocol is significant in that it serves to inform each party of the other's lineage and pays homage to each person's ancestors. Though there are varying degrees of this practice, from the highly ritualized to a less formal and indirect inquiry into one's family background, the practice remains strong. In Hawaii, for example, the typical first questions of a stranger are "what high school did you attend" and "are you related to so and so" (with the same surname). These questions tie a person to a community or island and gather important information on their family background. Such contextualization is a means to appraise the person. Researchers are not immune to this practice. Despite having credentials that reflect academic qualification, indigenous residents are keen to learn more about the researcher's values and motives that are often linked to place and family of origin. For many indigenous people, credibility is derived from the integrity of the individual and less so from academic degrees.

Trust and social bonding are contingent on the extent to which people share common features. Behaviorally disparate parties must overcome huge obstacles in order to know enough about the other to trust them. Establishing trust is facilitated by behavioral and semantic concurrence. Fluency in the native language, when it is the first language of residents, removes major logistical problems related to translation and conceptual equivalence and breeds trust.

Striving for Authenticity

Researchers working in indigenous communities must recognize that society is indoctrinated with a colonial version of historicity whose rendition serves to justify colonial mastery. Much of the accepted narratives on indigenous people are really the narratives of colonialists and cultural hegemons (Touraine, 2001). In the Pacific, indigenous claimants have emerged to assert contending visions of the cultural past. There is a revitalized struggle occurring globally among indigenous people to manage, define, and promulgate their own histories and cultural realities.

This legacy, and subsequent movements to alter previous conceptions, has politicized the research process. Indigenous communities are becoming aware of the power of research and its utility and are assuming greater control over who is involved and how it is conducted. Past attempts to document the life ways of indigenous people were fraught with cultural biases, misinterpretations, and even deliberate efforts to deceive foreign observers as a form of mockery. Communities are taking corrective action by supporting research that promotes authenticity.

Authenticity has many different attributes. It is about peoples' interpretations of and reactions to phenomenon that are drawn from deeply imbedded values and culturally constructed notions of reality. Researchers bent on finding "truth" must reconsider mythology, lore, and superstition as terms used to describe and denigrate indigenous beliefs. That is, a phenomenon that is not easily demystified and apprehended through measurement is often deemed to be imaginary.

In many Pacific cultures, spirituality and metaphysics are essential elements in an ecology that supports human well-being. Western social science does not have available methodologies capable of apprehending indigenous spirituality and other empirically elusive phenomenon. Authenticity is brought to bear through methods that are adapted to capturing the inherent qualities of spirituality and other phenomenon.

While objectivity may be viewed as critical in any research venture, maintaining personal distance impedes the comprehension of authentic culture. Even researchers who manifest excellent rapport and behavioral sensitivity must spend volunteer time with subjects of inquiry in order to observe a spectrum of behaviors. Behavior is situational and multidimensional. Immersion in a context provides researchers with an opportunity to understand the social interactions. Relying on multiple data sources enable researchers to coalesce empirical themes and draw whole and more complete impressions.

Appropriate Research Methods

The positivism that emerged during the modern era is gradually being replaced with heuristic paradigms promoting notions of data discovery and triangulation (Bolland & Atherton, 2000). This multimethod approach is well suited for securing rich descriptions of indigenous life conditions. Statistics drawn from multivariate analysis are useful in determining broad relational patterns between factors. Statistical results represent the tip of the phenomenon and should be placed amid other forms of empirical data as a way to cross-validate impressions.

Some researchers who subscribe to a multimethod research approach use survey results as the central force that drives the acquisition and interpretation of qualitative data. This is problematic if measures are unreliable across cultures, data processing is prone to systematic error, samples are unrepresentative of indigenous populations, and so on. Methods used in data gathering should not be staged as an incremental process with one method taking precedence over another. Rather, they should be "stand alone" activities contributing to a broad, multidimensional dataset that is triangulated or woven together into mosaic-like community profiles. After all, communities are nested, layered, and multidimensional systems, and single data source profiling is reductionistic.

Other than the typical quantitative survey and qualitative key informant methods, there are highly viable research methods used with indigenous communities (Turner, Beeghley, & Powers, 2002). One of which is Geographic Information Systems (GIS) mapping that we have used to chart behavioral patterns related to traditional and customary practices, subsistence patterns and resource areas, sacred sites, and population changes (Minerbi, McGregor, & Matsuoka, 2003). In other studies, GIS has been used to demarcate land ownership boundaries and jurisdictions, zone designations, service locations, and catchment areas. Data acquired in this manner is transformed into GIS maps and used to assist social planners and decision makers in determining the location and extent of cultural impacts related to proposed development projects. The technique resonates with indigenous informants because it is used to collect data that is "place based."

A major challenge in indigenous research is settling on a time frame that satisfies the expectations of funders/contractors and addresses community issues related to the time-consuming process of building trust and rapport (Morrow, 1994). Researchers must find a pace that moves the study process forward to meet contractual agreements and is sensitive to participant involvement. For indigenous participants not used to being subjects of scientific inquiry, it may require more time and persuading to garner a sample large enough to validate results. Westernized cohorts who understand the utility and power of empirical data are generally less resistant, and thus time requirements are easier to meet. Although research plans are posed at the outset of a study, it is critical to maintain a degree of flexibility. If a methodological approach is not resonating well with participants, then alternatives must be considered. In some cases, even pretesting instruments do not always provide investigators with enough predictive information regarding their applicability.

On multiple occasions, everyone has been a part of a larger communal research process that involved civic and indigenous leaders, heads of government agencies, and business leaders from the geographic areas of interest. The study or task group served to develop a conceptual framework, reviewed questionnaires for language and content, publicized the study, organized community involvement, assisted in interpreting study results, and helped develop an empirically based action plan. From beginning to end indigenous leadership was enmeshed in the research process. The depth of their involvement encouraged communities to assume ownership of the data and to realize the significance of research in terms of policy development and social planning.

The joint involvement of multiple stakeholders ensures objectivity and a government-facilitated planning and action process. Constituents sitting at the table create a context for multiperspectivism, mutuality, and buy-in, and ultimately, the validation of indigenous issues and practices.

EMERGENT METHODOLOGIES: TRANSFORMING COMMUNITIES

The transformation of communities, and particularly the people of indigenous communities, to achieve a stronger alignment with their own culture, beliefs, and values, is a formidable challenge. Of Smith's (1999) 25 identified projects to advance this transformation, six are mentioned in this chapter as central to the theme of generating knowledge and research to improve the well-being and health of special populations.

Claiming and Reclaiming

Guided by tribunals and international courts, indigenous people are called on to conduct systematic research resulting in the documentation of national, tribal, and familial histories. The purpose of this line of research is to establish the legitimacy of claims to land, resources, identity, language, and culture.

Storytelling and Testimonies

Scholarly work must capture the essence and identity of cultures that have depended on oral histories and life experience as the basis for the transformation and transfer of knowledge across generations. Testimonies provide the basis for claims by articulating the truth. Testimonies are also the process and means by which a person is afforded protection and space for expression.

Storytelling is a process for gaining the perspectives of native people, particularly the elders and women whose voices were silenced in the colonizing process. For many indigenous writers, storytelling is the means of passing down belief and values of a culture with the expectation that future generations will find meaning and a sense of place and identity. The storyteller is able to connect the past with the future. Storytelling is also a fundamental process of facilitating dialogue and conversations among indigenous people as people of the culture and the land. As suggested, research on storytelling indicates that it is a culturally appropriate tool "of representing the 'diversities of truth' within which the story teller rather than the researcher maintains control" (Bishop, 1996, p. 24). Storytelling is a process through which "the indigenous community becomes a story that is a collection of individual stories ever unfolding through the lives of the people who share the life of that community" (Bishop, 1996, p. 169).

Celebrating Survival

Scientific inquiry into indigenous communities has emphasized the demise and cultural assimilation of the people. Often these individuals' life experiences have been characterized as fragile in the wake of the historical trauma that resulted from the colonizing process. This trauma includes aspects of genocide, lost of identity, culture. language, and land. Survival is key process of indigenous nations, characterized by "the degree to which indigenous peoples have retained cultural and spiritual values and authenticity" (Smith, 1999, p. 145). Celebration may take the form of dancing, music, athletic events, a collective experience intended to create a sense of life of shared history, meaning, and identity. Critical to this process is the contemporary concept of resilience. This requires indigenous people, both as individuals and collectively, to acknowledge their strengths, capabilities, and commitment to the preservation and meaning of their history and past.

Intervening

Under the rubric of action research, intervening is a process of becoming involved and proactive in an effort to improve on current conditions, rectifying wrongs, and shaping policies and conditions for the benefit of indigenous people. Of greatest importance, intervening is characterized as a community process that invites an intervening process into the community and sets the parameters for the intervention. Intervening from this perspective is directed at changing institutions, policies, programs, educational experiences, and training of staff. This program is not about changing indigenous people, but rather the transformation institutions that serve the people.

Revitalizing

Crisis-oriented and problem-focused professions and related programs set their parameters and targets directed at the immediate issues that lead to resolution, reconciliation, and improved well-being. Revitalizing focuses on a crisis of loss, if not diminished, existence of culture and elements of culture that are vital to survival of special populations who have historically embraced these elements. Revitalizing calls for the expanded worldview of professionals and their approach to special populations. It also requires them to be inclusive of cultural preservation and revitalization as critical elements to the well being and development of special populations. Language and its revitalization have been, and will continue to be, critical elements in the preservation of many special populations. Strategies to support or cultivate policies directed at language revival, of promoting exchanges among native speakers, and promoting the publication of information in native languages are critical part of the revitalization process.

Discovering

This is a process of central importance to both Western and indigenous populations. Science has been an integral part of indigenous ways of knowing. Western science, however, has been neither sensitive to nor respectful of indigenous ways of knowing. The knowledge base of indigenous people, an untapped and underdeveloped resource of scientific information, has been relegated to being inconsequential and thus an antithesis to the advancement of knowledge particularly in the social, behavioral, biological, and medical sciences. Yet, discovering remains a priority in both worlds. The bridging concepts of ethno-science is among many ideas that can serve to foster the advancement of knowledge to better serve these special populations.

Sharing

The dissemination of knowledge among special populations about knowledge gained from and with special populations is vital to the continuous improvement in the well being of the people being served. Professional disciplines have emphasized the dissemination of knowledge among professionals and specialized audiences, thus leaving the populations being served outside of the loop of information sharing. The current emphasis on community-based research, the invitation of scientists to communities as a basic right of entrance will shape the future of research on special populations, but the preparation of professions to involve the community, before, during, and after the conduct of inquiries, must be given a higher priority in the training process. Dissemination, in the indigenous community, is more than the transmission of knowledge gained. It is also a process of "demystifying knowledge and information" and the presentation in plain terms. "Oral presentations must confirm to community protocols and expectations" (Smith, 1999, p. 161).

CONCLUSION

For indigenous populations, also classified as special populations, the future is today. The metaphor of a dormant volcano coming to life is appropriate for it depicts the once silent voices of colonized people throughout the Pacific, in the continental United States inclusive of Alaska, seething, seeking an outlet and expression, and claiming what was once theirs. The Western stereotypes and analytical categories we have come to depend on to characterize and explain the behavior of immigrant and indigenous people are being challenged; the theories used to guide our predictions, explanations, and interventions are being confronted and questioned, and the tried-and-true research methodologies are being reframed in the context of culture, beliefs, respect, and values.

This chapter has been about groups of special people whose eligibility was shaped by a history of immigration and colonization and exploitation that marginalized and nearly destroyed a community of people enriched by a past, language, traditions, values, beliefs, and expectations and that has come to life with a vengeance. But their demands are reasonable and serve as reference points, as a GIS if you will, to guide the profession of social work in its search for true and deep understanding of immigrant and indigenous people, to shape relevant theories and propositions, and to conduct research based on protocol and respect for cultures that expect to be partners in the scientific process. In this sea of change, the profession has aligned itself with best practices and has given new meaning to being culturally competent. The chapter highlights and introduces the elements of an indigenous strategy for understanding, explaining, predicting, and studying special populations in a culturally sensitive and respectful manner. While provocative in its confrontation of current practices, the indigenous strategy is inviting and calling for the profession to engage the population in its own quest for understanding and to search for ways to improve on its spiritual, social, emotional, and economic well-being.

REFERENCES

Benham, K. P. M., & Heck, R. H. (1998). *Culture and educational policy in Hawaii: Silencing of native voices*. Hillsdale, NJ: Erlbaum.

Bishop, R. (1996). *Collaborative research stories: Whatawhanaungatanga*, Palmerton North, New Zealand: Dunmore Press.

Bolland, K., & Atherton, C. (2000). Heuristics versus logical positivism: Solving the wrong problem. *Families in Society*, *83*(1), 7–13.

Denzin, N. K., & Lincoln, Y. S. (Eds.). (1998). *The landscape of qualitative research: Theories and issues*. Thousand Oaks, CA: Sage.

Freire, P. (2002). *Pedagogy of the oppressed*. New York: Continuum.

Kahakalau, K. (2004). Indigenous heuristic action research: Bridging western and indigenous research methodologies. *Hulili: Multidisplinary Research on Hawaiian Well-Being*, *1*(1), 19–33.

Kamehameha Schools/Bishop Estate (1983). *Native Hawaiian Educational Assessment*, Honolulu, Hawaii: Kamehameha Press.

Kim, U., & Berry, J. W. (1993). *Indigenous paychologies: Research and experience in cultural context*. Newbury Park, CA: Sage.

Minerbi, L., McGregor, D., & Matsuoka, J. (2003). Using geographic information systems for cultural impact assessment. In H. A. Becker & F. Vanclay (Eds.), *The international handbook of social impact assessment* (p. 16). Camberley, England: Elgar.

Morrow, R. A. (1994). *Foundations of metatheory: Between subjectivism and objectivism, critical theory and methodology*. Thousand Oaks, CA: Sage.

Smith, L. T. (1999). *Decolonizing methodologies*. London: Zed Books.

Stannard, D. (1992) *American holocaust*, London: Oxford University Press.

Touraine, A. (2001). *Beyond neoliberalism*. Cambridge, England: Polity Press.

Turner, J. H., Beeghley, L., & Powers, C. H. (2002). *The early masters and the prospects for scientific theory: The emergence of sociological theory* (5th ed.). Belmont, CA: Wadsworth.

Chapter 18

DIVERSITY

Iris B. Carlton-LaNey

The social work profession is an extremely diverse profession that has worked to embrace diversity throughout its existence. This has not always been an easy task and social workers, like other Americans, have sometimes struggled to be responsive and celebratory toward diversity. The social work profession, like society in general, faces discrimination in the form of sexism, racism, ageism, ableism, heterosexism, and ethnocentrism. In an effort to counter these societal ills, the social work profession has embraced diversity and culturally competent practice. Diversity of populations served, diversity of skills and knowledge, and diversity of services and programs provided characterize the mission of the social work profession.

Diversity has become essential to the social work profession's fundamental mission, which is to serve people in need and simultaneously to make social institutions more responsive to people and their problems (Bent-Goodley & Fowler, 2006; Morales, Sheafor, & Scott, 2007). Social workers view diversity favorably and acknowledge the variation within the profession as an enriching quality. Essentially, the diversity within the profession enables social workers to respond more adequately to human needs that exist within a fluid and dynamic world. Several definitions of diversity have been presented throughout social work literature. *The Social Work Dictionary* (Barker, 2003, p. 126) defines diversity as:

> Variety, or the opposite of homogeneity. In social organizations the term usually refers to the range of personnel who more accurately represent minority populations and people from varied backgrounds, cultures, ethnicities, and viewpoints. Environmentalists use term to indicate a variety of plant and animal forms in the area rather than a system in which only one or few species exist.

Lum (2003, p. 36) says that diversity focuses on the differences that make a person distinct and unique from another person. It offers an opportunity for a person to name those distinctions and invites another person to discover those particular qualities about that particular individual. It is an inclusive term that encompasses groups distinguished by race, ethnicity, culture, class, gender, sexual orientation, religion, physical or mental ability, age, and national origin.

Others, like William W. Chace (1989), laced their definitions with admonitions for the reader to act in a socially just way in order to embrace differences:

> Generally understood and embraced, is not casual liberal tolerance of anything and everything not yourself. It is not polite accommodation. Instead, diversity is, the action, the sometimes painful awareness that other people, other races, other voices, other habits of mind, have as much integrity of being, as much claim upon the world, as you do. No one has an obligation greater than your own to change, or yield, or to

> assimilate into the mass. The irreconcilable is as much a part of social life as the congenial. Being strong in life is being strong amid difference while accepting the fact that your own self can be a considerable imposition upon everyone you meet. I urge you to consider your own oddity before you are troubled or offended by that of others. And I urge you amid all the differences present to the eye and mind to reach out and create the bonds that will sustain the common wealth that will protect us all. We are meant to be together. (Berg-Weger, 2005, p. 112)

As noted by these various definitions, diversity in fields of practice, diversity of clientele, diversity in knowledge and skills, diversity of services, and diversity in social and political policy perspectives characterize social work. Clearly, the social work profession has a long history of involvement with issues of human diversity, albeit not always adequate or effective. Some would argue that the United States' and social work's "ambivalence to human diversity has been greater than its acceptance" (Burwell, 1998, p. 388). Likewise, others acknowledge that social work's concern with persons of various racial, cultural, and ethnic identification tends to "ebb and flow" (Leigh, 1998, p. 3).

The nineteenth edition of the *Encyclopedia of Social Work* published in 1995 highlights the existence of a global view that has had a concomitant effect on sensitivity to and appreciation for diversity (Edwards, 1995). The interconnectedness of a global village has resulted from many factors, including an increase in mobility of the world's citizens along with an easy, rapid flow of information and ideas.

As the United States is becoming a more racially diverse country, it is simultaneously aging. The United States recently celebrated reaching a population milestone of 300 million. By the year 2050, more than 392 million people are expected to inhabit the United States, with 206 million Whites, 88 million Latinos, 56 million African Americans, 38 million Asians, and 3.7 million American Indians (Ozawa, 1997).

When data like these are presented, it is important for social workers to remember what Schriver (2001) calls "diversity within diversity" or recognizing that there are numerous diverse groups with diverse qualities within each group. First Nations People typify this concept of "diversity within diversity." The United States is home to over 500 distinct Native American nations. Many of these nations are very small, with fewer than 100 enrollees, while others like the Cherokee and Lakota/Dakota/Nakota have over 100,000 members (Weaver, 2003). Size is only one of many variables that contribute to the diversity among American Indians.

The Lumbee Indians of North Carolina "challenge almost every perception of what Indians should be" (Bordewich, 1996, p. 63). The Lumbee Indians range in appearance from nearly African to blond hair and blue eyes. They do not have reserved lands, U.S. treaties, or medicine men. They are English-speaking, Baptists who have "an unflagging conviction that they are simply and utterly Indian" (Bordewich, 1996, p. 63). They have state recognition but have for over 100 years sought, but failed to receive full federal recognition.

Other groups that typify "diversity within diversity" are the disabled. Scholars who engage in research with this population find themselves studying a diverse group of people and an equally diverse set of problems or issues ranging from long-term care for or de-institutionalization of people with disabilities (Parish, 2005; Parish & Lutwick, 2005), to financial well-being of young children with disabilities and their families (Parish & Cloud, 2006), to health disparities for women (Parish & Huh, 2006).

Table 18.1 Rural Elderly African American Caregiver Paradigm

Personal Resources	Informal/Communal Resources	Formal/Professional Resources
Self	Church (elders, stewards, deacons, church mothers, choir members)	Social workers
Nuclear family	Church auxiliaries (Pastors' aid committees, sick and shut-in ministries)	Physicians
Fictive kin	Secret orders (Masons and Eastern Star, Daughters of Zion)	Health-care providers
Extended family	Natural/faith healers	Agricultural and home extension agents
Friends	General stores (feed stores, seed stores, rural diners)	Social welfare services
Neighbors	Home demonstration clubs	Nursing homes

Source: "Rural African American Caregiving" (pp. 381–389), by I. Carlton-LaNey, in *Handbook of Social Work in Health and Aging,* B. Berkman (Ed.), 2006, New York: Oxford University Press.

Further, diversity within all groups is anticipated as the population ages. The number of elders is expected to increase from 12.8% in 1995 to 20.7% in 2040. These elders will be more mobile than their predecessors and will relocate to new communities for various lifestyle opportunities. Social workers must understand that working with older people adds a special challenge to the diversity mix. They must understand family, local and community history, formal and informal resources, and the help-seeking patterns within each particular group. For example, Table 18.1 illustrates a helping-seeking paradigm that rural African Americans and/or their caregivers might utilize. The elderly face a range of problems and issues and their responses vary depending on available resources. Social workers must be knowledgeable and respectful of the history and methods of problem solving to which elders adhere.

The following vignette illustrates the type of issues that arise and the various problems to which social workers should respond with sensitivity, skill, and compassion as they work with these individuals. Since the population of elders is diverse, social workers must be diverse in their approaches. Advocacy for elders must be neither color- nor gender-blind. Instead, the unique lifestyles of various ethnic and racial groups require that their specific needs be acknowledged and served (Carlton-LaNey, 1997).

When Aunt Cullie Started to Wander

It was about 1:00 in the morning. It was late fall and starting to get cool outside. Mama and Daddy were asleep when someone knocked on the back door. People don't stop by this time of morning unless something real bad has happened. Giving each other that "wonder-who-that-could-be look," Mama and Daddy both got up together to answer the door.

(*continued*)

It was Aunt Cullie. She had a still, blank look in her eyes and she was trying to find her daughter Bonita. But Bonita no longer lived in our neighborhood. She had been living in New York for over 35 years. Aunt Cullie said that she heard Bonita call for her, and she believed that her daughter was there.

It was a scary time because we knew that Aunt Cullie was changing. When Mama called Aunt Cullie's husband, Uncle Bryant, to tell him that she was up at our house, he was alarmed and surprised because he hadn't heard her leave their house. He came up to get her to take her back home. He said that he had seen some changes in her lately, but he knew this wandering was very dangerous. He paused, shaking his head and looking downward, as if searching to find some answers in the cold faded linoleum on the kitchen floor.

That next week, Aunt Cullie made another early morning visit to her niece's house further up the road. Aunt Cullie was still looking for her only child Bonita.

Uncle Bryant telephoned Bonita.

About a month later, Bonita came home from New York and moved Aunt Cullie away. The following summer Bonita brought Aunt Cullie home for a visit. We all walked down the road to see her. She looked good; her skin was beautiful and flawless. She seemed more like her old self, but we were told that her mind would come and go. That was the last time we saw our aunt.

We knew that Aunt Cullie was leaving our neighborhood for good, but that reality was too burdensome, so we smiled any way and waved good-bye as we watched Bonita's station wagon head up the road taking Aunt Cullie to live out her days far away in New York (Carlton-LaNey, 2005, pp. 37–38).

As this vignette shows, many elderly have aged in place—staying in the same living situation for years as their personal competence has declined (Hooyman & Kiyak, 2005). They, in many instances, lack the resources of their counterparts who have been more mobile throughout their lives. Many of these individuals have few advocates since their children and often their siblings have long since migrated to urban centers seeking better opportunities.

We also note an increase in the elderly who relocate to the U.S. Sunbelt. Other states like North Carolina and Florida have also seen net gains in migrants over the years. As the elderly move to new communities for various amenities, they bring resources that are welcomed into the local economy. In North Carolina, those same resources create local housing booms, for example, that obstruct the mountain vista in the western part of the state or contribute to the coastal erosion and compromise of the delicate ecosystem in the east. Unfortunately, this increase in diversity adds to public expressions of ageism and other prejudices that contribute to discrimination.

Housing and independent living arrangements are critical issues for elders and their families. The vignette illustrates the circumstances that rural elders experience that, in turn, create crises for their families and communities. It is not uncommon for family members to provide informal care in such situations. Called assistance migrants, family members who have moved away but are forced to return to their place of birth to care for the ailing older relative find their lives altered. Or, as this case illustrates, the elder is relocated to the caregiver's home—removing him or her from familiar living arrangements and altering life for an entire family. This demands change from all involved and may lead to caregiver strain that sometimes causes resentment and bitterness among family members.

Essentially, the diversity that characterizes the United States has also created tensions. Opposing values, beliefs, and practices have vigorously interacted causing differential treatment and unequal access to resources. While the democratic principles that support equality for all people existed in theory and law, these principles paled when sociopolitical and economic competition and the whims of powerful people prevailed. Pinderhughes (1989) summarized the results cogently when she said, "Forces pressing for equality and for discrimination, for rights and privileges for all and for men only, for democracy and for slavery have interacted dynamically with the superior resources and power of the most influential—middle-class White Anglo-Saxon protestants—often determining the outcome" (p. 2). Essentially, a perspective that views the center of power and superiority as being among "White, males, middle-class, heterosexual, able-bodied, mentally healthy, church-going Christians" (Anderson & Carter, 2003, p. 13) marginalizes all others.

Those individuals who embraced the values, behaviors, and customs of the most influential group were rewarded. Others who refused or were unable to acquiesce have felt the raft of an unforgiving social system. The societal pressures to protect the status quo, to maintain an ordered society and to promote an environment of sameness remained firmly intact well into the 1960s.

DIVERSITY AND SOCIAL WORK PATERNALISM

Prior to the 1960s consciousness-raising, social justice meant a color-blind response to societal ills. Pinderhughes (1989) notes that the human service needs and problems along with targeted solutions were identified and promulgated by the White middle class. "The definition of problems, that is, what is pathological and deviant, the theoretical constructs that determine assessment and intervention methods, the strategies devised, the programming of services, and even the evaluation of outcomes had been developed in terms of what seemed appropriate for the White American middle class" (p. 3). These attitudes maintained and propagated a guiding ethic of paternalism. Social work's propensity toward paternalism has also helped to focus the profession on the imperative of diversity.

Embracing paternalism posed a problem that has taken the profession some time to overcome. As the profession emerged, the roots of paternalism served as the guiding principle for actions and sometimes inaction. Simon (1994) describes paternalism as a system of relations in which those in authority act on behalf of other people without their permission to do so, while maintaining a belief that their action was in the best interest of the person in need regardless of that person's belief and wishes. The social work profession's history is replete with examples of such paternalism. Progressive Era responses to poverty and need included many organizations that adhered to expressions of paternalism. For example, the Charity Organization Society (COS), the settlement house movement, the National League on Urban Conditions among Negroes (renamed the National Urban League; NUL), and the National Association of Colored Women's Clubs (NACW) illustrate this point.

COS pioneers like Josephine Shaw Lowell and Mary Richmond targeted individual shortcomings and moral weaknesses in their casework practice. The avoidance of duplication of services was paramount and changing individual behavior was entrenched in the

COS movement's work. The COS embraced several fundamental ideas including interagency cooperation, individualization, adequacy of relief, preventative philanthropy, and personal service (Axinn & Stern, 2005), all of which were couched in paternalism. The White middle-class women who dominated the COS visited low-income neighborhoods to share their advice and wisdom on living wholesome lives (Berg-Weger, 2005). They role modeled the wholesome living they espoused and liberally reprimanded women, and sometimes men, who strayed from their admonitions.

Settlement house leaders also embraced the notion of paternalism, albeit to a lesser extent. Less prone to directly reproach individuals for "inappropriate conduct," the settlement house leaders encouraged, cajoled, and massaged newcomers, both immigrants and migrants, to convince them of the merits of assimilation and acceptable public conduct. To become true Americans, immigrants were expected and often encouraged to give up old-country ways, change their names and time-honored customs, and learn to speak flawless English. Settlement houses provided classes and clubs such as English-speaking classes to facilitate this "Americanizing." Simon (1994) noted that some paternalism crept into the various clubs and programs of the settlement houses as leaders held themselves up as role models and stalwarts of the American dream. While settlement house leaders touted the notion that residing in communities demonstrated the idea that dependency of the classes on each other was reciprocal, their methods of direct practice reflected paternalism and role modeling for assimilation and protection of the middle and upper classes (Berg-Weger, 2005; Carlton-LaNey & Andrews, 1998).

National Urban League leaders viewed their work as a way to integrate African Americans into the mainstream of American life through social services and social programs. The NUL, founded in 1911, had become synonymous with social work in the African American community by 1916. The organization's goals included (a) demonstrating the advantages of cooperation to social welfare agencies, (b) securing and training social workers, (c) protecting women and children from deceitful persons, (d) fitting workers for/to work, (e) helping to secure boys' and girls' clubs and neighborhood unions, (f) working with delinquents, (g) maintaining a country home for convalescent women, and (h) investigating conditions of city life as a basis for practical work (Carlton-LaNey, 1996b; Parris & Brooks, 1971; Weiss, 1974).

Urban Leaguers, like Forrester B. Washington, for example, were described as "paternalistic" in their roles. Washington believed that African Americans who migrated to the city were "very vulnerable to bad influences because they were without the retaining influences of their families, friends, and those who knew them" (Barrow, 2001, p. 132). With this, Washington set out to shape the behaviors and attitudes of the new migrants so they could be acceptable to Whites and to the better classes of African American people. He printed and distributed guidance cards, called "Helpful Hints" cards that contained directives on acceptable behavior and dress (Barrow, 2001).

The NUL's methods, however, were not universally accepted as the best way to serve the African American community. A. Phillip Randolph and Chandler Owens used their socialist magazine, *The Messenger*, to criticize the NUL's work calling it an organization of, for, and by capital (Reisch & Andrews, 2002). They condemned the NUL and other social work organizations, noting that they were "stifling" the promising young college men and women who work for the organization, while "thwarting [sic] their energies and sapping their judgment" (Invisible Government of Negro Social Work, 1920, p. 176).

The National Association of Colored Women's (NACW) clubs' motto of "Lifting as We Climb" reflects the clubwomen's bond with their lower class sisters. It also reflected their elitist paternalism. The movement began in response to growing unmet social welfare needs in the African American communities, to the increased racial tension of the late nineteenth century, and to the need to build a social reform movement with African American women's leadership (Salem, 1993). The emphases on self-help and racial solidarity were prominent in the movement. In their zeal to make African American womanhood respectable, capable, and morally correct, the clubwomen did not hesitate to represent and speak for their lower class sisters. In fact, a sense of class superiority and privilege permeated the club movement. In their efforts to teach social and cultural improvement and moral uplift, they also tried to teach African American women how to make their "homes bulwarks in the defense of black womanhood" (White, 1999, p. 69). Published guides of conduct included books like Charlotte Hawkins Brown's *The Correct Thing: To Do, To Say, To Wear* (1941). Essentially, the clubwomen's constant stream of advice ran the gamut from Brown's all encompassing book to an array of specific admonitions such as "stop sitting on stoops and talking and laughing loudly in public," to choosing their husbands more carefully all served to make clear the clubwomen's "feeling that the masses of black women did not measure up to middle-class standards" (White, 1999, p. 71).

This brief historical review of pioneering social welfare organizations demonstrates that social work began as a profession dominated by Whites and Protestants, laced with the values that they espoused. It is critical to also note that Jews, Catholics, and African Americans, regardless of religious orientation, have a rich and respected history of social welfare service delivery for the poor and needy. Further, their efforts have also been essential to the development of the profession and its acknowledgment of the vital need to embrace diversity. Moreover, diversity among social work pioneers and their approaches to problem solving have helped to augment the diversity that characterizes the profession.

DIVERSITY AND SOCIAL WORK PIONEERS

Social work pioneers have included well-known White pioneers, such as Paul Kellogg, Jane Addams, and Grace and Edith Abbott. George Edmund Haynes, Eugene Kinkle Jones, Edna Jane Hunter, Ida Bell Wells-Barnett, and Janie Porter Barrett can be counted among prominent African American pioneers. These individuals' works included pioneering social work education and training, establishing housing for young, single African American men and women moving to cities and establishing organizations like the NUL to serve African Americans moving from the agrarian South to cities in the North, South, and Midwest. Social settlements like Hull House and the Locust Street Settlement helped immigrants in large cities and migrants from small towns, respectively. Each of these agencies, organizations, services, and programs was designed to serve a diverse population of individuals with diverse needs and diverse circumstances (Carlton-LaNey, 1999, 2001).

These individuals' diversity of race, gender, age, sexual orientation, class, and so on is an enriching quality that has helped to create a dynamic profession capable of responding to human needs in a vibrant, changing society. While discrimination and exclusion certainly existed within the profession, reflecting societal norms, social workers have continuously acknowledged the need to serve diverse clients with diverse needs in diverse settings.

Settlement house pioneer Lillian Wald, for example, wanted to provide health care to needy women and children in their homes and communities. Through the Henry Street Settlement, as well as through her involvement with the Lincoln House Settlement, which served African Americans, Wald helped to train visiting nurses, visiting teachers, and social workers to respond to community needs with respect and acceptance. While this was a time of strict segregation, Wald nonetheless identified ways to function within the accepted norms of the day and to simultaneously engage in policy practice. On one occasion, both African Americans and Whites were to gather at the Henry Street Settlement for a meeting. Racial etiquette presented a dilemma as to how to serve dinner to a mixed-race group. The solution was to forgo a sit-down meal and instead to serve a buffet, which would allow the races to "mix" while standing, a much more socially acceptable practice.

Intimately involved with a network of female pioneers throughout her career, Wald was among the group of women who advocated for gender equity within Progressive Era parameters. Part of these women's advocacy was to promote Frances Perkins' appointment as the Secretary of Labor under the Roosevelt administration. Perkins' appointment was a political "hot potato" since no woman had ever held a presidential Cabinet position. Even Perkins herself needed some persuading, which Wald and her brigade of lady leaders provided handily. Furthermore, Wald and other pioneers in social work adhered to the Cult of True Womanhood, which assigned women the roles of defenders of the moral order. This made it acceptable for them to work, whether as paid employees or volunteers, outside the home since their compassion, nurturance, and morality made them suitable to tackle societal uncleanness and immorality (Day, 1997). These social work pioneer women's goals included the importance of women practicing and modeling integrative roles for other women.

DIVERSITY AND CONTEMPORARY SOCIAL WORK ORGANIZATIONS

As the social work profession developed during the Progressive Era and beyond, its work toward embracing diversity continued. While the transition has not always been smooth and universally accepted, the National Association of Social Workers (NASW) and the Council on Social Work Education (CSWE) have both taken a stand supporting diversity, albeit not always with the desired fervor, rapidity, and zeal.

Today, the significance of diversity in social work is highlighted in the documents of both NASW and the CSWE—the largest individual member organization and the organization that shapes social work education curricula, respectively. NASW's 2006 to 2009 policy statements clearly demonstrate the profession's commitment to diversity and cultural competence. Policy statements supporting diversity include Affirmative Action; Civil Liberties and Justice; Cultural and Linguistic Competence in the Social Work Profession; Gender-, Ethnic-, and Race-Based Workplace Discrimination; Linguistic/Cultural Diversity in the United States; Racism, Transgender, and Gender Identity Issues; and Women's Issues. Several of these statements are summarized in Table 18.2.

The CSWE included a statement in its 2001 *Educational Policy Accreditation Standards* that mandates content on diversity in bachelor's and master's of social work programs. The impetus for this policy stems from a desire to produce students who are capable of practice

Table 18.2 NASW Policy Statements That Demonstrate a Commitment to Diversity

Affirmative Action—NASW is firmly committed to affirmative action and will vigorously pursue its development and implementation at all levels (organizational, local, state, and federal). Achieving an environment that values, respects, and reflects multicultural diversity will take deliberate and progressive action (p. 18).

Civil Liberties and Justice—NASW calls on the social work profession to reaffirm its long-standing commitment to individual liberties and social justice. NASW considers the protection of individual rights and the promotion of social justice essential to the preservation of our collective well-being as a society. Social workers and other policy makers are urged to focus on the areas of criminal justice reform, access to justice, first amendment rights, equal protection under the law, and the right to privacy/social services and civil rights (pp. 43–51).

Cultural and Linguistic Competence in the Social Work Profession—NASW promotes and supports the implementation of cultural and linguistic competence at three intersecting levels: individual, institutional, and societal. Relevant social policy should be developed at the local, state, and national levels. Collaboration with consumers, families, and cultural communities is a precondition for the creation of culturally and linguistically competent services, reasonable accommodations, interventions, programs, and policies. Practitioners and their host organizations must ensure that services are offered in the language preferred by the consumers and families receiving service (p. 81).

Gender, Ethnic, and Race-Based Workplace Discrimination—NASW supports a number of principles and strategies for change in legislative, administrative, and educational areas. NASW reaffirms its commitment to affirmative action in the public and private sectors (p. 176).

Racism—NASW supports an inclusive, multicultural society in which racial, ethnic, class, sexual orientation, age, physical and mental ability, religion and spirituality, gender and other cultural and social identities are valued and respected (p. 310).

Transgender and Gender Identity Issues—NASW asserts that discrimination and prejudice directed against any individuals are damaging to the social, emotional, physical, and economic well-being of the affected individuals, as well as society as a whole, and NASW seeks the elimination of the same both inside and outside the profession, in both the public and private sectors (p. 368).

Women's Issues—NASW is committed to advancing policies and practices to improve the status and well-being of all women. NASW believes that it is vital for social workers to develop a critical consciousness about gender or use a feminist policy analysis that enables the ramifications of gender to be made visible in every issue, in every policy and every practice, at all three levels—micro, meso, and macro (p. 390).

Source: Social Work Speaks: National Association of Social Workers Policy Statements 2006–2009, seventh edition, by National Association of Social Workers (2006). Washington, DC: National Association of Social Workers Press. Reprinted with permission.

within a diverse society. The accreditation standards (Standard 4.1) mandate that BSW and MSW social work programs have content that promote an understanding, affirmation, and respect for diversity along with the development of skills needed to define, design, and implement strategies for practice that embraces diversity (CSWE, 2001). These programs are encouraged to develop their curriculum to reflect the diversity in their regions. For example, a social work program in eastern North Carolina might reflect content about the Lumbee Indians—the largest tribe east of the Mississippi River. Because of the diversity within diversity, Lumbee Indians do not share the same history and response to oppression as their Plaines counterparts.

CSWE foundation curriculum content also required that social work programs address information on populations-at-risk (Standard 4.2) with an eye toward the development of strategies to redress these groups' exclusion and oppression. Mandated content on social and economic justice also require that social work programs prepare students to combat discrimination, oppression, and economic deprivation. The tremendous growth in the number of accredited social work programs indicate that an effort is being made to design curriculum that produce culturally competent social workers (CSWE, 2001) at both the BSW and MSW levels.

While the NASW *Code of Ethics* and the CSWE *Educational Policy Accreditation Standards* requirements are valuable instruments, the social work profession must also identify and present "diverse policy perspectives and explore the inequity within the social policy" if social and economic justice for a diverse society is genuinely desired (Davis & Bent-Goodley, 2004). Essentially, social workers must also actively engage in policy practice. Davis and Bent-Goodley's book *The Color of Social Policy* (2004), is a significant contribution that provides content for sound policy practice and social justice. In an effort to ground the concept of social justice in social work education, Davis (2004) provides the following cogent definition of social justice:

> Social justice is a basic value and desired goal in democratic societies and includes equable and fair access to all social institutions, laws, resources, opportunities, rights, goods, and services for all groups and individuals within arbitrary limitations or barriers based on observations or interpretations of the value of differences in age, color, culture, physical or mental ability, education, income language, national origin, race, religion, or sexual orientation. (p. 236)

According to Davis, when this definition of social justice is used as the "operating framework... in the curriculum," it means that social work education is "committed to building and implementing the curriculum... around this basic value" (p. 236). Davis notes that it also means "that a school's faculty is also committing themselves to action" aimed at the concrete achievement of social justice.

Davis' treatise has been met with some resistance. The contemporary political climate has postulated what he calls a "divisive and unproductive philosophical debate" regarding social justice and the government's role (p. 235). Some of this rejection has found its way into conversations among social work educators (Gerdes, Segal, & Ressler, 2003). While the CSWE standards are clear and the mandate generally accepted, there remains "little agreement within the social work literature regarding how and where to teach this content and the form that it should take" (Gutierrez, Fredricksen, & Soifer, 1999, p. 410). The extent to which faculty are comfortable with diversity content is critical and challenging (Nagda et al., 1999). Gutierrez and her colleagues argue that social work faculty must be both comfortable with the content and competent in teaching it for useful educational preparation to take place. They further caution that the content on diversity may be altogether excluded or covered inadequately if there is no genuine commitment to its inclusion. Noted feminist scholar Peggy McIntosh 1988 drew similar conclusions when she examined the inclusion of content on women's issues. She indicated that men were willing to admit that this content was important and worthy of inclusion in courses, yet were simultaneously unwilling to acknowledge their privilege. This would likely present a biased perspective if

Table 18.3 Four Principles for Curriculum Development

A multicultural perspective should be inclusive of all subcultural groups, viewed as distinct groups that are interdependent with mainstream U.S. culture.
A multicultural perspective should recognize that all people in the United States society identify with "multiple cultures," with varying degrees of affiliation and social involvement.
A multicultural perspective should recognize that all members of U.S. society engage in various types of relationships within their various cultures, and in relation to a mainstream U.S. culture. Biculturalism, acculturation, amalgamation, and assimilation, as forms of attachment and social relationships with these cultures, are proposed as options for members of U.S. society.
A multicultural perspective would recognize the changing nature of U.S. society, as it is continually influenced by all of its subcultures and by national demographic, social, and institutional trends.

Source: "Revisiting Multiculturalism in Social Work," by P. Fellin, 2000, *Journal of Social Work Education*, 36, 271–272.

the content is included at all. Essentially, opponents generally tout that there is no place to put additional content in an already overcrowded curriculum.

For content on diversity to be taught in social work education programs, junior faculty and members of oppressed groups must not be the only advocates for including the materials. Moreover, they should not be the only faculty called on to teach this content. Clearly, adhering to CSWE's standards presents a challenge for many social work educators. To rise to the challenge, it is necessary that social work faculty, especially those less inclined to be supportive of content on diversity, engage in greater honest dialogue about this issue (Fellin, 2000; Gutierrez et al., 1999).

Many scholars believe that multiculturalism is an overarching concept for the inclusion and study of content in social work education that deals with populations-at-risk and human diversity (Fellin, 2000). Understanding multiculturalism requires that you value and have knowledge of history. Group identity and ethnicity result from historical and social influences. Therefore, a knowledge and understanding of this history provides insights into a community's strengths (Gutierrez, 1997). Again, there is disagreement among social work scholars about the virtues of multiculturalism for achieving social justice and providing equal access to societal resources. It is critical that the dialogue on the merits of multiculturalism continue among social work educators. Fellin (2000) believes that multiculturalism provides a foundation for teaching about cultural groups in social work education. He has postulated four principles (Table 18.3) useful in human diversity curriculum development. Further, Fellin believes that to achieve multiculturalism in social work education, this organizing concept should guide the selection and generation of knowledge and information about diverse groups in the United States.

DIVERSITY AND THEORETICAL FRAMEWORKS

In addition to a historical perspective, it is also important to consider diversity and work with different groups from a theoretical perspective. Several theories have been set forth regarding work with diverse populations. Theoretical frameworks that enhance social workers' understanding and intervention with consumers include the ecological perspective, the strengths perspective, and the Afrocentric perspective. (See also Chapter 19, this volume.)

The ecological perspective views the client system within the context of the environment in which the client lives. The environment includes family, work, religion, culture, and life events. The social worker must consider every aspect of the client's life in the practice relationship. The ecological perspective also notes that the client's past and present life experiences have influenced his or her beliefs, behaviors, interactions, and emotions. With an emphasis on the environment, the ecological perspective dictates that the social worker maintain an awareness of the influence that cultural factors including race, place of origin, ethnicity, age, social class, religion, gender, and sexual orientation have on the client. Historical, political, and societal issues must also be taken into account in order to understand the client system and environment (Germain & Gitterman, 1995). If, for example, the client has experienced a history of racial oppression, it might help to explain the client's reluctance to develop an effective relationship with a worker who is from the majority group (Berg-Weger, 2005). Similarly, elderly individuals who have experienced an indifferent health-care provider may be reluctant to continue to seek health care when needed. Likewise, First Nations people who have experienced the removal and placement of their children outside their tribe/nation may fail to report suspected child abuse or neglect. Levy (1995) believes that the ecological perspective, with its focus on the "goodness of fit" between a person and his or her environment, also shares a close alignment with the feminist principle that the "personal is political" (p. 289).

The strength perspective is deemed important for working with diverse groups. The strength perspective has been presented as a central, fundamental part all social work practice with diverse populations. The strength perspective requires incorporating the consumers' culture into the social work strategy as a strength that is consistent with the social work value that touts respect for individual uniqueness. The strength perspective also focuses on solutions instead of problems and relies on strengths as the central organizing principles for practice (Saleebey, 1997). The strengths perspective requires that the social worker build relationship around the experience and life of the client system. In so doing, the social worker demonstrates an understanding of, and respect for, the client's culture, lifestyle, and right to self-determination.

The strengths perspective requires that social workers understand how a history of oppression has influenced the survival and adaptive resources of many groups in America. The source of these strengths include family and community structures that develop self-esteem and a network of psychosocial and economic resources, survival determination and skills and personal transformation qualities resulting from overcoming self-depreciating forces (Anderson & Carter, 2003; Billingsley, 1992; Chestang, 1982; Hopps, Pinderhughes, & Shankar, 1995).

The strength perspective embraces empowerment principles (Solomon, 1976) that say that people have a right to engage in actions that define their existence. Levy argues that the strengths perspective "reinforce[s] feminist practice principles of renaming, valuing process, and empowerment" (p. 290). In discussing practice implications for gay and lesbian elderly, Levy cites examples that note the multiple losses that this group incurs. The loss of life partners and friends often go unnoticed because of societal secrecy regarding sexual orientation. These people are often hospitalized or placed on long-term care facilities when their sexual orientation is ignored and their relationships disrespected. Even when living wills and health-care powers of attorney have been put into place, the urgency of the medical crises may render the documents meaningless. Ageism in the gay and lesbian community, and in society at large, can lower self-esteem and create a sense of powerlessness.

Social workers learn how to be more effective practitioners when they openly and honestly embrace the strength perspective, which creates a client-worker partnership. Principles in the strength perspective (see Table 18.4) guide social workers to truly embrace the client's belief system, coping patterns, and behavioral styles (Lum, 2003).

The Afrocentric paradigm has been presented as an alternative way to engage in social work practice, acknowledging and underscoring the connection between African Americans and traditional Africa. It is believed that African Americans' enslavement and subsequent racial segregation, along with a desire to maintain tradition, have helped to preserve African philosophies and traditions among members of this group (Franklin, 1980; Harvey, 2001; Martin & Martin, 1985).

Schiele (1996) provides three objectives of the Afrocentric paradigm: (1) promote an alternative social science paradigm more reflective of the cultural and political reality of African Americans; (2) dispel the negative distortions of people of African ancestry by legitimizing and disseminating a worldview that goes back thousands of years and that exists in the hearts and minds of many people of African decent today; and (3) promote a worldview that will facilitate human and societal transformation toward spiritual, moral and humanistic ends and will persuade people of different cultural and ethnic groups that they share a mutual interest in this regard (p. 286). Essentially, Schiele contends, theorists who embrace the Afrocentric paradigm do not believe in "social science universalism—that one theory or paradigm can be used to explain social phenomena among all people in all cultures" (p. 285).

Covin's (1990) five measures of the Afrocentric paradigm are outlined in Table 18.5.

Swigonski (1996) says that Afrocentric theory "shows how developing knowledge of another culture from the perspective of that culture can transform social work practice" (p. 156). Harvey and Coleman (1997) provide guidelines for an Afrocentric approach to service delivery for youth and their families who are in the juvenile justice system. They

Table 18.4 Strengths Perspective Principles

1. Client knowledge and experience are valued.
2. Client gifts and talents are emphasized.
3. Learned hopefulness is promoted.
4. The practitioner recognizes that people are more successful when moving toward something than when moving away from something.
5. The practitioner avoids labels and the victimizing effects of labels, and uses concepts such as resilience rather than at-risk.
6. Positive expectations are integral to the relationship.
7. In the client-worker relationship, the qualities of openness, clarity of expectations, genuineness, and supportiveness are emphasized.
8. Change in one area reverberates in other areas of life.

Source: Culturally competent practice a framework for understanding diverse groups and justice issues, (p. 173), D. Lum (Ed.), 2003, Pacific Grove, CA: Brooks/Cole-Thomson Learning.

Table 18.5 Measures of the Afrocentric Paradigm

1. People of African descent share a common experience, struggle, and origin.
2. Present in African culture is a nonmaterial element of resistance to the assault on traditional values caused by the intrusion of European legal procedures, medicines, political processes, and religions into African culture.
3. African culture takes the view that an Afrocentric modernization process would be based on three traditional values: harmony with nature, humanness, and rhythm.
4. Afrocentricity involves the development of a theory of an African way of knowing and interpreting the world.
5. Some form of communalism or socialism is an important component for the way wealth is produced, owned, and distributed.

Source: "Afrocentricity in O Movimento Negro Unificade," by D. Covin, 1990, *Journal of Black Studies*, 21, 126–145.

claim that, while no one approach is the answer, the Afrocentric approach is "a vehicle for helping to reestablish a sense of self-dignity self-worth, spirituality, and community among this youth population" (p. 210). Chipungu, Everett, and Leashore (1991) in their book, *Child Welfare: An Afrocentric Perspective*, provide guidelines for incorporating the Afrocentric perspective into the assessment, planning, and delivery of services to African American children and their families. They initially use the Afrocentric perspective to frame the cultural and sociohistorical context of African Americans while describing the values and worldviews of African. Chipungu and her colleague's work can be reflected in recent practice approaches in child welfare, such as family group conferencing, in which family culture and cultural responsiveness are critical for best practice with abused or neglected children. In family group conferencing, family members are the cultural amplifiers and cultural guides for the child welfare professionals involved with the at-risk child(ren) (Waites, Macgowan, Pennell, Carlton-LaNey, & Weil, 2004).

Based on recent scholarship in social work publications, many have embraced the Afrocentric perspective as a valuable approach to social work practice with various African Americans, such as women experiencing partner violence (Bent-Goodley, 2005a, 2005b; Harvey, 2001). Yet, others argue that this perspective may fall short in many ways. Anderson and Carter (2003), for example, contend that more conceptual work needs to be done for the Afrocentric perspective to emerge as a "widespread alternative" paradigm for social work. They believe that two important conceptual problems exist that involve the centrality of race versus the centrality of other defining features and the issue of differential adherence to the Afrocentric worldview within the African American community. As social work continues to embrace diversity as an essential element of best practice, we will continue to explore the veracity of Afrocentricity and its role in social work practice.

CASE STUDY

While the history and theoretical frameworks related to diversity are checkered and varied, the social work profession continues to advocate that attention be given to issues of social justice since discrimination, inequalities, and oppression continue as significant social problems in the United States. The *Case of Trent* demonstrates that attention to diversity and culture is essential. Jo, a White female graduate student working toward her master's degree in social work, engaged in culturally competent school social work practice with a young boy named Trent. Jo typified school social workers, a group consisting primarily of White women who use clinical practice as their primary method of intervention (Shaffer, 2006).

Working with Trent reinforced for Jo the importance of cultural awareness, self-awareness and respect for diversity. The following *Case of Trent* explains how Jo handled this challenge and demonstrates that her cultural competence helped to make a difference in a young boy's life.

The Case of Trent

Two weeks ago, Jo began her field placement at Cover Elementary School. She was excited about this opportunity, since she planned a career in school social work after completing her degree. She was also enthused about her new field instructor and wanted to learn his approach to working with children in a school setting. Jo was told she would be working closely with the school psychologist and a number of other professionals. The prospect of interdisciplinary collaboration also greatly appealed to her.

Because Jo had some beginning ideas about her role as a school social worker, part of her daily routine included a morning walk through the school to acquaint herself with the teachers and support staff, to learn children's names and have them recognize her, and to make herself available for referrals. As she was walking through the freshly painted and brightly decorated school halls, one morning, she noticed a small boy yelling and screaming loudly, begging for his mother. A somewhat frustrated looking teacher's aide hovered over the boy, responding to him with similar yells and screams and trying to force his small rigid frame into a chair placed in an isolated section of the corridor used for time-out.

Initial Engagement

Jo approached the teacher's aide quizzically, hoping to find out the nature of the problem. Trent, a small, attractive, bright-eyed 5-year-old African American child looked relieved that someone was coming to his rescue. The teacher's aide told Jo that throughout the day Trent was totally disruptive, rowdy, and aggressive toward other children in the classroom. She explained that the usual method of time-out, sitting quietly in another teacher's room, did not work for Trent. Therefore, placing him in the hallway was her only option. Jo spoke briefly to Trent, informing him about the time-out process and asking him to cooperate with the teacher's aide. She explained that his time-out would begin only after he stopped crying and could sit quietly. Jo said, "By the time I count to five, you should be perfectly still and quiet. Then your time-out will begin." Trent responded appropriately, and Jo stayed with him for the two-minute time-out session.

(*continued*)

The next morning, Jo spoke with Trent's teacher. She confirmed the aide's version of Trent's behavior. Both the teacher and the aide were certain the only option for Trent was to have him tested for behavioral and emotional handicapped (BEH) certification and evaluated for intensive services such as placement in a self-contained classroom.

Since school had been in session for only 2 weeks, Jo was both surprised and concerned that Trent's teacher had so quickly reached such a drastic conclusion about Trent's needs. She was also curious as to why such a young child was causing such uproar. Jo also found it difficult to understand how Trent could be described as "rowdy" and "aggressive," since his behavior seemed to her to be rather deliberate and slow. Jo wondered if Trent's teacher had tried any systematic interventions other than time-outs. Jo understood that African American children, especially boys, are often labeled very early in school and that these labels follow them throughout their education. She remembered that labels influence how teachers and other staff react to kids and could compromise the quality of education that children obtain.

Data Collection and Assessment

Jo's enthusiasm showed when her field instructor told her to pursue Trent's situation and see what she could do to help. She began by consulting the school psychologist. Together they decided that Jo should gather as much information as possible. This would help her test her idea that Trent was labeled in error. It was suggested that Jo try every possible alternative to get needed information before making a referral.

Further discussions with Trent's teacher revealed that she had not really tried other intervention strategies with Trent, nor had she talked with others at the school about ways to handle him. Jo was concerned that Trent's teacher, a White female, was operating with some preconceived ideas and stereotypes about African American male children. Since Trent was slow-moving, deliberate in his speech, and inattentive, Jo feared that his teacher had labeled him as a slow learner with behavior problems and was seeking confirmation for her assessment. Jo, who was also White, tried to be sensitive to her own role in working with an African American child. She expected that Trent's family would be more guarded in their interaction with her, and that the issue of race might need to be discussed with the family. She knew that it was important for her to develop an early positive relationship with them to understand the family dynamics and to help Trent. Jo was aware that for African American families there are often key decision makers and networks of support within the extended family. She concluded that it would be important to get to know the significant family members and include them in working with Trent.

Jo set her plans into action over the next 2 weeks. Her first actions included contracting a BEH specialist to observe Trent and determine if he should be tested for exceptionality, gathering information from the school on family background as a preliminary step to conducting an in-depth social history, and scheduling one-on-one sessions with Trent to complete a developmental evaluation.

The BEH specialist saw Trent within the week, and she and Jo discussed Trent's behavior since the beginning of the school year. The BEH specialist observed that Trent appeared to be a very intelligent child who was very slow in his movements and mannerisms. She felt that the crowded and visually stimulating classroom was too much for Trent to process quickly and easily. The specialist and Jo agreed that a plan could be implemented to help Trent be successful in kindergarten.

Jo began investigating Trent's family situation by reading the school record and speaking by telephone with Trent's father. It was revealed that, until recently, Trent had been living with his mother. A few weeks ago, Trent's mother enrolled in graduate school and decided Trent should live with his father and stepmother while she completed graduate work. Trent's stepmother had two older daughters who lived in the home, so Trent was introduced to a new family living situation. Trent's father tried to make the transition easy for him, often spending Saturday alone with Trent. To avoid imposing Trent on his new wife, Trent's father took full responsibility for his care. Unfortunately, Trent's father treated him like a toddler instead of a 5-year-old, requiring little responsibility from Trent. The stepmother did little for Trent and did not participate in his discipline.

Jo tried to complete a genogram to better understand the family dynamics. The genogram would allow her to collect and visualize data about several generations of family members, their significant life events, and other family patterns. As Jo suspected, the father and stepmother were responsive yet guarded during their first meeting at the school. The interview provided Jo with very little information and left her feeling frustrated and ineffective. Jo knew that African Americans sometimes feel alienated from formal systems, and she tried to convince her field instructor that this might explain some of the resistance to disclosing family information. The field instructor assured Jo that the school was the best place to schedule the second interview and cautioned her that a young White woman might not be safe doing an in-home interview in that neighborhood. Jo argued that because of the problems with the first interview, a home visit was the best strategy. Against her field instructor's judgment, Jo scheduled the second interview a week later in the father's home.

Jo arrived at the home a little late. The family greeted her warmly and appeared to be much more relaxed. Jo told the couple that she had gotten lost trying to locate their home, and she apologized for her tardiness. She also told them the route she had taken and admitted being a little scared. They empathized and said that they would have also been uncomfortable in that area and told Jo of a safer route to and from their home. Admitting that she was uncomfortable relieved Jo of much of her anxiety and simultaneously helped Trent's family see Jo as a sincere person genuinely concerned about Trent.

During the second interview, Jo explained the purpose of their meeting and discussed the genogram with them. The father and stepmother provided information. Jo knew a more complete picture was needed and later contacted Trent's mother for additional information. Upon completing her interviews, she was able to complete a genogram that revealed a stable and functioning extended family. It also showed a grandmother who played a significant role in Trent's life, providing child care while his mother worked. Jo remembered that grandmothers often play an intricate role in African American families and add major strengths to the family unit. Jo also found

(*continued*)

that prior to moving in with his father, other members of the extended family were routinely involved with Trent.

To complete Trent's developmental evaluation, Jo scheduled half-hour sessions with him twice each week. The sessions allowed Jo to further develop a helping relationship with him. During the meetings, Jo asked Trent to complete several activities that required him to use classification skills, to show evidence of understanding concepts of conversation, and to identify common symbols (e.g., letters of the alphabet, stop signs). Trent completed each task without difficulty. He was able to form patterns with various colored and shaped blocks, read simple words, identify the letters of the alphabet in various contexts. Trent showed no developmental delays in physical ability and was able to run, hop, skip, and gallop when asked. He was skilled at catching, throwing, and kicking a large rubber ball, and his fine motor skills appeared appropriate for his age. Essentially, Jo found no evidence of cognitive or physical developmental delays.

Intervention

After several meetings with the school psychologist, the teacher, the teacher's aide, Trent, and his parents, an intervention plan was devised. Jo helped identify goals for Trent including being able to maintain appropriate behavior at school, and being able to act responsibly at home. Jo decided to follow Trent's progress at school by using a chart illustrating four behaviors: (1) obeys the teacher and classroom rules, (2) keeps hands and feet to himself, (3) uses good manners, and (4) walks in line/sits in seat correctly. Trent participated in making the chart; including decorating it and deciding the types of stickers he would like to use to reward appropriate behavior. With his interest in animals, Jo was not surprised that Trent selected brightly colored zoo animals for his stickers. Participating in the construction of the chart and selecting stickers helped invest Trent in the behavioral change process.

In addition to the behavior chart and task list, Jo suggested that Trent's care plan include a small social skills group. Five other boys from Trent's class were in need of some special attention in the area of social skills, and Trent was included in this group. The members of the group also functioned as a potential source of friends for Trent, since he had not made many friends since moving in with his father. The group also provided an opportunity for Trent to learn and practice socially appropriate behavior through group interaction in a safe setting.

Jo paired Trent with a seventh grader who would act as his "lunch pal." This student, an African American youngster, would have lunch with Trent three times during the week, serving as an older role model and reinforcing appropriate social skills. Although Jo felt Trent's father was an excellent caregiver and role model, she was concerned that there was a lack of understanding and appreciation of African American culture within the school setting. Jo felt that choosing an African American youngster as a lunch pal might minimize the negative effort of the school "culture" on Trent and enhance his school survival skills. Jo also assigned Trent a science tutor. The science tutor could nurture Trent's extraordinary interest in science and nature by spending time with him in the science center at the school. This allowed Trent to explore his interest in animal life and learn new responsibilities.

Evaluation

Jo maintained regular contact with Trent's mother and father, teacher, and the other support personnel. The parents cooperated by maintaining behavior charts at home, while Trent's teacher followed Trent's progress by charting his behavior in the classroom. The teacher and Trent's parents reported positive changes in Trent's behavior and maturity level. By Christmas break, Trent was interacting with his classmates with much more ease and confidence. The teacher and the aide were relieved that Trent spent time outside the classroom in regular sessions with Jo and with the science tutor. They identified fewer disruptive outbursts and were better able to manage the ones that did occur. Jo felt confident that she had been effective in her work with Trent. Her plan helped him to modify his behavior and to adjust to kindergarten.

Jo remained skeptical and concerned that Trent was at risk in the public school system because of the history of discrimination African American males have faced within that system. She decided, as a long-range career goal, to address this problem by researching the extent to which African American males are treated differently within the schools. She suspected that differential treatment would be found and that a wider change effort would be necessary to remedy this condition. She wondered how she could help the school to be more sensitive to African American males (Carlton-LaNey, 1996a, pp. 3–5).

Jo's experience demonstrated that she engaged in ethnic-sensitive practice, acknowledging and respecting Trent and his family's racial/ethnic reality. According to Schlesinger and Devore (1995), the social worker must have multiple skills at the cognitive (knowledge of diversity history), affective (emotional), and behavioral (language and communication skills) levels in order to be culturally competent. Jo relied on her knowledge of African American culture and an honest, caring approach when working with Trent and his family. Her understanding and respect for diversity guided her intervention strategies.

Understanding diversity is essential when choosing to use a genogram for engaging in family exploration (McCullough-Chavis & Waites, 2004). Boyd-Franklin (1989) notes that information gathering, through mechanisms such as genograms, should come later in the treatment process when working with African American families. This is sometimes counter to the approach that many practitioners have been taught. Building trust must take place before families are receptive to this intensive information gathering. Jo's initial effort to construct the genogram was met with resistance. She recognized the resistance and delayed the information gathering until the family demonstrated a level of comfort with her and their environment. However, her initial problem-solving approach began before the completion of the genogram.

An understanding of, and respect for, diversity may not only dictate when the genogram is completed as Jo found, it may also need to be altered to become a culturally responsive instrument. Watts-Jones (1997) believes that expanding the concept of family when working with African Americans and other groups in which functional kinship relationships are important provides "a more accurate reflection of how 'family' is defined and functions in this population" (p. 6). Jo found that extended family was significant in Trent's life and that their rather abrupt departure from his everyday existence may have contributed to his acting-out behavior. It is important that social workers know that other groups, including Latinos and First Nations people, also embrace the notion of family broadly, relying much more on the functional concept of family.

With the *Case of Trent*, it was critical that the social worker be aware, as Jo seemed to have been, that African American students are disproportionately referred to school administrators for disciplinary action and are also more than twice as likely as their White counterparts to be referred for corporal punishment (Haynes, 2005). Furthermore, schools disproportionately suspend students of color and teachers and administrators use disciplinary practices as ways to express their racial and class biases (Cameron, 2006). School disciplinary action targets boys more than girls and impacts disabled students and students receiving special education services disproportionably. As a result, students with the most challenges are forced to experience even more challenges.

CONCLUSION

As demonstrated throughout this chapter, social work continues to struggle with the importance and inclusion of diversity in professional practice, research, and social work education. It is not unusual to find scholarship that completely ignores any discussion of diversity. Authors are aware that they can write manuscripts without including any content on diverse groups and have those manuscripts published in reputable social work journals and texts. Professionals continue to write about the dominant cultural group, including content on different racial and ethnic groups as a footnote, preferring to write about Asian Americans, Native Americans, or Latinos in separate articles, books, monographs, and so on. Furthermore, there is a propensity to discuss diverse groups in terms of pathology while ignoring the strengths that have sustained them in a country where racism, ageism, sexism, heterosexism, and ableism are institutionalized.

While practitioners continue to express our commitment to including diversity in every facet of the social work profession, a stronger emphasis on cultural competence is necessary. Further, that knowledge should be applied in practice, research, education, policy development, and policy implementation. Embracing diversity is laudable and the continued commitment to foster the concept of diversity is a challenge that the profession is prepared to meet. To be effective, social workers must continuously and aggressively assess and evaluate their performance in this effort.

REFERENCES

Anderson, J., & Carter, R. (Eds.). (2003). *Diversity perspectives for social work practice*. Upper Saddle River, NJ: Pearson Education.

Axinn, J., & Stern, M. (2005). *Social welfare: A history of the American response to need*. Boston: Allyn & Bacon.

Barker, R. (2003). *The social work dictionary*. Washington, DC: National Association of Social Workers Press.

Barrow, F. (2001). *The social work career and contributions of Forrester Blanchard Washington, a life course analysis*. Unpublished doctoral dissertation, Howard University, Washington, DC.

Bent-Goodley, T. (2005a). An African-centered approach to domestic violence. *Families in Society, 86*, 197–206.

Bent-Goodley, T. (2005b). Culture and domestic violence: Transforming knowledge development. *Journal of Interpersonal Violence, 20*, 195–203.

Bent-Goodley, T., & Fowler, D. (2006). Spiritual and religious abuse: Expanding what is known about domestic violence. *Affilia Journal of Women and Social Work, 21*, 282–295.

Berg-Weger, M. (2005). *Social work and social welfare*. Boston: McGraw-Hill.

Billingsley, A. (1992). *Climbing Jacob's ladder: The enduring legacy of African American families*. New York: Simon & Schuster.

Bordewich, F. (1996). *Killing the white man's Indian: Reinventing Native Americans at the end of the twentieth century*. New York: Doubleday.

Boyd-Franklin, N. (1989). *Black families in therapy: A multisystems approach*. New York: Guilford Press.

Brown, C. H. (1941). *The correct thing: To do, to say, to wear*. Boston: Christopher.

Burwell, Y. (1998). Human diversity and empowerment. In W. Johnson (Ed.), *The social services: An introduction* (pp. 385–398). Itasca, IL: Peacock.

Cameron, M. (2006). Managing school discipline and implications for school social workers: A review of the literature. *Children and Schools, 28*, 219–227.

Carlton-LaNey, I. (1996a). The Case of Trent. In R. Rivas & G. Hull (Eds.), *Case studies in generalist practice* (pp. 1–7). Pacific Grove, CA: Brooks/Cole.

Carlton-LaNey, I. (1996b). George and Birdye Haynes' legacy to community practice. In I. Carlton-LaNey & N. Y. Burwell (Eds.), *African American community practice models: Historical and contemporary responses* (pp. 27–48). New York: Haworth Press.

Carlton-LaNey, I. (1997). Social workers as advocates for elders. In M. Reisch & E. Gambrill (Eds.), *Social work in the 21st century* (pp. 285–295). Thousand Oaks, CA: Pine Forge Press.

Carlton-LaNey, I. (1999). African American social work pioneers' response to need. *Social Work, 42*, 573–583.

Carlton-LaNey, I. (Ed.). (2001). *African American leadership: An empowerment tradition in social welfare history*. Washington, DC: National Association of Social Workers Press.

Carlton-LaNey, I. (2005). *African Americans aging in the rural south: Stories of faith, family and community*. Durham, NC: Sourwood Press.

Carlton-LaNey, I. (2006). Rural African American caregiving. In B. Berkman (Ed.), *Handbook of social work in health and aging* (pp. 381–390). New York: Oxford University Press.

Carlton-LaNey, I., & Andrews, J. (1998). Direct practice addressing gender in practice from a multicultural feminist perspective. In J. Figueira-McDonough, E. Netting, & A. Nicholes-Casebolt (Eds.), *The role of gender in practice knowledge claiming half the human experience* (pp. 93–125). New York: Garland.

Chace, W. (1989). The language of action. *Wesleyan, 62*, 32–43.

Chestang, L. (1982). *Character development in a hostile society*. Occasional paper. Chicago: University of Chicago Press.

Chipungu, S., Everett, J., & Leashore, B. (Eds.). (1991). *Child welfare: An afrocentric perspective*. New Brunswick, NJ: Rutgers University Press.

Council on Social Work Education. (2001). *Educational policy and accreditation standards*. Alexandra, VA: CSWE Press.

Covin, D. (1990). Afrocentricity in O Movimento Negro Unificade. *Journal of Black Studies, 21*, 126–145.

Davis, K. (2004). Social work's commitment to social justice and social policy. In K. Davis & T. Bent-Goodley (Eds.), *The color of social policy* (pp. 229–241). Alexandria, VA: Council on Social Work Education Press.

Day, P. (1997). *A new history of social welfare*. Englewood Cliffs, NJ: Prentice Hall.

Edwards, R. (1995). Introduction. In R. Edwards (Ed.), *Encyclopedia of social work* (19th ed., pp. 1–5). Washington, DC: National Association of Social Workers Press.

Fellin, P. (2000). Revisiting multiculturalism in social work. *Journal of Social Work Education, 36*, 261–278.

Franklin, J. (1980). *From slavery to freedom: A history of negro Americans* (5th ed.). New York: Alfred A. Knopf.

Gerdes, K., Segal, E., & Ressler, L. (2003). Should faith-based social-work programs be required to comply with nondiscrimination standards if they violate the beliefs of these institutions. In H. Karger, J. Midgley, & C. Brown (Eds.), *Controversial issues in social policy* (pp. 263–282). Boston: Allyn & Bacon.

Germain, C., & Gitterman, A. (1995). Ecological perspective. In R. Edwards (Ed.), *Encyclopedia of social work* (19th ed., pp. 816–823). Washington, DC: National Association of Social Workers Press.

Gutierrez, L. (1997). Multicultural community organizing. In M. Reisch & E. Gambrill (Eds.), *Social work in the 21st century* (pp. 249–250). Thousand Oak, CA: Pine Forge Press.

Gutierrez, L., Fredricksen, K., & Soifer, S. (1999). Perspectives of social work faculty on diversity and societal oppression content: Results from a national survey. *Journal of Social Work Education, 35*, 409–420.

Harvey, A. (2001). Individual and family intervention skills with African Americans: A Africentric approach. In F. Fong & S. Furuto (Eds.), *Culturally competent practice: Skills, interventions, and evaluation* (pp. 225–240). New York: Harworth.

Harvey, A., & Coleman, A. (1997). An Afrocentric program for African American males in the juvenile justice system. *Child Welfare, 76*, 197–211.

Haynes, B. (2005). The paradox of the excluded child. *Educational Philosophy and Theory, 37*, 333–341.

Hooyman, N., & Kiyak, H. (2005). *Social gerontology: A multidisciplinary perspective*. Boston: Allyn & Bacon.

Hopps, J., Pinderhughes, E., & Shankar, R. (1995). *The power of care: Clinical practice effectiveness with overwhelming clients*. New York: Free Press.

Invisible Government of Negro Social Work. (1920). The National League on Urban Conditions Among Negroes. *Messenger, 2*, 174–177.

Leigh, J. (1998). *Communicating for cultural competence*. Prospect Heights, IL: Waveland Press.

Levy, E. (1995). Feminist social work practice with lesbian and gay clients. In N. Van Den Bergh (Ed.), *Feminist practice in the 21st century* (pp. 278–294). Washington, DC: National Association of Social Workers Press.

Lum, D. (Ed.). (2003). *Culturally competent practice a framework for understanding diverse groups and justice issues*. Pacific Grove, CA: Brooks/Cole.

Martin, E., & Martin, J. (1985). *The helping tradition in the Black family and community*. Silver Spring, MD: National Association of Social Workers Press.

McCullough-Chavis, A., & Waites, C. (2004). Genograms with African American families: Considering cultural content. *Journal of Family Social Work, 8*, 1–19.

McIntosh, P. (1988). *White privilege and male privilege: A personal account of coming to see correspondences though work in women's studies* (Working Paper 189). Wellesley, MA: Wellesley College, Center for Research on Women.

Morales, A., Sheafor, B., & Scott, M. (2007). *Social work: A profession of many faces*. Boston: Allyn & Beacon Press.

Nagda, B., Spearmon, M., Holley, L., Harding, S., Balassone, M., Moise-Swanson, D., et al. (1999). Intergroup dialogues: An innovative approach to teaching about diversity and justice in social work programs. *Journal of Social Work Education, 35*, 433–449.

National Association of Social Workers. (2006). *Social work speaks: National Association of Social Workers Policy Statements 2006–2009* (17th ed.). Washington, DC: National Association of Social Workers Press.

Ozawa, M. (1997). Demographic changes and their implications. In M. Riesch & E. Gambrill (Eds.), *Social work in the 21st century* (pp. 8–27). Thousands Oaks, CA: Pine Forge Press.

Parish, S. (2005). Deinstitutionalization in two states: The impact of advocacy, policy, and other social forces on services for people with developmental disabilities. *Research and Practice for Persons with Severe Disabilities, 30*, 219–231.

Parish, S., & Cloud, J. (2006). Financial well-being of young children with disabilities and their families. *Social Work, 51*, 223–232.

Parish, S., & Huh, J. (2006). Health care for women with disabilities: Population-based evidence of disparities. *Health and Social Work, 31*, 7–14.

Parish, S., & Lutwick, Z. (2005). A critical analysis of the emerging crisis in long-term care for people with developmental disabilities. *Social Work, 50*, 345–354.

Parris, G., & Brooks, L. (1971). *Blacks in the city*. Boston: Little, Brown.

Pinderhughes, E. (1989). *Understanding race, ethnicity, and power*. New York: Free Press.

Reisch, M., & Andrews, J. (2002). *The road not taken: A history of radical social work in the United States*. New York: Brunner-Routledge.

Saleebey, D. (Ed.). (1997). *The strengths perspective in social work practice* (2nd ed.). New York: Longman.

Salem, D. (1993). National Association of Colored Women. In D. C. Hine (Ed.), *Black women in America: An historical encyclopedia* (pp. 842–851). Bloomington: Indiana University Press.

Schiele, J. (1996). Afrocenricity: An Emerging paradigm in social work practice. *Social Work, 41*, 284–294.

Schlesinger, E., & Devore, W. (1995). Ethnic-sensitive practice. In R. Edwards (Ed.), *Encyclopedia of Social Work* (pp. 902–908). Washington, DC: National Association of Social Workers Press.

Schriver, J. (2001). *Human behavior and the social environment: Shifting paradigms in essential knowledge for social work practice*. Boston: Allyn & Bacon.

Shaffer, G. (2006). Promising school social work practices of the 1920s: Reflections for today. *Children and Schools, 28*, 243–251.

Simon, B. (1994). *The empowerment tradition in American social work: A history*. New York: Columbia University Press.

Social work speaks: National Association of Social Workers Policy Statement 2006–2009 (7th ed.). (2006). Washington, DC: NASW Press.

Solomon, B. (1976). *Black empowerment: Social work in oppressed communities*. New York: Columbia University Press.

Swigonski, M. (1996). Challenging privilege through Africentric social work practice. *Social Work, 41*, 153–161.

Waites, C., Macgowan, M., Pennell, J., Carlton-LaNey, I., & Weil, M. (2004). Increasing the cultural responsiveness of family group conferencing. *Social Work, 40*, 291–300.

Watts-Jones, D. (1997). Toward an African American genogram. *Family Process, 36*, 1–7.

Weaver, H. (2003). Cultural competency with first nations peoples. In D. Lum (Ed.), *Culturally competent practice* (pp. 197–216). Pacific Grove, CA: Brooks/Cole.

Weiss, N. (1974). *National Urban League 1900–1940*. New York: Oxford University Press.

White, D. (1999). *Too heavy a load*. New York: Norton.

Chapter 19

SOCIAL AND ECONOMIC JUSTICE

Tricia B. Bent-Goodley

> Identifying that social and economic justice is the organizing value of our profession is essential to our future, to our capacity to survive and thrive as a profession . . . not infrequently, people misunderstand or misinterpret what we do. In these times we must keep in mind that our competitive niche derives from the fact that there is no other profession that identifies social justice as its central organizing value; none with our rich heritage; none with our expertise or knowledge and research base; none with our active engagement in practice and policy development with the implicit and explicit goal of preserving and promoting social and economic justice. We have a well-articulated values base and a rich heritage upon which to build our future. (J. C. Marsh, 2005, p. 293)

Social justice is the organizing principle of the social work profession (Congress & Sealey, 2001; J. C. Marsh, 2005; Swenson, 1998). It establishes the profession as a unique entity centered around the empowerment of people and the eradication of injustice on multiple levels. Acknowledged as a core area of emphasis in the National Association of Social Workers (NASW) Code of Ethics (1999) and regarded as a staple within the Educational and Policy Accreditation Standards of the Council on Social Work Education (CSWE), social and economic justice is a critical component of what defines and shapes social work as a profession. Social justice is most often aligned with advocacy, empowerment practice, racial justice, oppression, individual transformation, human and civil rights, and is inclusive of economic justice (Caputo, 2002b; Reisch, 2002; White, 1984). Principles of social and economic justice, however, are evident in all forms of social work practice, research and education and are at the foundation of the values and ethics that shape the profession. As part of its commitment to a social justice approach, the profession has also embraced its role of confronting injustice (van Wormer, 2004).

> Social injustices are those conditions or situations that oppress, withhold information, limit full and meaningful participation, establish and or maintain inequalities, structure the unequal distribution of resources, inhibit development and, in other ways, deny equal opportunities for all. (Birkenmaier, 2003, p. 44)

Despite the challenges faced by the profession with defining and implementing these concepts, the profession has a long-standing tradition of including social and economic justice as one of its major tenets (Davis, 2004; Reisch, 2002). In recent years, there have

---

The author wishes to thank Dr. Rhonda Wells-Wilbon for her thoughtful comments on earlier versions of this manuscript.

been tensions with regards to teaching social and economic justice (Pelton, 2001; Scanlon & Longres, 2001). Some believe that promoting social and economic justice is a façade for the instructor to promote his or her own ideology on impressionable minds. Despite this, social workers have been encouraged to continue to promote social justice and to not take a neutral stance on issues (Kumashiro, 2004; van Wormer, 2004). "Claiming neutrality does not constitute neutrality; quite the contrary, it helps maintain the status quo" (Freire, 1995, p. 141). While the issue continues to be raised, social and economic justice continues to be a staple in the profession.

Unfortunately, faculty struggle with how to include social and economic justice in the curriculum. There are social work educators that are unclear as to what constitutes social and economic justice practices and, consequently, may question why they should try to fit it into a curriculum already bursting at the seams with the required content. The purpose of this chapter is to illuminate the definition, principles, types, and models of social justice and discuss how to operationalize social justice into contemporary social work practice and education. Consequently, the philosophical thinking behind social justice is provided, as well as the application of social justice as conceptualized by the social work profession.

DEFINITIONS OF SOCIAL AND ECONOMIC JUSTICE

Deciphering an agreed-on definition of social justice is a challenge (Caputo, 2002a; Reisch, 2002). The profession continues to struggle with agreeing on one definition that is conclusive and recognized as "the" definition. Therefore, a number of definitions are presented to include this diversity of thought. Barker (2003) defines social justice as:

> An ideal condition in which all members of a society have the same basic rights, protection, opportunities, obligations and social benefits. Implicit in this concept is the notion that historical inequalities should be acknowledged and remedied through specific measures. A key social work value, social justice entails advocacy to confront discrimination, oppression, and institutional inequities. (pp. 404–405)

Social justice has also been defined as creating "equal access to resources, employment, services and opportunities that [are] require[d] to meet their human needs and to develop fully" (NASW, 1999, p. 18). Economic justice focuses on the inequity in the distribution of wealth, poverty inequality and economic disparities (Bullock & Lott, 2001; Less & Stolte, 1994). "But more than sufficient data have accumulated to support the conclusion that inequality has far-reaching consequences for health, political power and education. Problematizing the poor while neglecting inequality legitimizes the gap between the rich and the poor in income and other resources, that is, in power, and strips poverty of the contextual factors that produce it" (Bullock & Lott, 2001, p. 150). While social and economic justice have been defined differently, they share central principles and components that make the two inseparable in presentation. Consequently, this chapter focuses on social and economic justice as one entity. The following definition of social justice, which encapsulates the definitions provided previously, is the one we use:

> Social justice is a basic value and desired goal in democratic societies and includes equitable and fair access to all social institutions, laws, resources, opportunities, rights, goods and services for all groups and individuals without arbitrary limitations or barriers based on observations or interpretations of the value

of differences in age, color, culture, physical or mental disability, education, gender, income, language, national origin, race, religion or sexual orientation. (Davis, 2004, p. 236)

SOCIAL JUSTICE AND THE SOCIAL WORK PROFESSION

The social work profession is often described as having its earliest roots in the Charity Organization Societies (COS), first established during the late 1800s as a means of addressing poverty (Day, 2005; Pumphrey & Pumphrey, 1961; Segal & Brzuzy, 1998). Those engaged in this work were called "friendly visitors" and their focus was on correcting character issues and moral deficiencies perceived to be at the heart of the reasons why individuals were poor. These women, who were largely Caucasian and from middle-class communities, genuinely felt that if they could correct the individual issues inherent within the poor, they could help them to lead noble lives. One of the most well-known members of the COS movement is Mary Richmond (Segal & Brzuzy, 1998). Mary Richmond advanced the idea of using principles of scientific diagnosis to determine the ills of the poor and to use the diagnosis as a means of addressing the individual's issues. At the turn of the century, the settlement house movement would advance a different perspective of poverty.

The settlement house movement promoted the idea that poverty was not a result of individual flaws but instead a consequence of social and political issues impacting individuals and relegating their status in society (Day, 2005; DuBois & Miley, 1996; Reisch, 2002; Segal & Brzuzy, 1998). Initially, settlement houses focused on socializing new immigrants to this country. The role of settlement houses evolved to include an emphasis on social change through political action, community organizing, and confronting environmental influences prohibiting justice. One of the most well known advocates in the settlement house movement is Jane Addams, who along with Ellen Gates Starr founded Hull House in Chicago (Segal & Brzuzy, 1998). Hull House was noted for providing vocational training, recreational programs, literacy programs, activities for children, and promoting the arts among the poor. See Reisch (2002) for a fuller discussion of the history of the social work profession and social justice. It is important to note that African Americans were not welcome in mainstream settlement homes (Carlton-LaNey, 1999; Day, 2005). Even as our pioneers advanced social justice principles, there was still injustice present.

African Americans had long created their own institutions to aid their survival (Martin & Martin, 1995). The Free African Society was founded in the late 1700s to help slaves and former slaves with finding food, insurance, childcare, and assistance with burials. These mutual aid organizations advanced to the creation of African American settlement houses, homes for the aged, and institutions for juveniles (Carlton-LaNey, 2001). In fact, the profession has a history of paradox within its emphasis on social justice. The schism between diagnosing social problems and the focus on the individual and addressing environmental injustice through strengthening the community has, and continues to be, a point of deliberation in the profession (Johnson, 1999). The paradox of advancing the social justice issues of segments of the population, while not promoting the social justice needs of others, is also an issue that continues to be ruminated in the profession.

Social justice has often been viewed as related to issues of racial and ethnic discrimination, structural violence, disparities of power, empowerment practice, income and wealth inequity, and human and civil rights (Abrams, 2005; Pearson, 1993; Reisch, 2002;

Swenson, 1998). Social justice as operationalized in social work, however, has roots in Rawl's principles of social justice (Banarjee, 2005; Perez-Koenig, 2001). Rawls 1971 focuses on distributive justice as its primary focus. It emphasizes that political, economic, and social resources should be fairly and equitably distributed. The assumptions of Rawl's perspective of social justice is that (a) we are free and equal, (b) government is responsible for maintaining a fair society, and (c) cooperation and reciprocity exists among citizens and institutions (Rawls, 1999):

> Rawls expects the government to adhere to two principles of justice to ensure distributive justice for all. The two principles of justice are: (1) each person has the same indefeasible claim to a fully adequate scheme of equal basic liberties, which scheme is compatible with the same scheme of liberties for all. (2) Social and economic inequalities are to satisfy two conditions: first, they are to be attached to offices and positions open to all under conditions of fair equality of opportunity; and second, they are to be the greatest benefit of the least advantaged members of society. (Banerjee, 2005, p. 45)

Rawls asserts that if something benefits the larger society but is harmful to one member of the society then it is unjust, yet the potential of the person is seemingly not regarded. Acknowledging the possibilities, it has been suggested that the profession consider a capabilities perspective that assesses social justice by virtue of people being able to utilize their social capital, skills, and attributes equally (Morris, 2002). Still, some wonder if social work is getting beyond its mission and commitment to social justice (Nagda et al., 1999). Others question if a commitment to social justice allows the profession to be truly objective, particularly when conducting research (Longres & Scanlon, 2001; Pelton, 2001).

The social work profession has long struggled with social justice as a function of the profession versus a cause for organizing and social action (Perez-Koenig & Rock, 2001). As a function of the profession, social justice is viewed as one element of profession's obligation. As a cause, social justice is viewed as one of the major thrusts of the profession and a major reason for its existence. The debate of cause and function continues within the profession. Still others question the profession's commitment to social justice as a theoretical principle or as an implemented focus. "Historically, the concept of social justice in social work has been easier to define by its absence and its potential rather than by its conceptual clarity or understanding. We seem to know social justice more intimately and passionately when it is absent, denied, reduced, circumvented, threatened or violently terminated" (Davis, 2004, pp. 232–233). The commitment to social justice must move beyond rhetoric and discourse to action and strategic planning. Challenges within and outside of the profession make this operationalization even more difficult.

SOCIAL WORK PRINCIPLES AND TYPES OF SOCIAL JUSTICE

The social work profession espouses a number of principles that support a social justice approach (DuBois & Miley, 1996). The profession advocates for the dignity and worth of every person. Each person is to be treated with respect and each is to be valued despite his or her circumstance or status. The profession also promotes the idea of equality and equal access to opportunities. Self-determination is another key value of the social work profession that, as an organizing principle, states that people have the right to decipher the course of their lives and make decisions for themselves despite the perspective or influence of the social worker. The profession also purports principles of freedom, that all people should be free of tyranny, free of violence, free of confinement, and free of stereotypes that hinder progress. The profession also supports the idea of autonomy, stressing that the role of the social work profession is to help people become self-sufficient and not reliant on outside resources to survive and thrive.

In addition, the profession has stated that respect for diversity is an organizing principle. As such, social workers are encouraged to connect to communities and be inclusive of diverse perspectives. "Social work practice promoting social justice needs to be grounded in the cultures of the participating communities" (Marsiglia, 2003, pp. 82–83). The profession has stated a special affinity for helping those who are at greatest risk and in highly fragile situations and environments. Another important organizing principle of the profession is to engage in social and political action that supports a fair and equitable response to disadvantaged individuals, groups, and communities. Reisch (2002) defines five principles of social justice as (1) holding the most vulnerable populations harmless in the distribution of societal resources, (2) mutuality, (3) emphasizing prevention, (4) stressing multiple ways of providing access to services and benefits, and (5) enabling clients to define their own situations and contribute to the development and evaluation of services. These principles form the basis for social work's stance on social justice.

The attributes that ascertain the social judgments and ways of thinking that are important to understanding social justice are called the types of justice (Chatterjee & D'Aprix, 2002; van Soest, 1994, 1995). The types of justice are important because they form the basis of the thinking behind the models of social justice. Nine types of justice reflect those social judgments and attributes related to social justice models. For a more in-depth discussion of the conceptual history of social justice, please see Jackson (2005). *Distributive justice* is discussed most frequently in the social work literature and has different interpretations (Birkenmaier, 2003; Gitterman, 2003; Longres & Scanlon, 2001; Reisch, 2002; van Soest, 1995) but fundamentally refers to fairness related to the distribution of resources. Essentially, distributive justice speaks to the equity of the disbursement of resources. *Procedural justice* refers to the process by which resources are distributed (Gitterman, 2003). Thus, procedural justice is specific to the way in which resources are allocated and whether that process is fair and just. *Retributive* or *corrective justice* is the consequences of breaking social rules (Gitterman, 2003). In an effort to prevent vigilantism and citizens taking authority into their own hands, the notion behind retributive justice is that individuals will be punished in a way that is fitting to or comparable to the crime they have committed.

Relational or *processual justice* is when justice is defined as occurring when particular subgroups, like people of color or women, are able to secure their rights through a fair and equal decision-making process (Longres & Scanlon, 2001). *Legal justice* is the expectations and rules that govern society (Birkenmaier, 2003; van Soest, 1995). *Commutative justice* is the expectations of community members generated within the community (Birkenmaier, 2003; van Soest, 1995). *Restorative justice* holds people accountable for harmful behaviors and acts and allows the victim to confront the perpetrator that caused him or her harm. "Both an ideal principle—belief in the importance of providing justice to the offender, victim, and community—and a method of dispensing justice when a violation has been committed, restorative justice can be considered a form of social justice because of its fairness to all parties" (van Wormer, 2004, p. 13). This form of social justice seeks to compensate the victim for the injustice that has occurred. *Representative justice* addresses providing each group with equal access to resources to prevent injustice. *Protective justice* seeks to prevent an injustice from occurring (Chatterjee & D'Aprix, 2002). It provides services to those at-risk populations in need of supports to prevent further injustices. These types of justice speak to those attributes critical to understanding the models of justice.

MODELS OF JUSTICE

Ten models of justice are presented in this chapter that present an orientation toward social justice. Social work thinking can be found in many of the models, particularly those emphasizing equality, liberty, addressing oppression, and challenging systemic issues impacting the disenfranchised. Each model, while distinct, shares commonalities. These distinctions and similarities are highlighted where appropriate. To understand and compare the models, we must be clear about the meaning or interpretations for the model and the process by which change occurs according to the model. Thus, each model is presented as it relates to its meaning and process:

1. The *classical utilitarian tradition* emphasizes that justice should be based on merit and the contribution of the individual (Caputo, 2002a; van Soest, 1994). The meaning of social justice for the utilitarian is derived from moral duty and justice is part of utility. The process to achieve social justice is articulated as working toward the preservation of the greater good. Consequently, the interest of the greater good may not be to provide particular supports to the poor. If so, justice is still seen as being served even if it didn't focus on the needs of those that are the most disadvantaged.
2. The *liberal utilitarian tradition* stresses that you should maximize the greatest good without making the most vulnerable worse off and that justice is not measured by market value but by the infinite possibility of the individual (Caputo, 2002a; van Soest, 1994). Social justice is then interpreted as having liberty to ensure the protection of basic rights. It is stressed that rights should be protected and that all should enjoy living in liberty. The process of obtaining social justice is to use minimal state influence focused on issues of justice and security.
3. The *social contract model* stresses the principle of equal liberty (McCormick, 2003). Social justice is interpreted as a process by which individuals work toward their self-interest. The difference principle is best utilized to describe the perspective associated with this model. By using a rationale process for decision making, social justice can be acquired.
4. The primary emphasis of the *complex equality model* is to prevent political domination (McCormick, 2003). To ensure social justice, as articulated by this model, you must have a decentralized government.
5. The *feminist ethic of care* emphasizes social justice as a moral duty (McCormick, 2003). This model does not purport that individuals should or do always act out of self-interest but instead are responsive to moral dilemmas. The emphasis of this model

is on principles of relational and social care. Those espousing this model believe that people are interdependent and that what affects one affects all of humanity. The model stresses a character of caring. Social justice is achieved by confronting those systems that support oppression and stereotypes.

6. *Christian realism* is a model of social justice that ascribes meaning through advancing equal justice (McCormick, 2003). This model stipulates that to ignore injustice is to, in fact, commit a sin. Consequently, injustice is viewed as sinful and social justice is viewed as an expectation of Christians that is in alignment with the primary teachings of the church. Shared power promotes social justice for this model (Tangenberg, 2005).
7. The *Catholic social thought model* emphasizes the importance of transforming oppressive structures through the political and economic discourse (McCormick, 2003). Human rights are reflected through civil and political liberty. Everyone should be provided with the minimum conditions for life. Social justice is advanced by social action.
8. The *liberation theology model* stresses the importance of liberation from oppressive structures (C. Marsh, 2005; McCormick, 2003). It is believed that God sides with the oppressed and that it is the duty of both the oppressor and the oppressed to work together for change. Liberation theology is advanced by challenging structural oppression and injustice.
9. The *biblical justice model* shows concerns for others through compassionate justice that is life affirming and places an emphasis on obtaining a peaceful and just society (McCormick, 2003; Pelton, 2003). Social justice is advanced through confronting oppressive structures.
10. The *Afrocentric approach* to social justice is advanced through the principles of *Ma'at*, which emphasizes truth, balance, order, and interdependence (Schiele, 2000). The Afrocentric perspective advances the idea of communalism, humanism, and that everyone is fundamentally good. Social justice is advanced by confronting oppressive structures and empowering the oppressed.

The nine practices to advance social justice, to be described later in this chapter, build on these models of justice by incorporating elements of the models into their conceptualizations for practice.

CHALLENGES TO SOCIAL JUSTICE IN SOCIAL WORK

> I began to understand that professional social work had become embedded in human behavior theories that rationalized and camouflaged oppression while rationalizing individual identities of practitioners, their practice models, and their agency or private settings. These ideas allowed us to believe we were being helpful . . . while permitting us to deflect knowing about oppression and its legacy of individual, population, and multigenerational suffering away from our core identities. We were effectively being diverted from our values and mission. We could sustain employability by deflecting attention away from the social structures containing our employers and their social control functions. (Rose, 2000, p. 410)

There are a number of challenges related to advancing social justice in social work practice, education, and research (Burkemper & Stretch, 2003; Longres & Scanlon, 2001). Many of these challenges are within the profession and some are outside of the profession. Some trends in the profession, particularly those that emphasize psychopathology and the limited inclusion of disadvantaged groups, are viewed as antithetical to the social work profession (Finn & Jacobson, 2003; Nagda et al., 1999; Pearson, 1993). Trends include increasing globalization, widening economic disparities, social exclusion and dislocation, and advances in technology that alienate people across the world (Finn & Jacobson, 2003). There is a call for a renewed emphasis on social justice and addressing the gap between what we say in our policy statements and what we teach and practice (Gibelman, 2000).

Focus on Theory-Based Practice

The focus on theory-based practice forces the profession to target practice accountability and producing tangible outcomes. Theory-based practice also presumes a more objective process that some believe is not necessarily consistent with having a social justice perspective or orientation. Social justice has been viewed as a subjective activity that is not necessarily derived from a theoretical base. Consequently, in a profession that is focusing on theory-based advances and outcome-based practice, you might view social justice work as outside of the current thrust.

Relevance of the Profession

The profession is also addressing issues of the relevance. As different professions are increasingly involved with work roles that once were defined as social work roles, the significance of the profession in addressing daily issues has come into question (Bent-Goodley, 2002). Increasingly, nurses are engaging in case management services and providing home-based care that was once seen as a domain of social work practice. Individuals with MBAs and JDs now frequently lead agencies once led or created by social workers, while social workers serve in more direct service capacities. Having to focus on the survival of the profession detracts from highlighting social justice.

Use of the Medical Model

The use of the medical model has also been viewed as a challenge to advancing social justice in the profession (McNicoll, 2003; Rose, 2000). The medical model presupposes a problem behavior is specific to the individual and less often addresses the environmental factors and issues of social justice. Consequently, the use of the medical model has been questioned as it relates to advancing social justice.

Professional Status

Some wonder if the profession can transcend the professional lines drawn that emphasize diagnoses and treatment and the increasing focus on professional status (Rose, 2000). The greater emphasis on professionalization has been viewed as increasing the disconnect between the profession and the larger community. The profession has increasingly focused on issues of licensure and credentialing as it relates to professional status. While important to focus on the professionalization of social work, it has also been seen as a challenge to the profession in that the focus has shifted to the survival of the profession as opposed to advancing social justice. This shift in time and effort is costly to advancing a social justice agenda.

An additional challenge to the profession, particularly as communities diversify, is a perceived disconnection between the profession and the community (Rose, 2000). Due to the social control function inherent within the profession, including mandatory reporting requirements, social workers are often viewed as breaking up families and communities, not as helpful to resolving problems and not necessarily in tune with what is happening in the community. Often focused on individual needs and less on developing more interventions that target societal and environmental problems, communities often don't view social workers as helpers or advocates for social change but instead as part of the problem. The disconnect from the community is critical, because we cannot advance social justice without community trust and participation.

Lack of Knowledge and Training

While social work students are told about the ethical mandates revolving social justice, they are given less specificity on how to operationalize social justice into practice, research, or even the educational process itself (Birkenmaier, 2003). Without having a clear understanding of what it means to engage in social justice, it will be difficult to advance social justice. Students are also challenged to move beyond the profession's ethical mandates, to buy into the significance of their role, regardless of the type of practice they are engaged in, as necessary to promote social justice across all levels of practice and in all settings.

Lack of Administrative Support

There are limited administrative and managerial supports in place to assist direct service level practitioners who want to address issues of social justice in their practice (Birkenmaier, 2003). Increasing agency demands are real. Organizations are confronted with rising costs for services, higher staff caseloads, shrinking salaries in a competitive economy, more complex and intricate client issues, and communities that are increasingly stressed and resource challenged. Consequently, it is difficult for administrators to release direct practitioners from their daily responsibilities, particularly to engage in social justice work that is not well defined. There are also limited models of how administrators have been able to support social justice work in daily practice.

Isolation of Social Work Practitioners

Social work practitioners are often isolated as a result of all of these stressors and, thus, less interactive with each other regarding daily challenges (McNicoll, 2003). Isolation makes it difficult to engage in collective problem solving, coalition building, and advocacy. Being isolated also creates compromised communication, strained relationships, competition, and less camaraderie. Isolation also does not allow social workers to focus on the heart of the community and understand the new trends.

Increasing Globalization

Globalization is not controlled for, nor created by, social workers, but it does present real challenges to the social work profession and advancing social justice (Polack, 2004). Globalization has created greater income disparities, less communication between diverse groups, competition, fewer resources available to local communities, and mistrust among neighbors locally, nationally, and across the world (Marsiglia, 2003). While acknowledging the challenges of globalization, the profession has not yet advanced any global campaign to address issues deriving from this amazingly complex issue.

Greater Social Exclusion and Dislocation

With an increase in displaced populations and populations that are left out of the mainstream dialogue, communities are more isolated and have fewer relationships between them (McNicoll, 2003). Instead of banding together, many communities are mistrustful of each other, not engaged in civic pursuits, not engaged in the life of the community, and not willing to socialize, particularly among diverse racial/ethnic and income groups. These barriers to communicate within communities furthers the isolation and disconnect social workers have within the community.

Advances in Technology

While advances in technology have been helpful in increasing communication and hastening the communication process, it has also created a great divide between those who can afford computers and those who cannot. While technology is available in public places, such as libraries, having access to more updated computers and software in the privacy of a person's home is a luxury and an opportunity to better understand how to negotiate and maneuver different systems. Those without this understanding can be marginalized by lack of information and reduced access to resources.

PRACTICES TO ADVANCE SOCIAL JUSTICE

The challenges to the profession are many, yet the profession continues to reiterate its stance on supporting the principles of social justice. To this end, contemporary practitioners and educators have further devised how to advance the legacy of the profession's commitment to social justice in practice and specific ways.

The social work profession has theories and practices that advance social justice. The profession is not a novice at understanding how to operationalize the principles of social justice into practice on multiple levels. These practices are rooted in four essential criteria as described by social work pioneer Bertha Capen Reynolds (see Reisch, 2002): (1) that each person should be treated with respect and not viewed negatively because of his or her situation, (2) that people should be treated with compassion and empathy, (3) that each person should be engage in reciprocity and contribute to the greater good when they are able, and (4) that supports should be provided without expectation of reprieves.

Based on these criteria, we next discuss nine selected theories and practices that advance social justice on both direct and macro levels.

Strengths Perspective

The *strengths perspective* is defined as "the belief that people have credible though often untapped or unknown, resources for transformation and development" (Saleebey, 1997, p. 176). When he encouraged practitioners to recognize the strengths of African American families over 30 years ago (Hill, 1997), Saleebey operationalized the utilization of the strengths perspective in contemporary practice. Instead of focusing on deficits, the strengths perspective encourages social workers to learn more about the community and its strengths (Swenson, 1998). The premise is that people have the wisdom and ability to advance their situation and that through self-determination change can occur (Browne & Mills, 2001; Rapp, 1998). The strengths perspective advances social justice in that it focuses on optimizing the better qualities of individuals and communities and creating more improved opportunities for them to build on their abilities.

Ethnic Sensitive Practice

Ethnic sensitive practice begins with the premise that there is great diversity among and within groups. It "suggests that social work practice needs to be grounded in an understanding of the diverse group memberships that people hold. Particular attention must be paid to ethnicity and social class and to how these contribute to individual and group identity, disposition to basic life tasks, coping styles, and the constellation of problems likely to be encountered" (Devore & Schlesinger, 1996, p. 155). In addition to understanding the importance of contemporary realities of the group, the social worker is encouraged to understand individual and collective history of the group. While ethnicity is a source of cohesion, it can also be a source of potential stress and strain. Consequently, the individual and collective experience must be understood in context. Ethnic sensitive practice provides an opportunity to engage in social justice work that builds on having a respect for diverse cultures and keying in on the strengths that will aid in their survival (Swenson, 1998; Wells-Wilbon & McDowell, 2001).

Feminist Social Work Practice

Feminist social work practice "goes beyond a nonsexist or women's issues approach to practice because it links the personal and political dimensions of human experience and is rooted in liberation movements. It is an evolving and collective endeavor" (Coholic, 2001, p. 34). It begins with the premise that there are sexist hierarchal practices and policies that are centered on preserving male supremacy through systemic inequity and discrimination. Feminist social work practice is not just centered on addressing the individual needs of women but includes addressing those societal and environmental factors that oppress women and girls (Van Den Bergh, 1995). As such, men are liberated to see beyond gender roles and embrace an expansion of possibilities that better reflects the strengths and contributions of the individual. Focusing on addressing inequity, particularly around gender issues, feminist practice provides an opportunity to engage in social justice work that attempts to liberate humanity from the oppression created by patriarchy (Swenson, 1998).

Mutual Aid Groups

Mutual aid is viewed as "a form of social justice" (Moyse-Steinberg, 2003) because it helps communities tap into their own traditions and networks to aid in their survival and development (Carlton-LaNey, 2001; Henry, 2003; Swenson, 1998). Mutual aid allows individuals and communities to maintain their sense of self and internal abilities to survive and thrive. "True liberation requires individual and collective empowerment, support of mutual aid within communities, and tactical citizenship" (Bent-Goodley, Mayo, & Gonzalez, 2004, p. 220).

Empowerment Practice

Empowerment is defined as "a process whereby persons who belong to a stigmatized social category throughout their lives can be assisted to develop and increase skills in the exercise of interpersonal influence and the performance of valued social roles" (Solomon, 1976, p. 1). Empowerment practice has evolved to include several facets, including understanding historical oppression, facilitating individual and community advocacy and helping people learn how to organize and advance their communities and social change as they define it (Gutierrez & Lewis, 1999; Lee, 2001; Swenson, 1998). The empowerment approach is centered around critical consciousness that "through group participation, individuals who have been alienated from their culture are encouraged to identify, examine and act on the root causes of their oppression" (Friere, 1995, pp. 82–83). Empowerment practice advances social justice as it gives people the tools to organize and advance equity in their communities and create new resources (Bent-Goodley et al., 2004). It allows people to feel that they can make a difference and that they have the power to change their circumstances.

Afrocentric Social Work Practice

Afrocentric social work practice is defined as "a method of social work practice based on traditional African philosophical assumptions that are used to explain and to solve human and societal problems" (Schiele, 1997, p. 804). Afrocentric social work practice helps people, particularly people of African ancestry, to understand that they have the ability to transcend their situation and to tap into their rich history and tradition to aid in finding solutions to historical and contemporary challenges. Afrocentric social work is not limited to people of African ancestry nor is it a response to Eurocentrism; instead it involves a humanistic approach to social justice that advances the ideas that people are connected and dependent on each other for growth and change (Graham, 2000; Harvey, 2001; Monges, 1999). In essence, Afrocentric social work unites social justice with the principles of *Ma'at* that call for truth, order, and balance to life and using that as the basis for working together to end injustice and those systems that support it (Bent-Goodley, 2005; Schiele, 2000).

Ecosystems Approach

The *ecosystems approach*, which stems from ecological theory and systems theory, is defined as "transactions between persons and the larger social environments" (Kondrat, 2002, p. 437). It stresses the importance of examining environmental influences and how subsystems interact to impact the lives and functioning of individuals and communities (Germain, 1978). The ecosystems approach encourages us to consider how to improve and strengthen systems, remove environmental and systemic barriers, and ensure access to systems that can aid in the equal treatment of individuals and communities (Finn & Jacobson, 2003). The ecosystems approach advances social justice by focusing on changing the systems and environmental influences that interact to oppress and disable populations from growing.

Advocacy

"Social work advocacy is the exclusive and mutual representation of a client(s) or a cause in a forum, attempting to systematically influence decision making in an unjust or unresponsive system(s)" (Schneider & Lester, 2001, p. 65). *Advocacy* encourages the use of strategic tactics to influence the thinking and actions of individuals and groups and the environment on local and global levels (NASW, 1999). Advocacy can be used to advance social justice because it can bring attention to an issue, educate and inform key decision makers about an issue, influence their thinking, and encourage them to work toward advancing a social justice agenda (Hoefer, 2006). Advocates work in collaboration with individuals and groups to fight injustice and advance ideas about social justice.

Throughout the profession's history, social workers have been encouraged to enhance their skills in political social work and serve in political positions (Fisher, 2001; Linhorst, 2002). Using the Code of Ethics as a basis for serving in political office, social workers can advance social justice principles from how information comes to the attention of lawmakers to how policies are transformed and adopted during the policy formation process. It also allows for social workers to engage in enhancing political influence through organized groups, such as think tanks and coalitions, to impact change. Advocacy advances social justice by providing a vehicle for groups to have input and provide direction on social justice issues.

Documenting Inequity

Documenting inequity is a key role that social workers play when advancing social justice. Both clinical and macro practitioners are in key positions to document inequity. The direct service level practitioner can provide information about populations that may not be known to persons in positions of power and authority. They can keep track of key issues through mechanisms, such as case studies or single subject designs. They can work in collaboration with policy makers and macro practitioners to document issues and problems within systems. Social workers can engage in policy analysis, coordinate survey research and focus groups, conduct interviews, and track primary data in an effort to document inequity. Documenting inequity is the first step to acknowledging that there is a problem. Further, it allows for an accurate way of developing solutions that are realistic and tangible.

FUTURE IMPLICATIONS FOR SOCIAL JUSTICE AND SOCIAL WORK

This chapter has defined social justice, outlined its attributes and models, and discussed the use of social justice as an organizing principle in the social work profession. Additionally, we defined the challenges associated with engaging in social justice work and the methods already available to contemporary social work practitioners, educators, and researchers that foster social justice. The challenge is to address the barriers and opportunities to fully embrace social justice as an organizing principle of social work and foster social justice as a force for social change and the eradication of injustice.

Solidify Commitment to Social Justice in Principle and Practice

While we can argue that the social work profession has a commitment to social justice in principle, as reflected in the profession's Code of Ethics and the accreditation standards for social work programs, we can question the authenticity of the principle and the practice. There are social workers who do not believe that social work should focus on social justice. There are social workers who do not believe that the role of a social worker is to engage in social justice work. There are also different ideas of the meaning of social justice.

Second, while the profession has social justice rooted in its documents, social justice practices are far more scarce. Some social work professionals do not feel that they have the appropriate tools to engage in social justice work. Some social work educators do not feel adequately prepared to teach social justice concepts in the classroom. There is no one definition for social justice, so it is difficult to rally behind something that may mean different things to different people. The profession must define some parameters around social justice, but it should also be flexible enough to incorporate the diversity of perspectives of what is just and what is unjust. For this reason, social justice must be approached from the vantage point of those involved. When we involve the oppressed, we advance self-determination and our ability to work collaboratively with others from their position of power. The profession must consider establishing a set of standards related to social justice that can be tangible and measured. Utilizing some of the practice approaches already outlined, perhaps the profession can reexamine how to use these principles to advance social justice in a way that can be shared with other groups interested in implementing these ideas in practice.

Create Tangible Social Justice Outcomes in Field Placements

Field placements are where students are first introduced to the myriad practice issues, dilemmas, and solutions. They are tested on tangible outcomes related to practice, including knowledge, skills, and values for professional practice, yet social justice is not equally as tangible and operationalized in field placement evaluations. Ensuring that social justice content is included in every field placement experience—measured, and evaluated as part of the appraisal process—is key to helping students understand the value of social justice. It reinforces the profession's commitment to social justice and helps them to understand specific techniques that they can use to aid social justice regardless of methods of practice. Providing such an experience in the field may also require that social work field education departments engage in training with field instructors for this purpose. Ensuring that field education includes opportunities for all students to engage in social justice activities will aid the profession in fostering professionals committed to social justice and able to utilize diverse tools to promote social justice.

Reexamining Professionalization and Social Justice

The disconnect between the profession and communities is further exacerbated through the professionalization process. Some argue that professionalization does not allow or dismantles those natural systems of care in communities, displaces indigenous helpers in the community, while simultaneously not creating pathways for indigenous helpers to become credentialed. Clearly, every helper should not inherently be able to use the title social worker. When a person comes to get help from a social worker, he or she should know that the person is a qualified helper. At the same time, we must minimally examine how professionalization further impacts social justice, particularly because social workers often enforce social control measures, such as mandatory reporting. If the emphasis on professionalization continues, the profession must concurrently consider viable means for indigenous helpers to become qualified in the professional community as well.

Communities of color are often weary of social workers, mistrustful of their motives, and questioning of their sincerity and willingness to help. Part of the problem lies in the social control function of the profession, but it also lies in the perception of professionalization taking away the empathy and personal nature of service provision. This is not to say that professionalization is not important, rather, the profession should consider how professionalization is perceived in diverse communities and how that impacts the helping process and the ability to engage in social justice.

Advocacy Skills for All Social Workers

Although social workers are required minimally to be introduced to advocacy in the social work curriculum, this does not ensure that social workers understand the myriad opportunities for advocacy across areas of practice. It also does not ensure their ability to put advocacy skills into practice across multiple levels of intervention. Advocacy skills should be required of all social work students and placed into each field evaluation of student performance. Students should be required to connect the ability to advocate with the execution of social justice acts. Students should be exposed to how one can intervene as an advocate on a direct service level. Skill sets should be provided for students to implement in direct practice in an effort to help them understand tangible methods of engaging in advocacy. Students should also be exposed to how they can intervene on a macro level, within communities, organizations, and on societal levels. Skill sets should be provided to help them understand tangible methods of how administrators can advance social justice through advocacy, how organizational policies can be established to advance social justice without risking nonprofit status, and how to serve as an advocate within an organization and within a legislative context. Having a variety of field placements that allow students to directly and indirectly focus on advocacy can support this focus.

Advocacy skill sets should be provided through continuing education for field instructors and other professionals interested in learning how to advance social justice. Social workers can be exposed to curricula content, specific exercises, and actual opportunities to engage in social justice activities using advocacy techniques. Finding creative ways of getting this content to social work professionals would be helpful and would expand the numbers of practitioners able to benefit from the learning process. Continuing the emphasis on social justice and social change beyond social work programs allows the profession to reinforce the importance of using a social justice perspective regardless of practice area or arena.

The Macro-Micro Distinction

When we examine the contributions of many early pioneers in social work, many of them did whatever work was necessary to advance social justice and its principles (Carlton-LaNey, 2001; Day, 2005; Reisch, 2002). They did not divide their work into micro level and macro level interventions. Instead, they focused on how to advance social change and they used the most appropriate method to address the particular problem, person, or circumstance before them. For example, when Ida B. Wells-Barnett was serving as the first female probation officer, she advocated for her clients to obtain supports to help them find housing, become literate, and engage in civic activities (Bent-Goodley, 2001). As she witnessed the systematic issues confronting the men as a result of their probation status, she knew that she needed to do more. Thus, she founded the Negro Fellowship League, which provided counseling but also educated the men on voting rights and how to be an active part of the civic process. She helped them understand why literacy was important by showing them specific reasons to turn their experiences into opportunities for advocacy and social change. She did not just help them for their own self-determination, she helped them understand how their actions and lives were connected to the advancement of a race of people and humanity.

As social workers whose history is rooted in this type of forethought and thinking, we must ask if the macro-micro distinction is serving the profession well at this time. With problems becoming more complex and interrelated, is it possible that an advanced generalist education with a focus on social justice and social change is not the message that the profession needs to adopt? This statement is not meant to suggest that specialization is not important, however, the answer is not as simplistic or realistic as a distinction between these two areas. Is it possible that the ability to negotiate between these two areas of practice is the heart of the social work profession (and, thus, a major reason why we need to maintain its presence in the profession)? Is it possible that our emphasis on the dichotomy has impacted our ability to emphasize social justice? These are questions that we must consider as we consider how we can advance social justice in the social work profession.

Evidence-Based Practice and Social Justice

Although the literature talks about the focus on outcomes as a challenge to advancing social justice in the social work profession, we must also consider how evidence-based practice and social justice connect. Evidence-based practice has swept the social work profession in a short period of time. It is the preferred method within practice and research. Educational programs have been reshaped to include evidence-based practice as a major focus. Little examination has occurred, however, as to how evidence-based practice connects with advancing social justice. For example, one of the major premises of evidence-based practice is that practitioners build on the use of science by identifying the empirical research that supports a particular intervention before adopting the intervention. Part of the consideration includes determining if the intervention is relevant to the population receiving the service and, if so, assessing if the intervention has sufficient clinical testing to determine that it is, in fact, evidence-based. Unfortunately, many interventions have not been tested with people of color. In other cases, they have been tested with insufficient numbers of people of color, or the methodology is questionable as it relates to diverse groups.

In these situations, is using an evidence-based approach best? Is it possible that indigenous populations have been using effective practices that are unknown to researchers? Does adapting a program to a population who was not initially conceived for the intervention negate social justice? Does this type of process diminish the self-determination of communities if they have interventions that have not been selected or if they are unwilling to test indigenous models for fear of how the research may be used? With funding streams increasingly attaching monies to evidence-based practice, how does this impact social justice? These questions must be considered because this practice has been adopted without sufficient examination for populations that are often resistant to trust formal service providers and researchers. Even as science is advanced, professionals must be mindful of, and vigilant about, ensuring that justice is served within the profession before social change can become a large contextual focus.

Finding Ways of Moving Out of Isolation

One of the major challenges, noted previously, is the isolation that exists both within, and outside of, the profession. The profession must create more useful and engaging methods of increasing communication and networking within the profession on the ground level. With practice becoming more isolated due to rising caseloads and increasing complexities, it is critical to consider how systems can create opportunities for social workers to become less isolated and more communal toward advancing social justice. Helping social work administrators to conceive of specific ways that both they and their staff can engage in collective work, team building, and cross collaboration is important and can aid the work of social justice. Again, these opportunities must be created on the ground level. Strong organizational policies can help facilitate this but, ultimately, agencies and organizations can best support moving practitioners out of isolation and into the lives of communities.

On a national and global level, social workers are called to educate others about the profession via word and action. The NASW Public Education Campaign has been an excellent concept to help other professions and communities see the diversity that comes with being a social worker. In addition, the education campaign reminds social workers of the myriad things that they offer and can produce based on their training and professional niche. Educating others about the skills that social workers bring creates opportunities to diffuse isolation and helps others view social workers as viable experts to have on their teams. Providing action and being key on social justice initiatives is an effective way of building public confidence in the professions commitment and ability to advance social justice. Professionals must be prepared to initiate new ideas that promote social justice, as well as position themselves to fully embrace emerging issues when they occur.

CONCLUSION

This chapter focused on understanding the nature of social justice in social work. By examining definitions, attributes, models, and practice theories of social justice, the chapter provides social workers with an understanding of social justice and how it has been considered in the profession. The implications lend themselves for future generations of social workers to consider their roles and their skills in advancing social justice with clients, in communities, the nation, and the world. Social work is a profession with a rich history of advancing social justice. Now there are, and will continue to be, opportunities to take knowledge and put it into practice for the benefit of those that are most in need. As stated by Ida B. Wells-Barnett on the eve of her death,

> Eternal vigilance is the price of liberty, and it does seem to me that notwithstanding all these social agencies and activities there is not that vigilance which should be exercised in the preservation of our rights. This leads me to wonder if we are not well satisfied to be able to point to our wonderful institutions with complacence and draw the salaries connected therewith, instead of being alert as the watchman on the wall. (Duster, 1970, p. 415)

In these times of great challenges and ever-evolving barriers to preserving and advancing social justice in communities, localities, the nation, and the world, social workers should be those individuals standing strong and prepared for future generations to come.

REFERENCES

Abrams, H. (2005). Linking health to social justice. *American Journal of Public Health, 95*, 1090–1090.

Banarjee, M. (2005). Applying Rawlsian social justice to welfare reform: A unexpected finding for social work. *Journal of Sociology and Social Welfare, 3*, 35–57.

Barker, R. L. (2003). *The Social Work Dictionary* (5th ed.). Washington, DC: National Association of Social Workers Press.

Bent-Goodley, T. B. (2001). Ida B. Wells-Barnett: An uncompromising style. In I. B. Carlton-LaNey (Ed.), *African American leadership: An empowerment tradition in social welfare history* (pp. 87–98). Washington, DC: National Association of Social Workers Press.

Bent-Goodley, T. B. (2002). Defining and conceptualizing social work entrepreneurship. *Journal on Social Work Education, 38*, 291–302.

Bent-Goodley, T. B. (2005). An African-centered approach to domestic violence. *Families in Society, 86*, 197–206.

Bent-Goodley, T. B., Mayo, Y., & Gonzalez, M. (2004). Building a common agenda: Charting a social policy agenda for people of color. In K. E. Davis & T. B. Bent-Goodley (Eds.), *The color of social policy* (pp. 219–228). Alexandria, VA: Council on Social Work Education Press.

Birkenmaier, J. (2003). On becoming a social justice practitioner. In J. J. Stretch, E. M. Burkemper, W. J. Hutchison, & J. Wilson (Eds.), *Practice social justice* (pp. 41–54). New York: Haworth Press.

Browne, C., & Mills, C. (2001). Theoretical frameworks: Ecological model, strengths perspective and empowerment theory. In R. Fong & S. Furuto (Eds.), *Culturally competent practice: Skills, interventions and evaluations* (pp. 10–32). Boston: Allyn & Bacon.

Bullock, H. E., & Lott, B. (2001). Building a research and advocacy agenda on issues of economic justice. *Analyses of Social Issues and Public Policy*, 147–162.

Burkemper, E. M., & Stretch, J. J. (2003). The right of justice: Contributions of social work practice-research. In J. J. Stretch, E. M. Burkemper, W. J. Hutchison, & J. Wilson (Eds.), *Practice social justice* (pp. 1–6). New York: Haworth Press.

Caputo, R. K. (2002a). Discrimination and human capital: A challenges to economic theory and social justice. *Journal of Sociology and Social Welfare, 29*, 105–124.

Caputo, R. K. (2002b). Social justice, the ethics of care and market economics. *Families in Society, 83*, 355–364.

Carlton-LaNey, I. B. (1999). African American social work pioneer's response to need. *Social Work, 44*, 311–322.

Carlton-LaNey, I. B. (Ed.). (2001). *African American leadership: An empowerment tradition in social welfare history*. Washington, DC: National Association of Social Workers Press.

Chatterjee, P., & D'Aprix, A. (2002). Two tails of justice. *Families in Society, 83*, 374–386.

Coholic, D. (2001). *Exploring spirituality in feminist practices: Emerging knowledge for social work*. Dissertation Abstracts. University of New South Wales.

Congress, E. P., & Sealey, Y. M. (2001). The role of social work ethics in empowering clients and communities. In R. Perez-Koenig & B. Rock (Eds.), *Social work in the era of devolution: Toward a just practice* (pp. 305–330). New York: Fordham University Press.

Davis, K. E. (2004). Social workers commitment to social justice and social policy. In K. E. Davis & T. B. Bent-Goodley (Eds.), *The color of social policy* (pp. 229–244). Alexandria, VA: Council on Social Work Education Press.

Day, P. J. (2005). *A new history of social welfare* (5th ed.). Boston: Allyn & Bacon.

Devore, W., & Schlesinger, E. G. (1996). *Ethnic-sensitive social work practice* (4th ed.). Boston: Allyn & Bacon.

DuBois, B., & Miley, K. K. (1996). *Social work: An empowering profession* (2nd ed.). Boston: Allyn & Bacon.

Duster, A. M. (Ed.). (1970). *Crusade for justice: The autobiography of Ida B. Wells*. Chicago: University of Chicago Press.

Finn, J. L., & Jacobson, M. (2003). Just practice: Steps toward a new social work paradigm. *Journal of Social Work Education, 39*, 57–78.

Fisher, R. (2001). Social action community organization: Proliferation, persistence, roots and prospects. In J. Rothman, J. L. Erllich, & J. E. Tropman (Eds.), *Strategies of community intervention* (6th ed., pp. 350–363). Itasca, IL: Peacock.

Freire, P. (1995). *Pedagogy of hope: Reliving pedagogy of the oppressed*. New York: Continuum.

Germain, C. B. (1978). General systems theory and ego psychology: An ecological perspective. *Social Service Review, 52*, 535–550.

Gibelman, M. (2000). Affirmative action at the crossroads: A social justice perspective. *Journal of Sociology and Social Welfare, 27*, 153–174.

Gitterman, A. (2003). The meaning, scope and context of the concept of social justice in social work with groups. In N. E. Sullivan, E. S. Mesbur, N. C. Lang, D. T. Goodman, & L. Mitchell (Eds.), *Social work with groups: Social justice through personal, community and societal change* (pp. 25–33). New York: Haworth Press.

Graham, M. (2000). Honouring social work principles: Exploring the connections between anti-racist social work and African centered worldviews. *Social Work Education, 19*, 423–436.

Gutierrez, L., & Lewis, E. (1999). *Empowering women of color*. New York: Columbia University Press.

Harvey, A. R. (2001). Individual and family intervention skills with African American families: An Africentric approach. In R. Fong & S. Furuto (Eds.), *Culturally competent practice: Skills, interventions and evaluations* (pp. 225–240). New York: Haworth Press.

Henry, S. (2003). Social group work, social justice. In N. E. Sullivan, E. S. Mesbur, N. C. Lang, D. T. Goodman, & L. Mitchell (Eds.), *Social work with groups: Social justice through personal, community and societal change* (pp. 65–77). New York: Haworth Press.

Hill, R. B. (1997). *The strengths of African American families: Twenty-five years later*. Washington, DC: R & B Publishers.

Hoefer, R. (2006). *Advocacy practice for social justice*. Chicago: Lyceum Books.

Jackson, B. (2005). The conceptual history of social justice. *Political Studies Review, 3*, 3–21.

Johnson, Y. M. (1999). Indirect work: Social work's uncelebrated strength. *Social Work, 44*, 323–334.

Kondrat, M. E. (2002). Actor-centered social work: Revisioning "person-in-environment" through a critical theory lens. *Social Work, 47*, 435–448.

Kumashiro, K. K. (2004). *Against common sense: Teaching and learning toward social justice*. New York: Routledge.

Lee, J. (2001). *The empowerment approach to social work practice: Building the beloved community* (2nd ed.). New York: Columbia University Press.

Less, J. S., & Stolte, J. F. (1994). Cultural and structural determinants of justice reactions in the economic domain. *Social Behavior and Personality, 22*, 319–328.

Linhorst, D. M. (2002). Federalism and social justice: Implications for social work. *Social Work, 47*, 201–208.

Longres, J. F., & Scanlon, E. (2001). Social justice and the research curriculum. *Journal of Social Work Education, 37*, 447–463.

Marsh, C. (2005). *The beloved community: How faith shapes social justice, from the civil rights movement to today*. New York: Basic Books.

Marsh, J. C. (2005). Social justice: Social work's organizing value. *Social Work, 50*, 293–294.

Marsiglia, F. F. (2003). Culturally grounded approaches to social justice through social work with groups. In N. E. Sullivan, E. S. Mesbur, N. C. Lang, D. T. Goodman, & L. Mitchell (Eds.), *Social work with groups: Social justice through personal, community and societal change* (pp. 79–90). New York: Haworth Press.

Martin, E. P., & Martin, J. M. (1995). *Social work and the black experience*. Washington, DC: National Association of Social Workers Press.

McCormick, P. T. (2003). Whose justice? An examination of nine models of justice. In J. J. Stretch, E. M. Burkemper, W. J. Hutchison, & J. Wilson (Eds.), *Practice social justice* (pp. 7–26). New York: Haworth Press.

McNicoll, P. (2003). Current innovations in social work with groups to address issues of social justice. In N. E. Sullivan, E. S. Mesbur, N. C. Lang, D. T. Goodman, & L. Mitchell (Eds.), *Social work with groups: Social justice through personal, community and societal change* (pp. 35–50). New York: Haworth Press.

Monges, M. M. K. (1999). Candace rites of passage program: The cultural context as an empowerment tool. *Journal of Black Studies, 29*, 827–840.

Morris, P. M. (2002). The capabilities perspective: A framework for social justice. *Families in Society, 83*, 365–373.

Moyse-Steinberg, D. (2003). Social work with groups, mutual aid and social justice. In N. E. Sullivan, E. S. Mesbur, N. C. Lang, D. T. Goodman, & L. Mitchell (Eds.), *Social work with groups: Social justice through personal, community and societal change* (pp. 91–102). New York: Haworth Press.

Nagda, B. A., Spearmon, M. L., Holley, L. C., Harding, S., Balasson, M. L., Moise-Swanson, D., et al. (1999). Intergroup dialogues: An innovative approach to teaching about diversity and justice in social work programs. *Journal of Social Work Education, 35*, 433–449.

National Association of Social Workers. (1999). *Code of ethics*. Washington, DC: Author.

Pearson, D. (Ed.). (1993). *Perspectives on equity and justice in social work*. Alexandria, VA: Council on Social Work Education Press.

Pelton, L. H. (2001). Social justice and social work. *Journal of Social Work Education, 37*, 433–439.

Pelton, L. H. (2003). Biblical justice. *Journal of the American Academy of Religion, 71*, 737–765.

Perez-Koenig, R. (2001). Actualizing social justice within the client/social worker relationship. In R. Perez-Koenig & B. Rock (Eds.), *Social work in the era of devolution: Toward a just practice* (pp. 3–16). New York: Fordham University Press.

Perez-Koenig, R., & Rock, B. (2001). Introduction. In R. Perez-Koenig & B. Rock (Eds.), *Social work in the era of devolution: Toward a just practice* (pp. xiii–xxiv). New York: Fordham University Press.

Polack, R. J. (2004). Social justice and the global economy: New challenges for social work in the 21st century. *Social Work, 49*, 281–290.

Pumphrey, R. E., & Pumphrey, M. W. (Eds.). (1961). *The heritage of American social work: Readings in its philosophical and institutional development*. New York: Columbia University Press.

Rapp, C. (1998). *The strengths model: Case management with people suffering from severe and persistent mental illness*. New York: Oxford University Press.

Rawls, J. (1971). *A theory of justice*. Cambridge, MA: Harvard University Press.

Rawls, J. (1999). *A theory of justice* (Rev. ed.). Cambridge, MA: Harvard University Press.

Reisch, M. (2002). Defining social justice in a socially unjust world. *Families in Society, 83*, 343–354.

Rose, S. M. (2000). Reflections on empowerment-based practice. *Social Work, 45*, 403–412.

Saleebey, D. (Ed.). (1997). *The strengths perspective in social work practice* (2nd ed.). New York: Longman.

Scanlon, E., & Longres, J. F. (2001). Social work and social justice: A reply to Leroy Pelton. *Journal of Social Work Education, 37*, 441–444.

Schiele, J. (1997). The contour and meaning of Afrocentric social work. *Journal of Black Psychology, 27*, 800–819.

Schiele, J. (2000). *Human services and the Afrocentric paradigm*. New York: Haworth Press.

Schneider, R., & Lester, L. (2001). *Social work advocacy: A new framework for action*. Belmont, CA: Brooks/Cole.

Segal, E. A., & Brzuzy, S. (1998). *Social welfare policy, programs, and practice*. Itasca, IL: Peacock.

Solomon, B. (1976). *Black empowerment*. New York: Columbia University Press.

Swenson, C. R. (1998). Clinical social work's contribution to a social justice perspective. *Social Work, 43*, 527–537.

Tangenberg, K. M. (2005). Faith-based human service initiatives: Considerations for social work practice and theory. *Social Work, 50*, 197–206.

Van Den Bergh, N. (1995). *Feminist practice in the 21st century*. Washington, DC: National Association of Social Workers Press.

van Soest, D. (1994). Strange bedfellows: A call for reordering national priorities from three social justice perspectives. *Social Work, 39*, 710–717.

van Soest, D. (1995). Peace and social justice. In R. L. Edwards & J. G. Hopps (Eds.), *Encyclopedia of social work* (Vol. 3, 19th ed., pp. 1810–1817). Washington, DC: National Association of Social Workers Press.

van Wormer, K. (2004). *Confronting oppression, restoring justice: From policy analysis to social action*. Alexandria, VA: Council on Social Work Education Press.

Wells-Wilbon, R., & McDowell, E. (2001). Cultural competence and sensitivity: Getting it right. *Cultural and Societal Influences in Child and Adolescent Psychiatry, 10*, 679–692.

White, B. W. (Ed.). (1984). *Color in a White society*. Washington, DC: National Association of Social Workers Press.

Chapter 20

PUTTING EVIDENCE-BASED PRACTICE INTO PRACTICE

James G. Barber

When trapped next to a stranger on a long plane trip, it is unwise to tell him that you are a social worker. If he asks what you do for a living, tell him that you are a plumber or a bar attendant, in fact, tell him just about anything but the truth. The problem is that everyone knows what to do about homeless kids, for example, and domestic violence, and drug addiction and all of the other social ills that beset us. The lady next door can tell you what to do to stem the tide of childhood mental disorder, and the bloke who delivers your mail knows how to stop parents from abusing their children.

Perhaps one of the reasons for this irritating phenomenon can be found in the very name of the profession—social work. These words are too common and the concept too self-evident. Everyone knows what social means and they also know perfectly well what work means, so they feel that the occupation to which these words refer must be a job for people who could not get into anything else at university. The problem is not just one of nomenclature, however. Social work has never succeeded in creating an obscure body of knowledge, preferably one that contains jargon constructed from Latin roots, with which to bamboozle the general public. That is not to say that some of us educators have not tried. Witness the plethora of introductory social work texts espousing theories that rejoice in titles containing terms like holistic, systemic and reflexive; or incorporating the quasi-technical word model (as in "the . . . model of social work"). The problem is that most of these "theories" and "models" consist of little more than mundane generalizations about the nature and purpose of social work itself. None provides much in the way of practical guidance to social workers in the field. None of them tells you what to do when your client is violent, suicidal, or marginalized, for example.

Experienced social work educators have come to understand that the reason why there are no textbook answers is because the problems practitioners confront are far too complex for simple solutions. The fact is that social work is an exceedingly difficult occupation. Part of the difficulty is that social workers deal with such a wide range of problems that it would be impossible to write a book, or even a shelf of books, on how to deal with them all. Added to this is the sheer complexity of the problems that are commonly referred to social workers. It is easy to say that the reason for social work intervention is *x* or *y*, but in most cases it is impossible to identify all of the relevant influences and hold each one constant while you work systematically through them all. Indeed many, or perhaps most, of these influences—structural forces like poverty, discrimination, and politics—are well beyond the reach of the workaday practitioner.

This does not mean that there is nothing that can be done to prepare aspiring social workers for the rigors ahead. It is just that there are no simple recipes to present to them. What can be done is to train them in ways of finding and applying the best available evidence when unfamiliar situations arise. This process is known as evidence-based practice and the purpose of this chapter is to examine the concept from the practitioner's viewpoint. After dealing briefly with the meaning of the term, the chapter turns to the questions of how to apply evidence to practice and what obstacles stand in the way of moving social work in this direction.

COMMON MYTHS ABOUT EVIDENCE-BASED PRACTICE

In view of the popular misconceptions about evidence-based practice (Gibbs & Gambrill, 2002), it is worthwhile to devote some space to what it is not. Perhaps the most common myth is that evidence-based practice involves extracting best practices from the scientific literature and turning these into practice prescriptions. Beware of this misconception whenever someone tells you that you ought to do this or that because it is "evidence-based." To be fair, the evidence-based practice movement has not always been clear on this point itself. Evidence-based practice is a term that originated in medicine where it was initially defined as "the conscientious, explicit and judicious use of current best evidence in making decisions about the care of individual patients" (Sackett, Rosenberg, Gray, Haynes, & Richardson, 1996). It was not long before Sackett and his colleagues realized that their definition was inadequate, yet like many an indiscrete comment, it has proven very difficult to take back. It is not that the statement is patently false; it is just that it is a half-truth, or to be more accurate, it is a third truth.

Evidence-based practice is about: (a) "the conscientious, explicit and judicious use of best evidence" to be sure, but it is also about: (b) the use of clinical judgment, and (c) the integration of best evidence with client values and preferences. The revised definition of evidence-based medicine (Sackett, Straus, Richardson, Rosenberg, & Haynes, 2000) now refers to, "the integration of best research evidence with clinical expertise and patient values" (p. 1). To the extent that the early definition of evidence-based practice omitted clinical judgment and client participation, it suggested an almost mechanistic approach to practice: go to the literature, identify what works best and apply it in every detail to the client no matter who the client is or what the context of the professional interaction.

Currently, at any social work conference where evidence-based practice is being discussed, you will encounter this caricature. The assumption is that the silver bullet is out there; the social worker just needs to find it and fire it. If this were so, it would be possible to develop a set of "evidence-based" practice manuals that lay out, step-by-step, what needs to be done whenever a problem requiring social work intervention arises. While evidence-based practice is certainly about identifying and applying the best available evidence, it is not about cookbook solutions. There is nothing wrong with cookbooks, of course, but the point has already been made that the field is unlikely ever to achieve an instruction manual for something as complex as social work practice. It is for this reason that it is referred to as "evidence-based" rather than "evidence-driven" practice. As Sackett and his colleagues recognize, there is a great deal of judgment, common sense, and skill involved in applying evidence to practice.

Another common objection to evidence-based practice is that it "privileges" certain ways of knowing over others—quantitative over qualitative, experimental over inductive, dominant over marginalized. The polemic often contains a moral overtone, as if some methods were somehow liberal, empowering, and good while others were conservative, oppressive, and bad. This is a tiresome and unnecessary debate. There are neither righteous nor evil research methods, there are simply a variety of questions requiring a variety of methodological approaches. Depending on the research question, the most appropriate method could be qualitative, quantitative, or a mixture of both. Problems only arise when researchers apply methods that are poorly suited to the question under investigation.

A good illustration of this is an informal study that has been carried out several times in this author's evidence-based practice classes. In the first lesson, a small white tablet and cup of water is placed in front of every student and they are asked to swallow the pill because there is reason to believe it will improve the quality of their learning. The students are given a few moments to comply with the instructions before being asked whether anyone has yet to take their medicine. Needless to say, almost none of the students ingests the pill, and when asked why, they present a barrage of objections to what Eileen Gambrill (2001) has called "authority-based practice" or the insistence that the students (read clients) submit to treatment merely because the instructor (read authority) tells them to.

Among the most common questions asked of the instructor are the following:

- What's in it (the pill)?
- What's it for?
- Does it work?
- Why do I need it?
- Even if it works on others, how do I know it will work on me?
- Are there any adverse side-effects?

These questions can be rephrased in methodological terms as indicated in Table 20.1.

Without utilizing the technical terms, students want to know precisely what the dependent variable is, what the independent variable consists of, what evaluation studies have been carried out and what threats to internal validity have been eliminated in the process. The students also demand to know about the external validity of any studies that have been conducted, whether that study has been independently replicated, what is known about individual differences, and so on. This is information that any thinking person would require

Table 20.1 The Nexus between Practice and Research

Practice Question	Research Issue
What's in it?	What is the independent variable?
What's it for?	What is the dependent variable?
Does it work?	Is there a causal connection between the independent and dependent variables?
Do I need it?	Do you have a valid and reliable means of establishing my need for treatment?
Will it work on me?	What is the external validity of your effectiveness research?

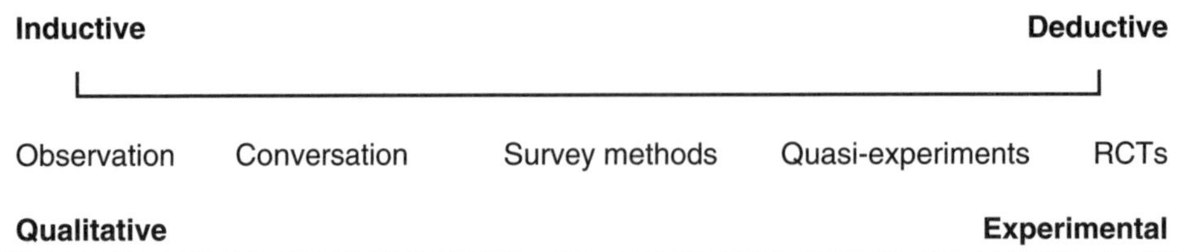

Figure 20.1 The Methods by Question Continuum

before agreeing to swallow an unknown substance. No academic debates about "ways of knowing." Just straight questions demanding straight answers. At its core then, evidence-based practice is about supplying clients with the best possible answers to commonsense questions and using that information to negotiate an intervention plan with them. In other words, evidence-based practice is ultimately about informed consent. It is about the client's right to know what is recommended and why, and it is also about treating the client as a collaborator rather than a recipient.

Not surprisingly, when the instructor offering the pill attempts to advance qualitative evidence, such as case studies and testimonials in support of the white pill, there are vigorous objections to the quality of the evidence. Students know intuitively that narratives drawn from small, unrepresentative samples are inadequate for dealing with most of their questions. Qualitative research methods have their place, but they are no substitute for experimental designs in the evaluation of practice outcomes. The fundamental idea is captured in Figure 20.1.

Figure 20.1 suggests that qualitative approaches are best suited to inductive, or theory-generating, questions. Qualitative methods work best when they are used to explore the subjective meanings and experiences associated with treatment effects and/or to generate hypotheses about what might work in the future. This is not to say that anecdotal information and testimonials derived from qualitative studies should never be used in program evaluation, but "evidence" of this kind is highly susceptible to the kinds of threats to internal and external validity that worry students when they are asked to submit to treatment. The main advantage of experimental method, particularly the randomized controlled trial, over qualitative methods lies in the strength of the causal inference. By a process of elimination of threats to internal validity, experimental designs lend far greater credibility to the conclusion that intervention x produces improvement in problem y than qualitative methods do. In a field where it can be difficult, if not impossible, to perform randomized controlled trials into the effectiveness of interventions (Barber & Dunstone, 2004; Sainz & Epstein, 2001), practitioners will sometimes have no option but to act with only anecdotal data to support their decisions. This does not, however, alter the fact that evidence of this kind is prone to very serious error, and clients have a right to know about the strength of the causal inference on which all interventions are ultimately based.

WHAT EVIDENCE-BASED PRACTICE IS

This issue of client rights is the ideal point for introducing the discussion of what evidence-based practice is. In a nutshell, evidence-based practice is a process; it is a way of going about practice. Certainly it is built on respect for evidence, but this is a necessary not sufficient condition for evidence-based practice. More specifically, evidence-based practice involves the following five steps:

1. Convert your practice problem into an answerable question.
2. Locate the best available evidence with which to answer that question.
3. Together with your client, critically appraise the evidence.
4. Use your clinical judgment and your client's preferences to apply that evidence to the present circumstance.
5. Evaluate the performance of your intervention according to the objectives you and your client had set out.

Thus, evidence-based practice is both art and science. There are technical skills involved in converting problems into tangible questions, searching databases, and evaluating methodological and statistical information. There are also skills in relating to clients, interpreting their subjective viewpoints and meanings, communicating complex ideas to them, and involving them in ways that are genuinely participatory rather than tokenistic.

The starting point for the process is with the frank admission that practitioners do not know in advance the best answer to the problems before them, if only because no two people and no two situations are identical. Evidence-based practice proceeds by converting the unknowns of a problem into one or more answerable questions that are capable of being pursued using electronic databases and search engines. In his excellent text on evidence-based practice, Gibbs (2003) lays out the essential components of answerable questions and demonstrates how to translate them into search terms for locating the best available evidence. A detailed discussion of this process is beyond the scope of the present chapter, but see Gibbs for a careful exposition of the procedures involved. Once the best evidence has been compiled, it can be appraised using structured instruments that assess the internal and external validity of the information and calculate the strength of any effects. The steps leading up to this point are operationally straightforward, so much of this work can indeed be expressed in the form of an instruction manual. As previously indicated, however, there is also an art in evidence-based practice, which consists of engaging with the client throughout the treatment process and in applying the evidence to practice. Perhaps because these aspects of evidence-based practice are so much more difficult to specify than the technical ones are, little has thus far been written about them in the social work literature.

Table 20.2 presents a framework for engaging the client in decision making and for encouraging practitioners to think systematically through the thorny task of converting research into action.

The first two questions in the checklist invite practitioners to compare their clients with those in the evaluation studies and also to compare themselves with the individuals who administered the intervention in question. As a profession, social work is very mindful of individual differences, and respect for diversity is enshrined in the codes of ethics of most, if not all, national associations (e.g., British Association of Social Workers, 1996; National Association of Social Workers, 1999). Differences between clients and participants in the research studies can be of degree or kind. Clients may be more or less distressed (difference of degree), for example, or they can be from a different social, ethnic, or religious background (difference of kind). Where individual differences such as these are apparent,

Table 20.2 The Application Checklist

Application Question	Decision Aids and Prompts
1. Is this case so different from those in the literature that I cannot apply the results?	Differences can be of: Degree Kind
2. Am I so different from the professionals in the literature that I cannot administer the intervention?	Differences can relate to: Skills Values Temperament
3. Is the intervention feasible in our setting?	Potential obstacles include: Agency policy, ethics, or mandate Cost (including time) Agency skill
4. What are the potential benefits and harms to the client(s)?	Taking account of cost, outcome valence, and NNT: Weigh the seriousness if you *do* intervene Weigh the seriousness if you *don't* intervene
5. How are the client's values relevant to the intervention and/or the outcome?	Assist the client(s) to weigh the intervention's: Acceptability Desirability
6. Taking account of the items mentioned previously, does the intervention need to be modified?	Modifications can be of: Degree Kind

Note: Questions 1, 3, 4, and 5 are based on *Evidence-Based Medicine: How to Teach and Practice EBM*, second edition (pp. 118–129), by S. L. Sackett et al., 2000, Edinburgh, Scotland: Churchill Livingstone.

one possible approach would be to dismiss research evidence as entirely irrelevant. In many (or most) instances, this would be a mistake, given that most humans tend to be more alike than they are different.

Nevertheless, differences of degree and/or kind between clients and subjects in research studies may well necessitate change in the content and/or mode of service delivery. Moreover, since the practitioner is an active participant in the process, it is just as important for social workers to reflect on the similarities and differences between themselves and the individuals who conducted the intervention. The worker may lack the requisite skills to administer the intervention or may harbor beliefs or values that are incompatible with the procedure, or the worker may merely be unsuited to the intervention by virtue of her or his temperament or personality. Various forms of group work or community organization, for example, require a level of self-confidence and leadership that not all workers possess.

The next question in the checklist follows logically from client and worker differences and directs the practitioner to consider organizational differences. Specifically, the third question asks the worker to reflect on whether the intervention is actually feasible in the work setting. Among possible reasons why the best-supported intervention may be unsuitable is that the procedure is inconsistent with agency policy, ethics, or mandate. Interventions that require the active participation of perpetrators, for example, will often be unacceptable to women's shelters or child protection agencies, no matter whether those interventions have been shown to work. Another potential organizational barrier is cost. Some programs can be too costly or too labor-intensive to implement. In these circumstances, the worker will be faced with a choice between doing nothing, referring the client somewhere else, or providing a modified version of the optimal procedure. A final organizational obstacle relates to the skill set of the agency as a whole. Child protection agencies may lack employees who are qualified to manage group work interventions or programs for the prevention of drug relapse, for example. Where the evidence suggests that specialized training or skill is required, some agencies may have to modify or even jettison the intervention altogether.

Assuming that no fatal obstacles were encountered in responding to the first three application questions, the fourth question prompts both social worker and client(s) to discuss the potential benefits and harms to the client(s) of acting and of not acting. In order to arrive at a judgment on this issue, social workers first need to reflect on the material and nonmaterial costs to client(s) and social worker of the procedure. Material costs include opportunity costs, direct service costs, and indirect costs, such as transportation and childcare costs incurred in participating. Nonmaterial costs include factors such as emotional distress, lost or impaired relationships, or social stigma. Material and nonmaterial costs must be weighed against the subjective importance of improving the situation (outcome valence) and the effect size of the intervention, which is normally expressed in evidence-based practice circles as the "number needed to treat" (NNT; Gibbs, 2003). Only when the social worker and client(s) have carefully examined all of these factors will they be in a position to make an informed judgment about whether or not the potential benefits of intervention outweigh the potential costs.

Next, the application checklist encourages practitioner and client to discuss client values and beliefs in relation both to the outcome produced by the intervention and the methods required to produce it. It is well established, for example, that medication can be very effective in the treatment of attention deficit hyperactivity disorder (ADHD; Pelham et al., 2002), but there will be parents who reject both the clinical label and the use of drugs to control behavior. Parents may also object to the implication that it is the child's behavior that needs to change, labeling the classroom environment as the culprit. A school social worker who is referred a child with a diagnosis of ADHD needs to explore the values and beliefs of the parents and their children regarding desired outcomes and methods before advocating a technique with solid supporting evidence.

Having worked through all of these application issues with the client(s), the practitioner should now be in a strong position to respond to the final question in the checklist: how, if at all, does the best supported intervention need to be modified in the present instance? Changes can be of degree—shorter, longer, or more or less intense—or they can be of kind. Changes in kind could include incorporating a more culturally appropriate component, or assigning a male rather than a female worker to the intervention. Through all of these changes, though, the objective of the evidence-based practitioner will be to adhere as closely as possible to the fundamentals of the intervention that combines the largest effect size with the most definitive research design.

OBSTACLES TO IMPLEMENTATION

Having considered the major tasks involved in performing evidence-based practice, it is important to recognize some of the obstacles that must be overcome before this approach to practice can take hold in the field. The first, and probably most formidable, of these obstacles involves the time, effort, and resources that are required to practice in this way. In evidence-based practice, each new case constitutes a new research problem requiring each of the five steps described earlier. While it is likely that workers who are experienced in a particular field of practice possess skills and knowledge that will greatly expedite the process, evidence-based practice places unavoidable demands on workers to continually research the evidence as new clients step forward and new knowledge is created. It has also been emphasized throughout this chapter that the evidence-based practitioner must take the client with him or her through this process of locating, appraising and applying the best available evidence. This way of working is a very tall order for social workers who are often weighed down by the sheer volume of active cases requiring their attention.

Moreover, the agencies that employ these social workers will be called on to provide resources and skills that not even all university departments posses: networked computers with access to costly online journals, in-house skills in electronic literature searches, and skills in statistics and research methods. It is unrealistic to expect individual workers laboring under pressurized conditions to embrace evidence-based practice if it places such burdens on them. One possible solution would be for social work agencies and universities to partner in the way that hospitals and medical schools have managed. By extending faculty status to key workers within agencies, the skills and infrastructure required to construct evidence-based solutions could be made available to practitioners. Such arrangements already exist in social work, of course, but they are rarely, if ever, focused on evidence-based practice. If one or more agency-faculty positions were created to act as consultants to front-line workers, the progress of evidence-based practice could be greatly expedited. With access to university library infrastructure and technical expertise, agency consultants would be in a position to take primary responsibility for the scientific aspects of evidence-based practice, while front-line workers could specialize in the more interpersonal tasks of involving and negotiating with clients. Both kinds of worker would require skills in all aspects of evidence-based practice, of course, but by collaborating in this way, some economy of effort should be possible.

Another kind of obstacle that must be overcome for evidence-based practice to succeed is attitudinal and this problem extends to both the funders and the providers of social work services. As previously indicated, there is a great deal of misunderstanding surrounding evidence-based practice and at least some of it is politically inspired. Some funders, in search of new ways of reining in costs, have enthusiastically embraced evidence-based practice because it appears to provide an apology for punitive outcome-based funding models. Whatever may be the merits of making funding contingent on performance, it is regrettable that financial accountability has become confused with evidence-based practice. If evidence-based practice is allowed to become code for overbearing funding policies, then practitioners are certain to reject the idea. Compounding the problem is social work's traditional resistance to the scientific method, which often manifests itself in the "ways of knowing" critique of evidence-based practice referred to earlier. For reasons that are not always clear to those of us in the evidence-based practice movement, there is a level of suspicion, even hostility, toward scientific method within social work circles that is impossible to reconcile with the miraculous contribution that science has made to humankind. This debate takes us well beyond the scope of the present chapter (see Barber, 1996, for a fuller discussion of this issue), but it is important to identify the issue as another attitudinal obstacle that must be surmounted if evidence-based practice is to win hearts and minds in this profession.

CONCLUSION

In summary, evidence-based practice is a promising new approach to social work that holds the profession to a very high standard of intellectual rigor and client self-determination. Far from being mechanistic or technocratic, evidence-based practice is an intensely consultative procedure that begins with the recognition that each new practice problem represents a new challenge requiring a unique solution. There are certainly technical aspects to evidence-based practice and these have now been clearly described in medicine, where the technique originated, and in social work itself. Much less attention has so far been paid to the slippery task of implementing evidence-based practice in the field. This chapter argued that these implementation challenges are intellectual, practical, and attitudinal, and it has endeavored to point the way to resolving each of them.

REFERENCES

Barber, J. G. (1996). Science and social work: Are they compatible? *Research on Social Work Practice*, *6*, 379–388.

Barber, J. G., & Dunstone, R. (2004). Evidence-based practice in Australia. In B. A. Thyer & M. A. F. Kazi (Eds.), *International perspectives on evidence-based practice in social work* (pp. 183–196). London: Venture Press.

British Association of Social Workers. (1996). *The code of ethics for social work*. Birmingham, England: Author.

Gambrill, E. (2001). Social work: An authority-based profession. *Research on Social Work Practice*, *11*, 166–175.

Gibbs, L. E. (2003). *Evidence-based practice for the helping professions*. Pacific Grove, CA: Brooks/Cole.

Gibbs, L. E., & Gambrill, E. (2002). Evidence-based practice: Conterarguments to objections. *Research on Social Work Practice*, *12*, 452–476.

National Association of Social Workers. (1999). *Code of ethics of NASW*. Washington, DC: Author.

Pelham, W. E., Hoza, B., Pillow, D. R., Gnagy, D. R., Kipp, E. M., Greiner, A. R., et al. (2002). Effects of methylphenidate and expectancy on children with ADHD: Behavior, academic performance, and attributions in a summer treatment program and regular classroom settings. *Journal of Consulting and Clinical Psychology*, *70*, 320–335.

Sackett, D. L., Rosenberg, W. M. C., Gray, J. A., Haynes, R. B., & Richardson, W. S. (1996). Evidence-based medicine: What it is and what it isn't. *British Medical Journal*, *312*, 71–72.

Sackett, E. L., Straus, S. E., Richardson, W. S., Rosenberg, W., & Haynes, R. B. (2000). *Evidence-based medicine: How to teach and practice EBM* (2nd ed.) Edinburgh, Scotland: Churchill Livingstone.

Sainz, A., & Epstein, I. (2001). Creating experimental analogs with available clinical information: Credible alternatives to "gold-standard" experiments? *Social Work in Health Care*, *33*, 163–183.

Chapter 21

MAKING SOCIAL WORK PRACTICE MORE SCIENTIFIC

Allen Rubin

As noted in the previous chapter, social work has traditionally resisted the scientific method. Nevertheless, throughout the profession's history, some social work leaders have endeavored to overcome that resistance. Mary Richmond's classic seminal text on social work practice (*Social Diagnosis*, 1917), for example, urged practitioners to use research-generated facts to guide both their social reform efforts and their direct practice with individuals and groups. An excellent book by Sidney Zimbalist (1977), *Historic Themes and Landmarks in Social Welfare Research*, documents how some factions within the profession aspired to make social work a science-based helping art throughout its early history. Perhaps most notable in that regard was the social survey movement during the early decades of the twentieth century, which marshaled descriptive data about deplorable living conditions—data that could be used by practitioners in their efforts to achieve social reform. The evidence-based practice movement can be viewed as the latest effort aimed at making social work practice more scientific and to bridge the gap between research and practice, but it faces the same barriers that previous efforts encountered. This chapter extends the previous chapter's treatment of evidence-based practice and looks more generally at the challenge of making social work practice more scientific.

THE RESEARCH-PRACTICE CHASM

Despite the efforts by scientifically oriented social workers to make the profession more scientific, most of the twentieth century was marked by a gap between research and practice. In fact, perhaps the term *gap* probably understates the situation. Perhaps *chasm* would be the more fitting descriptor, as study after study showed that social work practitioners rarely examined research studies as a basis for informing their practice (Casselman, 1972; Cheatham, 1987; Fischer, 1993; Kirk & Fischer, 1976; Kirk, Osmalov, & Fischer, 1976; Kirk & Penka, 1992; Richey, Blythe, & Berlin, 1987; Rosen, 1994; Rosen, Proctor, Marrow-Howell, & Staudt, 1995; Rosenblatt, 1968). Instead, they relied more on professional consensus and the "practice wisdom" of authorities, such as consultants, supervisors, and esteemed clinical gurus (Kirk & Reid, 2002; Mullen & Bacon, 2004).

The gap between research and practice has existed not only in the practice community, but in social work education as well. Throughout most of the twentieth century, research content was confined primarily to research courses that typically had inadequate content on the relevance of research for practice. Likewise, practice instructors typically relied on research courses to handle all the research content, and consequently made little effort to show how practice can, and should, be informed by research.

Empirically oriented leaders in social work education recommended various strategies to bridge the gap between research and practice in the social work curriculum (Briar, Weissman, & Rubin, 1981; Kirk & Reid, 2002; Rubin & Rosenblatt, 1979; Weinbach & Rubin, 1980). For example, a paradoxical strategy was implemented in 1968, when the Council on Social Work Education (CSWE) accreditation standard requiring the completion of a thesis or group research project for the MSW degree was abolished. The rationale was that relaxing research requirements would encourage schools to try innovative ways to strengthen the relevance of the research curriculum to practice and to students (CSWE, 1971; Kirk & Reid, 2002; Rubin & Zimbalist, 1979). Instead of improving the integration of the two curriculum areas, however, this change led primarily to a diminution of required research courses without any accompanying integrative efforts (Briar et al., 1981; Rubin & Zimbalist, 1979; Weinbach & Rubin, 1980).

The gap between research and practice attracted more concern during the 1970s, as reviews of studies evaluating the effectiveness of direct social work practice consistently concluded that it was not effective (Fischer, 1973; Mullen & Dumpson, 1972; Wood, 1978). Those reviews jolted the profession. Their findings, combined with the aforementioned findings about social workers not examining research to inform their practice, spurred the convening of several national conferences throughout the 1970s. The aim of those conferences was to initiate a dialogue between leaders in research and practice that would culminate in the development of effective strategies and tactics for bridging the gap between research and practice in both the practice community as well as in social work education. Those conferences were attended primarily by research-oriented academics, however, with very little representation from the practice community.

The Empirical Clinical Practice Model Emerges

At the same time, a new model of social work practice was emerging—the empirical clinical practice model (Jayaratne & Levy, 1979). Its aim was to provide a model of social work practice that would be integrated with research. As such, much of the discussion at the aforementioned conferences expressed enthusiasm for this model as a way to make social work practice more scientific (and, in so doing, make it ultimately more effective). The most significant (and, for its time, controversial) component of the model was its call for social work practitioners to employ single-case designs to evaluate their practice effectiveness in an idiographic manner with each of their cases. Single-case designs apply the logic of experiments to single cases so as to control for threats to internal validity without the need for experimental and control groups.

Two other components of the empirical clinical practice model are noteworthy. One was its recommendation that practitioners use scientifically valid measurement instruments in the assessment phase of clinical practice. The other was its call for practitioners to base their selection of interventions on reviews of experimental and quasi-experimental research studies in order to ascertain what interventions appeared most likely to be effective for their particular client in light of credible scientific evidence. Thus, the empirical clinical practice model resembles and overlaps with the evidence-based practice model in many ways, and clearly was its prime forerunner.

In fact, in light of those similarities, some might question the degree to which the evidence-based practice model is really new. Gibbs and Gambrill (2002), two pioneer luminaries in applying the evidence-based practice model to social work, provide an answer to that question. They cite the amount of detail in the model in each of its steps, including instructions for accessing and using the search engines and electronic bibliographic databases that have burgeoned in the twenty-first century. Likewise, they cite the model's attention to the use of systematic reviews (such as those of the Cochrane Collaboration and Campbell Collaboration) and meta-analyses that have mushroomed in recent years.

Throughout the 1990s, studies consistently showed that very few social work practitioners were using single-case designs to evaluate their practice. In fact, this was the case even for those practitioners who had been thoroughly trained in the use of single-case designs in several master's in social work programs that emphasized the empirical clinical practice model in their curriculum (Kirk & Reid, 2002). Various reasons were postulated for the disappointing use of the model in actual practice. Most prominent among those reasons were the lack of time and agency support practitioners had to carry out single-case evaluations.

Society for Social Work and Research and the Institute for the Advancement of Social Work Research

As optimism waned during the 1990s regarding the hopes that the empirical clinical practice model would close much of the gap between research and practice, two new developments arose aiming to make the social work profession (and social work practice) more scientific. One was the emergence of the Institute for the Advancement of Social Work Research, which, with seed money from the National Institute of Mental Health (NIMH), began implementing various efforts to enhance the preparedness and inclination of social work faculty members and doctoral students to conduct rigorous research and compete for research grants from federal funding sources.

The mid-1990s also witnessed the emergence of the Society for Social Work and Research (SSWR), the first professional membership organization for social workers dedicated to research. By the end of the decade, SSWR had initiated an annual conference, annual awards for outstanding research, and other activities aimed at improving the social work research enterprise and the scientific basis of social work practice. Those activities continue today, and SSWR's membership has quadrupled from its approximately 250 charter members in the mid-1990s. The implications of that membership growth, however, are unclear in light of the increased use of the SSWR conference as opportunities for faculty recruitment interviews, as opposed to attending research presentation sessions.

During the 1990s, in addition to supporting these developments, NIMH funded a Task Force on Social Work Research as well as research development centers in a handful of prestigious schools of social work. In funding those centers, NIMH sought to improve the research infrastructure in schools of social work and thus promote the submission of more competitive mental health research grant proposals from social work researchers. Several years later, the National Institute of Drug Abuse (NIDA) followed suit by funding several research development centers with a substance abuse research focus.

The impact of these initiatives to make social work better able to secure federal research funding left much to be desired. By and large, the centers encountered difficulty in getting their federal proposals funded as well as in renewing their NIMH funding for the centers after their 5-year initial grant period elapsed.

Recognizing social work's difficulty in competing for federal research funding, IASWR, SSWR, and several other leading professional organizations in social work formed a coalition in the late 1990s to lobby Congress to create a National Center for Social Work Research. The coalition, the Action Network for Social Work Education and Research (ANSWER), reasoned that the folks who comprised federal research grant review committees did not give social work research proposals appropriate consideration due to their pejorative views of social work and their lack of appreciation for the obstacles to carrying out pristine, randomized efficacy studies in real-world social work agencies with social work clients. To give social work researchers a fair shake, therefore, it was argued that federal money needed to be set aside exclusively for research proposals from social workers. The rationale for such a center also acknowledged that years ago such a center had been created for nursing research, and that it spurred a big increase in the number of federally funded nursing research projects. The nursing profession, however, apparently had more clout because to date ANSWER's ongoing lobbying efforts have not succeeded in the creation of such a center for social work research.

An Epistemological War Breaks Out

During the same hopeful decades that witnessed the emergence of the empirical clinical practice model and SSWR and IASWR, a philosophical challenge to the traditional positivist paradigm of scientific inquiry emerged. Alternative paradigms were proposed that came with different names (such as *postmodernism, social constructivism, relativism* or the *heuristic model*) but all reminded us that pure scientific objectivity is impossible to attain, that we all are influenced by our prior experiences and biases no matter how hard we try to use impeccable scientific methods and designs, and that there is no escaping the fact that we all have our own unique internal subjective realities that interfere with our ability to know an external objective social reality.

In its extreme radical form, however, this challenge to the philosophical underpinnings of the pursuit of objectivity and logic in science argued that there is no objective social reality to begin with, that not only does it not exist, it is utterly unknowable, and that we only delude ourselves when we use traditional scientific methods and designs aimed at maximizing objectivity and attaining the most objective possible understanding of social reality. Consequently, rather than pursue objectivity, it further argued that researchers should embrace subjectivity and merely inform those who read their works of the biases that guide their inquiries.

Those who espoused the new paradigms not only touted their merits, they attacked positivist efforts to be objective—calling positivism obsolete and arguing that it be replaced. In so doing, they depicted the contemporary positivistic pursuit of objectivity, logic and generalizations in straw man terms—as if contemporary positivism were really no different from the less sophisticated logical positivism of the nineteenth century. Unlike the logical positivism of the nineteenth century, however, contemporary positivism recognizes that while objectivity is worth striving for, complete objectivity is impossible to attain.

Researchers' predilections can and do influence what they opt to research, what and how they observe, and the conclusions they derive.

The strawman argument was not the only fallacy apparent in the more radical version of the attack on positivism. Another was the logical incoherence of the attack. It argued that there is no way to assess external reality objectively and that any individual's subjective take on external reality is just as valid as anyone else's. But if that is so, then there is no basis for them to proclaim their view of the nature of social reality as the correct view.

In their book, *Fashionable Nonsense*, Sokal and Bricmont (1998) criticized the way radical postmodernist attacks on positivism misuse terms from the natural sciences "displaying a superficial erudition by shamelessly throwing around technical terms in a context where they are completely irrelevant. The goal is, no doubt, to impress and, above all, to intimidate the nonscientist reader" (p. 5).

The radical postmodern notion—that there is no objective social reality, that all ways of "knowing" are equally valid, and that we should abandon efforts to pursue objectivity—has a special relevance for social work, given the profession's role in the fields of child abuse and domestic violence. Shall we just throw up our hands and say that since every individual's subjective reality is as valid as anyone else's, then the perpetrator's denial of abuse and/or justification of it cannot be questioned? Is it really not worth trying to be as objective as possible in attempting to ascertain the accuracy or legitimacy of the alleged perpetrator's subjective reality?

Sokal and Bricmont argue that "if all discourses are merely 'stories' or 'narrations', and none is more objective or truthful than another, then one must concede that the worst sexist or racist prejudices and the most reactionary socioeconomic theories are 'equally valid', at least as descriptions or analyses of the real world (assuming that one admits the existence of a real world). Clearly, relativism is an extremely weak foundation on which to build a criticism of the existing social order" (p. 209). In other words, how can we speak truth to power in advocating for the oppressed if the views of the oppressor are just as valid as our views? And if defenders of unjust social policies know that we espouse a radical postmodern epistemology, why can they not just say that we have no basis for saying that our take on reality is any better than theirs?

Contemporary positivism acknowledges that each person's take on alleged abuse (or other injustices) reflects their own subjective view of reality and that a social worker's investigation into the situation can be influenced by the investigator's own predilections and prior experiences. Although we cannot be completely objective and know for certain what happened, we can believe that there is an objective answer to the question of whether abuse occurred and that it is worth trying to maximize objectivity in the way we investigate things. A biased, inaccurate investigation could have tragic consequences for an endangered victim or for the person falsely accused as a perpetrator.

Inappropriate Conflation of Postmodernism with Qualitative Inquiry

During the same era that radical, relativistic postmodernists began attacking the promotion of positivistic calls for better controlled outcome evaluations of practice effectiveness, other voices emerged to remind the profession that quantitative inquiry is not the only way to make social work more scientific. The mission can also be advanced with qualitative studies that use flexible and subjective methods geared toward generating deeper insights into how the people of concern to the profession experience and interpret their circumstances or our efforts to help them.

Unfortunately, however, because qualitative methodologists recognize the advantages of subjective inquiry, the epistemological war between contemporary positivists and those who reject the pursuit of objectivity became mistakenly conflated as a battle between quantitative and qualitative methodologists. It was easy to make this mistake because those who attacked positivism typically praised qualitative methods as superior to quantitative methods. This led to a common misperception that the two lines of inquiry are incompatible—that researchers are either positivistic "quants" or anti-positivistic "quals." Accompanying this misperception was the erroneous notion that qualitative inquiry eschewed concerns about objectivity. If that were so, and since qualitative inquiry valued flexibility in research design, some apparently reasoned that perhaps virtually any qualitative study—no matter how blatantly biased or otherwise limited—could be justified on qualitative grounds.

Eventually, however, the profession learned that these perceptions were wrong. Some of the most highly respected qualitative methodologists actually are contemporary positivists who reject epistemological attacks on the pursuit of objectivity. Likewise, they reject the notion that claiming to do a qualitative study permits a cavalier, anything goes, disdain for methodological rigor. While they recognize the advantages of subjective inquiry, they also recognize the paradoxical need to try to combine subjectivity with objectivity. Thus, for example, if they sleep in a homeless shelter to try to generate in-depth, subjective insights as to what it is like to be homeless, they will have a colleague do the same thing independently and see if the insights generated by the colleague agree with their own insights. Agreement between the two sets of insights would support the notion that they are objective, accurate in-depth depictions of subjective experiences. Disagreement would suggest that one or both investigators perhaps erred in their subjective observations or interpretations.

Although some qualitative textbooks have been written in the context of an anti-positivistic epistemology (Denzin & Lincoln, 1994), others have spelled out standards for rigor in qualitative inquiry. Those standards call for using methods such as triangulation, prolonged engagement, and paper trails that permit audits as ways to improve and assess the objectivity and accuracy of subjective inquiry (Padgett, 1998). Indeed, the empirical clinical practice model now includes the use of qualitative methods as a component of well-controlled quantitative outcome evaluations (Bloom, Fischer, & Orme, 2003; Nugent, 1991). Moreover, general research methods texts now recognize the compatibility of the two lines of inquiry (Rubin & Babbie, 2005).

EVIDENCE-BASED PRACTICE MOVEMENT

Will evidence-based practice (EBP) be more successful than its forerunners? Those who think so might cite the many books and journal articles being published these days on EBP. They might also cite technological advances such as the advent of the Internet, its supply of search engines and bibliographic databases, and the consequent increasing ease of finding electronically sources of evidence as to what interventions are and are not effective for various problems. Likewise, they could cite the growth in meta-analyses and systematic reviews (such as from the Cochrane Collaboration and the Campbell Collaboration). Such works, which also are electronically retrievable, enable busy practitioners to learn what interventions are being supported by research without having to track down and critically appraise studies themselves.

Their optimism can be further buttressed by the allure of counterarguments to those who have characterized EBP as denigrating clinical expertise, ignoring client values and preferences, and instead advocating a cookbook approach to practice that requires practitioners to mechanistically employ manualized treatment procedures that have been supported by randomized clinical trials (RCTs) that have excluded the types of clients that social work practitioners are most likely to encounter in their real world day-to-day practice. As Barber explained in the previous chapter, such characterizations of EBP are based on the way it was defined originally, in medicine, and not on its revised definition which incorporates clinical judgment and client values and preferences. But as Barber also noted, the EBP movement must overcome some obstacles if it is to be more successful than its predecessors in bridging the gap between research and practice and making social work practice more scientific.

Just as enthusiasm for the empirical clinical practice model waned during the 1990s in light of the real-world agency-based practical obstacles to practitioner use of single-case designs to evaluate their own practice effectiveness, enthusiasm for EBP might wane in light of the "formidable" obstacles Barber mentions regarding "the time, effort and resources" practitioners need to implement EBP. Even if practitioners could find the time to search for evidence, their agencies might not have the resources needed to provide them access to Internet search engines and bibliographic databases. And even if that obstacle were overcome, agencies might lack the resources needed to provide practitioners with the training and supervision needed to implement properly the empirically supported interventions they find. Just how formidable these obstacles can be is indicated by the comments of one leader in the EBP movement, Edward Mullen, who has conducted a pilot project aimed at overcoming them in three New York City agencies:

> I am struck by how difficult this is to pull off in real live agencies due to such things as time, limited access to computers and the Internet (unlike universities where we have access to fee based databases, etc.). This says to me that a very major issue in the teaching of EBP is how to prepare students in EBP so that they will be prepared to function as EBP practitioners in real world agencies after graduation. A related issue is how to bring class and field work together in our efforts to teach students EBP. When I teach EBP to students they typically say it is an approach that they like and value but when they go into fieldwork the approach cannot be implemented because of agency barriers. (e-mail message to A. Rubin, April 12, 2006)

One of the issues often overlooked by those who are optimistic about overcoming practical obstacles of EBP in agencies is the fact that EBP is more ambitious than the empirical clinical practice model. The emphasis in that model was on using single-case design methods to evaluate one's own practice. In EBP, doing so is only one step, to be initiated after the other four steps that Barber lists in the previous chapter. If, as Barber and I have noted, the obstacles to completing the first four EBP steps are formidable, what does that imply about the feasibility of a model that contains a fifth step that—by itself—studies have found not to be used by practitioners who had been trained in its use (Kirk & Reid, 2002; Mullen & Bacon, 2004; Mullen, Schlonsky, Bledsoe, & Bellamy, 2005)?

With the aim of making EBP more feasible, some might be tempted to recommend dropping that fifth step from the EBP process. But dropping that step would be significant in light of the probabilistic nature of the findings of clinical outcome studies. Empirically supported interventions are not successful with all of their recipients. In fact, such interventions might not even be successful with *most* of their recipients. For example, if a new intervention effectively reduces the recidivism rate of sex offenders from 80% to 60% (hypothetically), it is being successful with less than half (40%) of its recipients. The significance of dropping step 5 also pertains to the argument against EBP regarding the shortage of quality research studies suitable for guiding practice with the kinds of problems and clients typically encountered by social workers. One counterargument by EBP advocates is that such a shortage is more of an argument for EBP than an argument against it. If practice decisions are being based on little or no evidence, all the more reason to "exercise caution and perhaps be even more vigilant in monitoring outcomes" (Mullen & Streiner, 2004, p. 115).

An alternative way to make EBP more feasible is to make the fifth step more feasible. In a forthcoming book that I've authored, *Practitioner's Guide to Using Research in Evidence-Based Practice* (Rubin, 2008), I've proposed the use of what I call the B+ design in the fifth step when monitoring outcomes of interventions that already have a strong evidence base. Using the B+ design, practitioners would not need to develop a baseline. (The baseline is the A phase of the AB design, and B denotes the intervention phase.) With the B+ design, only one data point would be needed at the commencement of treatment, followed by subsequent data points during the course of treatment. The goal would not be to ascertain whether the intervention was really the cause of any desired client outcome. Instead, the goal would merely be to see if a particular client achieved the desired outcome. The underlying rationale would be that previous studies have already established probabilistic grounds for considering the effectiveness of the intervention, and the practitioner's task therefore would be limited to seeing whether a particular client was or was not achieving success—recognizing that some clients don't benefit from interventions that have the strongest probabilistic evidentiary base.

Erosion of Evidentiary Standards

As Barber acknowledged in the previous chapter, internally valid experimental studies (such as RCTs) reside at the top of the EBP research hierarchy regarding what sources offer the "best evidence" to guide practice decisions about whether interventions are effective. Other types of studies—with less internal validity—might be more suitable than experimental ones when the research purpose is something other than verifying whether an intervention—and not some plausible rival explanation—is the *cause* of a particular outcome. Thus, qualitative methods might be placed at the top of a research hierarchy for exploring "the subjective meanings and experiences associated with treatment effects or to generate hypotheses about which might work in the future." Indeed, not all EBP questions pertain to testing causal hypotheses about intervention effectiveness. Some EBP questions are more suited for qualitative inquiry. For example, if the director of a homeless shelter wants to know why so many homeless people refuse to use the shelter, an RCT would be inapplicable, and a qualitative investigation would probably yield more useful information. However, when the EBP question asks about the effects of an intervention, evidence emanating from well-controlled experiments or quasi-experiments should take precedence over alternative sources of evidence, such as qualitative studies, pre-experimental pretest/posttest only studies, or anecdotal case reports.

Yet, as supporters of EBP counter arguments against it by emphasizing the role of clinical expertise in the EBP process, practitioners who are less scientifically minded might interpret this as license for citing lower sources of evidence as a basis for calling their favored interventions "evidence-based." According to the EBP model, if studies lower on the EBP research hierarchy happen to be the only evidentiary sources available, then evidence-based practitioners can be guided by them in a provisional manner (Thyer, 2004). Likewise, even if higher sources are available, they might not fit a unique practice context (such as regarding idiosyncratic client characteristics, values, and preferences). Thus, some authors advocate for increased emphasis on clinical judgment in the EBP process (Chwalisz, 2003; Messer, 2006; Priebe & Slade, 2002; Reed, 2006; Westen, 2006). They propose reasons why lower sources of evidence should sometimes outweigh experimental studies in influencing practice decisions about the effectiveness of interventions, even when experimental studies are available. For example, they cite the limited external validity of RCTs, the shortage of interventions found to be effective by RCTs for many areas of social work practice, the fact that RCTs tend to evaluate manualized treatments that cannot be applied in a manualized way with most social work clients, and the risk that a mechanical adherence to treatment manuals can harm the therapeutic alliance that some studies have found to be the most important factor explaining treatment outcomes (Messer, 2006; Mullen & Streiner, 2004; Reed, 2006; Westen, 2006; Zlotnik & Galambos, 2004).

While accepting the importance of clinical judgment in the EBP process, some EBP proponents have argued that inflated evidentiary claims are being made in promoting certain interventions as evidence-based (Gibbs & Gambrill, 2002). Likewise, Thyer (2004) cautions that the EBP concept "is subject to considerable misinterpretations, as those invested in the status quo attempt to distort this new and growing movement into existing practices" (p. 167). Shlonsky and Gibbs (2004) add that EBP "is in danger of becoming a catchphrase for anything that is done with clients that can somehow be linked to an empirical study, regardless of the study's quality, competing evidence, or consideration of clients' needs" (p. 137).

Empirical support for concerns about the erosion of evidentiary standards can be found in a recent study (Rubin & Parrish, in press). It found extensive reportage problems in published outcome studies that can mislead practitioners engaged in the evidence-based practice (EBP) search process. It assessed a purposive sample of 138 outcome studies published between 2000 and 2005. The sample included all outcome studies published in two social work research journals during that period, as well as outcome studies found in two searches of the PsycINFO database using the search terms "child maltreatment" and "domestic violence." The designs used in 69% of the studies had insufficient levels of internal validity to warrant conclusive causal inferences, but most of those weakly controlled studies contained statements that could be misperceived or intentionally exploited by readers as offering a basis for calling the evaluated intervention "evidence-based."

Some readers of weakly controlled outcome studies, for example, may lack adequate research design expertise to recognize why conclusive causal inferences are unwarranted. Others may have learned in research courses how to spot such problems, but may have become rusty in their ability to do so in the ensuing years as a practitioner. Still others, regardless of their acumen for critically appraising research, might be biased in their appraisals when they assess articles that evaluate interventions they favor or disfavor. Several studies have found such biases among practitioners (Henggeler, Lee, & Burnes,

2002; Huberman, 1994; Kirk & Fischer, 1976; Rogers, 1995). An increased emphasis on clinical judgment in the EBP process, combined with practitioner limitations and biases in appraising the bases for causal inferences, risks having EBP become a meaningless shibboleth in which some outcome studies—no matter how weakly controlled—can be cited as a rationale for calling virtually any intervention "evidence-based."

A national survey of social work educators provides similar grounds for concern about the erosion of evidentiary standards and its implications for the future of EBP (Rubin & Parrish, 2007). More than 40% of the respondents indicated, "positive findings from pretest-posttest studies without control groups would be a sufficient basis for conveying to students in their teaching that the supported intervention deserves special recognition as evidence-based." Those respondents were not solely acknowledging the potential utility of weak sources of evidence; instead, they apparently believe that virtually any outcome study with positive results is enough reason to call an intervention "evidence-based."

IMPLICATIONS FOR MAKING SOCIAL WORK PRACTICE MORE SCIENTIFIC

Many social work educators have high hopes that the EBP movement will succeed much more than prior efforts to make social work more scientific. But the foregoing concerns are reminiscent of an earlier era when the emergence of the program evaluation movement led some social workers to envision the dawn of an "age of accountability." This was during the 1960s and 1970s, when funding sources began to put more and more pressure on agencies to evaluate their services. In that era, the pressure to evaluate was not coupled with clearly defined, rigorous evidentiary requirements. This led to a cooptation of the program evaluation movement. Instead of carrying out rigorous evaluations, agencies were much more likely to conduct biased evaluations that produced findings promoting stakeholder interests and then to take credit for subjecting their services to an evaluation (Rubin & Babbie, 2005).

In light of this chapter's analysis, it is conceivable that we may be witnessing an analogous cooptation of the EBP movement. If so, what can be done to stem this unfortunate drift? Implications can suggest action in various spheres.

Educational Strategies

Educational strategies could be employed in efforts to increase the extent to which students, agency practitioners, and faculty colleagues are better informed about the EBP process and the appropriate use of evidentiary standards in appraising outcome studies. Extensive curriculum changes might be pursued so that the EBP process can be taught in all practice classes and reinforced in all field placements. Likewise, if practice courses were to emphasize interventions that have the best empirical support, students might be better able and more predisposed to provide empirically supported interventions after they graduate.

The George Warren Brown School of Social Work at Washington University, for example, has made EBP the organizational framework for its graduate curricula. Incoming students receive an overview of EBP at their student orientation, coverage of EBP in their introductory practice course, and are expected to prioritize empirically supported intervention models in their practice methods courses (Tonya Edmond, personal communication, January 9, 2006).

At the accreditation level, efforts could be undertaken to strengthen EBP content in the Educational Policy and Accreditation Standards (EPAS) of the Council on Social Work Education (CSWE). Indeed, as this book goes to press, a new EPAS document is in the works—one that promises to have a stronger emphasis on EBP than the previous statement, which only briefly mentioned the need to include empirically based interventions in practice content and to provide research content that prepares students to develop and use evidence-based interventions.

These efforts, however, may encounter significant resistance among faculty members. That resistance might appear as opposition to calls for more EBP content, or it might appear more subtly—in the way that such content gets distorted so that it fits the status quo. In a recent discussion of EBP in a meeting with faculty at a prestigious research university, for example, an argument was made against the EBP research hierarchy based on the relativistic notion that other ways of knowing deserve equal status with RCTs and well-controlled quasi-experiments when evaluating intervention effectiveness. A counterargument was also presented, suggesting that if all ways of knowing are equally valid—that all sources of evidence are equally valid—then the term *evidence-based practice* has no meaning. It distinguishes nothing and adds nothing. If one believes that all ways of knowing and all sources of evidence are equally valid, then one can deem everything that has ever been supported by any sort of "evidence" whatsoever as evidence-based.

Other faculty members averred that the EBP research hierarchy is not applicable to minority communities and that other designs such as participatory action research (PAR) should be higher than experiments or quasi-experiments on the hierarchy for evaluating the effectiveness of interventions in minority communities. Apparently, many scholars who resist the EBP research hierarchy do so based on the misperception that those who espouse it are advocating that RCTs and well-controlled quasi-experiments should be at the top of the research hierarchy regardless of the purpose of the research. If so, then those scholars need to be informed that proponents of the EBP research hierarchy do not mean to imply that the same hierarchy applies regardless of the question being asked.

For example, PAR might reside at the top of a research hierarchy if the question is how best to use research as a tool to empower disadvantaged or oppressed groups. In PAR, disadvantaged research participants define their problems, define the remedies desired, and take the lead in designing the research that will help them realize their aims. Advocates of PAR equate access to information with power. They argue that once people see themselves as researchers, they are better able to influence the policies and actions that affect their lives.

Likewise, qualitative methods might be placed at the top of a research hierarchy for exploring the subjective meanings and experiences associated with treatment effects or to generate hypotheses about which might work in the future. Qualitative methods would also be at the top of hierarchies pertaining to EBP questions about developing deeper subjective understandings of various phenomena or for generating insights about what it is like to walk in the shoes of members of various oppressed groups. RCT's and quasi-experiments would reside at the bottom of such hierarchies. They might also occupy a lower status on hierarchies pertaining to the kinds of research that can spur policy makers and the public to reform inhumane social policies. For example, studies using surveys, secondary analysis and ethnographic methods that describe inhumane living conditions might do more to influence policy changes than will RCTs, and thus might belong above RCTs on a hierarchy pertaining to EBP questions about what types of research will have the biggest impact in motivating the public to reform such policies.

If the EBP question pertains to verifying a cause-and-effect relationship between an intervention and an outcome, however, then the best studies are those that eliminate alternate explanations for the observed outcome. Those alternative explanations typically are referred to as threats to internal validity—such as measurement bias, history, passage of time, selectivity biases, and so on. The most internally valid studies for verifying cause and effect are RCTs and well-controlled quasi-experiments. Other types of studies—with less internal validity—might be more suited than experimental ones when the research purpose is something other than verifying whether an intervention—and not some plausible rival explanation—is the *cause* of a particular outcome. However, experiments and quasi-experiments (as well as systematic reviews and meta-analyses of such studies) reside at the top of the EBP research hierarchy when the we seek the "best evidence" to guide practice decisions about whether interventions are effective.

The logic of the rules of evidence for making causal inferences applies regardless of whether we seek to evaluate the effectiveness of interventions in minority communities or other communities. Nevertheless, the likely *feasibility* of successfully conducting RCTs and well-controlled quasi-experiments can be affected by the nature of the study population. If sources of evidence at the top of the hierarchy are not available for certain populations—perhaps due to feasibility constraints making it difficult to conduct RCTs and well-controlled quasi-experiments with them—then the evidence-based practitioner will seek the next best source of evidence on the hierarchy.

The statement that the logic of the rules of evidence for making causal inferences applies regardless of the type of population being studied does not imply that cultural differences should be disregarded when generalizing the results of a study conducted with one culture to other cultures. An RCT that supports the effectiveness of an intervention with Caucasians, for example, would have to be replicated with members of a minority group before the logic applies to that minority group. Moreover, when replicating that RCT, the intervention might have to be modified to make it culturally competent before experimentally evaluating its effects.

Professional Publications

In addition to educating students, practitioners and scholars about EBP, strategies also could be directed at our professional publications—to improve the ways in which inferences and implications are drawn from weakly controlled studies. Perhaps watchdog committees comprised of leading practice research scholars could examine each new article, book, and review dealing with the effectiveness of interventions, programs, or policies. They could scrutinize each publication as to the appropriateness of its causal inferences and implications and disseminate their assessments perhaps through a regular feature of a prominent research journal. For example, the SSWR could develop such a watchdog committee and disseminate its findings in each issue of its affiliated journal, *Research on Social Work Practice*.

In addition, members of journal editorial boards could advocate tightened publication standards to require articles that report weakly controlled outcome studies not to use wording in their abstracts or discussion sections that can be perceived by practitioners as implying that the results show the evaluated intervention to be effective or evidence-based. Instructions for authors perhaps should be developed that can guide them as to how best to word conclusions when weakly controlled studies have positive outcomes. For example, they can be required to eschew words like "effective" or "evidence-based"—even in a cautionary or preliminary sense—when interpreting what their findings mean about the evaluated intervention. Furthermore, they should be informed that no matter how extensively they acknowledge their study's limitations, that acknowledgment does not permit them to make guarded causal conclusions—in the abstract or elsewhere—such as, "Our findings tentatively support the notion that the intervention is effective," or "Our findings offer preliminary basis for considering the intervention to be evidence-based." A more appropriate statement would be, "Our design limitations preclude making causal inferences about the intervention's effectiveness, but our encouraging results provide a basis for future outcome research evaluating the effectiveness of this intervention using more rigorously controlled designs."

Editors of journals that publish outcome studies also could add as a regular feature a reminder to readers engaged in the EBP process that they should exercise caution when reading even the most rigorously controlled study. No single study, by itself, is sufficient to warrant calling an intervention "evidence-based." Other, perhaps equally rigorous, studies may have reported (or might soon report) contradictory findings. Moreover, perhaps editors should insert such a caveat before each outcome study. They also could require authors of outcome studies to accompany their conclusions with a mention of any incompatible conclusions found in other outcome studies.

Recent methodological advances have been made for improving the internal validity of quasi-experiments—especially regarding better controlling for or detecting selectivity biases. These include the use of techniques such as multiple pretests, switching replications, nonequivalent dependent variables, and propensity score matching (Fraser, 2004; Guo, Rose, & Bowens, 2006; Shadish, Cook, & Campbell, 2001). Moreover, some preexperimental pilot studies also can be strengthened using some of these techniques (Rubin & Babbie, 2005). Consequently, the publication of weakly controlled studies—on grounds that stronger controls are not feasible—may be becoming harder to justify.

CONCLUSION

The foregoing recommendations are just some small steps that can be tried to alleviate some of the problems regarding how the reportage, utilization, and exploitation of weakly controlled studies might lead to EBP becoming a meaningless shibboleth. But even if these recommendations get implemented and prove to be successful, they will not overcome all of the barriers to making social work practice more scientific. Social work research instructors are reminded every semester of how the bulk of students studying to become social work practitioners have little interest in producing research or utilizing it to guide their practice. Moreover, many of them fear quantitative methods and have neither an appetite, nor much of an aptitude, for such methods. Study after study also has found analogous problems among social work practitioners. It is not uncommon to find doctoral students who have weak research aptitudes or who reject contemporary positivism. Most of these students manage to find like-minded dissertation chairs and committee members who approve their dissertations and perhaps reinforce their relativistic epistemological paradigms. Consequently, the struggle to make social work more scientific seems likely to continue to be an uphill battle far into the future.

Despite the grounds for skepticism expressed in this chapter, I'll end on an optimistic note. I spearheaded an international symposium on improving the teaching of EBP, which took place in Austin, Texas, in October 2006 (sponsored by the University of Texas at Austin School of Social Work and my endowed professorship). The symposium proceedings produced many promising recommendations, and the symposium speakers formed an ad hoc task force, called the *Austin Initiative*, to work on their implementation. Leaders of the Austin Initiative are well aware of the daunting challenges that must be surmounted if we are to be more successful than prior efforts to make social work more scientific. But recognizing those challenges should neither reduce our chances of success nor dampen our enthusiasm. Remembering that the ultimate aim of EBP and scientific practice is to improve on our profession's track record of dubious effectiveness in helping people in need, there simply is no acceptable alternative to trying to make social work more scientific, no matter how daunting the obstacles we may face.

REFERENCES

Bloom, M., Fischer, J., & Orme, J. (2003). *Evaluating practice: Guidelines for the accountable professional* (4th ed.). Boston: Allyn & Bacon.

Briar, S., Weissman, H., & Rubin, A. (Eds.). (1981). *Research utilization in social work education* (pp. 48–58). New York: Council on Social Work Education.

Casselman, B. (1972). On the practitioner's orientation toward research. *Smith College Studies in Social Work, 42*, 211–233.

Cheatham, J. M. (1987). The empirical evaluation of clinical practice: A survey of four groups of practitioners. *Journal of Social Service Research, 10*, 163–177.

Chwalisz, K. (2003). Evidence-based practice: A framework for twenty-first-century scientific-practitioner training. *Counseling Psychologist, 31*, 497–528.

Council on Social Work Education. (1971). *Manual of accrediting standards*. New York: Author.

Denzin, N. K., & Lincoln, Y. S. (1994). *Handbook of qualitative research*. Thousand Oaks, CA: Sage.

Fischer, J. (1973). Is casework effective? A review. *Social Work, 18*, 5–21.

Fraser, M. W. (2004). Intervention research in social work: Recent advances and continuing challenges. *Research on Social Work Practice, 14*, 210–222.

Gibbs, L., & Gambrill, E. (2002). Evidence-based practice: Counterarguments to objections. *Research on Social Work Practice, 12*, 452–476.

Guo, S., Rose, R. A., & Bowens, G. L. (2006, January 14). Quasi-experimental strategies when randomization fails: Propensity score matching and sensitivity analysis. Paper presented at the annual conference of the Society for Social Work and Research, San Antonio, TX.

Henggeler, S., Lee, T., & Burnes, J. A. (2002). What happens after the innovation is identified? *Clinical Psychology: Science and Practice*, 9(2), 191–194.

Huberman, M. (1994). Research utilization: The state of art. *Knowledge, Technology, and Policy*, 7(4), 13–33.

Jayaratne, S., & Levy, R. L. (1979). *Empirical clinical practice*. New York: Columbia University Press.

Kirk, S. A., & Fischer, J. (1976). Do social workers understand research? *Journal of Education for Social Work, 12*, 63–67.

Kirk, S. A., Osmalov, M., & Fischer, J. (1976). Social workers' involvement in research. *Social Work, 21*, 121–124.

Kirk, S. A., & Penka, C. E. (1992). Research utilization and MSW education: A decade of progress. In A. J. Grasso & I. Epstein (Eds.), *Research utilization in the social services* (pp. 407–422). New York: Haworth.

Kirk, S. A., & Reid, W. J. (2002). *Science and social work practice*. New York: Columbia University Press.

Messer, S. B. (2006). What qualifies as evidence in effective practice? Patient values and preferences. In J. C. Norcross, L. E. Beutler, & R. F. Levant (Eds.), *Evidence-based practices in mental health: Debate and dialogue on the fundamental questions* (pp. 31–40). Washington, DC: American Psychological Association.

Mullen, E. J., & Bacon, W. B. (2004). Implementation of practice guidelines and evidence-based treatment: A survey of psychiatrists, psychologists, and social workers. In A. R. Roberts & K. Yeager (Eds.), *Evidence-based practice manual: Research and outcome measures in health and human services* (pp. 210–218). New York: Oxford University Press.

Mullen, E. J., & Dumpson, J. R. (Eds.). (1972). *Evaluation of social intervention*. San Francisco: Jossey-Bass.

Mullen, E. J., Schlonsky, A., Bledsoe, S. E., & Bellamy, J. L. (2005). From concept to implementation: Challenges facing evidence-based social work. *Evidence and Policy, 1*, 61–84.

Mullen, E. J., & Streiner, D. L. (2004). The evidence for and against evidence-based practice. *Brief Treatment and Crisis Intervention, 4*, 111–121.

Nugent, W. R. (1991). An experimental and qualitative analysis of a cognitive-behavioral intervention for anger. *Social Work Research and Abstracts, 27*(3), 3–8.

Padgett, D. K. (1998). *Qualitative methods in social work research*. Thousand Oaks, CA: Sage.

Priebe, S., & Slade, M. (2002). *Evidence in mental health care*. New York: Brunner/Mazel.

Reed, G. M. (2006). What qualifies as evidence of effective practice? Clinical expertise. In J. C. Norcross, L. E. Beutler, & R. F. Levant (Eds.), *Evidence-based practices in mental health: Debate and dialogue on the fundamental questions* (pp. 13–23). Washington, DC: American Psychological Association.

Richey, C. A., Blythe, B. J., & Berlin, S. B. (1987). Do social workers evaluate their practice? *Social Work Research and Abstracts, 23*, 14–20.

Richmond, M. (1917). *Social diagnosis*. New York: Sage.

Rogers, E. M. (1995). *Diffusion of innovations* (4th ed.). New York: Free Press.

Rosen, A. (1994). Knowledge use in direct practice. *Social Service Review, 68*, 561–577.

Rosen, A., Proctor, E. K., Marrow-Howell, N., & Staudt, M. (1995). Rationales for practice decisions: Variations in knowledge use by decision task and social work service. *Research on Social Work Practice, 5*, 501–523.

Rosenblatt, A. (1968). The practitioner's use and evaluation of research. *Social Work, 13*, 53–59.

Rubin, A. (2008). *Practitioner's guide to using research for evidence-based practice*. Hoboken, NJ: Wiley.

Rubin, A., & Babbie, E. R. (2005). *Research methods for social work* (5th ed.). Belmont, CA: Brooks/Cole.

Rubin, A., & Parrish, D. (2007). Views of evidence-based practice among faculty in MSW programs: A national survey. *Research on Social Work Practice, 17*(1), 110–122.

Rubin, A., & Parrish, D. (in press). "Problematic phrases in the conclusions of published outcome studies: Implications for evidence-based practice." *Research on Social Work Practice*.

Rubin, A., & Rosenblatt, A. (Eds.). (1979). *Sourcebook on research utilization*. New York: Council on Social Work Education.

Rubin, A., & Zimbalist, S. E. (1979). *Trends in the MSW research curriculum: A decade later*. New York: Council on Social Work Education.

Shadish, W. R., Cook, T. D., & Campbell, D. T. (2001). *Experimental and quasi-experimental designs for generalized causal inference*. Boston: Houghton Mifflin.

Shlonsky, A., & Gibbs, L. (2004). Will the real evidence-based practice please stand up? Teaching the process of evidence-based practice to the helping professions. *Brief Treatment and Crisis Intervention, 4*(2), 137–153.

Sokal, A., & Bricmont, J. (1998). *Fashionable nonsense: Postmodern intellectuals' abuse of science*. New York: Picador.

Thyer, B. (2004). What is evidence-based practice? *Brief Treatment and Crisis Intervention, 4*, 167–176.

Weinbach, R. W., & Rubin, A. (Eds.). (1980). *Teaching social work research: Alternative programs and strategies*. New York: Council on Social Work Education.

Westen, D. I. (2006). Patients and treatments in clinical trials are not adequately representative of clinical practice. In J. C. Norcross, L. E. Beutler, & R. F. Levant (Eds.), *Evidence-based practices in mental health: Debate and dialogue on the fundamental questions* (pp. 161–171). Washington, DC: American Psychological Association.

Wood, K. M. (1978). "Casework effectiveness: A new look at the research evidence." *Social Work, 23*(6), 437– 458.

Zimbalist, S. E. (1977). *Historic themes and landmarks in social welfare research*. New York: Harper & Row.

Zlotnik, J. L., & Galambos, C. (2004). Evidence-based practices in health care: Social work possibilities. *Health and Social Work, 29*, 259–261.

Chapter 22

ISSUES IN SOCIAL WORK

Stanley L. Witkin and Roberta Rehner Iversen

Imagine for a moment that you were asked to write a chapter on issues in social work. What words or terms come to mind? Homelessness? Child abuse? Low salaries? Managed care? Globalization? Or perhaps poverty, advocacy, an aging population, research, and unemployment seem like the most salient issues. Indeed, all of these topics might be plausible candidates for your chapter. Given social work's considerable breadth and problem focus, a lengthy list would not be surprising.

Not every topic will be an issue for every social worker. What looms large for some will seem less significant to others. Inevitably, what is chosen for an issues chapter reflects the authors' interests and values. These in turn are influenced by professional positions, geographic, cultural and historic locations, and political leanings. This is certainly the case here although we have tried to be mindful of others' concerns. With so many candidates for inclusion, any select group of issues will likely generate agreement and disagreement among readers. Therefore, we do not claim that the issues identified and discussed in this chapter are *the* definitive ones in the profession. Rather, our aim is simply to demonstrate their importance to current and future social work understandings and practices.

WHAT IS AN ISSUE?

Before embarking on this undertaking, it may be useful to clarify what we mean by "issues." To label something as a social work issue suggests an unresolved matter germane to the profession that merits attention. Such an assessment may reflect the existence of differing views or unanswered questions about a topic. Thus, to acknowledge an issue is to accept a particular state of affairs. For example, by identifying globalization as an issue for social work, we are asking readers to accept (at least conditionally) that this topic is an important one whose influence on the profession, now and/or in the future, deserves attention.

Sometimes the viability of an issue can itself become the issue. For example, the percentage of social workers whose primary work is individual psychotherapy may be an issue for some members of the profession, such as those believing it is a peripheral function, but not for others. In this case, the disagreement reveals another underlying issue: the place of psychotherapy in social work.

This example suggests that issues do not exist in a vacuum and are often interdependent. Issues that appear independent, on closer inspection, may reveal shared assumptions. For example, common assumptions about research underlie issues of evidence-based practice and professionalism. Finally, the level of generality in which issues are expressed may obscure their relationship. For example, identifying child welfare and kinship care as separate issues overlooks how the latter issue is a subset of the former one.

It follows from our conceptualization that issues are relational and arbitrary. They are relational in requiring some type of agreement about a perceived state of affairs and arbitrary in the sense of not being inevitable. What counts as social work issues are negotiated through various means (e.g., journals), by various actors (e.g., professional organizations), in different locales and settings. Those topics considered issues function as highlighters—foregrounding matters that need to be addressed. Collectively, the identified issues generate a framework for understanding and influencing social work.

As noted, the social work issues discussed in this chapter reflect our assessments of the profession, its aims and practices, and the social contexts within which it functions. Rather than presenting a compendium, the chapter focuses on five interrelated topics that we believe have important implications for the profession: postmodernism/social construction, globalization, evidence-based practice, ethics, and the profession. In each case, we explain why we see the topic as an issue for social work and articulate some challenges it poses. A brief synopsis of our approach to each issue follows.

Postmodernism/Social Construction

In this section, we discuss changes in the intellectual landscape over the past 50 years associated with postmodernism. In particular, we examine the postmodern expression known as *social construction* in terms of the changes it invites in our understandings and practices. From this particular stance, social work and social construction are highly congruent. This leads us to wonder why social construction has not been embraced by the profession and to consider the implications of this situation.

Globalization

Global interdependencies among economic, political, environmental, cultural, and technological spheres have changed the social work landscape. Many of the local conditions that social workers seek to ameliorate are linked to global trends and actions. Although the term *globalization* is often used to explain these trends and actions, it has multiple meanings. We attempt to "unpack" some of these meanings and to explore how social workers can adopt global perspectives and use global processes for the betterment of the people they serve.

Evidence-Based Practice

Social work's status as a research-based profession has been a subject of concern for much of its history. Should social work be a research (i.e., scientifically) based profession? If so, what does that mean? In recent years, the ascendance of evidence-based practice across several professions has had an important influence on social work research, education, and practice. We consider this development in light of the profession's aims and values and alternative ways of making sense of our practices.

Ethics

Values and ethics are part of the fabric of social work. The profession's code of ethics serves as a statement of its values, as a guide for professional conduct, and as a form of protection for clients. While these functions have provided some benefits, the code also reflects ways of understanding that exclude certain perspectives. Drawing on previous discussions of postmodern thought and globalization, we explore these topics and their implications for the profession.

The Profession

Social work's status as a profession has long been a topic of concern. Historically, social work has occupied a space in the interstices between society's dominant institutions and those marginalized by those institutions. Attempts to increase professional status, such as by becoming more research-based, have, in the opinion of some, moved social work closer to becoming a representative of the very institutions that generate the problems it aims to eliminate. Alternatively, moving toward a more "radicalized" position leaves social work more vulnerable to sanctions by these institutions and with less resources and legitimation. Thus, we consider how this tension affects social work's ability to fulfill its mission, the plusses and minuses of professionalism and alternative models that might be considered.

FROM THE MODERN TO THE POSTMODERN: SOCIAL CONSTRUCTION AND SOCIAL WORK

In this section, we discuss some basic ideas connected with postmodernism and social construction and how they relate to social work. Although only a cursory exegesis of these complex topics is possible here, it provides an important context for the other issues addressed.

Unlike other helping professions (such as psychiatry), whose development was closely aligned with science, social work developed from a moral and philanthropic tradition (Lubove, 1965). Rather than lay claim to a particular area of expertise, social workers focused on addressing broader social ills and providing relief for those who were marginalized and disenfranchised. While these are noble aims, they are not associated with professional or academic status. One consequence has been an ongoing tension between social work's historical mission and its aspirations for professional and social recognition.

Two well-known, perennial examples of this tension concern the appropriate balance between individual and social change and the importance of a distinctive social work knowledge base. Social workers' perceptions of these tensions—their salience, interpretation, and proposed solutions—have varied with broader social and intellectual trends. Thus, the development of medical education and the scientifically based practice of medicine in the early twentieth century influenced social work's professional orientation. Similarly, the advent and popularity of psychodynamic theories and therapies in the 1930s and 1940s created the "psychiatric social worker" who focused on individual change. More recently, the intellectual and artistic movement associated with the term *postmodern* has generated new tensions about social work's foci and knowledge base. In particular, new understandings of science, knowledge production, and the status of knowledge have led to alternative visions of the future of social work.

Postmodernism

Postmodernism is a complex notion that defies precise definition; some might even say that resisting definition is one of postmodernism's "defining" qualities. Simply put, the word suggests something that came after, or is different from, modernism—a term usually associated with ideas derived from a period in history known as The Enlightenment (roughly the eighteenth century). The Enlightenment emerged in Europe as a reaction to the authority of the Church and the power of the aristocracy.

Enlightenment thinking was characterized by the belief in reason as the path to progress and the perfection of man. The "modernist project" extended this thinking through the quest for truth through science. O'Farrell (1999) described the modernist creed as "the judicious use of reason and our powers of rational science will eventually solve all our political and social problems as well as allow us to master our physical environment in the form of our own bodies as well as the broader natural environment" (p. 11). This led to an epistemology where "knowledge is first, scientific and, second, absolutely knowable and truthful" (Ladson-Billings, 2003, p. 6).

Postmodernism represents disillusionment with these beliefs. It rejects "meta-narratives" (overarching beliefs or stories about history or humanity that are assumed to be universal and true) such as the inevitable march toward progress. In their place, it posits multiple ways of knowing that are local and changing. Singular "Truth" is replaced by plural truths that are historically and culturally contingent. Language is not viewed as a transparent conveyer or reflection of facts about the world, but as constituting what is taken to be real. Therefore, the study of language and language use can reveal assumptions and beliefs that are not readily apparent.

For many social work practitioners these differences may be barely visible or if they are, not particularly pressing. Like the proverb about not seeing the forest for the trees, modernist understandings represent the paradoxical case of something being so broad and pervasive that it is difficult to perceive. But without awareness, there is no opportunity to analyze or choose alternatives. Parton (2002), drawing on the philosopher Nicholas Rose (1996), expressed succinctly the importance of postmodern perspectives for social work: "Perhaps most centrally, such perspectives have reactivated a question which has lain dormant in social theory for many years but which touches the heart of much social work—what kinds of human being have we become" (p. 237).

The status of science as the authoritative source of truth about the world and its expression in activities known as research make its relationship to social work an important issue. Our beliefs about science and the nature of knowledge form the backdrop for education, practice, and research. More specifically, they influence how and what social workers are taught, the problems they consider relevant, appropriate ways to address those problems, and how to assess their usefulness.

For a long time, it was assumed that science used a particular method ("the scientific method") and that the proper application of this method would lead to Truth, that is, empirical facts or generalizations about the world. Practitioners of science ("scientists") were revered for their superior intelligence, logical adroitness, and dispassionate pursuit of Truth. Their use of the scientific method was considered a neutral way of discovering objective knowledge free of bias or the values and preferences of researchers. Science itself was believed to progress in a cumulative fashion with each generation of scientists building on the work of their predecessors. Thus, the rational pursuit of knowledge through science was believed to lead to inevitable progress and betterment in the world.

These views made the scientific establishment very powerful and relatively immune from most kinds of criticism. Research-based knowledge was difficult to dispute on grounds other than its own internal criteria. Other sources of critique were "nonscientific" and by definition not relevant or authoritative. Having a scientific base was an important claim for any profession seeking wide recognition and legitimacy. Thus social work sought to portray itself as based on scientifically derived facts about society rather than simply the expression of altruistic impulses.

Despite the authority attributed to scientific discourse, alternative perspectives emerged. Philosophical and social analyses questioned the underlying assumptions of science and proposed new accounts of knowledge development (e.g., Hanson, 1958; Knorr-Cetina, 1981; Weimer, 1979; Winch, 1958). During the 1960s, a time of social upheaval in the United States, alternative histories of science began to achieve notice. A landmark publication was Thomas Kuhn's *The Structure of Scientific Revolutions* (1962) in which he proposed an account of knowledge development that did not follow an upward linear trajectory (the progressive piling up of facts), but rather was characterized by periods of relative quiet and upheaval in which competing groups of scientists vied for theoretical ascendancy. The victors of such contests (i.e., paradigm clashes) were decided in large part by social and cultural factors rather than by neutral, objective assessments of the truth value of the competing viewpoints. This led Kuhn to conclude that, "We may have to relinquish the notion, explicit or implicit, that changes of paradigm carry scientists and those who learn from them closer and closer to the truth" (p. 171). Soon, scholars in more applied fields like psychology began to question the authority of scientifically established truths, even the mythology around scientists themselves (Mahoney, 1976).

Social work was slow to take up these issues. This made sense for a profession aspiring toward mainstream acceptance as a legitimate profession and a field of academic study. Also, other social developments such as the formalization of program evaluation during the 1960s and early 1970s encouraged a closer association between social work and mainstream science.

Fueled by national legislation mandating evaluations for government-funded projects and "sunset" regulations requiring programs to periodically justify their need for continued funding, program evaluation developed as a separate field. Early models of evaluation were based on fairly straightforward extrapolations of scientific research (see, e.g., Suchman, 1967), an area in which social workers were not considered highly proficient.

Around this same time period, the field of family therapy, begun in the late 1950s, became established as a separate field of practice and research with its own professional associations and academic journals. Despite social work's long-standing, pioneering work with families, it was never seen as a leader in this area. This may have been due to its lack of research and publications and to its close and hierarchical connection to psychiatry (Gurman & Kniskern, 1981).

In light of these developments and dwindling program resources, social work's efforts to align itself more closely with scientific research was a good political strategy. Still lacking, however, was a way to get ordinary practitioners involved in research. The development of single-case designs (or single-system designs as they were later called) seemed to address this problem.

Originally developed in psychology, single-case designs were advocated as a vehicle for creating a scientific, practitioner-driven knowledge base for social work practice (Kirk & Reid, 2002). Characterized by repeated measurements and the manipulation of interventions with individual clients, these designs were seen as clinical analogies to conventional research. They quickly became the defining feature of what became known as the scientist-practitioner movement in social work. Proponents of this movement envisioned social work practitioners using single-case designs en masse to generate a wealth of empirical data on the efficacy of their interventions. However, despite various attempts to make these designs more flexible and responsive to practice realities, this vision was not realized. Nevertheless, the scientist-practitioner movement remains strong, reincarnated as evidenced-based practice, an issue that is discussed later in this chapter.

Tensions associated with social work as science continue to exist. While proponents point to improved ability to compete for external research funds and increased recognition from institutions such as the National Institute of Mental Health, critics question the cost of such gains, for example, the ability of social work to fulfill its less popular but crucial mandate of social change. For social workers with postmodern sensibilities, the continued adherence to modernist concepts such as universality and objectivity exacerbate or generate problems instead of reducing them. Rather than being value-free, mainstream scientific approaches are considered value-denying and too often these values reflect and perpetuate those of historically dominant cultures (Western), genders (males), and races (Caucasian).

Social Construction

Postmodern perspectives represent, in part, responses to these concerns. Within social work, social construction has been particularly influential. As Kirk and Reid (2002) noted, "Social constructionism has emerged as the dominant epistemology in postmodern thought in social work" (p. 13). Although there is no one definitive version of social construction, most focus on the social processes—from the interpersonal to the historical—that give rise to and maintain beliefs and values.

The version of social construction developed by Kenneth Gergen (1994) integrates three strands of critique associated with postmodern thought. These include: (1) The literary critique concerned with how knowledge is bounded and shaped by textual traditions, rhetorical strategies and tropes, and the meanings of texts; (2) the social critique that explores the historical, social, and cultural dimensions of knowledge production; and (3) the ideological critique that exposes ways in which knowledge and power are intertwined and how the control of knowledge maintains dominant-subordinate relationships. Drawing on these different critiques, constructionist analyses often reveal previously unrecognized aspects of commonly held beliefs. By exposing implicit assumptions of beliefs and the social forces that maintain them or silence others, social workers can assess their appropriateness or utility and consider alternatives.

Like most postmodern-oriented scholars, social constructionists consider language of central importance. From a constructionist perspective, there is no necessary connection between a "thing" (i.e., an object or event) and what it is called. For example, there is nothing intrinsic to two people interacting that demands their encounter be labeled in a particular way. Rather, depending on their facility with language and other contextual factors, the same interaction may be labeled credibly as hostile, friendly, tense, calm, therapeutic, or a host of other descriptive adjectives. This suggests that the relationship between things and what they are called can, and often will, vary over time and across different social and cultural contexts. The implications for social work are enormous. For example, this position implies not only that what we call things may have important consequences, but that we have choice in the names we apply to people and situations. Consider, for example, the differences between homeless person and hobo, borderline personality disorder and abuse survivor, withdrawn and socially excluded, depressed and oppressed. This also suggests that we can challenge much that is taken for granted, such as ways of "languaging" people as well as objects and events that are presumed and unquestioned.

Social Construction and Social Work

In our view, social construction and social work have much in common. "From its origins as an alternative voice to the hegemony of the dominant knowledge establishment to its emphasis on the social dimension of human life, social constructionism echoes social work's values and mission" (Witkin, 1999a, p. 6). Other common features include an emphasis on contextual understanding, questioning what is taken for granted, and valuing multiplicity (Iversen, Gergen, & Fairbanks, 2005).

Both social work and social construction highlight the word "social" in their names. Although not used identically, the primacy of the social in practice and analysis is an important area of commonality. Related to this is the recognition that understanding must be contextual. People cannot be understood apart from their environments. The ecological perspective (Germain, 1979) is a well-known social work expression of this principle. Social constructionists expand the idea of environment to include historical and cultural traditions and language.

When social work is aligned with those who are marginalized, it tends to question the warrant for dominant understandings and institutionalized practices (e.g., traditional definitions of marriage or family). Similarly, social constructionists are concerned with how we have come to understand ourselves and others and to explore alternative constructs. These questionings rely on creating space for, and listening to, diverse voices. For social workers, it means recognizing the importance of diversity. For social constructionists, it stems from the position that no one perspective can claim universal truth. Establishing truth is less important than knowing how truth claims or understandings function—what problems and interventions are rendered visible or credible and which are obscured or devalued. For example, how do psychological theories make possible certain mental disorders? What maintains these beliefs? Who benefits and who is disadvantaged? What understandings about children support practices such as foster care? Such questions are relevant both to social work and social construction.

It is important to note that addressing the issue of social work's relationship to postmodern and social construction perspectives does not require claiming one position as victor and eliminating all others. Rather, a challenge is to create adequate space for all perspectives to be seen, heard, and considered. One way to do this is to extend the profession's commitment to diversity beyond that of socially defined categories to the intellectual realm.

As with other forms of diversity, social workers recognize that marginality is not a measure of worth or desirability; individuals everywhere can benefit from a richness of perspectives. This leads us into consideration of social work from a global perspective.

GLOBALIZATION AND GLOBAL SOCIAL WORK

According to the *Oxford English Dictionary,* the word *globalization* first appeared in 1962. By the 1980s, globalization was being used with increasing frequency in the professional and popular literature (e.g., Levitt, 1983). In July 2006, a Google search on the word globalization resulted in 101,000,000 hits. Thus, in a relatively short time, globalization went from a nonexistent concept to one considered by many to describe an important dimension of contemporary life. Exactly what it describes, however, is less certain.

What do you think of when you hear the word globalization? Multinational corporations? The Internet? McDonaldization? Increased opportunities? Terrorism? These were some of the responses to this question given by social work students from different countries who were attending a course on social work from a global perspective (cf. Witkin, 1999b). Similarly, social work practitioners and academics surveyed at an international social work conference often expressed ambivalence about globalization, noting its potential benefits and negative consequences. For example, to a social worker from Australia globalization represented "The collapse of economic and cultural boundaries between nation states. This can have the impact of encouraging the dominance of one global culture (primarily an American one!) or recognizing and celebrating cultural differences." A social worker from Palestine stated that: "Globalization for me has two conflicting sides: easy communication and exchange of experiences and research findings in all professional fields on one side; and lack of balance when being exposed to the influences and interests of the super powers" (Rowe, Hanley, Moreno, & Mould, 2000, p. 71). Brennan (2002) links this potential for positive and negative consequences as the unknown potentials of globalization for extended community and connectedness, or the expansion of corporatization and Americanization. Clearly, globalization is an important term that has many meanings. In this section, we explore ways of understanding globalization and the implications of those understandings for social work.

Thinking about Globalization

The association of the term *globalization* with economics and technology contributes to the perception that it is a recent phenomenon originating in the West. However, both of these beliefs have been challenged. The process of globalization—at least as the exchange of ideas, goods, or technology—has a lengthy history. Urmetzer (2005) cautions that "presenting the word's etymology as equivalent to its history constitutes too literal an interpretation, as it ignores the fact that the concept of global markets has existed for a long time" (p. 39). In addition, major scientific and technological achievements of the first millennium, such as the invention of the clock, the magnetic compass, gunpowder, and mathematics originated in China and Arabia and spread from East to West (Sen, 2002b).

What does seem new about globalization is the scale and intensity of supraterritorial relationships; that is, relationships that are not linked to territory. Advances in transportation and communication technologies have made it possible to quickly, even instantaneously, interact with others anywhere on the planet. Scholte (2002) noted that in centuries past technological changes, such as railroads, reduced distances "*within* territorial geography" (emphasis in original), whereas "In cases of supraterritoriality, place is not territorially fixed, territorial distance is covered in no time, and territorial boundaries present no particular impediment" (p. 19). These changes have transformed our understanding of the concept of distance. Rather than being an objective concept, distance, according to Bauman, (1998) "is a social product; its length varies depending on the speed with which it may be overcome" (p. 12). One consequence of the transcendence of distance is the polarization between those who can move freely among localities and those who "watch helplessly the sole locality they inhabit moving away from under their feet" (Bauman, p. 18). Such changes represent new challenges for social workers as when jobs are "outsourced," creating unemployment.

Another aspect of supraterritoriality has been an increased sense that we are living in one world in which there is a greater and deeper interdependence among geographical regions such that small events in one place can lead to greater consequences somewhere else (Nye & Donahue, 2000). Healy (2001) discussed four categories of interdependence—environmental, cultural, economic, and security—in relation to social work. Although she presents these forms somewhat independently, it is important to remember that the forms themselves are interdependent; for example, environmental interdependence will affect economic interdependence and vice versa. These forms are briefly discussed next.

Environmental Interdependence

All humans depend on the earth's resources: plants, animals, air, and water. Almost daily, it seems, reports about global warming, migrating diseases, and toxic chemicals underscore our environmental interdependence. Although awareness of this interdependence has increased, it remains selective and muddled by political and economic rhetoric.

Cultural Interdependence

Supraterritoriality has blurred geographic boundaries. Cultural contacts and exchanges are frequent and intense. For some, this is a welcome development leading to enhanced diversity and opportunities, while for others it means increased uniformity and economic exploitation. One concern is the imbalance of power that characterizes many cultural contacts and how imports and exports are decided on economic factors and control of media outlets. For example, Ramsaran and Price (2003) argue that the ideology of consumerism is transmitted via the media to select groups in capitalist countries through "niche marketing" that creates dissatisfaction and demand for new goods. In emerging markets the goal of this ideology is to convert even remote parts of the globe into a "transnational middle class."

Economic Interdependence

Martin Luther King once stated that "Before I finish breakfast I have depended on half the world." Unfortunately, "half of the world's largest economic units are not nations but multinational corporations" (Healy, 2001, p. 110). Internationalization of the economy means that jobs can be moved, depending on availability of labor markets, costs, and profits.

These developments have important implications for social workers. The search for cheap labor changes the relationship of industry to community. Bauman (1998), for example, discussed how globalization has led to the disconnection of power from obligations, which creates a new type of absentee landlord. This "disconnection of power from obligations [includes] duties toward employees, but also toward the younger and weaker, toward yet unborn generations and toward the self-reproduction of the living conditions of all; in short, freedom from duty to contribute to daily life and the perpetuation of the community" (p. 9).

Security Interdependence

Media reports of international terrorism and nuclear proliferation are grim reminders of our security interdependence. Violence is no longer confined to conflict between or within nation states, but to anyone seen as representing a threat to a particular group or way of life. Conflicts over resources such as oil also illustrate how various forms of interdependence (e.g., security, economics, environment) are themselves interdependent. In a similar vein, Kellner (n.d.), analyzing global terrorism, writes, "As different groups gain access to technologies of destruction and devise plans to make conventional technologies, like the airplane, instruments of destruction, then dangers of unexpected terror events . . . proliferate and become part of the frightening mediascape of the contemporary moment" (p. 17).

Such incidents suggest that the notion of global interdependence itself may need further analysis. True interdependence, that is, interdependence between equals, encourages cooperation—a quid pro quo relationship. Dependence, on the other hand, encourages manipulation, exploitation and often anger. Social workers, more than most professions, understand the dynamics of power imbalances and can help ameliorate their negative impact.

The above discussion reveals the inescapable political dimension of globalization. The consequences, positive and negative, of global forces are not experienced equally. Thus it is not surprising that globalization has both proponents and opponents. Disputes regarding the benefits or losses of globalization are difficult to resolve because indicators of both are readily available. For example, in a recent article in the *Hong Kong Journal of Social Work,* Shanti Khinduka (2001) noted that life expectancy has increased, but more than 300 million people will not live past the age of 40; health-care advances are extolled almost daily, yet one million children in Africa die each year of malaria, a preventable disease; global literacy has increased yet more than 800 million adults cannot read or write; and despite enormous advances in agriculture, millions live in states of perpetual hunger.

Although identifying specific globally related trends is important, general debates about globalization tend not to be constructive. Often such debates assume a relatively unidimensional, deterministic view of globalization. An alternative, suggested by Kellner (2002), is to retain the complexity of globalization, seeing it as neither good nor bad, but a site of struggle between different views. From this perspective, globalization can be thought of as a discourse—a way of understanding and talking about the world. Globalization as discourse invites us to think of globalization as a construct—a way of making sense of complexity—rather than as a "thing." It reduces globalization's aura of inevitability and its status as a causal agent.

A discourse perspective also encourages examination of factors that influence how the word globalization is used. It helps us move beyond dichotomous explanations such as good/bad or global/local to consider "both/and" positions. For instance, rather than talking about global problems or local problems, we have global/local problems requiring global/local solutions (Kellner, 2002).

Practice Implications

Social workers need to enter these sites of struggle between competing discourses if they are to influence the directions and impacts of global developments. One way of conceptualizing this struggle has been "globalization from above" and "globalization from below." The former refers to corporate capitalism and instruments of the capitalist state such as the World Trade Organization. It is characterized by a consumerist ethos and a Westernized world view (Falk, 1992). The latter refers to ways in which marginalized or socially excluded groups resist global developments promulgated by dominant groups. More affirmatively, it also refers to how groups "use the institutions and instruments of globalization to further democratization and social justice" (Kellner, n.d., p. 11).

Holland (2005) provides an example of globalization from below in which the Internet was used to promote locally controlled economic development. Five hundred old computers distributed to remote rural villages in Nicaragua enabled teenaged daughters of poor, illiterate peasants to use the Internet to track price fluctuations in the global corn market. Using e-mail to connect with each other, these young women formed a marketing cooperative that helped them determine the best time to market their product and eliminated the need for traditional regional brokers. The result was a doubling of the sale price of the corn.

Social workers operating from a dual local/global perspective are more likely to recognize their interrelationship. Rather than simply decrying the effects of global forces on the plight of their clients or working solely at the local level, they seek to reconfigure the global-local matrix in ways that allow people to participate in the benefits of globalization and resist its negative aspects. In the example of Nicaragua, key tasks were getting resources (computers) into the hands of people, helping them learn how to use them, and helping them form empowering alliances—variations on well-known social work functions. By operating with global awareness, social workers can carry out these functions in new ways.

In a presentation on globalization, Nobel Prize winning economist Amartya Sen (2002a) stressed the importance of inequality in evaluating global trends. Similar to our earlier discussion regarding the futility of debating whether globalization is positive or negative, Sen proposed moving beyond the debate of whether the rich are getting richer and the poor getting poorer. Rather, he argued that even if the poor are getting a little richer, it does not necessarily mean they are "getting their fair share of benefits of economic interrelations and the potential rewards from global interaction." The central issue, according to Sen, is "the massive levels of inequality and poverty that exist in the world." This view is consistent with social work's position on social justice and suggests how social work values can inform the ways in which we understand, participate in, and respond to globalization discourse. As Ahmadi (2003) proposed: "By emphasizing social work's core values of human dignity, solidarity, democracy and the individual's right to adequate living conditions, at a level that exceeds the nation-state, and by directing its activities toward the whole of humanity instead of only the citizens of a specific society, international social work could play an important role in bridging the national and cultural gaps between people with whom it works" (pp. 18–19). Operating from a similar value context, the U.N. High-Level Panel on Globalization and the State (United Nations, 2001) noted the "need to promote broad social awareness about globalization," and that "Globalization must mean globalizing of human rights and of the struggle against deprivation and poverty" (p. 5). Taken together, these statements extend the discourse of globalization to ethics and human rights. Social workers are well positioned to make these considerations part of the public discourse on globalization. They can ask, as did Nelson Mandela: "Is globalization only for the powerful? Does it offer nothing to the men, women and children who are ravaged by the violence of poverty?" (cited in Kellner, n.d., p. 8).

Understanding and practicing social work from a global perspective requires an interest in and openness to the ways in which we are interdependent, respect for different cultural and knowledge traditions, and a willingness to engage in constructive dialogue across those differences. Such constructive dialogue cannot come from an orientation whose aim is to demonstrate the "rightness" of one position (and the "wrongness" of others), but from an appreciation of the rich resources that diverse understanding and practices make available to us. We can facilitate others' participation in globalization discourse by helping them gain access to resources (e.g., Internet), advocating for changes in policies and laws (e.g., more equitable distribution of resources and inclusion in decision-making processes), and helping others to mobilize and form empowering alliances. For some, evidence-based practice—the next issue we explore—can play a role in influencing social work around the globe.

EVIDENCE-BASED PRACTICE

As noted earlier, social work's relationship with science has waxed and waned over its history. In this section we examine more closely a current manifestation of that relationship: evidence-based practice (EBP). We reflect on EBP in light of social work's aims and values and by exploring alternative ways of making sense of its practices. Extending our discussion of "science" in social work that was introduced in the section on postmodernism, we consider the development and current state of evidence-based practice.

Science and the Social Work Profession

Social work's relationship with science dates back to the beginnings of the profession. For example, in the late 1800s advocates of the scientific charity movement looked to the systematic data collection and causal analyses of science as a model for charity efforts (Kirk & Reid, 2002; Lubove, 1965). "Being scientific" meant using science (i.e., the scientific method) as a model for practice and/or as a source of authoritative knowledge (Kirk & Reid, 2002). More broadly, an association with science was a way of demonstrating professionalism.

Around the same period, the professionalization of the field of medicine, with its science orientation, also influenced the orientation of social work. Abraham Flexner's (1915) noted report on whether social work was a profession outlined that "the unmistakable professions . . . derive their material immediately from learning and science" (p. 583). He further critiqued social work for its essentially "moral" character and polemic tendencies, holding that "When social work becomes thoroughly professional in character and scientific method, it will be perceived that vigor is not synonymous with intelligence" (p. 589). Despite Flexner's relative ignorance of social work (by his own admission), the "Flexner myth" has strongly influenced social work's relationship to science and its expression in research.

Science, medicine, social work research, and professionalism became further intertwined as the fields of psychiatry and psychology came into prominence in the early 1900s, particularly after Freud's lectures at Clark University in 1912. However, this entwinement was not a smooth one. As Austin (1983) wrote, "While Freudian theory appeared to satisfy one element of the Flexner model [a systematic, transferable body of knowledge], it did not deal directly with the model's strong emphasis on the importance of laboratory and experimental science" (p. 370). It is thus reasonable to conclude that this era culminated in the divergence of psychiatrically/psychologically oriented (later, clinical) social work practice from the development of a systematic, "scientific" research orientation. In contrast, the field of medicine continued to develop its evidentiary base. These divergent directions in social work did not re-converge until the scientist-practitioner movement of the early 1970s discussed earlier.

The place of theory in scientific social work was and remains another area of contention. Many sociologists and psychologists emphasized the importance of theory for science and research (e.g., Greenwood, 1957) and their theories were commonly appropriated by social workers to inform practice. Theory development in social work, while of great importance, was seen by some as nonscientific in that it was not based on empirical generalization (for a contemporary perspective see, e.g., Thyer, 2001). This contributed to an estrangement between the theoretical and empirical dimensions of science with the latter being a characteristic of EBP.

Evidence-Based Practice Movement

As noted previously, social work's involvement with the contemporary evidence-based practice movement began with its interest in making practice more scientific in order to legitimate its professional standing and compete for resources, Although not called evidence-based practice in the 1970s, many of the same values and standards characteristic of EBP (e.g., belief in the superiority of scientific knowledge, objectivity) were touted as necessary to improve social work practice.

The reincarnation of scientific practice as EBP in social work (and other disciplines), was facilitated by the increased demand for "accountability" of outcomes. As Gibbs (2001) characterized it, "Privatization, managerialism and neo-liberal politics have ensured that agency-based research agendas are now firmly focused upon effectiveness, evaluation and monitoring" (p. 693). Given this context, it is perhaps not surprising that positivist-oriented science, which emphasizes measurement, methods, and quantification, reemerges as the dominant qualities of EBP. Minimizing the complex social processes that constitute practice, EBP purges knowledge production of its culture, contexts and subjects, "a move that permits the use of evidence as a political instrument where power interests can be obscured by seemingly neutral technical resolve" (Goldenberg, 2005, p. 2). This seemingly straightforward, neutral approach gains more attraction in an environment "of research-based knowledge on the development and debate of public policy" (Gibelman, 1999,

p. 305). In other words, EBP gives the *appearance* of being neutral which, ironically, makes it vulnerable to political manipulation.

Another important influence on the widespread adoption of EBP was its development and popularity in the field of medicine. Notable, however, is the shift in emphasis from its original aims. According to Gambrill (2006), "Evidence-based decision making arose [in the field of medicine] as an alternative to authority-based decision making in which decisions are based on criteria such as consensus, anecdotal experience, or tradition" (p. 339). In an oft-cited article, Sackett, Rosenberg, Muir-Gray, Haynes, and Richardson, (1996) defined evidence-based medicine as "the conscientious, explicit, and judicious use of current best evidence in making decisions about the care of individual patients" (p. 71). They cautioned that "evidence" is multifaceted, requiring "a bottom-up approach that integrates the best external evidence with individual clinical expertise and patients' choice" (p. 72).

Thus originally, evidence-based concepts were more a "philosophy of practice and policy" (p. 340) than a hierarchy of research methods. This original position seems consonant with the philosophical underpinnings of the profession of social work: particularly, its values of social justice, inclusion, and mutuality. However, the translation of this philosophy into social work practice seems to have taken a restrictive turn (Gambrill, 2006).

Debate about EBP in Social Work: Pro and Con

The debate about evidence-based practice mirrors social work's historical relationship with science. Briefly, proponents argue that "EBP holds great promise for building stronger bridges between science and practice" (Jenson, 2005, p. 132). They characterize the history of social work and scientific research as insufficient and self-referential—"authoritarian" in Gambrill's (2001) terms. Instead they propose a hierarchical ordering "within the EBP model, [in which] all forms of evidence are not seen as equivalently informative. There is a clear and explicitly articulated hierarchy of research methods which science accepts as possessing the potential to provide credible answers to clinical questions" (McNeece & Thyer, 2004, p. 10). This hierarchy from highest to lowest is: (1) systematic reviews or meta-analyses, (2) randomized clinical trials (RCTs), (3) quasi-experimental studies, (4) case-control and cohort studies, (5) preexperimental group studies, (6) surveys, and (7) qualitative studies (p. 10). Similarly, Reid, Kenaley, and Colvin (2004) award primacy to social work interventions whose "efficacy has been demonstrated by controlled experimental research" (p. 71). "Nonscientific" sources of assessing efficacy, such as "practice wisdom, tradition, or common sense" are nowhere in evidence (McNeece & Thyer, 2004).

Underlying the commitment to evidentiary decision making is an ethical belief that practitioners' actions *ought* to rely on the best available evidence. Professionals have an obligation to be informed about the most efficacious practices because such practices will lead to better outcomes than with a less knowledgeable practitioner (Goodman, 2003). For some (e.g., Gambrill, 2006) this obligation extends beyond individual practitioners to the work environments of social service organizations.

Since presumably all practitioners rely on some criteria to inform their decisions, key issues become the types of information available (is all information "evidence"?) or used and how such information should be weighted. There appears to be a consequentialist ethic operating here; namely, that clients will fare better with practitioners who operate from an EBP framework than those who do not and social workers should maximize good outcomes.

Although such an ethical position might appear straightforward, there are several factors to consider. Many things besides a specific intervention influence practice encounters; for example, the practitioner-client relationship, how problems are defined, and environmental resources. Also, outcomes themselves can vary widely. Most EBP recommendations are based on particular outcomes measured in particular ways. These may or may not be most relevant for different clients. Some would argue that EBP favors outcomes that lend themselves to empirical, reproducible measures thereby restricting the field of possibilities (see the discussion that follows).

In addition to these concerns, those who feel guarded about or oppose EBP worry about how a positivist empirical framework fits with social work values of empowerment and inclusion. They assert that objectivity (in the sense of evidence as "facts" about the world) is more a cultural achievement than a phenomenological truth and that the privileging of randomized clinical trials is top-down and undemocratic.

For example, Gibbs (2001) argues that consumer-oriented research, with its increased attention to the voices of the service users, is often "tokenistic" (p. 691). Walker (2001) finds similarly that "consumers and service users are still largely absent from the centers of power and control in personal social service provision. Effectiveness studies that fully incorporate client evaluations are still rare, as is user-participation in the design and monitoring of teaching programs or service delivery systems" (p. 33).

Evidence is produced within particular contexts of questions, perspectives, and desired outcomes. "Translation [of the EBP form of evidence] across to social problems and issues is far from straightforward" (Webb, 2001, p. 71). A danger of EBP is that the range of questions, perspectives and outcomes considered will be truncated in order to facilitate their fit with the "requirements" (e.g., measurement, experimental manipulation) of evidence (Griffiths, 2005). Webb (2001) is concerned that "evidence-based practice entraps professional practice within an instrumental framework which regiments, systematizes and manages social work within a technocratic framework of routinized operations [like 3 pills a day]" (p. 71). In effect—persons are reduced to their diagnoses, to which evidence-based therapeutic interventions are targeted. In contrast to this instrumental orientation, Goldstein (2000) sees practice as engaging clients' moral narratives, the "morass of goods and bads, rights and wrongs, evils and virtues, bearing little resemblance to the diagnostic labels or the balance sheet of assets or liabilities that the client inevitably earns" (p. 349). Whether there is "room" in EBP for this position is uncertain.

A more general concern that may be drawn from these critiques is that EBP may simply be a scientized version of the earlier hegemonic period of "professional expertise." For example, in a study of the development of EBP guidelines for physical therapy of children with disabilities, Landsman (2006) noted that "To some extent, authority and power constrain the range of knowledge that can be transformed into evidence; the knowledge of established 'experts' is authoritative despite sincere and largely successful efforts to construct an egalitarian process" (p. 2679). Reliance on research instrumentalism such as monitoring, while in the putative interest of the client, seems more driven by the need of organizations and other stakeholders to justify their expenditures to their funding bodies, which tends to foster power hierarchies and potentially exploitive practices.

As noted earlier, research can also be construed as a political act (Ladson-Billings, 2003; Witkin & Harrison, 2001) reflecting a power-oriented, Western cultural practice (Cannella & Lincoln, 2004). Despite the idealistic aspirations of some of its proponents,

EBP, like other forms of research, is subject to political and economic influence and the competing interests of different stakeholders. Such factors, while themselves not considered evidence, may influence what is considered evidence and how it is understood and used. In an analysis of the policy context of evidence-based medicine, Gordon (2006) argues that: "Determinations as to whether information counts as evidence, whether evidence is deemed valid, the risks of using available evidence, and whether evidence should be used to justify health policies or clinical care are based on the values stakeholders attribute to evidence. Policymakers' decisions to use currently available evidence to enact legislation or alternatively, to seek further evidence through additional research, reflects their valuation of social problems, respectively, viewed as being either worthy of immediate attention, or not" (p. 2717). Similarly, in a social work context, Parton (2007) cautions that EBP "has been used in a quite specific way which has the impact of reinforcing the political instrumentalism and aspirations for greater central control which are being implemented by the modernisation agenda. It is consistent with attempts to manufacture a sense of certainty in an increasingly uncertain world" (p. 155).

Broadening the Vision of Evidence in Social Work Practice and Research

More recently, scholars have called for broadening the purview of acceptable evidence beyond that gathered by randomized clinical trials of, primarily, health and mental health interventions. These more inclusive and more expansive epistemological and methodological perspectives hold different names and originate in different countries: for example, "critical best practices" in the United Kingdom (Ferguson, 2003); "critical approaches to structuralism" in Australia (Hugman, 2005); and integrating the art of practice and science of EBP in the United States (Pollio, 2006). Many of these approaches invoke the original intent of the evidence-based movement in medicine. Ferguson's (2003) "critical best practice," for example, requires a broadening of the concept of evidence-based practice to include qualitative research methods and the experiences of professionals, service users, and the production of "practice-based evidence" (p. 1005). McDonald (2003) cautions against a "one-size-fits-all" model (p. 137), and Gilgun (2005) argues for the reincorporation of clinical judgment via her position that, "Research-based evidence informs but does not replace clinical expertise, which is the basis of judgments as to how research findings are used with individual clients" (p. 53). Similarly, Parton (2007) argues for a broadening of EBP to incorporate research's emancipatory potential. He writes, "Evidence and different types of research could well provide a vital vehicle for critically commentating upon and resisting some of the centralising and dehumanising elements of contemporary policy and practice, that is reducing practitioners to organizational functionaries and community members to 'service users.' As ever, the key issue is invariably related to power and knowledge and, crucially, who asks the questions and with what import" (pp. 156–157).

While these perspectives differ along dimensions of methodology, target sample, field of practice, and policy or service orientation, they are epistemologically similar in their desire to broaden the range of acceptable evidence—in fact, they demand it, in the name of the historic social work and social welfare values and principles of empowerment, inclusion, multiplicity, and flexibility (see Gambrill, 2006). Reminiscent of a social constructionist perspective, Gibbs (2001) adds that, " 'Evidence' must be viewed as a social construct and reflect the many meanings that practitioners and service users may put forward to indicate success. Concepts like culture, spirituality, warmth and empathy [and we would add 'relationship'] are difficult to measure as evidence, yet they are clearly linked to effective social work" (p. 700). A critical issue, as Landsman (2006) noted, is that we must consider not only the "question of whose evidence counts, but what type of evidence is believed to matter" (p. 2679).

Ultimately, the verdict on EBP is still out. Will it save the besieged social work profession? Will it result in tangible and valued benefits for social service users? Will it be a transient fashion or religious belief (Morrell, 2000)? Will the influence of values on decisions be accommodated or diminished (cf. Munro, 2002)? And what are the implications for social work's ethical understandings and commitments? It is to this issue of ethics that we now turn.

ETHICS

Ethics lie at the heart of the social work profession, translating professional values, such as social justice, into conduct. They add substance to a vision about the kinds of people social workers should be and what they should do. The preamble to the National Association of Social Workers (NASW) Code of Ethics states that social workers "promote social justice and social change with and on behalf of clients"... "are sensitive to cultural and ethnic diversity and strive to end discrimination, oppression, poverty, and other forms of social injustice"... "seek to enhance the capacity of people to address their own needs"... and "seek to promote the responsiveness of organizations, communities, and other social institutions to individuals' needs and social problems" (NASW, 1999). These defining features of social work touch all aspects of professional activities: practice, education and research. Such breadth leads Freud and Krug (2002) to argue that: "Ethical considerations should dictate our use of theoretical models and they should even outweigh our reliance on research findings; ... [taking] an extreme example, research might show that chain gangs in prison reduce recidivism, yet, as social workers, we cannot condone such practices" (p. 475).

Although the need for professional ethics may seem self-evident, their meaning and function are less straightforward. First, there are different ways to view what is ethical. Second, as with any theory, there are multiple ways of translating concepts into action. Third, various functions of ethics in social work may be differently emphasized. These differing perspectives, in conjunction with the significance of ethics, are what make this an important issue for social work. Here too, so-called modernist and postmodern conceptions of ethics frame some of the most important controversies.

Ethical Perspectives

Discussions of social work ethics generally express (to varying degrees) three classic perspectives on moral conduct: consequentialism, deontology, and virtues. Consequentialist ethics focus on evaluating the consequences of one's action. For example, the philosopher Jeremy Bentham believed that action should be guided by the assessment of its pleasurable or painful consequences (called utilitarianism). Deontological ethics focus on rules or duties that one ought to follow or carry out in any situation. Kant's categorical imperative—that one should be guided by principles that can be adopted by everyone—is an exemplar of this perspective. Virtue ethics stress the role of personal attributes or characteristics in ethical conduct. For example, Aristotle, the founder of this approach, was concerned with what kind of people we ought to be in order to live a life that would be considered "good" (Aristotle, 1947/1992).

Each of these perspectives provides a useful analytical frame for assessing the rightness or wrongness of actions; however, each is also limited in important ways. Although consequences are commonly considered when determining appropriate conduct, evaluating whether benefits outweigh harms can be difficult, particularly in situations involving nonmaterial goods such as health, life, or well being. Also, how particular outcomes are evaluated may vary depending on the social context and who is doing the evaluating. It is not uncommon, for example, for social workers and their clients to hold disparate views about the benefits and harms of particular actions, such as removal of a child from her or his home.

Rule-based (deontological) theories are limited by their insensitivity to contextual factors. Kant's universal ideals are problematic in today's pluralistic world. Ethical positions develop within particular historical and cultural contexts. What is touted as universally applicable may not seem so from a different cultural standpoint.

Virtues tend to be individualistic and subject to various interpretations across cultures, times and situations. What is a virtue in one context can be a vice in another. Aristotle's virtues, for example, described what he believed to be the ideal Athenian male of the fourth century B.C., not necessarily the archetype for contemporary life.

The Postmodern Critique

The previous perspectives are "modernist" in their belief that there exists a set of objective, ethical principles that have essential features and universal applicability and in the assumption of individuals as autonomous moral agents. For postmodern theorists like Zygmut Bauman (1993), the quest for "an ethics that is universal and 'objectively founded' is a practical impossibility; perhaps even an *oxymoron,* a contradiction in terms" (p. 10). It is the disbelief in this possibility, according to Bauman, that defines postmodern thought about ethics. Similarly, Gergen (1994) questions whether the search for "universal standards of the good" is the best way to "enhance the quality of cultural life" (p. 106). One problem he notes is that in declaring universals, one must also discount or suppress alternative perspectives. Positions of ultimate superiority can be used to justify disruptions or eliminations of cultural traditions that function in important ways in the host culture. Sadly, history is replete with acts of savagery and oppression that were given moral justification: for example, the treatment of indigenous peoples of North America. Such egregious acts become comprehensible when one's moral language renders the victims as nonhuman, such as by equating them with animals, children, or women (when "man" is equated with human being; Rorty, 1998).

Gergen (1994) also questions the necessity and desirability of moral discourse in the creation and sustenance of a "good society." While acknowledging the important role of the language of individual morality and moral languages in general to social life, he nevertheless questions whether such precepts and their linguistic referents, such as "should" and "ought," are indispensable to an agreeable social order. Rather than promoting morality, such languages, in Gergen's view, function as regulatory devices keeping potential transgressors in check. They do this by giving rhetorical authority to ways of acting that already are part of traditional social interchange.

In social work, this regulatory function is evident in the various codes of ethics promulgated by professional associations. Social workers are expected to adhere to these codes (e.g., the prohibition against dual relationships) and may be sanctioned if they do not. In fact, the threat of such sanctions and, somewhat paradoxically, the protection of social workers from accusations of wrongdoing, seem to be major aims of these codes (Freud & Krug, 2002). Codes of ethics also are intended to protect clients by providing them with information about proper professional conduct. Finally, they have educational functions: providing guidelines for social workers faced with ethically ambiguous or conflictual situations, orienting students into the profession, and informing the public about social work.

Despite these positive aims, codes have been criticized for their overemphasis on regulatory and sanctioning functions and their inability to inspire "morally active practitioners" (Husband, 1995). For some, their modernist orientation is problematic. For example, Briskman and Noble (1999) found that social work codes of ethics in various countries tended toward universalism, individualism, and in some cases, lack of definitions for key concepts such as social justice. They argued that social work needs a postmodern ethics that challenges broad categorizations of people and can be responsive to diversity and otherness. In their view, ethics should always be open to negotiation and therefore provisional. In particular, social workers would actively seek the perspectives of those toward whom social work services are directed and find ways to take account of their views on ethical practice, deprivileging any one position.

Witkin (2000) also discussed the consequences of universalism and regulation in social work ethical codes. He noted that, "Without alternative perspectives the limits of our own belief systems become more difficult to assess" (p. 199). Such limits, in his view, are expressed in ethics that are more reactive than proactive, more about acts of commission than omission, more about individual conduct than collective responsibility, more about right or wrong than issues of power, more about sexual improprieties than draconian economic policies, more about the poor than the rich, and more about those who suffer from physical and emotional pain than those who restrict and profit from their care (p. 199). In other words, without alternative perspectives, it may be difficult to see how our own ethical positions serve differential interests, even unintentionally supporting the very institutional arrangements we are attempting to change.

Similar concerns have been raised by some feminist scholars who argue that traditional ethics are gender-based and unresponsive to the realities of women's lives (e.g., Jaggar, 1992). Some of these analyses have focused on power, pointing out how acceptance of a male-centered ethic based on individuality, rationality, and males' experience in the world keeps women in a subordinate position. For these scholars, an ethic that does not focus on eliminating relationships of domination and oppression is morally vacuous. Other feminist scholars, while supportive of this position, have cautioned against reproducing a universalist orientation even for the purpose of redressing wrongs. Women are a highly heterogeneous group inclusive of diverse classes, cultures, and ethnicities among other group identities. From their perspective, any story that claims to be *the story* (of women) is suspect and reproduces the patriarchal view of a single and timeless "truth" (see Tong, 2000).

Broadening the Conversation: Communicative Ethics

The postmodern critique of traditional ethics has created space for new understandings of and approaches to professional ethics (e.g., Chambon & Irving, 2003; Hugman, 2003; Parton, 2003). Although space limitations do not permit an exposition of these alternatives, we briefly discuss one such perspective in order to provide a sense of this issue. This perspective, called communicative or dialogical ethics, seems particularly congruent with the relational nature of social work.

According to Arnett (2002), the distinction between communicative and philosophical (i.e., traditional) ethics is that the former is "concerned with the communicators, the historical moment, and the topic at hand. We move from viewing the standard as an ideal to the standard's being a rhetorical construct—composed of an ideal form of communication, historical moment, and topic. Communication ethics evaluates the connection between all these communicative ingredients" (p. 498). He also asserts that "what is philosophically ethical is different from what is ethically appropriate in a communicative setting" (p. 498). These differences stem from the focus of philosophical ethics on abstract principles, whereas communicative ethics is interested in the interplay of history, culture, and language. In addition, communicative ethics is concerned with performance—how we *do* ethics in our dialogic encounters.

These foci can sensitize social workers to previously unnoticed dimensions of ethical practices, such as power. They also encourage new areas of ethical questions not typically raised by traditional codes of ethics. For instance, although social workers are aware of the totalizing effects of domination and oppression on conceptions of self, our ethics tend to be silent about such situations, focusing more on transgressions of appropriate conduct by social workers in relation to philosophically derived principles. In contrast, social workers operating from a position of communicative ethics might ask: What is our ethical responsibility toward people whose domination has led them to form self-identities in terms of the dominant culture's depiction of them (cf. hooks, 1995) Further, they may consider how ethical social work practice might function with clients located within institutional structures, such as the welfare system or the medical-mental health industry, that further their own oppression and domination. Is it ethical to encourage individuals to conform to oppressive social systems rather than oppose them? In such situations, do we have an affirmative obligation to provide, following Freire, the skills and resources necessary "to question institutional power" (Arnett, 2002, p. 493)? And how do we carry out such tasks without being patronizing or imposing our own vision on others while, at the same time, recognizing how our self and professional identities also are shaped in similar ways? These are not easy questions; however, their consideration may generate the kinds of dialogue that will enhance social workers' views of ethics.

Communication is not only about speaking, but listening. Bauman (2000) believes that people often do not understand how their personal narratives express the public rhetoric of the media. Sensitivity to such rhetoric requires us to consider how we listen. Are we open to hearing different narratives? Can we listen in a way that hears "other plots, other constructions of heroes and villains, different crisis points, and alternative moral structures to the [received] narrative " (Bracci, 2002, p. 481)? Does our listening encourage self-reflexivity? A view of listening as "ethical communicative action," according to Bracci, "may require, for example, a form of humility with respect to narrative morals, an intellectual modesty with respect to knowledge produced from interested and imperfect claims." Bracci further urges inquiry into "ethical listening patterns that cultivate dialogical courage" (p. 481). Thus, a communicative approach to ethics encourages individuals to reconsider how we participate with others, through speaking and listening, in the construction of dialogic realities.

The performance emphasis of communicative ethics is consistent with social constructionists' eschewal of abstract universals in favor of pragmatic and practice approaches to ethical understanding. Gergen (1994) proposes three implications of this shift: (1) the replacement of absolutist claims with collaborative and communal dialogue. For example, social workers might inquire how to engage in dialogue on ethical issues with clients and others in ways that will encourage expression of and respect for diverse perspectives; (2) the relocation of moral action from individuals to language. For example, rather than view morality as property of persons, social workers may ask how moral language functions in the lives of clients and in the practices of social workers; and (3) a shift from theories or principles of the good to morality as a social achievement. For example, social workers might pay increased attention to issues such as identifying the conditions under which people are accepting of differences, or how alternative linguistic resources might facilitate collaborative practices.

Taking these implications seriously would require that social workers reanalyze existing ethical codes from the perspective of the people they serve. It would invite their participation in a mutual effort at defining "the good" in particular situations. Finally, it would encourage ongoing examination of how language shapes the parameters of moral discourse. Less emphasis might be placed on ethical codes as regulators of conduct and more on the meaning of ethics—how meaning is constituted in language and functions in social life and professional practice. Social workers are invited to understand and accommodate different ethical systems and develop a moral language that is reflexive and contextual. Such considerations might encourage ethical practices that are sensitive and responsive to local realities and global concerns. These considerations might also render the social work profession more versatile and inclusive for the multifaceted twenty-first century world, a topic explored in the next section.

THE PROFESSION, PROFESSIONALS, AND PROFESSIONALIZATION

As noted earlier, the status of social work *as a profession* has been a concern throughout the history of the field. Although all fields and disciplines contend with processes of establishment and confirmation, social work is among those fields that perseverate about their position in academic and professional venues.

Because language is often a central strategy for status positioning, we first consider the role of discourse and rhetoric in the formation, dissolution, and reintegration of groups called "professions." In effect, we, as scholars and/or practitioners, have adopted various linguistic patterns to legitimize our work as we construct ourselves as *professionals*. In like manner, Kimball (1992) notes how the meaning of the word 'profession' changed "reflexively and episodically over time as the nature of what was actually called a 'profession' changed" (p. 323). For example, over the past century, social work has been conceptualized in many ways, such as *a pseudo* profession (Flexner, 1915); as a "semi-profession" (Etzioni, 1969);

as "social care" (Richardson & Asthana, 2006); and as an "art" (Higham, 2005; Waters, 2001). Similarly, changing ideas of what constitutes a "professional" are coterminous with changing constructions of the "profession." In other words, social work came to call itself a profession through changing rules of knowledge production. Accordingly, this final section asks the following questions: What do these changing rules look like in the profession's past history? What do they look like now, in the early years of the twenty-first century? And what might we want them to look like in the future?

Early Languaging of the Profession[1]

A characteristic of professions is their use of specialist discourses. As social work shifted from a moral to a scientific base of knowledge, and from a general to a specific skill base of practice, it required the language of specialization (Kimball, 1992, p. 271). Early on, the difficulty of explaining and justifying social work as a practice to improve individual and social well-being and increase social justice served as a discursive rallying point around which specialization efforts gathered. For example, the language of anti-delinquency, civic improvement, and community health led to a more specific language of social diagnosis, investigation, and social therapeutics, which helped to establish the social casework, and later the clinical, traditions. Accordingly, for the past half century or so, social work has relied on the language of specialized professional expertise.

These developments took place in the context of attempts by other vocations, fields, professions, and academic disciplines to establish unique domains in the universities and broader society in order to gain the credibility, respect, and financing that would secure lifetime career paths as educators, researchers, and practitioners. The developments occurred in the further context of a society that became increasingly industrialized, was constituted by an increasingly diverse populace, endured two world and numerous partial-world wars, developed revolutionary communications technologies, and became increasingly reliant on market mechanisms in all sectors.

Over time, however, resistance to the hegemonic language of professional expertise emerged both within and outside the profession. From within, the civil rights and feminist movements and other social change movements and legislation fostered practices of democratization in the social work profession. For a period in the 1960s and 1970s, and persisting still in pockets of resistance, some educators and practitioners designed and implemented practice models to enhance client empowerment. Others expanded social work curricula to include diverse and multiple perspectives. Still others opened up research to active and reciprocal engagement with "clients" or "users" of services.

External resistance to social work, however, was stronger. This resistance included political backlash to rising social welfare expenditures, reactions to race- and class-based agitation and social unrest, bureaucratic failures and financial excesses, increased privatization of social services, and preoccupation with organizational and professional accountability. In other words, the feet of social work as a profession in the United States were increasingly being held to the institutional fire.

[1] We use the term "languaging" to indicate the constitutive function of words and their multiple meanings.

Languaging of the Profession in the Twenty-First Century

Over the latter decades of the twentieth century and persisting into the twenty-first, public confidence in "authorities" and "experts" eroded. Professions and professionals alike are subjected to increased external scrutiny, even across geographic borders (Clark, 2005; Kunneman, 2005). In many countries, social work is among other professions now mandated to be "accountable" for "results" or "outcomes" (Hugman, 2005; Lymbery, 2001; Woodcock & Dixon, 2005). Doubt and attacks originate both from consumers, in the form of medical and social work malpractice lawsuits, and financiers, in the form of required demonstration of performance outcomes as a criterion of federal and private funding organizations. Providers of funding for social services are also expected to be "accountable," thus effectiveness expectations, often called "quality measurement" or "quality management," encompass the activities of both public and private service providers. Such challenges take the form of "new public management" in the United Kingdom, New Zealand, and Australia (Barzelay, 2001), "risk management" in the United Kingdom (Parton & O'Byrne, 2000), and "performance- or outcome-based funding" in the United States (Iversen, 2004). At the same time, other groups who are constructing themselves as "helping professionals" are encroaching on social work's historic professional territory through both rhetoric and action. As Allen-Meares (2005) cautioned, "MSWs now compete for positions with more business-minded MBAs, legal and policy professionals with JDs, and researchers with MPHs" (p. 18).

One response to these threats to the profession, as discussed earlier, seems to be an intensified emphasis on modernist patterns of knowledge production, in part through renewed emphasis on the discourse of scientific expertise. In this context, the privileging of modernist discourses, such as "science," may be a strategy to keep the profession viable.

Gregory and Holloway (2005) are similarly "concerned with the power of language to shape and confirm social work's identity and to control its essential direction and task" (p. 37). In the spirit of these constructions and reconstructions, we examine the "scientization" of today's social work *profession* and processes of professionalization by looking at three constitutive elements: (1) Control over entry into the vocation and its related structure of organizations and associations; (2) exclusivity over knowledge and terminology; and (3) monopoly over a territory of clientele.

This issue reaches beyond the United States, and even in the United States, involves many more professions than social work—education and nursing in particular, but medicine and law as well. We confine our examination here, however, to how control, exclusivity, and territorial monopoly intersect with the discourses of professional expertise and scientific expertise in today's social work education, inquiry and practice in the United States.

Social Work Education

In looking at professional control, exclusivity, and territorial monopoly in social work education, we need to think about the structure of U.S. universities. Most academic institutions are organized in modernist fashion into departments and professional schools—that is, they are organized into disciplines, or they are "disciplined" (Foucault, 1995). Moreover, their operations are strongly influenced by the condition of the university's finances. Schools and departments strive to maintain monopolistic control over their exclusive brand of rhetoric and terminology in order to be considered deserving of their full share of university funds and academic promotions. To maintain their position in today's validation queue, schools and educators must increasingly be seen as part of the "speech community" (Kuhn, 1996) of science.

The prior emphasis on hegemonic "professional expertise" in social work education is thus now delimited by the structure of the academy, which itself is strongly influenced by the market forces of escalating costs and decreasing federal funding. Educators can no longer retire to their towers to think and write whatever they want. Faculty in research universities are under pressure to obtain grant money to pay part of their salaries, which means that the preferences and requirements of funding actors influence scholarly inquiry (see section on social work research that follows).

Other stakeholders also influence the educational project in social work. University administrators, faculties and scholars increasingly define what counts as "scholarship," and such definitions are usually in accord with the accepted rhetoric and discourse in scholarly publications of the time. Journal editors decide what scholarly knowledge is of value, through both epistemological stance and selection of editorial boards and reviewers. From a postmodern perspective, the blind review process is based on modernist assumptions of external expertise, it assumes "objective, unbiased" review responses, it is not democratic, and it is enacted under the paternalistic guise of "protection."

At the same time, in order for social work educators to maintain their territory during evaluative reviews by the profession's accreditation body, the Council on Social Work Education (CSWE), they often have to cede full control over their preferred pedagogy in order to conform to the prevailing pedagogical discourse of the accreditor. As in the academy more broadly, "scientific expertise" is the dominant trope in social work accreditation. The Council's *Education Policy and Accreditation Standards* (CSWE, 2004) requires social work students to be trained in the skills necessary to appraise and make use of research evidence. Yet different versions of the standards show suggestive shifts in language. As Webb (2001) describes, "The phrase 'using research evidence' to facilitate practice is increasingly replaced by the more monolithic [and, we add, 'scientific'] assertion that practice should be 'grounded in' evidence or show a 'commitment to' evidence-based practice" (p. 59).

Social Work Research

Similarly, social work educators often must relinquish exclusivity over knowledge and terminology within their disciplinary territories in order to obtain research funding. This is seen graphically in the United States and elsewhere in the evidence-based practice movement (discussed previously) as the rhetoric of empiricism and the so-called "gold standard" method of randomized clinical trials that are mandatory for many government research grants. Moreover, grantmakers (federal and private) and other funding sources increasingly define "quality" and control how "evidence," "results," and "outcomes" are defined and assessed. Methods such as action research, participatory research, ethnography, and life-history research, all of which foreground the "user's" voice through relationship with the researcher or researcher-practitioner, are generally considered not as rigorously scientific and are thus less likely to be funded.

Scholars' control over the research portion of knowledge production therefore becomes a terrain negotiated with multiple actors, such as university administrators, accreditation bodies, and research funders. Because each of these bodies is also held "accountable" to yet other actors, the privileged discourse of science and positivist empiricism predominates, which subjugates many scholars' voices and generally ignores the voices of "users," the very populace for whom the service that is evaluated as "best" is targeted. In the process, production of knowledge *about* customers/clients/users and services becomes increasingly defined by the professional and larger scientific bodies, rather than by the users themselves—a process that Foucault calls "objectifying the subject" (Rabinow, 1984).

Social Work Practice

Moving to the "front line," it appears that the hegemony of the autonomous professional expert in the practice of social work is over, for good and ill. For good is that under the cloak of mission and service expertise, some practitioners prioritized preservation of their professional territory over excellence in service delivery (Iversen, 1987, 2004), and that prioritization may now be reversed. Also for good is that voices other than those of the expert are now sometimes heard, and in the best cases, may influence policy and program design.

For ill is that market forces, whether academic, government, or private in origin, now increasingly define practice. In effect, this turns professionals into "functionaries" (Clark, 2005, p. 183). Also for ill, market forces increasingly define the production of knowledge, as such production in the United States is essentially lodged monopolistically in academic institutions.

Practitioners also participate in the discursive frenzy of professional control, exclusivity, and monopoly in order to keep their service organizations viable. Social service organizations, just like educators and researchers, are increasingly held accountable for "successful" results by their funders and sponsors, who also often define what success means. The organization can therefore no longer grant its professionals unexamined exclusivity over knowledge production, over the definition of client/user, or over program services, for fear of losing essential financial support. As such, the service user is still relegated to receipt rather than production of social work knowledge.

Languaging the Future for Social Work Professionals and the Profession

The historic challenge to social work in the United States is to defend its professional role in the social and political context of disdain for people who are poor or marginalized. As Lymbery (2001) argued from the British perspective, social work's "survival as a recognizable professional activity is dependent on the extent to which it can redefine its role within society and re-establish clarity about its overall purpose and function" (p. 369). Lymbery holds further that, "Social work is at the crossroads, with choices about how it chooses to define its core functions and tasks" (p. 370).

Similarly, social work education, inquiry and practice in the United States also seem to be at a crossroads. Will the modernist trope of control, exclusivity and monopoly continue to define the constitutive elements of the profession? If not, what will the replacement elements be, and how will they manifest in education, inquiry, and practice?

On the ground, multiplicity and versatility are what has made social work strong. Looking for a *single* "best" or "right" answer too easily leads to narrowness and rigidity. As Parton suggested (in Walker, 2001), "the particular challenge for social work in the (post)modern era is to respond positively and with imagination to the prospect of living without securities, guarantees, and order, and with contingency and ambivalence" (p. 31).

Might a postmodern perspective in education, inquiry and practice provide a more fertile epistemological framework for social work in the twenty-first century? Discourses of community, collaboration, multiplicity, dialogue, and relationship might serve as more fruitful sites to promote human well-being, social justice, and social development across the globe than discourses of control, exclusivity, and monopoly through either "professional expertise" or "scientific expertise." To "profess" would then be lodged in discourse that does not privilege any expert, but resolves into action through dialogue and relationship. Education and inquiry would be similarly dialogical, aided by participatory research methods that seek interpretation, meaning, and context—not instead of, but in addition to quantitative and other methods that are currently privileged as "scientific." As Webb (2001) argued, "We should cultivate a reflective understanding of its [evidence-based practice] empiricist presuppositions as one category of knowledge among others, and its technical rationality as one mode of action among many" (p. 73).

Most broadly, we need to keep thinking, imagining, and envisioning how social ills can be best countered. "Thinking" is the key here, especially in light of what Woodcock and Dixon (2005) described as "the weakening of social work's social science knowledge base in favor of the advancement of technical proficiency" (p. 954). Finally, whether it is called a vocation, semi-profession, art, profession, or some new nomenclature, those who "do" social work are well advised to use multiple vantage points, strategies, and discourses to produce knowledge toward the historic ends of equity, equality, and social justice.

REFERENCES

Ahmadi, N. (2003). Globalisation of consciousness and new challenges for international social work. *International Journal of Social Welfare*, *12*, 14–23.

Allen-Meares, P. (2005). The role of social work education in the academy. *Social Work Education Reporter*, *53*(3), 1, 17–20.

Aristotle. (1992). Nichomachean ethics. In R. McKeon (Ed.), *Introduction to Aristotle* (pp. 315–579). New York: Modern Library. (Original work published 1947)

Arnett, R. C. (2002). Paulo Freire's revolutionary pedagogy: From a story-centered to a narrative-centered communication ethic. *Qualitative Inquiry*, *8*(4), 489–510.

Austin, D. M. (1983). The Flexner myth and the history of social work. *Social Service Review*, *57*, 357–377.

Barzelay, M. (2001). *The new public management: Improving research and policy dialogue*. Berkeley: University of California.

Bauman, Z. (1993). *Postmodern ethics*. Oxford: Blackwell.

Bauman, Z. (1998). *Globalization: The human consequences*. New York: Columbia University Press.

Bauman, Z. (2000). *Liquid modernity*. London: Polity Press.

Bracci, S. L. (2002). Seyla Benhabib's interactive universalism: Fragile hope for a radically democratic conversation model. *Qualitative Inquiry*, *8*, 463–488.

Brennan, T. (2002). *Theories of globalization*. Retrieved June 2006 from http://cscl.cla.umn.edu/faculty/syllabi/globalization.html.

Briskman, L., & Noble, C. (1999). Social work ethics: Embracing diversity. In J. Fook & B. Pease (Eds.), *Transforming social work practice: Postmodern critical perspectives* (pp. 57–69). London: Routledge.

Cannella, G. S., & Lincoln, Y. S. (2004). Epilogue: Claiming a critical public social science: Reconceptualizing and redeploying research. *Qualitative Inquiry, 10*(2), 298–309.

Chambon, A. S., & Irving, A. (2003). "They give reason a responsibility which it simply can't bear": Ethics, care of the self, and caring knowledge. *Journal of Medical Humanities, 24*, 265–278.

Clark, C. (2005). The deprofessionalization thesis, accountability and professional character. *Social Work and Society, 3*(2), 182–190.

Council on Social Work Education (CSWE). (2004). *Educational policy and accreditation standards*. Alexandria, VA: Author.

Etzioni, A. (Ed.). (1969). *The semi-professions and their organization: Teachers, nurses, social workers*. New York: Free Press.

Falk, R. (1992). The making of global citizenship. In J. Brecher, J. B. Childs, & J. Cutler (Eds.), *Global visions: Beyond the new world order* (pp. 39–52). Boston: South End Press.

Ferguson, H. (2003). Outline of a critical best practice perspective on social work and social care. *British Journal of Social Work, 33*, 1005–1024.

Flexner, A. (1915, May 12–19). Is social work a profession? *Proceedings of the National Conference of Charities and Corrections*. Chicago: Hildmann Printing.

Foucault, M. (1995). *Discipline and punish: The birth of the prison*. A. Sheridan (Trans.). New York: Random House. (Original work published 1971).

Freud, S., & Krug, S. (2002). Beyond the code of ethics. Pt. I: Complexities of ethical decision making in social work practice. *Families in Society, 83*(5/6), 474–482.

Gambrill, E. (2001). Social work: An authority-based profession. *Research on Social Work Practice, 11*(2), 166–175.

Gambrill, E. (2006). Evidence based practice and policy: Choices ahead. *Research on Social Work Practice, 16*(3), 338–357.

Gergen, K. J. (1994). *Realities and relationships: Soundings in social construction*. Cambridge, MA: Harvard University Press.

Germain, C. B. (1979). *Social work practice: People and environments, an ecological perspective*. New York: Columbia University Press.

Gibbs, A. (2001). The changing nature and context of social work research. *British Journal of Social Work, 31*, 687–704.

Gibelman, M. (1999). The search for identity: Defining social work: Past, present, future. *Social Work, 44*(4), 298–310.

Gilgun, J. F. (2005). The four cornerstones of evidence-based practice in social work. *Research in Social Work Practice, 15*(1), 52–61.

Goldenberg, M. J. (2005). On evidence and evidence-based medicine: Lessons from the philosophy of science. *Social Science and Medicine, 62*, 2621–2632.

Goldstein, H. (2000). Joe the king: A study of strengths and morality. *Families in Society, 81*(4), 347.

Goodman, K. W. (2003). *Ethics and evidence-based medicine: Fallibility and responsibility in clinical science*. Cambridge: Cambridge University Press.

Gordon, E. J. (2006). The political contexts of evidence-based medicine: Policymaking for daily hemodialysis. *Social Science and Medicine, 62*, 2707–2719.

Greenwood, E. (1957). Attributes of a profession. *Social Work, 2*(6), 45–59.

Gregory, M., & Holloway, M. (2005). Language and the shaping of social work. *British Journal of Social Work, 35*, 37–53.

Griffiths, P. (2005). Evidence-based practice: A deconstruction and postmodern critique: Book review article. *International Journal of Nursing Studies, 42*, 355–361.

Gurman, A. S., & Kniskern, D. P. (Eds.). (1981). *Handbook of family therapy. Vol. 1*. Bristol, PA: Brunner/Mazel.

Hanson, N. R. (1958). *Patterns of discovery: An inquiry into the conceptual foundations of science*. Cambridge: Cambridge University Press.

Healy, L. M. (2001). *International social work: Professional action in an interdependent world*. New York: Oxford University Press.

Higham, P. (2005). Multi-professional practice and the art of social work. Retrieved June 13, 2006, from www.ssrg.org.uk/assembly/files/multiprofessionalpractice.pdf.

Holland, J. (2005). The regeneration of ecological, societal, and spiritual life: The holistic postmodern mission of humanity in the newly emerging planetary civilization. *Journal of Religion and Spirituality in Social Work, 24*(1/2), 7–25.

Hooks, B. (1995). *Killing rage: Ending racism*. New York: Penguin.

Hugman, R. (2003). Professional values and ethics in social work: Reconsidering postmodernism. *British Journal of Social Work, 33*(8), 1025–1041.

Hugman, R. (2005). Looking back: The view from here. *British Journal of Social Work, 35*, 609–620.

Husband, C. (1995). The morally active practitioner and the ethics of anti-racist social work. In R. Hugman & D. Smith (Eds.), *Ethical issues in social work* (pp. 84–103). London: Routledge.

Iversen, R. R. (1987). Licensure: Help or hindrance to employment of women in social work. *Social Casework, 68*, 229–233.

Iversen, R. R. (2004). Voices in the middle: How performance funding impacts workforce organizations, professionals and customers. *Journal of Sociology and Social Welfare, 31*, 125–156.

Iversen, R. R., Gergen, K. J., & Fairbanks, R. P., II. (2005). Assessment and social construction: Conflict or co-creation? *British Journal of Social Work, 35*, 689–708.

Jaggar, A. M. (1992). Feminist ethics. In L. Becker & C. Becker (Eds.), *Encyclopedia of ethics* (pp. 363–364). New York: Garland Press.

Jenson, J. M. (2005). Connecting science to intervention: Advances, challenges, and the promise of evidence-based practice. Editorial. *Social Work Research, 29*(5), 131–135.

Kellner, D. (2002). Theorizing globalization. *Sociological Theory, 20*(3), 285–305.

Kellner, D. (no date). Globalization, terrorism, and democracy: 9/11 and its aftermath. Retrieved from www.gseis.ucla.edu/faculty/kellner/.

Khinduka, S. K. (2001). Challenges of the social work profession in the 21st century: A global perspective. *Hong Kong Journal of Social Work, 35*(1/2), 1–11.

Kimball, B. A. (1992). *The "true professional ideal" in America: A history*. Cambridge, MA: Blackwell.

Kirk, S. A., & Reid, W. J. (2002). *Science and social work: A critical appraisal*. New York: Columbia University Press.

Knorr-Cetina, K. D. (1981). *The manufacture of knowledge: An essay on the constructivist and contextual nature of science*. Oxford: Pergamon Press.

Kuhn, T. S. (1962). *The structure of scientific revolutions*. Chicago: University of Chicago Press.

Kuhn, T. S. (1996). *The structure of scientific revolutions* (3rd ed.). Chicago: University of Chicago Press.

Kunneman, H. (2005). Social work as a laboratory for normative professionalisation. *Social Work and Society, 3*(2), 191–200.

Ladson-Billings, G. (2003). It's your world, I'm just trying to explain it: Understanding our epistemological and methodological challenges. *Qualitative Inquiry, 9*(1), 5–12.

Landsman, G. H. (2006). What evidence, whose evidence?: Physical therapy in New York State's clinical practice guideline and in the lives of mothers of disabled children. *Social Science and Medicine, 62*, 2670–2680.

Levitt, T. (1983). The globalization of markets. *Harvard Business Review, 61*(3), 2–11.

Lubove, R. (1965). *The professional altruist: The emergence of social work as a career, 1880–1930*. Cambridge, MA: Harvard University Press.

Lymbery, M. (2001). Social work at the crossroads. *British Journal of Social Work, 31*, 369–384.

Mahoney, M. J. (1976). *Scientist as subject: The psychological imperative*. Cambridge, MA: Ballinger.

McDonald, C. (2003). Forward via the past? Evidence-based practice as a strategy in social work. *Drawing Board: An Australian Review of Public Affairs, 3*(3), 123–142.

McNeece, C. A., & Thyer, B. A. (2004). Evidence-based practice and social work. *Journal of Evidence-Based Social Work, 1*(1), 7–25.

Morrell, P. (2000). Response to Sackett and colleagues. (1996). "Is EBM a belief?" *British Medical Journal*—online. Retrieved June 20, 2006, from http://proxy.library.upenn.edu:8513/cgi/eletters/312/7023/71/.

Munro, E. (2002). The role of theory in social work research: A further contribution to the debate. *Journal of Social Work Education, 38*(3), 461–470.

National Association of Social Workers. (1999). Code of ethics. Retrieved from www.naswdc.org/pubs/code/code.asp.

Nye, J., & Donahue, J. (2000). *Governance in a globalizing world*. Washington, DC: Brookings Institution Press.

O'Farrell, C. (1999). Postmodernism for the uninitiated. In D. Meamore, B. Burnett, & P. O'Brien (Eds.), *Understanding education: Contexts and agendas for the new millennium* (pp. 11–17). Sydney: Prentice Hall.

Parton, N. (2002). Postmodern and constructionist approaches to social work. In R. Adams, L. Dominelli, & M. Payne (Eds.), *Social work: Themes, issues and critical debates* (2nd ed., pp. 237–246). Basingstoke: Palgrave/Macmillan.

Parton, N. (2003). Rethinking professional practice: The contributions of social constructionism and the feminist "ethics of care." *British Journal of Social Work, 33*, 1–16.

Parton, N. (2007). Constructive social work practice in an age of uncertainty. In S. L. Witkin & D. Saleebey (Eds.), *Social work dialogues: Transforming the canon in practice, inquiry and education* (pp. 144–166). Alexandria, VA: Council on Social Work Education.

Parton, N., & O'Byrne, P. (2000). *Constructive social work: Towards a new practice*. London: Macmillan.

Pollio, D. E. (2006). The art of evidence-based practice. *Research on Social Work Practice, 16*(2), 224–232.

Rabinow, P. (Ed.). (1984). *The Foucault reader*. New York: Pantheon Books.

Ramsaran, D., & Price, D. V. (2003). Globalization: A critical framework for understanding contemporary social processes. Retrieved July 1, 2006, from http://globalization.icaap.org/content/v3.2/02_ramsaran_price.html.

Reid, W. J., Kenaley, B. D., & Colvin, J. (2004). Do some interventions work better than others? A review of comparative social work experiments. *Social Work Research, 28*(2), 71–81.

Richardson, S., & Asthana, S. (2006). Inter-agency information sharing in health and social care services: The role of professional culture. *British Journal of Social Work, 36*, 657–669.

Rorty, R. (1998). *Truth and progress*. Cambridge: Cambridge University Press.

Rose, N. (1996). Authority and the genealogy of subjectivity. In P. Heelas, S. Lash, & P. Morris (Eds.), *Detraditionisation: Critical reflections on authority and identity* (pp. 294–327). Oxford: Blackwell.

Rowe, W., Hanley, J., Moreno, R., & Mould, J. (2000). Voices of social work practice: International reflections on the effects of globalization. *Canadian Social Work, 2*, 65–87.

Sackett, D. L., Rosenberg, W. M. C., Muir-Gray, J. A., Haynes, R. B., & Richardson, W. S. (1996). Evidence-based medicine: What it is and what it isn't. *British Journal of Medicine, 312*, 71–72.

Scholte, J. A. (2002). *What is globalization? The definitional issue: Again* (Working Paper No. 109/02). Coventry, United Kingdom: University of Warwick, Centre for the Study of Globalisation and Regionalisation.

Sen, A. (2002a). Globalization and poverty, lecture given at Santa Clara University Institute on Globalization, 29 October 2002. Retrieved May 2004, from www.globalisationinstitute.org.

Sen, A. (2002b). How to judge globalism. *The American Prospect, 13*. Retrieved April 2005, from www.prospect.org/print/V13/1/sen-a.html.

Suchman, E. A. (1967). *Evaluation research*. New York: Sage.

Thyer, B. (2001). What is the role of theory in research on social work practice. *Journal of Social Work Education, 37*(1), 9–25.

Tong, R. (2000). Feminist ethics. In E. N. Zalta (Ed.), *The Stanford encyclopedia of philosophy*. Stanford, CA: Stanford University, Center for the Study of Language and Information. Retrieved April 17, 2007, from http://plato.stanford.edu.

United Nations. (2001). Report on 56th session of the United Nations General Assembly Second Committee, High-Level Panel on Globalization and the State. Retrieved April 2007, from http://unpan1.un.org/intradoc/groups/public/documents/un/unpan001917.pdf.

Urmetzer, P. (2005). *Globalization unplugged*. Toronto, Ontario, Canada: University of Toronto Press.

Walker, S. (2001). Tracing the contours of postmodern social work. *British Journal of Social Work, 31*, 29–39.

Waters, C. (2001). Interview with Robert Ayasse. Retrieved June 13, 2006, from http://socialwelfare.berkeley.edu/robert_profile.htm.

Webb, S. A. (2001). Some considerations on the validity of evidence-based practice in social work. *British Journal of Social Work, 31*, 57–79.

Weimer, W. B. (1979). *Notes on the methodology of scientific research*. Washington, DC: Erlbaum.

Winch, P. (1958). *The idea of a social science*. London: Routledge.

Witkin, S. L. (1999a). Constructing our future. *Social Work, 44*(1), 5–8.

Witkin, S. L. (1999b). Letter from Lapland. *Social Work, 44*(5), 413–415.

Witkin, S. L. (2000). Ethics-R-Us. *Social Work, 45*(3), 197–200.

Witkin, S. L., & Harrison, W. D. (2001). Whose evidence and for what purpose? *Social Work, 46*(4), 293–296.

Woodcock, J., & Dixon, J. (2005). Professional ideologies and preferences in social work: A British study in global perspective. *British Journal of Social Work, 35*, 953–973.

Author Index

Subject Index